# GENOCIDE

# GENOCIDE

# CRITICAL ISSUES OF THE HOLOCAUST

## A Companion to the Film GENOCIDE

Edited by
## ALEX GROBMAN and DANIEL LANDES

Associate Editor
SYBIL MILTON

Published by
THE SIMON WIESENTHAL CENTER
Los Angeles, California
and

ROSSEL BOOKS
Chappaqua, New York

**Library of Congress Cataloging in Publication Data**
Main entry under title:

Genocide, critical issues of the Holocaust.

Bibliography: p. 512
Includes index.
1. Holocaust, Jewish (1939-1945)—Addresses, essays,
lectures.   I. Grobman, Alex.   II. Landes, Daniel.
III. Milton, Sybil.   IV. Genocide (Motion picture)
D810.J4G47   1983      940.53'15'03924        83-3052
ISBN 0-940646-04-8

Editorial Consultants
SHELLY USEN
STUART KELMAN

First Edition

*The maps entitled "Two Thousand Years of Jewish Life in Europe," "Massacre,
Pogrom and Emigration, 1600-1920," "The Persecution of the Jews of Germany in the
First Five Years of Nazi Rule, 1933-1938," "German Official Plans for the 'Final
Solution,' 20 January 1942," "The Concentration Camps," "The Desperate Search for
a Country of Refuge, 1933-1945," "Jewish Revolts," "Jewish Partisans and Resistance
Fighters," and "The Righteous Among Nations, 1939-1945" are from* The Holocaust:
A Record of the Destruction of Jewish Life in Europe During the Dark Years of Nazi
Rule, *by Martin Gilbert, Copyright © 1978 by Martin Gilbert. Reproduced by
permission of Hill and Wang, a division of Farrar, Straus & Giroux, Inc. The map
entitled "The German Partition of Poland, 1939/41-1945" is from* The War Against the
Jews *by Lucy S. Dawidowicz, Copyright © 1975 by Lucy S. Dawidowicz; Copyright ©
1975 by Holt, Rinehart, and Winston. Reprinted by permission of Holt, Rinehart, and
Winston, Publishers. "The History of the Holocaust" by Yisrael Gutman, Copyright ©
1977 by Yad Vashem, is reprinted by permission of the author. The "Selected
Documents" are from* Documents on the Holocaust: Selected Sources on the
Destruction of the Jews of Germany and Austria, Poland, and the Soviet Union, *edited
by Yitzhak Arad, Yisrael Gutman, and Abraham Margaliot. Copyright © 1981 by Yad
Vashem. Reproduced by permission of Yad Vashem.*

Manufactured in the United States of America.

# CONTENTS

## 9 Aftermath

## 10 Implications

## Postscript:

\* *From testimony given at the Eichmann trial.*

\*\* *From Leon Kahn,* No Time to Mourn: A True Story of a Jewish Partisan Fighter *(Vancouver, B.C.: Laurelton Press, 1978).*

## List of Maps

# PREFACE

*Genocide: Critical Issues of the Holocaust* was initially intended to serve as a companion volume to the film, *Genocide*, recipient of the Academy Award for Best Documentary Feature of 1981. Selections from the script, written by Professor Martin Gilbert and Rabbi Marvin Hier, thus introduce the sections of the book. In addition, the first and last chapters are directed to exploring the Holocaust through film.

The book, however, stands on its own as a study of the critical issues of the Holocaust, many of which are raised in the film itself. It consists of specially commissioned articles, appearing for the first time, that survey the whole range of Holocaust scholarship. The essays are written by experts in the fields of European, American, and Jewish history, psychology, religion, and theology. While viewing the Holocaust as a unique event, we have attempted to show the context of Western and Jewish history. A number of essays trace the history and lifestyle of European Jews prior to 1939. Others consider aspects of modern antisemitism. The book continues to explore the postwar aftermath of the destruction of European Jewish life, including an essay on the establishment of the State of Israel. Although not every topic could be covered (for example, the persecution of homosexuals, the physically and emotionally disabled, and Gypsies), we have attempted to address issues that are frequently ignored; for example: Sephardic Jews, spiritual and physical responses to the persecution, and the problems of rescue.

Numerous individuals have contributed to the successful completion of this project. We wish to thank Simon Wiesenthal; Rabbi Marvin Hier, the founder of the Simon Wiesenthal Center; and the Board of Directors for their recognition that scholarship must always be the cornerstone of the Center's activities.

We are deeply grateful to Dr. Stuart Kelman, for his counsel and educational concerns; Ms. Shelly Usen, for her careful technical assistance in the preparation of the text; our friend and colleague Rabbi Abraham Cooper, who supported this work from its inception; Mr. Martin Mendelsohn, who saw to various legal considerations; and Mr. Seymour Rossel and his staff, for publishing and distributing this work. We thank Ms. Ruby Johnson for her assiduous and expert typing of the manuscript.

We could not have completed this book without the love, patience, and counsel of the following people. Daniel Landes would like to thank his wife, Sheryl Robbin; Alex Grobman would like to thank his wife, Marlene, and his sons Elon, Ranan, and Ari; Sybil Milton would like to thank Henry Friedlander.

DANIEL LANDES.    ALEX GROBMAN    SYBIL MILTON

Los Angeles
9th of Av, 5742
July 29, 1982

**1**

# Approaching
# the Holocaust

# At the Pit of Destruction

*. . . When it came to our turn, our father was beaten. We prayed,
we begged with my father to undress, but he would not undress,
he wanted to keep his underclothes. He did not want to stand
naked. . . .*

*Then they tore the clothing off the old man and he was shot.
I saw it with my own eyes. And then they took my mother. . . .
She said, let us go before her; but they caught mother and shot
her too. Then there was my grandmother, my father's mother,
standing there: she was eighty years old and she had two children
in her arms. And then there was my father's sister. She also had
children in her arms and she was shot on the spot with the babies
in her arms. . . .*

*And finally my turn came. There was my younger sister, and
she wanted to leave; she prayed to the Germans; she asked to run;
naked, she went up to the Germans with one of her friends; they
were embracing each other; and she asked to be spared, standing
there naked. He looked into her eyes and shot the two of them.
They fell together in their embrace, the two young girls, my sister
and her young friend. Then my second sister was shot. . . . and
then my turn did come. . . .*

*We were already facing the grave. The German asked,
"Whom shall I shoot first?" I did not answer. I felt him take the
child from my arms. The child cried out and was shot
immediately. And then he aimed at me. First he held on to my
hair and turned my head around; I stayed standing; I heard a
shot, but I continued to stand and then he turned my head again
and he aimed the revolver at me and ordered me to watch and
then turned my head around and shot at me. Then I fell to the
ground into the pit amongst the bodies; but I felt nothing. The
moment I did feel I felt a sort of heaviness and then I thought
maybe I am not alive any more, but I feel something after I died.
I thought I was dead, that this was the feeling which comes after
death. Then I felt that I was choking, strangling, but I tried to
save myself, to find some air to breathe. I felt that I was climbing
towards the top of the grave above the bodies. I rose, and I felt
bodies pulling at me with their hands, biting at my legs, pulling
me down, down. And yet with my last strength I came up on top
of the grave, and when I did I did not know the place, so many
bodies were lying all over, dead people. I wanted to see the end of
this stretch of dead bodies, but I could not. It was impossible.
They were lying, all dying; suffering; not all of them dead, but in
their last sufferings; naked; shot, but not dead. Children crying
"Mother," "Father"; I could not stand on my feet. . . .*

# Approaching Genocide and the Holocaust

## ALEX GROBMAN

The film *Genocide* is the story of millions of people who were systematically murdered during the most traumatic period in Western civilization. For us as viewers, it is difficult to comprehend these events and painful to witness human degradation of such magnitude. How this could have happened in an "advanced" society remains an enigma.

To convey this message, *Genocide* utilizes a variety of media techniques: Still photographs, movies, slides, sound, and words all combine to offer a unified experience which makes demands on us as viewers.

*Genocide* focuses on the destruction of European Jews because the Jews alone were singled out for total annihilation. Although millions of soldiers and civilians died at the hands of the Nazis during the Holocaust, there was never a master plan to kill all of the Poles, Czechs, Gypsies, or any other group.[1]

When the Nazis murdered approximately 10,000 Polish intelligentsia, in 1939-1940, and Polish Catholic priesthood in western Poland, for example, they were trying to prevent these groups from becoming a political and spiritual force that could unite the country against them. Similarly, when the Nazis murdered over two and one-half million Soviet prisoners of war, they were killing a military force that had fought them on the field of battle.

European Jews, on the other hand, were the only people marked for complete destruction. To the Nazi leadership, the Jews were a satanic force that controlled both the East and the West and, therefore, posed a physical threat to the German nation. There was no way to stop this alleged international Jewish conspiracy from gaining total control of the world, the Nazis reasoned, except to physically destroy every Jewish man, woman, and child. Failure to do so, Hitler believed, "would not lead to a Versailles treaty but the final destruction, indeed, to the annihilation of the German people."[2]

When the executioners questioned their superiors about the need to kill every Jewish woman and child, Heinrich Himmler, head of the SS, asserted that he would not have been "justified in getting rid of the men—in having them put to death, in other words—only to allow their children to grow up to avenge themselves on our sons and grandsons. We have to make up our minds, hard though it may be, that this race must be wiped off the face of the earth."[3] Yehuda Bauer concluded that, "In a very real sense, the Nazi attack on the world, costing millions of lives and causing havoc and destruction unequaled before or since, was at least in part an ideologically or pseudoreligiously motivated struggle against the imaginary Jewish adversary. Antisemitism was a central cause of World War II."[4]

Perhaps the best way to understand the difference between what happened to the Jews and non-Jews is to distinguish between genocide and Holocaust. According to Raphael Lemkin, who coined the term in 1943, genocide is "effected through a synchronized attack" on the political, social, cultural, economic, religious, and moral "aspects of life of the captive peoples." It also involves a "policy of depopulation, promoting procreation by Germans in the occupied countries, introducing a starvation rationing system for non-Germans, and mass killings, mostly of Jews, Poles, Slovenes, and Russians."[5]

What Lemkin described is what happened to many peoples in Nazi Europe, but not to the Jews. In countries under Nazi rule, political, social, cultural, religious, and economic institutions were transformed into serving the Germans, but in general the people running these organizations were not killed. Mass murder on a "selective" basis did occur, to be sure, within these countries, but it involved only those who posed a threat or were perceived as a danger to the Nazis. The majority of the people under Nazi rule were kept alive to help build the Third Reich.

Since Jews did not share the same fate as the other peoples in Nazi Europe, we need another term to describe their unique plight. The term "Holocaust," or *"Shoah,"* is often used to describe this phenomenon. It is important to note that by distinguishing between what happened to Jews and non-Jews, we are not trying to demean the suffering of any other group of victims. This is not a "contest to measure pain or degrees of victimization," as Henry L. Feingold notes. "What is being measured," he maintains, "is the importance of the event in history, and there clearly the Holocaust is an entirely different order of events in terms of its historical weight. History is not democratic, it does not assign equal import to like events. To forget that difference, to permit it to be subsumed in facile comparisons with every trespass human flesh has been heir to, is to risk losing the possibility of retrieving some meaning from the event. When that meaning is found, it will be in its specificity rather than in what it shares with other catastrophies."[6]

By focusing on the unique position of the Jew in the Holocaust, we can learn much about the nature of Western civilization and culture. European Jewry, after all, "was not a dissident minority in a remote corner of the world, but by virtue of its thinkers [Einstein, Freud, Marx, Kafka, Proust] an important component of European civilization which dominated the pre-Holocaust world. What died at Auschwitz was not merely the corpus of a people but Europe's hope that its social system can endure. . . .Who can escape the bitter irony that European Jewry was destroyed by a perverse use of the very industrial process which everywhere is the hallmark of modernity?"[7]

Ultimately, the Holocaust raises the question of whether our civilization will accept the existence of the Jews and other minorities living in its midst as distinct entities with their own group consciousness. It is clear that antisemitism and racism are still pervasive elements in American society and will continue to be so for the foreseeable future. While the Jewish people have succeeded in surviving antisemitism, the question that remains is whether the West can "survive its persisting nature."[8]

While *Genocide* compels us to learn from the past, it is not intended to engender hate or prejudice towards other groups or nations. Franklin Littell, a Protestant theologian, has suggested that we approach the study of the Holocaust as social pathologists studying a sick society in order to discover how people from practically all segments of German society participated in the destruction process. Indeed, what is so alarming about the Holocaust is the involvement of average people, many of whom participated not so much out of hatred of Jews, but because this was part of their job. Christopher R. Browning notes that the "Jewish experts" in the German Foreign Office, for example, were not forced by "any external physical threat" to carry out policies against the Jews and that antisemitism was only "a contributing factor but not the decisive one" in determining their actions. The main reason they complied was because "they were dominated by an internal compulsion to keep their records unstained. This compulsion was so strong that it blotted out any sense of individual responsibility. They viewed their activity... solely from the point of view of how it affected themselves, not what they were doing to others. In short," Browning concludes, "they became dehumanized."[9]

Equally frightening was the assertion by Heinrich Himmler that those involved in the annihilation of the Jewish people had remained decent. "Most of you know what it means to see one hundred corpses piled up, or five hundred, or one thousand," Himmler told a group of SS leaders in Posen on October 4, 1943. "To have gone through this and—except for instances of human weakness—to have remained decent, that has made us tough. This is an unwritten, never-to-be-written, glorious page of our history."[10]

As long as we allow this page of history to remain in the past as if it were unwritten, we will never be able to sensitize our fellow citizens to the dangers inherent within Western culture. The Holocaust is, after all, the most extreme example of what Western society—with its civil service bureaucracy, modern technology, advanced scientific and business communities, centralized government, and highly trained police force and military—is capable of doing when mobilized for destruction.[11] In the final analysis, we are not sure whether "Auschwitz has become an eternal warning, or merely the first station on the road to the extermination of all races and the suicide of humanity."[12]

**Notes**

1.   Jacob Robinson, *And the Crooked Shall Be Made Straight* (New York: Macmillan Co., 1965), pp. 92-99; Rudolf Hoess, *Commandant of Auschwitz* (New York: World Publishing Co., 1959), p. 137; Uriel Tal, "Holocaust and Genocide," *Yad Vashem Studies* XIII (1979): 24-46.

2.   Yitzhak Arad, Yisrael Gutman, and Abraham Margaliot, eds., *Documents on the Holocaust: Selected Sources on the Destruction of the Jews in Germany and Austria, Poland, and the Soviet Union* (New York: Ktav, 1981), p. 89. See also Lucy S. Dawidowicz, *A Holocaust Reader* (New York: Behrman House, 1976), pp. 32-33.

3.   Helmet Krausnick et al., eds., *Anatomy of the SS State* (London: Collins, 1968), p. 123. See also Hoess, *Commandant*, pp. 165-166.

4.   Yehuda Bauer, *American Jewry and the Holocaust* (Detroit: Wayne State University Press, 1981), p. 19.

5.   Quoted in Yehuda Bauer, *The Holocaust in Historical Perspective* (Seattle: University of Washington Press, 1978), pp. 34-35; Yehuda Bauer, "Whose Holocaust?" *Midstream* (November 1980): 42-46.

6.   Henry L. Feingold, "Determining the Uniqueness of the Holocaust: The Factor of Historical Valence," *Shoah* (Spring 1981): 10-11.

7.   Feingold, "Determining the Uniqueness," p. 6. See also Jacob L. Talmon, "The Jewish Component in World History," *Midstream* (March 1972): 8-26; Jacob L. Talmon, "Prophetism and Ideology: The Jewish Presence in History," *The Jerusalem Quarterly* 3 (1977): 3-16.

8.   Arthur Hertzberg, "Anti-Semitism and Jewish Uniqueness," *The B.G. Rudolf Lectures in Judaic Studies* (April 1973): 19-20.

9.   Christopher R. Browning, *The Final Solution and the German Foreign Office* (New York: Holmes & Meier, 1978), pp. 179-180.

10.   Karl Dietrich Bracher, *The German Dictatorship* (New York: Praeger Publishers, 1971), p. 423.

11.   Richard Rubenstein, *The Cunning of History: The Holocaust and the American Future* (New York: Harper Colophon Books, 1978), pp. 2, 6-7. See also Raul Hilberg, *The Destruction of the European Jews* (Chicago: Quadrangle Press, 1961); Henry Friedlander and Sybil Milton, *The Holocaust: Ideology, Bureaucracy, and Genocide* (Millwood, NY: Kraus International Publications, 1980).

12.   Jacob L. Talmon, *From Holocaust to Rebirth* (Jerusalem: Yad Vashem, 1974), p. 72.

**For Further Reading**

Bauer, Yehuda. "Whose Holocaust?" *Midstream* (November 1980): 42-46.

————. *The Holocaust in Historical Perspective.* Seattle: University of Washington Press, 1978.

Bracher, Karl Dietrich. *The German Dictatorship.* New York: Praeger Publishers, 1971.

Hertzberg, Arthur. "Anti-Semitism and Jewish Uniqueness." *The B.G. Rudolf Lectures in Judaic Studies* (April 1973).

Talmon, Jacob L. "Prophetism and Ideology: The Jewish Presence in History." *The Jerusalem Quarterly* 3 (1977): 3-16.

# Sensitive Issues about Holocaust Films

## SYBIL MILTON

The visual impact of film footage showing Nazi atrocities raises a number of sensitive issues for the viewing public. Confronted by piles of naked corpses, the onlooker must consciously come to terms with personal attitudes to violence and horror. The unpleasant immediacy of newsreel film showing women being herded naked into pits by the *Einsatzgruppen* (SS mobile killing units) raises issues which any audience must confront.

Nudity and naked corpses in Holocaust films are not used to evoke a macabre sense of sadistic sex. Nudity in the context of "selection" and "death" is part of the Nazi degradation of prisoners and the destructive set of rules aimed at intimidating the victims. One Polish artist, a survivor of Buchenwald, stated that issue perfectly:

> I would like to ask you to print as an absolute necessity the drawings where prisoners parade naked. Such was the reality of camp life. The first breaking of a human being depended on brutally stripping clothing off one's body, which began in the first hours of our arrival in the camp and ended with a pile of naked corpses near the crematorium. False prudishness is not needed here.[1]

Nudity in this context should evoke neither guilt nor shame, since it was intrinsic to the emotional and physical violence used by the SS for controlling prisoners. Film footage showing nude women covering their breasts and pubic hair surrounded by SS men with guns were unofficial films. They were often amateurish "home movies" of relatively poor quality made by the perpetrators before killing their victims. The presence of the camera held by the perpetrators influenced the behavior of the victims; they attempted to protect vital organs in the chest and stomach. The women's hands are not a reflection of shame, rather of self-protection. The films were not intended as newsreel footage, but for the private amusement of the cameramen, who were identical with the killers. Thus, the context of nudity in Holocaust documentary films raises important issues about false problems in extant historical footage.

Repetitive images of horror on the screen require audience outrage, rather than numbed surrender to the effect of piles of corpses, eyeglasses heaped in containers, and skeletons. In a broadcast from liberated Buchenwald on April 16, 1946, Edward R. Murrow stated: "I reported what I saw and heard, but only part of it. For most of it, I have no words. . . . If I have offended you by this rather mild account, I'm not in the least sorry."[2] It is very difficult for a post-World War II generation of younger Americans raised on televised situation comedies like "Hogan's Heroes" (portraying the humorous contretemps of life in a POW camp), or heroic battle films like *Patton*, or resistance epics like *The Counterfeit Traitor* to relate to documentary footage evoking the stench of decaying corpses in mass graves, starvation in the ghettos, and Jewish resistance. Even Hollywood horror films, with their contrived scares created by sophisticated special effects, do not prepare the average American viewer for footage of deportations, the concentration camps, and the heaps of corpses found by the Allied armies in 1945. It is harder to engage audience sympathy for 500 murder victims than for one carefully delineated person, but a conscious educational use of historical narrative accompanying the visual images of "horror" must transform the emotional impact of stunned silence and tears into a visceral and intellectual understanding of the scope and nature of Nazi criminality. Visual literacy and understanding of photographic footage must make the "unthinkable" events of Nazi Europe a part of current historical consciousness.

Holocaust footage also poses serious problems about the violation of the victims' and survivors' privacy. The victims did not give their consent to be photographed; they did not know that their private agony would be recorded for posterity. They felt that some record of their agony and passage should survive, but they did not live to screen or assent to the extant historical footage. The world of the camps involved the use of numbers, not names; the pervasive lack of privacy in daily functions like eating, toilet use, sleep; physical demoralization; and the terrorization of the victims. Even death occurred en masse, not as a private event. Stock shots of concentration camp scenes reveal that the inmates' survival depended on the ability to work and obey, the fear of pain, and the will to live. The depersonalization and deprivation imposed in the camps affected every survivor. Thus, sensitive texts and use of memoirs must accompany the film footage, which is more limited and repetitive. Few victims had cameras; Mendel Grossman's record of the Lodz ghetto is, perhaps, unique. The film footage was made by the perpetrator as a "home movie" or an offical record of his "victories." The victim was thus victimized doubly when the surviving record, however accurate, is one-sided and taken by Nazi cameras. Art done by victims provides a balance to the official Nazi photographic record.

It is important to analyze film footage on the Holocaust. Available material reveals a very selective visual remnant: deportations, synagogue burnings, ghettos, and concentration camps. There are no known film shots of partisan units, no images of Jewish survival by use of bribery, sabotage, smuggling, or passive resistance. It is a truism for analyzing film that the historian must augment photographic images by documents and historical information. But the moral shock of Auschwitz is all too real on film; audience sensitivity to the "incredible" must be taught. The immense significance of Holocaust footage is obvious, even though it deals with only a fraction of the material available in written, oral, and documentary form. The dimensions of the problem of studying the Holocaust and issues like privacy, horror, and nudity make the study of the Holocaust film footage a potent tool for the educator. Complex analysis about the historical dimensions of the event must supplement and enhance the use of visual images.

### Notes

1.   Karol Koniecny's letter to Janina Jaworska in *Art of the Holocaust,* by Janet Blatter, Sybil Milton, and Henry Friedlander (New York: W.H. Smith-Rutledge, 1981), pp. 141, 253-254. See also Bruno Bettelheim, *Surviving and Other Essays* (New York: Alfred A. Knopf, 1979), pp. 274-314.

2.   Edward R. Murrow, *In Search of Light* (New York: Alfred A. Knopf, 1967), p. 90.

### For Further Reading

Blatter, Janet; Milton, Sybil; and Friedlander, Henry. *Art of the Holocaust.* New York: W.H. Smith-Rutledge, 1981.

Craig, Gordon A. *The Germans.* New York: G.P. Putnam's Sons, 1982.

Freund, Gisèle. *Photography and Society.* Boston: David R. Godine, 1980.

Friedlander, Henry, and Milton, Sybil, eds. *The Holocaust: Ideology, Bureaucracy, and Genocide.* Millwood, NY: Kraus International Publications, 1981.

Leiser, Erwin. *Nazi Cinema.* New York: Collier Books, 1974.

Rubenstein, Richard. *The Cunning of History: The Holocaust and the American Future.* New York: Harper Colophon Books, 1978.

Smith, Paul, ed. *The Historian and Film.* Cambridge, London, and New York: Cambridge University Press, 1976.

# Modesty and Self-Dignity in Holocaust Films

## DANIEL LANDES

The issue of viewing the naked bodies of Jewish victims of the Holocaust takes on another dimension when one considers the religious background of a large percentage of this group. Traditional Judaism's attitude towards the body is decidedly neither Greek nor Victorian. It rejects the notion that beauty, being sacred and true, is best expressed in the nude, whether the human form is captured in classical statuary or in the gymnasium. Despite ascetic tendencies, it similarly rejects the approach that there is something either expressly or vaguely "wrong" with the human body that clothes are meant to hide and disguise.

The Jewish approach to the body is subsumed under a broader category of human deportment: modesty, or *tsniut*. To walk modestly with one's God and in society is a general religious imperative that permeates Jewish law in both its letter and its spirit. As applied to matters affecting the body, it has meant a valuing and treasuring of the body, as underscored by its creation by God. In much the same way that the Torah (scroll of law) is carefully encased within its *mantel* (cloth coverlet), the human body is also seen to need suitable garments.

The properly dressed religious man wears a four-cornered poncho, the *arba kanfot*, which has specially tied fringes, or *tsitsit*, at each of the four corners. It may be likened to a ritual vest. It is worn either under or over the shirt, with the fringes either tucked in or left out. The Westernized religious Jews, in Germany and Lithuania, for example, were not given to outward display and, therefore, wore the garment under the shirt with the fringes tucked in. The garment's purpose is to remind the Jew of his religious duties (Num. 15:37-41). His head is covered at all times with a *kipah* or a *yarmulke* (hat or skull cap). On the Sabbath and holidays, many—especially the Hasidim—wear the *streimel* (fur-lined hat). The covered head indicates submission to the divine yoke.

Other than work clothes, the religious man wears muted conservative clothes. Many Jews, for example, wore a *kapote* or *bekeshe* (long black coat or caftan). Males often wear long, curled earlocks, *payot*, either hidden behind the ear or left dangling, in fulfillment of the biblical injunction, and grow beards as a guard against "evil impulse." This distinctive dress doubtlessly serves to further group solidarity and cohesion—especially for those who wear the *kapote* or *bekeshe*, the *streimel*, let their *tsitsit* "out," and have long *payots* and beards; but its main purpose is to serve the specific aims of piety and modesty.

Women are also obligated in the laws of *tsniut*. Religious women are careful to keep their legs and arms covered and refrain from wearing sexually provocative clothing. Upon marriage, most women also keep their hair—symbolic of sexual attraction—covered in public. They usually wear either a *sheitel* (marriage wig) or a *tikhl* (cloth head covering). A minority have shaven heads under the head coverings. These self-imposed dress restrictions are not meant to make women shabby or dowdy. Indeed, Jewish women have never lost their desire to be eminently presentable. The goal is to mute one's public sexual identity.

A double nakedness and a double shame were imposed upon the Jews caught by the *Einsatzgruppen* or interned in the camps. The terrible effects of being stripped naked have been discussed by Sybil Milton in her article, "Sensitive Issues about Holocaust Films." But there was another nakedness: the violent removal of that "outer" religious garb which expressed the Jews' innermost spiritual convictions. This was a purposeful shaming. The Nazis knew how to assault one's self-dignity. To jeeringly pull the hair from the "glory of a man's face," the *hadrat panim* of his beard, was to serve notice, painfully, that this man no longer had a God to serve.

Ripping a woman's dress sleeve meant that her desire for modesty was meaningless because she was a "nonperson." This distinction between the stripping of religious garb and total nudity was, to a certain degree, of course, artificial. People tended to form a unified image of themselves. Simply put, although further and worse indignities awaited them, the Jew and Jewess, who stood for the first time in their adult lives with their heads forcibly uncovered, already felt themselves naked.

The viewer of a Holocaust film, sensitive to the religious standpoint of many of the victims, is in a quandary. Jewish tradition, in many places and in many ways, urges us not to gaze upon the shame of our fellow man. What right do we have to look at the shame of the wretched sufferers of the Holocaust? The making of *Genocide* reflects this problem. The amount of footage showing the naked women being driven to their deaths was reduced from the original script, and that which was used was put through a blue filter to partially mute the scene. Still, the naked image is not really obscured; the tableau of men and women shorn of their customary clothing is frequently present on the screen.

Perhaps we show and watch these film clips because we feel impelled to demonstrate—to ourselves, no less than to others—that this event *has happened.* Ironically, when we do see the evidence, the brutality and rawness of it all, it tends to make us distance ourselves from it, to avert our faces and "deny" that it is there. But somehow, movement from viewing to alienation does not prevent us from looking again. This dialectic continues until a resolution of sorts is achieved: We believe the unbelievable as we watch the unbearable.

I am not sure if even this need to know gives us the right to see the shame of others. As Sybil Milton indicates, we don't have the opportunity to request permission. Considering the exquisite care that so many of the victims took to guard their modesty, one can never glibly assure us that they would have given their permission. And if even only one person would be further shamed by our viewing, would we have the right to look?

If we do look—and we do—it must be through biblical eyes. The *Eikhah,* The Book of Lamentations, offers descriptive and graphic depictions of the slaughter and degradation of the Jews during the destruction of the First Temple. When one reads its lines and the rabbinic commentary, the shame of those who suffered in Jerusalem sears the imagination. The communal recital of the Book of Lamentations during the fast of Tishah be-Av (commemorating the destruction of the Temple) attempts to do more. Avoiding a possible "numbing" effect that such a litany of horrors may eventually cause in the reader, it moves one beyond sympathy to empathy. Anyone viewing *Genocide* must undergo a similar leap into identification, understanding that we may never really know what it was like to be there. Their shame in some small way must become ours.

### For Further Reading

Berkovits, Eliezer. *Crisis and Faith.* New York: Sanhedrin Press, 1976.

Soudet, Pierre. "Misuses of the Holocaust by the Film Industry." *Centerpoint* 4 (Fall 1980): 151-152.

**2**

# THE JEWS OF EUROPE

# The Life That Is No More

*A hundred years ago, the majority of the world's Jews lived in Europe in the Polish provinces of the Russian Empire, in the Austro-Hungarian Empire, and in the German Empire. To be sure, it was a world of poverty and hardship, of sacrifice and struggle, but it was also a world of scholars and poets, of impressionable matchmakers and philosophers. It was a world where each week men and women confronted new perils and hazards, and where each Sabbath they sat with their children around a table surrounded by song and joy. It was a world of synagogues and houses of study where young and old crowded together by the candlewick to study late into the night; where mothers and grandmothers rocked their loved ones to sleep with lullabies of hope and faith; where a neighbor's joy was a shtetl's day of rejoicing, and where his pain was its day of sorrow. It was a world where the price for respect was good deeds, but where the right to friendship had no prerequisites. Such a world were these 10,000 tiny dots on the map—Belz, where the Hasid hurried to be at his rebbe's table; Vilna, where the ordinary cobbler conversed in the Talmud; Pinsk and Lodz, where vendors rose at the crack of dawn on Monday and Thursday to hurry their wares to the marketplace; there was Warsaw, where writers leisurely sipped tea, and interpreted the life of the times. . . Vienna, her parks and broad streets bustling with artists etching out moments of memory and violinists transforming cafes into symphonic halls...*

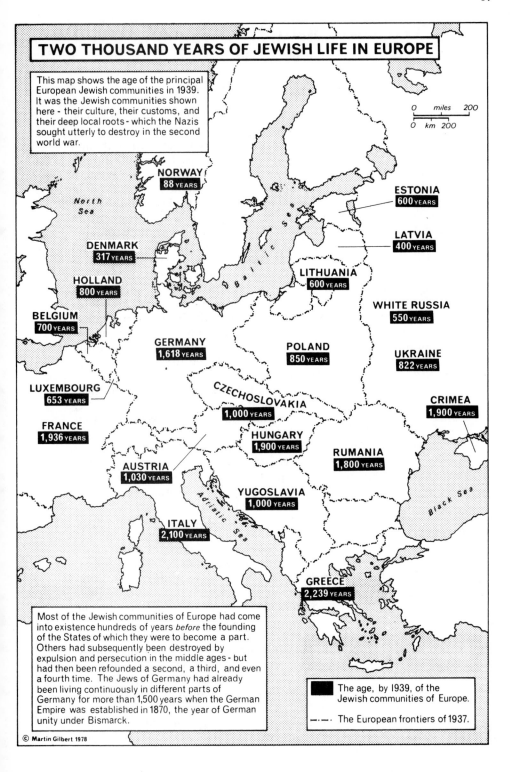

# TWO THOUSAND YEARS OF JEWISH LIFE IN EUROPE

This map shows the age of the principal European Jewish communities in 1939. It was the Jewish communities shown here - their culture, their customs, and their deep local roots - which the Nazis sought utterly to destroy in the second world war.

*North Sea*

0    miles    200

0    km    200

NORWAY
88 YEARS

ESTONIA
600 YEARS

LATVIA
400 YEARS

DENMARK
317 YEARS

*Baltic Sea*

HOLLAND
800 YEARS

LITHUANIA
600 YEARS

WHITE RUSSIA
550 YEARS

BELGIUM
700 YEARS

GERMANY
1,618 YEARS

POLAND
850 YEARS

UKRAINE
822 YEARS

LUXEMBOURG
653 YEARS

CZECHOSLOVAKIA
1,000 YEARS

CRIMEA
1,900 YEARS

FRANCE
1,936 YEARS

HUNGARY
1,900 YEARS

RUMANIA
1,800 YEARS

AUSTRIA
1,030 YEARS

*Adriatic Sea*

YUGOSLAVIA
1,000 YEARS

*Black Sea*

ITALY
2,100 YEARS

GREECE
2,239 YEARS

Most of the Jewish communities of Europe had come into existence hundreds of years *before* the founding of the States of which they were to become a part. Others had subsequently been destroyed by expulsion and persecution in the middle ages - but had then been refounded a second, a third, and even a fourth time. The Jews of Germany had already been living continuously in different parts of Germany for more than 1,500 years when the German Empire was established in 1870, the year of German unity under Bismarck.

The age, by 1939, of the Jewish communities of Europe.

—·—· The European frontiers of 1937.

© Martin Gilbert 1978

# Eastern European Jews Before World War II

## STEVEN M. LOWENSTEIN

Although there have been Jews in eastern Europe for about 1,000 years, the vast majority of the Jewish population there stems from the wave of central European migrants between the thirteenth and sixteenth centuries. At that time, Poland was by far the largest country in Europe. Because it was on the frontier of the Western Christian world, with an underdeveloped economy in need of merchants and farmers to help in its development, Poland welcomed foreign settlers. An especially large number of settlers came from Germany (both Jews and Christians). In addition to the economic opportunity that motivated many migrants, the Jews were also impelled by massacres and expulsions in Germany to seek a new home in Poland. The Jewish migrants brought with them from Germany their Ashkenazic[1] religious and communal traditions and their Yiddish language (which was based on Germanic dialects with Hebrew and Slavic admixtures). The peak of the Jewish immigration took place in the sixteenth century. By that time, the Jewish community of Poland had become far larger than the community remaining in Germany. By the eighteenth century, Poland would contain the majority of the world's Jews.

The Jews arriving in Poland found social and political conditions very different from those they had left in central Europe. Poland was a huge country with a weak central government that became progressively weaker. Unlike western and central Europe, Poland had a very weak native middle class which could do little to limit the commerce of the newcomers. The politics and economy of the country were dominated by the nobility, which owned the majority of the land in the realm and kept the peasants (the majority of the population) in a state of serfdom that often differed little from pure slavery. The nobles encouraged Jewish enterprise and settled Jews in private towns on their estates. In addition, they employed Jews to manage their estates as collectors of taxes, tolls, dues, and rents from the peasants and as concessionaires of the nobles' monopoly on liquor distilling and sales. Jews were also able to enter into all types of commerce and into many crafts (especially tailoring); they were not restricted to moneylending, as they had been in the West.

Because of the weakness of the Polish government, the Jews were permitted wide powers of self-rule. Since the Polish crown had almost no bureaucracy, the only way it could raise taxes from the Jews was to assess a lump sum on the Jewish community and then leave it to the community to decide how much each individual should pay. The Jews were not only permitted to have self-governing communities in each town, but they were also allowed a council of communal representatives in each of the two sections of the Polish Commonwealth—the Council of Four Lands in the west and south and the Council of Lithuania in the northeast. These councils existed from the late sixteenth or early seventeenth centuries until they were abolished in 1764. The Jewish communities and councils had powers that covered virtually all aspects of daily life—tax collecting, legal judgments in disputes between Jews, business regulations, upkeep of synagogues and religious schools—and the government permitted them to enforce their regulations with fines and excommunication. Most Jews, living in communities with large Jewish populations, had virtually no contact with the Polish government except through the intermediary of the Jewish community. Just as did other social and national groups in the huge amorphous Poland, the Jews lived lives of their own, differing from their neighbors in language, religion, and dress.

The weakness of the Polish government also had negative implications for the Jews. Although it allowed them autonomy, it also provided them with little security. The Polish nobleman whose word was law on his estate could favor Jews when it was in his interest and also, if he wished, treat them sadistically. In addition, the position of Jews as agents of the nobility exposed them to the hatred and violence of the peasants from whom they collected the dues and services owed to the landlord. The Jews' position was especially dangerous in the southeastern part of the Polish Commonwealth, the Ukraine. In this area, the Catholic Polish noblemen were lords of estates inhabited by Russian Orthodox Ukrainian peasants. The Poles sent in priests to spread Catholicism. Jewish settlements in the Ukraine grew tremendously in the eighty years preceding 1648. In that year, a tremendous revolt of the Cossacks and Ukrainians took place under the leadership of Bogdan Chmielnitski. The rebels not only attacked Polish noblemen and Catholic priests, but they also singled out the Jews for harsh treatment. Tens of thousands of Jews were massacred.

Poland never really recovered from the Chmielnitski uprising and the invasions of the Swedes and Russians that followed. The government was less and less able to govern, and Poland's neighbors interfered even more in its internal affairs. The Jews remained exposed to intermittent attacks from their neighbors, especially in the Ukraine. Finally, Poland's powerful neighbors, Prussia, Austria, and Russia, divided Poland into three partitions from 1772 to 1795, effectively eliminating it as a nation. After a brief interruption during the Napoleonic Wars, the division of Poland was confirmed in 1815. Most of Poland became a part of czarist Russia, with smaller sections going to the other two powers.

The fate of the Jews in the three successor states to Poland differed greatly. The Jews in Posen and West Prussia (the two provinces of Poland which went to Prussia) were at first subject to many restrictions, but by the second half of the nineteenth century they became Prussian (and later German) citizens. They soon began to adopt German culture and eventually were incorporated into German Jewry. In the late nineteenth century, they began to migrate to Berlin and other German cities; when Poland regained its independence in 1919, there were virtually no Jews still residing in the provinces of Posen and West Prussia.

Austrian Poland, known as Galicia, like Prussian Poland, initially restricted the rights of its Jewish inhabitants. In 1867, however, the Austro-Hungarian Empire granted the Jews full legal equality. The multinational Austro-Hungary differed greatly from the more monolithic Germany. Since the ruling Germans in Austria were a minority of the empire's population, they were unable to impose their culture on the provinces. Most Jews in Galicia remained traditional in religious practice and Yiddish-speaking in language. The backward economic conditions allowed traditional life to continue with little challenge in the small towns where many Jews lived.

Galician Jews were the largest single group of Jews in the Austro-Hungarian Empire, but they were not the only ones. Jews also lived in the Austrian provinces of Bohemia and Moravia (now western Czechoslovakia) and in western Hungary. (All of these groups resembled central European Jews as much or more than eastern European Jews.) In the course of the nineteenth century, the Jewish population of Hungary increased greatly as Jews migrated there from the West (Bohemia and Moravia) and from Galicia. The eastern and northeastern provinces of Hungary were inhabited mainly by Hasidic Jews from Galicia, while central and western Hungary were settled by more Westernized Jews.

Jewish communal and religious life, which in the heyday of the Polish commonwealth had been rather uniform under the domination of the powerful communal structures, began to become more differentiated in the eighteenth century. The first religious movement to call for a new type of religious life was Hasidism, founded in the mid-eighteenth century by Rabbi Israel Baal Shem Tov. The Hasidic movement, with its emphasis on individual prayer, a charismatic religious leader *(rebbe)*, and the possibility of religious greatness even for the unlearned, swept across the Ukraine and western Poland in the late eighteenth century. In the northeast (Lithuania), rabbinic opposition led by Elijah the Gaon of Vilna, who feared the Hasidic downgrading of learning and its minor liturgical changes, prevented the Hasidim from gaining the adherence of more than a minority of the Jewish population. The second challenge to traditional ways was the *Haskalah* (Enlightenment). Unlike Hasidism, which wished to make religious experience deeper and more personal, the *Haskalah* desired to bring the Jews closer to the secular culture, learning, and lifestyles of the non-Jewish world. Beginning in the late eighteenth century in Germany, the *Haskalah* affected a smaller group of Jewish intellectuals in eastern Europe who wished to see modernizing changes in Jewish education, dress, and religious life. The majority of rabbis opposed the *Haskalah*, and (at least until the late nineteenth century) so did the majority of the Jewish population of eastern Europe.

Czarist policy in Russia towards the Jews differed both from the policies formerly carried out by independent Poland and from those of Prussia and Austria. Until the partitions of Poland, Russia had excluded virtually all Jews and, when faced with this unexpected (and unwelcome) by-product of its expansion, decided to limit the size of the new population. Jews were allowed to live in the territories captured from Poland and in a few other provinces of southern Russia, but not anywhere else in the country. The restriction on Jewish settlement (Pale of Settlement) created in the 1790s continued in effect until the Russian Revolution of 1917. Czarist Russia, unlike Poland, was a strong centralized state with a large (if corruptible) bureaucracy. It was not willing to allow the Jews to retain their wide powers of self-government, but on the other hand was not willing to compensate them for the loss of autonomy by granting them equal rights and participation in the Russian government.

The policy of Russia in the first half of the nineteenth century was one of assimilating the Jews into Russian society without granting equality in return. Czar Nicholas I (1825-1856) ordered the drafting of Jewish boys at the age of twelve for at least twenty-five years of military service; the forbidding of traditional Jewish dress; the abolition of the Jewish communal executive *(kahal);* and the creation of secular schools for Jews. The Jewish community, except for a small number of supporters of the *Haskalah,* resisted all of these decrees, including secular schools. When Nicholas died, his somewhat more liberal son, Alexander II (1856-1881), instituted some reforms in Russian society and also removed some of the restrictions on Jews. Certain classes of Jews (such as merchants, ex-soldiers, and university graduates) were permitted to live outside the Pale. Political liberalization and the beginnings of industrial development encouraged some Jews to be optimistic about their future in Russia. Larger numbers of Jews attended secular schools and some abandoned traditional religious practice.

The assassination of Alexander II by revolutionaries in 1881 put an end to this brief liberal period. Pogroms (anti-Jewish riots) broke out in many parts of Russia. The reactionary government of Alexander III responded not by punishing the guilty, but by issuing new restrictions on the Jews. Residence restrictions were made stricter and quotas were enforced in institutions of higher learning and some professions. The last czar, Nicholas II (1894-1917), faced with growing unrest among the Russian people, turned to more and more explicitly anti-Jewish policies. The government supported organizations like the Black Hundreds, which incited pogroms and murdered Jews; the czarist secret police concocted the *Protocols of the Elders of Zion,* which charged that there was an international Jewish conspiracy; from 1911 to 1913, the government even staged a trial accusing the Jew Mendel Beilis of ritual murder.

The growing government hostility after 1881, coupled with growing economic distress, induced literally millions of Jews to leave eastern Europe, mainly for the United States. Many of those who had hoped that education would lead to the integration of the Jews into Russian society now came to feel that only the Jews themselves could solve their own problems. Although the majority of eastern European Jews were still traditional, the number of those who gained a secular education and abandoned traditional religion grew steadily. But those who gave up religious beliefs no longer looked for assimilation. Instead, a number of modern ideologies emerged, each claiming to have a solution for "the Jewish problem."

One of the new ideologies to emerge was early Zionism.[2] The Zionists argued that no solution could be found for the Jews while they remained in eastern Europe. They would never be accepted as equal citizens by either the government or the non-Jewish population because they were a separate nation. Only by returning to their homeland would they be able to have normal relations with the peoples of the world. The early Zionists found the *Hovevei Zion* movement, which helped found the first modern Jewish settlements in the land of Israel. When Theodor Herzl founded the political Zionist movement in 1896, the majority of his supporters were Russian Jews.

In its early days, Zionism was a minority movement opposed by a number of other strong ideologies. A particularly powerful movement was socialism, which argued that all problems in society were the result of exploitation of the workers by capitalists and noblemen. The Socialists desired a revolution to overthrow the czar and capitalism. Many Jews turned to socialism for a number of reasons. First, the Jews—more than many other groups—saw the existing government as especially hostile to them. Secondly, there were many well-organized Jewish workers. Finally, there were many Jewish students in the universities, the hotbeds of revolution. The Socialists opposed Zionism because it supported Jewish cohesion without regard to class distinctions. They also accused the Zionists of running away from the problems of Russia by looking for solutions in the far-off Middle East. The Socialists themselves were divided. The main Social Democratic party (divided between its Menshevik and Bolshevik, later Communist, wings) claimed that there were no special Jewish issues and no need for a separate Jewish culture. The Jewish workers' Bund (the popular Socialist party active in the workers' trade union struggle), on the other hand, was interested not only in revolution, but also in equal rights for the Jews and in the flourishing of a secularist Jewish culture in Yiddish.

As a compromise between socialism and Zionism, the Poale Zion was founded. It tried to combine the two movements by supporting the class struggle of the workers against the employers while simultaneously working for the creation of a new Jewish society in Palestine. Eventually, Poale Zion split over the issue of which of these two tasks was more important. Poale Zion was not the only ideological subgroup within Zionism. Orthodox Jews, dissatisfied with the secular nature of the movement, created the Mizrachi (religious Zionist movement) to promote a Zionist ideology based on Torah (Jewish teachings) and Jewish traditions.

Not all Jews agreed with either the Zionists or the Socialists. Some wished to create a Jewish society somewhere, but not necessarily in Palestine. These Territorialists showed interest in territories as varied as Uganda and Argentina. Others agreed that Jews needed to protect their cultural and national rights in addition to their civil rights, but opposed leaving Russia; they promoted the idea of autonomism. They hoped that once democracy came to eastern Europe Jews would gain (besides civil rights) recognition of self-governing Jewish communities and the right to use their own languages in schools, courts, and cultural institutions.

The supporters of the various ideologies disagreed not only about social revolution, religion, and the proper homeland for the Jews, but even about the language of Jewish culture. Although most agreed that Jews should use their own language and not the Polish, Russian, or Ukraninian of their neighbors, the supporters of Hebrew clashed with those who favored Yiddish. The Zionists tended to favor Hebrew, while the Socialists preferred Yiddish (the language of the common people); some were willing to find a place for "both national languages." Both languages developed a sophisticated and prolific literature in the years after 1881. Often, leading writers (like I.L. Peretz, Mendele Mocher Sforim, and Hayyim Nahman Bialik) wrote in both languages.

With the rapid growth of modern Jewish cultural activity after 1881, it no longer seemed necessary for those who left the Jewish traditional way of life to assimilate. Instead, they were able to create cultural or national alternatives which still stressed Jewish cohesion, even if on a secular basis.

Change was taking place not only in ideology, but also in daily life. However, in the 1880s, much of the traditional lifestyle still remained dominant. Jews made up about 10 percent of the population of the Pale of Settlement (and about the same percentage in Galicia), but they were not randomly spread in all settlements. In the mainly agricultural villages, the Jewish population was small or nonexistent. Many of the village Jews were innkeepers, and Russian government pressure tried to force them from the villages and from innkeeping. In the small commercial towns *(shtetlakh)*, on the other hand, the Jewish population was large indeed, sometimes even comprising a majority of the inhabitants. The *shtetl,* with a population of 500 to several thousand, was usually centered around a marketplace. The Jews tended to live in the center of town, where commercial activity was concentrated; peasants from the sur-rounding villages would come to the *shtetl* on market days to buy and sell. The *shtetl* generally had a well-organized Jewish community with its own synagogue, houses of study, charity organizations, schools, and other institutions. Within the *shtetl,* Jews could live a Jewish cultural and religious life with relatively little interference. This is not to say that all *shtetlakh* were alike or that they were immune to change. The secular ideologies made their entrance into *shtetl* life in the period from 1881 to 1914, and especially affected the younger generation.

Economic change affected both the life of the *shtetl* itself and the flow of migration from it. By the late nineteenth century, the trend of migration included not only the millions going overseas, but also the hundreds of thousands of Jews moving to the great cities of eastern Europe. Warsaw Jewry grew from 15,600 in 1816 to 130,000 in 1882 and 337,000 in 1914; Lodz grew from 2,775 in 1856 to 98,700 in 1897. By 1897, Odessa had 139,000 Jews, Kiev had 51,000, Vilna had 64,000, and Minsk had 47,500. Life in the cities was more varied and anonymous than in the *shtetlakh*. All the different trends in ideologies and tradition and the widest range of economic standing were to be found there.

The economic structure of eastern European Jewry was heavily influenced by the growth of railroads and industry after about 1880. A small number of bankers, manufacturers, and great merchants benefited from the changes, but the majority became even poorer than before. Changes in transport and trade routes took business from some of the *shtetlakh*; the many Jewish wagon-drivers were hurt by the competition of the railroad. Another common Jewish pursuit—crafts—was also affected. Small Jewish tailors, weavers, and other craftsmen could not compete effectively with factories. Many lost their independence and became workers in textile factories and other light industries. Numerous Jewish small businessmen saw their businesses decline; many lived from occasional work or business (they were known as *Luftmenshen*—literally, people living on air). The Jewish charity rolls grew. This trend of economic decline continued for the bulk of eastern European Jews until their destruction in World War II.

World War I, which broke out in 1914, led to tremendous changes in eastern Europe. At first, Jews tended to favor the German and Austrian forces who treated them better than the czarist government. This changed when the revolution of March, 1917, put a democratic government in place of the czar. The new government gave the Jews equal rights but was unable to maintain its power in the face of the continuing war and ongoing internal revolution. After eight months, it was overthrown by a Communist revolution whose leaders included many (highly assimilated) Jews. The Communist revolution led to a prolonged civil war between the Reds and the Whites (anti-Communists), much of it fought in areas heavily inhabited by Jews. Because the White armies in the Ukraine massacred tens of thousands of Jews in the towns they occupied, Jews were forced into the Communist camp.

The position of the Jews after the Communist victory was peculiar. On the one hand, the Red leadership contained many persons of Jewish origin, and Jews as a group had been supporters of the new regime. On the other hand, much of the policy of the Communists was bound to work against the Jews. First of all, the new regime took a stongly antireligious stand. Jewish religious activities were met by a barrage of obstacles and antireligious propaganda. Secondly, the regime could tolerate no rivals for power; it therefore forbade Zionism, the Bund, and all independent Jewish communal life. Finally, the Communists abolished private businesses and limited the civil rights of former business owners. A disproportionate number of Jews were affected by these measures.

Although the Communist regime had no room for businessmen, Zionism, or independent communities, it did have room, at least in theory, for minority national cultures. It claimed that communism would reverse czarist discrimination against non-Russian cultures and grant each nationality its own language, culture, and even its own provinces. After some debate, it was decided to recognize the Jews as a national group, even though they lacked their own territory. The Hebrew language was virtually forbidden, since it was associated with religion and Zionism, but Yiddish was permitted and even cultivated. It was to be used in theaters, schools, and even courts of law. Of course, by Soviet definition, all national cultures in the Soviet Union were to be "Socialist in content, national in form." This meant that the only thing it could express was Communist ideology, although it could use Yiddish or Jewish holidays to do so. The Jewish section of the Communist party (Yevsektsia) worked both to build up a "proletarian Jewish" culture and to destroy the forces of religion, Zionism, and "bourgeois nationalism" among the Jews. Non-Communist forms of Judaism were driven underground.

With the growth of Stalin's power in the late 1920s and early 1930s, even the legal Yiddish culture began to arouse suspicion. The Yevsektsia was abolished, in part because the government thought it was hampering assimilation by a too-strong defense of Jewish culture. The anomalous position of the Jewish nationality without a land led Stalin in 1928 to create the Jewish autonomous region of Birobidzhan, deep in Soviet Asia. The expected Jewish migration to this "Jewish" area did not materialize. Rather, there was a steady stream of Jewish population from the former Pale to big cities like Moscow and Leningrad. Meanwhile, Stalin began to purge and kill all his rivals for power. Many of the most prominent victims, including Trotsky, Kamenev, and Zinoviev, were Jews. The Jewish element in the Soviet leadership was radically reduced. Stalin also began to close many of the Jewish cultural and educational institutions. He became more and more distrustful of the Jews. (This was manifested openly during the period of liquidation of Jewish culture from 1948 to 1953.)

The situation in non-Soviet eastern Europe was very different, but hardly better. The treaties that ended World War I created a number of newly independent nations on territory formerly belonging to Austro-Hungary and czarist Russia. The new nations included Poland, Czechoslovakia, Yugoslavia, Lithuania, Latvia, and Estonia; the boundaries of the existing Austria, Hungary, and Rumania were adjusted to follow nationality divisions. All these nations, created on the basis of national self-determination, were to be democratically ruled and were treaty-bound to respect the cultural and political rights of minorities, including the Jews. Each of the new nations, however, having finally achieved national independence, wished to dominate the minorities. Slogans like "Poland for the Poles" became widespread, and every effort was made to evade the guarantees to the minorities.

Poland, with approximately three million Jews, was the best example of the way the new nations (except for Czechoslovakia) treated the Jews.[3] In contrast to Russia, Jewish communal life was left relatively free, but great economic and political pressure was put on the Jews. The Poles found it intolerable that the majority of merchants in Poland were Jews, and to change the situation they implemented tax policies and created monopolies which excluded Jews. Poland and most other countries in the area soon turned from democracy to dictatorship. Although the dictatorship of Marshall Pilsudski (1926-1935) treated the Jews better than most other Polish governments, his successors accentuated the anti-Jewish line. Right-wing parties like the Endeks (National Democrats), with much support from students and others, agitated against the Jews with calls for boycotts and violence. There were a number of pogroms in the 1930s, and in 1937 Polish universities bowed to student pressure and instituted segregated seating for Jewish students. Meanwhile, the economic situation of Polish Jews worsened; as many as one in three Polish Jews received their Passover *matzot* (unleavened bread eaten during the Passover holiday) from relief. Many depended on money from relatives in America.

Despite the ceaseless outside pressure, the Jews of non-Soviet eastern Europe developed a flourishing cultural life. The Jewish community was ruled by boards chosen democratically in elections, in which the ideological parties—from the Orthodox to the Zionists and Bund—ran candidates. Despite their deep divisions on principles, they were usually able to work together. A ramified system of modern Jewish schools was created in Poland and other countries. Besides government schools that closed on Saturday *(Szabatowka)*, there were the Hebrew *Tarbut*, the Yiddish *Cyszo*, and the Orthodox *Horeb* and Beth Jacob schools. Yiddish theater, newspapers, and magazines flourished; there was even a Yiddish institute for advanced research (YIVO). Although a considerable portion of the Jewish population remained traditional in dress, religion, and habits, modern Jewish institutions grew as never before and tackled problems (modern health care, school texts, etc.) that had never been faced before.

On the eve of World War II, eastern European Jews were already in the midst of a deep crisis. In the Soviet Union, Jewish cultural life was slowly being eliminated. Elsewhere in eastern Europe, there was a bustling, thriving Jewish cultural life, but the community faced economic disaster and physical threats. Yet, no one could have imagined that within a few years eastern European Jewish culture and communities would be virtually wiped out.

Although little remains of eastern European Jewry in its original location, its impact on Jews throughout the world continues to be immense. Most of the world's Jews are of eastern European background. Our ideas (especially in America) of what are typically Jewish foods, music, dress, and attitudes refer mainly to eastern European Jewish traits. Many of the ideological movements and religious trends still active in modern Jewry (Hasidism, Zionism, concern for social justice) owe much to their eastern European origins. The face of Jewish life would be hard to imagine without the imprint of the now destroyed communities that lived for a thousand years in the cold and often inhospitable climate of eastern Europe.

### Notes

1.   *Ashkenaz* was the medieval Hebrew name for Germany.
2.   Zionism, as a movement committed to the return of Jews to their ancient homeland, already existed in rudimentary form before Herzl formulated it as a political movement in 1896.
3.   The Jewish population in the various eastern European countries around 1930 was: Poland, 3,114,000; Czechoslovakia, 357,000; Hungary, 445,000; Yugoslavia, 68,000; Rumania, 757,000; Bulgaria, 48,000; Lithuania, 154,000; Latvia, 93,000; Estonia, 4,000; and the Soviet Union, 2,672,000.

### For Further Reading

Baron, Salo W. *The Russian Jew under Tzars and Soviets*. New York: Macmillan Co., 1976.

Dawidowicz, Lucy S., ed. *The Goldern Tradition: Jewish Life and Thought in Eastern Europe*. New York: Holt, Rinehart, and Winston, 1967.

Howe, Irving, and Greenberg, Eliezer, eds. *Voices from the Yiddish: Essays, Memoirs & Diaries*. New York: Schocken Books, 1975. (See especially Abraham Ain, "Swislocz, Portrait of a Shtetl," pp. 87-108.)

Roskies, Diane K., and Roskies, David G. *The Shtetl Book: An Introduction to East European Jewish Life and Lore*. New York: Ktav, 1975.

Singer, Isaac Bashevis. *In My Father's Court*. New York: Farrar, Straus & Giroux, 1966.

Weinryb, Bernard D. *The Jews of Poland: A Social and Economic History of the Jewish Community in Poland from 1100 to 1800*. Philadelphia: The Jewish Publication Society, 1973.

# Western European Jews Before World War II

## STEVEN M. LOWENSTEIN

Jewish settlement in western Europe dates back about two thousand years to the time of the Roman Empire. The Romans conquered all the lands surrounding the Mediterranean Sea, including Judea (Israel), and Jews soon spread to almost all parts of the empire. A substantial number of Jews settled in the city of Rome and in other parts of western Europe bordering on the Mediterranean, but some settled even further north in areas which would later be part of France and Germany. Although there were occasional persecutions, the Romans generally recognized the Jewish religion as legal and exempted the Jews from worshipping the emperor. Judaism made many converts, and a large proportion of the Roman population (one estimate is as high as 10 percent) was Jewish.[1]

Tremendous changes took place in western Europe in the fourth and fifth centuries because of two new factors—the conversion of the majority of the Roman population to Christianity and the invasion of Rome by barbarian tribes from the north. The invasions and fall of Rome seem to have put an end to Jewish settlement in northern Europe. The Christianization of Rome changed the position of the Jews tremendously. Judaism and Christianity were not only closely related, but they had become bitter rivals with diametrically opposed interpretations of their shared traditions. The new Christian rulers of the states that succeeded Rome usually allowed Jews (unlike pagans) to continue to live in their states, but they often imposed various restrictions and humiliations on them as punishment for their rejection of Christianity. Soon the Jews became virtually the only non-Catholic group in western Europe, a position which became increasingly dangerous.

The Jews in both the Roman and post-Roman (Middle Ages) era were recognized both as a separate religious group and as a separate nationality. They were granted a considerable amount of internal self-government in most of the places where they were permitted to live. The medieval social system, which granted different legal status to different social groups (nobles, merchants, craftsmen, peasants), was especially suited to giving the Jews a separate status, in which they were both treated as unequal to the other groups and granted the right to rule their own affairs.

In the course of the early Middle Ages, Jews from the Mediterranean area reestablished communities in northern France. From there (and also from Italy), Jews settled in England and in Germany. The settlement in Germany, which was quite small and insignificant when it was founded in the tenth century, became the ancestor of the Ashkenazic (of German descent) Jewish group (the name *Ashkenaz* comes from the medieval Jewish name for Germany). Ashkenazic Jews became the majority of the world's Jews by the seventeenth century and have remained so ever since.

In contrast to the Jews in Asia, North Africa, and Spain (which were conquered by the Moslems), who had broad intellectual interests (philosophy, poetry, Bible, Jewish law), the Jews of northern Europe concentrated almost exclusively on Jewish texts (especially the Talmud, the major work of rabbinic law and lore compiled between the third and fifth centuries C.E.*). Ashkenazic Jews in the Middle Ages developed an especially intense religious culture for which many were willing even to sacrifice their lives. Unlike Jews in the Moslem countries, who followed a broad range of occupations, almost all the Jews in northern Europe were merchants. As the non-Jewish merchant class grew and as legal restrictions against Jewish economic activity increased, northern European Jews were pushed more and more exclusively into moneylending as an occupation. In some places this was virtually the only occupation that Jews were legally permitted to follow.[2] It was not an occupation that made their popularity or physical safety any greater.

The position of Jews in northern Europe worsened between the eleventh and fifteenth centuries. Beginning with the First Crusade (1096), the Jews of northern Europe were subject to recurring massacres and religious persecutions. Various new accusations were made against the Jews in the thirteenth and fourteenth centuries, including charges of ritual murder, of desecration of the host (communion wafer), and of causing the bubonic plague by poisoning the wells. Hundreds of Jewish communities were massacred. The survivors were subject to growing government restrictions in occupation, to laws ordering them to wear special badges and live separately from Christians, and to special heavy taxation. Beginning in the late thirteenth century, Jews were expelled from one country after another (England—1290, France—1306, Spain—1492). Because Germany was not a united country, the Jews were not expelled from all sections of it. Nevertheless, many Jews left Germany for eastern Europe. After the sixteenth century, the center of world Jewry shifted to the East.

The relatively small numbers of Jews who still lived in western Europe after the sixteenth century suffered under a host of legal restrictions. Germany and Italy (neither of them united politically) were virtually the only places that still had Jewish communities. Although massacres were relatively uncommon after the fifteenth century, the position of the Jews was unenviable. Although Italian Jews did participate in some common cultural activities with their Christian neighbors during the Renaissance, they were restricted in many ways and, from the sixteenth century on, were strictly segregated in walled ghettos. The German Jews (perhaps 200,000 in number in the eighteenth century) were expelled from many of the major cities in the late Middle Ages and thereafter lived in small towns and villages, where they earned precarious livings as peddlers or agricultural middlemen. Although laws concerning Jews differed

* Common Era; equals A.D.

in various parts of German-speaking Europe, most states agreed to treat the Jews as outsiders whose permission to settle was a revocable privilege. Most Jews had to pay for their residence permits and often were not allowed to pass these permits on to their children. They were subject to special taxes, limited in their occupations, and they had little social contact or intellectual relations with the non-Jewish population. A considerable proportion of the German Jewish population consisted of beggars and wanderers who could not secure residence permits.

Despite the many restrictions, German Jews were permitted religious freedom in most places where they were allowed to settle, and the Jewish community had considerable power in regulating internal Jewish affairs. Most Jewish individuals had little to do with the government, since taxation, most judicial affairs, commercial regulations, and religious life were all controlled by the Jewish community. The community also cared for the Jewish poor. Although Yiddish-speaking Jews and German-speaking Christians could understand each other's language and did business with each other, they differed widely in manners, dress, occupations, and type of education. The overwhelming proportion of Jews was religiously traditional; their educational system still relied almost exclusively on Jewish religious texts and left very little room for secular knowledge.

In the course of the seventeenth and early eighteenth centuries, the trend of migration to the East began to reverse itself. Jewish communities were established (or reestablished) in England, the Netherlands, and parts of France. The Jewish settlement in the Netherlands, developing with fewer governmental restrictions than elsewhere, manifested traits that later would herald a major change in Jewish life in western Europe. Dutch Jewry, like the other new settlements, was made up of two population elements: Marannos, fleeing Spain and Portugal; and Ashkenazic Jews from Germany and Poland. The Marannos, who had masqueraded as Christians for generations,[3] were among the first Jews to know Christian culture, dress like non-Jews, speak and read their languages, and have far closer cultural ties with them than were found among Ashkenazic Jews. The influence of these Spanish and Portuguese Jews affected the Ashkenazim as well, although to a lesser extent.

A more widespread change in western European Jewry did not take place until after the attitude of European leaders towards the Jews began to change. First, the economic doctrine of mercantilism, in which the primary duty of governments was said to be the amassing of money, induced even some anti-Jewish rulers to favor those wealthy Jews who were economically useful to the state. Sometimes, the same ruler would favor wealthy Jews while expelling or restricting poor and "economically useless" ones. Slowly, in the course of the seventeenth and eighteenth centuries a small class of wealthy "Court Jews" grew up, some of whom began to adopt the lifestyle of Christian society. A second factor which became important by the middle of the eighteenth century was the philosophy of the Enlightenment, which spread through the educated classes of Europe. This worldview downgraded the role of the Church and of traditional Christian doctrines and proclaimed the idea that all human beings were created equal and had natural rights that no one could take from them. Although not all Enlightenment thinkers were favorable to the Jews, the doctrines themselves helped to undermine the legitimacy of treating one group as inferior to another. In Germany, the Enlightenment even affected some of the Jewish elite,[4] especially in Berlin. One Jewish philosopher, Moses Mendelssohn, even achieved recognition among German intellectuals as a leading Enlightened thinker, although he remained a practicing Jew.

A third factor leading to new policies towards the Jews was the general transformation in the European state, which began in the eighteenth century and carried over into the nineteenth. The old society, made up of different legal classes, each with their own different legal status, was being replaced by a society of national citizens with equal rights and duties. This new way of organizing society was desired by governments not so much because they believed in the Enlightenment principles of equality, but because it was more efficient to have one set of rules rather than a crazy-quilt of different regulations for each province, religion, and social group. Impetus for moving towards a more uniform state came both from rulers and bureaucrats in central European monarchies, like Prussia and Austria ("Enlightened Despotisms"), and from the revolutionaries in France, who overthrew the old regime and began a thorough change of all French institutions from 1789 on.

The French Revolution had an especially great impact, because revolutionary France began territorial expansion in a series of wars that lasted over twenty years. Under Napoleon, French troops dominated almost all of continental Europe and had great influence on policies well beyond the borders of France.

Although the French Revolution at first hesitated giving Emancipation (legal equality) to the unassimilated Ashkenazic Jews in the eastern French province of Alsace, it finally granted full rights to all Jews in 1791. In granting equality, one parliamentary leader stated that France would grant "to the Jews as individuals everything, to the Jews as a nation nothing."[5] Equality, thus, had two sides to it. Jews would be admitted into the French nation, but in return they were to give up the corporate status they had previously had. In exchange for the right to live where they wished, engage in all occupations, and hold government positions, the Jews were expected to cease being a separate group. Jewish communal courts were abolished; Jews were required to attend government schools, serve in the army, and identify with the nation in which they held citizenship. The old government policies of keeping the Jews separate were completely reversed. Now the governments hoped that all social and economic differences between Jews and Christians would disappear and that Jews would no longer feel national solidarity with Jews in other countries.

The emancipating governments were expecting a total transformation in Jewish life. They thought that eliminating the restrictions on Jews would make it possible for Jews to become like everyone else (except for religion) with little difficulty. In fact, the changes in occupation, education, and national identification, which would be required for the Jews to become so well integrated, were much more complex than the governments realized. For many Jews of the first generation after the Emancipation, the changing of government expectations must have been confusing. Often the governments were troubled at the slowness of the social transformation of the Jews and tried to intervene to speed up the changes. In 1806, Napoleon called an assembly of Jewish leaders and demanded to know if there was something in the Jewish religion which stood in the way of integration. Among other things, he asked whether Judaism permitted intermarriage, whether Jews considered France their homeland, and whether they considered French Christians to be their brothers. Although the Jews gave Napoleon the answers he desired, he nevertheless suspended some of their rights for a period of ten years. Despite Napoleon's ambiguous attitude, the French armies brought increased rights for the Jews in most of the countries they conquered. After Napoleon's defeat in 1815, some of the German states revoked some of the rights they had granted. In some cases they made rights conditional on changes in the Jewish social structure. They hoped (unrealistically) to produce a wholesale transformation of Jewish peddlers and middlemen into farmers and craftsmen. Those who did not change their occupations were subject to a host of restrictions. The final restrictions on Jews in Germany were lifted in 1871, when they finally achieved full legal equality.

Although the transformation of Jewish life in western and central Europe was neither as fast as the governments had expected nor of the type they wished, it was nevertheless quite thorough. Not only did Jewish political status change, but there were also important changes in Jewish economic life and in the very intellectual and religious definitions of what it meant to be a Jew. Exposure to secular culture in the schools that Jewish children now had to attend led to a new attitude towards traditional Jewish culture. Jews were quick to adjust to the new schools, and by the second half of the nineteenth century they were disproportionately represented in higher education. Jews began to participate in and contribute to the general culture as writers, musicians, and scholars. Often there was little specifically Jewish about their work. Many Jews wished to drop all features of traditional Jewish life that stood in the way of their integration into the larger society. Whereas Judaism had previously combined national and religious elements in an inseparable mixture, it now seemed necessary to many western European Jews to separate the two, eliminating the national Jewish and retaining only the purely religious. Even many Jewish religious practices, such as the dietary laws and the observance of the Sabbath, which seemed to many to stand in the way of social mixing or of economic advancement, were dropped by some Jews. Previously unknown religious problems, such as observing Jewish dietary laws in the army and compulsory school attendance on Saturday, troubled even the traditionalists.

For many of the educated and well-to-do, the traditional synagogue seemed too foreign and too old-fashioned to be of any value. Some Jewish leaders, especially in Germany, felt that the only way to prevent these people from being totally lost to the Jewish community was to make changes in Jewish liturgy and ritual. By introducing prayer in the vernacular and insisting on Western-style decorum and organ music, these Reformers hoped to make the synagogue more palatable to Westernized Jews and to their non-Jewish neighbors. By removing references in the liturgy to a return to the Promised Land and a restoration of the Temple in Jerusalem, they hoped to eliminate Jewish nationalism, which could conflict with hard-won citizenship rights. Whereas the early Reformers were more interested in specific changes than in an overall rationale for them, the university-trained Reform rabbis, who became prominent in the 1840s and thereafter, endeavored to create a Reform theology. Reform leaders, such as Abraham Geiger, argued that Judaism was a religion which had undergone historical evolution and would continue to do so. They argued that Judaism had progressed since the time of the original revelation and that some biblical and rabbinic laws relating to ritual had become outmoded. In creating their theory, many Reform leaders relied heavily on new methods of studying Jewish sources based on modern university research methods (Science of Judaism). Most Reformers in the nineteenth century argued that Judaism was purely a religious doctrine (ethical monotheism) and that its national elements were a thing of the past.

Not all German Jews accepted the arguments of the Reformers. The Orthodox theorist Samson Raphael Hirsch argued that the Torah (the Law) was eternal and divine and could be changed neither by human will nor by the "Spirit of the Times." Even Hirsch's followers, however, accepted the Emancipation and felt that Jews should participate in the life of the general society around them, providing they observed all the laws of the Torah. Although the Orthodox continued to have followers, Reform Judaism (in a fairly mild form) gained the adherence of the majority of German Jews by the 1870s. In most other western European countries there was no strong Reform movement, but there was still a decline in traditional religious observance. Although the synagogues in France and England remained rather traditional, there was a decrease in attendance.

Reform Judaism and the decline in traditional observance could be seen as direct consequences of the new Jewish education and the attempt by many Jews to fit into a society that now seemed to accept them. Economic changes, which were equally striking, were the result of a combination of the opportunities given by the Emancipation and those that came from the Industrial Revolution, which swept through western Europe in the mid-nineteenth century. The governments' hopes of Jews becoming farmers and craftsmen were frustrated, because industrial and commercial development provided greater opportunities for business pursuits in which Jews had traditionally been involved. Within commerce, the economic position of Jews improved substantially. By the late nineteenth century, Jewish beggars had virtually disappeared from western and central Europe; Jewish peddlers mostly had become shopkeepers or wholesalers, and many had built substantial businesses. Some, especially the children of those who had been successful in business, went into the professions, especially medicine and law. Western and central European Jews had become overwhelmingly middle class. These changes helped create a tremendous chasm between the Jews of western Europe (who constituted less than 1 percent of the population there) and those of eastern Europe (who were closer to 10 percent). Whereas the Emancipation and industrialization created Jewish communities in the West which were culturally integrated, often nontraditional in religious practice, and economically prosperous, eastern European Jews remained culturally self-sufficient and isolated, religiously traditional, and overwhelmingly poor.

Although western and central European Jews were very different by the 1870s from what they had been three generations earlier, they had not disappeared as a recognizable social group, nor had their organized communal life disintegrated. Most Jews still married other Jews, lived in neighborhoods near other Jews, had many Jewish friends, and supported Jewish charities; they still tended to concentrate in certain occupations (although not necessarily the same as those they had followed earlier). Often, because conservatives and supporters of Church control had opposed equality for the Jews, the Jews tended to support liberal causes. Nevertheless, it was clear that the Emancipation and social change had not eliminated Jews as a recognizable entity. Because the Jews now participated much more fully in the economic, political, and cultural life of the nations in which they lived, they now appeared more conspicuous and (in the eyes of those who distrusted them) more powerful than they had been before the Emancipation. When a period of economic slump followed the boom of the 1850s and 1860s, organized anti-Jewish feeling began to reemerge, arguing that the Emancipation had been a mistake, since it made the Jews stronger and more dangerous but had failed to cause them to merge and disappear into society as a whole.

The anti-Jewish forces were of two main types. The milder (and larger) of the two trends was Christian antisemitism. Followers of this trend wished to return society to its older Christian roots, in which each class knew its place and the rich helped the poor. They blamed capitalism and the secularized state (which they identified with the Jews) for eliminating all values except money. They saw the Jews as foreign to their Christian society and as a group which stuck together in order to dominate. This anti-Jewish feeling was directed not only against those unassimilated Jews who remained recognizably Jewish, but also against those who tried to fit in. This latter group, it was argued, was merely trying to penetrate European society in order to undermine it. Christian antisemites usually called for various types of restrictions to limit the political influence and economic activities of the Jews.

The second group was far more extreme. It claimed that Jews had not integrated (and could never do so) because they were racially different. The term "antisemite" was coined to show that the objection was not to the Jewish religion (since they wished to avoid being considered religious bigots) but to the morally inferior semitic race. Relying on pseudoscientific racist, anthropological, and linguistic ideas, they created complex theories showing the eternal opposition between the semitic and Aryan (a vague racist term which could mean blond northern European or be a mere codeword for non-Jewish) races. Some of the extreme racial antisemites even opposed Christianity because of its Jewish origin.

The new antisemitic movement spread in a number of countries, especially Germany, France, and Austria. Although it did not succeed in limiting the rights of the Jews, it did spread anti-Jewish ideas in the press, the universities, and in many political groups. Antisemitism became respectable in "patriotic" and conservative circles in all three countries. In France, the Dreyfus affair (1894-1906), in which a Jewish army officer was accused of spying on behalf of Germany, divided the country and led to intense anti-Jewish agitation. In some countries, even the medieval accusations of ritual murder were revived.

Jews reacted to antisemitic attacks in two main ways. The majority of western European Jews felt that Jews should defend their legal rights as citizens and should disprove the charges made against them through pamphlets and other types of literature. They resented accusations that they were not full-fledged and fully integrated Germans (or Frenchmen, etc.). Some Jews disagreed with this approach. The revival of antisemitism convinced them that Jews would never be accepted in the countries where they lived no matter how hard they tried to fit in. In their view, this was because the Jews were a nationality in exile from their homeland. They could never live a normal life in exile and would only be accepted when they again became an independent nation. This idea was promulgated by Theodor Herzl in his epoch-making book *The Jewish State* in 1896; the book helped lay the groundwork for the Zionist movement. Most of the western European Zionists were acculturated Jews who had once hoped for acceptance and now despaired of its achievement. They felt that the Emancipation had been based on false hopes and that assimilation was a mistake. Zionists called on Jews to look to their own culture and their own people rather than try to enter cultures in which they were not wanted. Zionism, in a way, represented the opposite of classical Reform Judaism. Whereas the Reformers wished to see Judaism as pure religion with no nationalist elements, the Zionists saw Judaism as primarily national. Although the Zionists remained a minority of western European Jewry (and were resented by many Jews as undermining the hard-won Emancipation), they slowly gained strength as antisemitism continued and Jewish settlement in Israel grew.

The nineteenth and early twentieth centuries were marked by

great migratory waves affecting western European Jews. From about 1820 through the 1860s there was a wave of emigration, especially from Germany to the United States. Within each country there was a continuous migration of Jews from the small towns to the cities. Around 1815, less than 2 percent of the Jews of Germany lived in Berlin; by 1925 over 30 percent of German Jews lived there. By the twentieth century most western and central European Jews were residents of the big cities, where they played an important and conspicuous role in economic, social, artistic, and cultural life.

Another wave of migration, which became especially important after 1880, brought increasing numbers of eastern European Jews to the cities of Germany, France, Holland, and England. In France and England, the new immigrants eventually outnumbered the older community, while in Germany their numbers finally reached about 25 percent of the total Jewish population. The new immigrants brought a more conspicuous Jewish life and more outspoken political views than were prevalent among the older residents. Often the "natives," who had a purely religious view of Judaism, were embarrassed about the Yiddish-speaking, Orthodox, or Socialist newcomers and feared that their presence would undermine the position of all Jews in the country.

World War I and the upheavals that followed it created an even more threatening political situation for western European Jews than had existed previously. Economic difficulties, frustrated nationalism, fear of communism, and dissatisfaction with democracy characterized the political attitude of many, especially young people. Often they turned to Fascist movements, some of which were blatantly antisemitic. In Germany, the Nazis were able to come to power by legal means, because the population had little respect for a democratic government that seemed to bring only economic disaster. In many countries the wave of hostility seemed to be mounting dangerously.

On the eve of the Holocaust, Jews represented only a small proportion of the population of western and central Europe. The largest community, Germany, had fewer than 600,000 Jews. France and Austria each had about 200,000. Other Jewish communities were even smaller (Netherlands—115,000, Belgium—50,000, Italy—45,000). Despite their relatively small numbers and their relative conspicuousness, many of these communities were the objects of intense hostility.

The Jews of western and central Europe were the first to face the challenge of modernity. It was in those countries (and especially in Germany), that Jews tried to find intellectual answers to the dilemma of participating in general society while retaining some kind of Jewish identity. Western European Jews experienced tremendous economic and cultural changes, which helped make them some of the most prosperous and culturally integrated Jews in the world. The cultural contribution of persons of Jewish origin in western and central Europe is immense. One need only mention the names of Albert Einstein, Sigmund Freud, Franz Kafka, or Heinrich Heine to demonstrate this fact. In most cases, there was little specifically Jewish about these men beyond their ancestry. Yet, despite the seeming integration and adjustment of western European Jews to their environment, they were not accepted. The disaster which would destroy much of European Jewry began not in eastern Europe, where Jews remained clearly and openly distinct, but in Germany, where Jewishness was rarely shown publicly. The tragedy of western European Jews was that they attempted to make the adjustments to European life that the Emancipation seemed to demand, but their very success in living within European society intensified hostility to such an extent that it led ultimately to their destruction.

### Notes

1.    Salo W. Baron, *A Social and Religious History of the Jews*, vol. 1 (New York: Columbia University Press, 1952), pp. 170-171: "Every tenth Roman was a Jew." Baron estimates that four million Jews lived in the Roman Empire outside of Palestine and that Jews made up 20 percent of the population in the eastern Mediterranean.

In contrast to more recent Jewish practice, Judaism was an actively proselytizing religion in Roman times. Several Latin writers refer to the conversion to Judaism of many Romans. At the time of the late Roman Empire, the decline in belief in the old Roman, Greek, and local gods, and the search for a spiritual way of life seemingly absent in the traditional religions, led many to turn to "Eastern" religions, including Judaism. Judaism made great inroads, but was eventually outstripped by Christianity, which did not require the observance of Jewish ritual (including circumcision) from its converts.

2.    The restriction of Jews to moneylending resulted in part, ironically, from the shared Jewish and Christian tradition that it was sinful to take interest from "your brother" but permissible to charge interest from "the stranger." Since Christians were forbidden by Church law to lend to other Christians on interest, the Jews became the natural source of potential credit. This fostered antisemitism in the following ways: 1) the Jews were accused of engaging in antisocial behavior by being in a business that was morally prohibited to Christians and 2) the high interest rates of the time gave rise to "normal" antipathy of those who owe to those who lend. Finally, the Jews also faced the problem of being coerced by local authorities to make high-risk loans. Often these went unpaid, and the Jews were expelled, empty-handed, from their homes.

3.    Since the expulsions of the Jews from Spain (1492) and Portugal (1497), the practice of Judaism had been illegal in those countries.

4.    Many wealthy Berlin Jews began to adopt the cultured lifestyle of bourgeois Christians, attending the theater and opera, going to coffeehouses, and giving up Jewish costume. They gave their children a secular education, often with a rationalist slant; some

also began to abandon Jewish religious practice.

5.   This statement by Clermont-Tonerre is quoted in numerous histories. One example is Raphael Mahler, *A History of Modern Jewry, 1780-1815* (New York: Schocken Books, 1971), p. 32, where it is translated: "Everything must be refused to the Jews as a nation; everything must be granted them as individuals."

### For Further Reading

Abrahams, Beth-Zion, ed. and trans. *Glückel of Hameln Written by Herself.* New York: Thomas Yoseloff, 1963.

Duker, Abraham G., and Ben-Horin, Meir, eds. *Emancipation and Counter-Emancipation.* New York: Ktav, 1974.

Hyman, Paula. *From Dreyfus to Vichy: The Remaking of French Jewry, 1906-1939.* New York: Columbia University Press, 1979.

Katz, Jacob. *Tradition and Crisis: Jewish Society at the End of the Middle Ages.* New York: The Free Press, 1961.

Marcus, Jacob R. *The Jew in the Medieval World: A Source Book, 315-1791.* Cincinnati: Union of American Hebrew Congregations, 1938.

Massing, Paul W. *Rehearsal for Destruction: A Study of Political Anti-Semitism in Imperial Germany.* New York: Harper & Brothers, 1949.

Mendes-Flohr, Paul R., and Reinharz, Jehuda. *The Jew in the Modern World: A Documentary History.* New York and Oxford: Oxford University Press, 1980.

Meyer, Michael A. *The Origin of the Modern Jew: Jewish Identity and European Culture in Germany, 1749-1824.* Detroit: Wayne State University Press, 1967.

Mosse, George L. *Germans & Jews.* New York: Grosset & Dunlap, 1970.

Pulzer, Peter. *The Rise of Political Anti-Semitism in Germany and Austria.* New York: Wiley, 1964.

Reichman, Eva G. *Hostages of Civilization.* Boston: Beacon Press, 1951.

Reinharz, Jehuda. *Fatherland or Promised Land?: The Dilemma of the German Jew, 1893-1914.* Ann Arbor: University of Michigan Press, 1975.

# The Life and Culture of Sephardic Jews Before World War II

## JANE GERBER

One of the main components of the Jewish people is the Sephardim, or Jews who trace their origin to medieval Spain. Living under Christian and Muslim overlords for over 1,000 years in Spain, the Jews of the Iberian Peninsula developed a unique culture, both secular and religious, and an articulated sense of a proud and brilliant history. Sephardic Jews in Spain, despite their many centuries of persecution, experienced periods of economic efflorescence and social integration, feeling quite at home in their Jewish culture as well as in the broader culture of the wider non-Jewish society. Open to philosophical concepts, receptive to Arab scientific and geographic discoveries, and enamored of the Hebrew language and its abilities to express lofty as well as mundane notions, Sephardic Jews developed an outlook and civilization unique in the annals of the Jewish people. This civilization was violently uprooted with the pogroms of 1391, the expulsion from Spain in 1492, and the expulsion from Portugal in 1497. Thousands of Spanish Jews sought refuge wherever possible, while smaller numbers chose to remain in Spain as clandestine Jews until escape was more propitious. But the doors of Europe were almost entirely shut to practicing Jews. Thus, the Jewish community of Spain was forced to flee to distant lands, bringing with them their cultural baggage and fierce nativist loyalties of a dispossessed people.

Sephardic Jews were warmly welcomed in the Ottoman Turkish Empire. Indeed, the Ottoman sultan is reported to have been incredulous that the king of Spain had ousted such a talented population element. From the 1490s, and in increasing numbers throughout the first quarter of the sixteenth century, boatload after boatload of Sephardic Jews arrived in the Ottoman Empire: Sephardim came to Rhodes after it was conquered by the Turks in 1523; the first documents attesting to a Jewish presence in Sarajevo date from 1565 and relate to Sephardic Jews; Sephardim quickly overwhelmed and dominated the old Ashkenazic and Romaniot (Greek-speaking) Jews of Bulgaria, so that the separate Jewish communities joined into a single Sephardic enclave in the sixteenth century. With the conquest of Belgrade by the Turks in 1521, older Jewish settlements in the city were revivified by Sephardic refugees. By far, the greatest concentration of Sephardic Jewish life and culture in Europe soon after the Spanish expulsion was in the city of Salonica in Greece (then part of Ottoman Turkish suzerainty).

For hundreds of years, Jewish culture in the Balkans emanated from the Sephardic cultural center of Salonica. On the eve of World War II, Salonica, with its 60,000 Jews, its printing presses and newspapers, its schools and scholars, its craftsmen and merchants, was the greatest Sephardic Jewish center in Europe. This premier place of Salonica had been established in the early sixteenth century, as waves of refugees settled there and dynasties of great rabbinic scholars and personalities issued legal decrees from its academies. While to the outside world these refugees were simply "Sephardim," internally they were divided by geographic origin, their synagogues bearing the names of Saragossa, Barcelona, Gerona, Gerush Portugal, Castille, Aragon, and a score of other Iberian place names. Each of the separate congregations boasted its own nexus of self-help institutions, such as alms chests, burial societies, sick care, and chests for orphans and widows. In addition, each congregation took pride in its academy of learning. Sixteenth-century Salonica was a center of learning of the Talmud that attracted students from abroad, its luminaries including such Jewish personalities as Solomon Alkabez and Samuel da Medina. It was also famed as a center of Jewish mysticism and provided instruction to Jews in medicine, natural sciences, liturgical poetry, and song. Although the city was weakened by successive plagues and conflagrations in the seventeenth century, its Jewish population still comprised half the population of the town throughout this period.

Salonican Jews were severely traumatized by the false messianic movement of Shabbetai Zevi in the seventeenth century, particularly as the impostor had preached in the city and had a strong personal following there. After Zevi's conversion to Islam and death, 300 Jewish families in the city converted to Islam, severely weakening the unity of the Salonican Jews. In general, the Jewish communities of the Ottoman Empire began to decline as the empire grew more anarchic.

The spread of European influence and consular protection of Jews in the Balkans ushered in a new era for Sephardic Jews. The nineteenth century witnessed many signs of Westernization among the Jews, the introduction of secular subjects in the newly founded schools of the French *Alliance Israelite Universelle,* and a quickening of Jewish political life, as Zionism captured the imagination of Sephardic Jews in Greece, Bulgaria, and Yugoslavia. So vital was the Jewish community to the economy of the city of Salonica that the whole town and its port were closed on the Sabbath at the beginning of the twentieth century. (It is interesting to note that fishermen, sailors, and stevedores of Salonica played a conspicuous role in the development of maritime life in Haifa and Tel Aviv in the 1920s and 1930s, encouraged to emigrate by Palestinian leaders Yitzhak Ben Zvi and Abba Khoushi.)

Sephardic Jews had not labored under the same restrictive economic system as their Ashkenazic coreligionists. While they distinguished themselves in commerce, utilizing their widely dispersed family connections to their commercial advantage, the Sephardim were an economically variegated community in Europe, equally distributed among rich and poor, modest blacksmiths and bankers or textile magnates. They were not housed in ghettos, but rather shared in the modernization and incipient industrialization of their states.

The cultural and communal life of Sephardic Jews, up until the eve of the Nazi onslaught, was richly textured and colorful. Despite differences among them, the Sephardim of the Balkan nations shared an underlying cultural unity. A lively Ladino and Hebrew press could be found in Sephardic lands, frequently tracing its origins back to the great Sephardic printing houses of Lisbon via Italy. Romances or ballads conveying vibrant, lyrical, and frequently courtly and sensual Iberian traditions could be heard at family and communal gatherings in Rhodes or Greece, Sarajevo or Sofia. Music and poetry were staples of community life.

Religious institutions and edifices were sources of pride in the Jewish communities. New and majestic synagogues dotted the communities, such as the great Sephardic synagogue built in Sarajevo in the late 1920s, and benevolent societies flourished. Zionist politics added lively debates to community discussions. The Sephardim of Sarajevo could even boast of a Jewish Workers' Union and a Jewish choir *(Lyra Sociedad de Cantar de los Judios-Espanoles)*. The great cemetery of Salonica's half-million graves was a living archeological treasurehouse of Jewish history in the area. This cemetery was desecrated and destroyed by the Nazis in the general pillaging of all the Jewish historical and cultural treasures of the city.

How does the historian measure the cultural and human loss when a community is wiped out? How does one comprehend the measure of destruction of communities that date their beginnings back to approximately 140 B.C.E.,* as was the case in Salonica? In the mosaic of Jewish communities, the dazzling jewels of the Sephardic Jews added a special luster to the whole. All that remains today are the oral traditions and ballads laboriously collected by anthropologists and folklorists among emigrés in Israel, Paris, and New York as literary testimony of the fidelity of Sephardic Jews to their Spanish heritage and Jewish patrimony.

* *Before the Common Era; equals* B.C.

**For Further Reading**

Angel, Marc D. *The Jews of Rhodes.* New York: Sepher-Hermon Press, 1978.

Benardete, Mair. *Hispanic Culture and Character of the Sephardic Jews.* New York: Sepher-Hermon Press, 1952, 1982.

Molho, Michael. *Usos y Costumbres de los Sefardies de Salonica.* Madrid: Conejo Superior de Investigaciones Scientificas, Instituto Arias Monto, 1950.

Rosanes, Solomon. *Korot ha-Yehudim be-Turkiyah ve-Artsot Ha-Kedem.* 6 vols. Tel Aviv: Sofia, 1930, 1948.

Tamir, Vicki. *Bulgaria and Her Jews: The History of a Dubious Symbiosis.* New York: Sepher-Hermon Press, 1979.

# And Under Every Roof They Would Sing

## DAVID G. ROSKIES

I cannot presume to speak for a civilization I know only secondhand through books and brief encounters. My time is discontinuous with theirs. Like the events recorded in the Scriptures—forever closed in the biblical canon, to be opened only with the rote repetition of the story as aided by the standard interpretive guides—I/we live outside the time scheme of 1939, minus all the years that came before, and most certainly outside 1939 and the six years that came after. Only through the study of its texts, or through attuning one's ears to its echoes, can the barrier of time be broken, revealing that part of ourselves which is lost forever.

A poet named Mani Leib anticipated our dilemma. He was from Nyezhin, the Ukraine, originally, but lived in New York most of his life. This is the sonnet he wrote sometime in his later years as he strained his fine-tuned ears for that echo.

There they were many, O God, so many
Such vital ones and unafraid,
Such noble ones, with beard and braid—
And talking in a marvelous strange way.

*Zey zenen dort, oy, Got, geven a sakh, a sakh,*
*Azelkhe lebedike un azelkhe brave,*
*Azelkhe shtaltne, berdike un kutsherave—*
*Un mit a vunderlekher oysterlisher shprakh.*

Their strength, they thought, lay in numbers. They always felt safer in towns and cities, crowded into the central business districts, in walking distance of each other. Village Jews, who lived among the peasants, came to town for the major festivals or during the periodic expulsions. Later, when the centers were no longer safe, when the towns were left empty on account of the trains, and poverty seeped through every crack of every home—such poverty that even statistics and the most compassionate reporting cannot begin to convey—when every Jew who could (and many peasants, too) sought every possible means of escape—to America, Palestine, the bigger cities, to the West, to social revolution—then, even then, the vast majority sought out groups of the like-minded, and these groups eventually grew into movements.

Once organized, there was no stopping them. Indeed, the Jewish Labor Bund of Russia and Poland was the first Socialist movement in eastern Europe with a real constituency. Zionists of every persuasion mobilized the scant financial resources and the vast reservoir of talent to make that impossible dream come true; there were those who fought for civil liberties and cultural autonomy on the spot, regardless of economic policy.

Every traveler from the West was struck by the sheer number of Jews that could be seen in the streets of the Eastern cities. Under closer inspection, the traveler might observe the vast network of inter-locking agencies that kept the Jews going even against incredible odds—the religious and educational network of synagogues; studyhouses; Hasidic *shtiblekh* (houses of prayer); adult study groups; private and community-supported elementary schools and *yeshivot* (talmudic acadmies), which later competed with secular Jewish schools where Yiddish, Hebrew, Russian, or Polish was the language of instruction; social and charitable services offering free loans, dowries for poor brides, hospitalization, visitation of the sick and burial; and the organization of Jewish trades into professional guilds that later evolved into effective unions. And if this traveler returned after World War I, he would also find Jewish libraries; theater groups; clubhouses; soccer teams; orchestras; and a dizzying array of political parties covering the entire spectrum—from the ultra-Orthodox Agudath Israel to communism.

Much of this activity was conducted in Yiddish, the language created by Ashkenazic Jews in their millennial history. Yiddish was, itself, a fusion of past and present, with a Hebrew-Aramaic base, and a repository of tradition, melding first with Germanic and then Slavic cultures. It was through Yiddish that Hebrew stayed alive, for Jewish vernaculars were always the vehicle for preserving and translating the classicial heritage; it was the proximity of Yiddish to German that helped the teachings of the Enlightenment spread in eastern Europe; and it was in Yiddish that a new and modern idiom evolved for the writing of fiction, poetry, and scholarship; manifestos, editorials, and cookbooks. Above all, it was the language of the folk.

> And under every roof they would sing—
> With Torah chant and Scripture cymbals—
> Such rare songs, proud and boastful:
> Of the golden peacock and Elimelekh the king.

> *Un zingen flegn zey fun unter yedn dakh*
> *Azelkhe hoferdike lider un tshikave:*
> *Fun meylekh Elimeylekh un der sheyner pave,*
> *Mit mayver-sedre-trop un tsimblen fun tanakh.*

The folk tradition was exceedingly rich, drawing freely and unselfconsciously from the Torah—not as the dead letter of the law, but as a living lesson, chanted each week and proclaimed anew each season; the Torah—as reinterpreted and revitalized by Hasidism, the greatest mass movement Judaism had produced in 1,700 years. With Torah as its foundation, there was nothing the folk could not assimilate: peasant proverbs and shepherds' tunes; marching songs and satires on the rabbis; expressions of erotic love and appreciations of nature. The modern poets, like Mani Leib, tried to forge a new language, using folksong as their source of inspiration, and hailed the Golden Peacock, *di goldene pave*, as the mascot of their trade. And all this flowed right back to the source, so that when Moyshe Nadir, who frequented the same writers' cafe on Second Avenue as Mani Leib, recast "Ol' King Cole" into the *"Rebbe Elimelekh,"* the folk accepted the song as authentic in every way! Between Hasidic ecstasy and mournful love laments, they sang of work ("This is how a tailor stitches, this is how he sews and sews, making other people's britches"); of play ("Have you seen my honey bears, honey bears, sitting up on wooden chairs?''); of childhood *("Afn pripetshik brent a fayerl");* of marriage ("I will dance with you, my dear, and you will dance with me. You can have the son-in-law, the daughter-in-law's for me!''); of protest ("Brothers and sisters, let's do it together. Let's bury Tsar Nicky along with his mother!"); and of warning ("Fire, brothers, fire! Our poor town is on fire!").

Modernity erupted in eastern Europe with explosive force, but the experience of modernity was channeled back into the popular culture, competing with and complementing the older forms of expression. Hasidim and marketwomen rubbed shoulders with pick-pockets and union organizers. Two women set out for Warsaw from the same town: one to get an abortion and the other to ask the Wonder Rabbi to bless her womb with male progeny. Anyone who has read a Yiddish family saga *(The Brothers Ashkenazi; The Family Moscat; Zelmenyaner)* remembers how radically the generation of the fathers was challenged by the sons. The grandchildren were already on their way back, to complete the cycle.

> But above their heads only the sun and its stare
> Saw the raw fury, the killer's cold blade,
> How with wild force it descended,
> And what massacres were there.
>
> Now they are but a trace of that fury:
> An axed forest, a couple of trees.

> *Nor iber zeyer kop—di zun hot nor gezen*
> *Di roye gvald, dem kaltn meser baym rotseyekh,*
> *Vi er iz iber zey arop, mit vildn koyekh,*
>
> *Un sara merderay iz dort geven!*
> *Itst zenen zey a zeykher nokh fun yener gvald:*
> *A tsvey-dray beymer fun an oysgehaktn vald.*

Those who were left were but a trace, not of the marvelous multitudes, but of the raw fury that descended upon them. There is no forest for lack of trees. So it is up to the rest of us to carry the echo and transform it back into song.

### For Further Reading

Dawidowicz, Lucy S. *The Golden Tradition: Jewish Life and Thought in Eastern Europe.* New York: Holt, Rinehart, and Winston, 1967.

Dobroszycki, Lucjan, and Kirshenblatt-Gimblett, Barbara. *Image Before My Eyes: A Photographic History of Jewish Life in Poland, 1864-1939.* New York: Schocken Books, 1977.

Howe, Irving, and Greenberg, Eliezer, eds. *A Treasury of Yiddish Stories.* New York: Schocken Books, 1973.

———. *A Treasury of Yiddish Poetry.* New York: Schocken Books, 1976.

Mlotek, Eleanor Gordon. *Mir trogn a gezang. The New Book of Yiddish Songs.* New York: The Workmen's Circle Education Department, 1977.

Roskies, Diane K., and Roskies, David G. *The Shtetl Book: An Introduction to East European Life and Lore.* New York: Ktav, 1979.

# Impressions of Religious Life of the Shtetl Before World War II

## ZALMAN F. URY

The following essay provides a succinct description of several aspects of religious life in eastern Europe, in the vanished world before the Second World War. I have limited the geographical areas to the *shtetlakh* (small towns) in Lithuania, Poland, and the ethnic White Russian provinces of northeastern Poland, which are representative of all eastern European Jews. The Jewish population of these provinces was approximately four million.

## The Family

Jewish family life in eastern Europe followed a traditional patriarchal structure. The home was seen as the woman's castle, and she was called *akeret habayit* (the lady of the house). The training of the young—boys and girls—was entrusted to the mother. Wives were respected and appreciated. Husbands followed traditional injunctions to "love their wives as themselves, honor them more than themselves, guide their sons and daughters in the ways of the upright, and marry off their daughters at an early age."[1] *Halakhah* (Jewish religious law), enforcing principles of modesty and sexual purity, restricted the role of women in the synagogue and in education, and denied them positions of religious and communal leadership.

The value of education was highly emphasized, even in lullabies. A popular Yiddish lullaby proclaimed: *"Toyre iz di beste skhoyre"* ("Torah [the Law] is the best commodity"). Daily observances of such *mitzvot* (religious commandments) as prayer and blessings were practiced at a young age. Some parents taught Hebrew reading to preschoolers so that they could pray from the *siddur* (prayer book). Children were also taught politeness, respect for elders, and responsibility. Learning and piety were highly valued.

Children were not pampered. They had to perform such daily chores as pumping and carrying water from the well, assisting with shopping, and supervising younger siblings. Toys were scarce; recreation and games were few. Children learned self-sufficiency and responsibility early in life.

For the family, the Sabbath (day of rest) was a blessed day. The father worked hard six days a week. He put in long hours whether he was a wagon-driver, shoemaker, tailor, blacksmith, watchmaker, or a small businessman. Unions, already active in the cities, were barely known in smaller *shtetlakh*. An eight-hour workday was not the norm. It was, therefore, natural that every member of the family looked forward to their only day of rest—*Shabes* (Yiddish for Sabbath). They longed for the physical rest, the special meals, the singing of *zemirot* (Sabbath songs) during each meal, and, of course, the sanctity of the Seventh Day.

Preparing for *Shabes* required planning and hard work. There were no canned, frozen, packaged, or convenience foods; every housewife had to bake the *hallah* (the traditionally braided white bread loaves) and cook the gefilte fish and the rest of the *Shabes* menu. Boys helped by shopping. Equipped with homemade shopping bags, they were dispatched to the general store to pick up flour, salt, sugar and spices, candles, and other required items. While one of the sons went to the grocery, another took a live chicken or two (depending on the family's income) to the *shohet* (ritual slaughterer). After plucking the feathers by hand, the mother would open the fowl and soak it in water and then salt it to draw out the blood (Jews are prohibited from consuming blood). Occasionally, a question would develop about whether the chicken was really *kosher* (ritually fit). If something about the fowl looked abnormal or unusual (a broken leg, a missing organ, or a needle inside of the chicken), one of the children would be summoned to take the chicken to the rabbi. The rabbi would examine the bird carefully and render his decision. When the rabbi pronounced *"kosher,"* the child would run home bringing the good news. If the verdict was unfavorable, the child would walk into the house with a sad face. The otherwise perfectly edible bird then had to be sold to a non-Jew for a fraction of its cost.

Preparing for *Shabes*—cleaning the house, getting washed (in the public bath house), and putting on one's best clothes—involved everyone. Some of the poorest families had dirt floors in their home. They prepared for the *Shabes* by sprinkling yellow sand on the floor to beautify the house. Older boys would help their father chop firewood. Often, especially in winter, the wood was wet and their mother had a hard time lighting a fire in the big Russian oven in which she cooked and baked. Girls would help cook, wash dishes, and do the laundry.

Just before lighting the Sabbath candles on Friday night, the mother would drop a few coins in the *pushke* (Yiddish for charity box) as she ushered in the Sabbath Queen (tradition has compared the Sabbath to a Queen). There was an expression of peace on her face. The children watched her with reverence. Standing by the table with her hands covering her eyes, she pronounced the blessing over the candles and whispered her private prayer. Mother wished her family *"gut Shabes"* (Yiddish for "good Sabbath"), and everybody joyously responded, *"gut Shabes!"* Often the older children thought that their mother was a *tsadeykes* (Yiddish for righteous woman); when she lit the *Shabes* candles, it would seem that the Divine Presence entered their home.

The father, dressed in his *Shabes* clothes, would go to *shul* (Yiddish for synagogue). The *shul* had also taken on a special appearance. The *davenen* (Yiddish for prayer) recited with the special *Shabes* chants was pleasant and relaxed. Almost every Friday night there were a number of itinerant beggars in the *shul.* The *shammash* (beadle) would assign them to families for the three *Shabes* meals. No matter how much food the family had prepared, no fellow Jew would be deprived of a *Shabes* meal.

During the Sabbath meals, the father often discussed with the children their studies during the week. The weekly chapter to be read in the *shul* was another regular topic for discussion.

During the *Shabes* day there was time for a *shpatsir* (Yiddish for a stroll) through the *shtetl* and the fields. Families visited relatives and friends and children played games. But, there was also some serious business. Schoolchildren faced the weekly *farher* (Yiddish for examination) by fathers and grandfathers in the presence of the child's *rebbe* (teacher). The boy who knew his subjects well would receive an approving *knip* (Yiddish for pinch) of the cheek, as well as candy and compliments.

After everyone had rested, the grandmother would read the *Tsenerene* (a Yiddish language anthology on the Torah) as the young gathered around her, enjoying the fascinating stories. This would add to the *Oneg Shabbat* (enjoyment of the Sabbath) of the reader and her predominantly female audience.

As the Sabbath drew to a close the following evening, when the stars were visible, grandmothers and mothers would recite the Yiddish folk prayer *Got fun Avrom. . . (God of Abraham, Isaac, and Jacob)*. Their subdued voices added to the sadness which descended on the house darkened by approaching night. The father returned from *shul* and recited the *Havdalah* (farewell to the Sabbath). Many people, particularly the Hasidim, wishing to delay the Sabbath Queen's departure, would gather for a *melavveh malka* (a Saturday night festive meal) to accompany her with song, storytelling, and cheerful comradeship.

Life in the *shtetl* on weekdays was often drab and monotonous. Religious parents did not allow their children to join secular youth groups. Religious youth organizations had not reached every *shtetl* and there was little opportunity for diversion and entertainment for either the young or adults. Children were busy. Long school days, homework, and household chores left little time for boredom. Besides the *Shabes*, family events (weddings, etc.) and holidays provided occasional excitement. Major holidays required weeks of preparation and generated anticipation and enthusiasm.

Even a minor holiday as Tu Bi-Shevat (Jewish Arbor Day) would stimulate the children. On a cold winter night, with snow blanketing everything, a knock at the door interrupted everyone's activity. Two boys, representing a Zionist youth group, brought a present from the Holy Land, a small bag filled with dry fruit. The father gave the boys a coin and thanked them. Once a year the family had a chance to eat fruit from *Erez Israel* (Land of Israel) and pronounce the special blessing of *She-Heḥeyanu* (traditionally recited when partaking of a new crop of fruit). Most intriguing were the carobs, hard fruits fit only for young teeth. Eating fruit from the Holy Land evoked nostalgia and yearning. It was a bittersweet experience. The family enjoyed the tangible evidence of the remote and inaccessible Promised Land, where they were unable to go.

Families produced law-abiding citizens. Juvenile deliquency was almost nonexistent. Drunkenness, murder, and rape were unheard of. The incidence of divorce, although legally permitted, was low. There were thieves, cheats, and quarrelsome people, but those individuals were a small minority.

Yiḥus (lineage) played a major role in community life. If a family was headed by a noted scholar, or had a grandfather who was a distinguished talmudist, it was a source of pride for the entire family. Such a family was respected and would receive lucrative marriage proposals. On the other hand, the people of the *shtetl* looked down on "ordinary" families (the tailors, shoemakers, wagon-drivers, etc.). The only way a son of a humble family could marry into a distinguished or wealthy family was if he enjoyed a reputation as a brilliant talmudic student. A daughter of a working class family could marry into a family with *yiḥus* or wealth if her father became rich and she had a good reputation. This class system must have imitated the caste and class structure of their Christian milieu, since in talmudic times, no shame was attached to menial work. Many sages of the Talmud were woodcutters, shoemakers, blacksmiths, and farm hands.

Families stayed together—even if husband and wife did not get along—because of the influence of the extended family. Most families lived in the same *shtetl* for generations with grandparents, aunts, uncles, cousins, and other relatives close by. A couple would receive solicited and unsolicited advice on many topics involving their marriage. The opinions of the extended family could not be easily ignored, for that might mean a loss of moral and financial support.

The mutual help available within the extended family was often substantial. For example, the extended family of a bride prepared weddings, including all cooking and baking. In times of illness or bereavement, the larger *mishpokhe* (Yiddish for family) provided counsel, comfort, and assistance.

## Schools

Historically, education has had a high priority in Jewish life. In keeping with the commandment "and you shall teach them [the words of Torah] diligently to your children,"[2] fathers were obligated to provide their sons instruction in Torah and Talmud. Mothers trained their daughters informally at home. Until recent times the schools were male-oriented. Girls did not attend religious schools. Many received a formal Jewish education from their parents or private teachers. Throughout history there were some notable women prophetesses, scholars, and leaders, but they were few in number.

This situation underwent a major change in the early twentieth century. Modernization, industrialization, and acculturation led to the loss of religious and family influence. The proliferation of newspapers, magazines, paperbacks, and radios contributed to the family's loss of influence. Although religious schools predominated in the provinces of Poland, Lithuania, and White Russia (excluding territory controlled by the Soviet Union after 1917), secular and antireligious movements and schools began challenging the traditional family. Formal religious education offered some protection against secular or demoralizing influences on boys, but the girls were not prepared to cope with new conditions. At the same time, the state required compulsory education, which exposed sheltered young girls to the alien environment of a non-Jewish public school. Thus, when an enterprising and inspiring educator, Sara Schenirer, organized in 1917 the first Beth Jacob school for girls in Cracow, the leading rabbis of that time approved and encouraged the establishment of such gender-segregated schools.[3] The Beth Jacob schools were an answer to this new situation. Jewish girls from observant homes were now provided with an intensely traditional and religious environment where they could study Jewish and secular subjects.

The changes wrought by increasing urbanization and subsequent modernization also affected boys' schools. Prior to World War I, when the provinces of Poland, Lithuania, and White Russia were ruled by the czarist empire, the old-style *ḥeder* prevailed. In this elementary school, no formal secular studies were offered. Competing modern schools were organized by *maskilim* (secular, "enlightened" Jews) with the encouragement of the authorities, but they were not accepted by the majority of the rural Jewish populace. Compulsory public school attendance after World War I and the growth of Socialist and Zionist secular Jewish schools, providing a general secular education, led to the decline of the *ḥeder*. The Orthodox community responded by establishing modern day schools, where intensive Torah studies were pursued alongside general studies.[4] These new elementary day schools, named *Ḥorev*, became the largest Jewish school system. The language of instruction was Yiddish and the emphasis was on Talmud. Teachers were trained at newly opened pedagogical institutions in Grodno and Warsaw. Simultaneously, *yeshivot* (talmudic academies) on a high-school and college level continued with Torah studies without a secular curriculum.[5]

The elementary schools were under the auspices of the World Agudath Israel Organization (non-Zionist Orthodox). The Mizrachi (the religious Zionist organization) opened a network of elementary and secondary day schools called *Yavneh*. In some cities, the lower grades, one through four, were coeducational, but were segregated after the fifth grade. In many schools, the language of instruction was Hebrew, even for arithmetic and science. These schools stressed the importance of living in *Erez Israel*. Bible and Talmud were studied, although Talmud study was generally less intensive than in the *Ḥorev* schools. The *Yavneh* network included a teacher-training seminar and developed into a large educational system.[6]

These developments occurred in the ethnic Polish-White Russian-Lithuanian areas. In Lithuania, which became a sovereign nation after World War I, the battle between Jewish secularists and religious Orthodox was similar to that in Poland, albeit with less ideological strife. The *Yavneh* schools were sponsored by all the Orthodox movements, although some independent Agudath Israel type schools were established in Telz and Kelm (Kelme). For a short period, the Jews of Lithuania had a large measure of autonomy and operated their own educational system. Only 10 percent of Jewish children attended public schools; the remaining 90 percent remained in elementary and secondary Jewish schools. The quality of education was very high.

# The *Yeshivah*

Technically, a *yeshivah* is a talmudic academy, a school of higher learning. A *yeshivah* is not, however, a professional school for the training of rabbis or other religious functionaries (although anyone who wishes to be a rabbi must study in a *yeshivah*). A *yeshivah* does not have graduation ceremonies, for one never completes studying Torah. There are no written examinations, although informal and indirect oral questions are used. There are no required courses, term papers, or dissertations. The Lithuanian and Polish *yeshivot* had neither formal registration nor tuition fees. Most students were poor, and the *yeshivah* provided them with study stipends.[7]

The scope, intricacy, and complicated language rendered the study of Talmud a formidable undertaking, requiring a master and the dialectics of associates. Without a *yeshivah*, headed by a venerable *rosh yeshivah* (dean), it would have been impossible to transmit the essence of Judaism's teachings from generation to generation.

*Yeshivot* existed in the communities of the Diaspora for many centuries. Whether in Babylonia, North Africa, Spain, France, Germany, Lithuania, Russia, Poland, Hungary, or America, all studied the same subject—Talmud. No matter what language the students spoke, and regardless of local customs and mores, the text remained the same.

In Europe, prior to the nineteenth century, each Jewish community had many students of the Talmud in local synagogues, where the rabbi or other local scholars could be consulted. Many famous rabbis would secure pledges from the community to set up and support *yeshivot*. The rabbi would serve in the dual capacity of spiritual leader and *rosh yeshivah*.

Around 1800, the local *yeshivah* was gradually replaced by larger, universal types of *yeshivot*. In the years from 1803 to 1807, two famous *yeshivot* were created. One academy in Volozhin, White Russia, was founded by Rabbi Chaim of Volozhin, the chief disciple of the Vilna Gaon. The second school was established in Pressburg, Hungary (Slovakia) and was headed by Rabbi Moshe Sofer, the illustrious *"Ḥatam Sofer."*[8]

In each *yeshivah*, the *rosh yeshivah* established its philosophy and curriculum priorities. Each *yeshivah* had its own style of instruction. Some stressed the analytical approach, with the student concentrating on the text; others emphasized the dialectic method, in which the student explored wide-ranging topics, seeking analogies, distinctions, contradictions, and underlying general principles. The *rosh yeshivah*'s regularly scheduled lectures sparked student reflections and further research. Students were expected to adhere to a rigorous schedule of study lasting from early morning to late night. Moreover, they were expected to discuss with the *rosh yeshivah* their ideas, insights, and questions.

In the Lithuanian *yeshivot*, which came under the influence of Rabbi Yisroel Lipkin-Salanter (1810-1833) and his disciples, the curriculum also included the study of *musar*. *Musar*, the Hebrew word for ethics, is a comprehensive term with a complex etymological structure. It is related to several roots and has a number of meanings and connotations. *Musar* refers to chastisement, reproof, admonition, exhortation, instruction, prohibition, transmission, discipline, politeness, and proper conduct.[9]

The religious ethic espoused by *musar*, especially as developed by Rabbi Yisroel Lipkin-Salanter,[10] was an all-embracing morality which recognized no distinction between moral law and statutory law. Morality and law were one.

Salanter developed the theory that the inconsistency between knowledge and belief, on the one hand, and conduct on the other, was caused, in part at least, by the formal study of ethics as if it were mere subject matter. To make ethics a decisive factor in human affairs, Salanter introduced a system of studying *musar* with ecstasy and employing unique methods of self-analysis and group analysis.

Salanter believed that his system of studying ethics, designed to involve the learner's emotion and hence evoke his commitment, would lead men to acquire actual beliefs. He maintained that the study of ethics as if it were cognitive knowledge at best resulted in professed beliefs. According to Salanter, only actual beliefs have a direct bearing on behavior.

The behavioral standards which *musar* maintained were indeed high. The numerous laws of the Torah governing human relations were apparently deemed insufficient, for there was an overriding moral requirement to go beyond the point of the Law.[11] The *Musar* Movement understood that the purpose of this injunction was to prevent people from following the letter of the Law while violating its spirit. Ethical behavior, then, was the constant and active striving to do more than was required; to seek to avoid any harm to others (especially that which may, through a loophole, be permitted); and to be willing to forego that which was rightfully one's own for the sake of helping others who are in need or distress. Ethical behavior meant also politeness of speech, proper manners, and the peaceful settlement of differences. But all of these had to be more than conventional mannerism; they had to flow from a sincere and abiding inner commitment to the worth of the individual and the equality of men. This sort of meaningful ethical behavior was expected of all students of the *musar yeshivot*.

The *Musar* Movement saw an element of vagueness permeating moral laws and moral situations, leaving many people confused as to the proper course of action in a given situation. Each human trait or inclination applied to an infinite number of situations, and each situation could be assessed and approached in many ways. In deciding what was moral and what was not in particular situations, each man had to be his own judge. Salanter was convinced that without full knowledge of and commitment to *musar*, one was incapable of rendering fair ethical decisions.

Underlying Salanter's theory of *musar* was an optimistic assertion that human nature can be improved. But, due to the complexity of human nature and the various environmental pressures and temptations, man must make *musar* a lifelong pursuit.

The study of *musar* was "bitter in the beginning but sweet in the end." The student of ethics sought first to relinquish frivolity and light-headedness and acquire sobriety and reverence. Only after a prolonged period of "bitterness" did he contemplate reaching the advanced "sweet" state of contentment and serenity epitomized by self-fulfillment.

In the *yeshivot* which espoused *musar*, students were expected to be critical of themselves. Disciples often kept a daily record of their achievements and failures, so that both the positive and negative elements in their behavior could be noticed and scrutinized. Recognizing that one's subjective judgment may weaken or impair self-analysis, the *Musar* Movement devised new methods of group analysis. Small groups of like-minded students would meet and evaluate the conduct of each member. No one escaped the group's evaluation, and each individual was under obligation to accept its recommendations for improvement.

The *Musar* Movement maintained that the group would be more objective than the individual could ever be regarding himself. Students were advised to exercise patience and to disregard pride when their behavior was discussed by the group. Members were also urged to take sufficient time for deliberation; not to mock anyone; and to consider the whole individual, his failures as well as his achievements.

The *musar* master, who, serving as *mashgi'ah (musar* mentor), would deliver lectures on ethics and theology and act as a mentor to the students, absented himself from the meetings, so that freedom of expression might be assured and the individual's rights and dignity safeguarded. There were no secret sessions, and the individual whose conduct was under discussion was on hand to clarify his position. Quite often the individual himself would present his "case" for discussion.

*Musar* was studied with ecstasy, "stirring the soul to seek self-improvement."[12] Ecstasy was engendered by reading aloud, and by projecting in one's mind the actual extent of the moral obligation he was studying as it pertained to his life. Asserting that the constancy of an emotionally charged study of *musar* would result in consistency of ethical conduct, regular periods for learning ethics were set aside daily.

The *rosh yeshivah*'s relationship with his students, in both *musar* and non-*musar yeshivot*, was also that of a mentor and guide.

Students respected and revered him, and would also consult him on personal matters. The general community also respected the *rosh yeshivah*. It was not enough that he was a man of great intellect, or a *gaon* (genius); he also had to be a *zaddik* (righteous one).

The *yeshivah* was the medium for the transmission of the rabbinic tradition from generation to generation. To this end, the curriculum consisted of Talmud and cognate studies; not history, language, literature, or other secular subjects. The *yeshivah* asserted that the transmission of this sacred heritage could only be accomplished through total commitment to Torah study and the interaction between masters and disciples, who sought no personal or material gain, but rather the perfection of their minds and personalities.

The *yeshivah* refused to integrate sacred and secular studies for two reasons. First, the study of the complex talmudic subjects must command the student's full attention. Success in Talmud study could only be achieved through total immersion. Second, secular culture was unacceptable to the talmudists, who predicted the moral decay of Western civilization and the bankruptcy of secularism. The *roshei yeshivah* (deans) were not opposed to natural sciences,[13] but to the humanities.

## Synagogues

The *shul* was the community center, study hall, house of worship, and a place to gather; it was home. *Davenen* (prayer) in eastern European synagogues would often elicit a *krekhts* (Yiddish for sigh), tears, ecstasy, and *kavvanah* (concentration) and would be accompanied by *shoklen* (Yiddish for swaying to and fro). Two characteristics resulted in an emotional style of prayer.

First, life in the *shtetl* had many difficulties. The standard of living was low and the environment was hostile. When people came to *shul* they sought relief and reassurance and found them in the *siddur* (prayer book). *Davenen* was thus an intensive emotional and therapeutic experience.

Second, an important factor which influenced eastern European worship and made prayer a regular daily activity was the homogeneous and organic Jewish lifestyle. *Yidishkayt* (Yiddish for Judaism) was a total experience. In larger cities, limited acculturation and assimilation existed, but the *shtetl* Jews were generally unassimilated. Although they spoke the vernacular, the rich and colorful Yiddish language constituted a *mehizah* (a separation) between the Jew and the Gentile; except for economic and governmental interaction, there was little or no social contact between them. It was, therefore, natural for people who lived a total religious life to consider the synagogue as their spiritual center.

The close ties between the *shtetl* Jews and their acute sensitivity to the problems of the Jewish people as a whole created a sense of community. Thus, they would come to *shul* to say *tehillim* (psalms) and shed a tear for any Jewish community, near or far, which had suffered from a pogrom or other calamity.

Besides prayer, the *shul* was used for other purposes. Funerals would originate in the courtyard of the *shul*, where the *hesped* (eulogy) was delivered by the rabbi. If the deceased was a *talmid hakham* (a scholar), the coffin would be taken into the *shul*. Customarily, the *hesped* did not concentrate on the virtues of the deceased. Most of the remarks were directed to evoking *teshuvah* (repentance) and the strengthening of the faith, the vanity of life, and the meaning of death.

The *shul* was also a place for regular and emergency communal meetings. Holiday celebrations, weddings, circumcisions, and the like, were also arranged in the *shul*. Individuals who faced personal crises would also turn to the *shul*. A mother whose child was critically ill would run into the *shul* shrieking that her baby was dying. She would open the *Aron Kodesh* (the Holy Ark), embrace the *Sifrai Torah* (scrolls of the Law), and beg for a *ness* (miracle).

A person who felt that he was denied justice would "stop the reading of the Torah" on the Sabbath. The man or woman would embrace the *Sefer Torah* (scroll of Law) as it was taken out of the ark, crying out for justice. No one would dare to use force against a fellow Jew holding a *Sefer Torah* in *shul* and demanding justice. Calling the police was unthinkable. Only after the leaders of the local *kehilla* (the official organized Jewish community) would promise to take action could peace be restored.

Occasionally, a well-known *hazzan* (cantor) was invited to a *shtetl*. He would conduct part of the *Shabes* morning service, in addition to giving a concert in the *shul* on a weekday. The concert featured religious selections from the *siddur* and other sacred texts. When the *hazzan* led popular prayer songs, such as *"Sheyiboneh Beit Hamikdosh"* ("May the Temple Be Rebuilt"), the audience joined in with gusto, as in community folk "songs".

Another diversion was the appearance of the *maggid* (itinerant preacher), who came to the *shtetl* once a year to preach in the *shul*. There were many *maggidim*. Some spoke on Saturday afternoons or on weekday evenings. Most *maggidim* were popular. Their stories and exhortations served a double purpose—instruction and entertainment. The more accomplished *maggid* spoke eloquently.

The *maggid* not only preached and entertained, but he also informed. Because he traveled from place to place, the *maggid* often disseminated news about outside events in the Jewish world. Whereas the *hazzan* was engaged in advance by the community for an agreed sum of money and, therefore, admission to his concert was by ticket only, the *maggid* arrived uninvited and admission was free. He passed a collection plate after his talk.

The *shul* was also used for Torah study. Seated at long tables, lit by candlelight (electricity had not yet reached most *shtetlakh*), informal groups of men of various ages would spend an hour or two learning. In *shul*, there was a *Hevra Shas* (a group studying Talmud), studying a Gemara, or talmudic text of their choice; a *Hevra*

*Mishnayot* (a group learning Mishnah, or talmudic text); a *Ḥevra Ḥumash* (a group engaged in the study of the Pentateuch); a *Ḥevra Ḥayei Odom* (a group studying Jewish laws); and a *Ḥevra Tehillim* (a group reciting psalms). When a *siyyum* (conclusion of study) of a text was celebrated by a group, they organized joyous festivities, much like Simḥat Torah (the holiday marking the end of the annual cycle of synagogal reading of the Torah).

## The Rabbinate

The eastern European rabbinate was divided into a number of different categories. The local rabbinate consisted of three distinct groups. First, there was the elected spiritual leader of the town. In some instances, his jurisdictional area included several smaller neighboring villages that could not afford to support their own rabbi. The elections of the *rav* (rabbi), ordinarily conducted by the *kehilla*, were free and democratic. In larger *shtetlakh*, the rabbi had two or more associates known as *dayyanim* (judges), who served on the *bet din* (rabbinical court). A *dayyan* would rule on *shayles* (Yiddish for queries), questions regarding *kashrut* (dietary laws), and other religious matters. The rabbi of the community was the *av bet din* (presiding judge) and official spiritual head of the *shtetl*. In Hasidic communities, especially in Poland, there was the *rebbe*. He was neither an official rabbi nor a *dayyan*. He was selected, rather than elected. Whether he was a scion of a distinguished dynasty of *rebbeyim* or a charismatic leader, the *rebbe* was the spiritual leader of his Hasidim. As a rule, the *rebbe* did not share in the official functions of the local rabbinate. However, as a prominent spiritual guide of many Jews, he would be invited to regional or national rabbinical conferences. A few of the well-known Polish Hasidic leaders were the *rebbeyim* of Ger, Belz, Sanz, Novominsk, and Tchortkov. The Lubavitch group was especially prominent in White Russia.

In addition, there was a less formal rabbinate. In some Lithuanian and White Russian communities, there were saintly individuals known either as a *ẓaddik* (a righteous one) or a *"guter yid"* (a good Jew). The local populace revered their *ẓaddik* and told wonder tales about him, considering him a miracle maker.[14] People would travel to see this *ẓaddik* for a *brokhe* (a blessing) in times of distress. In some instances the official rabbi himself would send people to the *ẓaddik* for his blessings and prayers. Some of these *ẓaddikim* had shunned publicity and spent most of their lives in private Torah study, *davenen*, fasting, and in ascetic practices. Others involved themselves in the affairs of the community. The hallmark of their communal service was *gemilut ḥasadim* (acts of kindness). A good example of such a *ẓaddik* is the legendary nineteenth-century sage Reb Nochumke of Grodno. Reb Nochumke was reportedly referred to by Rabbi Yisroel Lipkin-Salanter as "the pillar of *hesed*" (kindness) of his generation. It is known that the *Ḥafeẓ Ḥayyim* (a leading sage) traveled to Grodno to learn *hesed* and piety from Reb

Nochumke.

Eastern European Jews looked towards a series of a *manhigai hador* (leaders of the generation) for inspiration and direction. They were often communal rabbis, such as the late Rabbi Yitzchok Elchonon Spektor of Kovno (1817-1896), Rabbi Chaim Ozer Grodzenski of Vilna (1863-1940), or Rabbi Meir Shapiro of Lublin (1888-1934), who founded the well-known *yeshivah* in Lublin, served in the Polish Sejm (parliament), and conceived the idea of the *Daf Yomi* (daily page of the Talmud), studied to this day the world over. Quite often these men were neither communal rabbis nor *dayyanim*. Representative of such types were Rabbi Elija of Vilna (1720-1797), known as the Vilna Gaon, Rabbi Yisroel Lipkin-Salanter (1810-1883), and Rabbi Yisroel Meir Ha-Cohen (1839-1933), universally known as the *Ḥafez Ḥayyim*, the title of his first book. These saintly "uncrowned" leaders served the Jewish people by convening regular and emergency meetings,[15] lecturing to large audiences, and guiding scholars. They were viewed as a court of last resort and were besieged by people in distress seeking advice and blessings.

Leadership of the Jewish community was not the sole province of the rabbi. He was engaged by the *kehilla*. Between the two world wars, the governments of Poland and Lithuania recognized the *kehilla* as a legal entity. The *kehilla* was empowered to levy taxes on the Jewish community. The *kehilla* tax was a head tax, collected from every Jewish resident, and also an income tax, where the rich paid more than the poor. An additional tax was added to the price of *kosher* meat. The *kehilla* leadership was elected democratically. It is noteworthy that representatives of Socialist and Zionist movements, who had a considerable following in the cities, served on the *kehilla* together with Mizrachi and Agudath-Israel councilmen. The *kehilla* council members elected the president of the community. The *kehilla* had jurisdiction over the religious institutions and activities. Thus, the *shul*, school, *mikveh* (ritual bath), slaughterhouse, the home for the aged, the orphanage, the guest house for poor transients, and philanthropic drives were controlled by the *kehilla*.[16]

The cemetery was also under the auspices of the *kehilla*. Funerals were arranged by a volunteer group called *Ḥevra Kaddisha* (burial society) without charge. Cemetery plots were provided to the poor without cost. Wealthy families were taxed so that there would be sufficient funds for the upkeep of the cemetery.

The *kehilla* was also charged with the responsibility of engaging a rabbi and paying his salary and those of other religious functionaries. Some *shtetlakh* had two rabbis, each accepted by his followers only. Disputes over rabbis, which often lasted for a long time, developed because of ideological differences, personal likes and dislikes, or the recurring question of *ḥazakah* (tenure).

The principle of *ḥazakah* was often a perennial source of dissension. It was generally accepted that a rabbinical position was held for life. When the rabbi died, his son, if qualified, traditionally had priority, or *ḥazakah*, over other candidates. At times there were those who wanted a new rabbi and a controversy would ensue.

The rabbi in a large *kehilla* was paid a relatively comfortable salary. This was not true of the rabbi of the small town, who received an inadequate salary. To supplement his income, the *shtetl kehilla* granted the rabbi some exclusive business concessions, which, usually, were managed by the rabbi's wife, the *rebetsn*. That monopoly generally included the sale of candles, yeast, or wine. To be sure, sales did not generate much money and the rabbi rarely was rich. It was assumed that a rabbi did not need material wealth.

The rabbi's functions were varied. Since the *kehilla* had to register births, weddings, divorces, and deaths, it was the rabbi who kept the official records. The rabbi supervised the *shehitah (kosher slaughtering)*, the religious schools,[17] the *mikveh*, the synagogues, and all other aspects of religious life. The adjudication of litigation in civil or marital matters, in conjunction with the *dayyanim*, was another important responsibility. The rabbi would also have to *paskenen shayles* (Yiddish—to rule on *halakhic* questions) with regard to *kashrut*, the synagogue, or other areas of religious life.

As spiritual leader of the community, the rabbi was expected to be both student and teacher. He had to be humble so that even widows, orphans, and the poor saw him as their protector and as the embodiment of Jewish justice and morality. The rabbi often made rounds on behalf of needy families. And, finally, the rabbi was the spokesman for the Jewish community to local government officials and visiting state dignitaries.

The communal rabbi's relationship with other rabbis was guided by traditional etiquette. Even a great rabbi, when visiting the *shtetl*, would pay a courtesy call on the local rabbi, as he was the *mara de-atra* (the local master). The communal rabbi, in turn, would afterwards visit the famous guest at his hotel to show his respect. The local *rosh yeshivah*, even if he was of greater stature, would acknowledge the authority of the communal rabbi. Thus, when a religious question would occur in his home, the *rosh yeshivah* would submit it to the rabbi for a decision. Similarly, the local rabbi maintained tactful relations with the *rebbe* and the *ẓaddik*.

The rabbi was not required to give weekly sermons on *Shabes*. He delivered two major addresses a year, one on *Shabes* Hagadol, before Passover, and the other on *Shabes* Teshuvah, before Yom Kippur. If the rabbis were not overly involved in public speaking, many of them spent considerable time writing *Responsa* (rulings on questions of religious law) and *Hiddushei Torah* (new insights in Torah interpretation). Over the centuries there developed a massive *Responsa* literature, known as *she'elot u'teshuvot*, which may be classified as applied *halakhah*. In their *Responsa*, rabbis applied old principles to new situations created by scientific or medical advances and changing social conditions. The *Responsa* literature addresses practical new problems generated by changing circumstances of life. Whereas the *rosh yeshivah* was the academician and theoretician, the local rabbi was the practitioner. On the other hand, the theoretical issues, the *Hiddushei Torah*, were written mostly by *roshei yeshivah*.

The rabbi, himself a product of a *yeshivah*, brought the richness of his knowledge to bear upon the life of the entire community. The *yeshivah* transmitted the Torah from generation to generation, and the practicing rabbi, by applying *halakhah* to actual life, brought the word of Sinai to the people.

## Concluding Note

Nurtured by the warm and inspiring traditions of the family, and guided by the *shul*, school, *yeshivah*, and the rabbinate, the religious eastern European Jew developed an iron faith in Judaism and an intense pride and identity in being Jewish. Thoroughly pragmatic, he directed his life to the affairs of this world. At the same time, he yearned with all his being for the coming of the Messiah. The ultimate value of Judaism and its covenant were well understood and gladly accepted. These characteristics of the religious eastern European Jews were powerful weapons against assimilation and secularism and provided him with the inner strength to endure. To understand, therefore, the survival of the Jew, one must comprehend his religion.

New Jewish centers emerging in our time, although they seek to recapture the legacy of the vanished *shtetlakh*, will not be able to re-build on the ruins of the Holocaust. Contemporary conditions and attitudes are generally antithetical to those of the *shtetlakh* so that a similar, rich Jewish life most likely will not be duplicated. The *shtetlakh* had warmth, beauty, a wholesome and sanctified life, the grandeur of eastern European scholarship, and much more. That which took a thousand years to build cannot be restored in a short time. Some aspects of *shtetlakh yidishkayt* will be reproduced, but not the great totality of eastern European Jewish life. The losses have not been replaced and the wounds have not yet healed. We pray to the One who heals the sick of Israel that He should soon in our days bring comfort to His people and eternal joy.

### Notes

1. *Yevamoth*, p. 62 *(Babylonian Talmud)*.
2. Deut. 6: 7.
3. Aaron Suraski, *Toldot Ha-Hinukh Ha-Torati* [Hebrew] (Bnai-Brak, Israel: Or Haḥayim Publishers, 1967), pp. 427-431.
4. Miriam Eisenstein, *Jewish Schools in Poland, 1919-1939* (New York: King's Crown Press, 1950), pp. 71-82.
5. Suraski, *Toldot*, pp. 54-76.

6.   Tz'vi Scharfstein, *Toldot Ha-Ḥinukh B'Yisrael Badorot Ho-Aharonim* [Hebrew], vol. II (Jerusalem: Ruben Mass Publishers, 1960), pp. 131-160.

7.   In the nineteenth century, poor *yeshivah* students had to rely on *esn teg* (literally, "eating days"), whereby the student would dine each day of the week with a different family for the duration of one semester. This was discontinued for the college-age men, but until World War II, the younger boys of the Yeshivah Ketanah (preparatory school) continued to have "eating days."

8.   Suraski, *Toldot*, p. 281.

9.   Eliezer Ben-Yehudah, *Milon Ha-Lashon Ha-Ivrit* [Hebrew], vol. VI (Tel Aviv: La-Am Publishing House, 1948), pp. 2849-2853, 3137.

10.   Isaac Blazer, *Or Ysrael* (Tel Aviv: Israel-American Offset, 1959); Zalman F. Ury, *The Musar Movement* (New York: Yeshiva University Press, 1970).

11.   Deut. 6:18; Prov. 2:20; *Babylonian Talmud*, Tractates *Bava M'tzia*, 30b; *Bava Batra*, 12b, 88a,b.

12.   Blazer, *Or Yisrael*, p. 32.

13.   Some great rabbis in our history were physicians, astronomers, etc. They had acquired scientific knowledge outside of the *yeshivah*, after having mastered the Talmud.

14.   In the Hasidic community, such reverence would be accorded to the *rebbe*. The famous *rebbeyim* would attract adherents from far and wide.

15.   The Gaon of Vilna appeared less frequently in public than the other two rabbis.

16.   Harry M. Rabinowitz, *The Legacy of Polish Jewry* (New York and London: Thomas Yoseloff, 1965), pp. 108-125.

17.   There were some children who attended public schools. The rabbi, or his representative, would be invited once a week to give religious instruction to Jewish students.

### For Further Reading

Eisenstein, Miriam. *Jewish Schools in Poland, 1919-1939.* New York: King's Crown Press, 1950.

Garfunkel, Leib, et al. *Yahadut Lita.* [Hebrew] Tel Aviv: Am Hasefer Publishers, 1960.

Kariv, Avraham. *Lithuania Land of My Birth.* New York: Herzl Press, 1967

Mirski, Samuel K. *Mosdot Torah Be-Europa Be-Vinyanam U-Vechurbanam.* [Hebrew] New York: Ogen Publishing House, 1956.

Rabinowitz, Harry M. *The Legacy of Polish Jewry 1919-1939.* New York & London: Thomas Yoseloff, 1965.

Sachs, A.S. *Worlds That Passed.* Philadelphia: The Jewish Publication Society, 1943.

Scharfstein, Tz'vi. *Toldot Ha-Ḥinukh B'Yisrael Badorot Ho-Aḥaronim.* [Hebrew] Jerusalem: Reuben Mass Publishers, 1960.

Segal, Simon. *The New Poland and the Jews.* New York: Lee Furman, Inc., 1938.

Suraski, Aaron. *Toldot Ha-Hinukh Ha-Torati.* [Hebrew] Bnai-Brak: Or Hahayim Publishers, 1967.

# Aspects of Hasidic Life in Eastern Europe Before World War II

## NEHEMIA POLEN

Hasidism, the great revivalist and mystical movement in Jewish religion, arose in eastern Europe during the first part of the eighteenth century. The Jews had never fully recovered from the devastating aftereffects of the Chmielnitski massacres of 1648-1649; furthermore, the spiritual confusion resulting from the apostasy of the pseudo-Messiah Shabbetai Zevi (1626-1676) was still present. In a milieu combining Polish political instability, religious hatred, and economic deterioration, the Jewish masses needed hope and a new approach to rally and inspire them. Some of this was found in the movement and beliefs of the Baal Shem Tov.

Little is known about the early life of Rabbi Israel ben Eliezer (c. 1700-1760), also known as the Baal Shem Tov ("Master of the Good Name"), or Besht. Hasidic tradition tells us that he came from a poor and pious family and was orphaned at an early age. According to *Shivhei ha-Besht*, the earliest collection of stories about the Besht, his father's last words were ". . . my beloved son, remember this all your life: God is with you; you should therefore fear nothing."[1] These words made a firm impression on the young boy. His life's work was devoted to spreading the message of God's real presence in the world, and the consequent banishment of all fears, spiritual as well as material.

The Besht's message was simple and, in the context of the history of Jewish ethical thought, not particularly new. He emphasized the power of faith in God, the need for joyful enthusiasm in prayer, the performance of *mitzvot* (meritorious deeds), and the importance of love and good fellowship. One must ask what the Besht's originality and creative influence was. Part of the answer may be inferred from a story that describes the Besht's first encounter with a skeptical and hostile talmudic scholar and preacher, Rabbi Dov Baer of Mezhirich (1710-1772), known as the "Mezhiricher Maggid" (preacher), who later succeeded the Besht as head of the Hasidic movement. The Besht won over Dov Baer as his student by challenging him to interpret a certain mystical text. Dov Baer read the text in question, interpreting it in a formally correct but cold and detached manner. When the Besht recited the text, " . . . the house was filled with light, fire raged around it, and they saw with their own eyes the angels whose names were mentioned in the text." The Besht turned to the *maggid* and said, "The interpretation you gave is correct, but your study lacks soul...." Dov Baer, we are told, immediately cancelled his travel plans and "remained with the Besht, who taught him sciences great and profound."[2]

Leaving aside the supernatural elements of the story, a central point is clearly discernible: The Besht was able to attract mature rabbinic scholars to Hasidism because he could breathe fresh spirit into the dry words of ancient texts. This is precisely what he did with Judaism as a whole—penetrating traditional forms and rigid patterns, not to reject them but to make them glow with renewed human enthusiasm. One must always guard against performing religious acts reflexively and automatically, the Besht taught. Only by investing one's very self into one's words and actions could they be charged with life and inner power.

The generative core of the Besht's teachings is the emphasis on divine immanence—on God's presence in all creation and His accessibility to human beings. God may seem far from us, but this is only because we allow the material world to sustain the illusion of God's hiddenness. This point is brought out in the famous parable of the castle:

> There was once a very wise king. By employing optical illusion he made walls, towers, and gates, and commanded that he should be reached by way of the gates and towers. He further commanded that at each and every gate should be disbursed the treasures of the king. There were some individuals who went as far as the first gate, took money and turned back. Others [advanced further but then found some treasure and turned back.] Finally his son, his beloved, resolved firmly to reach his father the king. Then he saw that there is no partition separating him and his father, because all [the walls, towers, and gates] were merely illusion.[3]

Or, as the Besht's student Rabbi Jacob Joseph of Polonnoye (d. 1782) explained:

> . . . the whole earth is full of His glory; every movement and thought comes from Him, also all the angels and heavenly chambers—all these are created and made, as it were, from His very essence, like the snail whose garment is actually part of its body. [With this knowledge], there is no separation between the person and Him. . . .[4]

A related notion is that the secular and the sacred are not distinct domains. The profane has sparks of holiness; the secular can and must be sanctified. The eastern European Jew, socially isolated by walls of hatred and oppression, and by the self-imposed restraints of asceticism and exclusive devotion to study, was made to feel at home in the world of nature, and saw in its beauty a manifestation of the divine. Music, dance, and storytelling became expressions of religious creativity.

The Besht was not afraid of using mundane tools to arouse a spiritual ecstasy. If a morose heart could be made joyous by a joke, a prank, or even a shot of whiskey, then so much the better. The inner intensity of prayer was often sustained by wild gesticulations and by swaying to and fro (known in Yiddish as *shoklen*). Concentration in study and prayer was also maintained by a meditative focusing on the letters that comprised the words of the text. The point was to deflect attention away from the content in favor of perceiving the letters as pure spiritual forms serving as "vessels" for the flux of divine energy.[5]

One is struck by the earthiness of the stories about the Besht. He is often depicted as smoking a pipe or talking about horses. He heartily embraced the folk traditions of his people, healing with amulets and herbs as well as with prayer. He had a large mass following but was able to inspire an intellectual elite. He was a wonder-working folk hero—and also a teacher of esoteric doctrines to a devoted circle of religious sophisticates. Indeed, the transcendence of dualities, and the unification of disparate elements in the community's social and religious life, were key elements of his vision. They were the true test of the authentic teacher, the clear indication that his teachings came from the divine source of unity and not the fragmented "world of separation."[6]

The emphasis on unity was perhaps the key to the movement's success. Initially some Jewish communal and religious authorities opposed the Hasidim, suspecting that their emphasis on divine immanence and *devekut* (communion with God) might develop into a full-fledged antinomian heresy. The polemical literature of the Mitnaggedim (opponents of Hasidism) was emotional and vituperative.[7]

The early opposition to Hasidism came primarily from religious traditionalists, who saw Hasidic innovations as deviations from established customs. To them, the Hasidic adoption of a different liturgical rite, their ecstatic devotion, and their supposed neglect of the study of Torah threatened the continuity of religious life. Opposition also surfaced from the Jewish proponents of European Enlightenment, the Maskilim, who saw in Hasidism an anachronistic return to medieval superstition. The Maskilim valued critical rationalism and sober intellectual thought. The great nineteenth-century Jewish historian, Heinrich Graetz, lost his objectivity on the subject of Hasidism, characterizing it as "an unclear and irrational dream which to this day does its deeds in darkness." By mid-nineteenth century the Hasidin and Mitnaggedim had made peace with each other. They came to recognize that their real enemies were the Maskilim, who in their exteme manifestations opposed any form of traditional religious expression. Certain Hasidic leaders even acknowledged that the early opposition of the Mitnaggedim was good for the movement, in that it checked tendencies towards religious anarchy.

At the center of the Hasidic society was the *rebbe,* or master, also known as the *ẓaddik* (righteous one). The *rebbe* was their leader, teacher, emissary to God, and God's emissary to them. The *ẓaddik* was the channel through which both material and spiritual blessings flowed from heaven. The *ẓaddik* was prepared to risk all—his life, even his share in Heaven—for his people.[8] Opponents of Hasidism criticized the notion of the *ẓaddik* as the intermediary between God and the people. For the Hasidim, however, the *ẓaddik* became their guide even in matters of the world. Hasidim turned to their *rebbe* for advice in choosing a marriage partner, initiating a business venture, or purchasing a new home. Hasidim believed that their *rebbe*'s sagacity emerged from paranormal powers of clairvoyance; for others, it was primarily a matter of astute judgment sharpened by years of experience in dealing with the problems of his flock.

In any event, the Hasid felt a new infusion of energy and confidence when he received the blessing of his master. Hasidim would travel for weeks, sometimes by foot, to be with their master for a Sabbath or holiday. During the long and often arduous journey, the individual Hasid might meet others who, like himself, were traveling to visit their master. Their shared "pilgrimage" would be spent reciting Hasidic stories, anticipating the spiritual glories they would behold, and preparing themselves for the few moments when they might be granted a private audience with their master. Each individual wanted to make the most of the time he would spend alone with his master, and would mentally rehearse his every word. Of course, the meeting almost never went as planned; it would often seem to the Hasid that the *rebbe* penetrated to the core of his concerns rather than their superficial aspects, uncovering layers of which the Hasid was totally unaware.[9] The interview might conclude with the *rebbe* giving the Hasid a spiritual direction which the Hasid would attempt to implement in his daily life, for months or years, until the next time he might be privileged to visit with his master.

Besides the private audience with the *rebbe*, the Hasid would wait for those times when his master would "say Torah," or present an original homily. The discourse would elucidate the inner significance of a classical text, disclosing its relevance to the spiritual needs of the Hasidim. Usually delivered in Yiddish (but later recorded in Hebrew), the discourse would unfold an associative train of thought, building around key words and concepts and connecting unrelated passages of sacred literature with new creative insights. Featured frequently in the Hasidic discourse, as well as in the shorter epigrams for which some masters were celebrated, was the play on words, which often hinged on a semantic or syntactic shift in the sacred text. These plays were meant to startle the listener into new perceptions of familiar passages, as well as of their own personal situations. Many masters became famous not for miraculous powers, but for the ability to "say Torah" in an engaging manner. The Hasidim were especially captivated when it was clear that the master had not prepared his homily ahead of time, but was speaking from the inspiration of the moment. At such times it was believed that the master's speech was not under his conscious control, but was being used as an instrument of the Divine Wisdom.[10]

Hasidism bridged—but did not eliminate—the gap between rich and poor, between scholar and semiliterate.[11] Wealthier Hasidim generally supported their poorer brethren, and opened their houses to travelers needing lodging. In the Hasidic community everyone had a place, and each individual was an organic part of a unified body of believers. While the role of women followed traditional patterns, it was true that women had opportunities for creative religious expression which were unavailable elsewhere. Certain exceptional women recognized for their charismatic gifts attracted their own followers, in effect becoming independent Hasidic masters.[12]

While untutored Hasidim could not follow the learned discussions of scholars, they could—and did—participate equally in the life of prayer, the devotional recitation of psalms, the study of *Ein Ya'akov* (a collection of the homiletical passages of the Talmud), and the telling of stories of the masters. These activities were considered appropriate for even the greatest scholars. Thus, while Hasidism by no means eliminated social and class divisions, it definitely made them less sharp and divisive.

The softening of rigid lines of demarcation is evident, for example, in the laxity shown regarding fixed times for prayer. The Hasidic practice of offering afternoon prayer well after sunset scandalized the Mitnaggedim. The Hasidim replied by pointing out that while the king's ministers need an appointment to approach their monarch, the king's own children can approach him at any time. This attitude to prayer did not signify a lessening of commitment to the body of Jewish law. In fact, in most respects the Hasidim kept the Law with a vigorous enthusiasm. The Hasidic flouting of the fixed times for prayer was an attempt to enact on a symbolic level the interpenetration (though not the elimination) of separate domains, a softening of the sharp contours of the map of everyday reality. As some of their critics noted, this was closely related to the Hasidic theology of divine immanence, which lessened the perceived distance separating God and man, and undermined distinctions in general.[13]

The Hasidim also emphasized the need to transcend polar opposites even in the realm of human emotion. There must be reflective sobriety as part of greatest joy. On the other hand, even in tragedy one must search for a glimmer of light, and retain the ability to rejoice.

Psalm 126:5, which states:

They that sow in tears
—in joy they shall reap

was given a Hasidic twist. The verse was parsed differently, so that it read:

They that sow in tears [and] in joy
—they shall reap!

The Jew of eastern Europe was no stranger to tears, but Hasidism gave him the ability to mingle them with joy.

By the third generation of Hasidism—in the last decades of the eighteenth century—the movement had no central location. Disciples and descendants of the major leaders were constantly traveling to new areas carrying their message. Thus, the movement spread from its original location of Podolia in the Ukraine into Lithuania, Galicia, Central Poland, and the rest of eastern Europe. Each individual master became known for a particular style and approach. For the economically oppressed and politically disenfranchised Hasidim, who were treated as aliens in the countries they resided in, personal allegiance to a master became a means of identification and enabled feelings akin to patriotic national sentiments. At times, the inevitable disagreements between different dynasties would degenerate into serious internecine feuding; more often, however, there was mutual respect, or at least peaceful coexistence.

The latter half of the nineteenth century saw the dramatic growth of several Hasidic dynasties and the transformation of the movement's character. Hasidism had received its initial impetus from small circles of enthusiasts, and was originally confined to rural and remote towns of eastern Europe. By the turn of the twentieth century, however, it had become a genuine mass movement, with some of the major dynasties numbering adherents in the hundreds of thousands. World War I accelerated population trends and movement to the large cities. In the years between the two world wars, Warsaw was a major center of Hasidic activity. These changes led to the appearance of a new type of Hasid. The followers of some masters included physicians, journalists, and industrialists as well as craftsmen, scholars, and laborers. Certain Hasidic groups became politically sophisticated and organized political lobbies and parties for Orthodox Jews.

In evaluating the creative achievements of eastern European Jews in the 200-year period between the onset of the Besht's public ministry (1736) and the Holocaust, it is evident that Hasidism played a major role. It inspired a veritable explosion of religious, literary, and aesthetic creativity.

The losses to Hasidism during the Holocaust were substantial. It is a remarkable phenomenon that, one generation later, Hasidism is again flourishing in Israel, the United States, and elsewhere. The Hasidim themselves no doubt see Divine Providence as responsible for their regeneration. At the same time, it seems evident that certain aspects of the Hasidic ethos were specific to the eastern European period, and it is hard to see how these might ever be fully recaptured. Nevertheless, Hasidism insists that it is possible, at least in part, to recover a lost reality by telling its story. Telling a tale, in the Hasidic view, is very different than nostalgic reminiscence or folklore transmission. It charges the values embedded in it with new potency; it invests the transmitter, the audience, and most of all the heroes of the story itself with new life.

In that spirit, we shall conclude this brief essay with a story,[14] which touches on the three central themes of Hasidism: love of one's fellow, love of God, and love of the Torah. As is quite commonly the case, the story serves as a commentary on a biblical passage; the stage is set not by artistic evocation of a mood or ambience, but by pointing out a puzzling feature of the sacred text, which the story, in parabolic fashion, then proceeds to resolve and clarify. Also, this tale exhibits a rudimentary version of the story-within-a-story format, which often (though not here) involves many twists and concatenations of the story line. In addition, it should be noted that because of the oral character of Hasidic stories, most of them have no "canonical" form. Therefore, the same story may appear in a number of sources, with slight variation of detail; also, similar stories are often attributed to several different masters. In our case, the subject of the "outer" story is Rabbi Mendel of Rymanov (d. 1815), student of Rabbi Elimelekh of Lizhensk; the hero of the "inner" story is . . . ah, but perhaps it is best to let the reader decide that!

One year, on the High Holiday of Rosh Hashanah (Jewish New Year), just before the sounding of the *shofar* (ram's horn), Rabbi Mendel of Rymanov went to the pulpit of the synagogue and posed the following question to his congregation: "Why does the famous passage in Leviticus (19:18), which states 'And thou shalt love thy neighbor as thyself,' conclude with the words, 'I am the Lord'? What does the latter phrase add to the former? What does it mean in this context?"

The congregation agreed that the words "I am the Lord" seemed to be curiously unrelated to the beginning of the verse. No one could answer his question. Rabbi Mendel waited a few moments and then continued by telling a story:

Once, in a small Russian town, two children—let us call them David and Jonathan—became fast friends. They played together, they got into trouble together, and they always helped each other out. When, one day, it became clear that the responsibilities of young adulthood would force them to move to separate towns, they decided to enter into a bond of friendship. They promised that wherever life may lead them, they would never forget the fellowship they had shared.

Years later, Jonathan—who by that time had entered the world of business, and had a large family—was accused of a serious crime of a political nature, which involved the possibility of the death penalty if he were convicted. When news of the situation reached David, he traveled to the city where Jonathan was being tried, and demanded to see the prosecutor. He said, "I do not know why you are accusing my old friend Jonathan, but of one thing I am sure . . . he could not have committed that crime!" When it became clear that the prosecutor was utterly unimpressed by David's assurances regarding Jonathan's character, David found himself blurting out, "I'll tell you why I'm so sure that Jonathan is innocent—it's because I committed the crime myself!" Having a confession in hand, the prosecutor had no choice but to release Jonathan and imprison David. However, when Jonathan discovered the reason for his release from prison, he immediately reversed his own protestations of innocence and loudly declared that he was, indeed, the guilty party after all. At this point the prosecutor threw up his hands and, because of the political nature of the accusations, decided to refer the whole matter to the central government.

Eventually, the case came to the attention of the czar himself. The czar called both parties into his private chambers, and demanded that they tell him the truth. Both David and Jonathan told the czar of the bond of friendship they had made long ago, and each one explained how he had confessed in order to save his fellow. Suddenly, the czar began to cry. David and Jonathan were both puzzled and frightened. After a while the czar regained his composure and said, "I am the Czar of Russia, I can have anything I want. My servants are only too eager to do my bidding. But there is one thing I do not have, and could never get by demanding it. And that is . . . a true friend. Of course I have millions of subjects, as well as many advisors and counsellors. But that is all very different than a true friend.

"Your stories have the ring of truth, and I am sure that you are both innocent. So, you are free to go. But, may I ask a favor? Could you grant me the gift which no one else can give me? Will you take me in and make me the third partner in your bond of friendship?"

Rabbi Mendel of Rymanov looked at his congregants and said, "You see, God is an all-powerful ruler. The whole universe is His. But there is one thing, in all his awesome majesty, which, as it were, He does not have—a true friend. So whenever two people really love each other, and carry out in life the full meaning of the words "And thou shalt love thy neighbor as thyself," then God, as it were, gazes on them longingly and says, "I am the Lord—I created heaven and earth, all the angelic hosts sing my praises, but there is one thing they cannot be for me . . . a true friend. So, I ask you, will you allow Me to be the third partner in your friendship?"

### Notes

1.   S. A. Horodezky, ed., *Shivhei ha-Besht* [Hebrew] (Tel Aviv: Dvir, 1975), p. 41. An English translation of this work, by Dan Ben-Amos and Jerome R. Mintz, was published under the title *In Praise of the Baal Shem Tov* (Bloomington, Ind.: Indiana University Press, 1970).

2.   We present here the version of this story found in *Keter Shem Tov*, a collection of the Besht's teachings as found in the writings of his students, in particular Jacob Joseph of Polonnoye. The work, compiled by Aharon ben Zvi Hirsh ha-Cohen, appeared originally in 1794-1795. Most current editions are quite corrupt, with separate teachings running together in one section, and with some teachings arbitrarily divided and made to appear as separate and unrelated.

Many of these errors are corrected in the Kehot Publication Society edition (Brooklyn, 1972). In that edition, our passage appears on pp. 124-125, and is marked as no. 424.

3. *Keter Shem Tov*, p. 15, no. 51.

4. *Keter Shem Tov*, p. 15, no. 51.

5. See the discussion of J.G. Weiss, "The Kavvanoth of Prayer in Early Hasidism," *Journal of Jewish Studies* 9 (1958): 163-192. For Hasidic prayer in general, see Louis Jacobs, *Hasidic Prayer* (New York: Schocken Brooks, 1973).

6. Cf. *Keter Shem Tov*, p. 8, nos. 22-23.

7. Cf. Mordecai Wilensky, *Hasidim u-Mitnaggedim* [Hebrew] (Jerusalem: Bialik Institute, 1970).

8. Cf. Samuel H. Dresner, *The Zaddik* (New York: Schocken Books, 1974).

9. The material on the *rebbe* as spiritual counsellor has been extensively discussed by Zalman M. Schachter in *The Yehidut: A Study of Counselling in Hasidism*, (Ph.D. diss., Hebrew Union College, 1968).

10. Cf. J.G. Weiss, "Via Passiva in Early Hasidism," *Journal of Jewish Studies* 11 (1960): 137-155; also Rivka Schatz Uffenheimer, *Ha-Hasidut ke-Mistikah* [Hebrew] (Jerusalem: Magnes Press, 1980), especially Chapters 8 and 9.

11. The whole issue of the social significance of Hasidism is perceptively discussed by Shmuel Ettinger, "The Hasidic Movement—Reality and Ideals," in *Jewish Society Throughout the Ages*, eds. Haim Hillel Ben-Sasson and Shmuel Ettinger (New York: Schocken Books, 1973), pp. 251-266. Ettinger emphasizes the role of Hasidism as a unifying force.

12. Material on this force has been collected in Harry M. Rabinowicz, *The World of Hasidism* (Hartford, Ct.: Hartmore House, 1970), pp. 202-210.

13. For the Mitnaggedic attitude, see Hayyim Volozhiner, *Nefesh ha-Hayyim* (Vilna, 1834), especially Chapter 3. This work and its relationship to Hasidism has been discussed by Nahum (Norman) Lamm, *Torah Lishmah* (Jerusalem: Mossad HaRav Kook, 1972). See also Norman Lamm, *Faith and Doubt* (New York: Ktav, 1971), pp. 42-68; 212-246.

14. As recounted by Shelomo Carlebach.

### For Further Reading

Buber, Martin. *Tales of the Hasidim.* 2 vols. New York: Schocken Books, 1975.

Jacobs, Louis. *Hasidic Prayer.* New York: Schocken Books, 1975.

Rabinowicz, Harry. *The World of Hasidism.* Hartford, Ct.: Hartmore House, 1970.

Schatz Uffenheimer, Rivka. *Quietistic Elements in Eighteenth-Century Hasidic Thought.* [Hebrew] Jerusalem: Magnes Press, 1980.

Wiesel, Elie. *Souls on Fire.* New York: Vintage Books, 1973.

# Jewish Religious Leadership in Germany: Its Cultural and Religious Outlook

## DAVID ELLENSON

In November, 1938, immediately after *Kristallnacht* (Night of Broken Glass—1938 German pogrom), the *Rabbiner-Seminar fuer das Orthodoxe Judentum*, the Orthodox rabbinical seminary established by Rabbi Esriel Hildesheimer of Berlin in 1873, was closed by the Nazis. Similarly, the pogrom of 1938 led to the demise of the *Juedisch-Theologisches Seminar* of Breslau and on February 21, 1939, this institution of Positive-Historical Judaism, which had opened in 1854 and had initially been headed by Rabbi Zacharias Frankel, ordained its last two students as rabbis. Finally, on July 19, 1942, the *Hochschule fuer die Wissenschaft des Judentums*, established by Rabbi Abraham Geiger of Berlin in 1872 as a center for the academic study of Judaism and the ordination of Liberal rabbis, was also shut down by the Nazis. Thus, through the destruction of these three major spiritual centers of religious German Jewry, the Nazis brought an end to an important era in German Jewish history. However, the religious and cultural worldviews these institutions represented, and the models of Jewish religious leadership they produced, have been of lasting relevance to Jews in Western lands. Institutions such as Yeshiva University, the Jewish Theological Seminary, and the Hebrew Union College-Jewish Institute of Religion in the United States, and the Leo Baeck Rabbinical College in London are all, in several senses, modeled today after these three previous centers of German Jewish religious life. Their significance clearly extends beyond their own day into our own.

This brief essay will attempt to capture the essence of the religious worldviews—the differences and similarities—that marked the outlooks of the leaders of these three German Jewish religious institutions, and will draw a profile of the cultural and religious models of leadership they produced. In this way, something of the spirit of German Jewish religiosity can be evoked. This will also enable us to understand its legacy for the post-Holocaust Jewish world.

## I.

Alexander Altmann, a graduate of the Orthodox Hildesheimer Seminary in Berlin, has commented that graduates of the three major rabbinical institutions of German Jewry shared sufficient cultural and religious characteristics to be termed "colleagues." Essentially "intellectuals," these western European rabbis "all shared a common language"[1] and a German cultural milieu. Although there is some truth to the claim that a true German-Jewish dialogue never existed,[2] Altmann's observations point to the unique Jewish cultural and religious leaders produced in nineteenth- and twentieth-century Germany. In order to understand the background for this leadership cadre and its worldview, it is necessary to turn to the first decades of the nineteenth century and the phenomenon of *Wissenschaft des Judentums*—the academic study of Judaism—which was born in those formative years.

The term *"Wissenschaft des Judentums"* was first used by Leopold Zunz (1794-1886), perhaps the greatest scholar of nineteenth-century Germany, in the title, *Zeitschrift fuer die Wissenschaft des Judentums (Journal for the Scientific Study of Judaism)*, which he edited from 1822 to 1823 for the *Verein fuer Kultur und Wissenschaft der Juden* (Society for Jewish Culture and Science), an association formed by several outstanding Jewish students in Berlin in 1819. Immanuel Wolf, in the first article published in this periodical, "Concerning the Idea of a Science of Judaism," stated that *Wissenschaft des Judentums* embraced Judaism in its totality, "not in the limited sense of Jewish religion alone." Secondly, the purpose of the academic study of Judaism was to present Judaism in a systematic form by relating the particular item under discussion to underlying principles which formed the core of Judaism. Here, the Hegelian and German idealistic concern to define the essence of a phenomenon can be seen to have made a major impact upon these early pioneers. Moreover, this influence continued on German Jewish religious thinkers throughout the nineteenth century. Finally, every subject treated by *Wissenschaft des Judentums* was to be explored for its own sake, and not for some extraneous program or school.[3] *Wissenschaft des Judentums* thus aspired to an academic objectivity and presentation that conformed to contemporary standards of German scholarship.

All branches of Judaism in Germany—Liberal (which had a generally less ritually observant Reform wing and a more ritually observant Positive-Historical wing) and Orthodox (with the exception of Rabbi Samson Raphael Hirsch, 1808-1888, and his followers)—were equally wedded to *Wissenschaft des Judentums*. All were committed to explaining Judaism to German Jews and Gentiles in the language and style of contemporary German culture. Abraham Geiger, Zacharias Frankel, and Leopold Zunz embraced *Wissenschaft des Judentums*. Esriel Hildesheimer, in a letter to a supporter of his Orthodox seminary, emphasized that *Wissenschaft des Judentums* was practiced no less assiduously within the walls of the *Rabbiner-Seminar* than it was at Breslau or at the *Hochschule*.[4] The rabbinical candidates at all three schools were required to be graduates of German *Gymnasia* (university preparatory schools or the equivalent), and during their years at the seminary, each student also had to obtain a doctorate from a German university. Thus, men such as Fritz Bamberger and Abraham Joshua Heschel of the *Hochschule*, who later became leading scholars of American Reform and Conservative Judaism, and Eliezer Berkovits of the *Rabbiner-*

*Seminar,* a major contemporary spokesman of Orthodox Judaism in the United States, were students at the University of Berlin; this created collegiality and relationships between graduates of the different seminaries not found in other countries, such as the United States. Professors at each institution engaged in rigorous academic studies, and the results of their research were usually published in yearbooks printed by each institution. The spirit of the German rabbinical seminary led to a similarity of outlook and of spirit.

How, though, and why did this come to be the case? Moreover, having seen how Wolf defined *Wissenschaft des Judentums,* it is now necessary to ask how the leaders of these rabbinical institutions viewed the purposes of this study. The answers to these questions are interrelated and provide a key to understanding the spirit of religious Jewry in Germany—a spirit attracted to the worth of German culture—during the pre-Holocaust era.

First, it is essential to note that the political structure of the medieval world—the Jewish one included—dissolved in western Europe with the rise of the modern nation-state and the advent of modern notions of individual, not group, rights. Civil rights were now granted to individuals and not to corporate, semiautonomous bodies within the state. Clermont-Tonnerre, a leader of the French Revolution, articulated this position for the Jews when he stated, "The Jews should be denied everything as a nation, but [the Jew] granted everything as an individual." The political identity of the Jew, which in Europe during the Middle Ages had been derived from his position as a member of the Jewish community, was transformed. The Jew was now regarded as a citizen of the country or state where he resided, whose religious faith happened to be Jewish. The Jewish community was no longer semiautonomous, and the community no longer could impose police sanctions to enforce its will. Religious Jews in Germany did not protest these developments, but—from Hirsch to Geiger—applauded the opportunities that political emancipation afforded the Jews.

The Jews also began to participate in the life of German society and culture. During these post-Napoleonic years, Jewish life moved from a segregated ethnic-religious community, united by a common worldview and political structure, into fragmented communities stripped of their autonomy and eagerly seeking their place within European culture and society. Jewish identity was no longer monolithic, and Jewish religious leaders had to define a philosophy that would permit Jews to participate in Western life while still maintaining concepts and practices deemed essential to an "authentic Judaism." While responses to this challenge were variegated, *Wissenschaft des Judentums* and an affirmation of German culture on the part of the religious leaders of German Jews became an important, indeed, crucial means to responding to this dilemma of modernity.

*Wissenschaft des Judentums,* as understood by its nineteenth-century German practitioners, was designed as a weapon in the struggle for political emancipation and cultural equality. In 1836, and again in 1845, Abraham Geiger called for the establishment of a department of Jewish theology in a German university. All such attempts to establish Jewish theological departments at German universities failed and with it the hope that German universities—by including the academic study of Judaism within their curricula—would legitimate the integral role Judaism played in the development of the West. Despite this failure, the early years of *Wissenschaft des Judentums* also witnessed efforts on the part of Jewish religious leaders to replace the old talmudic rabbinical academies *(yeshivot)* with modern rabbinical seminaries that would train rabbis both in traditional rabbinic texts and the more contemporary scientific approaches to Jewish scholarship. Ludwig Phillipson (1811-1889), a major Reform leader, proposed the creation of a seminary in 1837, but only in 1854 was such a school created in Breslau; its head was Zacharias Frankel. Slightly less than two decades later the *Hochschule* and the *Rabbiner-Seminar* were founded.

The purpose of these seminaries, and their study of *Wissenschaft des Judentums,* was to lead the Jews into a harmonious relation with the age and nation in which they lived. By applying contemporary standards of scholarship to Judaism and to the study of the Jewish past, proponents of *Wissenschaft des Judentums* felt that they were extricating Judaism from its cultural isolation and thus earning a place of cultural parity within the intellectual milieu of nineteenth-century postrevolutionary Europe. The inclusion of *Wissenschaft des Judentums* in the training of German rabbis meant that these rabbis shared a common theological language and a positive attitude towards German culture. The embracement of *Wissenschaft des Judentums* was intended to improve the political, as well as cultural, position of the Jews in Germany. As Zunz explained, one of the purposes was "the winning of favor of those in power and the good will of sensible men."[5] It was this positive attitude towards German culture that marked all religious branches of German Jews. *Wissenschaft des Judentums* was seen as an ally in the political and cultural struggle of Judaism in its confrontation with modernity in Germany during the nineteenth and twentieth centuries.

Proof for this enthusiasm with which religious Jews in Germany welcomed political emancipation and Western culture can also be seen in the cultural mores and patterns of the leading German rabbis. German Liberal Judaism adopted nineteenth-century German aesthetic standards of decorum, order, and beauty and employed them in the cause of liturgical reform and synagogal architecture. Sermons in the vernacular, choirs, clerical gowns, and the abbreviation of services were introduced into German Jewish religious life in the nineteenth century. However, these reforms were not confined to Liberal synagogues alone, but became standard in many Orthodox synagogues as well (although prayers were not abbreviated). Decorum came to mark the German religious service, and rabbis such as Hirsch and Hildesheimer wore clerical gowns when attending services and preached sermons of moral edification and spiritual uplift in the same manner as their Reform colleagues. Moreover, as a picture of Rabbi Hirsch Hildesheimer—the son of Esriel and himself a professor at the *Rabbiner-Seminar*—in the lithograph collection of the Skirball Museum at Hebrew Union College in Los Angeles indicates, the German Orthodox rabbi dressed in contemporary German attire and would sometimes even go bareheaded. Indeed, Rabbi David Hoffman (1843-1921), Hildesheimer's successor as rector of the *Rabbiner-Seminar*, reports that when he first arrived in Frankfurt from his native Hungary, Rabbi Hirsch informed him that wearing a head covering in certain stituations in Germany would be regarded as a display of bad manners.[6] Orthodox Jews in other parts of Europe viewed their German colleagues with suspicion, and Rabbi Hildesheimer himself, in the responsum of one Hungarian Orthodox rabbi, was referred to as "an abominable troubler who intends to destroy the Jews."[7] Thus, it is evident that the positive affirmation of Western culture by the religious leadership of German Jews distinguished it from the majority of rabbis living in eastern Europe.

# II

Despite the common cultural bonds which united German Jewish religious leaders, there were also crucial differences between the religious outlooks of these men. A major purpose of *Wissenschaft des Judentums* was to aid the Jews in their struggle for political emancipation and entry into German cultural life, but the academic study of Judaism also had another purpose—to provide the basis for religious reform. Zunz said that *Wissenschaft des Judentums* would make it possible "to know and distinguish the old which is still of use, the antiquated which has become pernicious, and the new which is desirable."[8] This approach was designed to integrate the "genuine" and "essential" elements in the Jewish past into contemporary Judaism. Reform was to be based on historical investigation. History, the academic study of the past, was thus a major determinant for theology.

The respective attitudes towards history and the role of history in theology divided the Liberals from the Orthodox in Germany. Both Frankel and Geiger believed that all religions, including Judaism, were the products of history. Religions did not simply endure but evolved in history. One obvious implication of this view was that history produced certain forms and institutional expressions in one particular era and could eliminate or create new ones for different milieus. One radical (Reform) exponent, Rabbi Samuel Holdheim (1806-1860), applied this view to Judaism in the following declaration: "The Talmud speaks with the ideology of its time, and for that time it was right. I speak from the higher ideology of my time, and for this age I am right."[9] According to the Liberals' position, history legitimated the reforms they made in contemporary Jewish practice and theology.

However, it is crucial to note that the study of history could be used not only to abnegate certain traditional practices, but also to legislate the continuity of Jewish ritual and ceremonial law. Frankel was the most prominent non-Orthodox leader in Germany to adopt this view towards the study of Jewish past; Geiger, to a large extent, also shared this attitude. In his classic, *Darkhe HaMishnah*, Frankel asserted that the talmudic expression, "a tradition of Moses from Sinai," referred to those ordinances whose origins were unknown and which, because of their great antiquity, were regarded by the rabbis of the Talmud *as if* they had been received by Moses at Sinai. Frankel accepted the idea that Judaism had developed over time; and this work is one of the great contributions to the study of the development of Jewish law. Frankel stated that the academic study of the Jewish past could be used to demonstrate the developmental character of the rabbinic law, but it also showed the "Positive-Historical" and binding nature of the past. Law, revealed by the study of the Jewish past as the essence of Judaism, could not be dismissed. Ritual laws regarding the Sabbath and Jewish dietary laws had to be retained, and Frankel departed from his more Liberal colleagues in the 1840s through his insistence that the predominantly Hebrew character of Jewish prayer be maintained.

Geiger was not as conservative as Frankel in his approach to Jewish traditions and history, although he, too, spoke of "Positive-Historical" approaches to Judaism. Geiger described Judaism in Hegelian terms and saw the notion of one God as the essential ideal of Judaism, but he opposed Sunday Sabbath worship, observed Jewish dietary laws, and refused to serve separatist Reform congregations which were not affiliated with the general Jewish community. Liberal Judaism in Germany was much more traditional than in the United States and, in almost every Liberal community in Germany, men wore head coverings during prayer and men and women sat separately during services. German Liberal rabbis uniformly observed the dietary laws and—in the twentieth century—only in the largest cities would a Liberal rabbi have driven on the Sabbath. This display of traditional ritual practice by the Liberals allowed the Orthodox to be somewhat tolerant of their Liberal brethren and also sometimes permitted cooperation on such issues as conversion between Liberal and Orthodox rabbis in Germany.[10]

Finally, a distinctive Liberal approach to revelation emerged in Germany during the nineteenth and twentieth centuries. Influenced by liberal Protestant thinkers, Liberal Jewish theologians asserted that the revelation into which God entered with Moses and the Jewish people at Sinai was, "a nonpropositional one." God, in this view, revealed Himself as a presence to the Jewish people at Sinai and did not, initially, place any substantive demands (such as commandments) upon them. The Jewish people, when covenanting with God at Sinai, first said, "We will do," indicating their affirmation of His presence. Only later did they respond, "We will listen," availing themselves of the substantive content of His message.

This approach, most clearly stated by the great lay leader of

Liberal German Jewry, Martin Buber (1878-1965), has been important in liberal Jewish circles until today. Its importance in Germany, and its relationship to *Wissenschaft des Judentums,* can be seen most clearly in the life and thought of Buber's friend and colleague, another layman, Franz Rosenzweig (1886-1929). Rosenzweig believed in the dynamic quality of Jewish revelation and felt that a commitment to understanding that revelation necessitated an encounter with Jewish sources and history. Rosenzweig established an adult education program in Frankfurt and spoke of the need for the Jew—both as an individual and as a member of a community—to distinguish the Law *(Gesetz)* and commandment *(Gebot).* Law, to Rosenzweig, was impersonal and static. Commandment, however, was personal, an address by God to the individual Jew and the Jewish community. In Rosenzweig's view, the task of the Jew, through study and practice, was to transform the Law into commandment. In this way, individual autonomy—a modern concept—could be retained while yet maintaining a common sense of obligation. Indeed, this approach, which allows both the individual Jew and the Jewish community to study the Jewish tradition in order to extract God's message from it, remains one of German Jewry's most profound contributions to contemporary Jewish religious life.[11]

For the Orthodox in Germany, however, this approach to Jewish life and faith was considered inauthentic. In Rabbi Hildesheimer's words, Jewish authenticity consisted of continued allegiance to the principle that the Torah—both written and oral—was revealed "from the mouth of the Almighty." For Rabbi Samson Raphael Hirsch, this meant that "the Torah, both written and oral, was closed with Moses at Sinai."[12] In contrast to Liberal Jewish theology, the Orthodox rabbis saw Jewish tradition as codified in the rabbinic law and the writings of leading rabbinical authorities over the centuries as authentic. They labeled themselves *"Gesetztreuer,"* literally, "faithful to the Law [of the Torah]," and attacked all other denominations of Judaism as religiously inauthentic.

The Orthodox attitude towards history—not its positive response to German culture, language, patriotism, and style—distinguished it from the Reformers. The Orthodox denied historical development in Jewish law, and Hirsch excoriated Frankel for his work on the development of the rabbinic law. Similarly, Hildesheimer would not permit the academic study of the Jewish past to encroach upon the theological principle that Jewish law was divine and given by God to Moses at Sinai.[13] Thus, Hildesheimer and Hirsch proscribed any Jewish community from accepting a graduate of the Breslau Seminary as a rabbi and stated that if a community chose to accept such a rabbi, then a pious Jew was obligated, by religious duty, to secede from it. From the standpoint of theology, Hildesheimer saw little to choose between Frankel and Geiger. He wrote, "How little is the difference between these Reformers [the Breslau people], who do their work with silk gloves on their hands, and the Reformer Geiger, who strikes with a sledgehammer."[14] God's revelation to the Jewish people was seen as a "propositional one," and the ahistorical nature of Jewish law was defended by the Orthodox in accordance with the rabbinic statement found in the *Palestinian Talmud, Peah* 17a, "Even that which a distinguished disciple is destined to teach in the future before his master was already revealed to Moses at Sinai." The problem of individual autonomy and development in Jewish law, while sometimes alluded to in the writings of the German Orthodox, was not as important for them as for their Liberal colleagues. In this sense, the spiritual outlooks of German Orthodox and Liberal Jews diverged and the purpose of *Wissenschaft des Judentums,* to provide the scientific basis for religious reform, was rejected by the Orthodox in Germany.

# III

Moshe Schwarcz has commented that, "Cultural integration became one of the distinguishing marks of religious Jewry in Germany."[15] This observation is correct. German Jews were highly acculturated, and this led to similar cultural styles and worldviews on many facets of German Jewish religious life. The German rabbi, trained in *Wissenschaft des Judentums,* was uniquely the modern scholar-rabbi. There were, of course, real differences between religious trends in German Jewish life. Nevertheless, the spirit of cultural integration and loyalty to Judaism exemplified by the religious leaders of the German Jews remains instructive to Jews today and is an important part of the spiritual legacy bequeathed by German Jews to the contemporary Jewish world. The spirit of German Judaism, despite the physical destruction and dispersion of its people and institutions, continues today.

### Notes

1. Alexander Altmann, "The German Rabbi: 1910-1939," *Leo Baeck Institute Yearbook* (1974): 32.

2. Gershom Scholem, "Against the Myth of the German-Jewish Dialogue," in *On Jews and Judaism in Crisis,* Gershom Scholem (New York: Schocken Books, 1976), pp. 65-70.

3. For a translation of the Wolf essay, see Michael Meyer, *Ideas of Jewish History* (New York: Behrman House, 1974), pp. 141-155.

4. See Ismar Schorsch, "Ideology and History in the Age of Emancipation," in *Heinrich Graetz—The Structure of Jewish History and Other Essays,* ed. and trans. Ismar Schorsch (New York: Ktav, 1975), pp. 10-11.

5. Leopold Zunz, quoted by Nahum N. Glatzer, "The Beginnings of Modern Jewish Studies," in *Studies in Nineteenth-Century Jewish Intellectual History,* ed. Alexander Altmann (Cambridge: Harvard University Press, 1964), p. 39.

6. David Hoffman, *Melammed L'Hoyil, Yoreh Deah*, no. 56.

7. This description of Hildesheimer by Rabbi Hillel Lichtenstein (1815-1891) is found in Alexander Guttmann, *The Struggle Over Reform in Rabbinic Literaure* (New York: World Union for Progressive Judaism, 1977), pp. 289-291.

8. Leopold Zunz, quoted in Michael Meyer, *The Origins of the Modern Jew* (Detroit: Wayne State University Press, 1967), p. 161.

9. Cited by Noah Rosenbloom, *Tradition in an Age of Reform* (Philadelphia: The Jewish Publication Society, 1967), p. 18.

10. I would like to thank my colleague, Rabbi Wolli Kaelter, who immigrated to the United States in 1935 and whose father was the Liberal rabbi in Danzig prior to the Holocaust, for these insights into German Liberal Judaism.

11. For example, see Jakob J. Petuchowski, *Ever Since Sinai* (New York: Arbit, 1979); and Eugene B. Borowitz, *How Can a Jew Speak of Faith Today?* (Philadelphia: Westminster Press, 1969), for the influence Buber and Rosenzweig have had upon American Reform theologians. For further insight into the influence of Rosenzweig upon contemporary non-Orthodox Jewish thought in America, see Milton Himmelfarb's Introduction to *The Condition of Jewish Belief*, compiled by the editors of *Commentary* magazine (London: Macmillan & Co., 1966).

12. Cited by Rosenbloom, *Tradition in an Age of Reform*, p. 234.

13. A classic statement of the Hildesheimer circle's approach to academic scholarship and its limits can be found in David Hoffmann's introduction to his commentary on Leviticus. The translation of this introduction appears in Jenny Marmorstein, "David Hoffman: Defender of the Faith," *Tradition* (Winter 1966): 91-101. There, Hoffman writes, "Any interpretation of the Torah which opposes traditional interpretation . . . is to be rejected as . . . an un-Jewish explanation," p. 92.

14. See David Ellenson, "Modern Orthodoxy and Jewish Religious Pluralism: The Case of Rabbi Esriel Hildesheimer," *Tradition* (Spring 1979): 74-91.

15. Moshe Schwarcz, "Religious Currents and General Culture," *Leo Baeck Institute Yearbook* (1971): 3.

**For Further Reading**

Blau, Joseph. *Modern Varieties of Judaism*. New York: Columbia University Press, 1966.

Graupe, Heinz Moshe. *The Rise of Modern Judaism*. Huntington, NY: Robert E. Krieger Publishing Company, 1978.

Meyer, Michael. *The Origins of the Modern Jew*. Detroit: Wayne State University Press, 1967.

Schorsch, Ismar, ed. and trans. *Heinrich Graetz: The Structure of Jewish History and Other Essays*. New York: Ktav, 1975.

3

# ANTISEMITISM

# In Every Generation

. . . in every century, the non-Jewish world looked with suspicion on this people set apart; men who needed scapegoats for their own failure turned readily against the Jew.

In the earliest days of Christianity, St. John Chrysostom, frustrated by the Jews' refusal to convert, called them the most miserable of men. The great theologian, Martin Luther, encountering the same steadfastness, declared: "Their synagogues should be set on fire . . . their homes should likewise be broken down and destroyed . . . let us drive them out of the country for all time."

In every country the Jews were the convenient enemy. To the illiterate, they were knowledgeable; to the peasants, wealthy; to the rich, clever. The Romans saw them as political rivals; the Inquisitors saw them as Christ killers; the Cossacks saw them as squeezing out the wealth of the land. To them they were different; different in their looks, in their mode of dress, in their beliefs, in the observance of their holy days. . . .

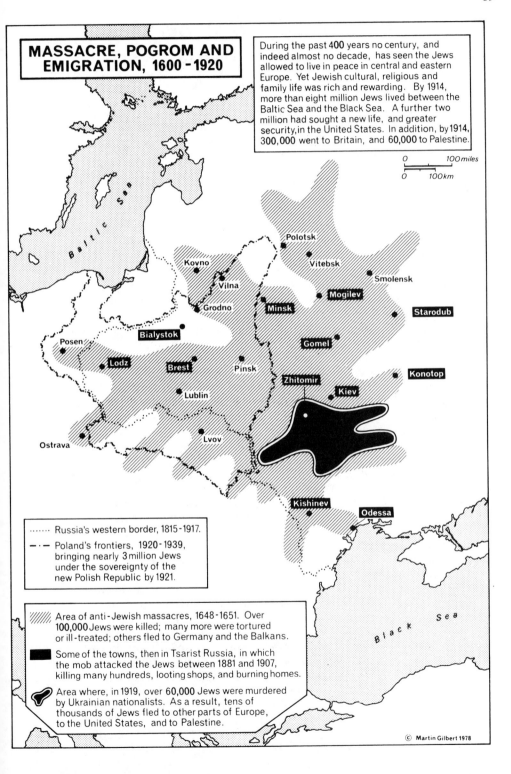

# MASSACRE, POGROM AND EMIGRATION, 1600-1920

During the past 400 years no century, and indeed almost no decade, has seen the Jews allowed to live in peace in central and eastern Europe. Yet Jewish cultural, religious and family life was rich and rewarding. By 1914, more than eight million Jews lived between the Baltic Sea and the Black Sea. A further two million had sought a new life, and greater security, in the United States. In addition, by 1914, 300,000 went to Britain, and 60,000 to Palestine.

0    100 miles
0    100 km

Polotsk
Vitebsk
Kovno
Smolensk
Vilna
Mogilev
Grodno
Minsk
Starodub
Posen
Bialystok
Gomel
Lodz
Brest
Pinsk
Konotop
Zhitomir
Lublin
Kiev
Ostrava
Lvov
Kishinev
Odessa

Baltic Sea
Black Sea

...... Russia's western border, 1815-1917.

—·— Poland's frontiers, 1920-1939, bringing nearly 3 million Jews under the sovereignty of the new Polish Republic by 1921.

///// Area of anti-Jewish massacres, 1648-1651. Over 100,000 Jews were killed; many more were tortured or ill-treated; others fled to Germany and the Balkans.

███ Some of the towns, then in Tsarist Russia, in which the mob attacked the Jews between 1881 and 1907, killing many hundreds, looting shops, and burning homes.

Area where, in 1919, over 60,000 Jews were murdered by Ukrainian nationalists. As a result, tens of thousands of Jews fled to other parts of Europe, to the United States, and to Palestine.

© Martin Gilbert 1978

# The Theological Roots of Antisemitism: A Christian View

## PAUL M. VAN BUREN

"Antisemitism" is a modern word, first coined in 1879 in connection with the contemporary pseudoscientific racial theory, but it also refers to a phenomenon with ancient roots. Stripped of modern racist overtones, antisemitism is the heir of an anti-Judaism as old as Western Christianity. Behind the antisemitism that played so large a role in Hitler's thinking and program lies a long and well-documented history of Jew-hatred developed and nurtured by the Church.

There is solid historical evidence of anti-Jewish acts and attitudes before Christianity came into prominence in the ancient world. From a sociopsychological perspective, it would be likely that any people resisting total assimilation into the Hellenistic culture of the Roman Empire would arouse some degree of suspicion. But anti-Jewish acts in the Roman Empire were not programmatic and lacked any cohesive rationale. The Roman Empire was not systematically antisemitic. On the contrary, the Jewish people had legal standing and the right to live according to their own traditions.

The Christian church, as represented by the surviving writings of its leaders, began before it was a century old to produce a systematic anti-Jewish teaching tied directly to its own theological affirmations. By the second century of the Common Era, a consistent theological rationale for disdain of Jews and contempt for Judaism had been developed and was to mark the whole course of Western civilization. As the Church became ever more politically powerful, beginning in the fourth century, theory was increasingly put into practice. Jews lost their favored status under Roman law, and a pattern of discrimination and harassment was set in motion, leading to the ghetto, physical expulsions, and pogroms. Hitler's "Final Solution to the Jewish Question" marked a radical new step, but it was a step on a road prepared by the Christian church. The failure of the Church to mount any serious resistance to Hitler's program becomes more understandable, if not excusable, when the theological roots of antisemitism are understood.

The beginnings of this tragic development lie in the first-century split between the Christian church and the Jewish people, an event documented by limited and indirect evidence. We can be certain that the initial Jesus movement was at first totally Jewish, and can be seen as a Jewish sect. We know little about that Jewish community, because there are no firsthand accounts. The apostle Paul is the only author of the writings comprising the Church's New Testament who was certainly a Jew, but he only wrote to Gentile Christians about Gentile problems, such as, how Gentiles can escape from the curse of Torah, a curse richly deserved for having rejected Torah (the Law) when it was offered at Sinai. If we can trust the Gentile author of the

Acts of the Apostles, Paul was thought to have taught that the Jews of the Diaspora should abandon Torah. That would have shocked any Jew, including those of the Jesus movement. There is no evidence from Paul's authentic letters to support this charge, but such a misunderstanding may have been the seedbed of distrust that led to the later split.

The future of the Church was not in the Jerusalem community. As it is continued in loyal Jewish practice and worship, the Diaspora movement was going in a different direction. It was drawing its members from the Gentiles. We may assume from Paul's letters that they were Gentiles well-versed in the Greek translation of Israel's Scriptures, for Paul based most of his teachings and arguments on those writings. It seems reasonable to conclude that these Gentile converts to the young Church were largely drawn from the so-called "God-fearers" of whom the first-century Jewish historian Flavius Josephus wrote—people attracted to Judaism, familiar with its teaching and Scriptures, frequenters of Diaspora synagogues, but not yet full converts. The Gentile mission of Paul and others, therefore, would seem to have harvested in fields well-planted and watered by the Pharisees and other agents of Jewish proselytism. What is certain is that the Church, originally a purely Jewish movement, in membership was well on its way by the middle of the first century to becoming an almost totally Gentile enterprise.

There were evidently those among the new Gentile converts to Christianity who thought that one could only be a member of this movement by becoming a full Jewish convert, accepting circumcision, and keeping Torah. Paul argued vehemently against that view, maintaining that in Jesus the God of Israel had done a new thing, opening the light of his love to Gentiles *as Gentiles,* to receive the blessing of Abraham alongside Israel. Paul, therefore, argued that his Gentile converts not seek circumcision nor follow the details of Torah observance, since this would be to deny God's new opening to them. Nowhere did Paul argue that *Jews* should abandon Torah, but after his death, an increasingly Gentile church was to read him as if he had spoken without respect to whether his audience was Jew or Gentile. What Paul wrote against Gentile imitation of Jewish practice was read later as an attack on Jewish practice by Jews. The grounds for Christian anti-Judaism were thus unwittingly prepared by one who was proud of his Jewish identity and heritage, convinced that God's covenant with Israel was eternal. It was planted and watered by Gentiles who failed to understand the complex understanding of Torah of the Pharisee Paul.

It is certain that Paul argued that *Gentiles* did not need to become Jews in order to know the love of God. It is equally certain that he was interpreted to have meant that *Jews* need not (and therefore should not) remain Jews in order to know the love of God. The question unfolds whether the theological roots of antisemitism lie within the New Testament itself, or whether they are to be found in a Gentile misreading of writings rooted in the Jewish character of the original Jesus movement. In the case of the authentic letters of Paul, a case can be made for the second answer. For the Gospels, it is not so clear.

The Gospel of Mark is generally considered the earliest; it was written about the time of the destruction of the Second Temple and the sack of Jerusalem (68 C.E.*). Most scholars believe that the other Gospels come from nearer the time of the split and reflect the growing animosity. It has been suggested that the Jerusalem church may have withheld support for the revolt against Rome, which would have contributed to hard feelings, but evidence on this is not reliable. The Gospels of Matthew and John portray especially hostile relations between Jesus and various groups. It could be that their authors assumed that their own conflicts with the Pharisees (by their day the dominant force in Jewish life) mirrored the conflict in which Jesus lost his life, but for whatever reason, or as Gentiles, they may simply have never shared the evident love and concern of Jesus for his people. Whatever the cause, they presented Jesus in conflict with his own people (in the process presenting the cruel procurator Pilate, whom the Emperor Caligula recalled from Palestine for his tyrannical ways, as a weak and generally kindly soul) so as to encourage any simple reader to see Jews generally as responsible for his death. Matthew has the crowd cry out, "His blood be upon us and upon our children," perhaps having in mind the destruction of Jerusalem in 68 C.E., but many Gentile readers for centuries afterward read this as a call to punish this self-condemned people in every way.

The Gospels are complex documents arising from a complicated tradition in a confusing time. There is more to them than the passages that have caused so much Jewish suffering. There can be no doubt that they contain words which have fed antisemitism for two thousand years, yet those very words, read with an understanding of their context, can be read as polemics understandable in our less-than-perfect world and so as no justification whatsoever for an anti-Judaic conclusion. What can scarcely be denied is that an anti-Judaic conclusion was the consistent result of the way in which the Gospels, and also Paul, were read and interpreted by Christians from the second to the twentieth centuries. They are still read by many in this manner. This reading is the foundation for the distinctive theological anti-Judaism of the Christian tradition. It is the theological root of antisemitism.

On this foundation, Christian leaders developed a theological polemic against the Jewish people that suggests that many of their flock may have gotten along quite well with their Jewish neighbors and found synagogue services worth attending. Reading between the lines of this polemic, one detects the signs of the continuing attraction of the intimacy and loftiness of the Jewish understanding of God, as well as of the moral worth of Jewish living, so different from the corruption of daily life in the empire. This polemic entered deeply into the theology of the Church and produced a vision of reality in which a negative view of Jews and Judaism was bound to

---

* *Common Era; equals* A.D.

the self-understanding of the Church.

The result of this development, already evident in the writings of the second century authors and elaborated over the following two centuries, was the theology of displacement: The Church was the true heir of the election of and promises to Israel. The Jews had turned their backs on their Messiah and killed him. Having rejected God's act for their salvation, God had rejected this people. They had now been displaced by the Church, which alone had God's favor. Israel's Scriptures had become the property of the Church, which alone understood them. Judaism, therefore, had no more reason to exist, and the Jews were maintained by God in their homeless, Templeless, wandering condition as an indirect witness to the truth of the Christian church. For the sake of this witness, they were not to be killed, but like Cain, they were destined to be "a fugitive and a wanderer on the earth." This theology of displacement thus built contempt for Jews and Judaism into the very structure of the Church's self-understanding.

In the fourth century, Christianity became the official religion of the Roman Empire, and the Church came increasingly to dominate the Western world. As it did so, it put theory into practice and Jews began to lose the civil rights that had been theirs under Roman law. They were not allowed to hold public office (Synod of Claremont, 535 C.E.); they were forbidden to have Christian servants or slaves (538), which effectively excluded them from agriculture; their books were burned (681); they were taxed to support the Church (1078); they were forced to wear a badge on their clothing (1215); they were forced into ghettos (1267); and they were denied university degrees (1434). In addition to these official decrees of Church synods and councils, there were unofficial persecutions, in which many Jews lost their lives; forced "conversions"; and mass expulsions from one country after another. Antisemitism became a common feature of all of Western culture and history, and it did so frequently using the continuing theological anti-Judaism of the Christian church. When Hitler said that he was only putting into effect what the Church had always taught, he was quite correct, until his decision to kill every Jew in Europe.

In the light of the Holocaust, the churches have begun to reverse their ancient tradition of anti-Judaism. Beginning with the Second Vatican Council, the Roman Catholic church has repudiated its charge of deicide and acknowledged the continuing validity of God's covenant with the Jewish people. With increasing clarity, Church statements, both Protestant and Catholic, European and American, have denounced antisemitism and repudiated the tradition of contempt for Jews and Judaism. Whether the Church at the grass roots level will succeed in making this aboutface remains to be seen. For six million Jews, the turn has come much too late, but for the future of the Jewish people, this reversal of "the teaching of contempt" may be of no small consequence, for it begins to get at the primary root of antisemitism. That root, however, is deeply embedded in the theology of the Church and eliminating it will be no easy matter. It will require of the Church a new reading of its own sacred texts and a new understanding of its own identity. Until that happens at the level of the ordinary Christian, the theological roots of antisemitism will not be dead.

### For Further Reading

Eckardt, A. Roy. *Elder and Younger Brothers.* New York: Schocken Books, 1973.

Hay, Malcolm. *Thy Brother's Blood.* New York: Hart, 1975.

Parkes, James. *The Conflict of the Church and the Synagogue.* New York: Atheneum, 1977.

Van Buren, Paul M. *The Burden of Freedom.* New York: Seabury Press, 1976.

———. *Discerning the Way: A Theology of the Jewish-Christian Reality.* New York: Seabury Press, 1980.

# Luther and the Jews

## FRANKLIN SHERMAN

Martin Luther did not really know what he was starting when he nailed his "Ninety-Five Theses" to the church door in Wittenberg that late October day in the year 1517. The effects of his action spread beyond his wildest imagining, and later ages would mark that event as the beginning of the Protestant Reformation.

Similarly, Luther could not know, as he published his writings on the Jews, that some four centuries later his words would be cited in support of the antisemitic measures of a violent neopaganism that had seized the heart of Europe. Yet, so sharp were his words, and so pervasive his influence, that he cannot be absolved of all responsibility for what happened, despite the vast historical gap between his time and ours.

It is ironic that Luther, in his later life, should have become known as a foe of the Jews (his major treatise on the subject was published in 1543, just three years before his death), for in his early years it was just the opposite. Jewish leaders hailed the work of Luther and the Reformation as the dawn of a new day, in which they might experience a greater freedom and justice than they had known in medieval Christendom. They noted the new interest in the study of Scripture in the original languages, and the establishment of professorships of Hebrew in the Protestant universities.

The young Luther, for his part, fully reciprocated this new sense of cordiality. This may be seen most clearly in his treatise of 1523, significantly entitled, "That Jesus Christ Was Born a Jew," in which Luther stressed the Jewish origins of Christianity and, especially, the Jewishness of Jesus. An appreciation of this indebtedness, he indicated, would induce an attitude of affection and respect towards contemporary Jews. "We are aliens and in-laws," he reminded his fellow Gentiles; "they are blood relatives, cousins, and brothers of our Lord."

A closer examination of the text of the treatise, however, reveals the deep ambiguity of Luther's attitude towards the Jews, even in this earlier period. On the one hand, he was sharply critical of traditional prejudices, and proposed, in effect, that Christendom make a fresh start, adopting policies based on an affirmation and appreciation, not a denigration and rejection, of the Jews and their faith. On the other hand, it is plain that his eventual hope was for their conversion. Note how these two motifs intertwine as Luther wrote, in his usual colorful style:

> Our fools, the popes, bishops, sophists, and monks . . . have hitherto so treated the Jews that anyone who wished to be a good Christian would almost have had to become a Jew. If I had been a Jew and had seen such dolts and blockheads govern and teach the Christian faith, I would sooner have

become a hog than a Christian. . . . I hope that if one deals in a
kindly way with the Jews and instructs them carefully from
Holy Scripture, many of them will become genuine
Christians. . . . They will only be frightened further away
from it if their Judaism is so utterly rejected that nothing is
allowed to remain, and they are treated only with arrogance
and scorn.

The same duality of motive—genuine human concern and the
hope for conversion—is evident in Luther's concluding
recommendations in the 1523 treatise:

Therefore, I would request and advise that one deal gently
with them and instruct them from Scripture; then some of
them may come along. Instead of this, we are trying only to
drive them by force. . . . So long as we thus treat them like
dogs, how can we expect to work any good among them?
Again, when we forbid them to labor and do business and
have any human fellowship with us, thereby forcing them
into usury, how is that supposed to do them any good? If we
really want to help them, we must be guided in our dealings
with them not by papal law but by the law of Christian love
. . . If some of them should prove stiff-necked, what of it? After
all, we ourselves are not all good Christians, either.

Compared to the foregoing, Luther's treatise, written twenty
years later, exhibited a very different attitude, from its title, "On the
Jews and Their Lies." Here, we find Luther treating the Jews with the
"arrogance and scorn" that he had earlier condemned. Rather than
"dealing gently" with them, he advocated exceedingly harsh
measures. As to the Jews' economic role, he overlooked the fact that
the restrictions which a Christian society had placed on them may
have forced them into usury; he now blamed solely their avarice and
cunning. In short, his image of the Jews and his recommendations
became almost entirely negative.

How is this transformation to be explained? A variety of theories
have been propounded to account for it. Reference has been made to
Luther's declining health in his later years; to his frustration over the
obstacles being met by the Reformation and the splintering of the
movement; to his fear of what he considered "Judaizing" tendencies
within the Church itself. The most important factor, however, was
clearly the disappointment of the hopes expressed in Luther's earlier
treatise, that is, *the Jews' failure to convert.*

Thus, the Jews fell afoul of Luther's wrath for the same reason
they had remained a "problem" ever since the emergence of
Christianity—their steadfast maintenance of the integrity of their
faith. Originally, of course, it had been the Christians who were the
minority, a small sect that had burst forth from the womb of Judaism.
But as the Christian mission advanced, transcending the ethnic base
of Judaism and appealing to all peoples, the proportions were

reversed, until in time Christianity was acknowledged as a separate religion in its own right, and eventually as the official religion of the Roman Empire. Now Christianity had at its disposal not only the sword of the spirit but also the sword—in the literal sense—of the secular power as well. This would remain true throughout the Middle Ages and down to the rise of modern democratic pluralism (far after Luther's time).

Within this framework, all the "dynamics of prejudice" were free to operate. Thus, the rivalry between Jews and Christians during this period can be viewed in several dimensions: (1) sociologically, it represented a classic case of in-group/out-group tension, one group in the possession of privilege and power and the other struggling to gain a share of it; (2) psychologically, it showed all the signs of scapegoating—the projection onto a hapless individual or group of the blame for untoward events for which there is no ready explanation, or for which others wish to escape responsibility. This was greatly intensified by the dark undercurrent of superstition in the late Middle Ages, which could attribute all sorts of demonic powers and practices to the Jews; (3) economically, there was the resentment of the Jewish role as moneylenders, and of the wealth that some Jews were able to achieve; (4) ideologically, the Jews suffered from being the one most glaring exception to an otherwise universally accepted set of symbols that served to give cohesion to the whole social order —in this situation, "heresy" was considered very close to "treason"; and finally, (5) religiously, the two faiths may be viewed as locked in a sibling rivalry, each claiming to be the true heir of the prophets and patriarchs of ancient Israel. To the Jews, the Christians were a people who, although sprung from Jewish loins, had forsaken the law of Moses, the Torah, for the sake of a messianic faith that lacked confirmation in reality (did the world look redeemed?). To the Christians, the Jews were those who, out of willful blindness, rejected and crucified the true Messiah.

Luther's treatise reflected all these factors. The greater part of it was taken up with the interpretation of numerous passages from the Hebrew Bible (the Old Testament) that Luther claimed must be interpreted as prophecies of Christ, but which the Jews interpreted in a different sense (hence their "lies," in Luther's view). Here, Luther was continuing a debate that had gone on for centuries between Jewish and Christian scholars; but he lent it the special harshness of his own rhetoric. Elements of superstition and half-truths about Jewish practices and alleged anti-Christian rituals were passed in review with mounting ire on Luther's part, until finally he issued his infamous list of proposals—that their synagogues and houses be destroyed, their prayer books seized, and their rabbis forbidden to teach, etc. Although many of these proposals parallel, in a chilling manner, the antisemitic measures later undertaken by the Nazis (not to speak of the many intervening persecutions and pogroms), it should be made clear that Luther did not envision anything like genocide. Luther advised pastors to admonish their parishioners to be wary of the Jews, but he added, "They should not curse them or harm their persons." His ultimate penalty was to expel them from the country.

Luther's treatise of 1543 has caused embarrassment and dismay from the first day of its publication; it is known, for example, that his closest colleague, Phillip Melanchthon, was unhappy with its severity. Fortunately, his proposals met with very little response among the authorities. In two nearby provinces, the right of safe conduct of Jews was withdrawn, and in another, Jews were prohibited from moneylending and were required to listen to Christian sermons. In no cases were his harsher suggestions followed. As to the treatise itself, it did not sell widely, in contrast to the more benign treatise of 1523. For the most part, it has remained buried in obscurity, although selected quotations from it—the worst parts, of course—have been circulated by antisemitic movements.

There is no way to undo what has been done or to unsay what has been said, but some comfort can be taken in the fact that this aspect of Luther's thought has been so vigorously repudiated by contemporary Christians, including official Lutheran church bodies. We live in a day of ever-deepening dialogue and the growth of mutual respect between Jews and Christians. Yet, we are living also just one generation after the Holocaust. Facing the stark facts of Jewish-Christian conflict in the past, such as in Luther's time, can serve to remind us of the need for eternal vigilance against the forces of racial and religious hatred.

### For Further Reading

Althouse, LaVonne. *When Jew and Christian Meet*. New York: Friendship Press, 1966.

Bainton, Roland. *Here I Stand: A Life of Martin Luther*. New York: New American Library, 1978.

Eckardt, A. Roy. *Your People, My People: The Meeting of Christians and Jews*. New York: Times Books, 1974.

Kirsch, Paul J. *We Christians and Jews*. Philadelphia: Fortess Press, 1975.

Pawlikowski, John T. *Sinai and Calvary: A Meeting of Two Peoples*. Encino, Ca: Glencoe Publishing, n.d.

Ruether, Rosemary. *Faith and Fratricide: The Theological Roots of Anti-Semitism*. New York: Seabury Press, 1974.

Talmadge, Frank P. *Disputation and Dialogue: Readings in the Jewish-Christian Encounter*. New York: Ktav, 1975.

Wouk, Herman. *This Is My God*. New York: Doubleday, 1959.

# Why the Jew?: Modern Antisemitism

## YISRAEL GUTMAN

Antisemitism as a manifestation of Jew-hatred and a motive for persecution and attack is a very ancient phenomenon. We find it for the first time in the Book of Esther in the following passage: "There is a certain people scattered abroad and dispersed among the peoples in all the provinces of your realm. Their laws are different from those of every people. They do not observe even the king's laws. . . ." (III:3) From that time until the present day, antisemitism has been a striking characteristic of the Gentile attitude towards the Jews, and throughout the centuries antisemitism has never been absent from Jewish existence in its dispersion among the nations.

It is natural that both Jews and non-Jews have attempted to investigate this phenomenon, to understand its origins and its tenacity, and to know why the Jewish people have become the target of never-ending hostility. Many have asked if there is not some element in the Jews themselves, their collective character, behavior, or actions, which has caused this hatred and repulsion. A dozen or so years ago, during one of the numerous discussions on this theme, Professor Benzion Dinur, an historian at the Hebrew University in Jerusalem, remarked that the Jews are indeed guilty, owing to their very existence. By this ironic remark, Dinur intended to point out that the Jews themselves are in no way responsible for this age-old animosity towards them, and that their only sin is their existence as human beings, as a religious community, and as a nation among other nations. But is antisemitism only visible in the presence of Jews; is it unknown; or, does it disappear in their absence?

It is interesting to note that a new appearance of antisemitism engulfed Poland in 1982, with the crushing of the Polish workers' union, Solidarity, and the imposition of martial law. Polish Jews, and Jews in general, were blamed for the demands for freedom and the rejection of a Soviet puppet regime. Did Jews really play any role in this affair? In 1939, on the eve of World War II, there were some 3½ million Jews in Poland. Ninety percent of them were murdered or perished in the Holocaust. The vast majority of the survivors emigrated to Israel or other countries, and during the last wave of antisemitism in Poland, in 1967-1968, approximately 20,000 of the few remaining Polish Jews escaped or were expelled from the country. In 1982, the Jewish population of Poland—once a thriving center of Jewish life—is no more than a few thousand, almost all of them elderly or apostates who have long since abandoned their Jewish identity and are totally estranged from their culture. It is, therefore, apparent that antisemitism can prevail even in a country without Jews, and that antisemitism in such a country can also constitute a factor in political conflicts in which Jews are completely uninvolved.

The case of Poland is, however, not the only, or most widely known, example of antisemitism without Jews. Shakespeare's play, *The Merchant of Venice*, which presented a fanatical and repulsive Jew by the name of Shylock as one of its main protagonists, was written at a time when there were no Jews living in Britain. Shakespeare was not actually acquainted with Jews, but created the character out of his imagination—a symbolic Jew conceived in his mind's eye.

The actual concept of antisemitism, or, more correctly, the term "antisemitism" is relatively new—in view, at least, of the extended period of time during which antisemitism has existed. The expression "antisemitism" for Jew-hatred was first used by a German during the 1870s. In what way does antisemitism differ from the hatred of, or opposition to, Jews that occurred before the term had been coined? The answer is clear. Anti (against) semitism indicates opposition to Jews not on religious or national grounds, but because of race. Anthropologists who have classified human races deny the existence of a semitic race, and mostly state that there is only a family of semitic languages to which Hebrew and Arabic, among others, belong. Even those who claim that a semitic race exists include in it both Jews and Arabs. Nevertheless, we know that antisemitism as a movement, or an ideological system, is not directed against Arabs but only against Jews.

The Nazis brought antisemitism to a level of unbounded fanaticism, denying the Jews the right to live and condemning them to death purely on the grounds of being Jewish. On the other hand, the Nazis hosted the Arab leader, the mufti of Jerusalem, and declared their pro-Arab attitudes on more than one occasion. The mufti himself was a rabid antisemite and we know that even today, there are extreme antisemitic segments among the Arabs. Moreover, tests carried out at the beginning of the century on groups of schoolchildren in Germany demonstrated that many Jewish children possessed facial and cephalic features and hair-coloring generally attributed to the Aryan, non-Jewish race, while a high percentage of German children had characteristics which, according to antisemites, typify the semitic race. Many *sabras* born in Israel are light-skinned and blond, in contrast to the semitic type traditionally depicted by the antisemites. Who is in reality a semite, and who is an Aryan? For the antisemites, the question is of no importance. As far as they are concerned, antisemitism is anti-Judaism, and they decide who is a semite and who is a Jew.

We began this article with a short description of racism and antisemitism, to which we shall return. This is only one of the chapters in the history of antisemitism. It was preceded by other versions and forms of antisemitism—during different periods of history, antisemitism focused on various arguments and accusations. That Jews were castigated and segregated as followers of a different faith has been mentioned above. It is common knowledge that Christianity is, to a certain extent, an offshoot of Judaism, and the Bible is sacred to both Jews and Christians. However, Christianity did not forgive Judaism and the Jews for failing to recognize Jesus as the

Messiah, and for rejecting the tidings he brought to his disciples. Christianity held the Jews responsible throughout the generations for the Crucifixion of Jesus, and claimed that Jews were a stiff-necked people who refused to recognize the true faith. Christians averred that Jews throughout the ages were guilty of strange misdeeds which could apparently be traced back to their distant ancestors. Moreover, Jews did not have equal rights with Christians, and Jews must be subordinate in order to ensure the sovereignty and preeminence of Christians over Jews; in turn, the inferior Jewish status would in itself prove that the Christian faith was the true faith.

This is not the forum to discuss the arguments and exegetics which form the principles and concepts of theology, but Christian anti-Jewish claims did not remain maxims of religious dogma, or subjects for sermons in Church. The negative and harmful impulses attributed to the Jews caught the imagination of the people, and during the Middle Ages, when frequent attempts were made to find a supernatural cause for events, superstitious and libelous horror stories concerning the Jews abounded. The most widespread were accusations that Jews murdered Christian children in order to use their blood to make *matzot* (unleavened bread) for Passover (the holiday commemorating the Exodus from Egypt). Jews, who were commanded to exercise the utmost care that their food not contain any blood, became the victims of this recurring libel that has not died out to this very day. Jews were accused of poisoning wells and spreading plagues. It may be asked how Jews poisoned wells from whose waters they, too, had to drink, and how they spread diseases which make no distinction between Jew and non-Jew. Another anti-Jewish charge was that Jews purposely trampled on the wine and communion wafers of the Christians, which were supposed to embody the blood and flesh of Jesus. Logic refutes this accusation. How should Jews, who did not believe in this mysterious union of the bread and wine, have attempted to conspire against it? The accusations against the Jews were not based on proven facts, nor made against guilty parties, but were directed indiscriminately against a social group. Such hatred is, to a great extent, an outlet for vicious inclinations, suffering, and despair in times of distress and disorientation. It must be stressed, however, that not all Christians were a party to this hatred or believed these libels. Alongside the persecutors and the Jew-haters were sincere and upright individuals who opposed the mudslinging and the indiscriminate and baseless accusations.

A later form of antisemitism developed at a time when the power of religious faith and its influence on the lives of the European people was declining, while the trend towards Enlightenment was becoming more widespread, and scientific knowledge reached the masses. During the second half of the eighteenth century and throughout the nineteenth century, bourgeois society opened up new avenues for economic initiative and talents, without regard for religious beliefs or social position. In various European countries, individual Jews and Jewish families became prominent, some accumulating vast fortunes in the fields of banking and commerce (for example, the Rothschild family, whose sons became bankers in the main European capitals). In reality, these Jewish families were comparatively few in number, but this did not hinder the dissemination of the charge that Jews were in control of the economy, banking, and important spheres such as railroad building—and that this alleged domination presented an ever-increasing danger to Christian society. Large numbers of professions had been closed to Jews for many generations, and they had been forced to concentrate mainly on moneylending and commerce. This was to their advantage when financial and commercial concerns began to play an increasingly important role. However, such opportunities were only open to some Jews in western Europe, while the multitude of Jews in eastern Europe (Russia, divided Poland, Rumania) were poor. In the East, the majority of Jews were impecunious and engaged in a constant struggle for their daily bread.

From the last third of the nineteenth century, a new trend became predominant—that of political antisemitism. The nineteenth century also resulted in the emancipation of Jews, i.e., the recognition of Jews as citizens with the same rights and duties as others. This recognition, which was achieved by the Jews or granted to them by their compatriots, constituted a vast improvement and total change in their status. For generations, Jews had been the vassals of kings and overlords. Jews had been permitted to dwell in certain countries as a privilege, i.e., by special permission of the local ruler. The power which had granted the Jews right of residence could also retract it, and the sovereign was even entitled to confiscate their possessions. As long as it was worthwhile to keep the Jew, they were given asylum, but when circumstances altered or the rulers' attitudes changed, the Jews were expelled. Thus, the Jews were forced to leave England, France, Spain, Portugal, and many German principalities during the Middle Ages. During modern times, Jews were permitted to dwell in Europe as a favor, not a right. Jews were subjected to restrictions and special laws which closed many professions to them, including the army and trade, agriculture and real estate. The gradual granting of equal rights to the Jews after the French Revolution slowly broke down the barriers between them and their fellow countrymen. Of course, Jews, particularly in eastern Europe, were required to pay a price for their rights: They were obliged to forego their uniqueness, their institutions, and many of their customs, since the non-Jews demanded a high degree of assimilation as a precondition to equal status and nauralization. Many Jews welcomed the changes, and renounced many of their ancient customs that did not conform to those of their patrons.

Here, perhaps, we should pause to consider the Jewish part of the question. We have already asked if there is some quality in the Jews which might serve as a pretext for antisemitism, or which stirs up hatred in their fellow men. The truth of the matter is that the Jews were and are different—not *alien*, but *different*. The two concepts require clarification. A Jew is different by virtue of the fact that he adheres to another religion, eats different foods, learns in his own way, and places his faith in the future when redemption will come to all mankind. The Jewish family and way of life, Jewish festivals and prayers are unique. But Jews are not alien, neither with regard to character nor to feelings, love, hate, or hope. In these respects, Jews are the same as others. Their differences increase their strangeness, which in turn engenders fear and suspicion. This, then, raises barriers between groups and individuals.

In the opinion of many Jews and non-Jews, Emancipation removed many barriers, and the Jews slowly became integrated in the everyday existence common to other Europeans. Many aver that a new era of progress and education began when people became more enlightened and tolerant of their fellow men. It was assumed that since all discrimination would be eliminated in this new age of equality, knowledge, and democracy, antisemitism would also disappear. What actually took place, however, was the development of a new type of hatred, far stronger and more dangerous than that which had previously prevailed: political and racial antisemitism.

How did it come about that, contrary to all expectations, a wave of unbridled, violent hatred developed which finally led to terror? There is no clear, unequivocal answer to this question. Perhaps it should be stressed that even this mounting tide of hatred did not occur in every country and among all individuals. When dealing with antisemitism, there is always a danger that Jews, too, will become subject to making generalizations. Just as antisemites regard one negative act by an individual Jew as the responsibility of the entire Jewish nation, so Jews also are sometimes apt to brand every non-Jew a potential antisemite, and hold him responsible for atrocities and murder. The truth is that countries such as Holland and Italy were to a wide extent not antisemitic, and were hardly contaminated to any degree by Jew-hatred during the decades preceding the two world wars. Moreover, there were long periods marked by an absence of violent antisemitism and even of striking tranquility in relationships between Jews and non-Jews.

There is generally a difference in this respect between western and eastern Europe. In the West, the Jews were granted full rights, particularly in Germany, where the Jewish community achieved a genuine emotional and cultural identification with their compatriots, and sought to become an integral part of the German nation. In eastern Europe, the Jews were not granted equal rights, and manifestations of general and popular antisemitism made it abundantly clear to the Jews that they were considered aliens in those countries. Harbingers of the Jewish national movement, and of Zionism in particular, insisted that there was a gap between Jewish expectations of acceptance by the European nations and the real attitude of the latter towards the Jews. Both in the West and, to a certain, if lesser, degree in the East, Jews did not perceive or correctly evaluate the significance of the gap between the equal rights granted them by law and public opinion. It is probable that the new legal status of the Jews did not root out antisemitism or remove barriers of mistrust, but sometimes aggravated existing suspicion and hatred. In France, for example, there was a large-scale outburst of hostile public opinion during the Dreyfus affair at the end of the 1890s, and in Russia, the trend was clearly discernible in the wave of pogroms nicknamed "Storms in the South" during the 1870s. Political antisemitism tended to lay responsibility upon the Jews for defeats and political and economic crises, while it sought to exploit opposition and resistance to Jewish influence as elements in political party platforms. Thus, antisemitism became a factor in the political arena. Jews were also accused of disseminating revolutionary Socialist ideas and creating revolutionary unrest.

The most devastating influence, however, was the racial element in antisemitism. Racism placed opposition to Jews on a new plane, far removed from any other version of antisemitism. Antisemitism in all its previous manifestations had confronted the Jews with onerous demands and challenges, had denounced their religion, forced them to adopt different professions, and attempted to oust them from various spheres of public activity. Naturally, had the Jews sanctioned the claims of their persecutors—and in certain cases they actually did so—antisemitism would still not have died out. It is now a proven fact that the Jews became a permanent, convenient target for psychologically unstable and embittered classes of modern society. This attitude was not based on facts, knowledge of, or acquaintance with the Jews, and the charges against the Jews bear no relationship to the truth. Thus, a stereotype of the Jews was created by the antisemite, entirely the product of his imagination.

Nevertheless, at least theoretically, the Jews were capable of reform, and the antisemites declared that if the Jews improved their ways, their own attitude would also change. Racism ascribed the Jews' defects and the danger which they constituted to the rest of society to their geneology and heredity. According to this view, the Jew was unable to change either through education or by accepting the judgment of those who condemned him. The fault lay in his very existence, in his physical presence. Racial antisemitism was not even appeased by the most radical step which the Jew could take in order to escape from his identity and position—conversion—since, in its view, even a converted Jew, and his children and even his grandchildren, remained Jews. Racial antisemitism, in conjunction with extreme political antisemitism, ascribed to the Jews a secret plan to rule the world; this led to Nazi racialism and the Holocaust. However, Nazi racism and the Holocaust, designed to destroy the Jewish people, also constituted a potential danger to the whole world. Racism, in addition, did not rest at categorizing Jews as an inferior and harmful breed that must be wiped out. It not only attacked the basic axioms of all religious faiths, and the concept of the unity of mankind, but it also classified other nations according to this system of superior/inferior nations and master/servant relationships. Thus, antisemitism facilitated the absorption of racist ideas in Europe and was the source and cornerstone of an ideology which threatened all mankind.

In summing up this survey, we are confronted by the disturbing question: Is there no escape from antisemitism? Is antisemitism a chronic social disease that does not, and never will, have any remedy? This is apparently the case from the historical point of view. But when one studies the importance of antisemitism, its development and influence in different cultures and at different periods, one discovers that its strength can be diminished, and that in certain societies and under certain circumstances it ceases to play any considerable role. It resurfaces particularly during periods of unrest and crisis, and in societies torn by conflict. Nevertheless, the fact that antisemitism is subject to change provides some hope for the successful struggle against antisemitism.

Paradoxically, the State of Israel, the Jewish State, regarded by many throughout the ages as a solution to the dilemma and a means to abolish antisemitism, has not led to the cessation of antisemitism. In fact, current antisemitic lines of thought, influenced by Arab propaganda, have arisen directly from Zionism and the existence of the State of Israel. We know that the United Nations, on the initiative of Arab and Communist states and their satellites, have brazenly passed senseless resolutions equating Zionism with racism. However, if Israel has not succeeded in abolishing antisemitism, it has nevertheless established a Jewish force which clearly demonstrates to its enemies that Jewish blood and lives are no longer to be trifled with. This important development, the consequences of which are perceived throughout the Diaspora, has placed the question of relations between Jews and antisemites in a totally different perspective, and has invested it with a new significance. What the State of Israel will mean for future manifestations of antisemitism remains to be seen.

### For Further Reading

*Anti-Semitism*. Jerusalem: Keter Books, 1974.

Ben-Sasson, Haim Hillel, and Ettinger, Shmuel, eds. *Jewish Society through the Ages*. Cambridge: Harvard University Press, 1976.

Cohn, Norman. *Warrant for Genocide: The Myth of the Jewish World Conspiracy and the Protocols of the Elders of Zion*. London: Eyre and Spottiswoode, 1967.

Flannery, Edward H. *The Anguish of the Jews: Twenty-Three Centuries of Anti-Semitism*. New York: Macmillan Co., 1965.

Gutman, Yisrael, and Rothkirchen, Livia, eds. *The Catastrophe of European Jewry: Antecedents, History, Reflections*. Jerusalem: Yad Vashem, 1976.

Katz, Jacob. *From Prejudice to Destruction.* Cambridge: Harvard University Press, 1980.

Littell, Franklin H. *The Crucifixion of the Jews: The Failure of the Christians to Understand the Jewish Experience.* New York: Harper & Row, 1975.

Mosse, George L. *Toward the Final Solution: A History of European Racism.* New York: Howard Fertig, 1978.

Parkes, James. *The Conflict of the Church and the Synagogue: A Study on the Origins of Anti-Semitism.* New York: Sepher-Hermon Press, 1974.

Tal, Uriel. *Christians and Jews in Germany: Religion, Politics and Ideology in the Second Reich, 1870-1914.* Ithaca, NY: Cornell University Press, 1975.

Trachtenberg, Joshua. *The Devil and the Jews: The Medieval Conception of the Jews and Its Relation to Modern Anti-Semitism.* New Haven: Yale University Press, 1943.

4

# OVERVIEW:
# 1933-1945

# Like Sheep to the Slaughter?

People often ask, "Why did the Jews go like sheep to the slaughter?" Sheep to the slaughter? How can they know what it was like, crowded together in a way that even animals are not treated—weakened by months of hardship and hunger, locked up in sealed wagons, without food, weapons, without friends— knowing that if even one escaped the Nazis, who was there that would welcome them, who cared! Who would lift a finger? . . . Sheep to the slaughter? What do those who use the phrase know about honor, about the thousands of parents who would not desert their little ones, who stayed behind to embrace them, cuddle them, to exchange glances with them just one more time? What do they know about reverence, about those who gave up their daily ration of food so that a father, a grandmother, a rabbi might live another day? What do they know of a people who refused to believe in the death of mankind, who in forsaken places called hell organized schools, prayed and studied Talmud, wrote poems, composed lyrics, sang songs of today, of eternity, of tomorrow, even when there was to be no tomorrow? . . .

Boundary of Poland up to September 1, 1939

Generalgouvernement of Poland after July 1941 (under German administration)

German-Russian border, September 1939–June 1941

Incorporated in the German Reich

Death camps (names underlined)

BALTIC SEA

LATVIA

Riga

LITHUANIA

Kovno

Vilna

Minsk

SOVIET

GERMANY

Danzig

EAST PRUSSIA

Grodno

REICHSKOMMISSARIAT OSTLAND

Incorporated in

UNION

WARTHELAND

Poznań

Chełmno

GENERALKOMMISSARIAT
Białystok
BIALYSTOK
(quasi-incorporated
with East Prussia)

Baranowicze

Treblinka

Brest Litovsk

Pińsk

Lodz

WARSAW

Sobibór

Radom

Lublin
(Majdanek)

Incorporated in
REICHSKOMMISSARIAT
UKRAINE

Breslau

Częstochowa

Bełżec

Dubno

PROTECTORATE
OF
BOHEMIA
AND
MORAVIA

Oświęcim
(Auschwitz)

Cracow

GENERALGOUVERNEMENT

Przemyśl

Lwów

Tarnopol

UKRAINE

SLOVAKIA

HUNGARY

(added to
Generalgouvernement
in July 1941)

Śniatyn

# The German Partition of Poland, 1939/41–1945

RUMANIA

Kotschar

# The Geography of the Holocaust

## HENRY FRIEDLANDER

The Nazis chose eastern Europe as the arena for the murder of the European Jews. With rare exceptions (for example, Yugoslavia) the killings took place in Poland, the Baltic states, and the Soviet Union. The Nazis chose these locations for a number of reasons: Most of the Jews resided there; it was far removed from neutral observers; the local population was hostile to the Jews; and the killings could be camouflaged as part of the ideological struggle against Bolshevism.

After the conquest of Poland in September, 1939, Germany annexed western Poland. These so-called incorporated territories included Danzig (Gdansk) and West Prussia; Posen (Poznan) and Lodz (renamed Litzmannstadt); and portions of Upper Silesia. The most populous region, containing the largest number of Jews, was the Posen-Lodz area, known after the annexation as the Wartheland. Its governor, Arthur Greiser, was a leading antisemite who wanted to expel all Jews. Unable to do so, he created ghettos long before the rest of Poland. Indeed, the first European ghetto was established in Lodz (Litzmannstadt) in April, 1940.

The remainder of Poland, except the eastern Polish territories occupied by the Soviet Union, was constituted as the General Government *(Generalgouvernement)* under German administration. Governor General Hans Frank established his regime in Cracow. His realm was divided into four districts: Warsaw, Radom, Cracow, and Lublin. The Jews in the General Government were also forced into ghettos, but these were established later than in the Wartheland: the ghetto in Warsaw was sealed late in 1940 and those in most other cities early in 1941.

Soon after the Nazis conquered Poland, they forced the Jews to wear an identifying mark. In the Wartheland, the Jews were required to wear a yellow star on the right side in front and in the back. In the General Government, they had to wear an armband with the Star of David. By contrast, the yellow star, worn in front on the left side and inscribed with the word "Jew" in the applicable national language (but in script designed to resemble Hebrew), was not imposed in Germany proper until September, 1941, and in the occupied West not until the spring of 1942.

After the invasion of the Soviet Union in June, 1941, Germany gained additional territories. First, the Nazis occupied the Polish areas and Baltic states that had been seized by the Soviet Union in 1939 and, second, they conquered large areas of the Soviet Union itself. From these so-called occupied eastern territories the Germans formed two administrative regions: Ostland and Ukraine. The Reich Commissariat Ostland, governed by Hinrich Lohse, included Lithuania, Latvia, Estonia, and Belorussia. The Reich Commissariat Ukraine, governed by the East Prussian Nazi leader Erich Koch, was also divided into a number of districts. The Polish territories taken from the Soviet Union in 1941 were not included in these commissariats; the Bialystok region was administered by Koch personally, and the region of Lemberg (Lvov) became the fifth district—named Galicia (Galizien)—in the General Government.

During the invasion of the Soviet Union, the SS *Einsatzgruppen* (mobile killing units), following the invading army, immediately commenced to kill the Jews in mass executions. In addition, the SS created ghettos for the Jews that survived these massacres; in the Ostland, for example, newly established ghettos included those in Kovno (Kaunas), Vilna, Riga, and Minsk. Unlike in Poland, the Germans killed the Jews in these newly conquered territories before, not after, the creation of ghettos. Thus, usually only Jews who were still able to work were placed in ghettos; all others were killed.

In the Ostland and the Ukraine, the SS shot the Jews in improvised places of execution near their homes. In Poland, however, the SS established special camps for the murder of the Jews. This started in the Wartheland. There, Greiser wanted to rid himself of all Jews; to this end, a special SS commando built and operated an extermination camp at Kulmhof (Chelmno). The Jews from the Wartheland, including those from the Lodz ghetto, were killed there. Kulmhof, the first extermination camp in Europe, started operations in December, 1941; with one interruption in 1943, it continued as a killing center until August, 1944, when the remaining Lodz Jews— approximately 60,000—were sent to Auschwitz.

The General Government soon imitated the Wartheland and established its own extermination camps. The Lublin SS and Police Leader Odilo Globocnik was commissioned by Himmler to arrange for the murder of the Polish Jews. For this purpose, he organized Operation Reinhard and established three extermination camps: Belzec, Sobibor, and Treblinka. In these camps the Jews of the General Government were killed. Their task completed, the camps (and Operation Reinhard) closed in 1943. The remaining Jews in labor camps in eastern Poland were killed late in 1943 in the Lublin camp Maidanek.

Jews native to eastern Europe were not the only ones killed. The Nazis deported Jews from Germany, Austria, and Czechoslovakia to the East. Transports of central European Jews arrived in Lodz, Kovno, Riga, Minsk, and a number of towns in the Lublin region including Nisko, Piaski, Izbica, and Trawniki. There, they shared the fate of the eastern European Jews. They were shot by the *Einsatzgruppen* or gassed in the extermination camps. Later, entire transports of Jews from France, Holland, central Europe, and Russia arrived directly at the extermination camps of Operation Reinhard.

Most Jews not native to eastern Europe were killed in the largest extermination camp built in the East: Auschwitz-Birkenau. Located in Upper Silesia near Kattowitz (Katowice), with excellent railroad connections, it eventually surpassed all other camps in its killing capacity. In 1944, after all other camps had closed, it became the only killing center for Jews. When the gas chambers of Auschwitz-

Birkenau ceased to operate in November, 1944, they had been used to kill more than two million Jews from Poland and all the occupied countries of Europe.

### For Further Reading

Dallin, Alexander. *German Rule in Russia.* New York: Octagon, 1957.

Gross, Jan Tomasz. *Polish Society under German Occupation.* Princeton: Princeton University Press, 1979.

Hilberg, Raul. *The Destruction of the European Jews.* Chicago: Quadrangle Press, 1961.

# The History of the Holocaust

**YISRAEL GUTMAN**

## Antisemitism and Hitler's Rise to Power

Antisemitism existed in Germany and other European countries for many hundreds of years. The racist doctrines which made their initial appearance in the nineteenth century added new momentum to the hatred of the Jews. In many countries, racist antisemitism was used as an instrument of political propaganda to gain the support of the masses. However, it was only in the 1930s, with the growth of the National Socialist party and Adolf Hitler's rise to power in Germany that racial antisemitism was adopted as a policy by a major political party.

Racism added new and substantial dimensions to traditional antisemitism. In the past, hatred of Jews had had specific grounds and certain lines of development. The hatred nurtured by ancient Christian concepts regarded the Jews as the people of Israel and the people of the Messiah, but also as the people who had rejected its Redeemer, Jesus, and thus had condemned itself to ostracism and the eternal enmity of the Christian world. The Jews had to be kept in a state of servitude, misery, and degradation. Moreover, their eternal wandering among the nations, forever at the mercy of the Christians, seemed to confirm the veracity of Christian teachings. Later, antisemitism was reinforced by a greater stress on economic, social, and political factors. Racial antisemitism, linked with a misinterpretation of Darwin's view of society, lent a new validity to traditional Jew-hatred. According to the Nazi theorists, the danger arising from contact with the evil, perverted Jews sprang not from their mistaken beliefs or their economic role, nor even from their tendency to live as a closed social group, but from their very identity, their tainted Jewish blood.

According to nazism, the German people constituted the highest stratum of the Nordic-Aryan race, while the Jews were a subhuman race who perpetually undermined the sound structure of world affairs and sought to usurp the authority and leadership of the superior race. Destiny demanded of the Germans that they wage an uncompromising struggle for their heritage, primacy, and power. Liberalism, democracy, socialism, and communism were regarded as destructive Jewish notions, whose only aim was the eradication of all that was right in the world, i.e. the concepts which glorified strength and beauty and invested the preordained race with wealth and power, and accorded it world domination. According to Nazi theory, humanity was not a homogeneous unit, and the human race had no common denominator. Those who spoke of the unity of the human race were intent upon falsifying the truth, as they denied the existence of races and refused to recognize the constant conflicts between them. Phrases about the common destiny of mankind were ridiculous, as absurd as talk of a partnership between men and insects. Marriage between Jews and non-Jews was the equivalent of the Trojan horse, an attempt to bring about the collapse of the superior race from within. When the Nazis came to power, the war of the races reached its climax. Should the Aryan race be defeated and fail to establish its dominion on earth, the victorious Jews would undoubtedly carry out their evil designs and the world would be doomed to decline and deteriorate.

This doctrine, which Hitler repeatedly and loudly affirmed, had its own laws and lines of development. The mere insistence upon a state of racial war in which there could be no compromise, helped create the background for the Final Solution. Obviously, if the Jews posed such a serious danger to society, then any measures taken against them, including extermination, were justified.

On the eve of World War II, in January, 1939, Hitler said: "Today I will once more be a prophet. If the international financiers inside and outside Europe should again succeed in plunging the nations into a world war the result will not be the Bolshevization of the earth and thus the victory of Jewry, but the annihilation *(Vernichtung)* of the Jewish race throughout Europe." Thus, Jews came to be regarded as "enemy number one," and the murder of Jews became one of the aims for which the war was being waged.

The economic and political circumstances in Germany between the wars facilitated Hitler's rise to power. Many Germans had refused to accept the fact that Germany had been defeated in World War I. They claimed that the German army had been "stabbed in the back" and that disloyalty at home had paralyzed the front and brought about the collapse of the German army. A significant portion of the blame for weakening the front was, of course, heaped upon the Jews. The Weimar Republic, which was established after the War, was unpopular in German nationalistic circles. In the eyes of the opposition, the democratic regime had been imposed upon them, and did not truly represent the German people. The Versailles Peace Treaty, and especially the clauses which called for the payment of heavy reparations, were regarded in Germany as measures of revenge. Naturally, there were only a few people who recalled that when Germany appeared in the role of victor at the negotiating table at Brest Litovsk, she had dictated far harsher peace terms to Russia than those imposed upon her by the Allies at Versailles. A sense of frustration, a refusal to accept the situation, and an evergrowing fear of communism created fertile soil for the growth of radical, rightwing groups in Germany. The N.S.D.A.P. (Nazi party) was founded during this period. The unstable economic conditions prevailing in Germany at the end of the war gave additional impetus to the extremists, who demanded many radical changes. In 1923, the National Socialist party attempted a political coup in Munich. Their intention had been to set out from the Bavarian capital to conquer the whole of Germany. The "putsch" failed, and Hitler and several of his associates were arrested. However, the court which tried them was unduly lenient in sentencing those responsible for the revolt. Moreover, Hitler exploited his appearance in court to make propaganda for his party. During the short period he spent in prison, Hitler wrote his well-known book, *Mein Kampf (My Struggle)*, in which he outlined the program of his movement. Hitler and his close associates displayed a remarkable talent for propaganda, organization, and political extremism, but they failed to gain sufficient influence and support to become a real threat to the Weimar Republic until the crisis of 1929. By then Hitler had learned the lesson of his attempted coup, and realized that he had to use the legitimate means afforded him by the democratic institutions in his struggle to gain power. Nevertheless, he and his aides made no secret of their contempt for democracy. They viewed democracy merely as a tool to be used to gain power, a tool to be discarded on the day of victory. In the 1924 elections to the Reichstag, the Nazi party received only 3 percent of the votes cast and had fourteen representatives in the Reichstag. In 1928, they had an even smaller percentage of the votes (2.6) and only twelve seats. However, 1929 saw the commencement of a world-wide economic crisis, which intensified both the social ferment and the political unrest in Germany. Thus, in 1930, in the first elections after the crisis, the Nazis made astonishing gains, getting 18.3 percent of the votes and 107 seats in the Reichstag. From then on they made steady progress, though it should be noted that in 1932, the last election before they took power, they suffered a setback, losing thirty-four of their seats in the Reichstag.

The Nazis never gained an absolute majority in a free election, not even in the election of March, 1933, when they were already in power. Ostensibly, the actual seizure of power was carried out in a legitimate and orderly manner. Hitler's appointment as chancellor had been preceded by frequent changes in the governments and leadership of the Weimar Republic. These changes were not based on any majority votes in the Reichstag, but were carried out by the president, Field Marshall von Hindenburg. These recurrent upheavals were accompanied by conspiracies involving right-wing politicians and senior military personalities who wished to exploit Hitler and the masses who flocked to his standard. They hoped that by appointing him chancellor they would be able to base their power on a majority of the electorate and thus secure their own positions. However, they underestimated Hitler, who soon showed that he was not prepared to serve any interests other than his own. Indeed, those who had hoped to exploit him for their own purposes, soon found themselves in his power.

In *Mein Kampf,* in the Nazi party press, and in Nazi publications, racist doctrines were openly espoused. Antisemitism was one of the most powerful propaganda weapons used by the Nazis to gain the support of the masses.

# Anti-Jewish Policy and Persecutions in Germany

Hitler came to power on January 30, 1933. From then on, the racist doctrine became an integral part of the totalitarian regime in which authority was exercised by a leader who regarded himself as sent by Providence to carry out a mission, one which was to exert a powerful influence upon future generations.

The official policy of the new government and the ruling party of the Third Reich was implemented immediately upon their ascent to power. The Nazis celebrated their victory with violent attacks on Jews. The chief victims were intellectuals and professionals. In addition, many Jews were arrested. During the first months of 1933, there was so much state-instigated brutality and disorder that there was a storm of protest in other countries. Germany had a longstanding tradition of order and discipline, much admired elsewhere, so that the chaos was all the more shocking. The heads of the new regime in Germany attributed the indignation expressed in other countries to agitation instigated by Jews, and they decided to retaliate against the Jews of Germany. They proclaimed a general boycott of Jewish shops and enterprises to commence on April 1, 1933. Julius Streicher, editor of the antisemitic periodical, *Der Stürmer*, was appointed to conduct the operation. A nationwide publicity campaign preceded the boycott, which lasted for only one day. On that day (April 1, 1933), armed guards picketed Jewish-owned shops, factories, and businesses. Placards were posted, and demonstrations were held to ensure the success of the boycott. The entire action was organized and carried out by members of the SA (Storm Troops) and SS.

In April the anti-Jewish policy of the Third Reich began to gain momentum. The first step was to deprive the Jews of their legal and civil rights. The next was to exclude them from the economy. Social barriers between Jews and Germans were set up, and many Jews were expelled from Germany. This initial phase, which was based on regulations and ordinances, and which led to the dismissal of all Jews from public offices and from the German army, reached a climax with the promulgation of the infamous Nuernberg Laws in 1935.

Besides dismissing the Jews from their jobs and depriving them of their civil rights, the Nazis also were intent on excluding them from German cultural life. In May, 1933, the works of some of the greatest thinkers in the world were burned for the sole reason that their authors were Jews. Minister of Propaganda Joseph Goebbels set about making the cultural life of his country uniform. He and his underlings decided who was a true artist and who was an impostor. The Jews, of course, belonged to the latter category, and as such were to be purged. All Jews were dismissed from the universities, the theater, the publishing industry, and the press. This phase of excluding Jews from all German cultural activity and stamping the party imprint on literature, art, and science received considerable support from many well-known Aryan artists and scientists. Scientists and doctors were recruited to expound the theoretical basis of racism, and in due course many of them took an active part in committing crimes against Jews under the cover of so-called "research" into race science.

The Jews reacted to this antisemitic policy by closing their ranks to face the emergency. Within six months of Hitler's taking office, a representative body of German Jews was established. This body included representatives of all the factions of German Jews, Zionists and non-Zionists, Orthodox and assimilationists. The Jews attempted to reconstruct their lives and to establish Jewish social and cultural circles. A fair proportion of the Jews of Germany believed that if they were content thus to remain apart, then the wicked men in power would ignore them and their activities. Others, mainly the Zionists, insisted that the only sensible solution to the problem was emigration. An immense effort was made to evacuate children and young people from Germany to Palestine by means of the Zionist movement "Youth *Aliya*" and pioneer training farms. Most Jews managed to retain their self-respect, and the title of an article by Robert Weltsch, "Wear It with Pride, the Yellow Badge" became, so to speak, the slogan of German Jews. It should be borne in mind that the character and status of German Jews was different than that in eastern Europe. For years, the Jews in Germany had been German citizens with all the rights, privileges, and obligations that such a status entailed. Many Jews had strong cultural and social ties with their non-Jewish fellow citizens and felt a strong sense of loyalty to what they considered to be their native country. They regarded themselves as patriotic Germans of the Jewish faith, and sought a basis for the common destiny and historic connection, which, they felt, bound Jews and Germans together. For such people the antisemitic decrees of the Nazi regime came as a terrible shock.

On the other hand, there were many German Jewish public figures who fully realized the meaning of the Nazi menace. These men warned their fellow Jews that nazism was not an ephemeral phenomenon, and that the base passions it evoked were liable to pervade the whole German population, so the Jews must prepare themselves to face hardships and suffering, humiliation and the desecration of all that they held sacred.

The Nuernberg Laws, decreed in September, 1935, comprised two basic laws which were accompanied by a series of regulations governing their implementation. The first, called the "Reich Citizenship Law," decreed that only persons "of German blood" (Aryans) could be citizens of the Reich, while persons of "impure blood" (non-Aryans) were of inferior status, and were "subjects" not "citizens." In effect, this law put an end to Jewish emancipation, and reduced Jews to being second-class citizens. The second law was called the "Law for the Protection of German Blood and Honor." It forbade marriage and sexual intercourse between Jews and "bearers of German blood," and the employment in Jewish households of German female domestics under the age of forty-five. In addition, it prohibited Jews from flying the flag of the Reich.

The result of these laws was that the Jews were left defenseless, and could not fight against their eviction from their jobs and the seizure of their property. Under these new circumstances, the Jewish community sought to safeguard their livelihood and material existence. They deluded themselves into believing that if their work in commerce and industry were essential to the German economy, then the Nazis would hesitate to replace them.

Racist ideology and antisemitism were preached and practiced throughout the period of Nazi rule. However, the implementation of this policy sometimes fluctuated, and waves of agitation, terror, and antisemitic enactments would sometimes be followed by periods of relative moderation. The comparative restraint, owing to a sudden need to consider world opinion, strengthened Jewish illusions and aroused hopes that better times lay ahead.

During the first three years of Nazi rule (1933-1935), 78,000 Jews left Germany. Almost half of these emigrated in 1935. The Nazi authorities, in particular the party and SS authorities, were anxious to speed up the emigration of Jews, but their desire to be rid of the Jewish inhabitants of Germany was surpassed by their desire to pillage Jewish property and reduce the Jews to poverty. In the early years, the Nazis were inclined to facilitate emigration by allowing "transfer" procedures, which enabled emigrants to transfer part of their property to Palestine in money or goods. After 1935, with the enactment of the Nuernberg Laws and the official end of emancipation, many Jews wanted to leave. However, the Nazi authorities began to put obstacles in the way of would-be emigrants, whose property was usually confiscated. By November, 1938, approximately 170,000 Jews had left Germany. Of the half million Jews living in Germany (about 0.8 percent of the total population) when Hitler took power, some 300,000 emigrated in time to escape the Final Solution of the Jewish Question.

The Zionist movement, international Jewish organizations, and various representative bodies of German Jews outside Germany played an important role in organizing Jewish emigration. Many more Jews could have been saved had the free nations of the world been willing to take in Jewish refugees (many of whom were professionals). In 1938, during the period when emigration from Germany was permitted, the Evian Conference was convened on the initiative of President Roosevelt. It was attended by representatives of many nations, but it brought no relief to those persecuted by the Nazis. On the contrary, the Evian Conference revealed the failure of the democracies to take any useful action, and emphasized the utter helplessness of international institutions, for all doors remained firmly closed. The Jews of Palestine were prepared to take in large numbers of their brethren and in fact did so, but British policy in Palestine prevented the rescue of many more Jews.

In 1938, the Nazis' anti-Jewish policy became even more oppressive. While the Nazis were annexing territories, they were also accelerating their preparations for war. Undoubtedly, their fanatic opposition to the Jews should be regarded as an intrinsic part of their political ideology. In 1938, many synagogues were destroyed (in Munich and Nuernberg, for example), there were mass arrests and the pillaging and wrecking of Jewish shops. All Jewish property had to be registered—a preliminary step to confiscation. The property was assessed at seven billion marks and Nazi Minister Funk boasted that by 1938 they had already succeeded in confiscating two billion marks worth of Jewish property. On October 5, 1938, passports held by Jews were invalidated. Jews who needed passports in order to emigrate were issued passports stamped with a capital "J" ("Jude," Jew). During the same year, Jews of Polish origin who lived in Germany were expelled en masse. Since Poland refused to accept these Jews, they were crowded together in a frontier area under inhuman conditions.

The expulsion of Polish Jews from Germany was directly connected to the so-called *Kristallnacht* (Night of Broken Glass) pogrom on the night of November 9-10. On November 7, Herschel Grynszpan, whose family had been expelled from Germany and were stranded in the camp of unwanted refugees near the Polish border—shot and killed Ernst vom Rath, third secretary of the German Embassy in Paris. In reality, the pogrom was not spontaneous and had already been planned in detail by the Nazis. The vom Rath assassination merely provided the ideal pretext for putting the evil plan into action. The signal to commence operations was given by Goebbels. SA gangs destroyed many synagogues and much Jewish property. Between 20,000 and 30,000 Jewish men were arrested and sent to concentration camps. In addition, ninety-one Jews were killed (according to official German figures) and some 7,000 Jewish shops and businesses were looted. Moreover, the German Jews were forced to pay a fine of one billion marks. The 1938 pogrom marked the culmination of the period of social segregation, exclusion from the economy, and promotion of emigration.

On March 13, 1938, the Nazis annexed Austria *(Anschluss)*. There the methods used in implementing their policies were far more expeditious and brutal than those they had used in Germany. In the wake of the *Anschluss,* the Jews of Austria suffered humiliations, maltreatment, and physical assaults even worse than those which had been meted out to their brethren in Germany. The legislation which had been gradually introduced into the Reich was immediately enforced in Austria. Masses of people were dispatched to concentration camps.

After Austria, the Nazis set out to seize Czechoslovakia. In 1938, the Allies had allowed the Germans to annex the Sudetenland, and in March, 1939, Germany seized the rest of Czechoslovakia. In addition to the Jews of that country, 15,000 Jewish refugees, former inhabitants of Germany and Austria, fell into their hands.

After the *Anschluss,* Adolf Eichmann, a member of the SS, was appointed to set up an "emigration office" in Vienna. This office very quickly became notorious for its efficiency. Eichmann turned voluntary emigration into what was in reality expulsion. He forced the leaders of the Jewish community to assist him in carrying out his plans and compelled those Jews who were in better circumstances to finance the expulsion of their poorer coreligionists. By the time that mass extermination was begun, about half the Jews of Austria had emigrated or been expelled. According to one Jewish source, by September, 1939, 110,000 Jews had left Austria and 35,000 had emigrated from Bohemia and Moravia. As a result of his highly successful "experiment" in Vienna, Eichmann was chosen to introduce his system in Berlin and Prague. He established his reputation as an "expert in Jewish affairs" and was later made head of the Jewish section in the Reich Security Main Office *(Reichsicher-heitshauptamt).*

## The Period of Restrictions and Internment of Jews: 1939-1941

With the outbreak of World War II on September 1, 1939, the Nazis initiated a new phase in their anti-Jewish policy. The years 1939-1941 marked a period of transition from a policy of forced emigration to the implementation of the Final Solution. It took the Germans three weeks to conquer most of Poland, and the western and northern districts of the state were annexed to the Reich. The eastern provinces, as previously agreed upon in the Molotov-Ribbentrop Pact, were annexed to the Soviet Union and Lithuania. Only the enclave in the center of Poland, which included the Polish capital Warsaw, became the General Government. There were some 3½ million Jews in Poland. These Jews were steeped in Jewish learning and represented the well-springs of Jewish creativity. According to the Nazis, they constituted the focus and chief biological basis of the Jewish people. It is estimated that there were about 1.7 million Jews in the German-occupied areas of Poland.

Before the war, the German government had been forced to exercise some restraint in their treatment of the Jews, but under wartime conditions, these considerations were no longer taken into account. Moreover, in Poland, the circumstances of the Jews were different from those of the Jews in Germany. In Poland, there were very few mixed marriages, and the Jews were not an integral part of the cultural and political life of the country. The Reich Security Main Office, set up in 1939 and headed by Reinhard Heydrich, an associate and close collaborator of Heinrich Himmler, was given the task of solving the Jewish Question. Since the Jewish problem was considered to be within the sphere of the fight against the enemies of the Aryan race and the Third Reich, the German police and the SS regarded themselves as competent to make and implement decisions concerning the Jews.

As early as September, 1939, Heydrich issued urgent instructions regarding the treatment of Jews in the occupied areas of Poland. Jews living in small towns were to be transferred to the ghettos which would be established in the large cities. At the same time a Jewish Council *(Judenrat)* was to be set up in every town and village to carry out the orders of the German authorities. Heydrich distinguished between these measures, which he regarded as a transitional stage in the solution of the Jewish problem and the final goal, the extermination of the Jews. It is unlikely that at this stage the Final Solution had already been decided upon and its program drafted.

Those in power probably only had very vague ideas of what they wished to achieve. While all desired a speedy and radical solution of the Jewish problem, they were not clear how to accomplish their goal.

Antisemitic decrees imposed on the Jews included: a) the wearing of a special Jewish badge; b) forced labor; c) looting of Jewish property; and d) expulsion to labor camps.

A series of decrees excluded the Jews from all branches of the economy, and prevented them from earning a living. Many were transported to labor camps, where, as a result of overcrowding, undernourishment, and lack of sanitation, a large number died. Clearly, it would appear that the Nazis were already intent upon creating such conditions which would render it impossible for any normal human being to survive.

Within a year, the Jews were isolated in ghettos. The first large ghetto was in Lodz; the largest of all, in Warsaw, was set up in the autumn of 1940. In due course, approximately half a million Jews were concentrated in the Warsaw ghetto.

In the large ghettos, the Jews suffered from overcrowding, starvation, and disease. The rations for the Jews were much smaller than those allotted to the Poles. Due to the overcrowding, the shortage of food, the lack of fuel for heating, and the absence of proper sanitation services, there were outbreaks of infectious diseases. The Warsaw ghetto in particular had many typhus epidemics. At first it seemed to the Jews that the Nazis were intent upon wiping them out by starving and working them to death. In the occupied areas of Poland, German soldiers and Nazi guards were allowed to take the Jews' property and mistreat them in any way they desired.

For generations, the Polish Jews had had to face hardships of every kind. Time after time they were forced to struggle more for survival, and stand firm against vicious manifestations of antisemitism. Inevitably, Polish Jews had become conditioned to withstand misfortune; when faced by the Nazis, they created various institutions to enable themselves to resist the onslaught upon their physical and spiritual existence. In spite of the prohibition against educating their children, they set up a network of clandestine schools. Lectures were delivered on cultural and political themes. Clandestine records were kept. Jews evaded many of the German decrees against them. Food and other supplies were smuggled into the ghettos. Though forbidden to undertake any gainful employment, Jews continued to work in a variety of camouflaged workshops.

Political parties continued their activities underground as did clandestine youth movements. Secret newspapers were published and these played an important role, as no uncensored newspapers appeared in the German-occupied areas and listening to Allied radio broadcasts was prohibited. Welfare societies were organized, and these grew into large-scale mutual benefit associations that collected funds from Jews within occupied territory and even from abroad. These welfare societies had a public standing; they were directed by well-known personalities who were in touch with the underground movements.

Immediately following the defeat of France, a new plan was proposed to solve the Jewish Question. This plan, which was to be under the aegis of the German Foreign Ministry and the SS, called for the concentration of all European Jews on the island of Madagascar under strict Nazi control. The Madagascar Plan did not materialize, however, because of the war with England.

The victories of their army in western Europe encouraged the Germans to tighten their stranglehold on the Jews under their control. In less than two years, from September, 1939 (the attack on Poland) to June, 1941 (the beginning of the campaign against Russia), the Nazis succeeded in overrunning the greater part of Europe, including Norway, Denmark, Belgium, France, Holland, Yugoslavia, and Greece. The countries of southeastern Europe, Hungary, Rumania, and Bulgaria were content to become Axis satellites.

The Nazis thought that the time was not far off when their "New Order" would enable them to decide the fate of all the European Jews. In the meantime, the methods of handling Jewish affairs had to vary according to the country. Certain western European governments still retained a measure of independence in their internal affairs, and in those countries the Nazis could not act with impunity, as the local population had to be considered. In much of western Europe, the mass of the people regarded the Jewish communities as an integral part of the nation, and this attitude was an obstacle that forced the Nazis to slacken the pace of their anti-Jewish measures in Western countries. In such cases they found it expedient to direct their first attacks against the "foreign" Jews (refugees and stateless persons) and then to gradually and systematically extend their influence until they could eliminate all the Jews of Europe. Even the Jews of western Europe were to be included in the "solution of the Jewish problem." At this stage, after the Madagascar project had been abandoned, the Nazis changed their attitude to Jewish emigration. Previously, it had been possible for Jews to leave for the free countries, but now Jews were categorically prohibited from emigrating.

The Nazi-occupied areas were almost completely cut off from the free world. Every possible obstacle was put in the way of the Jewish communities and international Jewish organizations who were anxious to make contact with the beleaguered Jews in order to supply them with some material help and, later, to help rescue them. Early in the war, various organizations succeeded in transferring supplies of food and sums of money to the occupied countries. During this period, some Jews managed to reach the free countries, but with the entry of the United States into the war, there was no longer any means of sending food or money to the Nazi-occupied territories. The frontiers of the occupied countries had long been sealed and no Jews could escape. The Jews of Palestine established a rescue committee *(Vaad Hatzala)* with offices in Istanbul, Turkey, and Geneva, Switzerland. These offices tried to maintain contacts with the Jews under Nazi rule. Transferring money involved incredible difficulties. The means at the disposal of this agency were limited and inadequate.

The Allied powers fighting the Nazis were unwilling to permit communication of any kind with enemy-occupied territory and regarded the shipment of food, clothing, or money as indirectly aiding the enemy. As time went on, the Jews in occupied Europe were more and more cut off from their brethren in the free world and no real help or guidance was given the Jews condemned to death.

## The Final Solution: 1941-1945

The third and last phase of the Nazi "Final Solution of the Jewish Problem" began in June, 1941, with the German invasion of the Soviet Union, and ended with the German capitulation in May, 1945. During these four years, Jews were savagely persecuted, subjected to every possible pain and humiliation, and murdered in mass shootings or in the gas chambers of extermination camps.

As far as is known, there is no document extant which shows who decided, when and how, to commence the total extermination of European Jews. Many historians believe that no such order was ever set down in writing. The slaughter began in occupied Soviet territory with the wholesale murder of "hostile elements," i.e. Jews and certain members of the Red Army. These operations, initiated in the East by the *Einsatzgruppen* (mobile killing units) were later expanded. Hitler decided that the "Final Solution to the Jewish Problem" was to murder every Jew who fell into Nazi hands. The German government offices and the SS carried out the diabolical Nazi plan with typical German attention to detail. They worked at their inhuman task with fanatical zeal and cruel precision. This singular precision was not inspired by sadism or the release of base instincts. Most of those who planned this genocide were seemingly ordinary members of society and educated men. They were, however, inculcated with the belief that every Jew was a powerful enemy of the German people and had to be destroyed. As a result, they planned the execution of a crime unparalleled in human history.

The *Einsatzgruppen*, which were under the orders of the *Reichsicherheitshauptamt*, were composed of men from the SS and police and auxiliary units recruited from among the local population. The size of such a group varied from 500 to 1,000 men. Four *Einsatzgruppen* (A,B,C, and D) operated in the rear of the German army on the Soviet front. Officially, the task of these "operational units" was the elimination of the "hostile elements" in the con-quered areas of the Soviet Union. According to Ohlendorf, comman-der of one of the *Einsatzgruppen* which murdered 90,000 Jews, the order to kill Jews was given verbally by Heydrich.

According to the figures submitted to the International Military Tribunal, the *Einsatzgruppen* murdered about a million Jews from the beginning of the Russian campaign until the end of 1941.

Killing "operations" were carried out according to a set routine. First a large hole or trench was dug, usually by the victims themselves. Then the Nazis lined up the victims on the edge of the hole and mowed them down with a volley of shots. The soil of Lithuania, Belorussia, and the Ukraine is scarred by many sites of slaughter and the mass graves of Jews.

As early as July 31, 1941, Reichsmarschall Hermann Goering sent an order in writing to Heydrich "to make preparations for the general solution of the Jewish problem within the German sphere of influence in Europe." On January 20, 1942, a conference was held in Wannsee, a suburb of Berlin. This conference, presided over by Heydrich, was of decisive importance. There were sixteen participants, all representatives of central authorities in the Third Reich. Here the *Reichsicherheitshauptamt* and the ministries and authorities concerned coordinated the plans for the extermination of the Jews. Heydrich gave the figure of eleven million as the number of Jews included in the plan for the Final Solution of the Jewish problem. This figure seems to indicate that he believed that additional territory would fall into Nazi hands, as the Jews of those areas were also included in the overall plan. The minutes of the Wannsee Conference state: "As a result of the war, the program for Jewish emigration has been changed for one of sending Jews to the East, according to the wish of Hitler. . ." In his autobiography, Rudolf Hoess, commander of Auschwitz, relates how he was summoned to Berlin in 1941 (the exact date is not given) by Himmler, who said that "the Führer has given the order for the Final Solution of the Jewish Question." Himmler added that it was the task of the SS to carry out the order. Hoess continues: "The exisiting extermination points in the east were inadequate for large-scale, long-term activity and I designated Auschwitz for this purpose."

In every country in Europe occupied by the Germans, the murder machine was put into operation. Wherever there were large concentrations of Jews, a special "commando" would be sent to supervise the expulsion and deportation of the Jews. The "commandos" were reinforced by SS units, by auxiliary Ukranian, Lithuanian, Latvian, and Estonian units, and by the local police in the various countries. Deportation was carried out on a variety of pretexts. In Poland, for example, the Jews were told that "superfluous elements, unemployed, were being 'resettled' in the East, where they would find work." In western Europe, they were told of Jewish "settlements" in the East. The pretense and deception continued to the end, to the very threshold of the gas chambers. Generally, the deportation was carried out in stages. The first to be expelled were from the lowest social stratum (the unemployed, sick, poor, and refugees). The others, meanwhile, were left with the illusion that they would not be affected. Sooner or later, however, a second and then a third series of deportations took place, until the area was *Judenrein* (clear of Jews).

No exceptions whatsoever were made in the Nazis' policy of racial discrimination and physical extermination of the Jews. However, local conditions had a marked influence upon both the rate of extermination and the methods used. The readiness or reluctance of the local population to cooperate with the Nazis was a factor of vital importance. The various conquered peoples were allowed different degrees of self-government. The Poles, for example, had no self-government, while the Danes retained relatively wide powers. Obviously, the attitudes of the people themselves were also an important factor. The Baltic peoples were eager to collaborate in the extermination of the Jews in their countries. For the most part, the Poles remained aloof and indifferent to the course of events. The Bulgarians saved most of their Jews, but the outstanding example of rescuing and helping Jews was shown by the Danes. Satellite states, such as Croatia and Slovakia, were headed by puppet rulers devoted to the Nazis and their ideology, who were only too ready to fulfill the requests of their overlords.

Two main factors influenced the Jews' reaction to the impending extermination. In the first place, during the preceding years, the Nazis had done their utmost to rob the Jews of their physical strength, strip them of their self-respect, paralyze their will power, break up their organizations, and completely isolate them from the outside world. In fact, the systematic humiliation, starvation, disease, and noisome conditions which faced them day in and day out weakened their ability to resist. Nothing mattered, save mere existence. Was it possible to cheat death? Could hunger be stilled? The catastrophe which had overtaken Jews was, so to speak, an amalgam of countless personal tragedies. The murder machine would descend without warning on towns and villages. The "action" would continue for days or weeks, during which the Jewish residents were often in a state of shock and anguish so great that there was no possibility of organizing any effective resistance. Another factor was the disbelief shared by most normal human beings. The Nazi pretense and camouflage were successful in deceiving the Jews until the very last moment. Rumors about the extermination camps were met with scepticism. No one with any common sense could believe such a gruesome possibility. Late in 1942, news of the extermination camps and the fate of the Jews deported from the ghettos of Poland spread. In view of the conditions under which the Jews were living and the attitude of their non-Jewish neighbors, it is little wonder that in many cases the Jews failed to resist.

The main extermination camps were established in Poland, and Jews from all the countries of occupied Europe were sent there to be murdered. Apart from a tiny minority (such as, for example, the Council for Aid to the Jews, Zegota) most Poles regarded the extermination of the Jews with total indifference. During 1942, some 70 percent of the Jews of Poland were annihilated, and most of the ghettos in the country were liquidated. Of the approximately 3½ million Jews in Poland in 1939, almost 3 million were murdered before the war was over.

In the countries of western Europe, the Nazis encountered greater difficulties in carrying out their antisemitic policy, so they resorted to more sophisticated tactics. In a few Western countries, Nazi antisemitism was regarded as part of the occupation policy of the foreign invader, and there were even instances of demonstrations of solidarity with the persecuted Jews.

There were approximately 300,000 Jews in France before the war, most of them inhabitants of long-standing. The country was divided into three zones—a German-occupied zone, the Vichy government zone, and a small enclave in the south under Italian rule. In March, 1941, the Vichy government set up a Commissariat for Jewish Affairs. The first victims of the Nazis were the "foreign Jews"—that is, those Jews who were not French citizens. Deportations began in the German-occupied zone, but before long were conducted from the areas under the Vichy government as well. Only in the tiny area under Italian control were Jews safe. In fact, many attempts to rescue Jews originated in this region. The sympathy of a large part of the French population enabled many Jews to remain in hiding and/or to join the French resistance movement. In all, about 90,000 Jews were deported from France to the extermination camps.

In Belgium, the home of some 90,000 Jews, nighttime roundups of Jews began in mid-1942. Residential neighborhoods were surrounded, streets were cordoned off, and the Jews were hunted out and dragged off to the transit camp at Malines. Here, too, the "foreigners" were the first to be deported. It should be noted that Catholic religious institutions endeavored to rescue Jews, especially children. About 40,000 Belgian Jews perished.

In 1941, the Jewish population in Holland numbered approximately 150,000. Early in 1942, Jews were sent to labor camps (inside Holland), and in March, 1942, they were concentrated in the Jewish quarters of Amsterdam. During July, August, and September transports were dispatched from there to the East, via the transit camp of Westerbork. In February, 1941, a general strike was held in Amsterdam, mainly as a demonstration of solidarity with the Jews. The Nazi terror machine was put into action and largely succeeded in halting the Dutch opposition. The great majority of Dutch Jews were deported to the extermination camps, and only 10,000 survived.

In September, 1943, the Nazis attempted to round up the 7,500 Danish Jews. This attempt was a failure, because the Danes not only warned the Jews but helped them to go into hiding and cross over to neutral Sweden. Of the 7,500 Jews in Denmark, only 467 old people were caught. They were sent to the Theresienstadt camp in the Protectorate of Bohemia-Moravia.

In Norway, where a collaborationist government was set up by Vidkun Quisling, the Nazis began to arrest Jews in 1942 and concentrated them in a camp at Berg. The Norwegian people and their church defied the Nazis, and exerted every effort to prevent the arrests and deportations. They succeeded in smuggling about 1,000 Jews into Sweden (half of the total Jewish population).

There were about 75,000 Jews in Yugoslavia, before the Holocaust. Most of the Jews of Serbia were killed immediately after the Germans' entry. In Croatia, where the Ustashe movement had set up a Fascist government, the Jews were herded into camps, where they were tortured and killed, or, with the active cooperation of the Ustashe, deported to the East. Only in the Italian sector of Croatia was any help extended to Jews. Italian officials prevented Jews from being handed over to the Nazis. Groups of Jews succeeded in escaping the Nazis, and joined Josip Tito's partisan units. Only 20,000 Yugoslavian Jews escaped extermination.

Most of the Jews of Greece fell into Nazi hands, since the majority lived in Salonica, which was in the German zone of occupation. Of the 75,000 Jews of Greece, 65,000 were deported to Auschwitz.

The Bulgarian authorities handed over the Jews living in those areas of Yugoslavia and Greece which they had annexed. However, in 1943, when the Germans ordered the deportation of the Jews who were Bulgarian citizens, the opposition aroused was sufficiently strong to prevent the plan from being carried out.

Rumania, a willing and obedient satellite of the Nazis, had a strong antisemitic tradition. Many Jews were expelled from Rumania across the Bug River and thus driven into the arms of the Nazis. About a quarter of a million Jews were kept in captivity in Transnistria (the area in the Ukraine located between the Bug and Dniester rivers) under appalling conditions of overcrowding, disease, and starvation. When a commission of the *Judenzentrale* (Jewish Center) succeeded in getting into Transnistria, only 77,214 Jews remained there. Later, when the defeat of the Nazis became apparent, the Rumanians refrained from continuing their collaboration in the murder of Jews. It is estimated that the victims of the Holocaust in Rumania numbered 425,000.

When Slovakia declared its "independence," the Jewish population numbered approximately 90,000. The program of deportations to the East was unanimously accepted by the Slovak government. "Hlinka Guard" men were detailed to escort the transports to the German frontier where the Jews were handed over to the Germans to be sent to Maidanek and Auschwitz. Jewish leaders made courageous, though vain, attempts to rescue the Jews of Slovakia. During 1942, 58,000 Jews were deported from Slovakia. At the end of 1942, the deportations were halted, but in August, 1944, after the Slovak uprising they were resumed, and an additional 13,000 Jews were deported.

In Hungary, there was widespread support for fascism, and the Horthy government was a staunch supporter of Nazi Germany. When Hungary joined in the war against the Soviet Union, the government handed over to the Nazis 20,000 Jewish, Polish, and Russian citizens who were deported and murdered. The policy of extermination was not applied in Hungary until the Nazis took over the country on March 19, 1944. Eichmann and his henchmen set to work and regular transports began to leave Hungary for Auschwitz. About 400,000 Hungarian Jews were deported (mostly from the provinces), some by train, but more by forced marches. The transports were directed to the extermination camps in Poland. Almost all the Jews brought to these places were murdered en masse. Most of the Jews were murdered at Maidanek and Auschwitz—camps which were combinations of concentration and extermination camps. This majority of the deportees, including the children and the aged, were dispatched without delay to the gas chambers. Only a very limited number were put to work, which was equivalent to murder, but in this case the process of killing was drawn out. The deportations and the mass murders continued until the end of 1944. After 1944, killings in the gas chambers were discontinued, but murder by other means continued unabated.

Throughout Europe, the Nazis set up a system designed to facilitate the pillaging of Jewish property. This property included not only real estate, goods, and chattles, but also the personal possessions carried by the victims, and even the gold fillings in the teeth of the corpses. In addition, the Nazis exploited the labor of camp inmates for their own financial gains.

# The Reaction of the Free World

Innumerable questions have been asked about the reaction of the free peoples of the West. How did they regard the campaign of systematic persecution, robbery, and murder carried out by the Third Reich?

Up to the outbreak of World War II, the press of the Western world consistently reported on the Germans' anti-Jewish policy and the brutal, deliberate victimization of the Jews of Nazi Germany and the areas annexed. The general public was, therefore, fully informed as to the Nazi persecution of the Jews of Germany, Austria, and Czechoslovakia. In many cases, the public was outraged, but the governments of the major European democracies judged it expedient to regard the Jewish problem as the internal affair of a sovereign state. Since the governments were eager to achieve a rapprochement with Germany, they adopted a conciliatory policy, denying themselves the right to intervene. Thus, no effective protest was registered when Jews were deprived of their civil rights, and even of their means of earning their daily bread.

Despite their desire to remain neutral vis à vis the emigration of Jews from the Reich, the free countries were forced to take a stand on the question of the Jews' entry to countries of refuge. The United States was not prepared to relax its stringent immigration quotas, which limited the number of central and eastern Europeans admitted each year. Great Britain was pitiless in blocking immigration into Palestine and strictly limited the number of entry permits. States with a substantial capacity for absorption, such as Australia, Canada, and most of the countries of South America, were willing to receive agricultural laborers, but refused to allow the entry of professionals, merchants, and skilled artisans. Indeed, in Britain and the United States protests were actually organized against the admission of immigrant doctors.

In July, 1938, the Evian Conference was convened due to the initiative of the president of the United States. Its purpose was to find ways and means of helping the emigration of refugees from Germany and Austria and their absorption elsewhere. Thirty-two countries sent representatives to the conference and hopes were high that a solution could be found. However, it soon became clear that the great powers that had initiated the conference were themselves reluctant to take any significant steps towards absorbing the refugees and so they failed to set an example for the smaller countries. Lengthy speeches and appeals were made but no single country committed itself to taking any practical measures. The conference set up an international committee for refugee affairs with headquarters in London. This committee lacked the necessary funds to enable it to function effectively and did not have the means of directing the flow of refugees to any specific destination. Consequently, the Evian Conference must be regarded as a complete failure.

The results of the Evian Conference supplied the Germans with opportunities for cynical comments on the attitude of the free world. Before the first session was held, Hitler jeered that he could "only hope and expect that the other world which is so sympathetic towards these criminals, would at heart be generous enough to turn this sympathy into actual aid." When it became clear that the conference had ended without even outlining practical measures, the Germans hastened to exploit the situation. They claimed that the condemnation expressed by all the democratic countries was mere propaganda; it was obvious that they, too, did not wish to accept Jews.

When the war began, the flow of constant comprehensive information on conditions in Germany and the occupied countries ceased. Until about mid-1942, the general tendency was to regard the constant persecution of the Jews as one part of the total complex of oppression in the occupied countries. Early in 1942, more news of the activities of the *Einsatzgruppen* in the East and the mass killings in the extermination camps filtered through to the West. By the middle of 1942, the horrifying rumors about the Final Solution and the gruesome operations being conducted had been verified.

In the major countries of the anti-Nazi alliance, the United States and Great Britain, the reactions were horror and indignation. However, once again not only was there a refusal to consider the plans put forward by Jews to combat the Nazi's persecution of their brethren (such as a demand for the exchange of Germans for Jews or the launching of retaliatory strikes against the Germans until the murders ceased), there was not even a willingness to cease the formal procedures governing the transfer of dollars abroad which could have saved the lives of many Jews. Moreover, the policies with regard to immigration quotas remained inflexible. Proposals, which, if put into action, could have saved thousands of children and other victims, were submitted to a ponderous administration incapable of dealing with the situation and thus produced no tangible results.

In April, 1943, at the precise moment when the Jews in the Warsaw ghetto were fighting for their lives, a conference of the major Allies convened in Bermuda to consider the problem of the refugees. This conference, like its predecessor at Evian, proposed no practical solutions. The only step it took was to revive the moribund intergovernmental committee, which had no executive powers.

The stand adopted by the Allies was that rescue and relief would be achieved only by a final victory over the Nazis. In the meantime, no military action should be taken which was not part of the purely military-strategic plan. This attitude was rigidly adhered to, and no operation for relief or rescue was undertaken, even when such an action did not conflict with military objectives or require the use of military power.

## Armed Resistance and the Stuggle for Survival

In spite of the terrible conditions in the ghettos, the Jews stubbornly resisted and fought for survival. They sought to help one another, often showing an amazing degree of self-sacrifice. Thousands of mothers refused to save their own lives by handing over their children. Thousands of people went to their death rather than abandon their families. In the ghettos, an organized underground movement was active in every sphere of life.

In the political underground, anti-Nazi activity was strikingly effective. The majority of the political parties and youth organizations, which had functioned in the Jewish community before the war, continued their activities clandestinely. The pioneer youth organization continued to train young people, striving to give them sound spiritual values and strengthen their ties with the Land of Israel. In some places training farms were actually established. They were camouflaged as economically productive enterprises. The underground press reported on events at the fronts and emphasized the need for opposing the Nazi enemy. From the early days of the war, youth organizations sent out messengers (mainly girls) who maintained contact with distant Jewish centers. These emissaries were the main source of information with regard to the Nazi killings and the plan for total extermination. Obviously, expulsions and mass killings greatly reduced the possibility of any kind of public activity in the underground.

Jewish armed resistance took three forms: a) armed rebellion in the ghettos and camps; b) formation of partisan units; and c) joining the resistance movements in occupied Europe.

The armed struggle of the Jews of Poland was headed by the Jewish Fighting Organization, which included members of the Zionist Pioneer Movements (Dror, Hashomer Hatzair, Akiva, Gordonia, Young Zionists), the two factions of Poale Zion (Socialist-Zionist), members of the Bund (Socialist labor party), and the Jewish Communists. The fighters of this organization led the uprisings in Warsaw, Bialystok, Cracow, and the Czestochowa region of Zaglembia. The most noteworthy feat of the struggle was the Warsaw ghetto uprising in April, 1943, under the command of Mordecai Anielewicz. During the Warsaw ghetto uprising, the Jewish Military Organization of Betar took an active part in the fighting.

The Warsaw ghetto revolt was the largest Jewish uprising against the Nazis and was the first armed revolt in occupied Europe. In general, the non-Jewish underground organizations did not help the Jews organize. The Jews had few or no weapons and only in the Warsaw ghetto did the Polish underground supply them with sixty pistols of poor quality together with a very limited amount of ammunition. For the Jewish combatants in the ghettos, there was no prospect of victory or being saved by fighting, but uprisings were nonetheless acts of national and human significance.

In August, 1943, an uprising broke out in the Bialystok ghetto. The majority of those who revolted fell in battle. The remnant of the fighters escaped to the forests and joined the partisans. There were Jewish uprisings in many other ghettos and camps. In Vilna, the F.P.O. (United Partisan Organization) included members of all the Jewish political parties. In June, July, August, and September, 1943, many of the underground fighters escaped from the Vilna ghetto, reached the forests, and established Jewish partisan units which fought against the Nazis and participated in the liberation of Vilna with the Red Army.

In 1942 and 1943, the number of Jewish partisans rose steadily. Jews played a considerable part in the partisan fighting and in the resistance movements in France. They also organized the rescue of children and helped many people cross the borders. Frontier crossings were also carried out from Holland. There were Jews in the Belgian underground and resistance units, and Jews had a notable share in the uprising which broke out in Slovakia in the summer of 1944. Most of the Jews who escaped to the mountains in Yugoslavia joined the ranks of the partisan army led by Tito. Thousands of Jews managed to reach the forests of Belorussia and the Ukraine, founded partisan groups and distinguished themselves in the fighting. Jews fought in special Jewish units and also as individuals in mixed units. In the thickly forested regions of Belorussia and the Ukraine, family encampments were set up for Jewish noncombatants who had escaped to the forest. The Jewish combatants provided for those in hiding and defended them.

Even in the extermination camps, revolts broke out. Jewish prisoners succeeded in blowing up one of the crematoria at Auschwitz and attempted to escape. In Sobibor, the prisoners revolted and killed some of the SS guards. Hundreds were shot, but many made their escape.

# Aftermath

Six million Jews of all ages, backgrounds, and affiliations were murdered in the Holocaust. The hundreds of thousands who escaped, whether by hiding or by joining the underground or partisan units and the few who survived the camps refused to return to their former homes. Those lands had become graveyards to them, and they could not face the prospect of resuming life in those countries. The very few who had survived the period of darkness, suffering, and death and who had returned to their native cities and villages in eastern Europe, were received with anger and hostility.

The survivors, unwanted in their former homes and weary of a life of tribulation and adversity, waged a stubborn struggle for the right to immigrate to the Land of Israel. They formed the vanguard of the "illegal immigration" and constituted a powerful force in the political campaign waged for the establishment of an independent State of Israel.

In fact, the majority of the survivors reached Israel. There, they have made new lives for themselves and their children.

### For Further Reading

Arad, Yitzhak; Gutman, Yisrael; and Margaliot, Abraham. *Documents on the Holocaust: Selected Sources on the Destruction of the Jews of Germany and Austria, Poland, and the Soviet Union.* New York: Ktav, 1981.

Dawidowicz, Lucy S. *The War Against the Jews: 1933-1945.* New York: Behrman House, 1976.

Friedman, Philip. *The Roads to Extinction.* Philadelphia: The Jewish Publication Society, 1980.

Gutman, Yisrael, and Rothkirchen, Livia, eds. *The Catastrophe of European Jewry: Antecedents, History, Reflections.* Jerusalem: Yad Vashem, 1976.

Hilberg, Raul. *The Destruction of the European Jews.* Chicago: Quadrangle Press, 1961.

Krausnick, Helmut, and Broszat, Martin. *Anatomy of the SS State.* London: Collins, 1968.

Mosse, George L. *The Nationalization of the Masses: Political Symbolism and Mass Movement in Germany from the Napoleonic Wars through the Third Reich.* New York: New American Library, 1975.

# The Fate of Sephardic and Oriental Jews During the Holocaust

## JANE GERBER

The enormity of the destruction of the Ashkenazic (of German descent) Jews of Europe has tended to obscure the tragic consequences of the Holocaust for the Sephardic (of Spanish decent) Jews of the continent. Sephardic Jews were deeply rooted in Europe, having settled in Slavic and Ottoman lands after the expulsion of the Jews from Spain in 1492 and the continuing migrations from Portugal in the sixteenth century. Moving eastward in search of a refuge, the Sephardic Jews rebuilt their shattered communities in the Balkans, Asia Minor, North Africa, and Greece. In Sofia and Salonica, Morocco and Monastir, Sarajevo and Rhodes, the Jewish exiles of Spain, a restless and talented émigré group, built new communities that retained the language, culture, and traditions of their Iberian roots. This Ladino-speaking civilization, with its schools, press, rabbincal authorities, and commercial prowess, was wiped out by the Holocaust. For those Sephardic communities that survived, Jewish life in Europe was no longer tenable. Thus, the Sephardic Jews of Europe are a community of the past; in the Nazi blueprint of destruction, all Jews were slated for death, the Sephardim of the East sharing the same destiny in Auschwitz as their Ashkenazic coreligionists.

The efficacy of the destruction of the Sephardic Jewish community depended upon a number of factors: geography, protection by the Italian Fascists, half-hearted compliance with Nazi orders on the part of the Bulgarians, or zealous persecution of Jews by the Croatian Fascist movement, Ustashe. In the case of North Africa, the vicissitudes of Vichy French policy were cut short by the American forces, but not before deportations from Tunis had actually commenced. This essay considers the separate fates of these communities as well as the reverberations of the Nazi triumphs on some of the ancient Jewish communities in the Arab world.

On the eve of the outbreak of World War II, the Sephardim in Europe numbered approximately 130,000. The jewel in the crown of Sephardic Jewry was the Jewish community of Salonica in Greece. Exceeding 50,000 in number, Salonican Jews constituted a dynamic segment of this port city of 240,000 people. Over 11,000 Jews resided in the Thracian and Macedonian portions of Greece, which were ceded to Bulgaria after it joined the German war effort. Bulgaria's approximately 50,000 Sephardim were almost entirely concentrated in the capital city, Sofia. Yugoslavian Jews lived in the capitals of the former Balkan ethnic kingdoms, with Jews heavily concentrated in Belgrade, Zagreb, and Sarajevo. Most of Yugoslavia's 10,000 Sephardim were in the Bosnian capital of Sarajevo in central Yugoslavia. Smaller Jewish communities on the islands of Rhodes, Corfu, and Crete, totaling 7,500 Jews, constituted outposts of

Sephardic culture and were also engulfed by the Nazi forces. The much larger Jewish communities of North Africa numbered more than one-half million Sephardic and Oriental Jews. While logistics and history spared the North African Jews from the fate of their European brethren, their travails under the Third Reich should be mentioned.

Greek Jews had enjoyed a flourishing communal life prior to World War II. Although emigration had reduced their numbers in the 1920s and 1930s, Greek Jews formed a cohesive enclave when the German occupation began on April 9, 1941. Nazi discriminatory legislation was immediately introduced, expropriations and economic spoliation began, and Jewish males were drafted into forced labor units where the mortality rate was exceedingly high. A Jewish Council, or *Judenrat,* was established by the Nazis to assure compliance with their orders under the leadership of Rabbi Dr. Zvi Koretz, a man who was not native to Salonica, but who spoke German and belived in a policy of Jewish accommodation and compliance.

The destruction of the great cemetery of Salonica in December, 1942, and the raid on Jewish cultural treasures were merely a prologue to more extreme measures. With the arrival of Adolf Eichmann's deputies, Dieter Wisliceny and Alois Brunner, in February, 1943, the Final Solution was set in motion. From March 14 to August 7, 1943, the Jews of Salonica were herded in the cattle cars to Auschwitz and its gas chambers. Those Jews who managed to claim Spanish protection (but were not wanted in Spain) were dispatched to Bergen-Belsen. Greek Jews of Italian nationality were sent to Athens from Salonica, but were deported soon after the fall of Mussolini. Of the Salonican Jews, 46,091 were deported, 45,650 of whom were murdered in Auschwitz. Echoes of their solidarity within the confines of the concentration camp, their physical stamina, and special cultural characteristics, even in Auschwitz, can be heard in some of the accounts of survivors.[1]

The distinctive Jewish community of the island of Rhodes had existed since at least the thirteenth century, boasting its native customs, folklore, and rabbinic luminaries, as well as a rabbinic academy in the twentieth century. While the Italian Fascist occupation, beginning in 1936, brought in its wake seven years of harsh restrictions, the Jews of Rhodes managed to survive until the Germans took over the island. On July 19, 1944, the 1,700 Jews of Rhodes were moved by ship to Pireaus and dispatched to Auschwitz. Only 151 Jews of Rhodes survived.

A similar fate awaited the Jews of the second largest Ionian island of Corfu. Only a handful of the 1,800 Jews deported to Auschwitz in June, 1944, managed to survive. The roundup of Crete's historic Jewish community also occurred in June, 1944. Placed on a ship, and then abandoned by their German crew, the Jewish community of Crete was drowned in its entirety.

The fate of Balkan Jews was more complex. As in the instance of the Jews of Greece, the Jews of Bulgaria and Yugoslavia were relatively small communities, well-integrated in their countries but also consciously proud of their Sephardic heritage. In both Bulgaria and Yugoslavia, the Jewish communities were an ethnic mosaic, comprised of refugees from Austro-Hungary, indigenous Jews whose ancestry extended back to Byzantine times and the late medieval influx of Sephardic refugees from Spain. The commercial prowess, historic pride, and high cultural level of the Sephardim assured them a dominant role in the communties of Sofia and Sarajevo. By the twentieth century, Ladino culture and Sephardic institutions typified the Yugoslav Jewish community of Sarajevo and the Bulgarian capital of Sofia. The Jews in both these predominantly argricultural countries formed a significant middle-class population element. But here the parallels between the two countries cease, for while Yugoslavia's 76,000 Jews began to reel under the impact of the virulent antisemitism from Croatia and the *Volksdeutsche* (natives of German ancestry with strong Nazi sympathies), Bulgaria's Jews were spared the implementation of the Final Solution through a combination of factors. On the one hand, the Jews from the recently acquired areas of Thrace and Macedonia were deported to Treblinka. On the other, the Jews of "Old Bulgaria," or prewar Bulgaria, were spared, although plans for their deportation were already in motion in the spring of 1943. While modern scholars have shown that Bulgaria's monarch and her parliament *were* willing allies of the Germans and were not averse to the deportation of Jews from Thrace and Macedonia, they did not implement the Final Solution against their Sephardic community, primarily as a result of Allied interest in the Bulgarian Jews and the changing tides of war. Saved from the Final Solution, the Bulgarian Jews migrated en masse to Israel in 1949.

The fate of the Yugoslav Jews was more tragic. Caught between the competing nationalisms of the country's ethnic regions and virulent antisemites in their native land (known as the Ustashe), most of the Yugoslav Jews were murdered on Yugoslav soil. As a result of shootings, gas vans, and deportations to Treblinka, 60,000 of Yugoslavia's 75,000 Jews were destroyed. Twenty-five thousand of the victims were the descendants of earlier Spanish expulsions. While Serbian and Croatian collaborators distinguished themselves in brutality, the Jews of Yugoslavia played a disproportionately prominent role in the partisan movement and resistance to nazism.

It is commonly believed that Oriental Jews were untouched by the Holocaust. It is a fact, however that reverberations of anti-Jewish policies were felt throughout the Muslim world where Arab populations heralded the victories of Hilter and Mussolini. Jewish life was actively endangered in Vichy-controlled North Africa and British-occupied Iraq. In comparison with the agony of European Jews, the plight of Oriental Jews during the 1930s and 1940s appears minimal, yet the Jews of Muslim lands suffered anxiety, economic discrimination, and more than one physical onslaught as a result of the deep emotional hold which nazism had on the native Muslim and Christian populations.

North African Jews had enjoyed a period of relative tranquility and prosperity in the twentieth century as a result of the colonial presence of the French forces. The spreading antisemitism in Europe in the 1930s was, however, sympathetically regarded by local French colonialists in North Africa. Especially in Algeria, Hitler's rise to power was greeted with jubilation. Soon after the defeat of the French in 1940, one of the first measures adopted by the Vichy French forces in Algeria was the abrogation of the Cremieux decree, an 1870 declaration which had granted French citizenship to Algerian Jews. Vichy laws were zealously applied in Algeria, and Jews suffered daily depredations. Algerian resistance to the Vichy French was almost Jewish in its entirety, the local Muslims offering no resistance to fascism. This resistance ultimately led to the insurrection of Algiers in November 8, 1942. Under the leadership of the Jew Jose Abulker this Algerian insurrection played a major role in neutralizing the country while American forces landed. After the victory, however, the French generals Giraud and Darlan, with Governor Yves Chatel and the compliance of the local American Chargé d'Affaires Robert Murphy, established detention camps for Algerian Jews. Jewish rights were not restored until October, 1943.

The fate of Tunisian Jews was even more precarious than that of the Jews of Algeria. Subjected to a host of anti-Jewish regulations after the Vichy government assumed control in November, 1940, Tunisian Jews barely escaped the full force of destructive German policies. Between November, 1942, and May, 1943, the German occupation of Tunis resulted in the establishment of a *Judenrat*; conscription of Jewish males into labor units to build trenches and airfields, which were decimated by Allied bombings; imposition of extortionary fines and confiscations; arbitrary executions; and, ultimately, the beginnings of deportations to the European extermination camps. Only the turning tide on the North African front rescued Tunisian Jews from annihilation.

The figure of Adolf Hitler exercised a strong appeal and deep emotional hold over Arab masses and leaders in the East. Not least among his attractions was his rabid antisemitism. From the mufti of Jerusalem to Anwar Sadat (then merely a junior cadet in Egypt), Muslims in the East regarded Germany with approval. Terrorist acts against Jews began before the outbreak of World War II, frequently without any connection to events in Palestine. In Iraq, for instance, anti-Jewish demonstrations assumed violent proportions in 1937 and again in 1938. A pro-Axis coup under Rashid Ali Ghailani was suppressed in the spring of 1941, but soon thereafter, a bloody pogrom engulfed the Jewish community of Iraq, killing 150, wounding 700, and destroying scores of Jewish businesses and almost 1,000 Jewish homes. Other Middle Eastern Jews also lived through a period of insecurity and anxiety as a result of the pro-Axis sympathies of native Arab populations.

When the ashes of the war had settled, the once colorful, generous, and optimistic Sephardic Jews of the Balkans were gone. With the exception of Bulgaria, the Jews and their cultural monuments were extinguished. Traces of their former presence can be found in the Street of the Martyrs in Rhodes or in a carefully preserved refrain in Ladino concentration camp ballads. The "remnants of fifteenth-century Spain in twentieth-century Europe" are no more.

### Notes

1.   See, for instance, Primo Levi, *Survival in Auschwitz: The Nazi Assault on Humanity* (New York: Collier Books, 1969).

### For Further Reading

Angel, Marc. *The Jews of Rhodes.* New York: Sepher-Hermon Press, 1978.

Avni, Chaim. "Spanish Nationals in Greece and Their Fate During the Holocaust," *Yad Vashem Studies* VIII (1970): 31-68.

Freidenreich, Harriet. *History of the Jews of Yugoslavia.* Philadelphia: The Jewish Publication Society, 1978.

Hilberg, Raul. *The Destruction of the European Jews.* Chicago: Quadrangle Press, 1961.

Michaelis, Meir. *Mussolini and the Jews.* New York: Oxford University Press, 1978.

Molho, Michael. *In Memoriam: Hommage aux Victimes Juives des Nazis en Grece.* Thessalonique, Greece: Communauté Israélite de Thessalonique, 1973.

Roth, Cecil. "The Last Days of Jewish Salonica," *Commentary* XI (July 1950): 49-55.

# TIMELINE

## EPHRAIM ZUROFF

## 1933

January 30.   Adolf Hitler appointed chancellor of Germany.

February 27.   Reichstag fire. Nazis unleash terror to ensure election results.

March 23.   First concentration camp—Dachau—established.

March 27.   Enabling Act—suspending civil liberties—passed by Nazi-dominated Reichstag.

April 1.   Boycott of Jewish shops and businesses. Jewish professionals barred from entering offices.

April 7.   First anti-Jewish decree: The Law for the Reestablishment of the Civil Service.

April 21.   Ritual slaughter of animals in accordance with Jewish dietary laws prohibited in Germany.

April 26.   Gestapo established.

May 10.   Public burnings of books by Jews, those of Jewish origin, and opponents of nazism.

Spring-Summer.   Universities and the arts "cleansed" of Jewish influence. Jewish professors expelled, Jewish writers and artists prohibited from practicing their professions.

Spring-Summer.   Jewish organizations in America and western Europe protest Nazi persecution of the Jews. A few call for boycott of Nazi Germany.

October 19.   Germany leaves the League of Nations.

## 1934

June 30.   "Night of the Long Knives": Nazis purge leadership of Storm Troops (SA) and opponents of nazism.

August 2.   Hitler named president and commander-in-chief of the armed forces following death of von Hindenburg.

# 1935

March 16.   Germany renews conscription, in violation of Versailles treaty.

May 31.   Jews barred from serving in German armed forces.

September 15.   "Nuernburg Laws": anti-Jewish racial laws enacted. Jews could no longer be German citizens, marry Aryans, fly the German flag, and hire German maids under the age of forty-five.

November 15.   Germans define Jew: anyone with three Jewish grandparents; someone with two Jewish grandparents who identifies as a Jew.

# 1936

February 4.   David Frankfurter, young Jewish student, assassinates Wilhelm Gustloff, leader of Nazi party, in Switzerland.

March 3.   Jewish doctors barred from practicing medicine in government institutions.

March 7.   Germans march into the Rhineland, which had been demilitarized according to treaty.

May 5.   Ethiopia occupied by Italy.

June 17.   Himmler appointed chief of German police.

July.   Germans and Italians join Franco's forces in Spanish Civil War.

October 25.   Hitler and Mussolini form Rome-Berlin Axis.

# 1937

July 16.   Buchenwald concentration camp opens.

# 1938

March 13.   *Anschluss:* annexation of Austria by Germany; all German antisemitic decrees immediately applied in Austria.

April 26.   Jews in Reich must register all property with authorities.

August 1.   Adolf Eichmann establishes Office of Jewish Emigration to speed up pace of forced emigration.

**August 17.**  Decrees revoke all name changes by Jews and force those Jews who did not have names recognized as Jewish by German authorities to add "Israel" (for males) and "Sarah" (for females) as middle names.

**September 29-30.**  Munich Conference: England and France agree to turn over Sudetenland (part of Czechoslovakia) to Germany.

**October 5.**  Following request by the Swiss authorities, Germans order all Jews' passports marked with large red letter "J" to prevent Jews from smuggling themselves into Switzerland.

**October 28.**  Jews with Polish citizenship living in Germany are expelled to Polish border. Poles refuse to admit them; Germans refuse to allow them back into Germany—17,000 stranded in frontier town of Zbasyn.

**November 9-10.**  *Kristallnacht* (Night of Broken Glass): anti-Jewish pogrom in Germany and Austria. Two hundred synagogues destroyed, 7,500 Jewish shops looted, and 30,000 male Jews sent to concentration camps (Dachau, Buchenwald, Sachsenhausen).

**November 12.**  Decree forcing all Jews to transfer retail businesses to Aryan hands.

**November 15.**  All Jewish pupils expelled from German schools.

# 1939

**January 30.**  Hitler threatens in Reichstag speech that if war erupts it will mean the *Vernichtung* (extermination) of European Jews.

**March 15.**  Nazis occupy part of Czechoslovakia (Bohemia and Moravia); make Slovakia independent satellite state.

**March 22.**  Germans occupy port of Memel.

**August 23.**  Molotov-Ribbentrop Pact signed: nonagression pact between Russia and Germany.

**September 7.**  Beginning of World War II: Germany invades Poland.

**September 17.**  Russia invades eastern Poland.

**September 27.**  Heydrich issues directives to establish ghettos in German-occupied Poland.

**November 23.**  Jews in German-occupied Poland forced to wear distinguishing badge.

November 28.   First ghetto in Poland established in Protrkow.

## 1940

April 9.   Germans occupy Denmark and southern Norway.

April 27.   Himmler issues directive to establish a concentration camp at Auschwitz.

May 7.   Lodz ghetto closed off: approximately 165,000 inhabitants in 1.6 square miles.

May 10.   Germany invades Holland, Belgium, and France.

May 20.   Concentration camp established at Auschwitz.

June 22.   France surrenders to Nazis.

August 8.   Battle of Britain begins.

September 27.   Rome-Berlin-Tokyo Axis.

November 15.   Warsaw ghetto sealed off: approximately 500,000 inhabitants.

November 20-24.   Hungary, Rumania, and Slovakia join Rome-Berlin-Tokyo Axis.

## 1941

January 21-26.   Anti-Jewish riots in Rumania by Iron Guard: hundreds of Jews cruelly butchered.

March.   Adolf Eichmann appointed head of Gestapo section for Jewish affairs.

April.   Germany occupies Greece and Yugoslavia.

June.   Vichy government deprives Jews of French North Africa of their rights as citizens.

June 22.   Germany invades the Soviet Union.

End of June-December.   Nazi *Einsatzgruppen* (special mobile killing units) carry out mass murder of Jews in areas of Soviet Union occupied by German army.

July 31.   Heydrich appointed by Goering as responsible for implementation of Final Solution.

September 1.    Jews in Third Reich obligated to wear yellow Star of David as distinguishing mark.

September 28-29.    Massacre of Jews at Babi Yar—ravine outside Kiev: 34,000 murdered.

October 23.    Murder of 19,000 Jews in Odessa.

October.    Establishment of Birkenau camp: site of mass extermination of Jews, Gypsies, Poles, Russians, and others.

December 7.    Japanese attack on Pearl Harbor.

December 8.    Chelmno extermination camp begins operation: 340,000 Jews, 20,000 Poles and Czechs liquidated there by April, 1943.

# 1942

January 20.    Wannsee Conference: Heydrich reveals official plan to murder all Jews on European continent.

January.    Jewish underground organizations established in Vilna ghetto and Kovno ghetto.

March 1.    Extermination by gas begins in Sobibor extermination camp; by October, 1943, 250,000 Jews murdered.

March 17.    Extermination begins in Belzec extermination camp; by end of 1942, 600,000 Jews murdered.

Late March.    Deportations to Auschwitz extermination camp begins.

June 1.    Treblinka extermination camp begins operation; by August, 1943, 700,000 Jews murdered.

June 30.    All Jewish schools in Germany closed.

June.    Jewish partisan unit established in forests of Belorussia.

July 28.    Jewish fighting organization (ZOB) established in Warsaw ghetto.

Summer.    Deportation of Jews to extermination camps from Holland, Poland, France, Belgium, Croatia. Armed resistance by Jews in ghettos of Kletzk, Wieswiez, Mir, Lackwa, Kremenets, and Tuchin.

November.    Allied forces land in North Africa.

Winter.   Deportation of Jews from Norway, Germany, and Greece to extermination camps. Jewish partisan movement organized in forests near Lublin.

# 1943

January 18-21.   Germans attempt to liquidate Jews in Warsaw ghetto; armed resistance by ghetto inhabitants.

February 2.   German advance in Russia stopped at Stalingrad.

March.   Liquidation of Cracow ghetto.

April 19.   Warsaw ghetto revolt begins as Germans attempt to liquidate 70,000 ghetto inhabitants; Jewish underground fights Nazis until early June.

June.   Himmler orders the liquidation of all the ghettos in Poland and the Soviet Union.

Summer.   Armed resistance by Jews in Czestochowa, Lvov, Bedzin, Bialystok, and Tarnow ghettos.

August 2.   Armed revolt in Treblinka extermination camp.

Fall.   Liquidation of large ghettos: Minsk, Vilna, Riga.

October 14.   Armed revolt in Sobibor extermination camp.

# 1944

March 19.   Germany occupies Hungary.

May 15.   Nazis begin deporting Hungarian Jews; by June 27, 380,000 sent to Auschwitz.

June 6.   Allied invasion of Normandy.

Spring-Summer.   Red Army repels Nazi forces.

July 20.   Group of German officers attempts to assassinate Hitler.

July 24.   Russians liberate Maidanek extermination camp.

Summer.   Liquidation of ghettos in Kovno (Kaunas), Shavli (Siauliai), and Lodz; inmates sent to concentration and extermination camps.

October 7.   Revolt by inmates at Auschwitz: one crematorium blown up.

October 31.  Remnants of Slovakian Jews deported to Auschwitz.

November 8.  Beginning of death march of approximately 40,000 Jews from Budapest to Austria.

November.  Last Jews deported from Theresienstadt model ghetto to Auschwitz.

# 1945

January 17.  Evacuation of Auschwitz: beginning of death march of camp inmates.

January 25.  Beginning of death march of inmates of Stutthof.

April 6-10.  Death march of inmates of Buchenwald.

April.  Red Army enters Germany from East; Allies enter from West.

April 30.  Hitler commits suicide.

May 8.  Germany surrenders: end of Third Reich.

5

# THE PROCESS
# OF
# DESTRUCTION

# The Cemetery

My brother and I were hiding by the old cemetery next to the gravel pit. Suddenly, around ten o'clock, we were startled awake. In the distance, we could hear the rumble of field wagons approaching, and the voices of a great number of people. Some seemed to be crying, and some were shouting orders, and over all this were shots and screaming and screaming, and more screaming.

The sounds came nearer and we held on to each other, uncertain whether to run or hide. Then we shrank lower into the grasses as we realized that the sounds came from the roadway leading to the cemetery. The terrible procession was coming here! When it passed the gates, we stood up among the bushes to peer over the wall at an unbelievable sight.

The women and children of Eisiskes were being herded along the road by the Lithuanian police, whipped and beaten to move them faster. Farm wagons were loaded with children and with the dead and dying bodies of women who had rebelled at their captivity. As we watched, the whole grisly procession turned in at the farthest entrance to the gravel pit.

Then began a day I can never forget, for every detail is drawn on my memory as if it had happened only yesterday.

Over the cries and moans of this mass of defenseless creatures, Lithuanian police barked orders, then pushed and prodded to separate the women from their children. Benjamin and I desperately scanned the lines of women to find our mother, grandmother, and sister, but we couldn't see them. There was my aunt and my cousin, and that neighbor lady and the woman from the newspaper kiosk . . . but we couldn't see our own family. We were afraid to hope that they had escaped.

"What are they going to do?" Benjamin hissed in my ear. But we both knew in our hearts what was going to happen.

The women were taken in groups of a hundred or so down the path into the gravel pit. When they reached the point where the bushes that grew there would hide them from the sight of the others, they were made to strip naked, and pile their clothing nearby. The young were separated from the others and dragged into the bushes to be raped and raped again by soldier after soldier and policeman after policeman. Then they were dragged off, marched to the bottom of the gravel pit, lined up, and coldly shot to death by the Lithuanian killers.

*I clung to the edge of the cemetery wall, as horror welled up within me. I wanted to hide, to run screaming from the cemetery, to make this hideous thing end. Didn't they know what they were doing? These were human lives! These were people, not animals to be slaughtered! My mouth opened to scream, but I could not. I wanted to close my eyes, but they wouldn't close. "Don't look, Leibke! Don't look!" Benjamin sobbed, and pulled at me to make me leave the wall.*

*I didn't want to look, but I couldn't stop looking. I saw the Lithuanians shoot the breasts off some women, and shoot others in the genitals, saw them leave others with arms and legs mutilated to die in agony, and some to smother as the next load of bodies fell upon them. I saw my aunt die in a volley of gunfire. I saw my beautiful cousin raped and raped until death must have been the only thing she longed for.*

*My fingers slipped from the wall and I fell beside my brother retching and sobbing. He clung to me.*

*"Don't watch anymore, Leibke," he pleaded. "Stay here!"*

*I wanted to, but I couldn't. It was as if I had no will of my own, as if I had to memorize every crime and horror, and the face of each murdered. Weeping, Benjamin sat on me, trying to hold me down. I heard hopeless screams for mercy. Shrieks of terror and agony. And gunfire. I felt each bullet enter my brain.*

*"No!" I whispered and fought to get up . . . "I've got to!" And I returned to the wall. . . .*

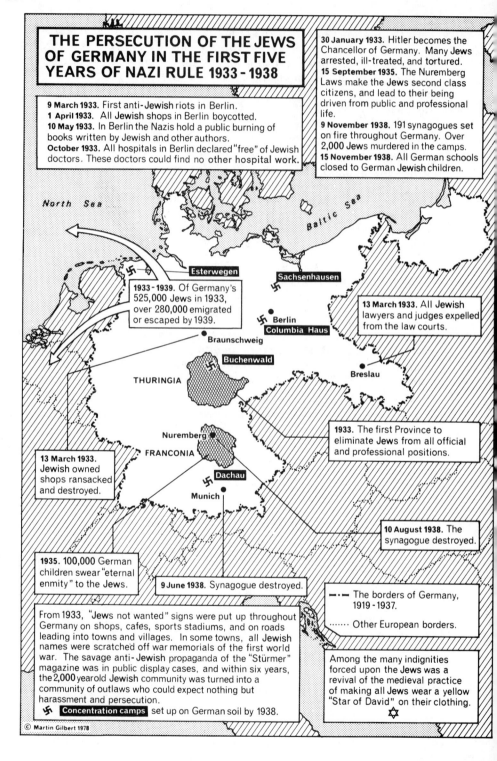

# THE PERSECUTION OF THE JEWS OF GERMANY IN THE FIRST FIVE YEARS OF NAZI RULE 1933 - 1938

**9 March 1933.** First anti-Jewish riots in Berlin.
**1 April 1933.** All Jewish shops in Berlin boycotted.
**10 May 1933.** In Berlin the Nazis hold a public burning of books written by Jewish and other authors.
**October 1933.** All hospitals in Berlin declared "free" of Jewish doctors. These doctors could find no other hospital work.

**30 January 1933.** Hitler becomes the Chancellor of Germany. Many Jews arrested, ill-treated, and tortured.
**15 September 1935.** The Nuremberg Laws make the Jews second class citizens, and lead to their being driven from public and professional life.
**9 November 1938.** 191 synagogues set on fire throughout Germany. Over 2,000 Jews murdered in the camps.
**15 November 1938.** All German schools closed to German Jewish children.

*North Sea*

*Baltic Sea*

Esterwegen

Sachsenhausen

**1933 - 1939.** Of Germany's 525,000 Jews in 1933, over 280,000 emigrated or escaped by 1939.

**13 March 1933.** All Jewish lawyers and judges expelled from the law courts.

Berlin
Columbia Haus

Braunschweig

Buchenwald

Breslau

THURINGIA

Nuremberg

FRANCONIA

**1933.** The first Province to eliminate Jews from all official and professional positions.

**13 March 1933.** Jewish owned shops ransacked and destroyed.

Dachau

Munich

**10 August 1938.** The synagogue destroyed.

**1935.** 100,000 German children swear "eternal enmity" to the Jews.

**9 June 1938.** Synagogue destroyed.

—·— The borders of Germany, 1919 - 1937.
······· Other European borders.

From 1933, "Jews not wanted" signs were put up throughout Germany on shops, cafes, sports stadiums, and on roads leading into towns and villages. In some towns, all Jewish names were scratched off war memorials of the first world war. The savage anti-Jewish propaganda of the "Stürmer" magazine was in public display cases, and within six years, the 2,000 year old Jewish community was turned into a community of outlaws who could expect nothing but harassment and persecution.

Concentration camps set up on German soil by 1938.

Among the many indignities forced upon the Jews was a revival of the medieval practice of making all Jews wear a yellow "Star of David" on their clothing.

© Martin Gilbert 1978

# The German Bureaucracy and the Holocaust

## CHRISTOPHER R. BROWNING

In his earliest recorded remarks on the Jews, Hitler emphasized the superiority of "rational" antisemitism over "emotional" antisemitism. The latter found its outlet in pogroms, while the former promised a "systematic legal opposition" to achieve "removal of the Jews altogether." Thus, despite the low regard in which Hitler held civil servants and jurists, the German bureaucracy was an essential component of the machinery of destruction which, in the words of Raul Hilberg, "infused" the other participants "with its sure-footed planning and bureaucratic thoroughness."[1]

Clearly, the anti-Jewish legislation produced by various ministries of the German government contributed significantly to the persecution of the Jews. Even before Hitler's assumption of power, schemes were being hatched in the Interior Ministry to purge the civil service, end the naturalization of *Ostjuden* (eastern European Jews), and prohibit the changing of names to disguise Jewish identity. Thus, the first major anti-Jewish legislation of the Third Reich, the Law for the Restoration of the Civil Service, enacted in April, 1933, was not forced upon a reluctant Interior Ministry by the triumphant Nazis but represented a convergence of their interests. This law, with its "Aryan paragraph" excluding Jews from the civil service, became the model for a continuing flow of legislation restricting Jewish participation in other professions and organizations. It was also significant in another way: By authorizing the dismissal of all officials whose behavior "did not offer the guarantee" of loyalty to the new regime, the law inhibited officials who were not particularly sympathetic to the Nazis from using their positions to obstruct the new regime and induced many to take out "employment insurance" in the form of party membership. The law was an effective weapon for nazifying the bureaucracy, thereby facilitating further legislative persecutions of the Jews.

If the wave of 1933 legislation meant a "civic death" for the German Jews by depriving them of equality before the law, the 1935 Nuernberg Laws (the Reich Citizenship Law and the Law for the Protection of German Blood and Honor and the decree defining the *Mischlinge*, or persons of mixed blood) constituted a "social death" by inhibiting contacts between Jews and non-Jews. Thereafter, the center of anti-Jewish legislative activity within the German bureaucracy shifted from the Interior Ministry to the Ministry of Economics. In 1938 the "economic death" of the German Jews was enacted. In April, the Jews were required to register their property. They were expelled from one area of the economy after another. "Compulsory Aryanization," forcing the Jews to liquidate businesses and assets at a fraction of their real value, was in reality expropriation. Finally, in 1939, all Jewish organizations were abolished and the Reich Union of Jews—subordinate to Reinhard Heydrich, deputy of SS Reich Leader Heinrich Himmler—was established as the sole Jewish organization in Germany. The German bureaucracy had, thus, ultimately delivered the German Jews into the hands of the SS. The "systematic legal opposition" advocated by Hitler as early as 1919 and pursued by the German bureaucracy after 1933 had indeed prepared the way for the "removal of the Jews altogether."

Legislation was, however, not the only way in which the German bureaucracy contributed to the persecution of the German Jews before the war. The German Foreign Office, perhaps the most prestigious and least nazified ministry before 1938, became the self-appointed apologist and defender of Nazi Jewish policy abroad. In the opening months of the new regime, and on its own initiative, the Foreign Office solicited antisemitic material from Reich Minister of Propaganda Joseph Goebbels. This material, which endorsed the Nazi theory of the Communist-Jewish world conspiracy in the crudest terms, was then distributed to German diplomatic missions abroad to help them provide a better "understanding" and defense of German Jewish policy. Not content to serve as apologist, the Foreign Office also proceeded to lobby against any amelioration of Germany's treatment of its Jews as an inadmissable sign of weakness to foreign pressure.[2]

What mentality prevailed among the bureaucrats of the German ministries to explain their complicity in Nazi Jewish policy? The upper echelons of the ministerial bureaucracy were products of pre-World War I Imperial Germany. Buffeted by defeat and national humiliation, by revolution, economic chaos, and the apparent collapse of traditional values, they longed to return to a bygone era. However disdainful these patricians were of the Nazis as social upstarts, they fully shared the Nazis' determination to reassert internal order through authoritarian measures and return Germany to the rank of a great power through national revival and rearmament. If the Nazis could be identified by the Old Guard of the German bureaucracy with these cherished goals, the Jews could be identified with all that was feared and opposed—liberalism and Marxism, internationalism and cosmopolitanism, financial speculation and economic disorder. The Old Guard perceived the Jews as aliens who had exploited German weakness after World War I to infiltrate and dominate German life. The reversal of this Jewish penetration was, therefore, part of a larger "restoration process." If the Nazis could be assured of Foreign Office defense of their Jewish policy by draping it in the flag of German patriotism, they could be assured of the participation of the Old Guard in a nostalgic "national revolution."[3]

The lower-echelon officals were of a younger generation, shaped by the turmoil and insecurity of post-World War I Germany. When the Nazis came to power, they rushed to gain party membership. For some, it was a chance openly to declare long-held political sympathies. For others, it was a matter of expediency, the most tangible demonstration of loyalty to the new regime that was now essential for successful career prospects. For many, it was undoubtedly a happy coincidence of conviction and self-interest. If the motives were mixed, the results were not. The civil servants soon reached the highest percentage of Nazi membership of any profession in Germany.

It was this younger generation of easily nazified civil servants that provided the cadres of "Jewish experts" (*Judensachbearbeiter*) to staff the Sections for Jewish Affairs, which became a mandatory feature of practically every governmental and party organization in Germany after 1933. The mere existence of a corps of Jewish experts created a certain bureaucratic momentum behind Nazi Jewish policy. Even when deportations and mass murder were already underway, decrees appeared in 1942 prohibiting German Jews from having pets, getting their hair cut by Aryan barbers, or receiving the Reich sports badge![4] It did not require orders from above, merely the existence of the job itself, to ensure that the Jewish experts kept up the flow of discriminatory measures.

The German bureaucracy adapted to the evolution of Nazi Jewish policy from legislative discrimination and expropriation to deportation and extermination. In fact, the bureaucracy proved itself capable not only of "systematic legal opposition" but also of mass murder. Himmler's SS and police, the primary instrument after 1939 for carrying out Jewish policy, was an amalgamation of party and state organizations, not just a collection of party fanatics. Himmler and Heydrich themselves had long supported a thorough and systematic handling of the Jewish Question, as opposed to violent outbursts by party radicals. Thus, SS ascendency did not mean the eclipse of the administrative-bureaucratic approach; it merely meant that ministerial bureaucrats were superseded in importance by police bureaucrats, many of whom had been civil servants long before the amalgamation of the police with the SS gained them SS rank.

Moreover, the SS could not carry out mass murder singlehandedly. At the Wannsee Conference of January 20, 1942, Heydrich assembled the state secretaries of the German ministries to coordinate their participation in the Final Solution. Adolf Eichmann, head of the Jewish section in the Reich Security Main Office, testified that prior to the conference, Heydrich was apprehensive about their reactions but subsequently was pleased and surprised by their readiness to cooperate. This cooperation was not insignificant. Even a single transport of German Jews required the involvement of many municipal authorities other than the local police. An assembly and loading area, usually in the cargo depot, had to be made available by local railway authorities. Officials from the Finance Office collected property inventories from the deportees, liquidated the property, and turned the proceeds over to the Tax Office. Personnel from the Labor Office collected work books, and the Housing Office disposed of vacant apartments. On a wider scale, officials of the *Reichsbahn* (German railroad) provided transport for deportations from all over Europe. The Foreign Office, anxious to preserve its dwindling influence within the Nazi regime, intensified its activity on behalf of Nazi Jewish policy by pressuring their allied and satellite countries to cooperate and by smoothing out complications involving Jews with foreign citizenship. This widespread participation in Nazi Jewish policy, even in the killing phase, has led Raul Hilberg to conclude: "The machinery of destruction, then, was structurally no different from organized German society as a whole; the difference was only one of function. The machinery of destruction *was* the organized community in one of its special roles."[5]

The Nazis' mass murder of the European Jews was not only the technological achievement of an industrial society, but also the organizational achievement of a bureaucratic society. The frictionless operation of the machinery of destruction required that the victims be dehumanized in the eyes of the perpetrators. This was achieved in part by ideological indoctrination that portrayed the Jews as vermin and bacilli, to be treated accordingly. But it was also achieved by a bureaucratic mode of operation, in which depersonalized and dispassionate behavior unprejudiced by human emotions was a fundamental and positive value of the civil service.[6] Many Germans viewed the Jews as aliens whose influence, and even presence in Germany and Europe, had to be curtailed or eliminated. But they also clung to deeply embedded values of law and order. Incidents, such as the boycott of 1933 and the *Kristallnacht* pogrom of 1938, meant a conflict of values between solving the Jewish Question and preserving law and order, which could only dissipate support for and acquiescence in Nazi Jewish policy. The bureaucratic approach of systematic but orderly discrimination was far more congenial, both to the bureaucracy and to the German public at large. Germans could take pride in their "legal revolution" and still deal with the Jews.

Moreover, when Nazi Jewish policy evolved into mass murder, fragmentation of responsibilities and routinization of operations enabled the German bureaucracy to continue its participation.[7] "Desk murderers" could shuffle papers, set rations, draft telegrams, schedule trains, and dispatch personnel, resulting in the deaths of millions, without once seeing their victims or perceiving themselves as involved in the taking of human lives. The German bureaucrats' involvement in the Holocaust revealed pervasive antisemitism, political myopia, opportunistic careerism, and the keen desire to preserve their bureaucratic "turf" against rivals. It also revealed the potential for depersonalized violence inherent in modern, bureaucratically organized society.

### Notes

1. Raul Hilberg, *The Destruction of the European Jews* (Chicago: Quadrangle Press, 1961), p. 39.

2. Christopher R. Browning, *The Final Solution and the German Foreign Office* (New York: Holmes & Meier, 1978), pp. 12-13.

3. On Germany's traditional elites and Hitler's "national revolution" see Karl Dietrich Bracher, *The German Dictatorship* (New York: Praeger Publishers, 1970), pp. 191-199.

4. Uwe Dietrich Adam, *Judenpolitik im Dritten Reich* (Düsseldorf: Droste Verlag, 1972), pp. 339-340.

5. Hilberg, *Destruction*, p. 640.

6. Richard Rubenstein, *The Cunning of History: The Holocaust and the American Future* (New York: Harper Colophon Books, 1975), Chapter 2.

7. George Kren and Leon Rappoport, *The Holocaust and the Crisis of Human Behavior* (New York: Holmes & Meier, 1980), pp. 140-141.

### For Further Reading

Adam, Uwe Dietrich. *Judenpolitik im Dritten Reich*. Düsseldorf: Droste Verlag, 1972.

Browning, Christopher R. *"The Government Experts."* In *The Holocaust: Ideology, Bureaucracy, and Genocide*, edited by Henry Friedlander and Sybil Milton. Millwood, NY: Kraus International Publications, 1981.

Hilberg, Raul. *The Destruction of the European Jews*. Chicago: Quadrangle Press, 1961.

———. "German Railroads, Jewish Souls." *Transaction, Social Science and Modern Society* (1976): 60-74.

Rubenstein, Richard. *The Cunning of History: The Holocaust and the American Future*. New York: Harper Colophon Books, 1975.

Schleunes, Karl. *Twisted Road to Auschwitz*. Urbana, Ill.: University of Illinois Press, 1970.

# The SS and Police

## HENRY FRIEDLANDER

The SS and the police implemented the so-called Final Solution of the Jewish Question. The development and role of these two organizations, and their relationship to each other, have often been misunderstood. The *Schutzstaffel* (Protective Squads) of the Nazi party was created in 1925 to serve as a praetorian guard for party leaders. At first, under the authority of Ernst Roehm's Storm Troops *(Sturmabteilungen,* or SA), they became virtually independent in about 1930. The name of the *Schutzstaffel* was abbreviated as SS, which was represented by two silver symbols on a black field: stylized S's resembling Teutonic runes and copied from the sign representing electricity.

In contrast to the plebeian brown-shirted SA, the black-shirted SS became an elite formation with a strict process of selection based on racial purity and physical stamina; this became especially pronounced after the appointment of Heinrich Himmler as Reich Leader of the SS *(Reichfuehrer* SS, or RFSS). After the liquidation of Roehm and his associates in 1934, the SS also replaced the SA as the private army of the Nazi party.

Most SS members belonged to the General SS *(Allgemeine* SS). Like the SA from which it grew, the General SS was a part-time formation, requiring service—for ideological and military training, collection drives and guard duties, demonstrations and parades— only for limited periods and special occasions. Members in the General SS held regular jobs and donned their uniforms only after working hours. Organized along regional lines, this large General SS army provided a manpower pool that could be mobilized in times of need. Only a relatively small number of SS leaders held regular full-time SS appointments in central offices or regional headquarters. Still, the General SS was structured along military lines, with units and ranks equivalent to those of the armed forces; only the names of units (e.g., *Standarte* instead of Regiment) and ranks (e.g., *Standartenfuehrer* instead of colonel) differed from those of the *Wehrmacht.*

In 1931, the SS began the process of specialization that would eventually make it the formation that possessed the greatest power and inspired the greatest fear. Himmler created a party intelligence apparatus and appointed Reinhard Heydrich to head it. The SS Security Service *(Sicherheitsdienst,* or SD) was designed to gather and interpret information about the enemies of the Nazi movement and to inform the party leadership about the intentions and capabilities of their opponents; it was prohibited from engaging in intelligence operations inside the Nazi party, but it obviously provided its chiefs with invaluable information that could be used in intraparty struggles. Heydrich built his SD along regional lines—but separate from the General SS—and staffed it with full-time officers as well as a large army of part-time intelligence agents.

After the seizure of power in January, 1933, the SS served to protect the achievements of the Nazi revolution. Like members in the SA, those in the SS served as auxiliary policemen and concentration camp guards; but while the SA was eliminated from these jobs after the murder of Roehm in June, 1934, the SS continued and enlarged its service to the Nazi state.

The SS *Verfuegungstruppe* (SS Troops for Special Disposition) was created as a military force to quell domestic disorders. Members enlisted for long periods, were quartered in barracks, and were trained for combat. The *Verfuegungstruppe* was viewed as a reserve army for use during civil war; the *Wehrmacht* accepted duty in these SS units as equivalent military service. Its most prominent unit—the Praetorian Guard *(Leibstandarte)* Adolf Hitler, commanded by Sepp Dietrich—served as headquarter guards in Hitler's Chancellery.

The SS Death Head Units (SS *Totenkopfverbaende*) were created to staff and guard the concentration camps. Like members of the *Verfuegungstruppe,* those in the Death Head Units were volunteers who enlisted for long periods and underwent combat training; however, duty as concentration camp guards did not excuse them from military service.

The seizure of power in 1933 led to a struggle among the Nazi leaders for control of the offices of the German state. The SS leaders infiltrated the police. Eliminating all rivals, the SS centralized and absorbed the police. In 1936, Heinrich Himmler completed the process by assuming command of the entire police, thus combining the offices of Reich Leader of the SS and of Chief of the German Police. This method of *Personalunion* (the union of two offices under one person) merged a party office, paid from party funds, and a government office, paid from the state budget.

The regular uniformed police—the metropolitan Protective Police *(Schutzpolizei,* or Schupo) and the rural Constabulary *(Gendarmerie)*—retained their organizational structure on the local level, but were combined on the national level to form the Order Police *(Ordnungspolizei,* or Orpo). The Central Office of the Order Police, headed by Kurt Daluege, assumed command over the uniformed police throughout Germany; it belonged to Himmler's growing empire of SS and police central offices. Although it was not a requirement to join the SS, most senior officers and large numbers of the rank-and-file joined; failure to do so made advancement less likely. Still, the police officers who joined the SS also remained civil servants *(Beamte).* In the uniformed Order Police, members of the SS continued to wear their green police uniforms, adding only a small insignia to indicate SS membership.

Alongside the uniformed police, there had always existed the nonuniformed detective squads. The Nazis transformed them into an instrument of terror. Himmler appointed Reinhard Heydrich to command the nonuniformed police. Heydrich, thus, headed the Central Office of the Security Service *(Sicherheitsdienst,* or SD) and the Central Office of the Security Police *(Sicherheitspolizei,* or Sipo). In doing so, he combined a party formation (the SD) and a state

Two agencies made up the Security Police. One was the Criminal Police (*Kriminalpolizei,* or Kripo); the other was the Secret State Police (*Geheime Staatspolizei,* or Gestapo). The Kripo, headed by the Prussian police officer Arthur Nebe, was the traditional detective force for the investigation of regular criminal offenses. The Gestapo, headed by the Bavarian police officer Heinrich Mueller, was a newly created political police. But both the Kripo and the Gestapo were staffed by regular police officers who had to pass civil service examinations to occupy their positions permanently. Although combined into the Security Police, the Gestapo and the Kripo retained their independent existence; the Central Office of the Sipo was only an administrative device symbolizing centralization.

The Kripo continued to fulfill the traditional tasks of fighting crime, and it thus took a number of years to separate it from the uniformed police on the precinct level. But at the same time, the Kripo began to use the methods of the Gestapo in accomplishing its goals, and the exchange of information and personnel between the Gestapo and Kripo increased. Slowly, the difference between the control of crime and the suppression of political opposition disappeared. Further, as the Gestapo and Kripo assumed the job of investigating and containing the enemies of the Nazi regime, the SS Security Service, which had previously attempted to do this job with fewer resources and men, no longer had an essential function to perform. Thereafter, the SD became the SS formation most attractive to academics; it served as a research institute to survey public opinion and formulate policy.

Like the members of the Orpo, those in the Kripo did not have to join the SS or the Nazi party, but most found it advantageous to do so; in the Gestapo it was virtually compulsory. But even when they joined the SS, members of the Security Police remained civil servants and retained their civil service ranks (for example, inspector or commissar) in addition to their SS ranks. They wore their SS uniforms only on parade; on duty, members of the Gestapo and Kripo wore only civilian dress.

In 1939, Heydrich combined his two central offices to ensure greater coordination and total control. The result was the Central Office for Reich Security (*Reichsicherheitshauptamt,* or RSHA). The RSHA was a mixture of party and state agencies, combining party and state budgets in one bureaucratic structure. Departments I and II dealt with administrative, technical, and legal matters. Departments IV and V were the Sipo: the former was Mueller's Gestapo; the latter was Nebe's Kripo. Departments III and VI were the SD: the former, headed by Otto Ohlendorf, was responsible for domestic affairs; the latter, headed by Walter Schellenberg, dealt with foreign intelligence. After the assassination of Heydrich in 1942, Ernst Kaltenbrunner headed RSHA as chief of the Sipo and the SD.

World War II changed Himmler's SS empire. Its members put aside the black uniform (except for ceremonial occasions), and henceforth only wore field gray with special SS insignias. The

*Verfuegungstruppe*, renamed the *Waffen* SS, served as a combat army; its divisions participated in all German campaigns. At the same time, the concentration camps increased in size and number, requiring an increase in the Death Head Units. Finally, members of the police served in special SS and Police Regiments *(SS-und Polizei Regimente)* to fight against partisans and pacify the conquered territories.

The large SS army of World War II needed soldiers. In Germany, the SS was prohibited from drafting freely; it was restricted by army rules to the pool of prewar volunteers. Thus, members of the General SS automatically entered the *Waffen* SS for combat duty. Additional men were recruited in the occupied countries where army rules did not apply. There, the SS drafted racial Germans (the *Volksdeutsche)* and other Germanic peoples (for example, Norwegians or the Dutch). In addition, the police recruited volunteers in the East to serve as SS auxiliaries: Lithuanians, Latvians, Estonians, and Ukrainians. These volunteer auxiliaries were known as Hiwis, or *Askaris.*

In the occupied countries, the SS achieved the ultimate amalgamation of party and state. In Germany proper, Gestapo, Kripo, and SD had still retained some of their independence at the local level. Heydrich created the SS *Einsatzgruppen* to follow the armies and pacify the conquered territories; in the West this meant terror, in the East mass murder. These mobile police units were staffed by Sipo and SD men; in the *Einsatzgruppen* party functionaries and government bureaucrats merged completely. After pacification, the *Einsatzgruppen* were transformed into stationary offices of the Security Police and Security Service, thus institutionalizing the amalgamation of state agency (Sipo) and party formation (SD). Moreover, members of the Gestapo and Kripo had worn no uniforms on duty in Germany. Outside Germany they had to wear uniforms; they were assigned SD uniforms even if they had never joined the SS.

Those who served in the SS could be assigned to any duty. It was common for individuals to be transferred from one SS unit to another. There was no real difference between the combat troops of the *Waffen* SS and the security troops in the police and concentration camps. Those wounded in combat were usually transferred to Security Police offices or concentration camps for duty behind the lines; at the same time, large numbers of camp guards and policemen served in the *Waffen* SS.

SS offices and units multiplied in the occupied territories. There were the *Waffen* SS, concentration camp Death Head Units, Sipo and SD offices, Orpo regiments and offices, SS courts, and a variety of other offices. To mediate between these competing units, Himmler appointed special representatives—SS and Police Leaders *(SS-und Polizeifuehrer,* or SSPF) and above them Higher SS and Police Leaders *(Hoehere SS-und Polizeifuehrer,* or HSSPF)—as coordinators. To supply and pay this growing empire, the SS built its own economic enterprises. These were managed by Oswald Pohl's Central Office for Economy and Administration (SS *Wirtschaftsver-*

*waltungshauptamt,* or WVHA). It absorbed the office that ran the concentration camps and eventually operated a vast slave labor empire.

After the attempt to assassinate Hitler in July, 1944, the powers of the SS increased. The SS extended its authority over the POW camps; the SD seized control of military intelligence (the *Abwehr*). Himmler became commander of the home army and, thus, was responsible for all manpower reserves; after that the SS could finally draft Germans. At the end, the SS empire came to rival all other state and party agencies. After the war, the Allied judges at Nuernberg condemned the SS as a criminal organization.

### For Further Reading

Höhne, Heinz. *The Order of the Death's Head.* New York: Coward-McCann, 1970.

Krausnick, Helmut, et al. *The Anatomy of the SS State.* London: Collins, 1968.

Reitlinger, Gerald. *The SS: Alibi of a Nation.* New York: Viking Press, 1956.

# The Perpetrators*

## HENRY FRIEDLANDER

No adequate study exists about the perpetrators of the Holocaust as a group. We know a great deal about the process of destruction, but we know far less about the perpetrators. At present, it is even difficult to give a precise definition of the group; we do not even have basic statistics: age, birth place, occupation, party membership, etc. We possess little information about the social and economic composition of the group. Until we have this kind of information, we cannot attempt to construct a psychological profile. Sources for this type of investigation do exist at least in part: SS personnel records and war crimes trial records. But it takes time to analyze this data; so far, attempts to accomplish this have been rare.

We know most about the men who initiated the murder of the European Jews. They were Hitler and his associates: Goering, Himmler, Goebbels, Bormann, and a few others. A great deal is known about these Nazi leaders. Trial records, political biographies, even psychohistorical studies are available.

Much is also known about the senior officials who implemented Hitler's orders. We know the names, ranks, vital statistics, educational levels, and careers of the senior SS and police leaders: department heads in the Central Office for Reich Security; commanders of *Einsatzgruppen* and *Einsatzkommandos;* chiefs of Gestapo, Kripo, and Orpo offices. The data concerning these men can be found in Nazi documents, SS personnel folders, and the records of postwar trials. But there have been few biographies of these men, and studies about the SS or the police have only reached very tentative conclusions about these perpetrators.

They were, in general, professional men who considered themselves members of the middle class. They had made a career in party or government service and looked forward to rapid advancement. They were young; few were older than forty. Many were lawyers, some held Ph.D. degrees in the humanities. Those without university degrees had advanced in the police administration through civil service examinations. They were members of the Nazi party and of the SS; but some had joined only after Hitler's assumption of power.

These senior officials did more than implement orders; they were efficient, inventive, and even zealous in the job of mass murder. None refused to cooperate, and none asked to be excused. Why did they do it? Some were undoubtedly fanatic Nazis who killed from ideological commitment. But most probably participated in mass murder only for one of the following reasons: opportunism (the desire for career advancement); obedience (the tradition of following orders); or peer pressure (the fear of being different).

* *Prior to reading this article, it is useful to read "The SS and Police," by Henry Friedlander, in this volume.*

Another group of perpetrators involved in the killings occupied a different social position. These were the concentration camp commanders. Unlike the majority of the senior SS and police officials, the camp commanders had no formal education and did not occupy higher civil service positions. They were usually veteran Nazis who had joined the SS before the assumption of power; after 1933, they drifted into the Death Head Units guarding the camps. During World War I, they had served as noncommissioned officers in the army; in the postwar period they had worked in blue-collar jobs, and many had been unemployed during the Depression years. In the SS, they rose from the ranks to the office of commandant; they considered that job the pinnacle of their careers. Trained to obey, they followed orders without hesitation. At the same time, they combined cruelty with sentimentality, and were capable of almost any crime. One of them—Rudolf Hoess—wrote a revealing memoir before his execution in Poland; others testified at their postwar trials. Their personnel dossiers have survived, and they provide a great deal of information about them.

The commanders of the extermination camps of Belzec, Chelmno, Sobibor, and Treblinka were younger versions of the concentration camp type. They came to their jobs of killing suddenly at the start of World War II, but they efficiently built and ran the killing centers. They came from similar social, educational, and economic backgrounds as did the concentration camp commanders, but they were younger and had no previous experience as soldiers. They had served in the police, and had been members of the Nazi party. They had been selected almost at random for work in the Euthanasia program (killings of German nationals deemed incurably ill, disabled, or mentally insane). From there, they had been sent to the extermination camps, probably because they had shown the required mixture of obedience and initiative. They ranked lower than the older concentration camp commanders: The former were usually colonels, the latter did not rise above captain. We know little about these men from documents; even their personnel records provide little information. All that we do know is based on postwar trial testimony. But we possess a penetrating analysis of one such commander, Franz Stangl; written by the journalist Gitta Sereny and based on interviews, it is the best available study of a perpetrator.

Aside from the SS, there were those who supported the killings and without whose aid genocide would have been impossible. These included civil servants, army officers, and industrialists. The senior civil servants directed the vast bureaucracy of the German state, essential for the success of the killings carried out by the SS and police. The Foreign Office, for example, negotiated with satellite leaders about the deportation of the Jews; the Railroad Administration provided the trains to carry the Jews to the extermination camps; the Ministry of Armaments issued the orders for Jewish concentration camp labor; and the Ministry of Finance collected the valuables from the murdered Jews.

The officers in the High Command of the Armed Forces

similarly collaborated with the SS and police in the killings. They turned over to the SS execution squads large numbers of Russian POWs; ordered the shooting of thousands of Jews as hostages in Yugoslavia; and permitted the *Einsatzgruppen* to kill millions in areas under the control of the *Wehrmacht*.

The industrialists participated in the killing process by exploiting the labor of millions. Using the camp inmates supplied by the SS, they disregarded all civilized forms of conduct in search after quick profits. They built factories near Auschwitz and other camps; there they used inmate labor and, when the prisoners were no longer able to work, they permitted the SS to exterminate them.

Some of these perpetrators—bureaucrats, officers, and capitalists—were tried by the Allies, but even those convicted were usually released before they had served their sentences. Most never faced any judges. They argued that they were innocent; they claimed that they had only done their duty. In the end, they retained their pensions and their properties.

Least is known about the rank-and-file perpetrators: the guard at Buchenwald, the policeman at Babi Yar, the Ukrainian auxiliary at Treblinka. These were the men and women who did the actual killings. After the war they disappeared; only a very small percentage were ever tried. The data to write a composite biography of this group do not exist at this time. Only isolated individuals are known from their postwar trials.

Feodor Fedorenko was one of these perpetrators. Captured as a Red Army soldier, he escaped from the harsh conditions of the POW camps by volunteering to serve as an SS auxiliary. Trained at Trawniki, he was eventually stationed in Treblinka. There, he participated in the murder of almost one million Jews. Surviving inmates later identified Fedorenko as one of the Ukrainian guards who tortured victims before they were gassed.

After the war, Fedorenko concealed his Treblinka record, and was thus able to enter the United States illegally as a displaced person (DP). He settled in Connecticut and found employment as a factory worker. In more than two decades of residence, he never broke the law and received only one parking ticket. Those who knew him in Connecticut described him as a "good neighbor" and as a "diligent worker." No one suspected his Treblinka past. He retired to Florida and lived peacefully there until the Supreme Court, ruling that he had entered the United States illegally, stripped him of his citizenship [Fedorenko v. United States, 449 U.S.—, 101 S.Ct. 737, 66 L.Ed. 2d 689 (1981)].

### For Further Reading

Arendt, Hannah. *Eichmann in Jerusalem.* New York: Viking Press, 1963.

Dicks, Henry V. *Licensed Mass Murder: A Socio-Psychological Study of Some SS Killers.* New York: Basic Books, 1972.

Hoess, Rudolf. *Commandant of Auschwitz: The Autobiography of Rudolf Hoess.* New York: World Publishing Co., 1959.

Merkl, Peter H. *The Making of a Stormtrooper.* Princeton: Princeton University Press, 1981.

Sereny, Gitta. *Into That Darkness.* New York: McGraw-Hill, 1974.

# GERMAN OFFICIAL PLANS FOR THE "FINAL SOLUTION", 20 JANUARY 1942

The number of Jews mentioned at the Wannsee Conference, country by country and area by area, for eventual deportation, and subsequent death. More than 14 million people were thus marked out for death.

One of the macabre features of the numerical list of the Jews submitted to the Wannsee Conference was the fact that no figure was given for the Jews of Estonia, merely a brief note that Estonia was 'Free of Jews'. This was true; the 1,000 Estonian Jews who had come under German rule in October 1941 had all been murdered during the three months before the Wannsee Conference.

ESTONIA
"Free of Jews"

USSR
5 million

NORWAY
1,300

DENMARK
5,600

LATVIA
3,500

LITHUANIA
34,000

HOLLAND
160,800

BIALYSTOK DISTRICT
400,000

WHITE RUSSIA
446,484

BELGIUM
43,000

Wannsee

GERMANY
131,800
Berlin

Chelmno

GENERAL GOVERNMᴺᵀ.
2,284,000

EASTERN TERRITORIES

420,000

UKRAINE
2,994,684

FRANCE OCCUPIED ZONE
165,000

BOHEMIA AND MORAVIA
74,200

SLOVAKIA

88,000

AUSTRIA
43,700

HUNGARY
742,800

FRANCE UNOCCUPIED ZONE
700,000

CROATIA
40,000

SERBIA
10,000

RUMANIA
342,000

ITALY
58,000

ALBANIA
200

BULGARIA

48,000

GREECE
69,600

0  miles  200
0  km  300

In December 1941, a month *before* the Wannsee Conference, the first Nazi extermination camp had already come into operation, at Chelmno, responsible for the mass-murder of Jews, Gypsies, and Soviet prisoners-of-war. After passing through corridors marked 'To the showers' and 'To the doctor', the victims were forced into a large truck which was in fact a gas-chamber, where they were killed within a few minutes. By the end of 1944 more than 360,000 Jews had been murdered in Chelmno alone.

The Wannsee Conference also specified the number of Jews in *unconquered* countries for eventual destruction, including 330,000 from Britain, 18,000 from Switzerland, 6,000 from Spain and 4,000 from Ireland.

© Martin Gilbert 1978

# Deportations

## CHRISTOPHER R. BROWNING

The physical removal of the Jews, in one way or another, was central to Nazi Jewish policy long before extermination. Until the outbreak of war, the Nazis sought to create a Germany "free of Jews" *(Judenrein)* through emigration. As expansion into Austria and Czechoslovakia increased the number of Jews in the German sphere, foreign countries raised even higher barriers against Jewish immigration, thus leading the Nazis to resort to forced emigration or expulsion. The techniques developed by a young SS officer in Austria, Adolf Eichmann, became the model for the rest of the Third Reich in this regard. The outbreak of war (in 1939) reduced Jewish emigration to a trickle, while German military successes once again increased the number of Jews under Nazi domination. Furthermore, German victories led to the recruitment of a growing list of subordinate allies with large Jewish populations, especially in southeastern Europe. European Jews were now trapped on a continent under German control and constituted a "problem" the Nazis were ideologically committed to solve.

As the old solution of emigration, inadequate even in the last years before the war, was not viable in this new situation, the Nazis first turned to various schemes for the mass deportation and resettlement of the European Jews. In the fall of 1939, following the lightning conquest of Poland, plans were made to resettle the Jews and Poles of the "incorporated" territories of western Poland (those annexed directly to the Third Reich) as well as from Austria and the Protectorate (Bohemia) on the so-called Lublin Reservation in southeastern Poland. In the winter of 1939-1940, some 200,000 people were deported, but the plans for the Lublin Reservation were canceled in the spring. The influx of vast numbers of deportees, without adequate housing or food supply, produced such chaotic conditions that the local Nazis prevailed upon Berlin to stop the deportations. Logistically, it would prove easier to murder than to resettle the European Jews, but this conclusion was reached only after the failure of a second and even more ambitious resettlement project—the Madagascar Plan.

The French territory of Madagascar had long attracted antisemitic polemicists, as well as various Polish, French, and German officials, as a possible resettlement area for Jews in the prewar period. When the conquest of France in June, 1940, placed the French Empire at Germany's disposal, a concrete plan for the resettlement of European Jews on the island of Madagascar quickly emerged, and was even discussed between Hitler and Mussolini. However, the prerequisite defeat of Great Britain and control of the seas never materialized, and the Madagascar Plan was shelved.

The decision to attack the Soviet Union raised the old dilemma that further military conquest would bring additional millions of Jews under German control, vastly increasing the magnitude of a problem whose solution had not yet been found. Hitler responded by ordering the extermination of the Russian Jews who fell into German hands. Systematic mass murder, now a reality in Russia, inevitably beckoned as a solution—indeed the Final Solution—for the European Jews as well, but the primitive mobile firing squad *(Einsatzgruppen)* methods used in Russia were not applicable in Europe. The European Jews could not be shot down on the spot in Amsterdam, Salonica, or even Warsaw. In a series of massive deportations they would have to be sent to secret assembly line killing centers in Poland. Half the intended victims were already concentrated in the Polish ghettos totally under German control. The administrative apparatus to carry out the deportations was in place; only the extermination camps remained to be built. But the rest of the intended victims were scattered among more than a dozen countries; some of these countries were occupied by Germany, while others enjoyed varying degrees of sovereignty. It was in these countries that the Nazis faced a problem not only of great magnitude logistically but also of immense complexity politically.

Direct responsibility for coordinating the deportation program outside Poland rested with the Gestapo's expert on evacuation and Jews, Adolf Eichmann, who had devised ingenious techniques for the forced emigration of Austrian Jews before the war. Eichmann was, above all, an organizer. He had only a handful of men directly under his supervision, and thus most of his work involved getting others to perform the functions vital to a successful deportation program. Eichmann's men, though small in number, formed an extensive, far-reaching network. In the territories under German military occupation, Himmler had established his own police agencies, and Eichmann could maintain direct contact with the Jewish experts of the local Gestapo units. In the allied and vassal states, where the facade of sovereignty had to be preserved, Eichmann's representatives were lodged with the German embassies as "advisers" on the Jewish Question to the local authorities.

Eichmann's tiny agency was the nerve center of the deportation program, but several other agencies were also of crucial importance. One of these was the German Foreign Office. The Jewish Desk of the Foreign Office had long offered its advice concerning the foreign policy implications of Nazi Jewish policy, especially when foreign Jews were involved. It had also initiated the first concrete preparations for the Madagascar Plan. Now, it secured the right to be consulted by Eichmann concerning the Final Solution in all European territories occupied or influenced by Germany. The Jewish Desk of the Foreign Office subsequently worked zealously to facilitate the frictionless implementation of deportations. This was done by urging preparatory anti-Jewish legislation on the German model, negotiating agreements on the fate of Jewish property, excercising intense diplomatic pressure to assist Eichmann's representatives in attaining final agreement to deport, and smoothing out complications arising from the presence of large numbers of Jews with foreign citizenship, who required special consideration if embarrassing incidents were to be avoided.

Even more important than this expert assistance from the German Foreign Office was the logistical support of the German railway, the *Reichsbahn*, and its Polish auxiliary, the *Ostbahn*. Without rail transporation, the deportations were physically impossible, yet in wartime there were immense demands upon Germany's rail capacity. The ability of the *Reichsbahn* to provide the necessary rolling stock to ship nearly one million Jews into Poland and to shuttle another two million within Poland from ghetto to extermination camp was an extraordinary feat under the circumstances, demonstrating a determination and professional pride to overcome all obstacles and conduct business as usual, despite the most unusual business (three million one-way group fares!) at hand.

But even the SS, the Foreign Office, and the *Reichsbahn* together could not have carried out the deportations on their own. In the areas not totally under German control, the task of rounding up the Jews required manpower far beyond that directly at Eichmann's disposal. Often, the Germans had to rely upon native collaborators. Allied and puppet regimes in France, Slovakia, Hungary, and Bulgaria rounded up Jews and turned them over to the Germans. The failure of deportations in those countries which refused to assist, such as Denmark, the Italian occupation zones, and Russia and Bulgaria, regarding their "own" assimilated Jews but not foreign or alien Jews, demonstrated how essential such collaboration was to the Germans.

In July, 1941, Goering ordered Heydrich to prepare an overall plan for "a total solution of the Jewish Question in the German sphere of influence in Europe." The outlines of this overall plan— deportation to extermination camps—emerged in the fall of 1941, but due to the time-lag between conception and construction of the extermination camps, the deportation program began in confusion. In mid-September, 1941, before either the plan or the camps were complete, Hitler suddenly ordered that Germany be cleared of Jews by the end of the year. Trainloads of German Jews were shipped to Lodz, Minsk, Kovno, and Riga. At the last two destinations, the Jews were shot on arrival, and gas vans at Chelmno began reducing the population of the Lodz ghetto, but nonetheless the reception capacity was inadequate to achieve Hitler's goal of a *Judenrein* Germany by the end of the year. Only when the extermination camps went into full-time operation in the spring and summer of 1942 could the deportation program begin in earnest.

Beginning with deportations from Lublin to Belsec in March, the onslaught against the Polish ghettos began. It reached its climax with massive deportations from Warsaw from late July on, after Treblinka had "come on line." Simultaneously, the Eichmann network began deportations from other parts of Euopre.

The Slovak government was requested in mid-February, 1942, to supply 20,000 strong, young Jews for labor in the East, a proposal it "eagerly snatched up," according to the German ambassador. In March, Eichmann requested the deportation of initially 1,000 and then an additional 5,000 Jews, from France, which also proceeded without difficulty. The first wave of full-scale deportations quickly followed. In late March, the Slovak government was informed of Germany's willingness to deport the rest of its Jews, and 56,000 were shipped to Poland by the end of the summer. In July, mass deportations from France, the Netherlands, and Belgium began. At first, they primarily were composed of foreign Jews to facilitate local cooperation and acquiescence. The deportations from these countries continued until 1944, but encountered gradually increasing difficulties. Collaborators became more reluctant, and native Jews themselves became aware of their impending fate and took desperate measures to evade the roundups. But, in the end, nearly 200,000 Jews were deported from France, the Netherlands, and Belgium. Small deportations from Norway and Croatia (where most of the Jews, however, were killed locally by native Fascists) also took place in 1942.

The second wave of deportations began early in 1943, as the center of German attention shifted to the Balkans. Bulgaria rounded up and delivered over 11,000 "alien" Jews of the newly acquired territories of Thrace and Macedonia, but subsequently backed out of an agreement to deport its "own" Jews from Old Bulgaria when domestic opposition surfaced and Germany's prospects of victory began to dim after Stalingrad. The Rumanians had cooperated with *Einsatzgruppe* D and had carried out their own deportation of alien Jews to camps in Transnistria, where most perished, but they, too, backed out of the final steps of deporting their "romanized" Jews to Poland. In Greece, the Germans had only to contend with Italy's refusal to adopt common measures in its own occupation zone. Unfortunately, the majority of the Greek Jews lived in the German zone around Salonica, and some 46,000 were deported between mid-March and the end of May. The German military provided all the assistance Eichmann's experts needed. The attempt to deport Jews from Denmark in October, 1943, failed when neither the German military authorities nor the native government would cooperate, and the local population first hid and subsequently smuggled the Jews out to Sweden. On the other hand, in the same month the Germans succeeded in rounding up and deporting to Auschwitz over 1,000 Jews in Rome, following the German occupation of Italy.

In 1944, the Germans completed "mopping up" deportations from Slovakia, northern Italy, the former Italian zone in Greece, and the last major ghetto in Poland, Lodz. But 1944 also witnessed the most stupendous and tragic deportation of the Final Solution— Hungary. In August, 1941, Hungary had handed over fleeing Galician Jews to the Germans for liquidation, but subsequently (like Bulgaria and Rumania) refused intense German pressure to deport its own Jews. Following German occupation of the country in March, 1944, however, Eichmann's entire team of experts descended upon the country, found willing Hungarian collaborators to concentrate the Jews who remained unwarned by their leadership, and deported 437,000 between mid-May and mid-July.

In the end, two of the three million Polish Jews who eventually perished in the Holocaust had been deported from ghettos to the extermination camps. Nearly a million additional Jews were deported to extermination camps from other European countries. Deportations were, thus, an essential step in the deaths of half the victims of the Holocaust.

### For Further Reading

Arendt, Hannah. *Eichmann in Jerusalem.* New York: Viking Press, 1963.

Browning, Christopher R. *The Final Solution and the German Foreign Office.* New York: Holmes & Meier, 1978.

Hilberg, Raul. *The Destruction of the European Jews.* Chicago: Quadrangle Books, 1961.

Reitlinger, Gerald. *The Final Solution.* New York: Beechurst Press, 1953.

**6**

# THE GHETTOS
# AND THE
# PARTISANS

# The Warsaw Revolt

*A year earlier, in the spring of 1943, the remnants of the Warsaw ghetto had themselves risen in revolt. Poorly armed but strong in spirit, their commander, twenty-four-year-old Mordecai Anielewicz proclaimed:* *

> *It is impossible to put into words what we have been through. One thing is clear, what happened exceeded our boldest dreams. The Germans ran twice from the ghetto. . . . Beginning from today we shall shift over to the partisan tactic. . . . It is impossible to describe the conditions under which the Jews of the ghetto are now living. Only a few will be able to hold out. The remainder will die sooner or later. Their fate is sealed. In almost all the hiding places in which thousands are concealing themselves it is not possible to light a candle for lack of air. . . . Peace go with you, my friend! . . . The dream of my life has risen to become fact. . . . I have been a witness to the magnificent, heroic fighting of Jewish men of battle.*

*In many other ghettos, men and women, often unarmed, also revealed the highest achievement of the human spirit.*

* *See Document 6 in Appendix: Selected Documents*

# The Ghettos

## YISRAEL GUTMAN

The ghettos in Nazi-occupied eastern Europe were established at the beginning of World War II, after the conquest of Poland in 1939, and the occupation of Soviet-annexed territories in June, 1941. There was no general directive to seal off the ghettos simultaneously. The first ghetto in occupied Poland—Piotrkòw Trybunalski—was set up in the autumn of 1939. The Lodz ghetto, which at the time of its isolation from the outside world had 165,000 inhabitants, was formed in the spring of 1940. The Warsaw ghetto, the largest, which at its peak period contained 450,000 Jews, was sealed in October, 1940. The administrations of the various ghettos were not identical. Thus, the Lodz ghetto was hermetically sealed: No one might enter or leave it, and no article was brought in or out without the knowledge and consent of the authorities. On the other hand, although the Warsaw ghetto was strictly isolated, quite a large number of Poles were permitted to enter it, and a few Jews were allowed, under specific circumstances, to leave its confines for limited periods of time. Most important of all, however, was the fact that during the entire existence of the Warsaw ghetto, a brisk trade existed in smuggled goods, in the course of which food was illegally brought into the ghetto in exchange for Jewish valuables, clothing, and various household utensils. Conversely, there were ghettos from which Jews were permitted to leave for a few hours to make purchases and arrange matters of essential importance. The Warsaw ghetto was isolated from the outside world by a wall 9.8 feet high, covered with fragments of glass and barbed wire. Other ghettos were closed off by barbed wire or wooden fences. The Lodz ghetto was guarded by German sentries; the gates of the Warsaw ghetto were patrolled by groups of German, Polish, and Jewish policemen.

The first ghettos separating Jews from the Christian population were located in Italy in the sixteenth century. During the nineteenth century, with the Emancipation of the Jews in most European countries, the ghettos were abolished. Even in the twentieth century, districts and quarters of eastern European towns inhabited mainly by Jews were often dubbed ghettos, but Jews were, in fact, not legally obliged to reside in those areas. The ghettos were simply mixed neighborhoods with a predominantly Jewish population, and they were not naturally isolated from the rest of the city by any physical barrier. The ghettos of the later Middle Ages were designed to give practical expression to the Christian doctrine that Jews should live among Christians under inferior and menial conditions and that, consequently, communities must be divided and the Jews isolated. At the same time, it must be noted that, to a certain extent, this isolation was in accordance with the security requirements of the Jewish community, as well as with its unique religious and cultural character.

In contrast to the ghettos of the Middle Ages, the ghettos during the Nazi period were not intended as a permanent framework, but simply as a stage in preparation for a future general solution to the "Jewish Problem." The Nazis gave several pretexts for the establishment of ghettos: For example, they wished to prevent the dissemination of diseases supposedly prevalent among Jews, or to suppress alleged black-market activities by Jews. While the Nazi authorities definitely aimed at establishing an impenetrable barrier between Jews and non-Jews, their main objectives were the creation of extremely harsh living conditions, isolation from the outside world, and the internment of Jews in vast prisons under conditions of total helplessness. These goals would, in turn, lead to the breakdown of their physical, mental, and social structure, destroying their resistance as a community.

These ghettos became miniature self-contained states. The Nazis claimed that the ghetto was autonomous. At first, some Jews were deluded into believing that a separate ghetto in which the Jews would be left to their own devices would actually be to their advantage, but the bitter truth became rapidly clear. The Jewish community in the ghetto was obliged to arrange and handle matters with which it had never dealt formerly. Before the creation of the ghettos, the communal authorities looked after religious affairs, welfare, and supplementary education. Occasionally, the community appeared as a representative body to defend Jewish interests in various sectors. In the ghettos, however, the situation changed. The Jewish administration was obliged to take charge of such matters as labor, food, and housing, usually handled by the government. Activities formerly the province of municipal, welfare, or educational institutions were given to the Jewish ghetto administration as the sole representative of the Jews to German military authorities and Polish municipal bodies. The ghetto administration was also forced to create a police force and prisons, institutions far removed from the traditional activities of the Jewish community and in which it had no experience.

The ghetto administration, or Jewish Council *(Judenrat),* is a term with very negative connotations. During the past few years, scholars have carefully reappraised the individual *Judenräte* and their activities, and have concluded that a totally negative picture is not always justified. The *Judenräte* were set up in accordance with a general decree by the Nazis, who did not conceal their intentions: They wanted a Jewish representation that would carry out German orders and commands to the letter and would be responsible to the Nazi authorities for the implementation of those orders. The Jews, on the other hand, assumed that the *Judenräte* would represent and protect Jewish interests as far as possible. The respective expectations of both sides towards the *Judenräte* were, thus, diametrical opposites. In most ghettos, the first *Judenrat* leaders were eventually removed from office or murdered and were replaced by men the Germans found more compliant to their wishes, who accepted their fate without protest, knowing that the penalty for any attempt at rebellion was death.

The primary and most disturbing problem that faced the Jews in the ghetto was food and provisions. Almost all sources of Jewish income had been seized or prohibited. Moreover, the Germans had separated the Jews from the general economy, and forbade them to engage in most professions. Jewish property was confiscated, and Jewish-owned shops and factories expropriated. Jews were forbidden to hold private stocks of merchandise or cash, and periodically the Nazis raided Jewish homes and stole whatever they wanted. The Germans instituted forced labor for the Jews, but the Jews received either no payment at all or a sum that did not even suffice to buy a loaf of stale bread. This struggle for life in the ghetto was called "sanctification of life" by Rabbi Yitzhak Nissenbaum in the Warsaw ghetto. He explained that previously, when those who persecuted the Jews wished to break their spirit and destroy their faith in God, the Jews' answer was "sanctification of the Name" (that is, it was permissible and preferable to die rather than deny the principles of Jewish law and faith). During the Nazi era, however, when the enemy planned the death of Jews, the answer could only be "santification of life"—one had to protect one's life and preserve the spark of life.

How did the Jews respond to Nazi persecution? Chaim Aharon Kaplan, a Jewish teacher in Warsaw who kept a diary in Hebrew, wrote on April 24, 1940:

> Lord God! Where do all these people find the money to support themselves? Any form of business or profession is forbidden to them. All businesses have been liquidated; all positions which yielded an income have been abolished; thousands of out-of-work officials roam the streets of Warsaw; there is no [economic sector] apart from grocery stores, which can manage to exist; everything has been shut and closed down, smashed and shattered; all sources of income are blocked; and to top it all a life of shame and humiliation; for there are streets whose right or left sidewalk is forbidden to Jews, and a notice in enormous letters informs one of this. Nevertheless, the multitude lives; the multitude is alert; the multitude declares the conqueror's decrees null and void as the dust of the earth, and does everything in its power to hoodwink him and to deceive him, and to carry out all its activities secretly and indirectly, and God supplies it with sustenance.[1]

What is the meaning behind Kaplan's words? What he, in fact, meant was that the Jews did not capitulate and did not succumb without resisting. The Nazis demanded that Jews hand over their money and movable possessions, but the Jews did not comply with the order. The Nazis forbade the Jews to engage in trade or work as artisans, but the Jews labored in secret and manufactured goods clandestinely. The Nazis prohibited communal prayer, but the Jews gathered despite the prohibition and held services on weekdays and festivals. The Nazis forbade the Jews to open schools, but the Jews organized clandestine kindergartens and schools for all age groups.

In Warsaw and the other ghettos, there was an incessant illegal trade in food to supplement the starvation rations imposed by the Germans. The Jews organized networks and individually smuggled contraband food into the ghetto. The ghetto wall was virtually a front line. Children and adults who were caught smuggling were killed at the wall, but trade did not cease. Approximately 80 percent of all food that entered the ghetto arrived illegally.

Should this tenacious regard for life shown by the eastern European Jews be considered solely the natural instinct of human beings in distress—to summon all of one's mental and physical powers in an effort to remain alive? It may well be that the powerful will to live in every person guided the Jews in their battle for life. But did the uniqueness of Jewish life in the ghettos lie solely in this desire for life?

From the communal and political points of view, the internal organization of eastern European Jews created a framework of unity and mutual responsibility. Despite the fact that prominent person-alities among Polish Jews left Warsaw during the first days of the war, political Zionist bodies and the Bund (Socialist labor party) began to operate as underground groups immediately after the Nazi occupation of Poland. The leaders of the Zionist *Ḥalutz* youth movement also left with the stream of refugees from the Polish capital, but they sent back a few of their activists on the assumption that their members would need guidance and leadership even under the occupation.

The political and social underground organizations were mostly concerned with mutual help and the acquisition of basic material necessities, but an argument speedily arose as to whether they should stop there. Following discussions, the political underground turned its activities in two directions—help and social aid on the one hand, and the organization of propaganda and political affairs on the other. Mutual aid, backed by prominent underground figures and heads of the American Jewish Joint Distribution Committee (JDC), was organized. The organization's legal public activities coexisted with illegal operations. Thus, for example, soup kitchens provided the needy with bowls of soup and slices of bread and simultaneously served as schools, clubs for underground organizations, and sites for covert cultural meetings. In the Kovno, Vilna, and Bialystok ghettos, various departments of the *Judenrat* aided clandestine cultural activities. In the Warsaw ghetto, there was an underground Jewish press. In view of the fact that Jews were forbidden to possess radios, and that the official Jewish-Polish language newspaper only carried bulletins issued by the Germans, the secret press—which carried reliable news from the free world and the *Yishuv* (Jewish community in Palestine), cricitism of the *Judenräte* and explanations of fundamental ideas—was a valuable organ which supplied the Jews with trustworthy information and encouragement. The secret press was operated by various political bodies, but the largest role in preparing and distributing the newssheets was played by members of youth movements from all political parties. These movements played a central role in the underground in the Warsaw ghetto; moreover, they initiated resistance in many other ghettos and maintained close contact among them by means of male, and particularly female, liaison officers, who concealed their Jewish identity and traveled on behalf of their organizations. The youth movements did not extend material help alone, or aim only at physical survival, but concentrated their efforts on creating spiritual and intellectual leadership for their young members, training them for their future roles. The youth movements established secret study circles and a *Gymnasium* (senior high school), organized seminars for youth leaders and secret national conferences, opened underground training centers, and established an organizational network that extended over all of occupied Poland.

In Warsaw, Emmanuel Ringelblum, the historian and Zionist communal worker, founded a secret archive code-named *Oneg Shabbat*. Workers in the archive collected many official documents, commissioned articles, and organized secret surveys in order to save the broadest picture of Jewish life under the Nazis. Much of the documentary material in our hands today comes from this source. A similar archive was founded later by Mordechai Tannenbaum-Tamrof, an active member of the Zionist *Dror-Heḥalutz* movement in the Bialystok ghetto. In Vilna, a group of writers and underground activists also supervised the collection of historically valuable material. Many Jews wrote memoirs in which, apart from personal and family events, they recorded data concerning the community and Jewish life in general. Some of these diaries have been preserved and have aided in the reconstruction of the struggle for life and clandestine activities of the Jewish underground.

### Notes

1. Chaim A. Kaplan, *The Warsaw Diary of Chaim A. Kaplan,* ed. Abraham I. Katsh *(Megillat Yesurin), [Hebrew]* (Tel Aviv: Am Oved/Yad Vashem, 1966), p. 221.

### For Further Reading

Arad, Yitzhak. *Ghetto in Flames: The Struggle and Destruction of the Jews of Vilna.* Jerusalem: Yad Vashem, 1980.

Donat, Alexander. *The Holocaust Kingdom.* New York: Holt, Rinehart, and Winston, 1963.

Gutman, Yisrael. *The Jews of Warsaw, 1939-1943: Ghetto, Underground, Revolt.* Bloomington, Ind.: Indiana University Press, 1982.

Hilberg, Raul; Staron, Stanislaw; and Kermisz, Josef, eds. *The Warsaw Diary of Adam Czerniakow*. New York: Stein and Day, 1979.

Kaplan, Chaim. *Scroll of Agony*. New York: Macmillan Co., 1965.

Korczak, Janusz. *Ghetto Diary*. New York: Holocaust Library, 1978.

*Patterns of Jewish Leadership in Nazi Europe, 1933-1945. Proceedings of the Third Yad Vashem International Historical Conference, April, 1977*. Jerusalem: Yad Vashem, 1979.

Ringelblum, Emmanuel. *Notes from the Warsaw Ghetto*. Translated and edited by Jacob Sloan. New York: McGraw-Hill, 1958.

―――. *Polish-Jewish Relations During the Second World War*. Edited by Josef Kermisz and Shalom Krakowski. Jerusalem: Yad Vashem, 1974.

Trunk, Isaiah. *Judenrat*. New York: Macmillan Co., 1972.

# Life in the Ghettos of Eastern Europe

## SOLON BEINFELD

The swift German defeat of Poland in September, 1939, and the extension of Nazi rule over the western half of the country, brought for the first time a mass Jewish population under the control of the most fanatically antisemitic regime in history. The Nazis, who had already destroyed Jewish life in Germany, Austria, and Czechoslovakia, were now faced with a situation both quantitatively and qualitatively different from the "Jewish Question" as they had known it before the war. Instead of a relatively small and assimilated Jewish population, they now confronted a dense network of Jewish settlements, with hundreds of preponderantly Jewish small towns and dozens of heavily Jewish larger towns and cities. The Jewish population, constituting 10 percent of the total in a still largely rural Poland, ran to nearly two million in the German zone of occupation, with another million and a half in eastern Poland under Soviet rule. Warsaw alone had some 350,000, not counting refugees, while Lodz had 200,000. The numbers alone do not tell the whole story. Polish Jewry, for all the assimilationist tendencies that had emerged in recent years, and despite the rise of major Jewish centers elsewhere, remained what it had been for centuries—the great biological and cultural reservoir of world Jewry. The Nazis, who had long reviled and caricatured eastern European Jewish life with particular venom, sensed that they had a chance to strike at the authentic core of their racial enemy, and did so from the start. The military campaign in Poland in September, 1939, was accompanied by atrocities against the Jewish civil population, which, however mild compared to what was to follow, nevertheless spread terror throughout the occupied area and provoked horrified protests throughout the Jewish world. A special historical commission was established as early as October, 1939, in Vilna—then part of neutral Lithuania—to collect materials concerning anti-Jewish outrages in occupied Poland.[1]

The terror of the opening weeks of the occupation was accompanied by a deluge of oppressive decrees—the yellow star, confiscation of property, restriction of movement—that went well beyond the anti-Jewish legislation already in force in the Reich. The most significant official document from this period is the *Schnellbrief* (express letter) of September 21, 1939, sent by Reinhard Heydrich, head of the Security Police, regarding the establishment of Jewish Councils *(Judenräte)* and the concentration of the Jewish population in the larger towns. In areas annexed to the Reich the Jewish population was to be expelled; only in the General Government (the unincorporated areas of central Poland) were a large number of Jewish "points of concentration" to be established— ominously along railway lines. Within these towns, Heydrich foresaw that local authorities might have to exclude Jews from certain neighborhoods, or prohibit them from leaving the "ghetto."[2] Although the word ghetto is used here for the first time, Heydrich did not explicitly require that ghettos be established, nor did he spell out what kinds of ghettos might be involved. In fact, the process of ghetto formation in Poland was a long one, with many local variations. In some cases it was never completed. A few communities had no formal ghettos at all, and some overwhelmingly Jewish towns were, in effect, ghettos unto themselves. The form of the ghetto—open or closed— was left to the initiative of local German authorities. Nevertheless, it was clear from the start that these would not be ghettos in the medieval sense of Jewish residential quarters from which Jews could emerge during the day to conduct their business.[3] The ghettos of Poland—and later of other Nazi-occupied and satellite areas of eastern Europe—have to be seen, rather, as urban concentration camps whose purpose was the control, exploitation, humiliation, and eventual liquidation of their Jewish inmates.

## Process of Ghettoization

After a few abortive local attempts at ghettoization in the last months of 1939 (including Warsaw, where the order was countermanded by the military authorities), the process began in earnest in 1940. In the annexed areas, the Lodz ghetto was established from February to April. In the General Government the great Warsaw ghetto, with its nearly half a million people (including refugees and expellees), was established by degrees. Individual streets were walled off, "quarantine" zones were established against "epidemics," and, finally, the last entrances were closed in November, 1940. The famous wall was not completed until several months later.

The pace of ghetto formation accelerated in 1941, both in the General Government and, after the invasion of the Soviet Union in June, in the newly conquered territories of eastern Poland, the Baltic States, Belorussia, and the Ukraine. A few ghettos were established as late as 1942. We will probably never know for certain how many ghettos existed in all; a significant number of smaller ones have probably left no survivors or records. The total number surely comes to over 200 and would run much larger if one included ephemeral ghettos in the former Soviet territories, where the Jewish population was briefly concentrated before being murdered. The composition of the ghetto network was, moreover, in constant flux, with a general tendency for smaller ghettos to be absorbed by larger regional ones. This process often involved great loss of life, as was the case in the spring of 1943, when the smaller ghettos of the Lithuanian-Belorussian border region were liquidated and some of their populations sent to Vilna and other larger ghettos.

There was a wide range of options in ghetto matters available to local German authorities. This led at times to the replacement of the usual *Judenrat* format by authoritarian regimes centering on a single "strong man." This was the case with the celebrated dictatorships of Chaim Rumkowski in Lodz and Jacob Gens in Vilna. As a general rule, however, the basic character of a ghetto depended on the wider administrative unit in which it was located. We distinguish, therefore, between the ghettos of the General Government into which the whole local Jewish population was herded, and those in the former Soviet territories, in which much—often most—of the Jews were murdered *before* the formation of the ghetto or very shortly afterwards. These latter ghettos were thus "pre-selected" and were supposed to consist entirely of workers and their families. The Lodz ghetto, in the annexed western region, was something of a cross between these two varieties because of its large labor force and industrial output.

All ghettos, however, shared certain basic characteristics. They constituted a type of urban community previously unknown in history: an incarcerated civilian population living, often for relatively long periods of time, in conditions of maximum deprivation and defenselessness, confronted with the threat and eventually the reality of total physical annihilation. All ghettos were located in the poorest and most dilapidated quarters of their towns. They were typically subject to fantastic overcrowding and inadequate provision of human necessities like food, fuel, clothing, and medicine. Most were tightly sealed off from the "Aryan" parts of town and even more so from other cities and ghettos. Where egress was permitted at all, it was only for the limited and closely supervised purpose of labor during the day. Unauthorized exit from the ghetto was punishable by death. Furthermore, unauthorized entry by non-Jews (other than German military and civilian authorities) was a serious crime. Smuggling, though widely practiced, was subject to the harshest penalties, including death.

As foreseen in the Heydrich *Schnellbrief* of 1939, the formation of ghettos was preceded by the creation of local Jewish Councils sometimes from among prewar community leaders, but often quite arbitrarily. Within the ghettos the Councils, or their successor regimes, became responsible in the first instance for the carrying out of German orders concerning the ghettos—including, eventually, their total or partial liquidation. They simultaneously had to undertake the maintenance of public order and the distribution of vital goods and services, to whatever extent possible. For these multiple and contradictory purposes the typical ghetto witnessed the creation of a Jewish police, often hated and feared by the population, as well as of a ghetto bureaucracy that was similarly (though with less justification) held in low esteem. The administrative apparatus in the larger ghettos, charged, in effect, with running the municipal services of a city within a city, tended to become very elaborate; in Lodz the bureaucracy was divided into seven major divisions subdivided into 73 agencies and offices employing 12,880 people as of August 1, 1942.[4]

A network of these forbidden cities stretched from the pre-1939 Polish-German border in the West, via the central Polish regions of the General Government to the *Reichskommissariat* Ostland (Baltic States), Belorussia, and the Ukraine on former Soviet territory, and spilled over into the lands of Germany's allies, Rumania and Hungary. Some lasted only a few weeks. Most endured for almost two years before their inmates were "resettled." The longest was Lodz, which existed for nearly five years, almost as long as the war itself.

In view of what we now know to have been the real purpose of ghettoization and the ultimate fate of all but a tiny minority of ghetto inhabitants, it is difficult to realize that in many cases the establishment of a ghetto was seen as a relative improvement. The brutality and lawlessness to which Jews had been exposed in the pre-ghetto period (in the ex-Soviet territories this meant mass executions as well), followed by the tensions and uncertainties leading up to the proclamation of a ghetto, and lastly the often nightmarish exodus to the ghetto itself, created in many cases a sense of relief at being among fellow Jews. A survivor from Vilna recalled the mood of the time:

> "As long as we are among Jews." So everyone consoled and encouraged himself. It seemed to each of us that though poor and hungry it would be possible to breathe freely in the Ghetto.[5]

This mood did not last long, though its shadow persisted in the hope that the ghetto might not be an entirely negative phenomenon, that it might somehow provide its population not only with some security but even with a modicum of social justice. This was, of course, in the tradition of eastern European Jewry, a tradition still fully alive in 1939 in all but Soviet-ruled territory. Although the Jewish *kehillot* (communal organizations) of Poland were nominally religious in character, in fact they were involved in the broadest range of cultural and charitable activities. There was a corresponding tradition of obligation to serve on the part of local Jewish elites, which explains the willingness of prewar community activists to serve on *Judenräte*. In part, the ghetto seemed an extension of the prewar community, with many of the same educational, social, and cultural functions. What was new for the ghetto administrations was the provision of municipal services—police, sanitation, and the like—which no prewar Jewish *kehilla* had to supply, and beyond this the delivery of basic necessities like food and fuel, which were not normally municipal responsibilities.

## Food

Food was probably the most difficult problem for the ghetto. In most cases the *Judenrat,* or other central administrative body, had to become the main agency for the purchase, storage, and distribution of foodstuffs. It tried, through strict rationing, the establishment of soup kitchens and other similar devices to provide for the feeding of its population. German allocations of food were minimal, in the case of fats and proteins negligible, and everywhere far below what would sustain life for long, especially under conditions of hard physical labor. The delivery of even these pitiful amounts was so erratic and so often in the form of food unfit for consumption that the task was hopeless in most ghettos. Only smuggling could alleviate the problem, and in closed ghettos like Warsaw this was a risky and dangerous enterprise. The inevitable result in many ghettos—and most notably in Warsaw—was slow and relentless starvation. In Warsaw in the first half of 1941, the caloric value of available food has been estimated at 10 percent of the prewar norm. Hunger in the Warsaw ghetto reached catastrophic proportions, with starving children begging in the streets and emaciated corpses left on the pavement to be collected like refuse. "Almost every day I see two or three people fall dead in the street from hunger," wrote the diarist and historian Emmanuel Ringelblum in March, 1941. By May, 1942, he was asking in despair: "What are we to do? Are we to dole out spoonfuls to everyone, the result being that no one will survive?"[6] It was even possible for a group of doctors to do a clinical study of hunger and its physiological effects in the unique context of a twentieth-century European metropolis.[7]

The case in most—though by no means all—ghettos was less extreme than in Warsaw. In Lodz, despite the ruthless campaign against smuggling, the caloric content of the food ration reached a high point of between one-half and two-thirds the minimum requirement. This "abundance" is misleading. The nutritional value of the rations was very low. In addition they were often badly distributed or in rotten condition, so that for over four years the majority of the Lodz ghetto inhabitants were in a constant state of hunger, leading from time to time to food demonstrations and riots.[8]

In some ghettos in eastern Poland, like Bialystok and Vilna, the food problem was comparatively less acute. In Vilna, at least officially, there were no deaths from starvation in the ghetto. Vilna, a "labor ghetto," had an unusually high percentage of inmates who worked by day for German institutions outside the ghetto. These workers not only received a "midday soup" at their places of employment, but also were able to smuggle in appreciable quantities of food for their families. This food was obtained from Gentiles in exchange for clothing or other personal possessions. The risks were high: flogging, arrest, even death. The popular singer Liuba Lewicka paid with her life for attempting to smuggle in a kilo of dried peas concealed on her person. At times, however, German or Lithuanian supervision at the ghetto gate was lax and the Jewish policewatch normally winked at smuggling. Indeed, at times the ghetto administration itself engaged in large-scale smuggling in wagons ostensibly to be used for garbage and snow removal, and even inside hearses.[9] The ghetto population and agencies of the ghetto bureaucracy showed great ingenuity in creating nutritious and even tasty preparations out of unpromising materials like frozen potatoes, and in extracting B-vitamin supplements from illegally obtained brewer's yeast. Supplementary rations were given to those who worked within the ghetto and thus had no opportunity to bring in food from outside. Some groups, e.g. the ghetto police, had access to special food cooperatives. Social cases of various kinds were at least minimally provided for by welfare agencies. But even in the "fortunate" Vilna ghetto, where such luxuries as horsemeat were occasionally to be had, deprivation was the rule. "Hunger knocks at the door," wrote the diarist Herman Kruk on April 20, 1942, during a "good" period in the history of the ghetto. "Misery grows from minute to minute."[10]

## Housing and Fuel

After food, shelter was undoubtedly the greatest problem. This was especially true in the early days of a ghetto, when whole populations were squeezed without adequate preparation, and often amidst panic and chaos, into the narrowly confined slum areas set aside for them. Boundaries might be changed several times (as in Warsaw) before being fixed. Those who were able to remain in their homes were fortunate both psychologically and materially, but they were in a minority. Newcomers, whether from better neighborhoods outside the ghetto area or refugees from other towns, had to find what accommodations they could. In Warsaw this meant, in practice, that most refugees were dependent on primitive shelter in public buildings. There was no other room for them in a ghetto whose population of approximately 450,000 in April, 1941 (70,000 of them expellees from the provinces) constituted a third of the population of Warsaw concentrated in 2.4 percent of the city's area. Population density in the ghetto was twenty times that on the Aryan side. Refugees and expellees lived huddled together, sometimes in groups of twenty to twenty-five people in a room six-by-four meters. One witness describes a hall housing seventy persons, a group of "filthy, lice-infested and hungry people" who had not changed their clothing in four weeks.[11]

The housing problem in the Warsaw ghetto was, in fact, never solved, except in the sense that the mass deportations of 1942 created "room" for those who remained temporarily behind. The same problem faced the authorities in other ghettos to a greater or lesser degree. All *Judenräte* had housing departments to deal with the allocation and maintenance of desperately scarce shelter. In Vilna, on September 6, 1941, the Jewish population had been given half an hour's notice or less to prepare for the march into the ghetto, with only such possessions as they could carry on their backs. Apartments within the seven small streets of the ghetto area rapidly filled up on a first-come, first-served basis, so that those who arrived later in the day had to camp in cellars and courtyards often for days until they could find someone to take them in, or until padlocked apartments whose owners had been taken away in pre-ghetto *Aktionen* (deportation roundups) were opened up.[12] The housing department eventually was able to find some sort of shelter for all, but even after the *Aktionen* of October and November, 1941, had cost the ghetto over half its population, the space available per capita came to no more than two square meters. Problems of overcrowding and friction among unrelated tenants crammed at random into tiny flats continued to plague the ghetto throughout its existence.[13]

Lodz seemed apparently better off in this respect with four square meters per person, but this was more than compensated for by the unusually dilapidated and even ruinous condition of the ghetto housing, a condition aggravated here (and elsewhere) by the demolition of premises by inhabitants desperately searching for wood to burn as fuel. The problem of fuel was particularly acute during the severe winters of eastern Europe. Warm clothing was scarce, and all furs were confiscated. Distribution of wood and coal for domestic heating was negligible or nonexistent, and thousands of ghetto inmates froze to death in their homes or on the streets. In the bitterly cold winter of 1940-1941 there were fuel riots in the Lodz ghetto and the demolition of dwellings and other structures led to severely repressive countermeasures on the part of the Rumkowski regime.[14] Vilna was fortunate to have its heating problem alleviated during the second of the two ghetto winters by the allocation of woodlots outside the city to which the ghetto administration sent laborers and, on occasion, its political opponents. The severe shortage of fuel affected not only the quality of home life in the ghettos, but also the functioning of important ghetto institutions like schools, bakeries, baths, and hospitals.

## Health

The catastrophic life situation of masses of the population in virtually every ghetto, with cruel shortages of the most elementary necessities, meant that the danger of disease and epidemics arose within a short time. The ghetto populations had reason to fear disease not only for its direct effects, but also for the pretext it might provide for the liquidation of the ghetto. The Germans had, in effect, created a self-fulfilling prophecy when they justified the creation of ghettos as a means of sealing off pestilential areas which threatened the non-Jewish civilian population and the German military with contagion. Epidemics of a type and intensity unknown in Europe in a century ravaged all but the most fortunate ghettos. The dirty, hungry ghetto dwellers, closely packed together, had neither the physical strength nor adequate medical and sanitary services to combat disease. When added to deaths from hunger and hunger-related diseases, epidemics of tuberculosis, typhoid, and especially lice-borne typhus caused astronomical mortality rates which at times were over ten times the prewar norm. It has been estimated that nearly one-fifth of all ghetto inmates died of "natural causes" and that the ghetto populations as a whole would have died out, without a shot being fired or a single deportation to an extermination camp, within a period of five or six years.[15]

All ghetto administrations did what they could to combat disease, but with limited success. The shortages of doctors, nurses, hospital beds, diagnostic apparatus, and medicines meant that, generally, only the most superficial assistance could be rendered. Sometimes the Germans insisted on measures, like the notorious disinfections in Warsaw, that helped spread the diseases they were supposed to prevent. In many ghettos, patients avoided the inadequate and makeshift hospitals where there lurked, in addition, the danger of early candidacy for deportation. Nevertheless, where circumstances were at all favorable, near-miracles were achieved in community medicine. In the Vilna ghetto no major epidemics occurred, though individual cases of typhus and other contagious diseases were fairly common. In general, the Vilna ghetto mortality rate, though of course much higher than before the war, was significantly lower than that in Lodz or Warsaw. The reasons for this lie in the energetic—even ruthless—sanitary and epidemiological measures taken by the appropriate agencies of the ghetto administration, which placed particular emphasis on child care and on the maintenance of standards of cleanliness of dwellings and persons. The results, in some respects, exceeded prewar norms. Lectures and posters popularized notions of hygiene, and special sanitary police carried out thorough periodic inspections of premises, with severe punishments for violators. Compulsory bathing was introduced, along with laundry and disinfection facilities, hot water dispensaries, immunization programs, and X-ray diagnosis. It was a great blessing that the prewar Jewish hospital was located within the ghetto boundaries and that a large number of devoted physicians, nurses, and pharmacists were available to the end to carry on the great medical traditions of Jewish Vilna.

## Social Dynamics

Hunger, cold, disease, and death were omnipresent realities for all ghetto inmates, but solidarity in the face of disaster proved difficult to achieve. Indeed, there could be no real social justice in the ghetto, where survival was always at the expense of someone else. Despite the levelling effect of ghettoization and periodic demands from the masses of the ghetto poor that all Jews must now be equals, new forms of stratification arose which bore little resemblance to the prewar structure of Jewish society. Fortuitous circumstances, like those surrounding the formation of a ghetto, at once gave rise to social cleavages between those who were able to remain in their homes and those who came into the ghetto from outside it. To be able to retain one's household possessions, clothing, and stocks of food was to have a reserve of immensely valuable commodities in the poverty of the ghetto. The same was true if one was fortunate enough to find shelter in the well-stocked apartment of a deportee, or if one had been daring enough to smuggle in unauthorized cash and valuables when entering the ghetto. Refugees from more distant places often arrived with very few possessions and quickly sank to the level of the deepest poverty. A particularly difficult problem was posed by expellees from western and central Europe, like the 20,000 German, Austrian, and Czech Jews who were deported to the Lodz ghetto in October-November, 1941. The foreigners, including many elderly without skills and resources, were never totally integrated into ghetto society, though Rumkowski's secretary was a German Jewess named Fuchs. The majority of the newcomers were deported to the Chelmno extermination camp in the first resettlements.

Once a ghetto had become somewhat stabilized, the social pyramid that emerged usually had at its apex the members of the *Judenrat* and the Jewish police, whose style of life, appearance, etc. often set them apart from the ghetto masses. Allied to them and a crucial support to the *Judenrat's* strategies of social welfare, bribery of German authorities, and the like, was a new financial elite of large-scale smugglers, speculators, and entrepreneurs who, at times, were even able to amass great wealth and the influence that went with it. The "free enterprise" economy of the Warsaw ghetto was especially notorious for its ghetto plutocracy, with its ostentatious patronage of restaurants, cabarets, dances, and so on. But this "upper class" was very small. The nearest thing to a "middle class" (which, naturally, under ghetto conditions had little in common with the standard of life of the prewar bourgeoisie) was represented by the employees of the *Judenrat* and the skilled workers. As ghetto bureaucracies and economic enterprises expanded, these came to be a fairly sizable segment of the population. They enjoyed at least some measure of economic security as well as temporary immunity from deportation. Skilled workers, especially those in occupations in great demand by German military and civilian employers, were a privileged group. This was especially true if they had friendly relationships with individual Germans who were in a position to do favors for "their" Jews. Unskilled workers, who included vast numbers of déclassé former white-collar workers, intellectuals, and shopkeepers, were not so fortunate, and were part of the enormous floating mass of ghetto misery that included the aged, the sick, abandoned children, refugees, "illegals" who had evaded deportation, and the numerous other victims of bad luck.

The struggle for material existence in the ghetto was a particularly brutal form of Darwinian battle; social antagonisms, fueled by bitterness and envy, and filled with accusations of favoritism, greed, and insensitivity, ran very high. At the same time, in justice to the sorely-tired inhabitants and administrators of the ghettos, it should be pointed out that manifestations of social solidarity and self-help were equally characteristic of ghetto life. Even the least socially conscious of the much-maligned *Judenräte* were supplemented and even overshadowed by the work of autonomous bodies like the JSS (Jewish Social Self-Help, known as ZTOS in Warsaw). This organization was an outgrowth of the prewar TOZ (health), CENTOS (orphan care), and other welfare organizations. The JSS had official status in the General Government and developed into a broad network of member agencies, with 412 branches in 1942. Its main source of funding was the American Jewish Joint Distribution Committee, which had itself grown out of the need to help eastern European Jews during and after World War I. This precious source of income was cut off after the United States entered World War II, and thereafter all funds had to be collected locally through voluntary donations, assessments, subsidies from the

*Judenräte,* and the like. The JSS placed special emphasis on work among children, supporting milk distribution programs, day care centers, and orphanages, including Janusz Korczak's famous institution in Warsaw. But all categories of needy and disadvantaged people benefited to some degree from what help the overburdened JSS agencies could spare. In Warsaw, a unique and significant JSS institution existed in the form of tenement committees, of which over 1,000 existed in January, 1942. These local neighborhood groups attempted to provide minimal food, clothing, furniture, etc. for the needy within their buildings.[16] In the tightly controlled Lodz ghetto, which lay outside the General Government, it was the ghetto administration itself which undertook major responsibility for soup kitchens, orphanages, a "summer camp" for youth, an old-age home, and other welfare institutions. The Rumkowski regime, in addition, decided on a direct cash subsidy program whose recipients at times included the majority of the ghetto population.[17] In Vilna the task of providing for the poorest sectors of the population, including the large number of hidden "illegals" whose names could not appear on welfare or ration rolls, was divided between public and private agencies. The Welfare Department of the ghetto administration, supported by taxation and the beneficiary of confiscated and abandoned property, subsidized charitable institutions like several orphanages and an old-age home. It took under its protection and care the labor camps in the Vilna region and provided for their inmates when they were transferred into Vilna proper. A semi-official Winter Assistance Committee, the favorite charity of the wives of the ghetto elite, occupied itself with the collection, repair, and distribution of clothing. But the most active and widely respected welfare organization was the autonomous GHK (*Gezelshaftlekher Hilfs-Komitet* or Social Aid Committee), whose sponsors were the major political groups in the ghetto. So broad was its base and so democratic its leadership that it was known as the "Ghetto Parliament" in pointed contrast to the *Judenrat* and its successor regime, the dicatorship of Jacob Gens. Workers in the many labor units that were employed outside the ghetto, as well as those working within the ghetto administration, pledged a percentage of their meager wages for the GHK. The two main responsibilities of GHK were the distribution of food parcels and the disbursement of millions of rubles in cash subsidies. These latter were especiall directed, as tactfully as possible, to the surviving members of the prewar intelligentsia. Thereby, the ghetto carried on the long tradition of respect for intellectual and cultural creativity that had earned Vilna the title of "Jerusalem of Lithuania."[18]

## Cultural Life

The Vilna ghetto did not limit itself to the dignity and welfare of its creative groups; it encouraged them to participate in the active cultural life of the ghetto. In all major ghettos we find a varied and colorful range of cultural activities—an astonishing phenomenon under conditions of maximum deprivation and terror. This would appear to be the most positive and uncontroversial aspect of the ghettos, but no aspect of ghetto life was without its ambiguities. There were those in the ghettos—and even after the liberation—who were uncomfortable with the very notion of "theater in a graveyard," and saw in public entertainment the twin dangers of desecration of ghetto suffering and narcotic lulling of the sensibilities of its inmates. Indeed, the Gens regime in Vilna consciously used cultural activities to soothe the population in times of panic. In the early days of the Warsaw ghetto much of the available entertainment was on a low level and catered to the *nouveaux riches,* whose cabarets and restaurants stood in shocking contrast to the prevailing squalor. But in Warsaw successful efforts were made to raise the level of cultural activity. *Yikor* in Yiddish and *Tekumah* in Hebrew sponsored lectures on literature. Three Polish and two Yiddish theaters were active. Musical life flourished in the form of a symphony orchestra, several choruses, and string quartets. In Lodz, the ghetto administration established a Culture House for musical and theatrical performances whose level impressed even sophisticated central Europeans. Indeed, the central European deportees in the Lodz ghetto included many talented performers who added to the quality and range of cultural programs.

Particularly impressive is the cultural life in the Vilna ghetto. The first concert, in January, 1942, coming only weeks after the loss of over half the ghetto population, was widely resented. But most critics were mollified by its elevated and serious tone. From this tentative beginning, until the abortive 1943 fall "season," which the liquidation of the ghetto interrupted, the remnants of Vilna Jewry were offered a variety of plays, concerts, lectures, symposia, etc. that would have done credit to a good-sized city in peacetime. A week in the Vilna ghetto might present the choice of a full-scale Yiddish play, a revue in a lighter vein with original songs and skits on ghetto themes, a symphonic concert, a pops concert, a jazz concert, and performances by the Hebrew or Yiddish chorus or by students of various ghetto schools. There might be lectures sponsored by the Literary Artistic Association on poetry or painting, or discussions on mathematics and physics by the Scientific Circle. The Teachers' Associations and the Council of Labor Brigadiers might be giving popular lectures on cultural subjects and there might be one of a series of talks on religious themes or one of the frequent popular medical discussions. The ghetto administration, in addition to maintaining a full-fledged Cultural Department as one of its major agencies, subsidized a variety of literary and scholarly projects for a future "ghetto publishing house" and announced a series of cultural competitions for new musical, artistic, and literary creations. Some of the prize-winning entries were of lasting value, like the poetry of Abraham Sutskever that has entered the corpus of classic Yiddish poetry.

The Vilna ghetto was exceptionally proud of its library, amassed laboriously and sometimes at great risk from sources inside and outside the ghetto. A third of the ghetto population—some 5,000 people—were subscribers, and in little over a year, by December, 1942, the library could celebrate the lending out of the 100,000th book. The reading room of the library provided an oasis of quiet and even relative comfort in the midst of the claustrophobic ghetto.[19]

Other ghettos had libraries, too, as circumstances allowed. Everywhere escapist novels were popular, but so too were serious works of history, especially those dealing with past Jewish suffering and past German defeats, in an attempt to create some context and meaning for the present.

News of the present was hard to come by in the isolated world of the ghetto. Outside newspapers were ordinarily not permitted. On those occasions when they were available they were eagerly read and commented on, although the newspapers involved were pro-Nazi organs filled with propaganda and antisemitism. A few ghettos had official, *Judenrat*-sponsored publications, usually weeklies, like the *Geto-Tsaytung* in Lodz and the mimeographed *Geto-Yedies* in Vilna. The weekly *Gazeta Zydowska* in Cracow was supposed to serve as the official Jewish newspaper for the whole General Government. These periodicals were not newspapers in the ordinary sense. They were essentially official bulletins providing news of German regulations, decisions, and activities of the *Judenräte* and their agencies. They also served as propaganda vehicles for the ideology of the ghetto administration, preaching discipline, order, and the need for productivity and hard work to ensure the survival of the ghetto. The *Geto-Tsaytung* in Lodz was filled with encomiums to Rumkowski, whose "cult of personality" eventually reached alarming proportions. In any case, the official ghetto press had to be exceedingly cautious and evasive in its reporting. The ghetto inhabitants treated these publications with considerable reserve, but read them, all the same, for the practical information they provided and for what could be surmised by reading between the lines.

Quite a different kind of journalism was represented by the widespread illegal or underground press. Unfortunately, we have very fragmentary information on this subject, since many publications were ephemeral, and readers, for obvious reasons, did not hold on to their copies of illegal printed matter very long. We know that leaflets, posters, and journals appeared in many ghettos, like the *Hechalutz Halochem* in Cracow and the *Biuletin Fun Bund* in Lodz. Sometimes, a ghetto might even produce illegal literature intended for the non-Jewish population, as was the case in Vilna.[20] But only for the Warsaw ghetto do we have anything like a full record of the underground press, thanks to the "Oneg Shabbat" archives of Emmanuel Ringelblum. Some fifty publications in all three of the ghetto languages—Polish, Yiddish, and Hebrew—are known to have existed at one time or another, sponsored by every underground political organization, and particularly by their youth groups. The major Zionist groups, and the Socialist Bund were especially active, but there were Communist, Trotskyite, and other publications as well. *Hashomer Hatsair,* the left-wing Zionist youth movement, published a monthly: *Neged Hazerem (Against the Current)* appeared in all three languages and there were several other monthlies and weeklies as well. The Right Poale Zion put out the weekly *Dror (Freedom)* in Yiddish and Hebrew, plus a weekly youth paper in Hebrew and monthlies in Yiddish and Polish. The Left Poale Zion had two weeklies in Yiddish and one in Polish. *Histadrut-Gordonia,* like the General Zionists and the Revisionist Betar, had weeklies both for the party and for its youth groups. The Bund, with a history of underground journalism dating back to the turn of the century, supported a full range of publications, including its weekly *Der Veker (The Alarm)* in Yiddish and weeklies and monthlies in Yiddish and Polish for youth and other groups.[21]

These publications naturally dealt in part with activities within their own movements, and perspectives on the present catastrophe and hopes for the future also varied, of course, with political orientation. But all publications, without exception, served to criticize not only the German policies but also very frequently, and with great sharpness, those of the *Judenrat* as well. They attempted to raise the morale and combat the apathy and despair of their readers through pro-Allied versions of war news. They must be given much of the credit for popularizing the idea of physical resistance and ghetto revolt. With the beginning of the mass "resettlements" in the General Government, the underground press provided the earliest reliable information about the true nature of the deportations. On April 18, 1942, most publishers and distributors of illegal journals in the Warsaw ghetto were arrested and executed. This was a heavy blow to the underground press, but did not put an end to it. The Bundist press continued to function during the ghetto even during the mass deportations from Warsaw to Treblinka starting in July, 1942, and ceased only with the liquidation after the ghetto uprising. A Polish-language Bund bulletin even appeared thereafter on the Aryan side.[22]

## Education

The prevalence of youth publications in the underground press is one of many indications of the persistent concern in the ghettos for the future of the young, however slim their prospects of survival. This concern is shown most explicitly in the struggle in all major ghettos to provide for the education of Jewish children. This traditional high-priority community responsibility took on a new urgency under ghetto conditions. It was now necessary not only to care for the physical survival of Jewish youth but also to combat widespread demoralization and lawlessness. It was urgent to provide vocational training that would make possible the employment of young people while adding to the labor force on which the continued existence of many ghettos was presumed to depend. The *Judenräte,* individuals, and political groups joined forces in attempting to create educational institutions in all the major ghettos. But the occupation authorities, particularly in the General Government, placed tremendous obstacles in their path. The reopening of Jewish schools in the General Government for the academic year 1939-1940, at first permitted by the military, was soon vetoed by the civilian administration of Hans Frank. Even after permission was finally granted on August 31, 1940, for the establishment of elementary and vocational schools, authorization was withheld in Warsaw (allegedly for health reasons) until April, 1941. In the interim, clandestine *Komplety* (private classes) were set up under the aegis of CENTOS and prewar educational organizations, and these filled the gap to some extent.[23] Beginning with the 1941-1942 school year, the *Komplety* could function as the nuclei of a legal elementary school system. Secondary education, as well as university- and professional-level courses had to continue in secret. Vocational education was tolerated, and thousands of older boys and girls attended such courses in the Warsaw ghetto. All schools operated under tremendous handicaps. Finding suitable teachers, premises, and educational materials was extremely difficult. The problem was complicated by the existence of many different kinds of schools—a legacy of the prewar period—and the need to supply instruction in all three ghetto languages. Nevertheless, cooperation among educators of varied political-cultural backgrounds was general and the level of instruction was high. Nutritional and medical assistance was supplied to the children in their schoolrooms. Jewish history, culture, and values were emphasized in an atmosphere of great warmth and dignity. The children, in turn, responded to their schools with unprecedented enthusiasm and zeal.[24]

Only a minority of Jewish children was able to attend school in Warsaw. In Lodz the ghetto administration faced somewhat fewer problems in this area. Jewish schools opened for the first wartime school year, but classes were interrupted by the creation of the ghetto. Within the ghetto a unified school system was established, but it was plagued by absenteeism on the part of children obliged to work by economic necessity, and by the difficulties in retraining the largely Polish-speaking corps of teachers to use Yiddish, the language of instruction insisted on by the Germans. Finally, in July, 1942, the Germans closed the schools altogether.[25]

The tradition of Jewish education was particularly strong in Vilna, where an unusually high percentage of children had attended Jewish schools before the war. Not surprisingly, the Vilna ghetto showed the greatest success in its educational efforts. Within days after the formation of the Vilna ghetto in September, 1941, while the population was still in a state of shock and terror, a group of educators began to discuss the creation of schools. When the first schools were opened, in ruined premises, parents initially feared to send their children at a time of ongoing deportations. But after the first difficult winter, and with the stabilization of the ghetto, the schools attracted increasing numbers of students and received stronger support from the *Judenrat*. The Gens regime, which supplanted the *Judenrat* in July, 1942, paid close attention to the schools, made attendance compulsory in 1943, and insisted on a more national-Zionist unitary curriculum, although Yiddish remained the language of instruction. All children of elementary school age and many of secondary school age—eventually some 2,000 in a ghetto of fewer than 20,000 people—were drawn into the school network, which included *gymnasium*-level courses and special *yeshivah* programs for religious pupils. In a speech on January 15, 1943, Gens boasted that, "For the first time in the history of Vilna we have achieved a purely Jewish school system."[26] Even one of Gens' harshest critics, the Bundist Herman Kruk, had to ask himself, in connection with the ghetto's educational system:

> Is all this possible in the Ghetto? Has this been achieved in the Vilna Ghetto of all places? The future historian . . . will have to rack his brains more than once over this cultural miracle of the Vilna Ghetto.[27]

All witnesses testify to the high standards and the atmosphere of mutual affection between teachers and students that marked the Vilna ghetto schools. Those few students who survived the war found themselves able to resume their studies with full credit for time spent in the ghetto schools.

Like the schools, the Vilna Ghetto Youth Club, for older boys and girls who had to work during the day, was filled with the spirit of solidarity, comradeship, and self-worth. In addition, the Youth Club inculcated the spirit of resistance and militancy, and became a major recruiting ground for the United Partisan Organization (FPO).

To the end, the inhabitants of the ghettos struggled for survival and hoped for a better world after the war, in which their young people could live freely as Jews and as human beings. This was to be the case only for a small number of exceptionally fortunate individuals. In the case of entire ghettos, there were to be no exceptions whatever. Every ghetto, no matter where it was located, was liquidated before it could be liberated. Most Polish ghettos met this fate in 1942, beginning with Lublin in March and culminating in the mass deportations from Warsaw from July to October. It was only a small remnant that was left to raise the standard of revolt in April, 1943, and to close the story of the Warsaw ghetto in a blaze of heroism. To the east, Bialystok was liquidated in August-September, 1943, followed three weeks later by Vilna. A few residual ghettos like Kovno continued to exist as labor camps until 1944. The liquidation of Lodz came in August-September, 1944, when the Red Army was almost at its gates. With the end of this last ghetto the Final Solution in Poland was complete. The ghettos, together with the masses of eastern European Jews who had clung tenaciously to life in them, had passed into history.

**Notes**

1.   Herman Kruk, *Togbukh Fun Vilner Geto* (New York: Yivo, 1962), p. 535.

2.   The full German text of Heydrich's letter is published in *Yivo Bleter* XXX: 2 (1947): 163-168.

3.   See the comment to this effect by the Nazi "expert" on eastern European Jewish Affairs, Heinz-Peter Seraphim, at a conference in March, 1941, quoted in Philip Friedman, *Roads to Extinction: Essays on the Holocaust* (New York and Philadelphia: The Jewish Publication Society and Conference on Jewish Social Studies, 1980), p. 64.

4.   Isaiah Trunk, *Lodzher Geto* (New York: Yad Vashem and Yivo, 1962), pp. 33, 69.

5.   Mark Dvorzhetski, *Yerusholaim de lite in kamf un umkum* (Paris: Yidisher Folksfarband, 1948), p. 64.

6.   Emmanuel Ringelblum, *Notes From the Warsaw Ghetto*, ed. and trans. Jacob Sloan (New York: McGraw-Hill, 1958), pp. 143, 285.

7.   See Leonard Tushnet, *The Uses of Adversity* (New York: St. Martin's Press, 1966).

8.   Trunk, *Lodzher Geto*, pp. 108-117.

9.   Dvorzhetski, *Yerusholaim*, pp. 165-168.

10.   Kruk, *Togbukh*, p. 239.

11.   Quoted in Isaiah Trunk, *"Milkhome gegn yidn durkh farshpreytn krankaytn,"* *Yivo Bleter* XXXVII (1953): 54.

12.   Yitzhak Arad, *Ghetto in Flames* (Jerusalem: Yad Vashem, 1980), pp. 120-122; Kruk, *Togbukh*, September 7, 1941, p. 74.

13.   Dvorzhetski, *Yerusholaim*, pp. 146-148.

14.   Trunk, *Lodzher Geto*, pp. 127-127.

15.   Isaiah Trunk, *Judenrat: The Jewish Councils in Eastern Europe Under Nazi Occupation* (New York: Macmillan Co., 1973), p. 155.

16.   Lucy S. Dawidowicz, *The War Against the Jews* (New York: Holt, Rinehart, and Winston, 1975), pp. 243-248.

17.   Trunk, Judenrat, pp. 123-124.

18.   Dvorzhetski, *Yerusholaim*, pp. 183-185.

19.   The Vilna ghetto collection at Yivo Institute for Jewish Research, New York, contains thousands of original documents dealing with cultural life.

20.   See Isaac Kowalski, *A Secret Press in Nazi Europe* (New York: Shengold Publishers, Inc., 1972).

21.   See Joseph Kermish, "On the Underground Press in the Warsaw Ghetto," *Yad Vashem Studies* I (1957): 85-123, and Yisrael Gutman, *The Jews of Warsaw 1939-1943* (Bloomington, Ind.: Indiana University Press, 1982), pp. 146-154.

22.   Kermish, "On the Underground Press," p. 95.

23.   Such a school is described in *The Warsaw Diary of Chaim Kaplan*, ed. and trans. Abraham I. Katsch (New York: Collier, 1973), p. 242 (entry for February 15, 1941).

24. See Anna Natanblut, *"Di shuln in varshevergeto,"* Yivo Bleter XXX:2 (1947): 173-187.
25. Trunk, *Judenrat,* p. 209.
26. Quoted in Ruzhka Korczak, *Lehavot Be-efer,* 3rd ed. (Merhavia: Moreshet Sifriat Poalim, 1965), p. 345.
27. Kruk, *Togbukh,* March 3, 1943, p. 465.

### For Further Reading

Arad, Yitzhak. *Ghetto in Flames,* Jerusalem: Vad Vashem, 1980.

Dawidowicz, Lucy S. ed., *A Holocaust Reader.* New York: Behrman House, 1976.

Donat, Alexander. *The Holocaust Kingdom,* New York: Holocaust Library, 1965.

Goldstein, Bernard. *The Stars Bear Witness.* New York: Viking Press, 1949.

Gutman, Yisrael. *The Jews of Warsaw, 1939-1943.* Bloomington, Ind.: Indiana University Press, 1982.

Trunk, Isaiah. *Judenrat: The Jewish Councils in Eastern Europe Under Nazi Occupation.* New York: Macmillan Co., 1973.

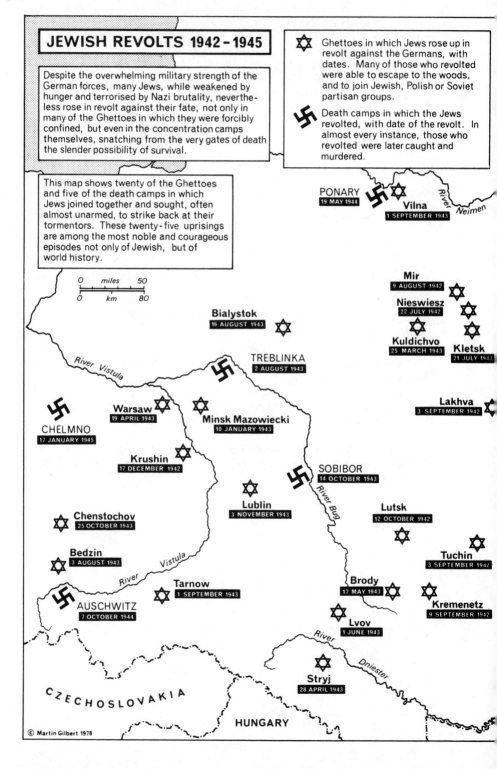

# JEWISH REVOLTS 1942–1945

Despite the overwhelming military strength of the German forces, many Jews, while weakened by hunger and terrorised by Nazi brutality, nevertheless rose in revolt against their fate, not only in many of the Ghettoes in which they were forcibly confined, but even in the concentration camps themselves, snatching from the very gates of death the slender possibility of survival.

Ghettoes in which Jews rose up in revolt against the Germans, with dates. Many of those who revolted were able to escape to the woods, and to join Jewish, Polish or Soviet partisan groups.

Death camps in which the Jews revolted, with date of the revolt. In almost every instance, those who revolted were later caught and murdered.

This map shows twenty of the Ghettoes and five of the death camps in which Jews joined together and sought, often almost unarmed, to strike back at their tormentors. These twenty-five uprisings are among the most noble and courageous episodes not only of Jewish, but of world history.

PONARY
19 MAY 1944

Vilna
1 SEPTEMBER 1943

River Neimen

O miles 50
O km 80

Mir
9 AUGUST 1942

Nieswiesz
22 JULY 1942

Kuldichvo
25 MARCH 1943

Kletsk
21 JULY 1943

Bialystok
16 AUGUST 1943

TREBLINKA
2 AUGUST 1943

River Vistula

Lakhva
3 SEPTEMBER 1942

Warsaw
19 APRIL 1943

CHELMNO
17 JANUARY 1945

Minsk Mazowiecki
10 JANUARY 1943

Krushin
17 DECEMBER 1942

SOBIBOR
14 OCTOBER 1943

River Bug

Lublin
3 NOVEMBER 1943

Lutsk
12 OCTOBER 1942

Chenstochov
25 OCTOBER 1943

Bedzin
3 AUGUST 1943

Vistula

Tuchin
3 SEPTEMBER 1942

River

Tarnow
1 SEPTEMBER 1943

Brody
17 MAY 1943

Kremenetz
9 SEPTEMBER 1942

AUSCHWITZ
7 OCTOBER 1944

Lvov
1 JUNE 1943

River Dniester

CZECHOSLOVAKIA

Stryj
28 APRIL 1943

HUNGARY

© Martin Gilbert 1978

# The Battles of the Ghettos

## YISRAEL GUTMAN

Prior to 1942, armed Jewish resistance to the Nazis was not seriously considered by the Jewish underground in the conquered countries in eastern Europe. The Jews had few available resources for such an effort, and armed resistance would not have helped them in their ongoing struggle for immediate survival or for improving their future political position. It was apparent that Jewish armed resistance could not substantially undermine Nazi strength; it was also clear that any such attempt would result in mass reprisals, costing many Jewish lives.

From the start of the war, Jews were, individually and as a group, involved in saving their own lives by evasion or resistance to Nazi decrees. The Nazi regime was perceived by the Jews as one which robbed them of their civil rights, divided them from the rest of their countrymen, and confiscated their basic resources. In other words, the Nazis created conditions under which no human could survive; thus, the major effort of the Jews was the struggle to stay alive. The Nazi regime was seen as a temporary evil; Jews had to find ways to preserve their community so that once the Nazis were defeated they would emerge with the least possible harm. The possibility of mass murder never occurred to anyone before or even during the first stages of the occupation. It was not possible, therefore, for the Jews to prepare themselves for actual events. The mass murder of Jews began in Nazi-occupied Soviet territory immediately after the invasion in the second half of 1941.

The idea of organizing armed resistance was first raised among the members of the Zionist *Halutz* youth movements in Vilna, Poland. Jewish Vilna, "The Jerusalem of Lithuania," numbered 60,000 people before the war and had been notable for its internal unity and strong attachment to Jewish culture, religion, and Zionism. From July, 1941, to the end of the year, two-thirds of the Jewish community was uprooted and taken to unknown destinations. A few survivors, who were wounded and shaken to the core, managed to make their way back to the ghetto, where they spread the shocking news that all the deportees had been taken to Ponary, located near Vilna, where they all were shot.

In the first poster issued by the Vilna *Halutz* movement to the Jews of the city in January, 1942, it was stated:

All the roads of the Gestapo lead to Ponary.
And Ponary is death!
Doubters! Cast off all illusions. Your children, your husbands, and your wives are no longer alive.
Ponary is not a camp—all are shot there.
Hitler aims to destroy all the Jews of Europe. The Jews of Lithuania are fated to be the first in line.

> *Let us not go as sheep to slaughter!*
> It is true that we are weak and defenseless, but resistance is the only reply to the enemy!
> Brothers! It is better to fall as free fighters than to live by the grace of the murderers.
> Resist! To the last breath.[1]

This appeal stated that the events in Vilna were not local, but that Vilna was merely the first step in implementing the plan "to kill all the Jews of Europe." This was the first time that a Jewish source, which did not have any information from either German or other sources, mentioned the total annihilation of the Jewish people. Moreover, this was the first appeal to call for revolt. For the first time, the demand for Jewish armed resistance was openly stated. In January, 1942, the FPO *(Fareinikte Partizaner Organizatziye,* Yiddish for United Partisans Organization) was established in Vilna.

The Jewish communal leadership in Poland, and especially in Warsaw, did not accept the dire prediction that all Jews under Nazi rule were doomed. Only the members of the *Halutz* youth movement initially accepted this, whereas other members of the community very slowly came to the realization of the truth under the impact of the deportations.

From the beginning of 1942, there were attempts in the Warsaw ghetto to establish a fighting force. The major organization, the ZOB *(Zydowska Organizacja Bojowa,* Polish for Jewish Fighting Organization) was only established in July, 1942, in the midst of the great deportations from the city. The smaller fighting organization, the ZZW *(Zydowski Zwiazek Wojskowy,* Polish for Jewish Military Union), which also took part in the Warsaw ghetto revolt and was founded by members of the Betar movement (the activist Zionist youth movement), was organized only at the end of that year (1942).

The Jews who were sealed off in the ghetto did not have the means, the links, and the experience to build an armed force that would be ready for battle. They did not possess arms, an intelligence network, or links with allies outside the country. In addition, they did not have any military training, especially in urban guerrilla warfare. They were forced to appeal to the Poles, who had a strong underground military organization. Despite their considerable opposition to the Nazis, the Poles, who were generally antisemitic, were not willing to aid the Jews.

Only in Warsaw was there established contact between the Jewish Fighting Organization and the Polish underground. The Jews received a small number of arms and help in transmitting information from abroad; sometimes, they were given other types of assistance. The Jewish fighters were also aided by a number of individual Poles and certain factions within the underground, who disobeyed the orders of the central underground organization. Most of the arms that were gathered in the ghetto, however, were acquired from other sources. Thus, some weapons were stolen from factories or arsenals belonging to the enemy by Jews and members of the underground who were employed there. Components of weapons were smuggled into the ghetto, where they were subsequently assembled. Weapons—mostly handguns, which were inefficient for street fighting—were also purchased from merchants or soldiers through intermediaries. Furthermore, a small factory was established in the Warsaw ghetto to manufacture hand grenades; these were very important when the revolt began.

The timing of the battle was another problem. Usually, in warfare the strategic considerations of the fighters determine when the fighting begins, so that the timing will be as advantageous as possible to them and at the same time create the greatest possible difficulty for the enemy. In the ghettos, however, the Nazis dictated when the Jews would revolt. In order to ambush the Nazis, the Jewish fighters had to wait until the Nazis came in for the final sweep of the ghetto. Since the Jews were shipped away by the Nazis in stages, it was difficult to know when the end would come; this lack of knowledge added to the difficulties of resistance.

Another problem was the manner in which the ghetto fighters were regarded by the civilian Jewish population. In general, fighters use arms when continued existence through negotiation has failed. The struggle by the ghetto fighters could not end with victory over the enemy or with the achievement of security, succor, or even a postponement of their fate. The battle of the ghetto was a desperate cry to future generations, and was not regarded as a realistic struggle to ensure the future survival of the fighters. Mordecai Anielewicz, the commander of the Warsaw ghetto revolt, expressed the significance of this battle:

> The dream of my life has risen to become fact. Self-defense in
> the ghetto will have been a reality. Jewish armed resistance
> and revenge are facts.[2]

A battle of this sort, which does not alleviate present misery or offer any hope for the future, is an extremely rare phenomemon in history, and by its very nature cannot involve the masses. Most people grasped at the slightest excuse for not getting involved in this futile struggle, hoping thereby to save themselves and their loved ones. In many ghettos, the fighters were without broad support and were, therefore, isolated from the masses. This sometimes led to despair. The resisters chose to fight the battle within the ghetto because that was where Jews had lived for generations. All of them, however, were very disappointed by the passivity of the Jewish masses.

Despite the many difficulties, revolts did break out in several ghettos. In Bialystok, Vilna, Czestochowa, Sosnowiec, and elsewhere, the fighters resisted or attacked. The one revolt that attained the dimensions of a mass, stubborn, and protracted rebellion took place in the Warsaw ghetto. This lasted from April 19 to May 16, 1943. According to German statistics, there were incidents even after that time, and groups of rebels were found in the ghetto after May, 1943.

The Jews of Warsaw were able to organize a resistance which cost the Nazis prestige, materials, and casualties. Moreover, Warsaw was the first rebellion in any occupied city in Europe. It tied down sizable forces of the enemy for a longer period of time than did many sovereign countries overrun by the Germans in World War II.

The Warsaw ghetto revolt was unique for two other reasons. In Warsaw, the tens of thousands of Jews who had remained behind after the two great deportations of the summer of 1942 and January, 1943, supported the idea of resistance and rebellion. Ghetto residents did not heed the calls of the Germans, did not report for selections (for deportation to the concentration camps), and hid in bunkers underneath the ground. These underground hiding places and bunkers were built over months; their locations and entrances were well concealed. Food and medical supplies were stored in there for prolonged hiding. Many bunkers also had arms. In actuality, most of the Warsaw ghetto in its last stages was an underground city that accommodated tens of thousands of Jews. When the Nazi soldiers came in to carry out the final deportation on April 19, 1943, they found a deserted city, with the way barred by hundreds of armed fighters. The two fighting organizations—ZOB and ZZW— numbered about 750 fighters in various positions, with a plan of action worked out to the finest detail. The rest of the civilian population had taken refuge in the bunkers and assisted the fighters in whatever way possible. Thus, all of the central ghetto of Warsaw became a partisan battle zone. The Nazis needed days of street fighting to capture each bunker individually, with the inhabitants of each bunker refusing to leave and sometimes answering calls to come out and surrender with gunfire.

Secondly, the resisters in the Warsaw ghetto did not prepare a path of retreat or plan any action other than fighting in the ghetto. The Poles tried to persuade the fighters to desert the ghetto a short while before the revolt and to hide in the forests. The answer of the fighters was unequivocal: "This is where the battle will take place."

The revolt in the Warsaw ghetto had broad implications. The Poles were impressed with the revolt and realized that even a handful of people, with a minimal amount of weapons, could cause great damage to the enemy in city fighting, and could tie down large forces.

For the Jews, the revolt in the Warsaw ghetto motivated the underground cells and fighting organizations in other areas— Bialystok, Vilna, Cracow, Czestochowa, Bendin—to fight and maybe die rather than fall into the hands of the Nazi conquerors. It also inspired others to escape to the forests, where they joined the partisans.

The Nazis learned a lesson from Warsaw as well. If they believed that the Jews would not resist, they were suddenly aware that the Jews could organize and fight with great valor and sacrifice. This was one of the reasons why they took steps to prevent further large-scale revolts in the deportations of Jews from other ghettos.

The revolt in the Warsaw ghetto, and the revolts in the ghettos in general, became a symbol for those who fought for the independence of Israel, as well as a beacon for all of humanity. It has taught us how a small handful of people, without hope, in complete isolation and in a depressed physical and mental state, could overcome all obstacles and embark on a heroic struggle.

## Notes

1. Yitzhak Arad, Yisrael Gutman, and Abraham Margaliot, eds., *Documents on the Holocaust: Selected Sources on the Destruction of the Jews in Germany and Austria, Poland, and the Soviet Union* (New York: Ktav, 1981), p. 433.

2. Arad, Gutman, and Margaliot, eds., *Documents*, pp. 315-316.

## For Further Reading

Arad, Yitzhak. *Ghetto in Flames: The Struggle and Destruction of the Jews of Vilna.* Jerusalem: Yad Vashem, 1980.

———; Gutman, Yisrael; and Margaliot, Abraham, eds. *Documents on the Holocaust: Selected Sources on the Destruction of the Jews in Germany and Austria, Poland, -and the Soviet Union.* New York: Ktav, 1981.

Donat, Alexander. *The Holocaust Kingdom.* New York: Holt, Rinehart, and Winston, 1963.

Gutman, Yisrael. *The Jews of Warsaw, 1939-1943: Ghetto, Underground, Revolt.* Bloomington, Ind.: Indiana University Press, 1982.

Milton, Sybil, ed. and trans. *The Stroop Report: The Jewish Quarter of Warsaw Is No More!* Introduction by Andrzej Wirth. New York: Pantheon, 1979.

# Spiritual Responses in the Ghettos

## DANIEL LANDES

Jewish spiritual response to the Holocaust can best be understood by the term *"kiddush ha-Shem"*—sanctification of the Name of God. *Kiddush ha-Shem* is derived from the biblical commandment describing the ideal posture of the Jew: "And ye shall not profane my holy Name, but I will be sanctified among the children of Israel."[1] Traditionally, every action was to manifest this principle. In crises it meant that one should be willing to even forfeit his life for basic religious principles. *Kiddush ha-Shem*, expressed both as martyrdom and as service to God within life, was in evidence during the Holocaust. A new definition of *kiddush ha-Shem*, that of the struggle to preserve life in the face of destruction, was also introduced during this period.[2]

## Factors Allowing for *Kiddush ha-Shem*

Only some Jews were able to attempt a spiritual response amidst the terrifying conditions in the ghettos. As Isaiah Trunk has observed, "From our perspective and hindsight today, the ghettos were, of course, a lost position. But in that *unpredictable* situation, the ghettos were the only place where the tragic endeavors for survival and adjustment could manifest themselves."[3] Spiritual responses were possible in the ghettos where Jews could venture to see themselves within a context of community and religion. To be sure, those conditions that allowed for *kiddush ha-Shem* were more in evidence in the larger ghettos—Warsaw, Kovno, and Vilna as prime examples—than in the smaller ones, whose existences were of a shorter duration and more directly under the eyes of the Nazis and their native Fascist followers. We should also note that as the situation deteriorated in the larger ghettos, options and choices became even more circumscribed. Despite these two reservations, we can nevertheless distinguish several factors that contributed to creating a climate within which spiritual responses would occur.

1) The Jew in the ghetto often had a measure of time to consider his situation. This does not imply that he was fully aware of what his severely limited options were. This also does not deny the swiftness of death when it came, nor the terrible toll that malnutrition, hard labor, fear, and depression took on his decision-making capabilities. Many ghetto residents, nevertheless, did endlessly analyze their situation publicly in debate and discussion, and privately in the form of diaries, letters, and meditations. A number carefully formulated views and reactions to what was happening to them.

2) The Jew was within a community. In the circle of family and friends he could practice and be encouraged to maintain his religious principles. The familiar, if altered, context of the community elicited

the continued observance of the Sabbath, holidays, and public prayer. Even martyrdom could exert an attraction as the ultimate statement of faith when it was to be enacted "among the children of Israel" whom he knew and cared for.

The limited self-rule allowed Jews in many ghettos also had an effect upon spiritual responses. Some concessions, such as rest on Saturday or permission for public worship, were sometimes obtained from the Germans. Although tenuous and shortlived, they were encouraging while they were tolerated. Even the *Judenrat* (the Jewish Council), with an assimilated leadership that was hostile or indifferent to religious practices, as in Warsaw and Lodz, was often able to provide for certain religious needs, such as the baking of *matzah* for Passover.[4]

3) The ghetto was served well by its spiritual leadership. The rabbis' position, to be sure, was precarious. Some initially held positions in the local *Judenräte* of the smaller ghettos, but those rabbis usually did not last long. They acted in ways that ran counter to Nazi wishes and they refused to present lists of Jews to them for deportation. These rabbis were removed from office and, along with other colleagues, publicly shamed, deported, or immediately murdered. In the larger ghettos, many surviving rabbis went underground. A few others held relatively insignificant positions.

The rabbis, nevertheless, exerted an important influence. To understand this, one must note that Judaism has traditionally demanded a large measure of independence from its adherents. Every man stands directly before his Creator. But he does not stand alone. The rabbi interprets the demands of *halakhah* (Jewish law) in the given situation. An inspirational figure, he chastens and comforts as needed. In the Hasidic community, the rabbi (known as *rebbe*, the Hasidic master) has a fatherly role and is considered a special intercessor to God. These functions were desperately needed by the religious Jew in the ghetto, who sought out the remaining rabbis for guidance and comfort.

The rabbis of the ghettos were often men of unusual scholarship, piety, and communal experience. Serving as *roshei yeshivah* (deans of talmudic academies), rabbis of major cities, and Hasidic masters of large courts, they were accustomed to exercising leadership. While maintaining public office, their true authority had always been personal. Their own lives were extremely well-disciplined and usually ascetic. These elements, along with a deep faith, allowed many to respond fully, genuinely, and forcefully to the deprivations and upheavals that confronted their flocks.

4) The ghettos resulted in the worst conditions—apart from the concentration camps—that Jews faced throughout their long history of persecution. This experience, nevertheless, was understood by many within that context of suffering and struggle. Thus, the somber recitation of the Book of Lamentations on the Ninth of Av, commemorating the destruction of Jerusalem, and the liturgical elegies that memorialize medieval massacres evoked a feeling of common fate and identification with prior generations.[5] The joyous

holidays, celebrating victory over oppression, often encouraged hope for the future. Traditional theological formulations of good and evil, exile and redemption, developed in reaction to past travail, found renewed expression in sermons, talks, and writings produced in the ghettos.[6] The ghetto experience was sufficiently similar to prior Jewish experience to provide for the assumption of a common context. Evaluating their present situation in the light of previous persecutions doubtlessly provided insight and some hope and comfort; but, it should be noted, it also posed a danger. Previous persecutions were not as thoroughly implemented as the Holocaust. Overemphasizing analogies to prior experiences could also lead to self-deception.

5) *Halakhah* proved supple and strong enough to respond to the severe victimization of ghetto residents that took place in every aspect of daily life. An exhaustive ethical, social, and ritual code, *halakhah* regulated every area of the Jews' existence. The ghettos, which transformed personal lives and communal institutions, challenged Jewish law on every front. But rooted in a strong belief in a transcendent reality with rules considered timeless and unchanging, the application of *halakhah* to life has always been acutely situational and directed to the need of the hour. Even the abstract study of *halakhah* has focused on the unusual and on crisis situations. *Halakhic* authorities in the ghetto were, therefore, able to immediately and effectively use the traditional legal methodology to respond to a wide spectrum of moral and religious issues.[7]

*Halakhah* survived for another reason. For the religiously observant Jew, *halakhah* was fully integrated into his life. The two could not be separated. A Jew ate in a certain way, dressed in a particular manner, and related to people within a specific framework. Habit may be the enemy of religious devotion, but it is also the ally of religious practice. Even without the conscious decision to continue *halakhic* forms, the religious Jew was often propelled by the experiences of his life to remain faithful to those (religious) responses that came automatically to him.[8]

Thus, a spiritual response to ghetto conditions was possible for many Jews because they often had time to consider their situation and they possessed a context within which they could make decisions. This context had several dimensions: community, leadership, historical precedent, and religious language and discipline. This allowed for some to choose *kiddush ha-Shem.*

## *Kiddush ha-Shem* as Martyrdom

*Kiddush ha-Shem* as martyrdom is defined as the absolute refusal to transgress the cardinal prohibitions of idolatry, forbidden sexual union, and murder. Even lesser moral and religious practices, however, are included within this category if the intent is to publicly disparage Judaism.[9] In the medieval period, Jews suffered martyrdom rather than convert to Christianity or Islam. This became the dominant form in which *kiddush ha-Shem* took place.

The Holocaust seems to deny the possibility of *kiddush ha-Shem*. First of all, the Nazis did not despise the Jews because they embraced the wrong religion. Indeed, even their conversion to Christianity proved to be no protection. More importantly, nothing that the Jews could do would appease the Nazis. They consequently appear as tragic victims, not as proud martyrs.[10]

This conclusion is hasty. It is true that Nazi anti-Jewish legislation and policy was not primarily directed against Jewish religious institutions and observances.[11] The Nazi SS and soldiers, along with the local Fascists employed in controlling the ghettos, however, responded violently to manifestations of Jewish religion. They frequently vented their rage against Judaism. Religious Jews often had to look on while synagogues burned or while rabbis were defamed. At times, they were compelled to participate in such sacrilege for fear of their lives and those of their families and neighbors.

Despite the dangers, however, many refused to stand by. Two cases are illustrative. In Bendin (Bedzin, northwest of Cracow), the Nazis set fire to the synagogue and to the adjoining houses. Any Jew leaving his home was shot. A Mr. Schlesinger, along with his son and son-in-law, broke into the burning synagogue, each rescuing two Torah scrolls. As they left, they were shot to death by the Nazis. In Vidava (Widawa, southwest of Lodz), Nazi officers found a Torah scroll hidden in the house of Abraham Mordecai Maroco, the young married town rabbi. They ordered him to tear it up or they would burn him alive. When he refused, they poured benzine over him and set him afire along with the Torah scroll.[12]

The Nazis and their followers also targeted the bearded pious Jews for special treatment. They compelled them to shave in public displays or have their beards painfully pulled off their faces. Some were shot or deported. In Rava (Rawa Mazowiecka, east of Lodz), Rabbi Rappaport, the elderly town rabbi, was taken to be shorn publicly of his beard in the town square. The local priest, an old friend, interceded on his behalf. The Nazi officer offered Rabbi Rappaport a choice of either receiving 100 blows or having his beard shaved off. The rabbi accepted the beating, which sent him to the hospital and eventually resulted in his death.[13]

In the above stories, martyrdom takes place in a sudden and almost spontaneous manner. In a number of other instances, Jews knew that death awaited them. Many attempted to perform the last act of *kiddush ha-Shem* with full dignity, in accordance with Jewish tradition and before the community. Thus, the martyrdom of the Jews of Kobilnik (Kobylnik, now Narutch, northeast of Vilna), who were thrown to their knees in front of the open graves before they were shot. Their rabbis gently ordered them to rest on their toes and fingers so as not to kneel (a posture only assumed by Jews in a solemn part of the High Holiday service) and to recite the *Shemah* ("Hear, O Israel, the Lord is our God, the Lord is One").[14] A similar case is that of Rabbi Nehemiah Alter—the son of the *Rebbe* of Gur, who authored

*Sefat Emet* (a classic work of Hasidic thought). He served as *halakhic* authority in Lodz, where he declared at a public meeting: "One does not have to sanctify the Name of God specifically with guns. Each one should perform *kiddush ha-Shem* according to his own ability. Let us not lower ourselves in front of the Gentiles. Also, let us not fulfill their orders which brings us to death." When Rabbi Alter was deported, he donned his clothes for the Sabbath and carried his prayer shawl and phylacteries. Under his arm was a copy of the *Sefat Emet*. Entering the railroad car, he sang with great enthusiasm a section of the Sabbath morning liturgy: "The soul of every living being shall bless Thy Name." He was shoved to his death by an enraged Nazi officer, who cried, "This is surely a Jewish leader. Let him go there. Even there they need Jewish leaders. . . . "[15]

These religious Jews were convinced that death at the hands of the Nazis was an act of *kiddush ha-Shem*. One of those who believed this was Rabbi Menaḥem Zemba, one of the three last rabbis of Warsaw. Ironically, on the day his wife was murdered by the Nazis, he concluded a monograph on the subject, which he dedicated to her.[16] Many rabbis taught special lessons to their students and others on *kiddush ha-Shem*. Rabbi Ephraim Oshry, during a selection in the Kovno ghetto, decreed the proper formulation of the blessing before undergoing martyrdom to be: "Blessed art thou, O Lord, King of the Universe, who has commanded us to sanctify His Name in public," as opposed to "who has commanded us upon sanctification of His Name." The latter form is reserved for actions that can be done through an agent. *Kiddush ha-Shem*, rather, is a deed that one must perform himself. Therefore, one should use the former, the infinitive, form.[17]

The significance of Rabbi Oshry's opinion is that these religious Jews did not feel that they were passive victims. Surely, they did not wish to die, but their willingness to meet and interpret their death as an act of *kiddush ha-Shem* indicates a choice and an action. They believed that they must ensure by the proper intention, as indicated by the recitation of the blessing, that their cruel end would not be in vain. Rabbi Elhanan Wasserman, famed for his righteousness as well as his scholarship, expressed this attitude when he urged his twelve companions as they were led away by the Lithuanian Fascists from their hiding place in the Kovno ghetto:

> It is incumbent upon us to repent now, at this moment, and on this spot, for time is short. . . . We shall walk with our heads up without a blemished thought that would befoul and spoil our sacrifice. We are now fulfilling the greatest commandment: *kiddush ha-Shem*. The fire that will consume us is the same fire from which the Jewish people will rise anew.[18]

# Breakdown of Religious Life

Despite the strong commitment to religious ideals on the part of large sections of the Jewish population, ghetto life—disease, poverty, hard labor, and the ever-present fear of deportation or murder—proved destructive to spirituality. The Sabbath was an early casualty. In many ghettos, the Germans ordered that stores be open on that day. The work battalions also did not allow for Sabbath rest. As conditions worsened, even very observant Jews could be seen begging on the streets on the Sabbath. Special food was not available with which to celebrate the day. Many religious women, not being able to differentiate between the profane week and the holy Sabbath, did not light Sabbath candles on Friday night. For others, candles were a luxury they could not afford. Poverty caused other changes. *Taliyot* (prayer shawls) minus their ritual fringes were dyed and sold as dresses to Gentile women. Torah scrolls, formerly valued heirlooms, were sold far below their value along with prized sets of the Talmud.[19] Chaim Aharon Kaplan, a Hebrew teacher, reports in his Warsaw diary that during Passover of April, 1942, *matzah* was too expensive for the entire eight-day holiday: "On the other hand, large amounts of bread [absolutely forbidden by Jewish law on Passover] were prepared for the first days of the holiday. Everyone bought it secretly. A grocer would hand a loaf to a customer discreetly, adding in a whisper, "On *hol-ha-moed* [intermediate days of the festival] you'll be able to get more bread if you need it. Don't be shy!"[20]

The breakdown in religious life extended to all areas of life. Fear of deportation forced the religious Polish Jew to give up his distinctive *kappata* (caftan) and *streimel* (fur hat), as well as his beard. The Polish woman was deprived of her *sheitel* (marriage wig). The advanced *yeshivot* (talmudic academies) and Hasidic *shtiblekh* (prayer and learning centers) were closed, with many students deported in the early days of the ghettos' establishment. Synagogues were closed, although in some ghettos, a few were reopened for a short period. One observer also noticed a decline in public morality brought about by the uncertainty of life.[21]

The story of one *shtibl*,[22] while atypical, is illustrative of the drastic distortions that ghetto life could cause. The *shtiblekh* in prewar Warsaw enrolled approximately 3,500 students between the ages of fourteen and twenty-eight. They were unique learning centers developed by the Hasidim. There were no administration, curriculum, or teachers. The *shtibl* was essentially a large study room with benches, tables, and books. Students (a *shtibl* could have up to 230 students; most were considerably smaller) studied together, in small groups or on their own, whatever classic talmudic, ethical, or Hasidic text they wished. Guidance was provided by the older fellows. Periodically, *bahurim* (lads) would visit the scholars of the city and engage in talmudic discussion, but basically, they were on their own. The *bahurim* were known to be very independent, not caring what others in the Jewish community thought of them. Ultimately, they recognized only the authority of the *rebbe* to whose court they were attached, and whom they visited as often as possible. They dressed and acted in a distinctive Hasidic style. The *shtibl* produced outstanding Hasidim but, academically, they were far inferior to the students of the *yeshivot*.

Two thousand of the *bahurim* were Hasidim of the *Rebbe* of Gur. Some of these *bahurim* were *harifim* (zealots). They virtually lived in their *shtiblekh*, only returning home late at night to sleep. They generally did not speak with their mothers and sisters, and limited conversation with their fathers. During the week and even on the Sabbath, they ate in the *shtibl*, sharing in a communal meal that all contributed to from their homes. Unlike the other *shtiblekh*, they would expel any member once he sought employment.

With the establishment of the Warsaw ghetto, the *shtiblekh* were disbanded. Several older *harifim*, with some fifty *bahurim*, sought to reestablish a *shtibl* in an apartment at Mila Street. They resumed their former life but with further self-imposed restrictions: *Bahurim* now slept in the *shtibl;* when at home, they would refer to their mother and sister, respectively, as "the housemate of father" and "father's daughter." Members from wealthier homes provided food that was shared by the entire group. The *shtibl* supplemented this with begging on the outside. Their devotion to learning lessened with the need for increased begging to provide essentials.

The shared meals became festive Hasidic celebrations accompanied by song and dance. Eventually, they wished to include the drinking of hard liquor in their meals. Moderate drinking was a traditional Hasidic means of relaxing in the company of friends, allowing one to open himself to the joy of the song, dance, and words of Torah recited at the table. Liquor was enormously expensive in the ghetto. In order to pay for it, the *bahurim* began to take and pawn their parents' possessions. Later, they extorted money from wealthy Hasidim. They threatened those who would not comply with informing upon them to the authorities. Supposedly, in some cases, they made good their threats. The *bahurim*'s neighbors were appalled at their constant celebrations during this tragic period in Jewish history. The neighbors eventually were able, after several ugly incidents, to evict them. At the same time, the Hasidic community tried to exert pressure upon them to curb their extreme behavior.

The *bahurim*, however, were uncontrollable. They were confident that their *rebbe*, who had escaped Poland, would approve of their actions. At last, the *rebbe*'s brother, Rabbi Moshe Bezalael Alter, who was in Warsaw, addressed them in a letter, urging them to devote at least eight hours a day to the study of Talmud. He also strongly disapproved of the fact that:

> . . . many of you are slighting the most severe of all [commandments] and a pillar of Judaism—to honor one's parents . . . taking things out of the house without their permission. . . . It is also improper that you have increased festive meals and especially the drinking of liquor. Even in normal times, my saintly brother our Master, may he live

long and happily, warned that such events should take place no more than once a month. And now even that would be precluded given the present situation. . . . The collection of *tzedakah* [charity] on your behalf should not be a steady practice but should be reserved for exceptional circumstances. And it should be performed in an honorable way.

Your present practices are causing neglect of the Torah, and heaven forbid, a profanation of the glory of my saintly brother our Master, may he live long and happily. And for many reasons, both obvious and subtle, I should warn you to sleep only in the home of your parents, may they live.[23]

The *bahurim,* of course, ignored the letter. The brother of the *rebbe,* after all, is not the *rebbe!* They remained convinced that he would agree with their practices. They moved to 30 Muranowska Street. We are not informed of their subsequent fate.

How does one understand this "outlaw" *shtibl* that was shunned by the rest of religious Jewry? They were victims of the ghetto's corrosive impact upon their particularistic mode of life. Relying on their *rebbe* only, they could not effect a transfer of authority when contact with him was cut. As members of a subgroup that was closed and sectlike, they drew further inward when confronted by the hostile conditions on the outside. Their continued distinctiveness set them apart even from other Hasidim who compromised their dress in order to survive. The *shtibl's* religious activities turned more to the escapist tendencies of their practices as the general situation continued to worsen. One must also question whether an apocalyptic element [24] is revealed in this group's behavior. Facing a terrible end, there is often a release from certain normal societal constraints coupled with a desire to celebrate the little life that remains. In any event, criticized and alone, they sought ways to keep their group together. Accustomed to support from their parents and from their Hasidic group, they felt that they deserved this continued support, as now they were the last of the "true" Hasidim. If it was not given to them, they would take it. The story of this *shtibl* is, then, the story of a group of young men living together who could not translate their religious lives to the radically altered, oppressive, and finally destructive conditions of ghetto life.

## *Kiddush ha-Shem* in Life

Despite the deleterious effects of ghetto life, many remained faithful to Judaism, continuing to learn Torah and observe its ritual and moral precepts. Earlier in this essay, we discussed the factors present that enabled many Jews to seek to sanctify the Name of God within the ghetto—namely, the time needed to make a decision and the proper communal and religious contexts in which these decisions could be implemented.

At this point it would be logical to pursue the reasons why Jews clung tenaciously to religious practices and how they understood and perceived this effort. A clear answer is not forthcoming. Many of the religiously observant ghetto inmates did not survive the Holocaust. Others who did survive often tend to interpret their actions in light of later experiences in the camps or after the Holocaust. In addition, the experience of being religiously observant was not the same for everyone—it varied from ghetto to ghetto and by year, circumstance, and, of course, personality. In the accounts of religious observance in the ghetto, one can, nevertheless, detect several recurrent motifs that elucidate the varying manifestations of spirituality.

The first motif was the desire to escape the terrible reality of the ghetto for a transcendent realm. This was clearly articulated by the last spiritual director of the Slabodka Yeshivah, Rabbi Abraham Grodzinsky, who taught his students in the Kovno ghetto the verse "The Lord is on my side; I will not fear: what can a man do to me?" (Psalm 118:6):

> Normally, we explain this to mean that if God comes to someone's aid, there is no power that other men can evoke to hurt him at all. But in truth, the verse has a deeper idea. If a man merits to reach the spiritual level where he is close to God, is he not the most blessed of anyone in the world? Compared to this [blessedness] what is the evil that man can do to him?[25]

To this end, Jews created havens where they could be "safe" for a time from the evil of man. After the *yeshivot* were disbanded, Dr. Hillel Seidman made this entry in his Warsaw diary concerning one such effort:

> I visited today the strange underground world. In the morning, two young men came to me . . . Moses Rosenstreich and Handels who told me that today at 6:00 P.M. there would be a meeting at 35 Nalewki Street . . . and so at five to six, I arrived at the gate of 35 Nalewki Street. A young man wearing a Jewish hat stood at the gate and waited. He went in first and I followed. We entered a room on the first floor. There was an [empty] *bet midrash* ["house of study," room for the learning of Torah]. From there we passed into an adjoining room that contained a stove. My guide entered the stove and disappeared. I remained standing outside. Immediately I heard a voice: "Come in." Crawling, I entered after him into the stove. From there was an opening leading to the cellar. I descended a rope ladder that seemed never to end. Finally my feet touched ground. I looked around. I saw a clean spacious room well lit by electric lights, with a long table. . . . From the distance came a sound like that of a beautiful choir. The *nigun* [melody] was familiar; it was the *nigun* of the learning of Talmud. I was astonished. Instead of

offering explanations, they brought me into a second *shtibl.*
What my eyes beheld there reminded me of the descriptions of
the *tannaim* [early rabbinic authorities] who learned Torah
in caves, and of the period of the Marranos in Spain [both
groups had to hide in order to practice Judaism]. What lay
before my eyes was completely real. Around a long table in
front of open talmudic tomes sat some twenty young men
learning with desire, intensity, and full mental acumen.
They were focusing on the Tractate of *Nedarim* [vows], folio
52, in the *Ran* [classical commentator on the page] . . . pale
faces, their eyes flashed. . . . They dwelt completely in another
world. The majority of these young fellows were without
parents or families and even without a *rebbe.*[26]

There are many other examples of Jews recreating their Torah
academies. In a Warsaw shoe repair shop sat the remaining elite of
Polish scholars, including the last dean of the famed Yeshivat
Chachmei Lublin and the Piazesne *Rebbe,* who spoke Torah as they
hammered nails into leather. Similarly, in the Kovno ghetto, the
intellectual elite of Lithuanian Jews—Rabbis Elhanan Wasserman
and Abraham Grodzinsky, among others—devoted days and nights to
the study and teaching of Torah. A young woman known as the
"Preacher" of the Vilna ghetto organized fellow teachers and students
of the Beth Jacob schools (a network of religious schools for girls) for
study, prayer, and the saying of psalms. Also, in the Lodz ghetto there
were classes for young women in Torah, the Prophets, and the
theological works of Samson Raphael Hirsch. A group of young
Hasidim in the Cracow ghetto, who retained their traditional ways
completely, refused to join a friend who had passed as a Gentile in the
Aryan sector of the city: "How could we pray and learn there? And
without that, how can we live? And what worth would such a life
have?"[27]

The reported instances of those who created a parallel life of
transcendence rooted in study are impressive. Obviously, however,
only a relatively small number could take this path. A wider
population was able to share through *Shabes* (Yiddish for the
Sabbath), holidays, and prayer in glimpses of transcendence. One
Warsaw woman, in addition to her daily twelve-hour shift in a factory
kitchen, worked extra nights to free herself and a friend from working
on the Sabbath: "No matter what I will not sell *Shabes!*"[28] During the
eight-day joyous festival of Succot in 1940, Rabbi Menaḥem Zemba of
Warsaw built a small *succah* by poking a hole in the roof of his
apartment which he covered with branches. The *succah* signifies the
impermanence of life and the need for reliance on God. Hundreds of
Jews testified to this reliance by visiting Rabbi Zemba's *succah* every
day to sit for a moment and recite the blessings over a small piece of
bread. In the Kovno ghetto, there was no wine for the *seder* (the home
ceremonial meal held on the first two nights of the Passover holiday);
normally, even the poorest Jew was required to sell the shirt off his
back to acquire wine. Rabbi Ephraim Oshry allowed the most

important drink in the ghetto, tea sweetened with saccharin, to be substituted. His students distributed this "wine" so that all could be able to drink the "four cups of liberation."[29] Rivkah Cooper, in her testimony at the Adolf Eichmann trial, concluded, after listing the punishments meted out for observing the Jewish religion in the Cracow ghetto: "With all this we observed *Shabes*, the holidays, prayer, the lighting of the Hannukah *menorah* and the reading of the *Megillah* [scroll recounting the story of Queen Esther's saving of the Persian Jews during the reign of Ahasuerus in the fifth century B.C.E.*] on Purim. We did not pass over any holiday. Quite the opposite—we had the aspiration to guard it as one guards his last glowing coal."[30]

Preservation of the Torah was not only a means of escaping the degradation of daily life in the ghetto. Many believed that their spiritual practices had an ultimate significance. This motif was articulated by Rabbi Nahum Yanchiker, the last dean of the Slabodka Yeshivah, to his students right before the Germans overtook Kovno. He had continued to exhort them in the way of *musar*—the quest for moral and spiritual perfection through introspection and special discipline. The students felt this effort to be incongruous with their new situation. Rabbi Yanchiker demurred:

> Were the world to behave in a fit and proper manner, we here in Slabodka might allow ourselves to ignore the task of moral improvement and withdraw from continual combat against the obstinate arrogance of the evil impulse; but, at this moment when wickedness is so universal who will preserve humanity if not Slabodka?[31]

Rabbi Yanchiker's words were part of the traditional Jewish belief that the Torah was the very purpose of the universe. Without the study and practice of its precepts, the world would return to the primordial chaos that existed at Creation—"and the earth was without form and void; and darkness was on the face of the deep" (Genesis I:2). In the ghetto, many who faced the darkness of the deep sought the light of creation. Rabbi Menaḥem Zemba reminded the religious leadership of Warsaw on Hannukah, 1941, that "even a small cruse of oil, if sufficiently pure, can light the entire world."[32] To this same end, Rabbi Abraham Grodzinsky met weekly with ten advanced disciples, who pledged to pursue the highest levels of righteousness, in order to review their progress. At the same time, scholars wrote new works and buried their manuscripts for future students.

Jews refused to be drawn into the darkness. *Se'udah shelishit*, the third meal eaten at the sunset of the Sabbath day in a mood of great yearning for the divine, was celebrated by a group of young Hasidim in the *Umschlagplatz* (loading platforms) as they awaited deportation from the Warsaw ghetto. Women in all the ghettos risked

* *Before the Common Era; equals B.C.*

their lives to go to the *mikveh* (ritual bath) to preserve the Jewish laws of family purity. A scholar from Nyitra (Nitra, in Czechoslovakia), who made a very modest living from raising chickens, shouted excitedly to a friend from the train as he was deported to a death that he knew awaited him: "Cruelty to animals is prohibited by the Torah! Water and feed the chickens!"[33] These Jews believed that it was not futile to strive for holiness, purity, and moral sensitivity.

In concluding this section, we should again emphasize that the texture of religious life changed in many ways in the ghetto. Few questions, for example, were posed to the rabbis regarding *kashrut* (dietary laws). The reason for this noticeable omission is simple. Meat, fowl, and dairy products eventually were unavailable in the ghetto. *Shehitah* (ritual slaughtering of animals) was also banned by the Nazis, even though slaughterers went to great lengths and considerable risks to provide *kosher* (ritually fit) meat when there were cattle and chickens to kill. For a period of time, several slaughterers were even able to escape the ghetto through a complicated ruse, spend a week at a Polish farm, and return with smuggled meat they had prepared.[34]

The rabbis also performed few divorces. In the ghetto, where people relied upon each other for survival, most reasons to separate seemed rather trivial. In contrast, there were a great many weddings. A large percentage were fake—mother and son or sister and brother— in order to preserve a ration card or other vital papers in a family when a working member died or was deported. Many, however, were quite legitimate. The rabbis welcomed and encouraged marriage as an expression of faith in the future, even when their celebration could, at best, be minimal.

Finally, the rabbis functioned in a judicial capacity. Many Jews continued to take their monetary claims to the traditional *bet din* (court). This court was famed for its impartiality and sense of equity that sought to find a solution all parties could live with. Not all problems involved conflict. Rabbi Oshry, for example, allowed the destitute neighbors of a family that was killed to sell the latter's possessions once he had determined that there were no family heirs in the ghetto.[35]

## *Kiddush ha-Shem* and Survival

*Kiddush ha-Shem* in the ghetto was also defined as the effort to survive. It is worth noting that Polish and Lithuanian Jews, who were either religious or heavily influenced by Jewish tradition, did not surrender. Allowing for the fact that under certain extreme conditions, it may be permitted by Jewish law to kill oneself (an act usually abhorred by Judaism; an intentional suicide could not be buried in a Jewish cemetery), Rabbi Oshry maintained:

Nevertheless, one is certainly not permitted to declare it in public as a clear decision that one may commit suicide in

> such circumstances as through this action support is given to
> our enemies, who many times wondered why the Jews did not
> commit suicide. . . . Such an action is a *hillul ha-Shem*
> [profanation of the Name] because it shows that the Jews do
> not trust in God to save them. . . . It should be noted with
> pride that in the ghetto of Kovno there were no cases of
> suicide save in three instances. All the other inmates of the
> ghetto believed with perfect faith that God would not forsake
> his people. . . .[36]

Rabbis and religious Jews were active in various forms of mutual
aid and rescue attempts. Some also supported revolt in the hope that
this would help to save lives. Rabbis also encouraged their fellow
Jews not to forfeit their lives when it was clearly impossible to observe
certain dictates of Judaism. As one example, the rabbis of Kletzk
(Kletsk, southwest of Minsk) visited each home in the ghetto urging
everyone to report for work the next day, which was Yom Kippur.
Rabbis in the ghetto allowed for Jews to attempt to save themselves by
passing as Christians in seeming violation of Maimonides' (the first
*halakhic* codifier) dictum: "Even if a tyrant tries to compel us by force
to deny Him, we must not obey, but must positively rather submit to
death; and we must not even mislead the tyrant into supposing that
we have denied Him while in our hearts we continue to believe in
Him (exalted be He)."[37] The Holocaust, however, was perceived to be
a radically different situation:

> Maimonides is dealing in a situation where they [the
> Gentiles] know and recognize that he is a Jew, but in order to
> save himself he . . . denies the faith of his fathers. This
> Maimonides forbids. But here where the Gentiles do not
> recognize him and they do not know that he is a Jew—it is
> permissible to fool them with any ruse, even to say that he has
> always been one of them. . .[38]

Rabbis often participated in agonizing life-and-death decisions.
On October 26, 1941, the Kovno *Judenrat* was informed that on
October 28, all ghetto residents were to assemble at Democratic
Square with their work papers. Those found unsuitable for hard
labor were to be taken to "another location." The *Judenrat*
understood this to mean death. It asked the rabbi of the city, Abraham
DovBear Schapiro, whether it should comply or resist. The ill and
aged rabbi had to be revived when he heard this question. After
ascertaining that resistance would be futile and may result in the
death of all, he replied:

> If a decree has been made to destroy the Jewish community,
> and there is the possibility through different ways to rescue a
> portion of them—it is incumbent upon the leadership of the
> community to gather their strength and to fulfill their
> responsibility. They must use all possible means to save those
> they can.[39]

In a somewhat parallel situation, a distinguished rabbi discusses the actions of a man who hid with others in a bunker.[40] A baby started to cry as the Nazis approached. All attempts to quiet the baby proved fruitless. Despite the protests of the others, the man smothered the child. Rabbi Shimon Efrati justified this action. The baby had become the potential cause of the death of them all, including his own.

The tragedy of the Holocaust is revealed in this episode. The Nazis and their collaborators created a situation which in prior Jewish history would have seemed preposterous—a Jewish child in the role of a *rodef* (pursuer) bringing certain destruction upon his family and community.

At this point the interpretation of *kiddush ha-Shem* as the attempt to survive confronts *kiddush ha-Shem* as martyrdom. Rabbi Shimon Efrati, who defended the actions of the man who smothered the baby to save the others, recounts the parallel story of his brother, Rabbi Yitzhak Zevi Efrati. He also hid in a bunker along with his own family and others from his hometown. As the Nazis approached, there too a baby began to cry. Rabbi Yitzhak Zevi refused to let anyone harm the baby. The bunker was discovered by the Germans, who took its inhabitants away to be shot. According to an eyewitness, they went to their death singing with great devotion from Maimonides' principles of faith: "Though the Messiah may tarry, nonetheless I shall wait every day for His arrival."

The two stories mirror each other with different images of tragic irony. It seems impossible to consider one without its twin. Nevertheless, despite our dread, the question is somehow asked: Which was the correct path? In one case, in order to survive, a baby's life was ended. In the other, in order to preserve life, all in the end forfeited their own lives. The first story, under "normal circumstances," would not be considered the preferred path; indeed, the rabbi must defend and justify the action of killing the child. The second story seems to exemplify the "higher" road—dependence upon mercy from heaven even at the last moment. But mercy was not forthcoming. It was not the Jewish people, nor was it the *halakhah*, which created the situation in which such choices had to be made. The choices made were in accordance with the letter of Jewish law and in tune with the deepest spirit of Judaism. One can only acknowledge that here, as in all instances where *halakhah* allows for two different and paradoxical paths: "Both of these are the words of the living God."

## Notes

1. Lev. 22:32.
2. See "The Ghettos," by Yisrael Gutman, in this volume.
3. Italics are author's emphasis. Yehuda Bauer and Nathan Rotenstreich, *The Holocaust as Historical Experience* (New York: Holmes & Meier, 1981), p. 268.

4.   Ísaiah Trunk, *Judenrat* (New York: Stein and Day, 1977), pp. 186-215.

5.   Michael Dov-Ber Weissmandel, *Min ha-Mezar* [Hebrew] (Jerusalem: published by the sons of the author, 1960).

6.   Peter Schindler, *Responses of Hasidic Leaders and Hasidim During the Holocaust* (Ph.D. diss., New York University, 1972).

7.   Irving J. Rosenbaum, *The Holocaust and the Halakhah* (New York: Ktav, 1976); H.J. Zimmels, *The Echo of the Nazi Holocaust in Rabbinic Literature* (New York: Ktav, 1977).

8.   Eliezer Berkovits, *With God in Hell* (New York: Sanhedrin Press, 1979), pp. 49-60.

9.   Moses Maimonides, *Mishneh Torah: Hilkhot Yesodei ha-Torah*, V, 1ff.

10.   Alexander Donat, "Erand in Search of God," *Yalkut Moreshet* 21 (June 1976): 105-138.

11.   Zimmels, *Echo*, p. 250.

12.   Shimon Huberband, *Kiddush ha-Shem: Writings from the Holocaust Period* (Tel Aviv: Zachor, 1969), pp. 27-29.

13.   Huberband, *Kiddush ha-Shem*, p. 32.

14.   Mordekhai Eliav, *Ani Ma'amin* [Hebrew] (Jerusalem: Mossad HaRav Kook, 1965), pp. 26-27.

15.   Eliav, *Ani*, p. 23.

16.   Hillel Seidman, *Diary of the Warsaw Ghetto* (New York: The Jewish Week, 1957), pp. 281-285.

17.   Ephraim Oshry, *Mi-Ma'amakim* II (1963): 28-30.

18.   Eliav, *Ani*, p. 24.

19.   Huberband, *Kiddush ha-Shem*, pp. 94-98.

20.   Chaim A. Kaplan, *The Warsaw Diary of Chaim A. Kaplan*, ed. Abraham I. Katsh (New York: Macmillan Co., 1965), p. 307.

21.   Huberband, *Kiddush ha-Shem*, pp. 114-117.

22.   Huberband, *Kiddush ha-Shem*, pp. 79-82.

23.   Huberband, *Kiddush ha-Shem*, p. 81.

24.   This point was suggested to me by Sybil Milton.

25.   Dov Katz, "Gaon ve Gibor ha-Musar," *Tevunah* 9 (1949): 82.

26.   Samuel K. Mirsky, ed., *Jewish Institutions of Higher Learning in Europe: Their Development and Destruction* (New York: Ogen Publishing House, 1956), p. 361.

27.   Eliav, *Ani*, p. 150.

28.   Seidman, *Diary*, p. 125.

29.   Oshry, *Mi-Ma'amakim* III (1969): 51-55.

30.   Eliav, *Ani*, pp. 108-109.

31.   Joseph Gutferstein, "The Indestructible Dignity of Man: The Last Musar Lecture in Slabodka," *Judaism* 19 (Summer 1970): 262.

32.   Seidman, *Diary*, pp. 281-285.

33.   Weissmandl, *Min ha-Mezar*, p. 32.

34.   Huberband, *Kiddush ha-Shem*, pp. 100-111.

35.   Oshry, *Mi-Ma'amakim* III (1969): 48-50.

36.   Zimmels, *Echo*, p. 85.

37.   Charles Chavel, *Sefer ha-Mitzvoth of Maimonides*, vol. I

(New York: Soncino Press, 1967), pp. 12-13.
   38.   Oshry, *Mi-Ma'amakim V* (1978): 36-50.
   39.   Oshry, *Mi-Ma'amakim V* (1978): 13-24.
   40.   Shimon Efrati, *Mi'gei ha-Haregeah* [Hebrew] (Jerusalem: Yad Vashem, 1961), chapters 1-3.

### For Further Reading

Bauer, Yehuda, and Rotenstreich, Nathan. *The Holocaust as Historical Experience*. New York: Holmes & Meier, 1981.

Efrati, Shimon. *Mi'gei ha-Haregeah*. [Hebrew] Jerusalem: Yad Vashem, 1961.

Eliav, Mordekhai. *Ani Ma'amin*. [Hebrew] Jerusalem: Mossad HaRav Kook, 1963.

Huberband, Shimon. *Kiddush ha-Shem: Writings from the Holocaust Period*. [Hebrew] Tel Aviv: Zachor, 1969.

Kaplan, Chaim A. *The Warsaw Diary of Chaim A. Kaplan*. Edited by Abraham I. Katsch. New York: Macmillan Co., 1965.

Meisels, Zvi Hirsch. *Mekadeshei ha-Shem*. [Hebrew] Vol. 1. Chicago: published by the author, 1955.

Oshry, Ephraim. *Mi-Ma'amakim*. [Hebrew] 5 volumes. New York: 1949, 1963, 1969, 1975, 1978.

Rosenbaum, Irving J. *The Holocaust and Halakhah*. New York: Ktav, 1976.

Schindler, Peter. *Responses of Hasidic Leaders and Hasidim During the Holocaust*. Ph.D. Dissertation, New York University, 1972.

Seidman, Hillel. *Diary of the Warsaw Ghetto*.[Hebrew] New York: The Jewish Week, 1957.

Zimmels, H.J. *The Echo of the Nazi Holocaust in Rabbinic Literature*. New York: Ktav, 1977.

# JEWISH PARTISANS AND RESISTANCE FIGHTERS

This map shows some of the areas in which Jewish resistance fighters were particularly prominent and active in destroying German military stores and communications, and in seizing whole regions from German control.

As well as the Jewish revolts in Ghettoes and Death Camps, many Jews fought in resistance and partisan units throughout Nazi-occupied Europe. Some fought as individuals within local resistance groups, while others formed specifically Jewish units, working closely with local and national underground groups.

FINLAND

SWEDEN
neutral

North Sea

Baltic Sea

S O V I E T

Pskov

U N I O N

GREAT BRITAIN

Berlin ◎

GERMANY

BELGIUM

Mogilev

Vilna

Gomel

P O L A N D

Koniecpol

*NAZI-CONTROLLED EUROPE*

SLOVAKIA

Gorodenka

SWITZ

HUNGARY

FRANCE

Lyons

RUMANIA

Toulouse

YUGOSLAVIA

Black Sea

SPAIN
neutral

I T A L Y

BULGARIA

GREECE

TURKEY
neutral

0    miles  150

0    km  100

GREECE

*FROM PALESTINE*

*Mediterranean Sea*

Areas in which specifically **Jewish** partisan groups attacked and harassed the German occupation forces.

• Thirty-eight of the towns and villages in eastern Europe near which **Jewish** partisan groups were active in the behind-the-lines struggle against the German occupation forces, attacking German troops, cutting railway lines, and forming focal points for local anti-Nazi resistance. Those who were captured were all tortured and shot. Several thousand **Jews** also fought in Soviet and Polish partisan units.

➤ Jewish soldiers from Palestine and Britain who were parachuted *behind* enemy lines, in order to link up with resistance groups.

—·—· European boundaries of 1937.

© Martin Gilbert 1978

# Eastern European Jews in the Partisan Ranks During World War II

## DOV LEVIN

European Jews fought the Nazis in partisan groups in the forests, villages, and other nonurban locales. The terrain included many dense and large forests, wide, marshy swamps, and other inaccessible hideouts. These broad areas, covering thousands of square miles, were mostly conquered in the early stages of the war by the Nazi armies. Some partisan units were under the authority of the Polish government in exile. Most units were connected to the Soviet partisan movement, from whom they received aid, directions, and orders. Finally, they acceded to the Soviet command completely. The military and political activities of these units occasionally brought them near to the largest concentrations of the Jewish population in eastern Europe.

At the outset of the war between Germany and Russia (1941-1942), this population was imprisoned in the ghettos and in the camps. Under these conditions of brutal oppression, and in constant danger of destruction, groups of rebels organized underground units to resist and to fight the Nazis. A prime goal was to bring out large numbers of Jews from the ghettos and camps to join the partisans. Much effort was expended in that direction, but only 30,000 Jews actually succeeded in joining the Soviet partisan movement. These Jews later numbered in their ranks senior officers, outstanding heroes, and many who received decorations. The partisans—with the exception of regular armies—were one of the best known, strongest, and inventive of the European resistance movements, and Jews participated in inflicting damage upon the Nazis. Despite this record, the question must be asked: Why during the Holocaust did proportionately so few Jews join the partisans?

There is no one simple explanation for this phenomenon. Much has to do with the nature of the partisan struggle in eastern Europe that did not allow many to join. There were also specific problems with Jewish participation.

First, it must be emphasized that the Soviet partisan movement arose and operated from military and political necessities. These criteria were decisive in deciding whether to provide refuge for the local population oppressed by the Nazis. In any event, the partisan movement did not, in general, delegate to itself as a special task the rescue of Jews, despite the fact that the latter were the prime candidates for murder by the Nazis. Jews were only allowed in partisan ranks if they could contribute to furthering the goals of the partisan movement. These included: conducting rear-guard actions against the Nazis; terrorism, with all the military force it could generate; operations to diminish the enemy's strength; and conquering territory in preparation for a return to Soviet sovereignty. All of this was coordinated with the regular Soviet army and the political institutions of the Soviet Union. The Nazi occupation government and its collaborators made every effort to wipe out the partisans. They were not particular about the methods they used. They usually executed those suspected of collaborating in the partisan operations. Often they executed the families of suspects after torturing them.

The ammunition and light equipment of the partisan units could not compare with that of the German army and their allies. The partisans, nevertheless, were able to strike hard at their enemies because of their flexibility and mobility, expert knowledge of the terrain, and ethnicity, which permitted them to merge with the local population. Every partisan, moreover, was expected to be battle-experienced, in superb physical shape, patient, trustworthy, and devoted to the cause. These conditions were often waived for a candidate who brought with him a weapon.

In general, the Jews were not good candidates for the partisan ranks. Predominantly urban, they generally lacked several of the essential attributes required of a partisan: military experience, familiarity with the local terrain, typical outer appearance, absolute command of local languages, and other attributes that would promote and facilitate relationships with the villagers, the partisans' most important allies. The Jews also did not have the option of presenting a weapon as a ticket of admission to the partisans. Obtaining and possessing arms was not only personally dangerous, but could lead to reprisals upon their households, relatives, and the entire ghetto.

There were instances when Jews—from the villages, for example—with weapons and with several of the necessary qualifications—succeeded in making it to the forests. Even then, however, they were often compelled to retrace their steps (in the best of circumstances) because of the prevailing situation in the forests. On this point, it is essential to distinguish between two main periods.

During the initial period of partisan activity (1941-1942), the number of units was minimal and military strength was ineffective. The personnel consisted mostly of former Red Army soldiers, who had remained in the forests, and a mixture of farmers and city dwellers, including criminals who found sanctuary in the woods. Their order and discipline were weak, and a significant number were little more than bands of robbers. For example, a large portion of these units was not subservient to the partisan high command, and every local commander operated independently. During this period, Jews who had the necessary qualifications and the desire to join the partisans had no one to whom they could turn, due to the weak and ineffectual partisan movement. Moreover, a number of these partisan units were violently hostile to Jews.

A good example of the prevailing conditions may be seen in the story of Jews of the Tutshin (Tuczyn) ghetto, in the western Ukraine. On September 22, 1942, the German and Ukrainian forces decided to eliminate the ghetto and destroy its inhabitants. The Jews revolted, burned their houses, and used a barrage of gunfire to cover their escape into the nearby forests. At the time of the breakout from the ghetto, approximately 1,000 Jews were killed. Approximately 3,000 Jews reached the forests, where they roamed about, suffering from exposure and hunger. About 300 of them returned to the ghetto and were immediately shot. About 1,000 to 1,500 of the Jews from the ghetto were recaptured in a short time and suffered a fate similar to those who returned. The remainder, among them husbands separated from their families, survived longer. However, most of them were ultimately killed, either when they were robbed or murdered outright, or were informed upon by the virulently antisemitic Ukrainian population. From the entire Jewish community only fourteen people survived. It is no wonder that many Jews preferred to take their chances and remain in the cities rather than escape to the forests.

The partisans underwent a change during the second period of activity—1942-1944. During these years the supreme partisan commander in Russia exerted authority over most partisans in the area, except for Polish and nationalistic Ukrainian units. The local commanders, certified by virtue of their ability, were placed under the jurisdiction of the representatives of the staff of the partisan high command. What is important for this study is that these changes in all phases of the functioning of the units came too late. By then, a significant portion of eastern European Jews had already been murdered. When the Jewish multitudes were still alive, they could not find any partisans to whom they could flee. When partisans would accept them, there were hardly any Jews left to escape and join. While this tragic paradox may be considered as the decisive factor for the nonparticipation of the Jewish populace in the partisan movement, it was not the only one.

The intense, deep-seated hatred of the local population towards the Jews also had a great deal of significance. This hatred expressed itself in the betrayal of the Jews attempting to reach the forests in order to locate the partisans. Jews were alternately robbed, murdered, or turned over to the authorities resulting in their execution.

Closely linked to this hatred were the negative opinions of Jews regularly heard in partisan ranks, whose personnel were often drawn from natives of the area. In addition, many former Soviet soldiers, especially those who escaped from prisoner-of-war camps, were already infected with antisemitic opinions absorbed from Nazi propaganda. Partisans accused their Jewish comrades-in-arms of spoiling their relationship with the local population, thereby causing substantial damage to the cause. Some local commanders and their superiors also had negative opinions about the Jews. Thus, the Jewish partisans suffered not only from persecution and discrimination at the hands of their fellow fighters, but also from the commanders.

Reports of these conditions reached the ghettos and work camps and strengthened the hesitation of individuals and groups to escape into the forests. They struggled over the difficult personal decision to escape the ghetto, thereby abandoning a wife, children, elderly parents, or younger siblings to an unknown fate. Thus, there were individuals and groups in the ghettos who preferred to make a stand at the time of the final Nazi assault, rather than leave for the forests.

However, faced with mass murder and destruction of the ghettos, without even an opportunity for resistance, it became clear to many who hesitated that despite the drawbacks, the partisan-held forest was a real alternative.

A significant phenomena, which blunted antisemitism and presented Jewish fighters with a focus for their organizational and military capabilities, were the Jewish national units. Most were formed in the partisan forests in 1943. These units were composed of determined and highly motivated fighters. They were led by able commanders, almost all of whom had a strong national Jewish consciousness. These Jewish units were imbued with rich Jewish traditions and made extensive use of the Yiddish language. They fostered relations with the Jews in the nearby ghettos, helping them to join the partisans. Ten units totaling about 1,000 individuals were established, including one under the leadership of Abba Kovner, later a leader in Israel's War for Independence and a renowned poet. These units were soon disbanded, with their fighters scattered throughout other units. The reason for this action by the partisan command appears to have been political. Despite the dissolution of the Jewish units, other national units, such as Ukrainians, Russians, Belorussians, Lithuanians, and Moldavians, were allowed to exist until the end of the war.

More effective than the Jewish partisan units was the plan by which Jewish citizens and their families, who had escaped to the forests, were sheltered and maintained. The basic function of the twenty Jewish family camps, which were spread throughout eastern Europe and the western territories of Russia, was to serve as a refuge for thousands of men, women, and children, both individuals and families. The size of the camps varied, from camps of a few families to those with hundreds of families. The two largest family camps were in the dense forests of Belorussia. One was commanded by Tuviah Belski and contained 1,200 Jews; the second was under the command of Shimon Zorin and held 800 people. Army units composed of partisans defended the camps both from Nazi forces that had besieged the forests and from the non-Jewish partisans. An additional function of the units was to locate food for the camps' inhabitants by utilizing partisans' methods. This was accomplished through confiscation by threat or by force. Here it should be mentioned that while farmers were generally ready to allow the seizure of food by non-Jewish partisans, they rebelled against confiscation attempts by the Jewish partisans for their family camps.

Even though the family camps came into existence in scattered locations through Jewish initiative, they eventually became a reality with which the partisan high command had to come to terms. These family camps were an independent and original Jewish response, through which thousands of men and women, old and young, were saved from the enemy and from starvation. In a few cases, Jewish survivors of the ghettos were integrated into nearby partisan units so that they would not have to be sent into the interior regions of Russia.

During the Holocaust, partisan units, in actuality, rescued only a relatively small number of Jews. Yet considering the tremendous losses of the Jewish people and the limited means of escape, we must not belittle any effective rescue. Furthermore, we must not forget that for many Jews the partisan struggle was an end in itself: a contribution to the general anti-Nazi resistance and a personal revenge for the murder of loved ones.

### For Further Reading

Arad, Yitzhak. "Jewish Armed Resistance in Eastern Europe." In *The Catastrophe of European Jewry: Antecedents—History—Reflections*, edited by Yisrael Gutman and Livia Rothkirchen. Jerusalem: Yad Vashem, 1976: 490-517.

Bar-On, Zvi. "The Jews in the Soviet Partisan Movement." Edited by Shaul Esh. *Yad Vashem Studies* IV (1960): 167-190.

Cholavsky, Shalom. "Jewish Partisans: Objective and Subjective Difficulties." In *Jewish Resistance During the Holocaust. Proceedings of the Conference on Manifestations of Jewish Resistance, April 7-11, 1968*, edited by Moshe M. Kohn. Jerusalem: Yad Vashem, 1970.

Friedman, Philip. *"Jewish Resistance to Nazism."* In *Roads to Extinction: Essays on the Holocaust*, edited by Ada June Friedman. Philadelphia: The Jewish Publication Society, 1980, pp. 387-408.

Kahanowitz, Moshe. "Why No Separate Jewish Partisan Movement Was Established During World War II." *Yad Vashem Studies* I (1957): 153-156.

Levin, Dov. "Jews in Soviet Lithuanian Forces in World War II. The Nationality Factor." *Soviet Jewish Affairs* (1973): 57-63.

"Partisans." In *Encyclopedia Judaica*. 13 (1972): 140-144.

# 7

# THE CAMPS

# "Hazak V'Amatz" — "Be Strong and Brave"*

*Rosa Robota from Ciechanow was twenty-one as she watched her family taken to the gas chambers in a selection at Birkenau in November, 1942. Her opportunity to avenge came two years later. Able to make contact with some of the slave laborers, she and a group of girls working with her at the Krupp munitions plant at Auschwitz arranged to smuggle out dynamite to the resistance organization in the camp. Hiding the little wheels of explosives in their bosoms or in special packets they had sewn into the hems of their dresses, the material was passed to a Russian prisoner of war, Borodin, who converted them into bombs. Some of the girls were caught and hanged. But the smuggling went on. Then, on October 7, 1944, everyone at Auschwitz heard and saw something unbelievable—one of the crematoria, in which the bodies of so many of their mothers, fathers, and young had been burned, was blown to pieces. Five SS men were killed. As the flames burst forth, more than 600 people escaped—most were hunted down and shot in a few days. In an investigation that led to the arrest of Rosa, the SS used all their sadistic methods of torture on her. She betrayed no one. Her last words scribbled on a piece of paper just before she was hanged in front of the assembled inmates at Auschwitz were* "Hazak V'Amatz"—"Be Strong and Brave."

* An account of this story may be found in "Rosa Robota—Heroine of the Auschwitz Underground," in Yuri Suhl, ed. and trans., They Fought Back: The Story of the Jewish Resistance in Nazi Europe (New York: Crown, 1967), pp. 219-225.

# THE CONCENTRATION CAMPS

Between 1939 and 1945, six million unarmed and innocent Jewish civilians - men, women, children and babies - were murdered in Nazi-controlled Europe, as part of a deliberate policy to destroy all traces of Jewish life and culture. As many as two million of these were killed in their own towns and villages, some confined in ghettoes where death by slow starvation was a deliberate Nazi policy, others taken to be shot at mass-murder sites near where they lived. The remaining four million Jews were forced from their homes and taken by train to distant concentration camps, where they were murdered by being worked to death, starved to death, beaten to death, shot, or gassed.

North Sea

Vaivara

Klooga
ESTONIA

LATVIA

LITHUANIA

U S S R

Stutthof

Neuengamme
Bergen - Belsen
Sachsenhausen
Ravensbrück
Chelmno
Treblinka
POLAND

Mittelbau Dora
Buchenwald
Gross Rosen
Sobibor
Auschwitz
Maidanek

GERMANY
Flossenberg
C Z E C H O S L O V A K I A
Plaszow
Belzec

Natzweiler
FRANCE
Dachau
Mauthausen
AUSTRIA
HUNGARY
RUMANIA

Gospič
Jasenovac
YUGOSLAVIA
Sajmište

Adriatic Sea

ITALY

Among the hundreds of thousands of non-Jews sent by the Nazis to concentration camps were anti-Nazis, Jehovah's Witnesses, homosexuals, the mentally ill, and the chronically sick. In addition, more than 250,000 Gypsies were murdered, in a Nazi attempt to eliminate Gypsies as well as Jews from the map of Europe.

**Auschwitz** concentration camp in which more than 2 *million* people were murdered between 1941 and 1944, including Jews, Gypsies, and Soviet prisoners-of-war.

Camps set up solely for the murder of Jews.

Other camps in which Jews and non-Jews were put to forced labour, starved, tortured, and murdered in conditions of the worst imaginable cruelty. Most of these camps had "satellite" labour camps nearby.

In many of the camps shown here so-called "medical" experiments were carried out, without anaesthetics, solely to satisfy the curiosity and sadism of the doctors. Hundreds of otherwise healthy "patients" were tortured and murdered during these experiments.

0    100 miles
0    100 km

© Martin Gilbert 1978

# The Nazi Camps*

## HENRY FRIEDLANDER

The Nazis established camps for their political and ideological opponents as soon as they seized power in 1933, and they retained them as an integral part of the Third Reich until their defeat in 1945. During the 1930s, these concentration camps were at first intended for political enemies, but later also included professional criminals, social misfits, other undesirables, and Jews.

During World War II, the number of camps expanded greatly and the number of prisoners increased enormously. Opponents from all occupied countries entered the camps, and the camps were transformed into an empire for the exploitation of slave labor. Late in 1941 and early in 1942, the Nazis established extermination camps to kill the Jews, and also Russian POWs and Gypsies. These camps had only one function: the extermination of large numbers of human beings in specially designed gas chambers. The largest Nazi camp, Auschwitz-Birkenau, combined the functions of extermination and concentration camp; there, healthy Jews were selected for labor and, thus, temporarily saved from the gas chambers. In this way, small numbers of Jews survived in Auschwitz and other Eastern camps. In 1944-1945, as the need for labor increased, surviving Jews were introduced into all camps, including those located in Germany proper.

In the United States, the term "death camp" has frequently been used to describe both concentration and extermination camps. It has been applied to camps like Auschwitz and Treblinka—killing centers where human beings were exterminated on the assembly line. But it has also been applied without distinction to camps like Dachau and Belsen—concentration camps without gas chambers, where the prisoners were killed by abuse, starvation, and disease.

## The Nazi Concentration Camps Before World War II

Six Nazi concentration camps existed on German soil before World War II: Dachau, near Munich; Sachsenhausen, in Oranienburg near Berlin; Buchenwald, on the Ettersberg overlooking Weimar; Flossenbürg, in northern Bavaria; Mauthausen, near Linz in Austria; and the women's camp Ravensbrück, north of Berlin. Other camps like Esterwegen, Oranienburg, or Columbia Haus had existed for a few years, but only the permanent six had survived; they had replaced all other camps. Dachau opened in 1933, Sachsenhausen in 1936, Buchenwald in 1937, Flossenbürg and

---

* Prior to reading this article, it is useful to read "The SS and Police," by Henry Friedlander, in this volume.

Mauthausen in 1938, and Ravensbrück in 1939.

These camps, officially designated *Konzentrationslager* or KL, and popularly known as Kazet or KZ, were originally designed to hold actual or potential political opponents of the regime. A special decree had removed the constitutional prohibition against arbitrary arrest and detention, permitting the political police—the Gestapo—to impose "protective custody" *(Schutzhaft)* without trial or appeal. The protective custody prisoners—mostly Communists and Socialists, but sometimes also liberals and conservatives—were committed to the camps for an indefinite period. The camps, removed from the control of the regular prison authorities, were not run by the Gestapo; instead, they were administered and guarded by the Death Head Units of the black-shirted SS *(Schutzstaffel)*, a private Nazi party army fulfilling an official state function.

Reich Leader of the SS Heinrich Himmler appointed Theodor Eicke as Inspector of the Concentration Camps and Commander of the Death Head Units. Eicke had been Commandant of Dachau; he had built it into the "model camp." Eliminating unauthorized private murders and brutalities, he had systematized terror and inhumanity, training his SS staff and guards to be disciplined and without compassion. From the prisoners, Eicke demanded discipline, obedience, hard labor, and "manliness"; conversion to Nazi ideology was neither expected nor desired. Eicke issued rules that regulated every area of camp life and that imposed severe punishments for the least infraction. His petty rules were a perversion of the draconic training system of the Prussian army. This system accounted for the endless roll calls (the *Appell*), the introduction of corporal punishment (the *Pruegelstrafe*), and the long hours of enforced calisthenics. The SS added special refinements to this torture: suspending prisoners from trees, starving them in the camp prison (the *Bunker*), and shooting them while "trying to escape." In this system, labor was only another form of torture.

When Eicke became Inspector, he imposed the Dachau system on all concentration camps. Every camp had the same structure; every camp was divided into the following six departments:

1. The *Kommandantur*. This was the office of the commandant, a senior SS officer (usually a colonel or lieutenant-colonel and sometimes even a brigadier general) assisted by the office of the adjutant. He commanded the entire camp, including all staff, guards, and inmates.

2. The Administration. The administrative offices were charged with overseeing the camp's economic and bureaucratic affairs. Junior SS officers directed various subdepartments, such as those for supply, construction, or inmate properties.

3. The Camp Physician. This office was headed by the garrison physician and included SS medical officers and SS medical orderlies. The camp physician served the medical needs of the SS staff and guards; he also supervised medical treatment and sanitary conditions for the inmates.

4. The Political Department. This office was staffed by SS police

officers (not members of the Death Head Units), who were assigned to the camps to compile the dossiers of the prisoners and to investigate escapes and conspiracies. They took their orders from both the commandant and the Gestapo.

5. The Guard Troops. These were the military units assigned to guard the camp. Quartered in barracks and trained for combat, they served under their own SS officers. They manned the watch towers and the outer camp perimeter. Officially, they had contact with the prisoners only when they accompanied labor brigades as guards.

6. The *Schutzhaftlager*. The protective custody camp was the actual camp for the prisoners; surrounded by electrified barbed wire, it occupied only a small fraction of the entire camp territory. It was headed by a junior SS officer (captain or major) as protective custody camp leader. He was assisted by the senior SS noncommissioned officer; this roll call leader *(Rapportführer)* supervised the day-by-day running of the camp. Under him, various SS men served as block leaders in charge of individual prisoner barracks and as commando leaders in charge of individual labor brigades.

The SS hierarchy of the protective custody camp was duplicated by appointed inmate functionaries. But while the SS were always called "leader" *(Führer)*, the inmate functionaries were called "elders" *(Aeltester)*. The chief inmate functionary, for example, was the camp elder, corresponding to the SS roll call leader. The functionary corresponding to the block leader was the block elder, who was in charge of a single barrack. He was assisted by room orderlies, the so-called *Stubendienst*. The functionary corresponding to the commando leader was the *kapo* in charge of a single labor brigade. He was assisted by prisoner foremen, the *Vorarbeiter*. In large labor brigades with several *kapos*, the SS also appointed a supervising *kapo (Oberkapo)*. (The unusual title *kapo*, or *capo*, meaning head, was probably introduced into Dachau by Italian workers employed in Bavaria for road construction during the 1930s. During World War II popular camp language, especially as spoken by non-German inmates, transformed *kapo* into a generic term for all inmate functionaries.) In addition, inmate clerks, known as *Schreiber*, performed a crucial task. The camp clerk assisted the roll call leader and supervised the preparation of all reports and orders. Clerks also served in labor brigades, the inmate infirmary, and various SS offices.

Until 1936-1937, the prisoners in the concentration camps were mostly political "protective custody prisoners" committed to the camps by the Gestapo. At that time, the category of "preventive arrest" *(polizeiliche Vorbeugungshaft)* was added to that of "protective custody." The Criminal Police, the Kripo, and not the Gestapo, thereafter sent large numbers of "preventive arrest prisoners" to the camps. These included the so-called professional criminals *(Berufsverbrecher)*. They were rounded up on the basis of lists previously prepared; later, the police simply transferred persons who had been convicted of serious crimes to the camps after they had served their regular prison terms. The Gestapo and Kripo also used preventive and protective arrest to incarcerate the so-called asocials, a group that included Gypsies, vagabonds, shirkers, prostitutes, and any person the police thought unfit for civilian society. Finally, the Gestapo sent to the camps those whose failure to conform posed a possible threat to national unity; this included homosexuals as well as Jehovah's Witnesses.

In the concentration camps, the inmates lost all individuality and were known only by their number. Shorn of their hair and dressed in prison stripes, they wore their number stitched to their outer garment (during the war in Auschwitz non-German prisoners usually had this number tattooed on their forearm). In addition, the arrest category of each prisoner was represented under his number by a color-coded triangle. The most common were: red for political prisoners, green for professional criminals, black for asocials, pink for homosexuals, and purple for Jehovah's Witnesses. Inmate functionaries wore armbands designating their office. The SS used mostly "greens" for the important offices, but during the war the "reds" often replaced them and in some camps even non-German inmates were appointed *kapos* and block elders.

Before 1938, Jews usually entered the camps only if they also belonged to one of the affected categories. In the aftermath of the *Kristallnacht* in November, 1938, the police rounded up the first large wave of Jewish men. Approximately 35,000 Jews thus entered the camp system, but most were released when their families were able to produce valid immigration papers for them.

In 1938, after the roundups of criminals, asocials, Jews, and Jehovah's Witnesses, and after the waves of arrests in Austria and the Sudetenland, the camp population reached its highest point for the prewar years. But after the release of large numbers, it sank again to approximately 25,000 by the summer of 1939.

# The Nazi Concentration Camps During World War II

World War II brought substantial changes to the Nazi concentration camp system. Large numbers of prisoners flooded the camps from all occupied countries of Europe. Often entire groups were committed to the camps; for example, members of the Polish professional classes were rounded up as part of the "General Pacification Operation" and members of the resistance were rounded up throughout western Europe under the "Night and Fog Decree." To accommodate these prisoners, new camps were established: in 1940, Auschwitz in Upper Silesia and Neuengamme in Hamburg; in 1941, Natzweiler in Alsace and Gross-Rosen in Lower Silesia; in 1942, Stutthof near Danzig; in 1943, Lublin-Maidanek in eastern Poland and Vught in Holland; in 1944, Dora-Mittelbau in Saxony and Bergen-Belsen near Hanover.

By 1942, the concentration camp system had begun to develop into a massive slave labor empire. Already in 1939, the SS had established its own industries in the concentration camps. These included the quarries at Mauthausen, the Gustloff armament works at Buchenwald, and a textile factory at Ravensbrück. During the war this trend continued; every camp had SS enterprises attached to it: forging money and testing shoes at Sachsenhausen, growing plants and breeding fish at Auschwitz, and producing fur coats at Maidanek. In addition, the SS rented out prisoners for use as slave labor by German industries. The prisoners were worked to death on meagre rations while the SS pocketed their wages: Both SS and industry profited. I.G. Farben established factories in Auschwitz for the production of synthetic oil and rubber; Dora-Mittelbau was established to serve the subterranean factories of central Germany. However, the largest expansion came with the creation of numerous subsidiary camps, the *Aussenkommandos*. For example, Dachau eventually had 168 and Buchenwald 133 subsidiary camps. Some of these—like Mauthausen's Gusen—became as infamous as their mother camp. The growing economic importance of the camps forced a reorganization. Early in 1942, the Inspectorate of the Concentration Camps, previously an independent SS agency, was absorbed by the agency directing the SS economic empire. It bcame Department D of the SS Central Office for Economy and Administration (SS *Wirtschafts-Verwaltungshauptamt*, or WVHA); chief of WVHA Oswald Pohl became the actual master of the camps.

After 1939, the concentration camps were no longer the only camps for the administrative incarceration of the enemies of the regime. They lost their exclusivity to a variety of new institutions: ghettos, transit camps, and different types of labor camps. In eastern Europe, the German administration resurrected the medieval ghetto, forcing the Jews to live and work behind barbed wire in specially designated city districts. These ghettos served as temporary reservations for the exploitation of Jewish labor; eventually everyone was deported and most were immediately killed.

The Germans did not establish ghettos in central or western Europe, but a variety of camps existed in most occupied countries of the West. In France, camps appeared even before the German conquest. There the French government incarcerated Spanish Republican refugees and members of the International Brigade. After the declaration of war, these camps received large numbers of other aliens: Jewish and non-Jewish anti-Nazi German and Austrian refugees; Polish and Russian Jews; Gypsies and "vagabonds." The largest of these camps was Gurs, in the foothills of the Pyrenees; others included Compiègne, Les Milles, Le Vernet, Pithiviers, Rivesaltes, and St. Cyprien. After the German conquest, these camps were maintained by the French and the inmates were eventually deported to Germany or Poland.

Most Jews from western Europe went through transit camps that served as staging areas for the deportations to the East: Drancy in France, Malines (Mechelen) in Belgium, and Westerbork in Holland. Theresienstadt, established in the Protectorate of Bohemia and Moravia, served the dual function of transit camp and "model" ghetto.

Captured Allied soldiers found their way into POW camps: the Oflags for officers and the Stalags for the ranks. Their treatment depended in part on the status of their nation in the Nazi racial scheme. Allied soldiers captured in the West, even Jews, were treated more or less as provided by the Geneva Convention. Allied soldiers captured in the East, however, did not receive any protection from international agreements. Camps for Red Army POWs were simply cages where millions died of malnutrition and exposure. Prisoners identified as supporters of the Soviet system—commissars, party members, intellectuals, and all Jews—were turned over by the *Wehrmacht* to the SS Security Police, who either shot them or sent them to concentration camps.

Labor camps had appeared immediately after the start of the war. Hinzert in the Rhineland was opened for German workers and was later transformed into a Buchenwald subsidiary for former German members of the French Foreign Legion. Similar camps appeared in Germany for workers imported from the East *(Ostarbeiter)* and in most European countries for a variety of indentured workers, such as those for Jews in Hungary.

Most important were the Forced Labor Camps for Jews in the East. Hundreds of these camps, ranging from the very small to the very large, were established in Poland, the Baltic states, and the occupied territories of the Soviet Union. These forced labor camps were not part of the concentration camp system, and they were not supervised by WVHA. Instead, they were operated by the local SS and Police Leaders, Himmler's representatives in the occupied territories. While executive authority rested with the SS Security Police, the camps could be run by any German national: police officers, military officers, or civilian foremen. Although the supervisors were always German, the guards were usually non-German troops. Some of these were racial Germans *(Volksdeutsche)*, but most were Ukrainians, Latvians, and other eastern European nationals recruited as SS auxiliaries.

Conditions varied from labor camp to labor camp. Some were tolerable and others resembled the worst concentration camps. Like the Jews in the ghettos, those in the labor camps were eventually deported and killed; some labor camps, like Janowska in Lemberg, also served as places for mass executions. Only a few camps, economically valuable for the SS, remained in operation. In late 1943, WVHA seized them from the SS and Police Leaders and turned them into regular concentration camps: Plaszow near Cracow in Poland, Kovno in Lithuania, Riga-Kaiserwald in Latvia, Klooga and Vaivara in Estonia; other camps, like Radom, became subsidiaries of these or older concentration camps.

World War II also changed the function of the concentration camp system. On the one hand, it became a large empire of slave labor, but on the other, it became the arena for mass murder. During the war, persons sentenced to death without the benefit of judicial proceedings were taken to the nearest concentration camp and shot.

Large numbers of inmates no longer able to work were killed through gas or lethal injections. Thousands of Russian POWs were killed in the concentration camps, while millions of Jews were systematically gassed in Auschwitz and Maidanek.

In 1943 and 1944, large numbers of Jews entered the concentration camp system. Many had been selected for labor upon arrival at Auschwitz; others had been prisoners in labor camps and ghettos that were transformed into concentration camps. These Jewish prisoners were retained only in the East. Germany itself was to remain free of Jews, and this included the camps located on German soil. But as the front lines advanced upon the Reich and the need for labor increased, Jewish prisoners were introduced into all camps, including those located in Germany proper. Eventually, Jews made up a large proportion of inmates in all concentration camps.

The end of the war brought the collapse of the concentration camp system. The approach of the Allied armies during the winter of 1944-1945 forced the evacuation of exposed camps. The SS transported all prisoners into the interior of the Reich, creating vast overcrowding. On January 15, 1945, the camp population exceeded 700,000. Unable to kill all the inmates, the SS evacuated them almost in sight of the advancing Allies. Inmates suffered and died during the long journeys in overcrowded cattle cars; without provisions and exposed to the cold, many arrived at their destination without the strength necessary to survive. Others were marched through the snow; those who collapsed were shot and left on the side of the road.

As the Russians approached from the East and the Anglo-Americans from the West, cattle cars and marching columns crisscrossed the shrinking territory of the Third Reich. The forced evacuations often became death marches; they took a terrible toll in human lives, killing perhaps one-third of all inmates before the end. Even camps like Bergen-Belsen, not intended for extermination, became a death trap for thousands of inmates. Thus, the Allies found mountains of corpses when they liberated the surviving inmates in April and May, 1945.

## The Nazi Extermination Camps

In 1941, Hitler decided to kill the European Jews and ordered the SS to implement this decision. After the invasion of Russia, special SS operational units, the *Einsatzgruppen*, killed Communist functionaries, Gypsies, and all Jews. These mobile killing units roamed through the countryside in the occupied territories of the Soviet Union, rounding up their victims, executing them, and burying them in mass graves. The units consisted of members of the Security Police and of the SS Security Service, recruited for this purpose by Reinhard Heydrich and his Central Office for Reich Security *(Reichsicherheitshauptamt,* or RSHA). They were supported by units of the German uniformed police and they used native troops whenever possible; local Lithuanian, Latvian,

Estonian, and Ukrainian units participated in these massacres whenever possible. To increase efficiency, the Technical Department of RSHA developed a mobile gas van, which was used to kill Jewish women and children in Russia and Serbia. But the troops did not like these vans; they often broke down on muddy roads.

The *Einsatzgruppen* killings were too public. Soldiers and civilians watched the executions, took photographs, and often turned these massacres into public spectacles. The killings also demanded too much from the SS troops. They found the job of shooting thousands of men, women, and children too bloody. Some were brutalized; some had nervous breakdowns. To maintain secrecy and discipline, the SS leaders searched for a better way. They found the perfect solution in the extermination camps, where gas chambers were used to kill the victims. These killing centers were installations established for the sole purpose of mass murder; they were factories for the killing of human beings.

Murder by gas chamber was first introduced in the so-called Euthanasia program. Late in 1939, Hitler ordered the killing of the supposedly incurably ill. The program was administered by the Führer Chancellery, which established for this purpose the Utilitarian Foundation for Institutional Care, whose headquarters was located in Berlin at Tiergartenstrasse 4 and was known as T4. The victims (the mentally ill, the retarded, the deformed, the senile, and at times also those with diseases then considered incurable), chosen by boards of psychiatrists on the basis of questionnaires, were transferred to six institutions—Bernburg, Brandenburg, Grafeneck, Hadamar, Hartheim, and Sonnenstein—where specially constructed gas chambers were used to kill the patients. This radical ideological experiment in murder involved German nationals, and public protests forced the Nazi leadership to abort it in 1941. However, the program continued for adults and particularly for children on a smaller scale throughout the war, especially for the murder of ill concentration camp prisoners under the code designation 14f13.

Killing centers using gas chambers appeared late in 1941. In western Poland, the governor of the annexed area known as the Wartheland established a small but highly efficient killing center at Kulmhof (Chelmno) for the extermination of the Lodz Jews. A special SS commando, formerly occupied with killing mental patients in East Prussia, operated the installation. Using gas vans and burning the bodies, the commando killed at least 150,000 persons. In eastern Poland, the Lublin SS and Police Leader Odilo Globocnik headed the enterprise known as Operation Reinhard. Its object was to concentrate, pillage, deport, and kill the Jews of occupied Poland. He established three extermination camps: Belzec, Sobibor, and Treblinka. To operate these killing centers, he requested the services of the T4 operatives. A number of these, including the Kripo officer Christian Wirth, traveled to Lublin to apply their know-how to the murder of the Jews. Augmented by SS and police recruits with backgrounds similar to those of the T4 personnel, and aided by Ukrainian auxiliaries serving as guards, they staffed the extermination camps and, under the overall direction of Wirth, ran them with unbelievable efficiency.

Belzec opened in March, 1942, and closed in January, 1943. More than 600,000 persons were killed there. Sobibor opened in May, 1942, and closed one day after the rebellion of the inmates on October 14, 1943. At least 250,000 persons were killed there. Treblinka, the largest of the three killing centers, opened in July, 1942. A revolt of the inmates on August 2, 1943, destroyed most of the camp, and it finally closed in November, 1943. Between 700,000 and 900,000 persons were killed there. These three camps of Operation Reinhard served only the purpose of mass murder. Every man, woman, and child arriving there was killed. Most were Jews, but a few were Gypsies. A few young men and women were not immediately killed. Used to service the camp, they sorted the belongings of those murdered and burned the bodies in open air pits. Eventually they, too, were killed. Very few survived. Kulmhof and Belzec had only a handful of survivors. Sobibor and Treblinka, where the above-mentioned revolts permitted some to escape, had about thirty to forty survivors.

The method of murder was the same in all three camps (and similar in Kulmhof). The victims arrived in cattle wagons and the men were separated from the women and children. Forced to undress, they had to hand over all their valuables. Naked, they were driven towards the gas chambers, which were disguised as shower rooms and used carbon monoxide from a motor to kill the victims. The bodies were burned after their gold teeth had been extracted. The massive work of mass murder was accomplished by unusually small staffs. Figures differ (approximately 100 Germans and 500 Ukrainians in the three camps of Operation Reinhard), but all agree that very few killed multitudes.

Thus, mass murder was first instituted in camps operated outside the concentration camp system by local SS leaders. But the concentration camps soon entered the field of mass murder, eventually surpassing all others in speed and size. The largest killing operation took place in Auschwitz, a regular concentration camp administered by WVHA. There Auschwitz Commandant Rudolf Hoess improved the method used by Christian Wirth, substituting crystalized prussic acid—known by the trade name Zyklon B—for carbon monoxide. In September, 1941, an experimental gassing, killing about 250 ill prisoners and about 600 Russian POWs, proved the value of Zyklon B. In January, 1942, systematic killing operations, using Zyklon B, commenced with the arrival of Jewish transports from Upper Silesia. These were soon followed without interruption by transports of Jews from all occupied countries of Europe.

The Auschwitz killing center was the most modern of its kind. The SS built the camp at Birkenau, also known as Auschwitz II. There, they murdered their victims in newly constructed gas chambers, and burned their bodies in crematoria constructed for this purpose. A postwar court described the killing process:

Prussic acid fumes developed as soon as Zyklon B pellets

seeped through the opening into the gas chamber and came into contact with the air. Within a few minutes, these fumes agonizingly asphyxiated the human beings in the gas chamber. During these minutes horrible scenes took place. The people who now realized that they were to die an agonizing death screamed and raged and beat their fists against the locked doors and against the walls. Since the gas spread from the floor of the gas chamber upward, small and weakly people were the first to die. The others, in their death agony, climbed on top of the dead bodies on the floor, in order to get a little more air before they too painfully choked to death. [21 JuNSV 428]

More than two million victims were killed in this fashion in Auschwitz-Birkenau. Most of them were Jews, but others also died in its gas chambers: Gypsies, Russian POWs, and ill prisoners of all nationalities.

Unlike the killing centers operated by Globocnik and Wirth, Auschwitz combined murder and slave labor. RSHA ran the deportations and ordered the killings; WVHA ran the killing installations and chose the workers. From the transports of arriving Jews, SS physicians "selected" those young and strong enough to be used for forced labor. They were temporarily saved.

Those chosen for forced labor were first quarantined in Birkenau and then sent to the I. G. Farben complex Buna-Monowitz, also known as Auschwitz III, or to one of its many subsidiary camps. Periodically, those too weak to work were sent to Birkenau for gassing from every camp in the Auschwitz complex; they were simply replaced by new and stronger prisoners.

A similar system was applied in Lublin-Maidanek, another WVHA concentration camp with a killing operation. But it closed much earlier than Auschwitz; it was liberated by the Red Army in the summer of 1944. Auschwitz continued to operate even after all other extermination camps had ceased to function. But when the war appeared lost, Himmler ordered the gassings stopped in November, 1944. Only a few hundred thousand Jews survived as slave laborers in Auschwitz and other concentration camps. Those who survived the evacuation marches of early 1945 were liberated by the Allied armies.

### For Further Reading

Broszat, Martin. "National Socialist Concentration Camps." In *Anatomy of the SS State,* by Helmut Krausnick et al. London: Collins, 1968.

Friedlander, Henry. "The Nazi Concentration Camps." In *Human Responses to the Holocaust,* edited by Michael Ryan. New York and Toronto: Edwin Mellen Press, 1981.

Kogon, Eugen. *The Theory and Practice of Hell.* New York: Farrar, Straus & Giroux, 1950.

Sereny, Gitta. *Into That Darkness.* New York: McGraw-Hill, 1974.

# Surviving

## HENRY FRIEDLANDER AND SYBIL MILTON

The Nazis killed almost six million Jews; only a few hundred thousand survived the ghettos and camps of Nazi-dominated Europe. From the beginning, survival was a matter of pure chance; the Jews did not control their own fate. Those caught in the machine of destruction—roundups and deportations—could do nothing to alter their fate. At that point, survival depended on two factors: luck and the ability to do hard labor.

Pure chance—what we may call luck—governed survival at the crucial point where the victims entered the world of camps and executions. There, survival was virtually impossible in any of the following situations:

1. Roundups by the SS *Einsatzgruppen*. Practically every Jew caught by these SS mobile killing units in the occupied territories of the Soviet Union was killed. There was virtually no possibility of escape once the roundup had been completed.

2. Deportation to the camps of Belzec, Chelmno, Sobibor, and Treblinka. Almost all Jews arriving at these extermination camps were killed. There was almost no chance to survive. From Belzec and Chelmno, only five persons are known to have survived; from Sobibor and Treblinka, where revolts took place, less than one hundred survived the war.

Thus, the chances for survival were often determined by the pure chance of geography. Few Jews from Denmark, Italy, or Bulgaria perished; even large numbers of Rumanian Jews survived. In contrast, almost all Jews were killed in Holland and Poland. In these countries, the chances for survival depended on factors outside the control of the victims; the degree of German control (direct rule in Poland, as opposed to indirect rule in Vichy France); the nature of German administration (rule by the SS in the *Ostland* [the Baltic states and Belorussia] as opposed to military administration in Belgium); the attitude of local governments (hostility towards Jews in Croatia as opposed to refusal to harm them in Bulgaria); the availability of escape routes (the proximity to Sweden in Denmark and the distance from any neutral country in Holland).

The logistics of the deportations also determined one's ability to stay alive. Those deported to Auschwitz, where the able-bodied were selected for labor, had a chance to live. Those deported to the other extermination camps, where no such selections took place, had no chance to survive. Few German Jews deported to Lodz or Minsk survived; a somewhat larger proportion of those deported to Riga escaped death.

The date of the deportations also influenced the chances of survival. Those deported later in the war had a better chance to live, since they had fewer years to spend in the camps, and conditions improved slightly as the Germans needed labor for their war industries. In Auschwitz, few Jews deported from Slovakia in 1942 survived, while a somewhat larger number of Jews deported from Hungary in 1944 lived to see liberation.

Even Jews with a chance for survival faced enormous odds. Those arriving in Auschwitz had to undergo a "selection" on the railroad platform known as the *Rampe*. SS physicans "selected" those able to work, sending all others to their death in the gas chambers. Similar selections of those able to work took place elsewhere. Again, chance governed survival. Entire categories of people were automatically sent to the gas chambers: children, mothers with small children, old people, and invalids. The remainder had a chance to survive the selection process. Still, even for the young and able, various extraneous factors influenced survival: health (a temporary illness could be a death sentence); size (the tall had a better chance than the short); strength (weakness led to rejection and thus death); and, as always, luck.

Only those selected to work in Auschwitz or other concentration camps could, in a small way, influence their eventual fate. Even here, chance (or the whim of the Germans) played its role: Higher authorities could decide to kill entire labor brigades, or epidemics could kill entire barracks. But those lucky enough to escape those dangers had a chance to survive. For them a number of factors influenced survival:

1. Physical strength. The camp inmates had to perform hard labor under adverse conditions; this favored those with the physical strength to endure. And those with physical strength were then rewarded with better treatment because they were stronger.

2. Special skills. Those with training as craftsmen—masons, plumbers, electricians, and the like—were able to join favored labor brigades with better conditions. The same applied to physicians. Most other professions—lawyers, accountants, and historians, for example—received no special consideration. However, the SS, preoccupied with the preparation of reports, valued persons with the ability to do calligraphy.

3. The ability to speak German. Those able to communicate with the SS and the German *kapos* had a better chance to be chosen for jobs and functions. The ability at least to understand German commands was crucial, since the failure to follow orders could be fatal. Thus, Jews from countries where neither German nor Yiddish was spoken were at a great disadvantage. This was particularly true for those from Greece or Italy.

4. The ability to withstand the climate of Poland. The location of many of the camps was important. Jews from Poland or Slovakia, used to the cold climate, had a far better chance to survive than Jews from Salonica, who were used to the mild climate of the Mediterranean.

5. Membership in a group. In the camps, the lone individual had less of a chance to survive than the member of a group that extended aid to its members. Thus, the prisoner could get help from his political party (Communist or Socialist), his religious group (Jehovah's Witnesses and Jews), national unit (Poles and the French),

or family.

These factors were all actually outside of the control of the victim. No one could change his or her physical strength, acquire a skill overnight, learn languages immediately, get used to climates, or join a group without a great deal of time. But there was no time available. One technique for survival, however, could be learned: the will to survive. Those determined to survive, and willing to make all the needed adjustments through compromise and adaptation, had a chance to survive if all other factors—luck and skills—were also in their favor.

### For Further Reading

*Apart from individual memoirs, three volumes deal with the broad issues of survival:*

Bettelheim, Bruno. *Surviving and Other Essays.* New York: Alfred A. Knopf, 1979.

Cohen, Elie. *Human Behavior in the Concentration Camp.* New York: W. W. Norton, 1953.

Des Pres, Terrence. *The Survivor: An Anatomy of Life in the Death Camps.* New York: Pocket Books, 1977.

# Life in the Camps: The Psychological Dimension

## SHERYL ROBBIN

A perennial question in discussions of the concentration camps is: How did anyone survive? Survivors have written accounts describing their own experiences. Most of them indicate, as previously detailed in the above article "Surviving," by Henry Friedlander and Sybil Milton, that chance played a major role in individual survival. We must also take into consideration that if liberation would have been significantly delayed, very few would have survived at all. Yet, between chance and liberation, what psychological mechanisms were people able to mobilize for their own defense? Any answer requires an understanding of the conditions and the nature of the assault against the incarcerated victims. We must remember that conditions in concentration camps differed and the experiences of the inmates varied depending on the date and their origin.

The assault upon the inmates commenced before arrival at the camp itself. After experiencing the traumatic occurrences of the Nazi occupation, the individuals were then uprooted from familiar surroundings, to be deported to an unknown location.[1] After an exhausting trip, typically lasting several days, packed in railroad cars like cattle and deprived of adequate food and water, they arrived at the camp. Later in the war, some inmates arrived after a forced march on foot.

Upon arrival, they were immediately intimidated by the SS and their savage dogs, and by hardened *kapos*. Many of those at the extermination camps were immediately taken to the gas chambers;[2] others often were beaten or witnessed violence, even murder, inflicted upon fellow inmates. Whatever comfort was derived from being together with family or friends was now lost as they were separated into different groups.

The inmates were first stripped of all their material possessions, including the clothes off their backs. Naked, they were physically searched to see if money or jewelry were hidden in any part of the bodily orifices. Shaved of all bodily hair, they were then given showers at extreme temperatures. Afterwards, they were provided with ill-fitting, often tattered, clothes. Many new inmates were also subjected to beatings.[3] Women faced possible sexual abuse. It was also at this point that veteran inmates, who usually had little comforting news to offer, were met for the first time.

Another part of the dehumanization process in the camps was the living conditions. The beds were often slats of wood covered with straw, where several inmates were "shelved" together. Toilet facilities were inadequate and access to them was usually strictly limited. Showers were allowed only at rare and infrequent intervals. Conditions were overcrowded, devoid of any and all privacy.[4]

Camp life often involved assignment to harsh slave labor designed to break the backs and the souls of the inmates. The inmates, in fact, were "less than slaves," for their masters had no interest in keeping them alive.[5] Some died in accidents. There were twice daily roll calls, which were held outdoors, even in the cruelest weather, and were often excruciatingly prolonged for the slightest whim or infraction of the rules. The inmates were subject to selections (for slave labor or extermination), wanton killing, and constant physical harassment. They were surrounded by death—everywhere.[6]

Inadequately clothed, often without proper footgear, the inmates were also starved. The food—usually a watery gruel and bread—was not enough to sustain life, and was often adulterated.[7] Malnutrition, combined with the unsanitary, overcrowded living conditions[8]—lice and vermin abounded—and lowered physical resistance, led to epidemics of typhus and dysentery.[9] Medical treatment in the camps was almost nonexistent; there was also savage experimentation on human subjects. Illness could mean selection for the gas chambers.

Conventional language fails to describe the horrors of the concentration camps.[10] One survivor put it this way:

> Just as our hunger is not the feeling of missing a meal, so our way of being cold has need of a new word. We say "hunger," we say "tiredness," "fear," "pain," we say "winter" and they are different things. They are free words, created and used by free men who lived in comfort and suffering in their homes. If the *Lagers* had lasted longer, a new, harsh language could express what it means to toil the whole day in the wind, with the temperature below freezing, and wearing only a shirt, underpants, cloth jacket and trousers, and in one's body nothing but weakness, hunger and knowledge of the end drawing near.[11]

What has been discussed above is only meant to indicate those conditions which placed an enormous psychological strain that inmates had to endure. Again, noting that people live through experiences differently, there are certain commonalities. The arrival and the first brutal hours at the camps caused the newcomers to be shocked, dazed, listless, and apathetic. After separation from loved ones, many felt intense despair, abandonment, and isolation. Many were alone for the first time, creating a strong sense of hopelessness.[12]

Usually, the changes in a person's life are somewhat gradual, enabling the person to reorient himself and to adapt to a time continuum. The changes the inmates experienced in the camps were swift and massive. Some responded by denial—refusing to fully comprehend what was taking place.[13] Many had difficulty making decisions or pursuing whatever severely limited actions they could on their own behalf. The spiritual and physical violence, the perpetual fear, and poor physical conditions of the inmates contributed for many to a lack of self-care or self-worth. In extreme cases, one became a *musselman*, a man whose eyes were dead and who was a walking corpse. His time was limited and he would die from either disease, starvation, or the selection.[14]

As mentioned earlier, the camps were designed to destroy the life and autonomy of the inmates. It is not surprising that on a psychological level, many were indeed shattered.[15]

But many individuals survived. Those who overcame the first few days of selections and brutality had a chance to reintegrate (reestablish) their "shattered" personalities. They could adapt—within severe limitations—to the realities of the camps. In an environment designed to destroy their humanity, personality reintegration involved a conscious decision to retain their dignity.

For many inmates, there was a particular moment when they decided to resist destruction.[16] A crucial component of this resistance was to care for appearance by remaining clean.

Primo Levi, upon entering Auschwitz, remembers the advice given him by a fellow inmate:

> . . . Precisely because the *Lager*. . . [is] a great machine to reduce us to beasts, we must not become beasts; . . . So we must certainly wash our faces without soap in dirty water and dry ourselves on our jackets. We must polish our shoes, not because the regulation states it, but for dignity and propriety. We must walk erect, without dragging our feet, not in homage to Prussian discipline but to remain alive, not to begin to die.[17]

A key to survival was the desire to bear witness.[18] Within this desire, there was an implied belief that if mankind knew the horror, future atrocities could be prevented.[19] Some wished to survive out of a feeling that someone—from their family or city—had to live. Others fought for survival out of a sheer will for life over death.

One way of increasing the possibility of survival was the dyad,[20] a unit of two people. The inmate needed another person as a friend—someone who would be concerned about him and, simply, someone who would talk to him. This provided emotional support at a time when all other support systems had been destroyed. Thus, inmates shared bread and even presented small gifts of food or articles of clothing to each other. This support system was certainly also of great "practical" significance. An inmate could help nurse a friend through an illness or support him from collapsing from exhaustion through a prolonged roll call.

Survivors' accounts while depicting the horrors also detail the inmates' mutual assistance. In Maidanek, for example, Alexander Donat's name was placed on a list to receive twenty-five lashes, a punishment he felt he could not survive. A fellow inmate, whom he barely knew, gave the panic-stricken Donat four cubes of sugar to bribe the *kapo* to remove his name from the list. Later, after diligent trading in the camp's black market, he repaid this "debt of honor" to his benefactor by presenting him with two cigarettes. In another instance, Donat's wife, Lena, a pharmacist in the Auschwitz hospital, exchanged beds with her friend Judith when the latter contracted typhus. By hiding her in this manner, Lena saved Judith from the selection. Sleeping in her friend's lice-infested bed, Lena knew that she would become ill within the disease's two-week incubation period. During Lena's subsequent bout with typhus, friends protected her. In this case, as in others, mutual assistance did not insure survival for all. While Lena recovered, her childhood friend and fellow worker, Ola, caught the disease and died.[21]

Some survived through collaboration with the enemy, and others engaged in brutality to other inmates. There were also thefts of food and clothing and violent fights.[22] This type of ruthlessness was not the whole story. Many inmates were helped by and contributed to the larger group. While complying with camp rules on the surface, many used unauthorized means to subvert the system.[23] Smuggling, stealing supplies from work areas, bartering on the camp's black market, transferring work assignments, and tampering with lists were all inmates' means to aid in their own and in the group's survival. At times, news or rumors from the front spread through the camps, encouraging many.

A number of inmates were aided in their survival through a belief in someone or something which existed outside of their immediate circumstances. Although the inmate could not be expected to focus upon his belief with any consistency, it still provided a measure of support. Viktor E. Frankl, a psychiatrist who survived Auschwitz, spoke one night to his barracks, which had gone without food that day rather than inform upon a fellow inmate. Frankl encouraged each man to find his own significance in his suffering, whether a loved one, one's life work, or a belief. They needed to feel both that their death would have a meaning and, conversely, that they had a reason to survive.[24]

It is pertinent to note that religious Jews, Zionists, and Communists often seemed to survive better than assimilated Jews. The individual who possessed a religious or political ideology often resisted Nazi horror through placing his experiences within a context. In contrast, the assimilated, humanistic intellectual was unable to do so. He suffered the physical hardships of the camp worse than even the nonintellectual inmate, as he saw his belief in man collapse. Jean Améry, the western European intellectual, in reviewing his own experiences in Auschwitz, states that: " . . . whoever is, in the broadest sense, a believing person, whether his belief be metaphysical or bound to concrete reality, transcends himself. He is not the captive of his individuality; rather he is part of a spiritual community that is interrupted nowhere, not even at Auschwitz."[25]

A cautionary word must be expressed. The camp did not offer good choices[26]—a positive action for oneself or for a comrade could have negative consequences for another person. If one inmate's name was removed from a list, then someone else's would have to be added. Often the choices implied tragedy: the mother who had to select one of her three children to live; the nurse who drowned a newborn infant so that the mother would not be gassed. We must be careful lest, in order to make sense of what took place in the camps, we overstate or romanticize the mechanisms by which people survived.

In detailing their experiences, survivors often expose brutalized inmates who would do anything to survive. Yet, there are also portraits of people who held firm to their values[27]: comradeship and social organization; religious[28] and political beliefs; and the memory of a loved one.[29] In their daily lives in the camps, survivors tell of being obsessed by hunger, cold, constant terror, and uncertainty. Although to have lived their lives at this level of debasement was the purpose of the perpetrators, the survivors were able, in some circumstances, to function at another level of human dignity and transcendent values. It is this duality of their survival which must be remembered.

### Notes

1.   See Christopher R. Browning's article, "Deportations," in this volume; Rahmil Bryks, *Kiddush ha-Shem*, trans. S. Morris Engel (New York: Behrman House, 1977), pp. 49-54.

2.   Primo Levi, *Survival in Auschwitz: The Nazi Assault on Humanity* (New York: Collier Books, 1969), pp. 18-32.

3.   Alexander Donat, *The Holocaust Kingdom* (New York: Holocaust Library, 1978), pp. 161-190.

4.   Terrence Des Pres, *The Survivor: An Anatomy of Life in the Death Camps* (New York: Oxford University Press, 1978), pp. 55-80.

5.   Benjamin B. Ferencz, *Less Than Slaves* (Cambridge: Harvard University Press, 1979).

6.   Professor André Stein, "The Wasteland of Speech," unpublished manuscript.

7.   Raul Hilberg, *The Destruction of the European Jews* (Chicago: Quadrangle Press, 1961), pp. 581-582.

8.   Anna Pawelczynska, *Values and Violence in Auschwitz* (Berkeley: University of California Press, 1979), pp. 24-43.

9.   Wieslaw Kielar, *Anus Mundi: 1,500 Days in Auschwitz/Birkenau* (New York: Times Books, 1980), p. 84; Richard Rubenstein, *The Cunning of History: The Holocaust and American History* (New York: Harper & Row, 1978), pp. 48-67.

10.   George Steiner, *Language and Silence* (New York: Atheneum, 1979), pp. 118-126, 155-170; Lawrence L. Langer, *Versions of Survival* (Albany: State University of New York Press, 1982), pp. 1-65.

11.   Levi, *Survival*, pp. 112-113.

12. Viktor E. Frankl, *The Doctor and the Soul* (New York: Vintage Books, 1973), pp. 94-103; Bruno Bettelheim, *Surviving and Other Essays* (New York: Vintage Books, 1980), pp. 274-314.

13. Bruno Bettelheim, *The Informed Heart* (Glendale, Ca: The Free Press, 1960), pp. 120-130.

14. Pawelczynska, *Values and Violence*, p. 76.

15. Des Pres and Bettelheim refer to this as "personality disintegration," the process by which the usual coherence of an individual's actions, thoughts, and self-perception is destroyed. See Des Pres, *The Survivor*, pp. 81-108.

16. Des Pres, *The Survivor*, pp. 27-54.

17. Levi, *Survival*, p. 36.

18. Yisrael Gutman, "Kiddush ha-Shem and Kiddush ha-Hayim," *Yalkut Moreshet* 24 (October 1977): 7-22.

19. Des Pres, *The Survivor*, pp. 109-174.

20. Levi, *Survival*, pp 70-78.

21. Donat, *Holocaust Kingdom*, p. 308.

22. Filip Müller, *Eyewitness Auschwitz: Three Years in the Gas Chambers* (New York: Stein and Day, 1979), pp. 120-171.

23. Des Pres, *The Survivor*, pp. 95-147.

24. Frankl, *Man's Search*, pp. 128-133.

25. Jean Améry, *At the Mind's Limits: Contemplations by a Survivor of Auschwitz and Its Realities* (Bloomington, Ind.: Indiana University Press, 1980), p. 14.

26. Lawrence L. Langer, "The Dilemma of Choice in the Death Camps," *Centerpoint: A Journal of Interdisciplinary Studies* 4 (Fall 1980): 53-59.

27. Eliezer Berkovits, *With God in Hell* (New York: Hebrew Publishing Co., 1979).

28. Müller, *Eyewitness*, pp. 113-114.

29. Frankl, *Man's Search*, p. 58.

**For Further Reading**

Améry, Jean. *At the Mind's Limits: Contemplations by a Survivor of Auschwitz and Its Realities.* Bloomington, Ind.: Indiana University Press, 1980.

Bettelheim, Bruno. *The Informed Heart.* Glendale, Ca: The Free Press, 1960.

————. *Surviving and Other Essays.* New York: Vintage Books, 1980.

Birenbaum, Halina. *Hope Is the Last to Die.* New York: Twayne Publishers, 1971.

Des Pres, Terrence. *The Survivor: An Anatomy of Life in the Death Camps.* New York: Oxford University Press, 1978.

Donat, Alexander. *The Holocaust Kingdom.* New York: Holocaust Library, 1978.

Ferencz, Benjamin B. *Less Than Slaves.* Cambridge: Harvard University Press, 1979.

Frankl, Viktor E. *The Doctor and the Soul.* New York: Vintage Books, 1973.

―――. *Man's Search for Meaning.* New York: Beacon Press, 1959.

Kielar, Wieslaw. *Anus Mundi: 1,500 Days in Auschwitz/Birkenau.* New York: Times Books, 1980.

Langer, Lawrence. *The Holocaust and the Literary Imagination.* New Haven: Yale University Press, 1975.

―――. "The Dilemma of Choice in the Death Camps." *Centerpoint: A Journal of Interdisciplinary Studies* 4 (Fall 1980): 53-59.

―――. *Versions of Survival.* Albany: State University of New York Press, 1982.

Levi, Primo. *Survival in Auschwitz: The Nazi Assault on Humanity.* New York: Collier Books, 1969 (Originally appeared under the title, *If This Man Be Man,* Orion Press, 1959).

Müller, Filip. *Eyewitness Auschwitz: Three Years in the Gas Chambers.* New York: Stein and Day, 1979.

# Attempts at Resistance in the Camps

## ALEX GROBMAN

The response of the Jews to Nazi persecution in the concentration and extermination camps has remained largely an unexplored area marked by rhetorical exaggeration, confusion, and misunderstanding. Considering the vast literature that exists on the Holocaust, it is astonishing how little we actually know about Jewish resistance or the lack of it, about whether the Jews rebelled against their oppressors or, as has been alleged, walked like sheep to slaughter. To be sure, the memoirs of survivors have furnished some valuable data, but a truly comprehensive study of the Jews' reaction to the Holocaust remains to be done. To fully understand how the Jews responded, one needs to examine the conditions under which they lived, the manner in which they were deported, the dilemmas they faced, and Nazi efforts made to thwart resistance.

## Deportations

In eastern Europe, and to a lesser extent in western Europe, the Jews already had endured years of physical and mental abuse prior to deportation to the camps. They had suffered from hunger, disease, and exposure to the elements in eastern European ghettos, and throughout all of Europe, from anxiety, fear, and grief for lost family and friends. The roundups and process of deportation by the Nazis, calculated to break down whatever will the Jews had to resist, thus culminated in further demoralization.

For example, in 1942 Jews living in ghettos within a 120-mile radius of the Belzec extermination camp were rounded up by armed SS units, supported by Polish and Ukrainian auxiliaries, who, after breaking into Jewish homes, burned them, killed large numbers of Jews, and herded the remainder onto trains headed for the Belzec gas chambers.[1] In Rowne, Volhynia, the SS used hand grenades to blast open the doors of the Jews' homes.[2] In Sluck, Belorussia, and elsewhere, these scenes were repeated. According to the territorial commissioner Karol, "The appearance of the town was shattering. The German police . . . drove the Jews out of their homes with a cruelty and brutality that are indescribable. Echoes of shooting came from all parts of the city, and heaps of Jewish corpses lay about everywhere."[3]

After the roundups in eastern Europe, and prior to deportation, Jews often had to remain at collecting points, where they were locked up in synagogues, schools, and churches or left without shelter for the entire period, exposed to all kinds of inclement weather. Under these circumstances, many Jews died even before deportation to the camps.[4]

Elsewhere, Nazi measures differed. In Greater Germany (Germany, Austria, Bohemia, and Morovia), for example, deportations were carefully organized so that they would arouse no hostility from the local population. As a result, there were few brutalities. Nonetheless, the possibility of finding refuge or taking flight was limited, and only about 5,000 Jews (out of 250,000) survived in hiding in Germany and Austria.

Whether they were brutally or more humanely treated before being forced on the trains, the Jews often found the trip itself traumatic. One survivor from eastern Europe described the trip in this way:

> The temperature started to rise, as the freight car was enclosed and body heat had no outlet. . . . The only place to urinate was through a slot in the skylight, though whoever tried this usually missed, spilling urine on the floor. . . . When dawn finally rose . . . we were all quite ill and shattered, crushed not only by the weight of fatigue but by the stifling, moist atmosphere and the foul odor of excrement. . . . There was no latrine, no provision. . . . On top of everything else, a lot of people had vomited on the floor. We were to live for days on end breathing these foul smells, and soon we lived in the foulness itself.[5]

To prevent escape from the trains, guards were stationed on the top of the box cars or in other areas where they could shoot anyone attempting to escape. On some trains, the guards continually fired shots past the windows to discourage escape. The Germans were especially concerned about eastern European Jews, who might have heard rumors about the true nature of the transports and the camps. Jews from central and western Europe were of less concern, since they were far enough away from the camps and were thus possibly more persuaded by propaganda. Also, Jews from these regions arrived in passenger cars with some of their personal belongings, which induced them to believe they were being resettled in the "East."

In some transports Jews found escape opportunities, prying window frames loose with brute force or with tools they had brought on board. The decision to escape was in itself difficult. Aside from the risk of injury or gunshot wounds, reluctance to leave family members behind and the absense of proper identity papers and prepared places of refuge created severe hindrances. The local population was either hostile or afraid of getting involved. The penalty in eastern Europe, for aiding or harboring them was death; in western Europe, a fine, arrest, or confinement in a concentration camp. Moreover, rewards were offered to those who informed on Jews. In addition, since Jewish homes had been plundered and expropriated by non-Jews, the latter were not eager to have the Jews return. Still, in some cases Jews did receive help and asylum.

The decision to escape was frequently made in haste and confusion. For example; panic ensued when Jews in transit from Opoczno, Poland, realized they were not traveling westward on their way to Palestine as the Nazis had promised. "It was as though there had been an explosion and a collapse in the carriage," observed one survivor. . . . "I looked at members of my own family and it seemed . . .

as though they had all grown old within a single moment."[6]

Throughout the box car "there were images of dread and horror. Some people tore out their hair, others flung themselves about in despair, and still others cursed with all their might." One man tried to commit suicide. A woman pressed her baby to her breast with tremendous force. While the child struggled, she whispered to him and pressed him to her with even greater force. When her fellow passengers saw what she was doing they cried out for her to stop. "It's my child, mine," she shouted back, "and I want him to die a holy death. Let him die a holy death." By the time the people succeeded in freeing the baby, he was already dead.[7]

Amid this scene, one family considered an appropriate response. The father urged his children to escape at once while there was still a chance. The mother, however, counseled that they stay together. "No, no, no, there's no escape," she warned. "There's nowhere to run to, and with whom will we leave Rochele [twelve years old] and Malkale [nine years old] . . . We must stay together, to the last breath."[8] This was a routine dilemma for many Jews, and often either alternative—to split up the family or stay together—ended in death for all.

There is no way of establishing precise figures for those who escaped the transports and survived for a while or until the end of the war. We do know that the Nazis went to great lengths to deceive the Jews about the destination of the deportations. They were assured that work would be waiting for them. Physicians would tend the sick, tailors make dresses, and shoemakers make shoes. This was especially reassuring to the Jews, since they had learned from their experiences in the ghettos that only the "useful" had a chance to survive.[9]

From items found in their clothing and shoes—toothbrushes, toothpaste, candles, toys, knives, forks, spoons, sweaters and stockings—it is clear that whether the Jews came from the ghetto of Sosnovits, a short distance from Auschwitz, or from Hungary, most Jews did not expect to be killed at the end of their journey. The Jews from Hungary even brought winter coats and expensive furs with them, anticipating the cold winter ahead.[10]

The deception was so successful that some people voluntarily joined the transports to be with their families.[11] In 1943, a number of unmarried Jews from Greece even contracted fictitious marriages to be eligible to join a transport. The Germans offered to exchange *drachmas* for *zlotys* in the form of special receipts which could then be used to buy land near Cracow. The Greek Jews saw the offer as a unique opportunity and innocently took advantage of it.[12]

"We were helpless," remarked one survivor. "Our morale was completely broken. They had prepared us for months on end, so that on hearing their very voices we began shaking and trembling. It was a veritable collective psychosis which one could not overcome."[13]

## Arrival at the Camps

When they reached the camps, some Jews were already dead; the rest disoriented, exhausted, and dehydrated from voyages without anything to drink. Deceptions designed to allay their fears occurred as often as brute force; both hindered organized resistance, despite the numerical superiority of inmates over guards.

At Treblinka, deception began as the train arrived at the sham railway station. The Nazis erected this fake depot, complete with a large clock, baggage-check windows, waiting rooms, and posted train schedules. They created the illusion that this was a transit camp, a place en route to a final destination.

But deception to prevent resistance was used only when transports of unsuspecting Jews from the West arrived at the camps. The transports from the East, carrying Jews who suspected their fate, were met by brute force, designed to induce shock and thus make revolt impossible. When those transports arrived, SS and Ukrainian police lashed out at the Jews with whips to hasten their departure from the trains. Those who fell behind were immediately shot. As they passed the large number of piles of clothing scattered everywhere, they became suspicious. They were never given time to think, discuss, or plan a response. Within hours of their arrival, the selection for extermination, the separation of men from women, the stripping of clothes and valuables, and the marching or running to their deaths was completed.

At Treblinka, invalids, and others unable to move quickly, were not killed in the gas chambers, since this would have slowed down an otherwise efficient operation. Instead, they were taken to the so-called *Lazaret* or infirmary. This, too, was camouflage. The *Lazaret* was surrounded by a high, barbed-wire fence, with brushwood hiding it from view. There was a hut with a Red Cross symbol and the sign *LAZARET*. Inside was a "waiting room" with upholstered couches. Outside was a large pit, which became a mass grave. Most of the time a flame burned in the ditch. Those who entered the *Lazaret* were shot in the neck by the SS and thrown into the ditch. The bodies of both those who had died on the trains and those killed on arrival were also thrown there.

An additional attempt to confuse the Jews was a large Star of David on the gable of the front wall of the building that housed the gas chamber. A heavy curtain screening the entrance had the familiar Hebrew inscription: THIS IS THE GATE THROUGH WHICH THE RIGHTEOUS SHALL ENTER[14]

Another ploy creating disorientation was the Treblinka orchestra, which played its "concert in the square" every day. "The music had a devastating effect on the Jewish workers and on the people who were being driven to their deaths," observed one survivor. "It shattered what was left of their emotional stamina. But for the Germans, it was a 'boost,' a tonic for tired nerves."[15]

In other extermination camps, the Jews were also subjected to similar forms of deception. At Auschwitz, Filip Müller, a survivor, reported that:

> . . . those who arrived at night looked into the glare of thousands of lamps spreading over the lifeless landscape, a

pale and ghostly light, the somber effect enhanced by the SS guards on their watchtowers with their machine guns at the ready. So bleak was the sight which met new arrivals day or night that somehow it plunged them into a state of apathy. In addition, they were invariably plagued by raging thirst, particularly during the summer heat, and the thought of water so preoccupied them that they seemed no longer able to think of anything else, or of paying more than the most cursory attention to the usual surroundings in which they found themselves.[16]

For some of the new arrivals, another factor that contributed to this state of mind was the manner in which they were greeted at the Auschwitz station. As one survivor noted:

The carriage doors were flung open and a small detachment of prisoners stormed inside. They wore striped uniforms, their heads were shaved, but they looked well fed. They spoke in every possible European tongue, and all with a certain amount of humor, which sounded grotesque under the circumstances. Like a drowning man clutching a straw, my inborn optimism . . . clung to this thought: These prisoners look quite well, they seem to be in good spirits and even laugh. Who knows? I might manage to share their favorable position.

In psychiatry there is a certain condition known as "delusion of reprieve." The condemned man, immediately before his execution, gets the illusion that he might be reprieved at the very last moment. We, too, clung to shreds of hope and believed to the last moment that it would not be so bad. . . . Nearly everyone in our transport lived under the illusion that they would be reprieved, that everything would yet be well.[17]

The deception continued until the gas pellets were released. In the so-called changing rooms at Auschwitz there were signs in several languages reading TO THE BATHS and DISINFECTING ROOMS. In addition, there were slogans on the wall, such as ONE LOUSE CAN KILL YOU, or CLEANLINESS BRINGS FREEDOM. Moreover, numbered clothes hooks and wooden benches, as well as notices urging people to hang up their clothes and shoes and to remember their numbers for after their showers, created an aura of normality.[18] At Chelmno, the signs read TO THE PHYSICIAN and TO THE WASHROOM; at Belsec, the entrance to the gas chambers had signs reading WASHING and INHALATION EQUIPMENT. At some camps people were given soap and a towel as they entered the gas chamber; at Maidanek, children were given candy.[19]

If the SS guards sensed that the deceptions were not working, they responded with brute force. They beat the Jews and yelled at them to undress. At Auschwitz, a group from the Sosnovits ghetto who had undoubtedly heard rumors about the camp was handled this way. This "brutal action . . . completely unnerved [them]. They were confused, frightened, unable to communicate with each other and incapable of anything." As the SS continued their abusive behavior, the group quickly undressed. They were then chased into the crematorium. Once inside, the same procedure was repeated with another group until about 600 people were crammed into the gas chamber.[20]

With another group at Auschwitz, the Nazis chose a different tactic. Instead of beating and shouting, the guards were friendly and acted like traffic police. The Jews were uneasy, however, after they were taken to a yard that was locked behind them. The Nazis sensed their uneasiness and several senior SS men addressed this group of inmates. They assured the inmates that they were there to work and that those who were willing to do so would be all right.

The inmates were then told to undress for a shower, because their health was of primary concern. Afterward, the SS men added, they would find a bowl of soup waiting. Some of the inmates were asked about their trades, and the SS seemed pleased that they had skills which could be utilized in the camp.

During this discussion, the prisoners' "fears and anxieties vanished—as if by magic. Quiet as lambs, they undressed, without having to be shouted at or beaten." They tried to undress as quickly as possible so they could be the first in the shower. Thus "cozened and deceived," hundreds of men, women, and children then "walked innocently, and without a struggle, into the large windowless chamber of the crematorium."[21]

On another occasion, the SS dispensed with the deception when they realized that the Jews knew they were about to be murdered. As the SS surrounded the yard of the crematorium, the Jews understood there was no escape. Resigned to their fate, they began undressing, trying not to cry in order to avoid upsetting their children. After undressing, someone in the crowd led them in the *Viddui* (death bed confession). A Jew who witnessed this scene recalls that as they finished this prayer almost everyone wept. "Their tears were not tears of despair. . . . They put themselves in God's hands. Strangely, . . . the SS . . . did not intervene, but let the people be."[22]

There were Jews who were so shattered and traumatized by their experiences that they welcomed death as a relief from torture. Many people, having lost their families, saw no purpose in enduring pain, suffering, and torture any longer. At the Janowska concentration camp, for example, a number of women did not wait to be shot. They threw their children into the large pit and jumped in after them. After one woman spit in the face of a guard, he took her child by the legs, knocked its head against a tree and threw the child into the fire. The woman was then held upside down over the fire.[23]

Little, perhaps nothing, could be done by those who were taken to the gas chambers or killed immediately upon arrival. Members of the *Sonderkommando* at Auschwitz, who worked in the gas chambers and crematoria, learned from experience that it was pointless to inform unsuspecting people about their impending doom, unless they could provide them with possible ways of escape. Warnings caused fear and panic without saving a single life.

In the summer of 1943, a member of the *Sonderkommando* at Auschwitz recognized the wife of one of his friends in a transport that had just arrived from Bialystok, Poland. In the changing room, he informed her that the entire group would be gassed. She believed him, and as the impact of his words began to register, she started tearing her hair, beating her breast, and scratching her face with her fingernails. After a few minutes, she ran to the women around her and told them what she had learned. When they refused to listen, she ran to the men and repeated her story.

At first, all the people—men and women alike—were reluctant to acknowledge this information from a half-crazed woman. Then the group of about 1,000 began dressing and tried to leave the building. Although unsure of where to go, they at least tried to get out. But there was no way to escape; the building was completely surrounded by the SS. Anyone who tried to leave would have been shot.

During the first few minutes, the SS was unsure how to respond; then one of the officers blew his whistle several times. The noise frightened the crowd. Temporarily it also diverted the prisoners from moving towards the exits. After the SS had assured them that nothing was going to happen to them, the door was opened. SS guards, pistols in hand, stood ready to fire. They were flanked by barking dogs who bared their teeth and strained at their leashes only yards away from the crowd. The show of force succeeded. As long as the Jews were promised that no harm would come to them, they were willing to go to the showers. Perhaps even at this point there were some who still hoped that a miracle might occur.

The woman who had warned the group was not sent to the gas chamber, but taken out and shot. Her friend in the *Sonderkommando* was pushed into an oven and burned alive.[24]

In spite of the multiplicity of obstacles, there were occasional, spontaneous acts of resistance. At Auschwitz, a beautiful young dancer attracted the attention of two SS men as she undressed. As they came closer to ogle her, she struck one of them in the forehead with her high-heeled shoes and grabbed his gun. She aimed at him, missed, but then shot and killed his colleague. The SS guards responded by firing machine guns at all the people who remained inside the changing room. A small number who managed to survive the attack were taken outside and shot. Those who had entered the gas chamber and been shielded from the massacre were then gassed.[25]

At Treblinka, a transport of Jews from Grodno, Poland, refused to enter the gas chambers; one threw a hand grenade at the Ukrainian guards. The latter then opened fire on the group and chased them, while they were still fully clothed, into the gas chambers.[26]

Those not selected to be killed immediately upon arrival were subjected to all forms of degradation and humiliation. Random beatings, medical experiments, starvation, inadequate sanitation, and extremely harsh working conditions in all types of weather became part of everyday life in the camps. Under these circumstances, it was extremely difficult to organize any opposition. Moreover, there were the problems of building trust, communicating with people of different nationalities and languages; securing weapons; developing contacts within the camp and with the outside world; and establishing an organization for planning and implementing the rebellion. All this with the SS scrutinizing the inmates' every move. In addition, no matter how well-organized an operation might be, there was always the danger of betrayal, of key members becoming ill, transferred to other camps, murdered by guards, or sent to the gas chambers. Despite these seemingly overwhelming obstacles, resistance often culminated in major rebellions.*

## Individual and Group Responses

Lesser acts of resistance also occurred. Their existence and nature probably will never be fully known, but it is clear that gestures of resistance just short of open revolt took place everywhere. Escape was one such form of resistance. One Jew who escaped had worked at Kulm with a group that was in charge of burying the dead. After coming upon the bodies of his wife and children, he asked an SS guard to shoot him. The guard refused. That evening he tried to commit suicide, but his friends stopped him. Finally, three days later, he escaped from a work detail. Very few individual escapes from the camps, however, were successful.[27]

Individual attacks on guards constituted another form of resistance. At Treblinka, Meir Berliner was despondent after his wife and daughter were murdered in the gas chambers. On September 10, 1942, he stabbed and killed the SS officer Max Vielas to avenge the death of his family. In retaliation, the SS killed Berliner and ten other Jews and deprived the other inmates of dinner that evening. [28]

This was the first instance of open resistance at Treblinka, but it was not the last in which collective punishment was used to inhibit further occurrences. In another instance, mother and son from Kielce were separated shortly after arrival. When the son tried to say good-bye to his mother, he was stopped by a Ukrainian guard. The son then stabbed the guard with his pocket-knife. Before the day ended, all the Jews from Kielce had been shot in reprisal.[29]

Collective punishment probably inhibited individual attempts at escape or resistance. Moshe Beisky, reports that 2,000 people were incarcerated in his labor camp. At first, those assigned to outside work were heavily guarded. When the threat of escape decreased, the number of guards was reduced. Beisky noted that the reason for the changed attitude was simple: "If anybody escaped, his whole group, or most of it, was shot." Each group contained seventy to ninety people and no one wanted to be responsible for their deaths.[30]

* See Rebellions in the Camps: Three Revolts in the Face of Death," by Yisrael Gutman in this volume.

At the Janowska concentration camp, preparations had been made for a revolt, but the inmates failed to carry it out because they feared reprisals would be made against members of their families. Only when it became clear that the Germans would kill all the Jews was the idea of rebellion entertained.[31]

The absence of secure hiding places also inhibited large numbers of escapes. Some Jews did find a refuge among Gentiles, but many were beaten and robbed or betrayed to the SS by the local inhabitants. Clearly, there was no place of hiding adequate for millions of Jews. Even in Denmark, the Danish Resistance insisted on smuggling Jews out of the country to Sweden rather than risk hiding them in Denmark under the German occupation.

The need to bear witness was a powerful force among the Jews, prompting many of them to escape, despite the obstacles. In early 1942, one Jew escaped from Chelmno to the Warsaw ghetto. He met with members of the underground and told them how the Jews had been murdered in Chelmno. He made his report shortly after the underground received information from another source that tens of thousands of Jews from Vilna were being deported and killed. As a result, the underground stopped its cultural activities and devoted its energies to armed defense.[32]

Information about Treblinka was reported to the Jews inside the Warsaw ghetto by Abraham Krzepicki and David Nowodworski. On August 25, 1942, Krzepicki was deported to Treblinka from Warsaw; eighteen days later he escaped and returned to the ghetto. His report on Treblinka was the first eyewitness account the Jews in the ghetto had received. During the April 1943 revolt, his report was buried in milk cans in the ghetto—cans that were part of Emmanuel Ringelblum's archives. Krzepicki joined the Jewish Fighting Organization and was killed in the 1943 uprising.[33] Nowodworski also escaped from Treblinka and in April 1943 led a squad of the Jewish Fighting Organization.

Seventy-six Jews escaped from Auschwitz; all but a dozen were caught and returned to the camp.[34] Almost all were hanged or shot, their corpses displayed publicly as a warning to others. One young Belgian Jewess who tried to escape and failed was Mala Zimetbaum. Together with a Polish inmate, she fled to Slovakia in order to alert the world to the murder of Hungarian Jewry. To document her charges, she brought papers from the camp. But at the Slovakian border, she and the Polish inmate were arrested after the guards discovered the Auschwitz tatoo on Mala's arm. Both prisoners were returned to the camp and killed.[35]

Other escape attempts from Auschwitz were successful. Three photographs of the crematoria complex, including one of a pit with burning bodies, were taken by a member of the Auschwitz underground and smuggled to London. On April 5, 1944, Siegfried Vitezslav Lederer, a Czech Jew, escaped and reached Bohemia. He informed the Berlin Rabbi Leo Baeck, a member of the Theresienstadt *Judenrat*, about Auschwitz. Although Baeck believed Lederer, he decided not to share this information with the ghetto inhabitants. As he later explained:

> . . . I finally decided that no one should know it. If the Council of Elders were informed, the whole camp would know within a few hours. Knowledge of death by gassing would only be harder, and death was not certain at all. There was also selection for slave labor and perhaps not all transports went to Auschwitz. So I decided not to tell anyone.[36]

On April 7, 1944, Rudolf Vrba and Alfred Wetzler, two Slovakian Jews who worked in the administration at Auschwitz, escaped. They fled to Slovakia and tried to warn the leaders of Slovakian Jews about the imminent danger to the Jews of Hungary. Meetings were held with the Slovakian Jewish leaders, who asked them to prepare a report on Auschwitz with the Orthodox Slovakian leader, Rabbi Michael Dov-Ber Weissmandel.

These reports, along with accounts from Arnost Rosin and Czeszek Mordowicz, who escaped from Auschwitz on May 27, 1944, and information from a Polish officer, who also escaped at that time, were sent to the Swiss authorities, and the Vatican in June 1944. Hungarian Jewish leaders received copies in April and May; the American and British governments received abridged reports during the third week in June.

In a letter of May 18, 1944, Rabbi Weissmandel demanded that the Allies bomb the murder installations at Auschwitz as well as the railroad lines leading to the camp. Nothing was done, although in the late spring of 1944 the Allies flew over Auschwitz several times and photographed the camp.[37]

In summary, it is clear that when the Jews entered the camps, their options for resistance were few. For those who were taken to the gas chambers immediately, nothing but a dignified death was possible. They were trapped and, if deceptions failed, the SS used force. Those Jews who were spared during the initial selections faced almost insurmountable obstacles. Yet despite these, some Jews managed to escape, inform the world, and even start revolts.

Significantly, when Russian and Polish prisoners of war were about to be murdered, they reacted much like the Jews. On several occasions, Filip Müller, a member of the *Sonderkommando*, talked with the former in the dressing room at Auschwitz:

> Many of them had been newly arrested and the majority were strong, well-nourished men in their prime. Not a few had bruises, an indication that they had been beaten or tortured. When asked to undress, they realized at once what fate awaited them. [Helplessness] and fear, but also defiance, could be read in their eyes when, from the execution room, they heard the muffled sounds of shots and the dull thud of falling bodies. But at the last moment, even hardened old soldiers and partisans began to tremble. Many shook hands

or embraced, others crossed themselves and prayed, although they had not believed in God for a long time. Now, forsaken, and with nothing left to cling to, they turned to God and prayed to him.[38]

For the most part, these were trained soldiers, yet they went to their deaths like millions of Jewish civilians. Moreover, they often did not have to worry about the survival of their families if they disobeyed.[39]

## Notes

1.  Leon Poliakov, *Harvest of Hate: The Nazi Program for the Destruction of the Jews of Europe*, translated from the French (New York: Holocaust Library, 1979), p. 150.
2.  Isaiah Trunk, *Jewish Responses to Nazi Persecution* (New York: Stein and Day, 1979), p. 53.
3.  Trunk, *Jewish Responses*, p. 53.
4.  Trunk, *Jewish Responses*, p. 53.
5.  Cited in Terrence Des Pres, *The Survivor* (New York: Oxford University Press, 1976), p. 53.
6.  Cited in Azriel Eisenberg, *Witness to the Holocaust* (New York: Pilgrim Press, 1981), p. 210.
7.  Eisenberg, *Witness*, p. 210.
8.  Eisenberg, *Witness*, p. 211.
9.  Filip Müller, *Eyewitness Auschwitz: Three Years in the Gas Chambers* (New York: Stein and Day, 1979), pp. 26-27, 36.
10.  Müller, *Eyewitness*, pp. 32-34, 143.
11.  Olga Lengyel, *Five Chimneys: The Story of Auschwitz* (New York: Ziff-Davis Publishing, 1947), pp. 4-5.
12.  Poliakov, *Harvest of Hate*, pp. 158-59.
13.  Proceedings of the Trial of Adolf Eichmann (English Version), 2 May 1961, Session 24 Rrl IEM.
14.  Alexander Donat, ed., *The Death Camp Treblinka* (New York: Holocaust Library, 1979), p. 229; Attorney General's Opening Address, chapter IX, in Proceedings of the Trial of Adolf Eichmann, n.d., pp. ix 2-3.
15.  Donat, *Death Camp Treblinka*, p. 45.
16.  Müller, *Eyewitness*, p. 134.
17.  Viktor E. Frankel, *Man's Search for Meaning* (New York: Washington Square Press, 1963), pp. 14-16.
18.  Müller, *Eyewitness*, p. 61.
19.  Attorney General's Opening Address, Chapter IX p. 2.

20.   Müller, *Eyewitness*, pp. 32-33.
21.   Müller, *Eyewitness*, pp. 36-38.
22.   Müller, *Eyewitness*, pp. 69-71.
23.   Proceedings of the Trial of Adolf Eichmann, 2 May 1961, Session 23 N1 BG.
24.   Müller, *Eyewitness*, pp. 75-80.
25.   Müller, *Eyewitness*, pp. 87-89. See also Wieslaw Kielar, *Anus Mundi: 1500 Days in Auschwitz-Birkenau*, translated from the Polish (New York: Times Books, 1980), pp. 177-78.
26.   Attorney General's Opening Address, Chapter IX, p. 3.
27.   Gideon Hausner, *Justice in Jerusalem* (New York: Schocken Books, 1968), p. 169.
28.   Donat, *Death Camp Treblinka*, pp. 127-32.
29.   Donat, *Death Camp Treblinka*, p. 84.
30.   Hausner, *Justice*, pp. 162-63.
31.   Leon W. Wells, *The Death Brigade* (New York: Holocaust Library, 1978), pp. 83-85. Reprint of *The Janowska Road* (1963).
32.   Proceedings of the Trial of Adolf Eichmann, 3 May 1961, Session 25 JL IEM.
33.   Donat, *Death Camp Treblinka*, p. 77.
34.   Reuben Ainsztein, *Jewish Resistance in Nazi Occupied Eastern Europe* (London: Paul Elek, 1974), p. 685.
35.   Hausner, *Justice*, p. 191; Yuri Suhl ed., *They Fought Back: The Story of the Jewish Resistance in Nazi Europe* (New York: Schocken Books, 1967), pp. 182-88.
36.   Cited in Eric H. Boehm, *We Survived* (New Haven: Yale University Press, 1949), p. 293. See also Albert H. Friedlander, *Leo Baeck: Teacher of Theresienstadt* (New York: Holt, Rinehart, and Winston, 1968), pp. 46-48; and Randolph L. Braham, "What Did They Know and When?" in *The Holocaust as Historical Experience*, eds. Yehuda Bauer and Nathan Rotenstreich (New York: Holmes & Meier, 1981), pp. 109-31.
37.   Rudolf Vrba, *I Cannot Forgive* (New York: Grove Press, 1964), pp. 248-61; David Wyman, "Why Auschwitz Was Never Bombed," *Commentary* 65 (1978): 37-46.
38.   Müller, *Eyewitness*, p. 74.
39.   Hausner, *Justice*, p. 183.

### For Further Reading

Hausner, Gideon. *Justice in Jerusalem*. New York: Harper & Row, 1966.

Hoess, Rudolf. *Commandant of Auschwitz: the Autobiography*

*of Rudolf Hoess.* New York: The World Publishing Co., 1959.

Kielar, Wieslaw. *Anus Mundi: 1500 Days in Auschwitz-Birkenau.* New York: Times Books, 1972.

Kogon, Eugen. *The Theory and Practice of Hell.* New York: Berkley Windhover Books, 1975.

Müller, Filip. *Eyewitness Auschwitz: Three Years in the Gas Chambers.* New York: Stein and Day, 1979.

Trunk, Isaiah. *Jewish Responses to Nazi Persecution.* New York: Stein and Day, 1979.

# Rebellions in the Camps: Three Revolts in the Face of Death

## YISRAEL GUTMAN

The rebellions in the extermination camps were not initiated by the thousands of Jews who arrived at the camps each day. Stunned from their long and crowded train trip, the passengers were greeted by the guards with a hail of shouts and blows. There was no time to think, to become oriented, or to plan ahead. In an atmosphere of terror and shock, no organized or planned resistance could take place.

The Jews involved in the uprisings were those who had worked in the camps for long periods and knew what awaited them. Only they had the time to plan and implement rebellions.

## The Treblinka Rebellion

In the spring of 1943, transports to Treblinka were few in number. Inmates came to the conclusion that the Nazis were no longer in need of many workers at the site and that, consequently, their own end was near. This general sense of impending doom gave added impetus to the planning of an organized revolt and escape. An attempt was made to purchase weapons from the Ukrainian guards, whose own attitudes were changing after the Soviet victories on the Eastern front. The Ukrainians readily took the money, but they did not supply the promised weapons. In several cases, these contacts even led to the execution of members of the camp underground. The secret committee in charge of preparing the rebellion managed to obtain a key to the German arsenal, which would supply the weapons for a revolt. The underground committee also contacted the Jewish inmates working near the gas chambers.

In July, 1943, when the planning of the Treblinka uprising reached the stage of implementation, roughly 850 Jews were in the camp, about one-third in the area of the gas chambers/crematoria. The inmates intended to begin the revolt on a day when the SS guards were relatively few in number, and towards evening, when pursuit would be more difficult. They had to acquire the weapons, attack selected targets, including the camp headquarters, and kill the Germans as they arrived to relieve the earlier shift. Telephone and electrical lines had to be cut, observation towers attacked, the Ukrainians disarmed, and the camp set afire and destroyed before a mass escape to nearby forests could be staged. Treblinka was located about 37 miles east of Warsaw, and most of the inmates intended to reach the city or other urban centers in the heart of Poland.

August 2 was to be the day of the uprising. From noon onwards the plans were set in motion. The removal and transfer of arms from the arsenal began as planned. Even though only the resisters were apprised of the planned revolt, the news quickly spread throughout the general inmate population. Many armed themselves with makeshift weapons and prepared to break out. The leaders of the underground, Galewski (a *kapo*), Zev Kurland, and others gathered in the camp area, thus ensuring their control. The plan proceeded smoothly until three o'clock, when one of the SS men unexpectedly appeared in the camp area, stopped an inmate, and found money on him that he had prepared for his escape. Despite the fact that some of the weapons had not yet been distributed, that various preparatory stages were not yet completed, and that it was still too early in the day, the resisters decided to kill the SS officer and begin the uprising immediately.

The shooting marked the start of the uprising. From that point on, the revolt proceeded spontaneously. The prisoners set fire to the fuel tank, and all the adjacent camp structures began to burn. Shots were fired and grenades were thrown from all parts of the camp. The Ukrainian guards in the observation towers opened fire, which the rebels returned in a disorderly fashion. The inmates stormed the fences, struggled to break through the obstacles that surrounded the camp, and began their escapes.

Most of the rebels, including the leaders of the uprising, were killed in the fighting inside the camp while breaking through the fences and the obstacle-strewn area. About half managed to flee no-man's land, the outer perimeter of the camp. They had to cross approximately 3 to 5 miles to reach the woods. After the camp commandant, Franz Stangl, alerted the SS and the police stations in the vicinity, ambushes were set up and an extensive pursuit was initiated. Most of the Poles who encountered the escapees robbed them of their money and turned them over to the Germans. In some cases, however, the escapees were aided by Poles, despite the great danger inherent in this deed. It is estimated that sixty to seventy escapees were still alive at liberation; twenty to forty more hid in the cities or forests but perished before the end of the war. One of the escapees who reached Warsaw, "Yankel" Wiernik,[1] was the contact man between the resistance in Treblinka No. 1 (the regular camp) and Treblinka No. 2 (the extermination section). His testimony served as the basis of the publication on Treblinka issued by the Polish underground, which eventually reached other countries in the middle of the war. The Treblinka uprising resulted in the closing of this camp.

## The Sobibor Revolt

Sobibor was smaller and more tightly run than Treblinka. Consequently, escape was more difficult. Nevertheless, several individual and group escape attempts were made, and there were even attempts to rebel when transports arrived. With the change in the course of the war in the middle of 1943, there were cases of organized flight by armed Ukrainian guards, who crossed over to the Soviets. In response, the Germans mined all approaches to the camp.

Since escape attempts, successfully or otherwise, resulted in collective punishment, individual prisoners and groups began to consider the possibility of organizing a mass escape. Escape plans included digging a tunnel at night leading to the other side of the fence. These plans were contingent upon Ukranian cooperation. Since the camp was located on the eastern part of the *Generalgouvernement,* the inmates assumed they would be able to join partisans after escaping.

A number of attempts failed and many lives were lost. In October 1943, the camp underground was reorganizd after the arrival of the Soviet-Jewish POW, Lieutenant Alexander (Sasha) Perchersky from the Minsk ghetto. This shipment included a unit of about 100 POWs. Contracts between this group and the veteran Polish and Dutch underground members in the camp, renewed the impetus to organize an uprising. Pechersky became the leader and Leon Feldhendler, a Polish Jew who had long sought to devise a comprehensive plan for escape, became his deputy. Feldhendler served both as an instructor and as a contract man in the camp.

Two plans were formulated. The first was a variation of previously unsuccessful attempts to dig a tunnel under the fences and mined areas. The second plan entailed killing SS officers, gaining control of the weapons, and organized flight in an area apparently free of land mines.

The tunnel was begun, but it collapsed in a sudden rain storm. With time running out, the conspirators decided to initiate the revolt immediately. They planned to kill the SS men and take their weapons after luring them into the workshop where various jobs ordered by the SS were being carried out. Detailed plans were drawn for raiding arsenals, cutting telephone and electrical cables, sabotaging vehicles, and so on. The inmates intended to carry out these actions secretly, with only active underground members involved. They planned to order, at gunpoint, the officer who usually convened the inmates to lead the group to the camp gates. There they would inform everyone of the escape and direct them to the path free of landmines.

The uprising was set for October 4, 1943. The first stage took place as planned. All but one of the nearly twelve SS who were successfully lured to the workshops were killed. The SS arrived at the parade ground, noted that one of their comrades was murdered, and opened fire. A Ukrainian guard who turned up at the parade ground was killed in full view of the inmates by the underground. Panic ensued, with everyone running for the fences and the gates. Despite fire from the guards on the ground and on the observation towers, about 300 inmates succeeded in escaping. Many were killed or wounded by mines or by German and Ukrainian bullets. Almost all of the SS guards and a group of Ukrainian guards were wiped out. Knowledge of the uprising and the escape made a strong impression on the Germans, especially since the camp was relatively close to partisan bases. Hundreds of soldiers and police pursued the escapees. Even airplanes were used in the hunt. During the next few days, approximately 100 inmates were caught. The others escaped the camp area, with many joining partisan units. Pechersky survived and, in a pamphlet he later published, described the organization of the uprising and the story of the escape.[2] Most of those who successfully fled the camp fell or were killed later in the war. Only a small number lived to see liberation.

As with Treblinka, following the uprising and the escape, Sobibor ceased to function as an extermination camp.

## The Revolt in Auschwitz-Birkenau

In 1943, the International Auschwitz Resistance Organization was established at the camp. Included in this group were Jewish and non-Jewish inmates from Poland, Russia, Austria, Germany, France, Yugoslavia, and Belgium. Together, they sought ways to revolt against the Nazis with the help of the Polish resistance fighters outside the camp. As part of these preparations, explosives were smuggled out of the Weichsel-Union-Metallwerke ammunitions factory located within the confines of Auschwitz, where both male and female inmates were employed. Some explosives were smuggled into Auschwitz by Jewish members of the camp underground. Others were secretly transferred to Birkenau by young Jewish girls and entrusted to the mostly Jewish *Sonderkommando* workers.

After the transport of Jews from Hungary to Auschwitz ceased in the summer of 1944, the Germans began to reduce the size of the *Sonderkommando*. It had reached a peak of almost 1,000 men during the gassing of Hungarian Jews. The *Sonderkommando* members realized that their utility had ceased and with it their chances of survival. They urged the international underground to begin the uprising. The underground, however, adhering to its own schedule and calculations, did not consider the time ripe for a general rebellion. It is possible that the underground was not really interested in an insurrection, in view of the rapid advance of the Red Army towards the area in which Auschwitz was located.

Since the *Sonderkommando*'s demand was repeatedly rejected, it decided to proceed on its own. Over a period of time, the Jews of the *Sonderkommando*—including Hungarian, Polish, and Greek Jews, in addition to a few Russian POWs—planned for the uprising. Improvised weapons were prepared, explosives were planted under the crematoria, and grenades were constructed.

Details of this preparation are unknown, because the participants did not survive. Notes buried at Birkenau by Zalman Lewental, a member of the underground, reveal that among the activists there were two Polish Jews, Ya'akov Handelsman and Yosef Warszawski. A Russian named Timofei Borodin was engaged in constructing the bombs.

When the *Sonderkommando* heard of a planned selection of 300 of their number in October, 1944, they decided upon immediate insurrection. The revolt broke out on October 7. One unit of the *Sonderkommando* killed a *kapo* and the SS in their vicinity, destroyed crematorium No. 2, broke through the camp fence, and fled. Large German mechanized units immediately set out in pursuit of the escapees. No participants of this revolt are known to have survived.

The Germans opened an investigation to discover the source of the explosives and uncovered the Union factory. Four Jewish girls headed by Rose Robota, the organizer of the Birkenau cell, were executed, having never revealed the names of additional conspirators or activists.

Rose Robota smuggled a letter out of the "Bunker," the camp prison, to her friends in the Jewish underground. She wrote that it was difficult to take leave of life, but that she would not turn traitor. She left behind those whom she hoped would be fortunate enough to eventually live in freedom and to avenge her. Her note ended with the words: *"Hazak V'Amatz"*—"Be Strong and Brave."

### Notes

1. Jankiel Wiernik, "One Year in Treblinka," in *The Death Camp Treblinka,* ed. Alexander Donat (New York: Holocaust Library, 1979), pp. 147-188.
2. Alexander Pechersky, *The Sobibor Revolt* (Moscow: Emes, 1946).

### For Further Reading

Ainsztein, Reuben. *Jewish Resistance in Nazi-Occupied Eastern Europe.* London: Paul Elek, 1974.

Donat, Alexander, ed. *The Death Camp Treblinka: A Documentary.* New York: Holocaust Library, 1979.

Müller, Filip. *Eyewitness Auschwitz: Three Years in the Gas Chambers.* New York: Stein and Day, 1979.

Novitch, Miriam. *Sobibor: Martyrdom and Revolt.* New York: Holocaust Library, 1980.

Rashke, Richard. *Escape from Sobibor.* Boston: Houghton Mifflin Company, 1982.

# Spiritual Responses in the Camps*

## DANIEL LANDES

The subject of Jewish spiritual responses in the concentration camps is difficult to analyze. In general, we do not possess contemporaneous diaries, journals, newspapers, or other sources from the camps as are available for the ghettos. In addition, corroboration of many stories cannot be obtained. The principal reason for this difficulty in discovering and verifying proper information is that spiritual response in the camps was either entirely impossible or truncated. Furthermore, spiritual and religious factors are difficult to identify under normal circumstances and even more so under conditions of extreme duress.

In the extermination camps, large numbers of Jews were murdered almost instantaneously. Many others went to their death soon thereafter. Those who were able to survive longer, or who were interned in a labor camp, faced adverse conditions that caused severe damage to body and soul. The camp offered no respite for reflection or the performance of any act beyond that needed for survival. Survival itself was precarious and was never assured. Where life is denied, it is not surprising that spirituality also faces a rapid death or painful diminution. This bitter reality is hard to accept for those of us for whom religious values are of paramount significance. In attempting to discover and understand those incidents where religious observances were attempted, we must be careful lest we join those who, in the words of one survivor, "try to sanctify God's Name with false facts about the victims because it helps them to believe."[1]

In truth, there are numerous accounts of those who came to deny God and renounce His Torah (Law) in the camps. For many, the hellish life of the camps "crushed, shattered, [and] pulverized"[2] their faith. It would be patronizing, however, to assume that for all of them, this "disbelief was not intellectual." Some inmates reconsidered their theological position in light of their current situation, and *made a decision* to reject a long-held system of belief.

This process can be recognized in the story that Yisrael Aviram tells about his father, Yosef. Scion of a distinguished Hasidic family, Yosef was himself pious and a fine scholar of the Talmud. In the Lodz ghetto, the entire family responded to the Nazi persecution with renewed adherence to religious observances. Father and son were able to remain together through Auschwitz and later deportations to the work camps. From memory, Yosef taught his son Talmud during the short rest pauses. On Rosh Hashanah, Yosef served as cantor since he knew the entire service by heart. One night during the Ten Days of Penitence—between Rosh Hashanah and Yom Kippur—Yosef woke up his son, who was sleeping in the bunk tier below, and spoke to

---

* Prior to reading this article, it is useful to read "Spiritual Responses in the Ghetto," by Daniel Landes, and "Life in the Camps: The Psychological Dimension," by Sheryl Robbin, in this volume.

him. Yisrael reconstructs his father's words:

> A man never knows the day of his death—how much more so
> in our situation. Any minute could be our last; therefore, I
> wish that you know my feelings, thoughts and conclusions
> concerning that which stands at the center of my experience
> as a Jew and as a man. All my life I have believed in perfect
> faith in the omnipotent God of Israel. I have been convinced
> that He is omnipresent—"the whole world is full of His
> glory"—and everything obeys His command, as it says: "A
> man does not bruise his finger unless it has been decreed from
> above." And so, He is also here in this valley of the shadow of
> death; and all that is done here, He has decreed from above. I
> have reached a conclusion: Whichever way you look at it—
> either there is no God and all that I have been taught and have
> learned is a figment of the imagination and without
> foundation; or the other possibility is that there is a God and
> all this has occurred according to His will and due to Him. If
> so, this God is not my God. I do not desire Him; I shall not
> serve Him; I shall not turn to Him; and I shall not listen to
> His commands. To Him, I certainly shall not supplicate nor
> shall I pour out my prayers and requests before Him.[3]

One does not have to agree with the method and conclusion of
this theological analysis in order to recognize its utter seriousness and
cogency. According to his son's account, the father continued for
several hours to elucidate his view with many biblical and talmudic
citations. Based on his understanding of Judaism and his present
situation, this man, whose "whole being" formerly was suffused with
beliefs in the Holy One, rejected Him. On Kol Nidre eve
(commencing Yom Kippur), the holiest night of the year, inmates
from the block requested that he once again lead them in prayer.
"Pray?" Yosef responded. "To whom? I, presently, am going to eat."[4]
Taking a piece of bread that he had saved from the morning, Yosef—
not for reasons of malnutrition or starvation—intended to break the
holy fast just as it had begun. In obvious pain and sorrow, he
swallowed the bread.

It is not irrelevant to add that both father and son survived the
Holocaust to found a secular *kibbutz* (communal settlement) in the
emerging and embattled State of Israel. Yosef's participation in this
utopian social project bespeaks, I believe, an attachment to
communal values originating in the religiously observant life he had
rejected. In any event, the obvious sincerity in which Yosef
confronted both tradition and the camp, along with the great pain in
reaching and acting upon his decision, places this account within the
spectrum of spiritual responses.

The focus of our investigation, however, will be the experience of
those inmates who made a positive religious response (in terms of
traditional Jewish spirituality) in the extreme milieu of the
concentration camps.

Three qualities emerge from an analysis of the spiritual responses. They were, first of all, episodic. Religious observances were usually performed individually or in small groups. Done hurriedly, under fear of discovery, there was little or no expectation that they could or would be repeated. Acts of spirituality, therefore, had little continuity with each other. Religion did not serve as an ever-present possible "haven" from the harshness of the camp, unlike its role in the ghetto.

Spiritual acts were also fragmentary in nature. Observant Jews who in the pre-Holocaust years tried to fulfill the Law according to the strictest of interpretations, with complete attention to all details, were unable to peform rites and rituals in full in the camps. The performance of religious duties, if discovered, could result in death, mutilation, or severe punishment. At best, inmates were able to observe a limited portion of a *mitzvah* (commandment), usually in a very different form from the way it was normally performed.

Finally, the episodic and partial quality of religious acts in the camps determined that spirituality was usually disguised and not obvious in the camp. Observances were restricted in time and form, and often hurried. Exhausted and fearing discovery by camp guards, or *kapos*, inmates performed religious observances without any attendant drama, spectacle, or aesthetic care. The need to be inconspicuous was paramount. Indeed, they fortunately often went unnoticed by fellow inmates or guards.

## Martyrdom

*Kiddush ha-Shem* (sanctification of God's name in one's life) expressed as martyrdom reflects the partial and hidden nature of spiritual responses in the camps. There were, of course, exceptions. Among those selected immediately for death after the arrival of the transports, in the company of their families and fellow townsmen, many were said to have cried out the *Shemah* ("Hear O' Israel, the Lord is our God, the Lord is One!"). At times, this affirmation of faith was preceded by a last-minute exhortation by their rabbi or other religiously inspired individual.[5] In general, however, the accounts of death of those who survived longer in the camps lack any semblance of dignity or of drama in the retelling. The victims generally were ill, exhausted, and weak. They had been physically broken by their ordeal.[6] They often met their death not in the company of family members or those with whom they had been close. Words of Torah did not grace their last minutes. One surviving member of the *Sonderkommando* ("special unit" of inmates who transported bodies to the crematoria) in the Janowska (Poland) camp testified:

> Being witness to many thousands and hundreds of thousands of Jews just before they were killed, I never heard them crying out the *Shemah*. I personally witnessed all the tragedies in Lvov, Galicia, the cradle of Hasidism.

In Jewish tradition one had to say the *Shemah* in the loudest possible voice, but one did not even hear the rabbis of Europe screaming out the *Shemah*.[7]

This stark testimony should discourage an overly romantic portrayal of martyrdom in the camps. It is not convincing, however, as a refutation of the existence of consciously intended martyrdom. A surviving member of the *Sonderkommando* in Auschwitz reported that in the face of death, there were many who continued to affirm a strong religious belief:

Suddenly from among the crowd a loud voice could be heard: An emaciated little man had begun to recite the *Viddui* [Confessional]. First he bent forward, then he lifted his head and his arms heavenward and after every sentence, spoken loud and clear, he struck his chest with his fist. Hebrew words echoed round the yard: *bogati* (we have sinned), *gazalti* (we have done wrong to our fellow men), *dibarti* (we have slandered), *heevetjti* (we have been deceitful), *verhirschati* (we have sinned), *sadti* (we have been proud), *maradti* (we have been disobedient). "My God, before ever I was created I signified nothing, and now that I am created I am as if I had not been created. I am dust in life, and how much more so in death. I will praise you everlastingly, Lord, God everlasting, Amen! Amen!" The crowd of 2,000 repeated every word, even though perhaps not all of them understood the meaning of this Old Testament confession. Up to that moment, most of them had managed to control themselves. But now almost everyone was weeping. There were heartrending scenes among members of families. But their tears were not tears of despair. These people were in a state of deep religious emotion. They had put themselves in God's hands. Strangely enough the SS men present did not intervene, but let the people be.[8]

Similarly, a number of nonobservant Jews confided to a rabbi that they understood their imminent death to be an act of *kiddush ha-Shem*.[9] Continuing to believe in God and in the significance of being Jewish, they achieved an anonymous and lonely martyrdom.

## Re-Creation of the Community

Despite the episodic, fragmentary, and hidden nature of spirituality in the camps, religious observance had a powerful effect upon many. It often meant, first of all, the re-creation of a sense of community. In our discussion of spiritual responses in the ghettos, we considered the community as a vehicle or means for the expression of spirituality. Traditionally, however, the community itself is considered to have inherent spiritual value.[10] This is evident in analyzing religious behavior in the camp. To be sure, the community that was formed around the performance of a *mitzvah* was usually small in number and short-lived in duration. In that sense, it was as episodic and fragmentary as the performance of the religious deed itself. Survivors, nevertheless, testify to the genuineness and intensity of those contingent and hidden communities. One account relates an incident that took place in an Auschwitz barracks made up of Polish Jews and Greek Jews from Salonica, who did not share a common language. In the dead of night, lying on his tier, Ya'akov Habib began to chant a penitential prayer recited the week preceding Rosh Hashanah in the distinctive and plaintive Greek style. Soon the entire barracks, including the *kapos*, broke into cries of their shared fate that the prayer evoked.[11]

There were several reasons why the *mitzvah*-centered communities came into existence. To begin with, people with religious concerns would either actively seek each other out or sense the other's presence. A man, for example, who sorely missed putting on the ritual *tefillin* (leather boxes containing scriptural passages worn by men during morning weekday prayers) would notice a fellow inmate who quietly and secretively would rise early and move to a corner in the barracks with a small pouch concealed in his hands. The observer would sense that this was the man that he could approach in order to take part in the performance of that commandment.[12]

A second factor in the creation of these communities was that the performance of certain religious practices necessitated the cooperation of several people. Thus, one woman might steal a potato into which she would scoop out two holes. Another woman would make wicks out of cloth, while a third would offer a few drops of margarine. Together, they would kindle the Sabbath lights (candles). In a similar fashion, the procuring of *matzah* (unleavened bread eaten on Passover), which took place in many of the camps, involved the cooperation of a relatively large number of people, who would obtain flour, produce baking equipment, and see to the baking itself.[13]

Finally, communities were created due to the compelling nature of the religious practices themselves.[14] Even nonobservant Jews were drawn to the kindling of the Hannukah lights. High Holiday services were "conducted" in predawn services in barracks, in an abandoned shed to which people snuck away at great risk, or even on the march. In one camp, the normally hostile antireligious members of the *Sonderkommando* stood guard to insure the safety of their religious cohorts as they prayed.[15] They, too, had a need for the prayers to be recited, even if they themselves could or would not participate. They formed a community with their brethren, centered around this religious event.

An apparent significance of this *mitzvah* community is its resistance against the design of the Nazis to dehumanize the inmates and render them a mere number prior to their final physical destruction.[16] These spiritual responses, performed under adverse and hostile conditions, were an affirmation of both one's personal autonomy and the significance of his community. One had to exhibit cooperation, cunning, psychic strength, and personal courage. The acceptance—even if episodic and partial—of the yoke of the Torah could mean the momentary casting off of the yoke of the camps.

## The Experience of Spirituality

It is necessary to analyze the different experiential modes of this fragile and very limited sense of freedom granted by the performance of religious observances and adherence to religious belief. Spirituality in the camps manifested itself in self-denial, transvaluation of observances, the positing of a different reality, and use of classic theological formulations.

The desire to observe religious practices at times meant self-denial of essential resources. This seems highly paradoxical, considering that the Nazi program for the inmates was one of systematic denial of medical care, adequate clothing, rest, and especially food. In order to have a chance at survival one had to break out of the cycle of deprivation and secure additional rest and sustenance.[17] A spiritual response, however, could lead in the opposite direction. Religious members of the *Sonderkommando* in Janowska, for example, refused cigarettes (which were also a form of currency and could be traded for food, shoes, or clothing) on the Sabbath.[18] In Auschwitz large numbers of religious men rose earlier and washed their hands with the morning ersatz coffee before standing in line to put on *tefillin* for a moment in prayer. On Yom Kippur a large group of young women in a work camp by a ruse threw away their food (they had been given purposely special portions that day by the Nazis who desired that they break the holy fast).[19] In Maidanek, a rabbi working in the camp kitchen regularly traded all his food for watery soup and bread so that he could guard himself from breaking the dietary laws.[20] During Passover of 1945, in a German work camp, Rabbi Samson Stockhamer incredibly refused to eat bread for the eight-day festival with the intention that at least one Jew of the 2,500 interned there should properly observe the dictates of the holiday.[21]

There are numerous other instances in which the restrictive life in the camps was met by a greater self-limitation on the part of the inmates. Their goal was not self-deprivation, but in order to maintain certain spiritual practices this was often their only option. As this conflicted with the self-preservative need to secure survival by acquiring more, it was a manifestation of self-control and autonomous behavior. *Halakhah* (Jewish law), under normal circumstances, instructs man to observe a wide spectrum of restrictions in life in order to demonstrate man's mastery over life.[22] In the camps, the inmate was cast between the twin poles of ever-present death and the need to stay alive. Self-denial in service of the *halakhah* showed that spirituality could, even if for the briefest of moments, rise above that dualism.

Self-denial, however, was not a program. It could not be followed even periodically—except by a few dedicated and disciplined individuals—without tipping the balance in an already *in extremis* situation. There was a need, therefore, to reorient spirituality to the struggle to preserve life. Witness these words—written in the form typical of prayers recited prior to the performance of a *mitzvah* in order to elicit the proper intention—to be said "with great devotion" before the eating of leavened bread *(ḥamez)* on Passover in Bergen-Belsen concentration camp.

> Our Father in Heaven. It is open and known before You that it is our will to do Your will to celebrate the festival of Pesah by eating *matzah* and refraining from leavened bread. With aching heart we must realize that our slavery prevents us from such celebration. Since we find ourselves in a situation of *Sakkanot Nefashot*, of danger to our lives (should we not eat this bread), we are prepared and ready to fulfill Your commandment "'And thou shalt live by them' [by the commandments of the Torah], but not die by them";[23] and we are warned by Your warning: "Be very careful and guard your life."[24] Therefore, we pray to You that You maintain us in life and hasten to redeem us that we may observe Your statutes and do Your will and serve You with a perfect heart. Amen![25]

This prayer was not intended as an excuse for the eating of bread. Virtually everyone did, under duress, so no excuse was needed. Its purpose, rather, was to take the religious fervor that normally accompanied the eating of *matzah*, the symbol of freedom from slavery, and transvaluate it to the eating of bread. In the camps, bread meant life and survival. The full weight of tradition now was brought to bear to support this struggle. Survival was transformed into the prime spiritual value in the camp. Only with survival was there the promise of a future of full observance of His statutes "with a perfect heart."

Participation in Jewish spirituality frequently provided an alternate perspective, which helped inmates to deal with their plight. Jean Améry, a survivor of Auschwitz, understood the believing inmate to be:

> . . . both more estranged from reality and closer to it than his unbelieving comrade. Further from reality because in his finalistic attitude he ignores the given contents of material phenomena and fixes his sight on a nearer or more distant future; but he is also closer to reality because for just this reason he does not allow himself to be overwhelmed by the conditions around him and thus he can strongly influence them. For the unbelieving person reality, under adverse circumstances, is a force to which he submits; under favorable ones it is material for analysis. For the believer reality is clay that he molds, a problem that he solves.[26]

It is possible that Améry, confessing the despair of a

nonbelieving intellectual in the camps, overstated the case for the believer. At the same time, it is clear that the severely limited religious observances one could attempt in the camp offered the vision of a better reality that provided the strength to deal with the shattering reality facing the inmate. It created lines to personal past memories and future hopes so that the present was endurable. This was the strength of religious symbols such as the *seder* (festive ritual meal celebrated on Passover) or the Hannukah lights, which promised an end to oppression as well as a connection to the memory of a better normal time in the past.

This alternate perspective at times was formally articulated. In the ghetto, many Jews employed theological formulations conceived during previous tribulations in Jewish history in order to make sense of their present situation. One would not expect a similar attempt in the hell that was the concentration camp—a realm so brutal that it appears discontinuous with prior Jewish experience. Astonishingly, even in Auschwitz there were a few who sought to place the suffering of their people within a traditional context. They turned, obstinately, to Jewish history and teachings for understanding and for comfort.

One rabbi had the rare situation of working with fourteen other strictly Orthodox Jews in a work assignment of the *Sonderkommando* in Auschwitz. This religious "community" evidently supported and reinforced their religious beliefs. They were, however, frequently challenged by other members of the brigade—many of whom were religious before the Holocaust—for continuing to affirm a faith in Providence. The rabbi bore the brunt of the bitter attacks. He understood Auschwitz within a biblical context: "What happened to the fathers is an omen to their descendants."[27] Filip Müller, himself a nonreligious Jew, reports the rabbi's explanation of this principle to his cynical and hostile audience:

> . . . the pious Jew does not read the Bible like a legend, but applies its content to the present. A few years ago when I read in the synagogue from the Book of Esther, which describes the cruel annihilation of the defenseless Jewish people, I had the same feeling as now. When on the eve of the *seder* I hear the biblical verses on the more than 300-year long oppression by the Pharaohs, I experience again the earlier events as our fathers experienced them in the time of the Roman dominion or in the dark days of the Middle Ages. And if the *Haggadah* commands man in each generation to look at himself as if he himself had migrated from Egypt, the brothers who perhaps by a miracle will manage to survive will read the *Haggadah*, made whole by their experiences in Auschwitz, Maidanek or Treblinka. In every generation, my brothers, there were Pharaohs who wanted to exterminate us, but—praise be the Most Holy—He has always rescued us from their hands.[28]

The rabbi understood Jewish history as a whole fabric, that is, ahistorically. Under normal conditions, the Jew enters the past vicariously through the reading of Scriptures and commemorative ritual observances. In times of hardship and suffering, however, one experiences with his own physical self a reenactment of previous travail. The rabbi maintained that in a mystic sense Egypt and Auschwitz are the same event, occurring to the same people, Israel, only in different centuries and in different geographical locales. He saw this contemporary bondage as the bondage of Egypt. This is not a denial of the horror of their circumstances. Indeed, one can only survive, the rabbi tells us, "by a miracle." But he hoped that as redemption followed the Egyptian bondage, this same redemption would find them here.

## Reflection of the Reality

Religious observances also operated on an *elemental* level, reflecting the present reality of the camp and the contemporary situation of the inmate. Thus, survivors undramatically note that in attempting to procure the customary symbolic foods for the Passover *seder*, they had no need to eat the bitter herbs which traditionally represented the bitterness experienced in bondage, for they had their own experience of bitter servitude.[29] In the same fashion, those few who were able to construct a makeshift *sukkah* (hut in which observant Jews reside during the eight-day festival of Sukkot, commemorating God's providence over the Israelites in the desert) *knew* that they had possessed no other protection over their heads than that which would be provided by Heaven.[30] Praying in Auschwitz on Rosh Hashanah, inmates did not have to imagine a Day of Judgment:

> To be perfectly frank I must report that these [prayers] were not the outpouring of the heart that they should have been. They were rather restrained cries and groans as those which escape the mouths of beasts encaged in a zoo. We clearly knew and felt that "behold this was the Day of Judgment for the entire world"—how much more so for us swallowed alive in the belly of the lion. Our lives dangled by a single hair. We had the legal status of one *in extremis* [who could expire by the slightest touch]. We, therefore, should have cried out, for all forms of weeping pressed on our hearts. We should have stormed Heaven [with our sobs]. . . . I did not detect even a trace of a tear shed by anyone. Not I or anyone else. . . .
>
> We recited the verses "all mankind passes before thee like a flock of sheep. [As a shepherd seeks out his flock, making his sheep pass under his rod, so dost Thou make all the living creatures pass before Thee; Thou dost count and number Thy creatures, fixing their lifetime and inscribing their destiny.] On Rosh Hashanah their destiny is inscribed . . . [who shall live and who shall die; who shall come to a timely end, and who to an untimely end;] who shall perish by fire

[and who by water; who by sword and who by beast; who by hunger and who by thirst; . . .] who by strangling . . ."

We recited all this while we were in the pudendum. To our sorrow we saw these verses fulfilled. After only an hour, at the time when the children of Israel [normally] depart [from their homes] for *Tashlikh* [the ceremony of "casting" on Rosh Hashanah when Jews throw crumbs into a body of water and recite "and You will cast all their sins into the depths of the sea" (Mic. 7:19) as a sign of repentance] came the destruction known as the Selection [for extermination]. It did its work. The verses were fulfilled for us in the full sense of their meaning.[31]

The author of the above account was a loyal Hasid. His reflections on that Rosh Hashanah service must be understood in light of traditional Jewish piety. Under normal circumstances, tears and sobs accompany the religious Jew's recitation of the High Holiday liturgy. Doubtlessly, these outpourings are often only *pro forma*—an expected and affected emotional stirring. Nonetheless, it is clear that in the intense spiritual life of European Jews, even induced tears soon evoked and aroused genuine feelings. The service led the worshipper to understand that his stable and secure world faced a crisis—judgment by its Creator. The service meant to confront the worshipper with the contingency and fragility of all that he possessed, experienced, and of his own existence. Innermost fears and hopes for the future were brought to the fore. The worshipper wept as he realized that his life could either be renewed "for good" in the new year, or be tragically ended or diminished. The holiday liturgy instructs man that he can cancel any "evil decree" for his fate only through a resolute penitence *(teshuvah)* that means a true turning towards God and the paths of moral righteousness.

With this background in mind, we can attempt to understand the absence of tears in the Rosh Hashanah service in the camp. These Jews had already witnessed the contingency and fragility of their lives. Their innermost fears had been realized with the destruction of all they knew and loved. In such a situation, one could not imagine, much less construct, a clear picture of what hope for the future could be. *Teshuvah* itself could hardly seem a possibility—what paths of righteousness were there to trod in the camp? And, in truth, what was left of man himself to effect even a purely spiritual return? These worshippers did not need symbolic, aesthetic, or emotional inducements to consider a judgment that lay *before* them. As religious men in Auschwitz, they understood themselves to stand naked *within* a terrible and exacting judgment.

## Moral Questions

Our discussion has focused upon those aspects pertaining to ritual and the general relation of man to God. Turning to the other major section of Jewish spirituality, the relation of man to man, presents a daunting challenge. The experience of the concentration camps raises serious and painful questions concerning the moral universe of the inmates. We shall not take up, first of all, the *kapos* and others who, in order to attain some advantage, victimized less powerful fellow inmates. Despite the ugliness of this phenomenon, it is to a certain degree understandable. The same brutal conditions which resulted in the creation of physical and emotional musulmans—"little more than walking automatons"[32]—also formed moral musulmans, whose "innate humanity was pulverized under the crushing weight of the juggernaut of Nazi barbarism."[33] We shall also exclude from our discussion those spontaneous acts of theft and violence produced by starvation and acute physical need.

The fact which we shall deal with, and which strikes the observer as truly disheartening, is that the very struggle for life was a morally complicated issue. To survive, one generally had to assume a state which in normal circumstances would be considered radically self-centered. In a situation where opportunities for sustenance and safety were subminimal, a personal success could be harmful to someone else. An extra potato obtained for oneself, for example, was denied another who also desperately needed it. Evasion of a selection meant that one's place would be filled by another inmate. Existence in such a world implies the death of community, of all notions of responsibility to others, and of generosity of spirit—factors which support any system of morality.

Given this scenario of moral confusion amidst human breakdown, an attempted analysis based upon the expectations and demands of Jewish spirituality seems strangely quixotic. The classic injunction "do not judge your fellow man until you have been in his position"[34] would certainly rule out any moral judgment of inmates' behavior. We must also consider that few pious Jews surely had the opportunity or presence of mind to consider the subtleties of Jewish law as they performed slave labor in Auschwitz or were being herded to the gas chamber in Sobibor. Understanding the inmates' moral responses would seem more properly the subject for psychologists, social behaviorists, and ethical philosophers than that of *halakhists*.

That conclusion is, however, shortsighted. Yaffa Eliach has expressed the necessity for the study of the Jewish background of the victims of the Holocaust:

> A comprehensive knowledge of Jewish history and its cultural values is of paramount importance for the scholar who is investigating any aspect of Jewish reactions during the Holocaust. One may assume that the cultural heritage of the Jewish victim was an important factor in shaping his reactions . . . the exclusion of the Jewish factor creates a one-dimensional study of the Holocaust.[35]

It is in this context that we must consider the major role that *halakhah* played in Jewish life before the Holocaust and the effect it had upon even many Jews estranged from religious observances. *Halakhah* was a force that shaped the character of the Jewish people and dialectically a system which itself was molded by the living experience of the people.[36] More than formal law, *halakhah* was "the way" in which the Jews walked, which reflected their ethos—the "tone, character, and quality of [their] life, its moral and aesthetic style and mood; it is the underlying attitude towards themselves and their world that life reflects."[37] Even in a situation where technical legal analysis was impossible, one expects this ingrained set of values and behavior to play a role in the manner that many reacted to crises. *Halakhah*, as the traditional self-perception of the Jew, must be considered as one of the operative elements in the conduct of his life, even *in extremis*.

The classic talmudic discussion of contesting interests in survival is related in Tractate Baba Metzia, Folio 62a:

> Two are walking on the road. In the hand of one of them is a canteen of water. If they both drink—both will die. If [only] one drinks—he will reach his destination [alive]. Ben Petura learned: Better that both drink and they both die, rather than one see the death of his fellow. [This was the accepted teaching] until Rabbi Akiba came and interpreted [the verse from Leviticus 25:36] "That thy brother may live with thee," [to mean] your life precedes the life of your fellow.

Ben Petura's position is highly idealistic, reflecting the idea that each "one shall not be anguished by the death of his friend. And this falls in the category of a complete love where one loves his fellow more than he loves himself."[38] Better that both should die rather than either live at the expense of the other's death. Rabbi Akiba's position—normative in the *halakhah*—affirms that man has the responsibility to afford his fellow the opportunity for life even at great financial and material cost to himself. This responsibility, however, is predicated upon one's own life not being denied. In our case, therefore, the first obligation of the owner of the canteen is to himself. In situations where the outcome is less assured, there is a measure of disagreement amongst the authorities. All agree that *halakhah* does not mandate that one must enter a situation of *actual* danger to himself on behalf of his fellow. Some authorities do hold that one must enter a *potentially* dangerous situation when the danger to one's fellow is already *actual*. Others deny the significance of the distinction between potential and actual, maintaining that one's own life takes precedence whenever a measure of risk is involved.[39] The *halakhah* should not be construed, however, as prohibiting the taking of a mortal risk for one's fellow. It, rather, understands it as an act of supererogation—going beyond the normal requirement of the Law.[40]

Normative *halakhah* does not demand an idealistic or unattainable heroism. Adherence to Ben Petura's position during the Holocaust would have led to a disasterous reductionism, in which

personal survival would be disallowed in the face of the death of
others. In the camps, this position taken to its logical conclusion
would have meant the death of all. In truth, the struggle for personal
survival in the concentration camps is sustained by the *halakhah* as
articulated by Rabbi Akiba. In this context, we must remember the
crucial distinction between the hypothetical talmudic case of the
canteen of water and the camp experience. In the latter, there was no
guarantee of survival even if one concentrated only on his own
survival. Danger to life was constant and actual. It was not a
possibility at which one could reckon the odds on taking a calculated
risk. Where rules could change at the whim of a guard, even
reasonably safe and cautious behavior could end in death.

Despite the danger, inmates often took risks and made sacrifices
to help their fellows. They shared food and offered gifts and succor.
Acts of benevolence are recorded in survivors' memoirs.[41] Many
inmates went to great lengths to render needed aid. In searching for
the sources of this behavior one cannot ignore the life of generosity
and mutual aid that was the shared experience of two millennia of
Jewish life in the Diaspora. This life was imbued by a tradition which
viewed man as being "in the image of God." Enhancement of human
well-being was a major objective to be pursued by the individual and
the community despite economic limitations and other constraints.
The help proffered by inmates was an act of supererogation beyond
the demands of the Law. It was also a response to moral expectations
rooted in Jewish tradition and life.

The impressive nature of these acts of generosity and courage
notwithstanding, they shared the same limitations as other spiritual
responses. These acts were fragmentary in nature—an inmate could
not ensure, after all, his fellow's well-being. At best, he could help
stave off hunger or other immediate dangers. These acts also occurred
episodically as conditions forced everyone to primarily concentrate
on getting himself through the day and the hour. Help to others could
be proffered only fitfully, usually unsystematically, and in a partial
fashion. Morality, finally, was not necessarily consistent. In the
confusing maelstrom of camp life, a number of inmates alternated
deeds of spontaneous selflessness with thefts or violence bred from
desperation.[42]

Another difficult problem in the moral universe of the camps is
the "impossible choices"[43] to which a number of inmates were
subjected. The concentration camps produced situations where either
alternative facing the inmate, under normal circumstances, would
have been considered the wrong one. One such instance took place in
Auschwitz on Rosh Hashanah eve. A large selection of boys was taken
to barracks guarded by Jewish *kapos.* They were to remain there
without food or water until the following night, when they were to be
sent to the crematoria. Surviving fathers—and other relatives—
attempted to bribe the *kapos* with secreted valuables. As this was
going on, a Jew from Oberland posed a moral dilemma to Rabbi Zvi
Hirsch Meisels, who had served as both the Hasidic *rebbe* and town
rabbi in Veitzen, Hungary. Rabbi Meisels records the question and

his response:

> "Rabbi, my only son, who is dearer to me than the apple of
> my eye, is among the boys destined to be burned. I have the
> possibility of redeeming him; however, as I know the *kapos*
> would, no doubt, seize another boy in his place, I ask you,
> Rabbi, to give me a decision in accordance with the Torah
> whether I am permitted to redeem my son. Whatever your
> decision, I shall comply with it."
> When I heard that question trembling took hold of me. I
> had been asked to decide a matter involving life and death. I
> replied: "My dear friend, how can I, in my position, give you
> a clear decision on this question, seeing that also in the time
> when the Temple was standing a question concerning
> capital cases had to be brought before the *Sanhedrin* [the
> ancient Jewish supreme court]? I am here in Auschwitz
> without any books on *halakhah* [codes], without any other
> rabbis, without peace of mind, owing to the travails and
> troubles. . . "[44]

Rabbi Meisels refused to render a decision even after further
adjurations from the distressed father, even though the former, in his
pre-Holocaust vocation, was a well-known *halakhic* authority
accustomed to responding to the personal and communal needs of his
flock. Even in the camps he was able to perform many acts of piety
and of benevolence. Now a Jew voluntarily approached him for
guidance. Surely, no more crucial question has ever been posed to
*halakhah* and to its interpreters; surely, no man was more fit to
respond than this rabbi. The rabbi, however, could not respond. This
agonizing situation seemed beyond him and the resources of
Judaism. The convenant between God and Israel, which demands
that man follow God in all ways, had reached a crisis that was bereft of
resolution.

It is striking that Rabbi Meisels refused to condemn the choice of
many fathers to redeem their sons. Those fathers who saved their sons
did not consult the tradition in making their decision. Their choice,
however, has a strong echo in Jewish legal thought. *Halakhah*
teaches that a third party is not to ransom a captive when we know
that another will be substituted in his place. One major authority,
nevertheless, allows for a captive's natural right to save himself
disregarding whatever probable effect this would have on others.[45]
The point which Rabbi Meisels silently pondered was whether these
fathers could be identified with their sons as the "same person" and
therefore allowed to effect the ransom.[46] We may reflect that it is
highly likely that these men—the rest of their families gone—did feel
this identification and acted automatically upon it.

At the same time, Rabbi Meisels could not permit this father to
ransom his son. The reason was that the *kapos* would seize another
boy as a replacement before they would let the ransomed one go.
There was no chance at all of the *kapos* relenting and not making up

the required number. Certain harm, therefore, would occur to another boy even before his own son could be saved.

Rabbi Meisels conducted the above analysis silently. He refused to render a decision for the father. The latter finally concluded:

> Rabbi, I have done what the Torah commands me to do, i.e., to ask a Rabbi for a decision, and there is no other Rabbi here whom I could consult. If you cannot give me a reply whether I may redeem my child, it appears you yourself are not certain that I may do so, for were it permitted, without doubt you would have told me so. Therefore, I take it for granted that the decision is I must not do so according to the *halakhah*. This is sufficient for me. Therefore, my only child will be burned according to the Torah and *halakhah*. I accept this with love and joy. I shall do nothing to redeem him, because the Torah has so commanded me. . . .

The father refused to allow Rabbi Meisels to escape his role as a *rav* (legal authority) and as a Hasidic *rebbe*. He refused to allow the *halakhah* to be stymied and confounded. The father extracted from the silence that hidden decision too terrible to be pronounced by a rabbi in Israel committed to a Torah of life in the midst of the kingdom of death. The father alone gave utterance to the tragic decision. He did so, and thereby renewed the convenant between Israel and God.

Rabbi Meisels ends his account with the following observation:

> All my words that I did not wish to have the responsibility remained fruitless. He was adamant and did not redeem his son. The whole days of *Rosh Hashanah* he walked about happy, repeating to himself that he had the merit to offer his only son to God, although he had a chance to redeem him. . . . His attitude would be highly valued by God like the binding of Isaac which also took place on *Rosh Hashanah*.

The moral dilemma and the *halakhic* analysis of it lay within the realm of the relations of man to man. The father's acceptance of the decision lay in the realm of his relation to God. The father was correctly linked to the patriarch Abraham, who on being ordered by God to sacrifice his son, Isaac,[47] proceeded without contesting the command. This Jew from Oberland, in a similar fashion, did not request the reasons why Rabbi Meisels refused to permit him to ransom his son. In truth, no reason could be sufficient or logical to a father. On the moral plane, the choice would always remain "impossible." It only became possible when perceived as compelled by God.

The account in Genesis of the binding of Isaac upon the altar and his subsequent last-minute rescue is a highlight of the liturgy of the second day of Rosh Hashanah. The "Isaac" of our story was taken to his death on that same day in Auschwitz. We know even less of his emotions than we know of the biblical Isaac as his trial unfolded. We carefully examine Rabbi Meisel's story as the exegetes[48] have analyzed the biblical account, searching for clues to Isaac's feelings. Unlike the masters of old, we can find no hints. Our thoughts, nevertheless, are not stilled. The son surely must have known that his father had a gold coin. What did he think as he witnessed other boys redeemed by their fathers? We shall never know if the father was able to exchange a few words with his son that fateful day and if the son had accepted the decision as his father had. If there is an impenetrable mystery in the Holocaust, it lies in the heart of this anonymous Isaac.

### Notes

1.   Leon W. Wells, "I Do Not Say Kaddish," *Conservative Judaism* XXXI (Summer 1977): 5.

2.   Eliezer Berkovits, *Faith after the Holocaust* (New York: Ktav, 1973), p. 5.

3.   Yisrael Aviram, "A Testimony Concerning a Serious Topic" [Hebrew], *Yalkut Moreshet* 28 (November 1979): 124.

4.   Aviram, "A Testimony," p. 125.

5.   Eliezer Berkovits, *With God in Hell: Judaism in the Ghettos and Death Camps* (New York: Sanhedrin Press, 1979), p. 110.

6.   Filip Müller, *Eyewitness Auschwitz: Three Years in the Gas Chambers* (New York: Stein and Day, 1981), pp. 32-34.

7.   Wells, "I Do Not Say Kaddish," p. 4.

8.   Müller, *Eyewitness Auschwitz*, pp. 70-71.

9.   Zvi Hirsch Meisels, *MeKadeshei ha-Shem*, vol I (Chicago: Published by the Author, 1955). See "Zer Zahav," section 32, p. 26.

10.   Joseph B. Soloveitchik, "The Community," *Tradition* 17 (Spring 1978): 7-24.

11.   Mordekhai Eliav, *Ani Ma'amin* (Jerusalem: Mossad HaRav Kook, 1965), pp. 199-200.

12.   Yisrael Harpnes, *Bikaf HaKelah* (B'nei-Brak: Heihal HaSefer, 1981), pp. 118-120.

13.   Irving J. Rosenbaum, *The Holocaust and Halakhah* (New York: Ktav, 1976), pp. 106-108.

14.   Berkovits *(With God)*, Eliav, and Rosenbaum cite numberous accounts.

15.   Leon W. Wells, *The Death Brigade* (New York: Holocaust Library, 1978), p. 201.

16.   See "Life in the Camps: The Psychological Dimension," by Sheryl Robbin, in this volume.

17.   See "Surviving," by Henry Friedlander and Sybil Milton, in this volume.

18.  Wells, *The Death Brigade,* p. 202.

19.  Leah Neuman-Weiss, "Jewish Women in German Camps" [Hebrew], *Yalkut Moreshet* (No. 6): 57-58.

20.  Alexander Donat, *The Holocaust Kingdom* (New York: Holocaust Library, 1978), pp. 196-197.

21.  Eliav, *Ani Ma'amin,* pp. 220-221.

22.  Eliezer Berkovits, *God, Man and History: A Jewish Interpretation* (New York: Jonathan David Publishers, 1959), pp. 85-132.

23.  *Babylonian Talmud Yoma* 856 commenting on Lev. 18:5.

24.  Deut. 4:9.

25.  Berkovits, *With God,* p. 32.

26.  Jean Améry, *At the Mind's Limits: Contemplations by a Survivor on Auschwitz and Its Realities,* transl. Sidney Rosenfeld and Stella P. Rosenfeld (Bloomington, Ind.: Indiana University Press, 1980), p. 14.

27.  Chayim Henoch, *Nachmanides: Philosopher and Mystic* [Hebrew] (Jerusalem: Harry Fischel Institute, 1978), p. 437. See also *Tanhuma Lech Lecha* 9.

28.  Müller, *Eyewitness Auschwitz,* p. 67.

29.  Eliav, *Ani Ma'amim,* p. 226.

30.  Harpnes, *Bikaf HaKelah,* pp. 148-151.

31.  Harpnes, *Bikaf HaKelah,* pp. 120-122.

32.  Yehuda Bauer, *A History of the Holocaust* (New York: Franklin Watts, 1982), p. 218.

33.  Berkovits, *Faith,* p. 79.

34.  *Pirke Avot* 1:6.

35.  Yaffa Eliach, "Defining the Holocaust: Perspectives of a Jewish Historian," in *Jews and Christians After the Holocaust,* ed. Abraham J. Peck (Philadelphia: Fortress Press, 1982), p. 16.

36.  Avraham Yitzhak Hacohen Kook, *Orot HaTorah* (Jerusalem, 1961).

37.  Clifford Geertz, *The Interpretation of Cultures* (New York: Basic Books, 1973), p. 127.

38.  Korban Aharon on *Sifra Bechar* 5:3.

39.  See discussion of *Pithei Teshuvah* and *Beit Yosef* on *Tur Hosen Mishpat* 426. I plan to deal more extensively on these issues in a forthcoming work on *Responses to Violence in Jewish Law.*

40.  On the concept of supererogation, see Aharon Lichtenstein, "Does Jewish Tradition Recognize an Ethic Independent of Halakhah?" in *Contemporary Jewish Ethics,* ed. Menachem Marc Kellner (New York: Sanhedrin Press, 1978).

41.  Terrence Des Pres, *The Survivor* (New York: Pocket Books, 1976), pp. 109-174.

42.  Conversation with a survivor of Auschwitz and the labor camps (May 1982), on record at the Simon Wiesenthal Center, Los Angeles.

43.  Lawrence L. Langer, *Versions of Survival: The Holocaust and the Human Spirit* (Albany: State University of New York Press, 1982), pp. 67-129.

44.    H.J. Zimmels, *The Echo of the Nazi Holocaust in Rabbinic Literature* (New York: Ktav, 1977), pp. 113-115.

45.    *Yad Avraham Yoreh Deah* 157.

46.    Meisels, *MeKadeshei ha-Shem*, pp. 8-9.

47.    Gen. 22:1-24.

48.    Louis Ginzberg, *The Legends of the Jews* (Philadelphia: The Jewish Publication Society, 1909), pp. 279-286.

### For Further Reading

Berkovits, Eliezer. *With God in Hell: Judaism in the Ghettos and Deathcamps.* New York: Sanhedrin Press, 1979.

Eliav, Mordekhai. *Ani Ma'amin.* Jerusalem: Mossad HaRav Kook, 1965.

Meisels, Zvi Hirsch. *MeKadeshei ha-Shem.* Vol. I. Chicago: Published by the Author, 1955.

Rosenbaum, Irving J. *The Holocaust and Halakhah.* New York: Ktav, 1976.

Zimmels, H.J. *The Echo of the Nazi Holocaust in Rabbinic Literature.* New York: Ktav, 1977.

8

# THE
# BYSTANDERS

# Raoul Wallenberg

*It all seemed futile. Nobody cared about us. We were the world's extra baggage. We had given up hope until one day we heard this fantastic story about a prominent Swedish diplomat, Raoul Wallenberg, who had come to Hungary on a mission to save the Jews. Soon this man became our Moses. Every day, at great personal risk, he delivered people from the hands of the Nazis. He talked to us, and showed that there was one human being who cared—one angel in this hell. "I came to save a nation," he said. He would print his own Swedish passports, and then run off to the train depots—the trains that were leaving for Auschwitz—and he would reach out to the desperate group of outstretched hands, giving them their tickets to life. He saved thousands of people—one man!—and then, after the liberation of Budapest, the Russians kidnapped him. This is the irony of it all: This noble being who did so much for others may be rotting there somewhere—all alone.*

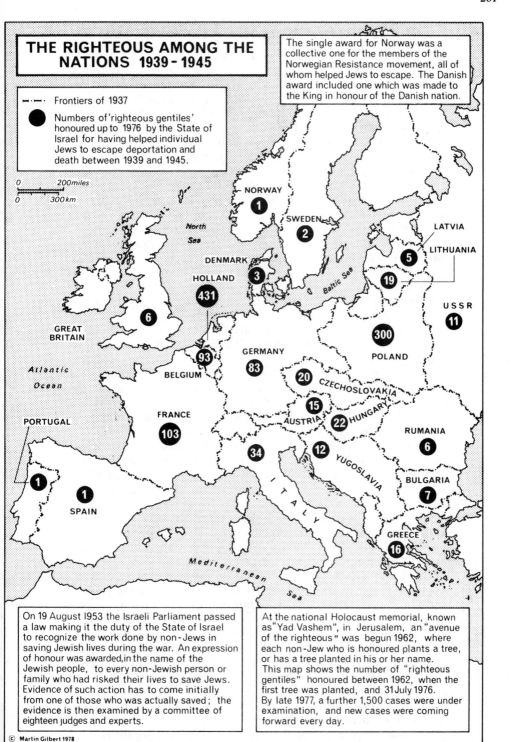

# THE RIGHTEOUS AMONG THE NATIONS 1939-1945

—·—· Frontiers of 1937

● Numbers of 'righteous gentiles' honoured up to 1976 by the State of Israel for having helped individual Jews to escape deportation and death between 1939 and 1945.

0    200 miles
0    300 km

The single award for Norway was a collective one for the members of the Norwegian Resistance movement, all of whom helped Jews to escape. The Danish award included one which was made to the King in honour of the Danish nation.

North Sea

NORWAY **1**

SWEDEN **2**

LATVIA

LITHUANIA **5**

DENMARK **3**
HOLLAND **431**

Baltic Sea

**19**

USSR **11**

GREAT BRITAIN **6**

GERMANY **83**
POLAND **300**

**93** BELGIUM

**20** CZECHOSLOVAKIA

Atlantic Ocean

FRANCE **103**

**15**
AUSTRIA

**22** HUNGARY

RUMANIA **6**

PORTUGAL

**1**
SPAIN **1**

**34**

**12** YUGOSLAVIA

BULGARIA **7**

I T A L Y

GREECE **16**

Mediterranean Sea

On 19 August 1953 the Israeli Parliament passed a law making it the duty of the State of Israel to recognize the work done by non-Jews in saving Jewish lives during the war. An expression of honour was awarded, in the name of the Jewish people, to every non-Jewish person or family who had risked their lives to save Jews. Evidence of such action has to come initially from one of those who was actually saved; the evidence is then examined by a committee of eighteen judges and experts.

At the national Holocaust memorial, known as "Yad Vashem", in Jerusalem, an "avenue of the righteous" was begun 1962, where each non-Jew who is honoured plants a tree, or has a tree planted in his or her name. This map shows the number of "righteous gentiles" honoured between 1962, when the first tree was planted, and 31 July 1976. By late 1977, a further 1,500 cases were under examination, and new cases were coming forward every day.

© Martin Gilbert 1978

# The Righteous Who Helped Jews

## SYBIL MILTON

It is generally assumed that an individual was powerless against the Nazis. It is true that there were genuine limitations to what could be done to thwart the Nazi aim of mass murder. Nevertheless, many ordinary men and women in every country of occupied Europe showed great courage and compassion in helping the Jewish victims of Nazi terror. For the most part, these individuals did not plan to become heroes; the names of the rescuers are largely unrecorded and their good deeds remain anonymous and unrewarded, except in the emotions of those they saved. They helped by providing hiding places, false papers, food, clothing, money, contact with the outside world, underground escape routes, and sometimes even weapons. Their decency exposed them to the dangers of discovery and denunciation. If caught, they faced torture, deportation to concentration camps, or execution. Their behavior was atypical even in their own communities, where the attitude of the majority was characterized by inertia, indifference, and open complicity in the persecution and mass murder of Europe's Jews.

It is impossible to analyze the multiple reasons for individual heroism and ethical behavior under Nazi occupation. Explanations for heroism and creativity rest in the individual psyche and character; however, it is clear that compassion and simple decency played as large a role as bravery. Impartial and reliable information about the number of rescuers and the number of Jews aided or saved is not available. Very rough statistics indicate that about 2,000 non-Jews participated in the rescue of Jews and that they saved between 20,000 and 60,000 children and adults. There is no postwar institution specializing in either World War II or the Holocaust that has collected systematic data about the righteous or about Christian-Jewish relations during the war years. Postwar historiography has given scant attention to this subject, except for biographies of heroes like Raoul Wallenberg in Budapest. Individual episodes are recorded in numerous published memoirs or hidden within the histories of the Jewish communities under German occupation. Others are found in some survivor testimonies, oral histories, and depositions.[1]

The rescuers can be broadly divided into two categories: 1) individuals acting autonomously in haphazard isolation, and 2) individuals acting as part of organized groups—for example, Christian clergy, Socialists, and Communists, among others. Both groups of rescuers faced certain common problems. They were dependent on the general political and military situation. Helping Jews was thus more successful as liberation approached than in the early days of the war. Later in the war, the time required in hiding was shorter, support from local resistance movements was better organized, and the degree of popular hostility to rescue was muted by imminent military defeat.

The geographical patterns of local hostility to Jews influenced receptivity to their rescue. Thus, western Europe (France, Belgium, and the Netherlands), Scandinavia (Denmark and Finland), and southern Europe (Italy and Greece) adapted rapidly to the problems of hiding and rescuing Jews, whereas eastern and central Europe (Poland, the Ukraine, and Austria) remained a more hostile environment to rescue efforts. As the war continued, the rescuers learned to adapt and work around the Nazi network of informers and collaborators. However, they were never able to develop effective strategies to combat the Nazis' rapid organization of mass deportations and population transfers. As the war progressed, rescuers were able to identify sympathetic local groups, individuals, and organizations in every country of occupied Europe: for example, low-level clergymen, Socialists, Communists, and nationalist anti-Nazis. At all times, however, the success of Jewish rescue depended upon fate and chance.

Individuals faced greater pressures than did groups. Many Christian professionals (writers, artists, doctors) saved their Jewish colleagues; Christian employees aided Jewish employers; Jewish employees were helped by Christian bosses; and Gentile wives helped save their Jewish husbands and children. Despite the overwhelming odds, individual rescue sometimes succeeded, especially if the Jewish fugitives could pass as natives in language, manner, and appearance; if the hideout was skillfully camouflaged; if the local population was sympathetic; if geography and distance from neighboring homes aided concealment; and if organized groups or sympathetic friends provided additional safehouses and forged ration papers for essentials like food and clothing. Notwithstanding the mortal risks, many individuals became "their brothers' keepers," were able to overcome their realistic fears, and forged an ethical and practical identification with the persecuted.[2]

Despite the Vatican failure to act, many priests, nuns, and laymen hid Jews in monasteries, convents, schools, and hospitals and protected them with false baptismal certificates. However, as Saul Friedländer's memoirs show,[3] many Catholic priests proselytized and converted their "guests." Moreover, after the war, many Jewish children were never returned to Jewish families, even after lengthy court battles. Nevertheless, some clergymen went to great lengths to protect the Jewish education and observances of their wards. Catholic, Protestant, Quaker, and Unitarian relief organizations cooperated with the Catholic church in France to rescue 12,000 Jewish children; they arranged safehouses and smuggled small numbers into Switzerland and Spain.

In Lvov, the Metropolitan Andreas Sheptitsky defended the Jews against the Nazis, and he and his Ukrainian compatriots hid about 150 Jews in monasteries in eastern Galicia. Furthermore, the French Huguenot Pastor André Trocmé converted the small French Protestant village of Le Chambon into a mountain hideout for 1,000 Jewish persecutees. Le Chambon was as unique as the mass rescue of Danish Jews, because the entire town supported the rescue and accepted arrest and torture rather than betray the Jews they hid. The

tradition of French Catholic persecution of the Huguenot minority
led to absolute identification with the Jewish fugitives, and
unambiguous anti-Nazi behavior was identified with moral survival
and ethical integrity in the town. The Confessing Church in
Germany also provided temporary asylum for Jews, becoming, in
effect, stations on an underground railway leading to the safety of
neutral Switzerland.

Lay Catholics, such as the German Dr. Gertrude Luckner, who
headed the *Caritas Catholica,* also extended help to Jews and non-
Aryan Christians in Germany. She was deported to Ravensbrück for
her aid to the persecuted. After the war, Dr. Luckner was honored for
her courage by the Israeli government. It must be noted that much of
this Christian help was actually rendered to fellow Christians
(converted Jews), who were classified as Jews due to their descent
under Nazi racial laws.

In addition to active help, many clergymen also protested the
mistreatment and deportations of Jews as violations of divine and
human laws. The Catholic pastor of St. Hedwig's Cathedral in
Berlin, Bernard Lichtenburg, prayed publicly for the Jews until his
arrest and death on the way to Dachau. The rescue work of priests of
all Christian denominations is well-documented in postwar literature.[4]

Spectacular rescues by mass resistance also occurred, as for
example, the rescue of 7,000 Danish Jews in October, 1943. The
combination of a mass resistance, the proximity of receptive neutral
Sweden, advance warnings of Nazi deportations, and identification
with the persecutees by a whole nation made this episode almost
unique. Similar smaller rescue operations occurred in Greece, where
Jews were hidden in the mountains or on islands. Later, Greek Jews
were smuggled into Turkey. Similar popular aid to the Jews was
rendered in Finland and in Holland, there was a protest strike in
February, 1941, against the deportation of Dutch Jews. The Italian
army also helped Jews in their occupation zones in France and
Yugoslavia, and they played an important role in rescuing Italian
Jews before the Germans occupied Italy in September, 1943.

Even policemen aided the persecuted against their Nazi
oppressors. Dr. Giovanni Palatucci, the chief of police in Fiume, was
deported to Dachau and killed there for having helped Jews. He was
posthumously honored, when the town of Ramat Gan dedicated a
street in his name in 1953. The Roman police officer Mario di Marco
was arrested and beaten by the Gestapo for helping the Jews of Rome.
Sympathetic policemen in Greece issued false identity papers for
almost 6,000 Jews, helping them escape the Nazi deportation dragnet.

Resistance movements also helped Jews. Sometimes, this aid was
intended to help the Jews; often it was rendered in the context of the
general anti-Nazi resistance. In Yugoslavia, Serbian partisans
attacked a concentration camp near Nish in 1941, freeing a small
number of Jews. On April 19, 1943, the Committee for Jewish
Defense, aided by Christian railroad workers, attacked a Belgian
transport leaving Malines for Auschwitz. Several hundred Jewish

deportees escaped with the help of the Belgian resistance. A unique example of anti-Nazi resistance occurred in the Bialystok ghetto, where several anti-Nazi German and Austrian soldiers were sentenced to death for smuggling weapons and wireless sets to the Jewish resistance. One of these men, Otto Busse, survived and settled in the Kibbutz Nes Amin in 1969, devoting his life to Israel as a concrete example of "Christian atonement."[5]

Many Jews were saved by hiding and also by illegal frontier crossings. Anne Frank's family hid in the concealed annex of an Amsterdam office building with the help of a Christian friend, and the family of Emmanuel Ringelblum (the Warsaw ghetto historian) hid in Warsaw in a specially prepared underground bunker camouflaged by a Polish gardener's greenhouse. Both the Franks and the Ringelblums were caught and perished. About 20,000 Polish Jews, however, did survive hidden in Aryan Warsaw. Likewise, 5,000 Dutch Jews and several thousand German Jews were hidden in the heart of the Nazi Empire, in Berlin and Hamburg. Gentiles, like the teacher Joop Westerweel, smuggled about 100 Jewish children (Palestine Pioneers) across the Dutch border through the French Pyrenées to safety in Spain. He worked alongside Yehoyahim Simon ("Shushu") in the Zionist *Halutzim* (pioneer) movement. Both Shushu and Westerweel were eventually caught by the Germans and executed. Spontaneous gestures by supportive Christian neighbors and friends led to aid for Jews in hiding and on the run. Although the Jewish underground railway to Palestine continued with difficulty throughout World War II, some Jews did escape the European arena and made it to safety in Palestine, Turkey, Sweden, Switzerland, and Spain.

Although Yad Vashem (Israel's Memorial to the Six Million) has honored over 1,200 "righteous of the nations" since 1953, it is impossible to generalize about the motives, deeds, and actual numbers of these rescuers. Some rescuers acted within the planned context of guerrilla units and resistance movements; others used the buildings and funds of the Roman Catholic church to aid Jews. The rescuers were able to use the national humiliation caused by the German occupation to build limited popular support and help the Jews. They were few in number but ethically and morally strong. Although the number of Jews they saved was small, they provide a beacon of victory for posterity, a victory over the capitulation and collaboration of the majority of their compatriots.

### Notes

1.   Philip Friedman, "Righteous Gentiles in the Nazi Era," in *Roads to Extinction: Essays on the Holocaust,* by Philip Friedman.

(New York and Philadelphia: The Jewish Publication Society and Conference on Jewish Social Studies, 1980), pp. 409-421.

2. Philip Friedman, *Their Brothers' Keepers* (New York: Holocaust Library, 1978); Arieh Bauminger, *The Roll of Honour* (Jerusalem: Yad Vashem, 1970).

3. Saul Friedländer, *When Memory Comes,* trans. Helen Lane (New York: Avon Books, 1980).

4. Philip Hallie, *Lest Innocent Blood Be Shed* (New York: Harper Colophon Books, 1980); Philip Friedman, "Was There an Other Germany During the Nazi Period?" in *Roads to Extinction,* pp. 422-464.

5. Reuben Ainsztein, *Jewish Resistance in Nazi-Occupied Eastern Europe* (New York and London: Barnes and Noble, 1974), pp. 898-899.

### For Further Reading

Ainsztein, Reuben. *Jewish Resistance in Nazi-Occupied Eastern Europe.* New York, London: Barnes and Noble, 1974.

Bauminger, Arieh. *The Roll of Honour.* Jerusalem: Yad Vashem, 1970.

Bejski, Moshe. "The Righteous Among the Nations and Their Part in the Rescue of the Jews." *Rescue Attempts During the Holocaust,* eds. Yisrael Gutman and Efraim Zuroff. Jerusalem: Yad Vashem, 1977.

Bertelsen, Sage. *October 43.* New York: American Jewish Committee, 1973.

Bierman, John. *Righteous Gentile.* New York: Viking Press, 1981.

Chary, Frederick B. *The Bulgarian Jews and the Final Solution.* Pittsburgh: University of Pittsburgh Press, 1972.

Friedländer, Saul. *When Memory Comes.* Translated from the French by Helen Lane. New York: Avon Books, 1980.

Friedman, Philip. *Their Brothers' Keepers.* New York: Holocaust Library, 1978.

Gross, Leonard. *The Last Jews in Berlin.* New York: Simon and Schuster, 1982.

Hallie, Philip. *Lest Innocent Blood Be Shed.* New York: Harper Colophon Books, 1980.

Hellman, Peter. *Avenue of the Righteous.* New York: Atheneum, 1980.

Keneally, Thomas. *Schindler's List.* New York: Simon and Schuster, 1982.

Leuner, H.D. *When Compassion Was a Crime: Germany's Silent Heroes, 1938-1945.* London: Oswald Wolff, 1966.

Yahil, Leni. *The Rescue of Danish Jewry.* Philadelphia: The Jewish Publication Society, 1969.

# The Holocaust: Failure in Christian Leadership?

## JOHN T. PAWLIKOWSKI

Since the end of the Nazi era, there have been continual reassessments of the roles played by Christian leaders during that tragic period. The actions of Pope Pius XII have been scrutinized in a special way. Generally speaking, Jewish scholars have tended to place considerable responsibility on many of the heads of the Christian communities inside and outside of Germany for the success of the Nazi effort. This has elicited rather uncritical defensive responses from postwar church representatives, but has also led an increasing number of church historians and theologians to probe the issue more deeply. An annual series of scholarly conferences, involving both Christians and Jews, has developed around the theme, "The German Church Struggle and the Holocaust."

By and large, the Christian scholars who have seriously studied the churches' stance during the Holocaust wind up with a reasonably critical evaluation of their Christian witnesses. They, of course, acknowledge the heroic efforts of righteous Gentiles, such as Dietrich Bonhoeffer. But, while these figures remain sources of Christian hope today, their miniscule number only serves to dramatize the general indifference to, and even cooperation with, the Nazi destruction of the Jewish people. Father Edward Flannery and Professor Franklin Littell are two such critical Christian voices. While recognizing the complexity of any investigation of the root causes of the Holocaust, Flannery clearly affirms that:

> ... in the final analysis, some degree of the charge [against the church] must be validated. Great or small, the apathy or silence was excessive. The fact remains that in the twentieth century of Christian civilization, a genocide of six million innocent people was perpetrated in countries with many centuries of Christian tradition and by hands that were in many cases Christian. This fact in itself stands, however vaguely, as an indictment of the Christian conscience. The absence of reaction by those most directly implicated in the genocide only aggravates this broader indictment.[1]

Professor Littell speaks in similar terms about the general state of the churches and their leadership in Germany. "It is quite wrong," he says,

> ... to assume that the Church Struggle was a battle to defend Christian Germany against the false teaching of neobarbarians. ... The tragedy is the wholesale apostasy of the baptized—their eagerness, in the name of "saving the world from atheistic communism" and "reestablishing law and order" ... to countenance the most brutal and anti-

Christian of political measures to reconstitute a lost age of religious monism.[2]

Concerned Christians like Littell and Flannery have bluntly challenged the churches for their part in the Final Solution. In the last decade, a growing number of Christian scholars, especially church historians, have tried to confront this issue in a more dispassionate, but equally serious, way. They have looked into the position of the churches in Germany as well as at the response of the international church. In the latter area, they have focused attention on the Vatican and Pope Pius XII.

None of the new generation of church historians dealing with the Holocaust in any way desires to whitewash the actions of Christian leaders. But a general consensus has also emerged that no simplistic blanket indictment of the churches will stand the test of historical evidence. Hence, we have slowly moved to a more balanced approach in the discussion of the Church Struggle from the situation several years ago, when unqualified accusations and equally uncritical defenses tended to predominate. There is also an additional caution that is now sounded by most Christian interpreters: Substantial archival materials still remain to be examined. Until many of these relevant church archives are made available by the churches themselves, the assessments of direct and indirect collaboration with the Nazi effort must remain open to future judgment. Furthermore, differences have emerged among those Christian scholars who have taken the Littell/Flannery challenge to heart. In part, these differences of opinion lie in disagreements as to how effective the churches could have been, even if their leaders had taken a much more outwardly hostile stance towards nazism.

One perspective that has gained acceptance from most church historians involved with this subject is that the Church Struggle in Germany cannot be evaluated without some understanding of the prior half-century of that nation's history and the churches' reaction to it. This is true with respect to both the Protestant and Catholic communities, even though their social roles were somewhat different. The churches, more than any other major component of German society, had become conscious that their continuing social role could no longer be upheld by mere appeals to tradition. It was commonly believed by many Christian leaders that the loss of faith following the debacle of World War I could be counteracted only by a vigorous and vibrant engagement with the social order. The Weimar Republic, despite its constitution, which granted the churches greater self-rule in their internal affairs, was viewed more as a foe than as a friend. There was the need to preserve Christian society in a social setting where the state apparatus was indifferent or even hostile to religion.

This was certainly the feeling which prevailed within the principal Protestant community, the Evangelical church of Germany. As the church historian John S. Conway has noted:

. . . the emphasis on the need for unity, continuity, and

nationalistically conditioned conservatism was inimical to the idea of the growth of alternatives. Indeed, strong opposition was raised against the idea of pluralism in society, which was presumed to lead to a false sense of freedom and to encourage immorality. Like other prominent figures in society, the ecclesiastics were wholly convinced of the danger of Bolshevism, which threatened both the institutional and spiritual heritage of German Christianity. Consequently the appeal of a political movement which combined nationalistic devotion to *das Volk*, a popular relevant social activism, and a strong aversion to Bolshevism achieved rapid growth among wide sections of the Evangelical churches.[3]

Recent research has shown that well over three-quarters of the Protestant pastors in Germany supported right-wing political parties. The churches issued official condemnations of left-wing political options, isolating pastors with Socialist leanings and excommunicating those who espoused communism. Church spokespersons became strongly nationalist in their language and frequently refused to support the "weak" and "antireligious" Weimar political leadership. As Professor Frederick O. Bonkovsky states:

> . . . fearful of the threat from the left they welcomed the Nazis as a strong force which might be able to end economic and social chaos. As Niemöller stated after the Ruhr crisis, "we lacked leaders, we lacked a real goal, and above all, we lacked the inward and moral urge to national action."[4]

Like its Protestant counterpart, the Roman Catholic church was also afflicted with serious ambiguity during the Weimar Republic. Its psyche still bore the scars of Bismark's *Kulturkampf*, which attempted to throttle the Roman church's influence in the newly established German Empire. A feeling of second-class citizenship frequently pushed Catholics into an exaggerated display of national loyalty. It also provoked Catholic leaders to take legal steps to guarantee Catholic prerogatives through concordats with individual provinces and then, finally, with the Reich government itself in 1933.

The growth of nazism in the predominantly Catholic region of Bavaria proved a special challenge to the Roman bishops. Various dioceses released early condemnations of the new Nazi racial theories. But then fear began to grow within the Catholic hierarchy that the popularity of nazism, if opposed, could result in widespread defections from Catholic ranks and to possible confrontation with the government and the Protestant Evangelical church. Public opposition by the Catholic leadership decreased and the ban on Catholic membership in the Nazi party was rescinded in March, 1933. This action on the part of the Catholic leadership motivated the Reich government to quickly conclude the negotiations for the

Concordat. The Catholic church had finally achieved the domestic safeguards it had long wanted. As John Conway indicates:

> Like their Protestant counterparts, the Catholic leaders had no sympathy for a pluralistic society. They looked with favor on a movement that promised national renewal and restoration, and readily indulged in the wishful thinking that the more radical and revolutionary elements of the Nazi creed would be jettisoned once the accession to power brought with it an acceptance of responsibility.[5]

But both Catholic and Protestant leaders soon realized that their hopes for nazism were mistaken, and that a myriad of administrative decisions—rather than frontal attacks on religion—by the Reich government were undercutting the churches. Protests began to emerge, but were muted by fears that the bulk of the Christian faithful could not be counted upon in an all-out confrontation with the political authorities.[6]

From the Protestant side, the basis for opposition to nazism was developed in the 1934 Barmen Theological Declaration approved at the first synod of the United Evangelical church (or Confessing Church) in Germany. Its aim was to counteract the errors of the so-called "German Christians" (those Christians who positively identified themselves with the Nazi programs on religious grounds) and the Reich church government. There have been varying analyses of the effectiveness of the Barmen Declaration.[7] They have been conditioned by various expectations of what opposition was possible by the churches and by evaluations of the churches' protest based on Barmen in isolation or together with other social groups. Frederick Bonkovsky's assessment of the opposition it engendered within the Confessing Church is rather positive. He feels that the indigenous Confessing Church (far more so than the "foreign" Roman Catholic church) was the only effective opposition group in any sector of German society during the height of the Nazi period. That it could not do more was due to the fact that it no longer held the kind of total sway over its membership that was true for the church in previous times.[8] Eberhard Bethge[9] is somewhat more critical in his judgment, as is John Conway. Conway does agree with Bonkovsky that members of the Confessing Church resisted Aryanization more than any other professional group in Germany. But he faults the Barmen Declaration for lacking any specific response to the Jewish Question and the proposed Final Solution:

> Defense of purity of doctrine was stressed over concrete Christian action. Later on [Karl] Barth [the famous theologian], the Barmen Confession's principal author, admitted that he had failed to make the Jewish Question a decisive issue at that time.[10]

On the Catholic side, evaluation of the church's leadership is equally diverse. Guenter Lewy is exceedingly harsh in his judgment.[11] Gordan Zahn[12] is critical but admits that the churches were the only social institutions willing to oppose the Nazis to any degree. Zahn also stresses the need to examine more fully possible Catholic resistance at the grass-roots level, even if the hierarchy appears timid. He suspects that more occurred at this level in opposition to the Nazis than has thus far been reported.

Zahn notes that official Catholic resistance appeared less than a year after the signing of the Concordat. The June, 1934, pastoral letter of the combined German hierarchy meeting at Fulda was a public and formal protest against the restrictions on the Catholic press and the church's organizational activity. This pastoral letter served to galvanize Catholic opposition in a way similar to the Barmen Declaration for the Protestant churches. It provided the justification for a steady, albeit unsuccessful, campaign of opposition to the growing attacks of the Third Reich against the Catholic church. Zahn criticizes the Fulda pastoral letter and subsequent Catholic pronouncements, including the papal encyclical *Mit brenneder Sorge* (1937), for the same reasons Conway objects to the Barmen Declaration: The Nazis' Final Solution to the Jewish Question is scarcely mentioned. Zahn feels that the Catholic protest failed because it could not match the power of the Third Reich and it was unwilling to push its supporters into total resistance and mass martyrdom.

Beate Ruhm von Oppen, another leading Christian interpreter of the Holocaust who has worked extensively on German records, believes both Zahn and Lewy are far too negative. She argues that the meaningful survival of the church today demands giving greater attention to the Catholic resistance that did exist. She is not urging a manufactured defense or the dismissal of significant collaboration and indifference, but she insists that a mere examination of the response of Catholic bishops must yield to a study of Catholic (and Protestant) military chaplains whose resistance, attitudes, and influence increasingly worried Nazi leaders like Goebbels.[13]

One must also consider the behavior of the Christian clergy in the rest of Europe. There are instances where priests, nuns, and pastors helped in the rescue of Jews (see Sybil Milton's article, "The Righteous Who Helped Jews" in this volume). But the possibilities of further organized and effective opposition to the anti-Jewish decrees, on the part of the clergy, must also be considered. The Chief Rabbi of Palestine posed this option to Monseignor Hughes (a representative of the pope) in 1944, in Cairo, when the deportation of Hungarian Jews to the extermination camps commenced in earnest:

CHIEF RABBI: If Hungarian Bishops were to go into the camps and announce publicly that, if deportation of Jews went on, they [the Bishops] would go and die with them, I think it would be difficult for the Germans to continue the deportations.

MONSEIGNOR HUGHES: The Bishops in France and other

countries have carried out demonstrations of that kind. When the Germans began deporting Jews, they [the Bishops] went into the streets wearing a yellow star. This action made a considerable impression and, in some places, rendered deportation impossible. But Your Honor will understand that realization of your proposal would require "unity of action."[14]

As Saul Friedländer notes: "Now there never was such a demonstration by French Bishops, as Monseignor Hughes must have known. The Chief Rabbi . . . had no means of judging whether or not these details were true."[15] We really do not know of any public protests on the part of Catholic or Protestant clergy, anywhere in Europe, during this period, including protests directed to the local population.

One must also consider the cooperation and complexity of clerical involvement in the destruction of European Jews. An example is Slovakia, "a heavily Catholic country with a priest as president and prime minister who prided himself on being a practicing Catholic,"[16] and who finally cooperated in the persecution of the Jews, leading to their deportation to the concentration camps. Before Passover in 1942, Rabbi Michael Dov-Ber Weissmandel, a leader of the Jewish underground, approached his old acquaintance Archbishop Kametko. He begged the archbishop to intervene with the latter's former personal secretary, President Tisso, regarding the expulsion of the Jews from Slovakia. The archbishop replied:

This is no mere expulsion. There—you will not die of hunger and pestilence; there—they will slaughter you all, young and old, women and children, in one day. This is your punishment for the death of our Redeemer. There is only one hope for you, to convert to our religion. Then I shall effect the annulling of this decree.[17]

It is interesting to note that a number of Jews did convert to Christianity in order to save their lives. As Raul Hilberg observes:

[Even though] . . . the Jews were primarily concerned with the protection, such protection could best be rendered by the Catholic Church. The Jews were not interested in theology just then. But therein, precisely, lay the reason for the imbalance of conversions—the Catholic Church was not primarily interested in the saving of lives; it wanted to save souls. Of course the Church protected its converts. The priesthood was angry when the state presumed to nullify the sacred baptism and turn Christians into Jews. But for exactly that reason the Catholic Church did not bestow lightly. The applicant had to be "sincere." If it took a catastrophe to make him "see the light," well then, all right, he could be admitted. However, if he was suspected of merely wanting to save his life, perhaps to revert to Judaism after the end of the war, he was turned away. When the wave of deportations overtook the Jewish community in Slovakia, there was little time for religious instruction, preparation, and meditation. That is, Orthodox Churches converted a disproportionately large number of Jews.[18]

Although Weissmandel knew of these conversions, he refused to accept them as an option. After escaping from a deportation to Auschwitz in the fall of 1944, he approached the papal *nuncio* (papal delegate) to plead once again for help. The delegate replied: "This, being a Sunday, is a holy day for us. Neither I nor Father Tisso occupy ourselves with profane matters on this day." What Weissmandel did not understand was how the blood of infants and children could be considered a profane matter. The archbishop told him: "There is no innocent blood of Jewish children in the world. All Jewish blood is guilty. You have to die. This is the punishment that has been awaiting you because of that sin [the death of Jesus]."[19]

The role of Pope Pius XII has also long been the subject of controversy among scholars. Earlier works by Jewish and Christian writers tend to be highly critical. Saul Friedländer,[20] Rolf Hochhuth,[21] Friedrich Heer,[22] and Nora Levin[23] are especially so. Few would accuse Pius of outright hatred for Jews. But a combination of a long-standing Catholic antisemitic tradition, coupled with his desire to preserve the Catholic community in Germany and to fight the onslaught of Bolshevism, rendered Jews "unfortunate expendables," in the pope's calculations.

Official Catholic responses to these charges tend to be highly polemical and defensive. Some have urged the canonization of Pius as a rebuff. Some Jewish defenses of Pius also surfaced, mainly Joseph L. Lichten's *A Question of Judgment: Pius XII and the Jews.*[24] Based on personal experiences and conversations, Lichten maintains that Pius did more in behalf of Jews than someone like Rolf Hochhuth allows. He quotes Dr. Nahum Goldmann, president of the World Jewish Congress, who offered a positive assessment of Pius' activities on the Jewish Question on the occasion of the pope's death. Whether a formal condemnation of the pope, as opposed to diplomatic initiatives, would have curtailed the mass murder of Jews, remains an open question for Lichten. Most critics of Pius assume that it would have, with the evidence leaning against any real results.

Beate Ruhm von Oppen and Father Flannery also believe that the focus on Pius has been to the detriment of a wider investigation of the Catholic church's role. Flannery says that "the centralization of the charge on the pope has unfortunately deflected attention from the scope of a silence that affected many churches, governments, and people."[25] Even Rolf Hochhuth, in a later interview, indicates that Pius' silence and consequent guilt on the Jewish Question was no greater than that of other religious and political leaders like Churchill and Cordell Hull.[26]

Recently, the controversy over Pius' papacy has once more received widespread attention. Father John Morley, in a recent study of Vatican diplomacy, argues that, generally, in all the important countries of Europe where mass Jewish deportations were occurring, the interventions by Vatican diplomats and papal *nuncios* were sporadic and reluctant, at times apologetic, and lacking the force of condemnation that the circumstances required. Yet, they had acted forcefully when church rights were at stake. . . .[27] And while not directly a response to the new evaluation by Morely, a recent volume by Father J. Derek Holmes of Great Britain has been used by some as a response to Morley. Holmes speaks of Pius' efforts in behalf of the Jews of Rome and feels that a public denunciation of the Nazis might have endangered the Vatican's work to save Jews.[28]

The case of Pius XII is still far from closed. Catholics and other scholars need to probe further, with an open mind, into his activities and those of the Vatican bureaucracy. It may be that the final judgment on the pope's stance will never reach a consensus, for how does one finally prove or disprove the possible effect of a hypothetical public stance by Pius? It is my contention, however, that the whole concept of the church that dominated the thinking of Pius XII and his associates, especially how it related the security of the Catholic church to the well-being of non-Catholics, needs to be studied far more thoroughly. Ultimately, Pius' accomplishments and failures were buried with him. There is no way we can change his record. But contemporary Christians are in a position to change their understanding of the church's relationship to Jews and others outside its community and beliefs, especially in times of profound social crisis.[29]

Despite the different interpretations, a few directions seem clear: (1) an overwhelming majority of Christian clergy acquiesced in the destruction of European Jews; (2) church leaders were unable to mount a successful effort against the Nazis. This bears serious reflection for the continuing struggles which the churches face in the contemporary world; (3) the church's self-understanding and its own sufferings under the Nazis were far too isolated from the sufferings of non-Christians, Jews in particular, to whom suffering meant death. Why did the churches raise the issue of Nazi murder of "baptized" Jews to the exclusion of the Jewish people at large?; (4) the churches were far too connected with the dynamics of German society to really stand in judgment against it; (5) the Jewish Question could not be adequately addressed because of the long-standing theological tradition of anti-Judaism in the churches. This tradition must be obliterated once and for all by the post-Holocaust Christian community; (6) the churches, which will never regain the kind of control over society they once had, must reflect anew on how to combat totalitarian power. Where are their primary resources in such a context?; and, finally, (7) the churches' fear of communism blinded them to all other forms of totalitarian oppression. Is there danger of repetition in our day?

## Notes

1. Edward Flannery, "Anti-Zionism and the Christian Psyche," *Journal of Ecumenical Studies* 6 (Spring 1969): 174.

2. Franklin Littell, "Church Struggle and the Holocaust," in *The German Church Struggle,* eds. Franklin H. Littell and Hubert G. Locke (Detroit: Wayne State University Press, 1974), p. 16.

3. John S. Conway, "The Churches," in *The Holocaust,* eds. Henry Friedlander and Sybil Milton (Millwood, NY: Kraus International Publications, 1980), p. 200. See also John Conway, *The Nazi Persecution of the Churches* (Toronto: Ryerson Press, 1968).

4. Frederick O. Bonkovsky, "The German State and Protestant Elites," in Littell and Locke, *The German Church Struggle,* p. 130.

5. Conway, "The Churches," p. 201.

6. See Gordon Zahn, "Catholic Resistance? A Yes and a No," in Littell and Locke, *The German Church Struggle,* p.228.

7. For one evaluation, see Arthur C. Cochrane, "The Message of Barmen for Contemporary Church History," in Littell and Locke, *The German Church Struggle,* pp. 185-202.

8. See Bonkovsky, "The German State."

9. Eberhard Bethge, "Troubled Self-Interpretation and Uncertain Reception in the Church Struggle," in Littell and Locke, *The German Church Struggle,* pp. 167-184. See also Eberhard Bethge, *Dietrich Bonhoeffer, Man of Vision* (New York: Harper & Row, 1970).

10. Conway, "The Churches," p. 205.

11. Guenter Lewy, *The Catholic Church and Nazi Germany* (New York: McGraw-Hill, 1964); Zahn, "Catholic Resistance," in Littell and Locke, *The German Church Struggle,* pp. 203-240.

12. Gordon Zahn, "Revolutionism and Counterrevisionism in the Historiography of the Church Struggle," in Littell and Locke, *The German Church Struggle,* pp. 56-68.

13. Zahn, "Catholic Resistance?" p. 233.

14. Saul Friedländer, *Pius XII and the Third Reich* (New York: Alfred A. Knopf, 1966).

15. Friedländer, *Pius XII,* p. 235.

16. John Morley, *Vatican Diplomacy and the Jews During the Holocaust: 1939-1943.* (New York: Ktav, 1980) p. 101.

17. Michael Dov-Ber Weissmandel, *Min Hamezar,* in *Faith After the Holocaust,* Eliezer Berkovits (New York: Ktav, 1973), pp. 16-17.

18. Raul Hilberg, *The Destruction of the European Jews* (Chicago: Quandrangle Press, 1961), p. 466.

19. Eliezer Berkovits, *Faith,* pp. 16-17.

20. Friedländer, *Pius XII.*

21. Rolf Hochhuth, *The Deputy* (New York: Grove Press, 1964).

22. Eric Bentley, ed., *The Storm Over The Deputy* (New York: Grove Press, 1964), p. 173.

23. Nora Levin, *The Holocaust* (New York: Schocken Books, 1973), pp. 687-693.

24. Joseph L. Lichten, *A Question of Judgment* (Washington,

D.C.: National Catholic Welfare Conference, 1963).

25. Flannery, *Anti-Zionism,* p. 175.
26. Bentley, *The Storm,* p. 43.
27. John Morley, *Vatican Diplomacy,* p. 201.
28. J. Derek Holmes, *The Papacy in the Modern World* (London: Burns & Oates, 1981).
29. See John T. Pawlikowski, *The Challenge of the Holocaust for Christian Theology* (New York: Anti-Defamation League, 1978), and "Method in Catholic Social Ethics: Some Observations in Light of the Jewish Tradition," in *Formation of Social Policy in the Catholic and Jewish Tradition,* eds. Eugene J. Fisher and Daniel F. Polish (Notre Dame, Ind.: University of Notre Dame Press, 1980), pp. 162-192.

### For Further Reading

Bentley, Eric, ed. *The Storm Over The Deputy.* New York: Grove Press, 1964.

Bethge, Eberhard. *Dietrich Bonhoeffer, Man of Vision.* New York: Harper & Row, 1970.

Conway, John. *The Nazi Persecution of the Churches: 1933-1945.* Toronto: Ryerson Press, 1968.

Friedlander, Henry, and Milton, Sybil, eds. *The Holocaust: Ideology, Bureaucracy, and Genocide.* Millwood, NY: Kraus International Publications, 1980.

Friedländer, Saul. *Pius XII and the Third Reich: A Documentation.* New York: Alfred A. Knopf, 1966.

Hochhuth, Rolf. *The Deputy.* New York: Grove Press, 1964.

Holmes, J. Derek. *The Papacy in the Modern World.* London: Burns & Oates, 1981.

Levin, Nora. *The Holocaust.* New York: Schocken Books, 1973.

Lichten, Joseph. *A Question of Judgment: Pius XII and the Jews.* Washington, D.C.: National Catholic Welfare Conference, 1963.

Littell, Franklin H., and Locke, Hubert G., eds. *The German Church Struggle and the Holocaust.* Detroit: Wayne State University Press, 1974.

Morley, John. *Vatican Diplomacy and the Jews During the Holocaust, 1939-1943.* New York: Ktav, 1980.

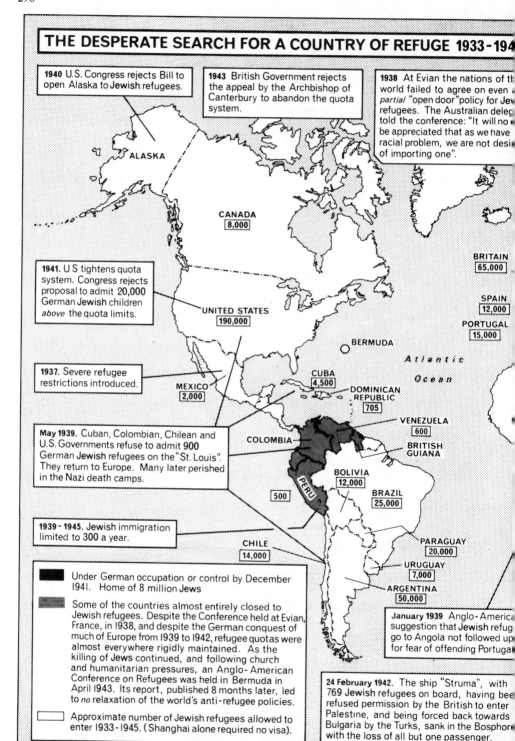

# THE DESPERATE SEARCH FOR A COUNTRY OF REFUGE 1933-194[5]

**1940** U.S. Congress rejects Bill to open Alaska to Jewish refugees.

**1943** British Government rejects the appeal by the Archbishop of Canterbury to abandon the quota system.

**1938** At Evian the nations of th[e] world failed to agree on even [a] *partial* "open door" policy for Je[wish] refugees. The Australian deleg[ate] told the conference: "It will no[t] be appreciated that as we have [no] racial problem, we are not desi[rous] of importing one".

ALASKA

CANADA
8,000

**1941.** U S tightens quota system. Congress rejects proposal to admit **20,000** German Jewish children *above* the quota limits.

UNITED STATES
190,000

BRITAIN
65,000

SPAIN
12,000

PORTUGAL
15,000

BERMUDA

*Atlantic*

*Ocean*

**1937.** Severe refugee restrictions introduced.

MEXICO
2,000

CUBA
4,500

DOMINICAN REPUBLIC
705

VENEZUELA
600

**May 1939.** Cuban, Colombian, Chilean and U.S. Governments refuse to admit **900** German Jewish refugees on the "St. Louis". They return to Europe. Many later perished in the Nazi death camps.

COLOMBIA

BRITISH GUIANA

PERU
500

BOLIVIA
12,000

BRAZIL
25,000

**1939-1945.** Jewish immigration limited to 300 a year.

CHILE
14,000

PARAGUAY
20,000

URUGUAY
7,000

ARGENTINA
50,000

■ Under German occupation or control by December 1941. Home of 8 million Jews

▨ Some of the countries almost entirely closed to Jewish refugees. Despite the Conference held at Evian, France, in 1938, and despite the German conquest of much of Europe from 1939 to 1942, refugee quotas were almost everywhere rigidly maintained. As the killing of Jews continued, and following church and humanitarian pressures, an Anglo-American Conference on Refugees was held in Bermuda in April 1943. Its report, published 8 months later, led to *no* relaxation of the world's anti-refugee policies.

□ Approximate number of Jewish refugees allowed to enter 1933-1945. (Shanghai alone required no visa).

**January 1939** Anglo-America[n] suggestion that Jewish refug[ees] go to Angola not followed up [ ] for fear of offending Portugal[.]

**24 February 1942.** The ship "Struma", with 769 Jewish refugees on board, having bee[n] refused permission by the British to enter Palestine, and being forced back towards Bulgaria by the Turks, sank in the Bosphor[us] with the loss of all but one passenger.

© Martin Gilbert 1978

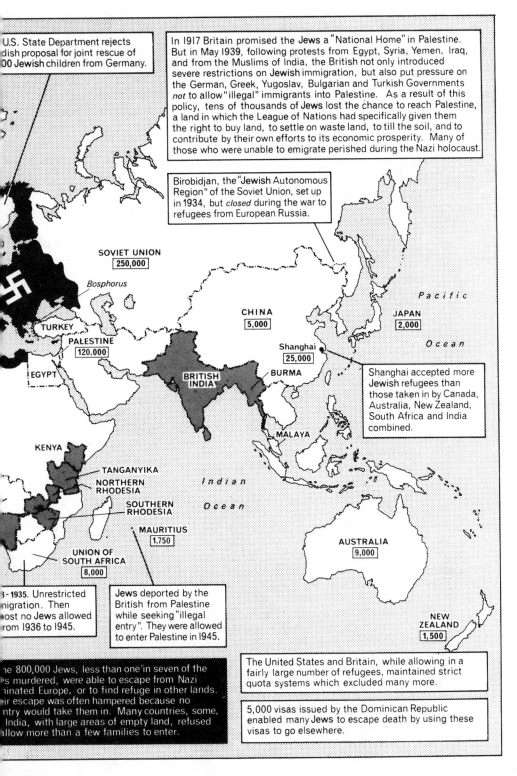

U.S. State Department rejects ⌐dish proposal for joint rescue of ⌐0 Jewish children from Germany.

In 1917 Britain promised the Jews a "National Home" in Palestine. But in May 1939, following protests from Egypt, Syria, Yemen, Iraq, and from the Muslims of India, the British not only introduced severe restrictions on Jewish immigration, but also put pressure on the German, Greek, Yugoslav, Bulgarian and Turkish Governments *not* to allow "illegal" immigrants into Palestine. As a result of this policy, tens of thousands of Jews lost the chance to reach Palestine, a land in which the League of Nations had specifically given them the right to buy land, to settle on waste land, to till the soil, and to contribute by their own efforts to its economic prosperity. Many of those who were unable to emigrate perished during the Nazi holocaust.

Birobidjan, the "Jewish Autonomous Region" of the Soviet Union, set up in 1934, but *closed* during the war to refugees from European Russia.

SOVIET UNION
250,000

*Bosphorus*

*Pacific*

CHINA
5,000

JAPAN
2,000

TURKEY

*Ocean*

PALESTINE
120,000

Shanghai
25,000

EGYPT

BRITISH INDIA

BURMA

Shanghai accepted more Jewish refugees than those taken in by Canada, Australia, New Zealand, South Africa and India combined.

MALAYA

KENYA

TANGANYIKA

NORTHERN RHODESIA

*Indian*

SOUTHERN RHODESIA

*Ocean*

MAURITIUS
1,750

AUSTRALIA
9,000

UNION OF SOUTH AFRICA
8,000

⌐-1935. Unrestricted ⌐nigration. Then ⌐ost no Jews allowed ⌐rom 1936 to 1945.

Jews deported by the British from Palestine while seeking "illegal entry". They were allowed to enter Palestine in 1945.

NEW ZEALAND
1,500

⌐e 800,000 Jews, less than one in seven of the ⌐s murdered, were able to escape from Nazi ⌐inated Europe, or to find refuge in other lands. ⌐ir escape was often hampered because no ⌐ntry would take them in. Many countries, some, ⌐ India, with large areas of empty land, refused ⌐llow more than a few families to enter.

The United States and Britain, while allowing in a fairly large number of refugees, maintained strict quota systems which excluded many more.

5,000 visas issued by the Dominican Republic enabled many Jews to escape death by using these visas to go elsewhere.

# The Importance of Wartime Priorities in the Failure to Rescue Jews

## HENRY L. FEINGOLD

In any study of the Holocaust, the role of the bystander is questioned. "Why did the witnessing agencies not do more to rescue the Jews during the Holocaust?" For those emotionally involved with the Holocaust, there can only be one response: The witnesses failed to properly play their historical role. This response assumes that nation-states and international agencies like the Red Cross were able to make humanitarian responses in situations like the Holocaust and that they had an interest in doing so. If we make the question more precise, the answers are more revealing of the complexity of the role of the witness. In this essay, we ask the following question: Considering the growing significance of Auschwitz in the lexicon of the West today, why was the rescue of the Jews given such a low priority during World War II? The response is often deeply troubling.

We must first determine what priority the rescue of the Jews had during World War II. Even to say that rescue had a low priority may be an overstatement, for, in fact, it had no priority at all. Some would even say that it had a negative priority. They would agree with Nazi Propaganda Minister Joseph Goebbels that the Allies were actually relieved to see Berlin liquidate the Jews. They might note, for example, that the Jewish Question was never discussed at any of the wartime conferences: Cairo, Teheran, Yalta, or Potsdam. It was also not mentioned in the Atlantic Charter of August, 1940, which declared the war aims of the Allies. In addition, the several agencies established to rescue the Jews (the Intergovernmental Committee on Political Refugees, the Presidential Advisory Committee on Political Refugees, the War Refugee Board) never mentioned the word "Jew" in their titles. The charter of UNRRA (the United Nations Relief and Rehabilitation Administration), headed by a Jew (Herbert Lehman), never made any special reference to the Jews, even though its mission concerned relief and rehabilitation. To this very day, nations under Soviet hegemony do not acknowledge the high priority Berlin gave to the liquidation of the Jews. There is no reference to Jews in the Soviet memorial at Babi Yar, or at any of the thousands of war memorials in that vast country. In Poland, the main arena for the slaughter of the Jewish people, the murdered Jews constituted 10 percent of the population of Poland; they have become in death what they were never allowed to be in life—honored citizens of that nation. Rescue, an agonized preoccupation for students of the Holocaust, was barely considered by the would-be rescuers at the time. Is there any way we can explain the low priority and reluctance to save lives? The question deserves our attention because the answer has inherent in it a bitter lesson regarding the nature of the nation-state.

The most obvious reason for the low priority given to the rescue of the Jews is antisemitism, but this is strangely unsatisfactory. Of course, there were antisemites in the State Department and in the Foreign Office. Antisemitism was undoubtedly a *sine qua non* in Stalin's Kremlin. The plight of the Jews in the ghettos and the extermination camps did not make the antisemite contrite. He did not see the Final Solution as the end-product of such hatred. Men like Breckinridge Long, the undersecretary of state who controlled the programs which made up the meager American rescue effort, or Richard Law, who headed the British delegation to the Bermuda conference, and others who found themselves involved in a movement to save lives for which they cared little, rarely gave public expression to their distaste for Jews. They were also sincerely appalled by Nazi behavior, but their class background somehow inured them from fully sensing the agony of the mass slaughter. They were probably incapable of the rage and the passion necessary to save lives that the moment demanded. Antisemitism served as background noise to the indifference and inertia of the witnessing governments and agencies. While it has always been present, its existence is almost impossible to detect in laws or regulations. There are no government edicts or statutes that ordered Jews specifically to be kept out or ignored. Rather, Jews were simply not mentioned. This silence could be juxtaposed to Nazi propaganda, which never stopped talking about Jews.

Directly connected with that silence was the fear among Allied decision-makers to focus on the Jews lest the war be converted into one to save the Jews. This would have only confirmed Berlin's propaganda line which perpetually sought to link the Jews and the war together in the hope that the residual antisemitism in the Allied camp would be aroused and thus interfere with mobilization for victory. Washington, Moscow, and London went to great lengths to conceal the fact that within the general war there was a separate "war against the Jews," which, for Berlin, often took precedence over the physical war. This war within the war slaughtered millions and spent millions implementing the Final Solution, human and financial resources that might have contributed to the hard-pressed German war effort. Roosevelt insisted on calling a "refugee" problem what the Nazis called the "Jewish" problem. He changed the name and therefore the nature of the problem as easily as the Nazis changed his name to "Rosenfeld."

Another reason for the low priority given to the rescue of European Jews stems from the nature of large modern bureaucratic institutions like the nation-state, or agencies like the League of Nations or the International Red Cross. There is a tendency to forget that they are man-made institutions, not man himself, and possess no human characteristics like conscience or soul or a sense of morality or even the ability to feel concern. Sometimes, such a coloration can be given to them by the men who run them, but that is very rare, especially in wartime. There is only one human attribute which such institutions have. It is the will to exist, to permit nothing to interfere with their institutional survival. Sovereignty cannot only not be divided; perpetuating its life takes precedence over the lives of its subjects.

During the Holocaust, which was itself implemented by a government apparatus, the governments called upon to rescue Jews felt that their own survival was in danger until well into 1943, after the battle of Stalingrad broke the back of a seemingly invincible Nazi juggernaut. Their first priority was to save themselves, then to win the war. If the rescue of the Jews could be accommodated to that objective, it could be achieved. But everything suggested by rescue advocates, whether sending packages to concentration camps, bombing the camps and the rail lines leading to them, or simply facilitating the admission of those in danger to receiving countries, was judged as militating against the first priority of winning the war. Jews were considered so much excess cargo on an overloaded lifeboat. They were allowed to drown while everyone averted their gaze. Jewish leaders who dared to argue against these priorities ran the risk of facing accusations of disloyalty or lack of patriotism. Most American Jews did not want special pleading on such terms and accepted the oft-repeated notion that the most practical way of saving their brethren was to win the war as quickly as possible. Those who accuse American Jews of not doing enough would do well to keep in mind that all government agencies involved with the Holocaust held their own survival to be the first order of business. In the Soviet Union, the war was dubbed "the Great Patriotic War," and among the Allies it would ultimately be called "the Great Crusade." It was never a war to save the Jews.

The pope's position in relation to the Final Solution did not depart from these normal priorities, despite the fact that in his person he embodied the moral spirit of much of the Christian world. The survival of the temporal institutional body of the Church received the highest priority. The Catholic flock of Europe had been split by the war. Catholics were fighting on both sides and calling upon the pope for succor. Moreover, 42 percent of the SS and much of the Nazi leadership were at least nominally Catholic. The Church had ample evidence of the threat posed by Nazi and Soviet totalitarianism to its existence. The Communists and the Nazis had demonstrated considerable ability to "persuade" millions of believers to abandon the Church. The Russian Orthodox church was but a relic of its former self. During the crisis, the Vatican walked a delicate tightrope. Pius XII did not dare speak out on the crucible of the Jews, which he knew to be the *bête noire* of Nazi leadership. Those priorities were echoed in Geneva, the home of the International Red Cross. Here, too, the leadership became convinced that the effectiveness and the survival of the agency depended on absolute neutrality and balance. Thus, little things which today seem of little importance but then might have saved thousands—insistance on inspection of the camps, the sending of food packages to inmates, the change of designation of certain inmates to prisoner-of-war—were either not attempted at all or were so reluctantly and tardily implemented that their promise was never fulfilled.

Evidence of these priorities can also be gleaned from the posture of the neutral countries—Sweden, Switzerland, Spain, and Portugal. These nations simply did not feel that what was happening to the Jews in the extermination camps had any relationship to their well-being. Although Sweden, Portugal, and Switzerland were limited havens of asylum for over 20,000 Jews, they felt it was not a momentous enough issue to risk the neutral posture. The Allied belligerents had, after all, not made the rescue of the Jews a wartime priority.

The inability to sense that the Final Solution had some bearing on their own existence is, in fact, a major question which the student of the Holocaust must confront. How were the witnessing governments and agencies able to so objectify the victims and the murder process that what was happening simply did not seem to matter? Had six million cattle been slaughtered, a rabbi once explained to Representative Emanuel Celler of the House Judiciary Committee, there would have been some outcry, at least from animal lovers. But, in the case of fellow human beings, there was only an eerie silence. They simply refused to believe that the inversion of the industrial process to produce death on a mass production basis, if allowed to proceed without objection, could mean the doom of their own systems as well. The Nazis had discovered a secret in the extermination camps: Those for whom society was organized—the weak, the vulnerable, the dependent, those who required the protection of the herd—could henceforth be liquidated rather than cherished, and organized society would not cry out. It is a fact that is now understood by every powerless group. It is no longer necessary to live in harmony with those who are different—they can be eliminated. But men like Roosevelt were not only unable to understand the implications of the Holocaust, they were also confined by the priorities of the state. The first priority was to win the war. Roosevelt, who was an assistant secretary of the navy in the Wilson administration, was fully aware of what could happen when a president forgets that first priority. Wilson tried to be both a belligerent and a peacemaker at the same time and ended by confusing his friends and the electorate and signaling to the vanquished Germans that they had not really lost the war.

Students of the Holocaust cannot fully understand the indifference of the witnesses without a good grasp of the domestic political situation. In the case of the Roosevelt administration, for example, its indifference during the crucial refugee phase (1933-1941) reflected a popular consensus. The American people were opposed to the admission of refugees during the Depression and, thereafter, were so preoccupied with the war in Europe and the Pacific that they did not believe or understand what was happening in the extermination camps. In order for Roosevelt to take some action, popular pressure was required; but mass support was not available to rescue advocates. Roosevelt's superb political antennae informed him that the division within his own administration and within Congress on the refugee issue reflected a public opinion that did not favor a more active rescue policy. This was obvious in public reaction to attempts to adjust the quota system or circumvent the immigration law; in the reaction to the admission of Jewish refugee children in 1939 and 1940 outside the quota system (the Wagner-Rogers Bill); in the opposition to admitting refugees to Alaska; in the establishment of other temporary havens in the American interior; in the issuing of threats of retribution against the Nazi anti-Jewish depredations; and, finally, in the adamant opposition of the military to the proposed bombing of the camps and the rail lines leading to them. All these proposals faced strong opposition from within the administration and often considerable opposition from the public.

In retrospect, it seems clear that American Jews simply did not possess sufficient political power to overcome all opposition to rescue efforts. It is surprising how much they did achieve. The distribution of life-saving visas went from a rejection of over 98 percent of the applicants in 1933 and 1934 to almost 50 percent approval in 1938 and 1939. In April, 1944, the impossible was achieved. The American immigration law was circumvented for refugees in need by the establishment of a special temporary refugee haven in Oswego, New York, outside the immigration laws. It was hoped that other nations would follow the American example. In January, 1944, the War Refugee Board, a special agency to rescue Jews and other civilians, was established by executive order. Those Hungarian Jews who survived owe their good fortune in some measure to the active American rescue policy followed in 1944. Prominent refugees in the cultural and academic life of Europe, many of them Jews, were admitted outside the quota system. This concession was wrung from a reluctant administration during wartime. It was, of course, not enough, considering the immensity of the disaster. Furthermore, as has been noted, it came too late, it took too long to change the administration, and that happened only after victory was assured. Even then, the rescue of the Jews was never allowed to interfere with the Allies' first priority—to win the war as quickly and with as few casualties as possible.

Finally, perhaps the most intriguing question that has been raised about rescue is the issue of bombing the gas chambers and crematoria of Auschwitz and its connecting rail lines. There is no doubt that by the spring of 1944, the bombing of Auschwitz was possible. Thousands of Slovakian and Hungarian Jews might have been spared had the American Fifteenth Air Force, stationed in northern Italy, and already bombing the synthetic oil and rubber works only five miles north of the Auschwitz gas chambers, been directed to do so. Instead, the suggestion was dismissed by Assistant Secretary of the Army John J. McCloy because of its "doubtful efficacy."

The notion of stopping the death mills by bombing has an allure all its own. All that was required, it seemed, was to destroy the death chambers and the production of death would cease. The situation was, of course, not that simple. Until 1944, bombing was relatively ineffective in halting Nazi war production. Moreover, Jewish rescue advocates were late in picking up the signals coming from Slovakia and Hungary which suggested bombing the rail lines. There was little agreement on its effectiveness. A. Leon Kubowitzki, the representative of the World Jewish Congress, which made the request for bombing to the Roosevelt administration, had strong reservations about it. Others believed that German fanaticism on the Jewish Question would render precision bombing of the gas chambers insufficient to halt the killing. The *Einsatzgruppen*, the special killing squads that roamed behind the German lines after the invasion of Russia, killed greater numbers in less time than the extermination camp process. The Germans could always revert to that more primitive method. Auschwitz, moreover, was only one place where killing took place.

The alternative of bombing Auschwitz, an option so highly touted today, did not effectively counter the threat that Berlin would escalate the terror and involve the Allies in a contest of barbarism. It was a contest in which the Nazis held all the cards, since their imaginations seldom failed when it came to brutality. The Allies were afraid of "more vindictive action"; whereas rescue advocates might wonder what was a possibly more vindictive action than the extermination camps. The latter viewed the bombing alternative from the viewpoint of the Jewish victims, precisely what non-Jewish decision-makers could not do, given their different ranking priorities. Nevertheless, one can hardly escape the conclusion that bombing should have been attempted and might conceivably have saved lives. Aside from bombing the camps, this option could have been used in another way.

In December, 1942, the governments-in-exile, led by Poland, delivered a collective *démarche* to the Allied High Command. It called for "retaliatory bombing," the bombing of German cities specifically linked to the excesses of the German occupation. It was rejected for the same reasons that bombing Auschwitz was. However, in retrospect, it probably offered a greater hope of rescue than bombing the camps, because it did not concern war priorities. The rescue possibility of retaliatory bombing is clearly illustrated by what happened in Hungary. When Miklos Horthy, the Hungarian regent, halted the deportations on July 7, 1944, he did so partly for fear that Budapest would be the target of another heavy air raid, as it was on June 2. It was the bombing of Budapest, not Auschwitz, that had the desired effect. The Germans had already linked saturation bombing of their cities and the Final Solution. Expecting such a *quid pro quo*, Goebbels had prepared a massive propaganda countercampaign. Himmler, too, had made the link between the destruction of Germany from the air and what was being done in the extermination camps. On June 21, 1944, he told his officers that if their hearts were softened by pity for the Jews let them recall that the savage bombing of German cities "was after all organized in the last analysis by the Jews."

Yet, the connection between bombing and the Final Solution

made in Berlin was not shared by Allied leadership or by Jewish rescue advocates. Had they conceived of it, it is possible that the fear of disaffection among the German populace, spurred by the terrible casualties, would have convinced more rational Nazi leaders that the Final Solution was simply not worth the physical destruction of German cities. If priorities could not be changed on the Allied side, the high priority in Berlin given to the destruction of the Jews could probably have been altered. Germany could have been coerced into abandoning an insane and unjustifiable war aim. We will never know if that scenario was possible, because the idea of retaliatory bombing was not picked up by rescue advocates, and by the time the notion of bombing the camps and the rail lines leading to them was picked up in March, 1944, millions of Jews were already in ashes. That is why the twelve-point rescue program which came out of the giant Madison Square Garden rally in March, 1943, is as startling as McCloy's later response to the request for bombing. It was silent on the question of bombing and on the more practical possibility of linking the bombing of German cities, which was already occurring, to the destruction of European Jews. Stranger still is the notion, put forward by high-echelon Allied leaders, that linking the bombing of German cities to the extermination camps would expose the Allies to charges of illegality and war atrocities. It seems clear that future researchers into the role of the witnesses will have to place failure of mind next to failure of spirit in accounting for the indifference of those years.

Clearly, the establishment of priorities during World War II was linked to a preceding perception of what that war was all about. The saving of Jewish lives was simply not very important to the principal decision-makers, who were chiefly preoccupied with saving their own governmental instruments and then their communities. During the Holocaust, there existed no legal sovereignty whose primary objective was to protect and nurture Jewish communities, just as the American government did for America. Had there been one, Jewish leaders would not have been compelled to go, hat in hand, to world leaders to implore them to intercede for their coreligionists in Europe. They did not do so at Entebbe.

## For Further Reading

Abella, Irving, and Troper, Harold. *None Is Too Many: Canada and the Jews of Europe, 1933-1948*. Toronto: Lester & Orpen Dennys, 1982.

Bauer, Yehuda. *American Jewry and the Holocaust: The American Jewish Joint Distribution Committee, 1939-1945*. Detroit: Wayne State University Press, 1981.

Feingold, Henry L. "The Witness Role of American Jewry: A Second Look." In *Human Responses to the Holocaust*, edited by Michael D. Ryan. New York: Edwin Mellen Press, 1981: 81-91.

Morley, John F. *Vatican Diplomacy and the Jews During the Holocaust, 1939-1943*. New York: Ktav, 1980.

Wasserstein, Bernard N. *Britain and the Jews of Europe, 1939-1945*. London: Institute of Jewish Affairs, 1979.

# Could American Jews Have Done More?

### HENRY L. FEINGOLD

One measure of the impact of the Holocaust on Jewish consciousness and self-image can be gleaned from the controversy about the role of American Jews during the Holocaust. The lengthening indictment includes everything from the charge of indifference about the fate of their European brethren to outright betrayal. Is there substance to these charges, or are they an example of self-laceration commonly found when communities have experienced great losses?

Historians are not immune from such traumas. While they feel despair that more was not done, they are obliged to consider the realities of the political and social context. There is little agreement on the possibility of rescue at any given juncture. More importantly, we soon learn that the Holocaust is a catastrophe of such immense scale and such tragic proportions that enough could *never* have been done. What was done was overshadowed by the fate of those who perished.

In this essay, the role of American Jews during that agonizing period will be discussed. Many who view their actions from a contemporary perspective are convinced that they failed. They see American Jews wielding considerable organized power in Roosevelt's New Deal. American Jews, after all, were members of Roosevelt's "inner circle." Some belonged to the "Brain Trust": one was an outstanding cabinet member—Henry Morgenthau, Jr.—and Felix Frankfurther and Louis Brandeis were building substantial judicial reputations on the Supreme Court. For some, Jews had become so prominent in the administration, especially the upper reaches of the federal civil service, and the new regulatory agencies, that they labeled the New Deal the "Jew Deal." In addition, Jews chaired the three congressional committees directly concerned with immigration, which could have provided the most direct method for rescue in the early phase of the Holocaust: Representative Sol Bloom, House Foreign Affairs; Representative Samuel Dickstein, House Immigration and Naturalization; and Representative Emanuel Celler, House Judiciary Committee. American Jews also boasted of greater experience in influencing foreign policy, since they had a great need to do so from the time of the Damascus Blood libel of 1840, in which members of the Syrian Jewish community were falsely accused, and subsequently tortured and killed, for the murder of a Catholic monk, evoking worldwide Jewish outrage. American Jews also helped to make the cumbersome democratic system work by the type of citizens they were. They showed a relatively high interest in political issues, were better informed than other ethnic voters, and were more generous in supporting the candidates they favored. Most important of all was their loyalty and support of the New Deal. Jewish support went beyond other ethnic constituencies, especially after the election of 1936, when the enthusiasm of these minority groups began to wane.

On the surface, it appears that the American Jews of the thirties possessed considerable political leverage, so that their responsibility for rescuing their European brethren could be matched by their power to do so. Unfortunately, nothing could be further from the truth. The problem of how to measure the power of a subgroup in the pluralistic American society is surpassed only by the still more difficult problem of defining what power is and where it is located. For example: How necessary is cohesiveness and coherence for the maximum exercise of power? We can assume that at least a modicum of unity is necessary. Yet, we find that during those agonizing years, the delicate bridges which tenuously bound together the different factions of American Jews collapsed. Everything, from a boycott of German goods to the priority of rescue over the homeland in Palestine, became the source of bitter acrimony. Each faction, each division, based on cultural differences as well as political sentiment, felt compelled to send its own delegation to Washington to plead separately for its clients. Only in the minds of antisemites were Jews a unified people conspiring to rule the world. In reality, the Jews were divided on every conceivable issue and could never unite long enough to act for their European brethren, whom they all wanted to help. Those who blithely speak of the "Jewish community" must ultimately recognize that there was no *one* Jewish community in America of the thirties. Such a community did not develop until 1948, partly as a result of the Holocaust, and even then, it was united only on certain crucial issues like the centrality of Israel.

We have mentioned the prominence of Jews in the Roosevelt administration, but that did not necessarily translate into power. *Shtadlanut* (the tradition, originating in the Middle Ages, of having influential Jews, sometimes known as "court Jews" intercede for their fellow Jews during periods of trouble) in the American polity was a risky business. It was dangerous to express a goal which seemingly served an ethnic interest at the expense of the "American interest." Pleading for the special needs of European Jews was often made to appear as unpatriotic by the legions of minor bureaucrats who were antisemitic or simply unsympathetic. The rapid decline of the political fortunes of Henry Morthenthau, Roosevelt's secretary of the treasury, after he submitted the hard-nosed "Morgenthau plan" for the postwar treatment of Germany is a good illustration. The changes in the diplomatic career of Lawrence Steinhardt, the Jewish ambassador in Moscow and Ankara, whose antirefugee posture was used by State Department officials to convince the president that the gates should be locked, is another example.

Even the loyalty which American Jews felt towards Roosevelt, so powerful that some called it a "love affair," militated against their ability to influence policy. So powerful was Roosevelt's hold on the Jewish voter that not only could Jewish leaders *not* threaten Roosevelt with the loss of the Jewish vote, they felt themselves dependent upon the approval of Roosevelt even to hold their own positions. The archives are full of letters from Jewish leaders requesting such letters of support from the White House. Jewish leadership throughout the crisis was compelled to depend on these less certain rewards for political loyalty.

In the 1930s and 1940s, Jews were a relatively small minority, totaling perhaps 3.2 to 3.5 percent of the total population of the United States. They could not, with such a minor political voice, hope to have an impact on policy. The admission of refugees and, later, their physical rescue was, moreover, major policy. The former impinged on immigration policy during a depression; it was highly sensitive and there was a clear opposition. The latter related to wartime priorities, in which the rescue of Jews from the gas chambers was not only not considered, but for some—like Undersecretary of State Breckinridge Long, or Secretary of War Henry Stimson—was viewed as a deterrent to quickly defeating the Nazis, the major aim.

In order to influence policy, American Jews, somehow, had to find the means to amplify their political voice. Although Jewish leaders had some experience with the media, they were unable to use this vehicle effectively because the war muted the special cry of pain emanating from the Jewish world. For some, especially before the war turned in the Allies' favor after the battle of Stalingrad in February, 1943, the Jewish request for special attention to its plight sounded like "Jewish moaning" or "playing the air for the Jew string." The problem of being heard above the din of war was compounded by the failure of rescue advocates to prove the systematic murder of European Jews. More than any other single factor, this muted the Jewish political voice. Moreover, most Americans did not believe stories that sounded suspiciously like the atrocity tales of World War I, which also spoke of cadavers being processed into soap; they also never remotely understood the meaning of the murder techniques employed by the Nazis. The significance of using modern technology, which had given European civilization dominance throughout the world and which was now literally consuming its own people, was totally lost on Allied leaders like Roosevelt. The American people, who were busy winning the war and making considerable sacrifices towards this end, understood the significance of the catastrophe even less.

Jewish interests have customarily been heard by the skillful practice of coalition politics, achieved by linking Jewish group interest to similar-minded groups in the political arena. But the tense climate of the thirties deprived Jews of ethnic allies, especially the American Irish. The popularity of American Jews during the thirties was minimal, attributable, in part, to the dislocation and intergroup tensions triggered by the Depression. The emergence of Jews from the depths of the Depression at a more rapid rate than other groups created hostility and envy. Tensions were intensified by professional antisemitic propagandists like Gerald Smith, Fritz Kuhn, and Father Coughlin, whose pronouncements were similar to those of the Nazi Reich. Under normal circumstances, these voices from the lunatic fringe would have been fairly harmless, but during the thirties, the Depression, the resonances of Nazi antisemitism among like-minded American groups, and the possibility of gaining legitimacy by riding the tail of isolationist/restrictionist sentiment was ever-present. When, in September, 1941, Charles Lindbergh, the most popular man in America, linked Jews to those who would drag America into war, it seemed to many that the antisemitism of the radical right had been legitimatized.

Finally, a word needs to be said regarding American Jewish political culture. When social scientists speak of political culture, they are referring to the basic assumptions about society and those habits and styles that a group brings into the political arena. It is like a political fingerprint. American Jewish political culture is very distinctive and easily recognized. Jews assign a heavy moral responsibility to politics. They expect it to usher in a new and better day. They want politics to improve mankind's lot on earth and, through it, man himself. Jews, especially those of the postemancipation era, speak of justice, righteousness, and humanitarianism. They assume that there is a "civilized spirit of morality" at work in the world. Its locale varies. Sometimes it is located in the Oval Office, or the Vatican, or the United Nations; sometimes it is embodied in a single individual like Franklin Roosevelt or Pope John. The Jewish community calls upon that spirit to intercede on its behalf. It calls upon a "reluctant" world to behave better than it wants to behave. Yet, while such assumptions are perhaps the most noble part of the Jewish political personality, they are strangely inappropriate for the game of politics as it is played on the grass-roots level in America. The Irish-Americans, perhaps the most successful practitioners of politics, viewed it simply as a form of individual and sometimes group aggrandizement. Jews were relatively slow in mastering the earthy *quid-pro-quos* of American politics. More importantly, the nature of Jewish power was long-range and ideological. But until such an elevation in the moral spirit occurred, the Jews were destined to remain insecure and vulnerable. Their power proved singularly ineffective in the face of a demonic force such as nazism. What was required against such a force was physical armed power, as the Israelis have exhibited—precisely what Jews did not possess during the Holocaust. As it turned out, not even the much-touted Jewish political influence in the Roosevelt administration was able to be translated into a more active rescue effort.

Those that charge that American Jews did not do enough during the Holocaust continue to hold to the old assumption. They assume that in the thirties, there was a concerned spirit in the Oval Office, and in Roosevelt, that could have been mobilized to rescue Jews. "If only Jews had been more energetic and mobilized that spirit" is the belief. Yet, there is ample reason for those Jews who lived in the time between the Kishinev pogrom (the antisemitic riot of 1903) and Auschwitz to doubt the existence of such a spirit of concern. That so many Jews still blame American Jews for having failed to arouse and mobilize a spirit which may not have in fact existed at all is perhaps the latest exercise in self-flagellation.

What can we conclude? That not enough was done is a self-evident truth for which there are six million pieces of evidence. But it was also a time in which enough could *never* have been done. Although American Jews were more vigorous and more successful than other subgroups in pressing their political interest in the corridors of power, that power did not match their awesome responsibilities during the years of the Holocaust. Moreover, it was the wrong kind of power, since both American and Nazi politics were peculiarly immune to the human side of the Jewish crucible. From an historical perspective, reading the notion of betrayal back into American Jewish history serves neither the truth of history nor the interest of American Jews today.

### For Further Reading

*American Jewish History.* "America and the Holocaust" I and II. Vol. 68 (March 1979), and Vol. 70 (March 1981).

Feingold, Henry L. *The Politics of Rescue: The Roosevelt Administration and the Holocaust, 1938-1945.* New Brunswick, NJ: Rutgers University Press, 1970.

Laqueur, Walter. *The Terrible Secret: Suppression of the Truth About Hitler's "Final Solution."* London: Morrison & Gibb, Ltd., 1980.

Marrus, Michael R., and Paxton, Robert O. *Vichy France and the Jews.* New York: Basic Books, 1981.

Martin, Gilbert. *Auschwitz and the Allies.* New York: Holt, Rinehart, and Winston, 1981.

**9**

# AFTERMATH

# A Symbol of Hope

It was 10 o'clock in the morning, with a bright sun shining down to help us to celebrate the moment of liberation. The American tanks entered the camp, and every prisoner struggled to get to them. I was about 150 yards from the first tank. The soldiers who had come were surrounded by prisoners sinking into their arms, crying, laughing at the same time, exulted beyond their ordinary feeling. I covered the first 100 yards, but then I collapsed on the ground. I was lying there, trying to get up again, panting and staring, fascinated as the American flag fluttered on the top.

I could not take my eyes from the stars of the flag, symbols not only of the States of the Union, but of all the things we had lost in the Holocaust. Every star had acquired a meaning of its own: One was the star of hope, and that of justice, of tolerance, friendship, of brotherly love, of understanding, and so on.

A little later, we saw prisoners from other blocks marching by, carrying their national flags—Czechs, Poles, Italians, and many others. They had secretly prepared them for the day of liberation. I looked around me, we were all Jews; I asked: "Why don't have we a flag?" I was longing for such a symbol of liberty and national dignity for us Jews. One of us had a blue shirt, I had one which had once been white. We took them off, and another prisoner managed to make them into something like a blue-and-white flag.

We were much too weak to attempt a parade like the other nationalities, and so we just sat there in the sun, holding up, waving our makeshift flag. Jews from other blocks came over to us and cried, some of them kissed the flag, a symbol of hope amidst the dead and the dying.

—Simon Wiesenthal

# From the Holocaust to the Establishment of the State of Israel

## ALEX GROBMAN

At the end of the war, there were over ten million displaced persons (DPs) in Germany and Austria, including concentration camp inmates, prisoners of war, slave laborers, voluntary workers, and foreign volunteers who had been transported to the borders of the Third Reich during the last months of the war. The existence of these millions of displaced persons did not come as a surprise to the Allies, although estimates of the expected refugee population ranged from nine to thirty million.

In 1943, the United Nations Relief and Rehabilitation Administration (UNRRA) was founded to help the Western armies repatriate and resettle the vast number of uprooted people, since the Allies recognized that the task could not be accomplished by the military authorities alone. While UNRRA was to provide medical, welfare, and administrative workers to aid the DPs, they could not operate in the liberated areas without consent of the military authorities. The Soviet army was the only one, however, not to use UNRRA. Instead, it repatriated the DPs in its zone as quickly as they were able to travel.[1]

## The DP Camps

In an attempt to bring some order to the processing and care of the DPs, a special Displaced Persons Executive (DPX) was established at SHAEF (Supreme Headquarters, Allied Expeditionary Forces). SHAEF incorrectly assumed, however, that many of these people had left their homeland unwillingly, were eager to return, and that their governments and fellow citizens would welcome them back. While millions of non-Jews did return to their former homes, those who had collaborated with or worked for the German army or industry were reluctant to return. They feared prosecution for their involvement with the Nazis. Many who had left Soviet territory also refused to go home because they wanted to live in freedom.[2]

Of all the DPs, the Jewish survivors presented the Allied armies with especially difficult problems. The majority of Jews who had survived were found in concentration camps.[3] The consequences of many years of maltreatment included malnutrition and severe medical problems. When the American and British armies entered the concentration camps in Germany and Austria in April and May, 1945, they found rampant epidemics, above all widespread typhoid. In Buchenwald and other camps, the American Medical Corps worked to save everyone they could, but large numbers of former inmates died.[4]

Of the approximately 200,000 Jews who were liberated from the camps, about three-quarters of them returned to their former homelands. Jews from western Europe (France, Holland, Belgium, Denmark, Norway), Hungary (the largest group), Rumania, and Czechoslovakia were eager to be repatriated so that they could look for their families, reclaim their possessions, and reestablish themselves.

Most of the 65,000 surviving Jews from Poland and Lithuania were reluctant to go back home.[5] Many wondered what purpose would be served by returning "to streets empty of Jews, towns empty of Jews, a world without Jews. To wander in these lands, lonely, homeless, always with the tragedy before one's eyes . . . " would have been just too difficult to bear.[6]

Yet, some Jews—how many is not known—went back to Poland, Lithuania, and Latvia to search for family and friends. Wherever they went in eastern Europe, they found surprise and disappointment that they had survived. Also, they were subjected to absurd harassments, including arrests on the charge of collaborating with the Nazis. Most found that their homes and property, if they were intact, were in the hands of new owners; the possibility of restitution of such property was nonexistent.[7] Those who were "bold" enough to ask for the return of their possessions did so at the risk of their lives. Accounts of Jews being murdered throughout Poland were not uncommon, despite the Polish government's efforts to prevent such acts.[8]

Once their search was completed, these Jews often returned to Germany. According to an agreement reached by the Allies, Germany was divided into four zones: French, Soviet, British, and American. The French occupied the Rhineland and the Saar Valley; the Soviets occupied eastern Germany; and the British were in northwestern Germany. The American zone included the southern states of Bavaria, Hesse, and North Wurttemberg-Baden; Bremen and Bremerhaven in the British zone; and a portion of Berlin, which was under the joint authority of all four powers.[9] Austria was treated as a separate entity, also under four-power occupation.[10]

Except for the Russians, who refused to acknowledge that a DP problem existed in their zone, the other Allies assumed responsibility for the DPs in their areas.[11] Some of the problems that the Jews posed for the Allies included their legal status; their need for food, clothing, shelter, rehabilitation, and medical care; and their desire to reestablish contact with relatives and friends. After years of systematic persecution and mass murder by the Nazis, the Jews assumed that the Allies would provide special treatment for them. In particular, they expected separate camps where they would not have to share facilities with their former guards and tormentors. "How could we ever have believed that at the end of the war the surviving Jews would have no more worries, that everything would be fine!" asked one Buchenwald survivor. "The world, we had thought, would welcome our few survivors with open arms! We, the first victims of the Nazis. They would love us! Quickly enough, we saw that the world had other things on its mind than Jewish suffering."[12]

It soon became clear that the Allies had no intentions of treating the Jews any better than the other DPs. The British refused to do so lest the Jews use their special status as leverage to obtain visas to enter Palestine, which the British vehemently opposed.[13] The Americans also rejected the idea of special consideration, but for different reasons.

One reason was given in an American War Department pamphlet in 1944: "As a general rule, [United States] Military Government should avoid creating the impression that the Jews are to be singled out for special treatment, as such action will tend to perpetuate the distinction of Nazi racial theory."[14] The Americans thought this was a real danger; even some American Jewish soldiers were persuaded by this curious logic.[15]

To ensure that persons who had been persecuted "because of their race, religion, or activities in favor of the United Nations" were accorded the same treatment granted to the United Nations DPs, the DPX issued an administrative memorandum to its unit commanders on April 16, 1945.[16] This and similar memoranda were not heeded by the local commanders, which caused difficulties for Jewish survivors. Jews from Germany, Austria, and other Axis countries, for example, were not treated as United Nations DPs, but rather as belonging to former enemy nations. At the same time, Jews from nonenemy countries were often forced into DP camps and installations with their former guards and killers.[17]

In general, the survivors suffered from intolerable living conditions, inadequate food and clothing, and the lack of freedom to choose their own destinies. Rabbi Abraham J. Klausner, an American army chaplain who surveyed the plight of approximately 1,400 Jews in Bavaria during May and June, 1945, sent a report to the leadership of American Jews about conditions in Germany. At one camp, he found that Jews still lived behind double barbed wire fences that were electrically charged. Everywhere soap, linens, toothbrushes, and laundry facilities were unobtainable. Even at better camps, accommodations were overcrowded, people slept on the floors, and cellars were converted into dormitories. Plumbing, when available, was always inadequate.

Food was scarce in the immediate postwar period; people charged that they had received more in the concentration camps. The average intake per day was between 900 to 1,000 calories. The clothing situation was no better, since the majority of Jews were still clothed in their striped prisoner uniforms. Although responsible for assisting the survivors, UNRRA was unable to do anything at first, while the Red Cross helped for only a short period at the end of the war. A limited number of Jews received some clothes from the Dachau storehouse because of Klausner's intervention.

Another problem was the lack of any overall plan for the supervision or dissolution of the camps. One unnamed camp was under the control of the Military Government, another under the Dachau Command (of the American army), and a third was under the jurisdiction of still another military unit. American officers in charge of these camps had little or no training. At two camps, they operated under their own improvised rules. In Pensing, the commanding officer of the airport arbitrarily forced sixty Jews to leave an area requisitioned by the Military Government without the slightest concern about where they could go. Klausner summarized the predicament of the Jews: "Liberated but not free—that is the paradox of the Jew. In the concentration camp, his whole being was consumed with the hope of salvation. That hope was his life, for that he was willing to suffer. Saved, his hope evanesces, for no new source of hope has been given him. Suffering continues to be his badge."[18] Klausner's criticism was, in part, a response to United States military indifference and at times outright hostility to the Jewish survivors.

The negative attitude of the American military towards the Jews had several causes. Many officers could not comprehend why Jews would not return to their former homelands or why they wanted recognition as a separate nationality. Part of the problem, as already noted, was that the American army failed to understand the unique situation of the Jews and informed its officers not to treat Jews differently than other DPs. As a result, the soldiers perceived the Jews as an added burden and did not want to be responsible for providing them with food (which had to be confiscated from the Germans) or other necessities. In some cases, the soldiers feared that their careers would be damaged by adverse reaction from the military if they mishandled their involvement with the DPs.

Furthermore, many officers were combat soldiers uncomfortable in their new role as civilian administrators; they resented anyone who disturbed the status quo. As one authority of the American occupation has noted, "Some Military Government detachments conceived themselves as perfectly free agents and a few even boasted that they had thrown away their handbooks and read almost nothing which came to them" from the American army. Some officers expressed surprise that Washington was interested in Germany's problems and that there was any place in field operations for policy decisions made in Washington.[19]

These attitudes are not surprising, since the Military Government personnel had been trained "to get communication and transport going again, behind a front line, not to govern." With rare exception, they knew "nothing about Germany." They did not speak the language, had to rely upon "unreliable interpreters," and had not been taught German history, politics, or economics. Moreover, "they knew next to nothing about how to deal with the wreckage of human minds and spirits which was to constitute one of their major responsibilities in Germany."[20] It should be noted that there were many American officers and soldiers who were deeply moved by the plight of the Jewish DPs and tried to assist them. A few even helped Jews illegally to enter the American zone of Germany.

A large percentage of the "officers who had been trained went home in the first six months of occupation because they had sufficient 'points' to be discharged." Those who stayed were "disheartened by the chaotic conditions in which they had to work, by the absence of any clear idea of what they were supposed to do, and by the hopeless inadequacy of the 'teenage' replacements." Most commanders of tactical units and their troops did not understand the role of the Military Government and were reluctant to allow its personnel to function in territory under their control.[21]

These problems affected the survivors and were further exacerbated by UNRRA's inability to function effectively from the start. UNRRA workers were often chosen in haste and poorly trained; many were incompetent, inefficient, unable to adapt, and incapable of communicating with the DPs because they lacked knowledge of the requisite languages. Moreover, UNRRA policies were confused, programs were uncoordinated and poorly administered, and, in general, the organization was on poor terms with the army.[22]

The American Jewish Joint Distribution Committee (JDC), a social services agency that aided Jews outside the United States, wanted to assist the survivors immediately after the cessation of hostilities. The army, at that point, however, would not permit the JDC to enter Germany because it did not want civilian relief agencies not directly under its control to interfere with its own occupation and relief efforts. Once the military was ready for the JDC, it would be allowed into Germany and Austria. If the JDC entered earlier, the army feared, Protestant and Catholic relief agencies would also demand the same right.[23] Individual JDC representatives did enter Germany and Austria in 1945, but it took many months for them to provide substantial aid to the DPs. A study of the JDC's activities in Europe has not yet been published.

## The Role of the American Jewish Chaplains

The absence of any well-organized relief effort meant that survivors had to rely more heavily on American Jewish chaplains, members of the Jewish Brigade (made up of Palestinian Jews serving in the British army), and on self-help. Individual American Jewish soldiers also aided the DPs, but the extent and type of their involvement has not yet been fully documented. The chaplains who came to Europe were American military personnel and were among the first Jews in Europe to meet with survivors. Although their primary obligation was to American soldiers, a number of the chaplains chose to help the DPs. They were not official representatives of the American rabbinate or any other organization in this work.

Much of their work with the survivors involved helping them solve personal problems with the military, providing food and material goods, and trying to build morale.[24] Abraham J. Klausner was one of the few chaplains who recognized that the survivors needed some control over their daily lives and a role in choosing their future residence. The survivors also reached this conclusion on their own. Klausner helped them establish a committee to determine priorities and long-range goals for the DPs and deal directly with the American military. Through their combined efforts, the Central Committee of Liberated Jews in Bavaria was established in July, 1945, with headquarters in Munich. The committee represented both the larger camps in Munich and its suburbs and the *Landsmannschaften* (groups formed according to national and linguistic origin) in the region.[25]

Another project undertaken by Klausner was to bring together the Jews of Bavaria into separate Jewish camps and hospitals for those in need of medical care. At the end of the war, every individual who was released from a concentration camp was allowed to enter one of the DP camps that was established by the army. The need for separate Jewish facilities became clear to Klausner after his extensive visits to seventeen DP camps in Bavaria. He believed that some organization or group would come and take the Jews out of Germany and he wanted them to be prepared. By consolidating them into camps, Jews would no longer be subject to harassment and mistreatment by non-Jewish inmates.[26] There were also hundreds of Jewish survivors in German hospitals being cared for by German doctors, and Klausner understood that this was a traumatic experience.

Klausner ultimately succeeded in establishing three Jewish hospitals and a number of Jewish DP camps, but it took a great deal of work. He fought hard to achieve these objectives because he believed that it was an important step in the army's recognition of the Jews as a separate entity.[27]

## The Harrison Report

While Klausner and other chaplains worked to help ameliorate conditions for fellow Jews, they recognized that American Jews had to be made aware of what was transpiring in Europe. Their reports, and those sent by American Jewish soldiers, newspaper correspondents, DPs, and other observers in Europe, aroused the American Jewish community to question the American government's handling of the situation.[28] As a result, Earl G. Harrison, the dean of the University of Pennsylvania Law School, was sent to Europe by the State Department and President Truman to investigate what was being done for the survivors by military, governmental, and private organizations.[29]

Harrison's original itinerary would have bypassed most of the DP camps, but Chaplain Klausner persuaded him to change his route.[30] Harrison's report to President Truman made front-page news across the United States on September 30, 1945. In it, he charged: "As matters now stand, we appear to be treating the Jews as the Nazis treated them, except that we do not exterminate them. They are in concentration camps in large numbers under our military guard, instead of the SS troops. One is led to wonder whether the German people, seeing this, are not supposing that we are following or at least condoning Nazi policy."[31]

Harrison's somewhat exaggerated report was controversial and raised questions in Washington, D.C., about the effectiveness of Eisenhower's command. It also embarrassed Eisenhower and put him on the defensive.[32] Some changes in the army's approach towards survivors occurred as a result, but it was clear that only a resolution of the DPs' status would solve the real problems.

Harrison noted that the solution was for the United States to support a plan to settle the DPs in Palestine. "With respect to possible places of resettlement for those who may be stateless or who do not wish to return to their homes," Harrison declared, "Palestine is definitely and preeminently the first choice." He informed the president that "there is no acceptable or even decent solution for their future other than Palestine," although he pointed out that some people felt that the United States or other countries were options.[33]

In particular, Harrison asserted that "some reasonable extension or modification of the British White Paper of 1939," which limited Jewish emigration to Palestine to 75,000 over a five-year period beginning in that year, "ought to be possible without serious repercussions." In arguing for Palestine as the solution to the problems of Jewish statelessness, Harrison pointed out that "this is said on a purely humanitarian basis with no reference to ideological or political considerations so far as Palestine is concerned."[34]

A decision on this issue had to be made shortly, Harrison insisted, because certificates for immigration to Palestine would be exhausted by August, 1945. "To anyone who has visited the concentration camps and who has talked with the despairing survivors, it is nothing short of calamitous to contemplate that the gates of Palestine should be soon closed," he declared.[35]

He then noted that the "Jewish Agency for Palestine has submitted to the British government a petition that 100,000 additional immigration certificates be made available. A memorandum accompanying the petition makes a persuasive showing with respect to the immediate absorptive capacity of Palestine and the current, actual manpower shortages there. . . ."[36]

"While there may be room for difference of opinion as to the precise number of certificates which might under the circumstances be considered reasonable," Harrison observed, "there is no question but that the request thus made would, if granted, contribute much to the sound solution for the future of Jews still in Germany and Austria and even other displaced Jews, who do not wish either to remain there or to return to their countries of nationality. No matter is, therefore, so important from the viewpoint of Jews in Germany and Austria and those elsewhere who have known the horrors of the concentration camps as is the disposition of the Palestine question."[37]

He also proposed that the United States "should, under existing immigration laws, permit reasonable numbers of such persons to come here . . . particularly those who have family ties in this country." This was not a major issue because, he believed, "the number who desire emigration to the United States is not large." Harrison further declared that "the urgency of the situation should be recognized" because it was "inhuman to ask people to continue to live for any length of time under their present conditions."[38]

Even before Harrison's report reached Truman, the president

recognized the need for the British to remove Jewish immigration restrictions for Palestine. He reached this conclusion after hearing about the plight of European Jews and at the urging of American Jewish leadership to bring pressure on the British. Reinforcement came during the summer of 1945, when thirty-seven governors endorsed a proposal to open Palestine to the refugees.

In July, 1945, at the Potsdam Conference, Truman spoke to British Prime Minister Winston Churchill about rescinding immigration restrictions. A few days later, however, Churchill's Tory party was voted out of office and Clement Attlee became the new prime minister. Before returning to the United States, Truman conferred with Attlee about this matter but nothing was resolved.[39]

After Truman received Harrison's report, he sent a copy to Attlee. In an accompanying cover letter dated August 31, 1945, Truman stated that "no single matter is so important for those who have known the horrors of concentration camps for over a decade as is the future immigration possibilities into Palestine." He urged that the British government grant 100,000 entry certificates to the Jewish survivors and pointed out that "if it is to be effective, such action should not be long delayed."[40]

Although Attlee originally rejected Truman's request, the British decided to call for an Anglo-American Committee of Inquiry after Truman made his demands public on September 24, 1945. Foreign Secretary Ernest Bevin, who wanted the Jews to return to their previous homelands, hoped that the formation of the committee would enable the British to delay a resolution of the problem of what to do with the refugees and involve the United States in the process of finding a solution. After some discussion, the Anglo-American Committee was set up in November, 1945.[41]

## Jewish Efforts to Reach Palestine

The Holocaust survivors did not wait while the United States and Great Britain discussed their fate. In the spring of 1944, small groups of survivors began organizing in the first areas liberated by the Red Army to discuss their future. They decided that there was no longer any reason for them to return to their former countries and that emigration to Palestine was their only solution. They were convinced that antisemitism was still a threat to world Jewry, that another Holocaust would occur, that Jews in the Diaspora had to be warned and properly prepared for this event, and that Palestine had to be built "as an ultimate refuge . . . " for the Jewish people. Plans for revenge against the Germans were also discussed, but became moot under the pressure of events.[42]

In December, 1944, these liberated groups came to Lublin, where in January, 1945, they met the former Warsaw ghetto fighters. Together they formed a secret organization called Berihah (Flight). Berihah in Poland soon began smuggling Jews to points on the Mediterranean coasts, where they would be in a better position to reach Palestine.[43]

The Jewish Brigade was also involved in getting Jews out of Europe and in transit to Palestine. Established by the British in September, 1944, the Brigade was formed by absorbing a number of Palestinian units serving with the British army. Most of the members of the Brigade were also members of the Haganah, the Jewish armed underground in Palestine. At first, the Brigade began this work independently of the Berihah until they discovered each other.

As soon as the war ended, members of the Brigade began searching throughout southern Germany and Austria for Jewish survivors.[44] Everywhere they went, survivors greeted them as heroes. At one DP camp, a survivor tearfully exclaimed, "It is only a dream," while another thanked God "for letting us live to see this day. . . ." The sight of self-assured Palestinian Jews in military uniform had an uplifting effect on the survivors. Unlike the Allies who had liberated them, members of the Brigade had been eager to find them and give them hope and courage.[45] One JDC official noted that there was "hardly a camp" that did "not bear the imprint of a *hayyal*, a member of the Brigade, who would come and go without fanfare, who would remain for weeks and months at a camp, no one quite knowing how he could arrange his military leave to do it, who lived with and worked for the people."[46]

From now on, the *Yishuv* (the Jewish community in Palestine) and the *Shearit Hapletah* (the Saving Remnant) were inseparable members of the Brigade. In a speech to the leaders of the DPs, Major Yigal Kaspi of the Brigade declared: "You are bone of our bone, flesh of our flesh. Our families are overjoyed to know you have survived, and are waiting to welcome you with open and loving arms. . . . Unite! Be organized and disciplined!"[47]

The Palestinians recruited several chaplains to work in the Berihah; they were asked to provide material and logistical support. Other chaplains took an active part in helping the Berihah smuggle Jews out of Germany and Austria.[48]

The efforts of the Berihah resulted in the arrival of a large number of Jews into the American zone of Germany on their road to Palestine. Many had reached Italy, but there was no room for all of them there. The Palestinians decided to divert as many of them as possible to the American zones of Germany and Austria. They would remain there until they could be taken to Palestine, despite the British ban on Jewish immigration. The American zone was chosen because it was a temporary transit area for the refugees and because they would be treated better than in the other zones. It should be noted that the DPs were not always well treated in the American zone. The situation improved only after survivors protested about being treated badly by the American military. In the British zone no additional refugees with a DP status were accepted.[49]

The American army was disturbed by this influx of Jews because it was responsible for their care. It claimed that it did not have enough supplies and that there was constant pressure to provide Jews with the best accommodations possible. To reduce the confusion, the army wanted the United States government to establish a long-range policy for dealing with these people and these problems.[50]

Until such a policy was established, "unofficial sources intimated" to American Jewish organizations "that if the monthly influx did not exceed five thousand, the army would make no difficulties at the border."[51]

The decision to allow 5,000 Jews to enter the American zone each month was motivated by the Harrison Report. After its publication, public opinion in the United States turned against the military's treatment of the Jews, and as a result the army decided not to thwart Jewish survivors' efforts to enter the American zone. The only effective means to stop the flow was by use of force, and this was not a realistic option for moral and political reasons. It should be emphasized, however, that this action by the army was decided at the highest levels of the Truman administration.

It seems that the army agreed in principle to allow Jews to enter the American zone as early as October, 1945. David Ben Gurion, then chairman of the Jewish Agency Executive in Palestine, was in Germany to meet with the survivors and representatives of the Jewish Agency as well as with Generals Eisenhower and Walter Bedell Smith, Eisenhower's chief of staff. He met the American generals in October to urge that the Jews be allowed to enter the American zone of occupation and be given the status of displaced persons. Ben Gurion hoped that by "concentrating a quarter of a million Jews in the American zone" it would "increase the American pressure [on the British] to allow them to enter Palestine." It was "not because of the financial aspects of the problem," he declared; "that does not matter to them—but because they see no future for these people outside of *Erez Israel* [Land of Israel]."[52] Ben Gurion's approach to Eisenhower and Smith, however, was that since a large number of Polish Jews were already infiltrating into the American zone it would be best to allow them officially to enter. Eisenhower and Smith agreed because of the Harrison Report and their concern over future adverse publicity with the DPs.

The American military was eager for the Jews in its zone to move on as rapidly as possible. The presence of these Jews in Germany thwarted America's increasingly pro-German policy. The upper echelons of the army sanctioned this movement of Jews but did not want United States troops compromised or bribed in the process. Moreover, they wanted this operation to be done quietly in order not to arouse British wrath, since the British vehemently opposed the Berihah. This meant that the Berihah's activities "had to be done around the American army, not through the American army."[53]

The Americans were not alone in their concern about the large numbers of Jews entering their zone. The Zionist leadership feared that the survivors might not wait until Palestine was open to them, but would seek admittance to the Western countries. Its fears were based on realistic considerations.[54] In a poll taken in early 1946 at the Landsberg DP camp, approximately 15 percent of the population indicated that the United States was their first choice for resettlement.

The number increased somewhat after the poll was taken, but the trend was halted only when it became clear that the United States was not facilitating DP immigration to America as President Truman had directed.[55] Given the choice between going to the United States or Palestine, it is estimated that 50 percent of the Jews would have opted for America.[56]

Despite these reservations of the Zionist leadership about bringing Jews into the American zone, there was virtually no alternative. In June, 1946, the Berihah increased the flow of Jews into Germany, putting pressure on the United States to allow larger numbers of Jews to enter its zone without being harassed. The Anglo-American Committee on Palestine, which submitted its report on April 22, 1946, recommended that Britain immediately admit 100,000 immigrants into Palestine. Haim Yahil, head of the official Jewish Agency mission for Palestine in Germany, feared that the Americans might make emigration of the 100,000 Jews to Palestine conditional on ending infiltration into the American zone. A significant increase of Jews, Yahil believed, might forestall the Americans from doing so.[57]

Many Jews were eager to enter the American zone of Germany because the committee's recommendations raised their hopes for reaching Palestine. Approximately 40,000 Jews were expected to infiltrate during the three months from July to September, 1946, according to Berihah estimates. Few people anticipated that Britain would refuse to implement the unanimous recommendations of the report, which it did because it "wanted an Arab Palestine with guaranteed rights for a permanent Jewish minority under British protection."[58] Various attempts were made by the United States government to arrive at an agreement with Britain over the committee's report, but without success. By early August, 1946, the report was no longer under serious consideration.[59]

The DPs were shattered by this event. Although they were initially upset that a committee was needed to investigate the problem, they expected that some of the committee's recommendations would be accepted. Now, the issues of Palestine and their own future were unresolved.

At the end of 1945, Truman attempted to admit some Jews into the United States. His efforts were unsuccessful. Despite the suffering endured by European Jews, the United States Congress was in no mood to relax restrictive immigration laws. Rather than initiate a protracted fight to change these statutes, Truman issued an Executive Order on December 22, 1945, which gave the Jews priority on existing quotas already available to DPs. The Polish, Austrian, and German quotas came to approximately 39,000.

Although large numbers of Jews were expected to enter the United States under this arrangement, lower-level bureaucrats in the United States government sabotaged this effort. Between late 1945 and the Displaced Persons Act of July 1, 1948, 45,000 DPs came to the United States zone. Of these, 12,649 were Jews who arrived between May, 1946, and October, 1948. During 1946, 9,000 Jews left Germany legally or illegally.[60]

The major factor contributing to the increased influx into the American zone was the Kielce pogrom. It has already been noted that assaults against Jews were not uncommon in Poland. Several hundred Jews had been murdered between November, 1944, and October, 1945; others were attacked and wounded. Anti-Jewish riots had broken out in several Polish cities in 1945, but in 1946 the number of riots increased dramatically. The worst occurred on July 4, 1946, with the pogrom at Kielce, in which forty-two Jews were murdered for allegedly using Christian blood for ritual purposes. The Kielce pogrom had a traumatic effect on Jews in Poland because it highlighted their vulnerability. Ominously, it took place in a city of 60,000 inhabitants where the local bishop resided. Moreover, members of the clergy and the local militia took part in this pogrom.

Within three months, 100,000 Jews fled Poland and the surrounding countries. This movement, led by the Berihah,[61] took Jews through Czechoslovakia to Bratislava and Vienna. From Vienna they were taken to Salzburg and then either to Italy or the American zone of Germany. Another Berihah route went from Stettin (Szezecin) to Berlin and from there to the West. Berihah operators from Poland, Rumania, Hungary, Czechoslovakia, and Yugoslavia continued into 1948, transferring approximately 250,000 survivors into Austria, Germany, and Italy. It was the "largest organized illegal mass movement in the twentieth century."[62]

Without access to Palestine, however, the Berihah's efforts were not complete. During 1945 and 1946, the Haganah, through the Mossad, its illegal immigration department, took control of all illegal activities in Europe. Shaul Avigur, the Mossad commander, with headquarters in Paris, assumed responsibility for the Mossad, the Berihah, and the Haganah in Europe, and for securing arms for the Haganah.[63]

Under extremely difficult conditions, the Mossad acquired ships, prepared them to take Jews to Palestine, and established a radio communications system. Thousands of survivors of all ages from Germany, Austria, Italy, Rumania, Bulgaria, North Africa, and elsewhere risked their lives on these small, overcrowded, and often unseaworthy vessels. In 1946, twenty-two ships brought 21,711 people to Palestine; between August, 1945, and May, 1948, sixty-five ships carried 69,878 Jews to the Holy Land. Without the vast network of camps, transports, and Palestinian Jews, as well as the support of Italians, French, Yugoslavs, and others who opposed British refusal to allow Jews to enter Palestine, this operation would have been impossible. The result was that only approximately 100,000 of the 300,000 Jews in central and western Europe decided to emigrate to countries other than Palestine.[64]

## Emigration to the United States

For those Jews left behind in Europe who were either unable or unwilling to make the voyage to Palestine, the failure to find a resolution to their statelessness compounded many existing problems. Leo Srole, an American sociologist who served as the UNRRA Welfare director at the Landsberg DP camp, observed that "their situation remains abnormal, laden with a heavy weight of anxieties and strains. . . . " Their dependent status lowered their self-esteem; their "subsistence" was "considerably below their needs, giving rise to constant insecurity, irritation, and a feeling of deprivation and degradation," and they were extremely apprehensive about being in Germany. They held the Germans collectively responsible for the Holocaust, regarded them as "still Nazi-minded," and feared that "if the Americans were to leave today, we all would be dead by morning."[65]

The survivors were also disturbed that "in the eyes of American military personnel their status as 'camp inmates' " had "fallen lower, while that of the Germans" had "risen rapidly." In addition, they "were haunted by the feeling that their time is running out, that the waste in their lives continues without end. 'The war broke our lives in 1939, and now seven years later the war is still not over for us alone. How long, oh Lord, how long?' "[66]

As already noted, in August, 1946, the British rejected the unanimous recommendations of the Anglo-American Committee of Inquiry to allow 100,000 Jewish survivors to enter Palestine. Recognizing that the British might not agree to these recommendations, President Truman began to look for ways to bring the DPs into the United States. In June, 1946, he informed the Grady Commission (a cabinet committee responsible for working with the British to implement the recommendations of the Anglo-American Committee) that the United States could accept 50,000 Jews if the British refused the committee's recommendations. Truman held exploratory discussions with members of the House and Senate committees and with diplomats from Latin America.[67]

On August 16, Truman announced that he would ask Congress to pass legislation allowing an unspecified number of DPs into the United States. While he thought of permission for 300,000 people, he did not disclose the number publicly. His decision to keep silent on the exact figure was wise. When the American public was asked in late August whether they agreed with Truman's proposal to let more Jews and other European refugees into the United States, 72 percent were against it; 16 percent approved; and 12 percent had no opinion.[68]

Truman's announcement that he would ask Congress to admit more DPs into the United States increased the quarrels among American Jewish groups over the issue of Palestine. Before the announcement, the non-Zionists, who opposed the establishment of the State, had supported the idea of 100,000 Jews going to Palestine as a humanitarian gesture. Once it appeared that they would not be allowed to go there, they launched a major initiative to bring these Jews to the United States.[69]

With the aid of many prominent non-Jews, the non-Zionists worked hard for the enactment of the DP acts of 1948 and 1950, which brought over 400,000 DPs to the United States by the end of 1952.[70] Approximately 68,000 of these DPs were Jews. Between this legislation and the Truman directive, less than 100,000 Jews reached the United States.[71] More might have come to the United States had it not been for Patrick McCarran, senior senator from Nevada. As chairman of the Senate Judiciary Committee, McCarran successfully delayed DP legislation so that by the time the DP law was ratified and the Jews were permitted to enter the United States, most had already left for Israel and other countries. McCarran opposed this legislation because he was an isolationist, did not like Jews, and did not get along with his fellow Democrat, President Truman.[72]

## Creation of the State of Israel

When it appeared to the Zionists that the president no longer believed that it would be possible to transfer the Jews to Palestine, they campaigned vigorously for the creation of a Jewish State. One of the first obstacles to this renewed drive appeared shortly after the British rejected the recommendations of the Anglo-American Committee of Inquiry. The British wanted to delay release of the report until they could discuss its contents with the Americans. The Americans refused and on May 1, 1946, when the report was made public, Truman announced his approval of the committee's recommendation that 100,000 DPs be admitted to Palestine. British Foreign Secretary Ernest Bevin immediately protested America's intervention "of unparalleled irresponsibility" during a time of great tension when British soldiers were "being killed by Jewish terrorists."[73] Clement Attlee demanded that the United States share the military and financial costs of implementing recommendations in the report; Attlee also stated that the British would not allow large numbers of Jews into Palestine until the illegal Arab and Jewish armies were stripped of their weapons and disbanded.[74]

These demands were viewed as a challenge in Washington, and when Bevin suggested that an Anglo-American committee of experts be appointed to reconcile the differences between the two countries, Truman agreed. The president, however, opposed the use of American military forces in Palestine and did not want the United States to act as trustee or co-trustee in Palestine.[75]

The British were eager for American involvement in Palestine, because their general position in the Middle East was eroding. With the anticipated loss of their bases in Egypt and Iraq, the British now needed Palestine. To ensure their continued rule, they felt they had to find a solution to the political future of the country that was acceptable to the Arabs, would suppress the Jewish resistance movement, and would curtail illegal immigration.[76]

Three different Jewish armed groups were involved in the fight against the British; each group had its own agenda. The largest was the Haganah, which in 1946 had approximately 40,000 members. Under the control of the Jewish Agency, the Haganah's goal was to make sure that the British understood that the *Yishuv* could thwart any solution against its interests. The IZL *(Irgun Zvai Leumi,* National Military Organization), with 300 fighters and a total membership of approximately 1,500 men, had declared war against the British in 1944. Led by Menachem Begin, the IZL wanted to force the British out of Palestine and establish an independent State. The Lechi (Fighters for the Freedom of Israel, also known as the Stern Gang, after its founder, Abraham Stern), with a force of about 300 men—of whom 120 were fighters—was the most violent of the three groups. It believed that only violence could drive the British out of Palestine.[77]

During the autumn of 1945, these three groups joined together to become the Jewish Resistance Movement *(Tnuat Hameri).* They concluded that the new British Labor government had no intention of allowing any significant number of Jews to enter Palestine or of permitting political autonomy for the *Yishuv;* therefore, they felt that military action against the English had to be intensified. From autumn, 1945, to July, 1946, these forces sabotaged airfields, railroads, radar stations, oil refineries, bridges, lighthouses, and other military targets. The IZL and the Haganah avoided attacking civilians and most of the time warned the British of an impending assault to prevent casualties.

After the Haganah destroyed most of the bridges connecting Palestine to its neighboring Arab countries on the night of June 17, 1946, the British retaliated with an intensive two-week search of houses, schools, and hospitals throughout the country. It began on Saturday, June 29 (Black Sabbath), and many Jewish Agency officials were rounded up and put into detention. However, the high-ranking leadership was not apprehended. The British also failed to uncover any significant arms caches.[78]

The British action, nevertheless, did succeed in convincing the Jewish Agency of the futility of continued armed struggle against a superior military force. The Haganah decided to channel more of its energies into illegal immigration. In July, 1946, the Jewish Resistance Movement was disbanded after the IZL blew up a wing of the King David Hotel in Jerusalem that housed the British administration offices. The IZL had warned the British before the explosion, but this information was not conveyed to the other building tenants. The Haganah agreed to the operation, but when more than ninety people died in the explosion, it ended its involvement with the IZL. Both the IZL and Lechi were not deterred by the British; if anything, Black Sabbath increased the IZL's tendency to use violence.[79]

The British further retaliated against the *Yishuv* in August by beginning to expel illegal immigrants to detention camps in Cyprus. Approximately 51,000 Jews spent nearly two years in these camps; the Jews were, however, not intimidated by British countermeasures. Their resolve to reach Palestine was only strengthened. Moreover, the image of crisp British naval uniforms rounding up a motley crew of starved and ematiated civilians (including women and children) rebounded against the British.[80]

While the British forces in Palestine were trying to quell Jewish resistance and place illegal immigrants in detention camps, the Anglo-American Committee of experts was completing its report. On July 31, the report and its recommendations, known as the Morrison-Grady Plan, after Dr. Henry F. Grady and Herbert Morrison (the heads of the two delegations), was released to the British Parliament. The committee proposed that the country be divided into separate Jewish and Arab provinces and that each community have self-rule in domestic affairs, but that the British retain control over foreign relations, defense, police, courts, customs, and communications. A hundred thousand refugees would be admitted to Palestine during the first year the plan was to be implemented, but the British would determine the extent of any future immigration.[81]

The British government reacted favorably to the Morrison-Grady Plan and initially it appeared that Truman might endorse this proposal. The Zionists recognized that acceptance of this plan would be disastrous, since it would preclude the establishment of a sovereign Jewish State. A meeting of the Jewish Agency Executive was called in Paris on August 2, 1946, to discuss the Zionist response. With the increased arrival of survivors into Germany, the growing demoralization in the DP camps, and the possibility that the Americans might stop trying to influence the British, the Zionist executive decided that a viable partition plan was their alternative counterproposal. This was an extremely difficult decision, but Dr. Nahum Goldmann of the Jewish Agency argued that it was the best of three possible options: bi-nationalism, trusteeship, and partition.[82]

Bi-nationalism was impractical, Goldmann asserted, because the Arabs would not agree to parity; and even if they did agree to this arrangement, there would be no unanimity on political decisions. Trusteeship would require a British presence, and the English were clearly anti-Zionist. Partition was, therefore, the only viable solution, he concluded, because it would separate the Jews and the Arabs, thus reducing conflict and simultaneously promoting economic competition.[83]

Goldmann took the partition proposal to the American government and convinced key members of the Truman administration and the American Jewish Committee that this was the only alternative. On August 12, 1946, Truman informed the British that he rejected the Morrison-Grady Plan because "the opposition in this country to this plan has become so intense that it is now clear it would be impossible to rally in favor of it sufficient public opinion to enable this government to give it effective support." Truman pointed out that he wanted to continue to search for a solution and that the American Embassy was prepared to discuss the partition plan advanced by Nahum Goldmann.[84]

On August 30, 1946, Goldmann asked for a statement from the president or Dean Acheson, acting secretary of state, endorsing partition. The State Department and the Joint Chiefs of Staff opposed the idea for fear of antagonizing the British and alienating the Arabs.

At first, Truman was also reluctant to issue such a statement, but on October 4, 1946, the eve of Yom Kippur (Day of Atonement), he issued a statement which suggested that a compromise between the two proposals would be supported by the American public.[85]

This statement frustrated the British because they recognized that they could not reach a joint solution with the United States. The British turned to the Jews and Arabs for a last attempt at imposing a new British plan. Both groups rejected the proposal; the Jews because it offered "neither an independent state nor an autonomous province"; the Arabs because it allowed for more Jewish immigration.[86] The British government "was caught on the horns of a dilemma," observed one historian. "It was unable to create the State desired by the Zionists for fear of losing its hegemony to one of its many rivals waiting eagerly in the wings; yet, unable either to redeem its promises to the Arabs to create an independent Arab state in Palestine and thus knowingly close the doors to hundreds of thousands of wretched Jewish refugees in Europe awaiting repatriation. With no obvious policy presenting itself, Britain under the new Labor government, drifted along aimlessly, improvising on the White Paper policy, giving no satisfaction to either party, yet arousing the ire of each."[87]

After this last effort failed, the British handed the problem over to the United Nations in February, 1947. In doing so, the British hoped that the United Nations would ultimately adopt their solution. They expected no western European opposition; furthermore, the Soviets, who were anti-Zionists, would be against a Jewish State, and Latin American countries would not want this new state, in line with the Vatican's opposition to Jewish sovereignty in Palestine.

The British had miscalculated. Public opinion in western Europe was sympathetic to the remnants of Europe's Jews as they struggled to get to Palestine. The Russians desired an end to British rule in Palestine and were willing to support the establishment of independent states in the region. As long as the holy places were accessible and internationalized, the Vatican was amenable to compromise. This meant that Latin American countries could decide for other reasons.[88]

During the summer of 1947, the United Nations Special Committee on Palestine visited Europe and Palestine to recommend a solution to the Palestine question. On August 31, 1947, the committee completed its report, which called for the partition of Palestine.[89] On November 29, 1947, the General Assembly of the United Nations voted by a two-thirds majority to approve the partition of Palestine.[90] The Arabs opposed this decision and the Israeli War for Independence began. On May 14, 1948, the State of Israel was established.

In early 1949, the war ended with an armistice. By that time, 6,500 Palestinian Jews, about 1 percent of the Jews in the country, had died. By 1950-1951, two-thirds of the survivors came to Israel; the rest went to other countries.[91]

The Jews paid dearly for their political independence and their return to world history. The establishment of the State of Israel in 1948 resulted from several factors. The United States, through President Truman, played a decisive role in keeping the British from implementing their anti-Zionist policy.[92] Truman was motivated by his desire to help the remnants of Europe's Jews.[93] American Jews, in turn, maintained pressure on American officials and cultivated American public opinion. This meant that the "establishment of the State of Israel and the consequent achievement of a political base for the Jewish people was made possible, to a large degree, by the Jews in the Diaspora: the survivors who organized groups like the Berihah, and American Jewry."[94] It also corrected "the impression that the main factor leading to statehood was the activity of the Jewish underground movements in Palestine. All these developments, of course, had built on the fundamental contribution of the prewar Zionist movement—the building up of the *Yishuv* by three generations of Zionist immigrants."[95]

This should also correct the unjustified belief that were it not for the Holocaust, Israel would never have been established. It is true that the presence of the DPs in Europe accelerated the formation of the State. At the same time, however, the Holocaust reduced the very possibility of statehood and weakened the new nation. Israel came into the world "smaller and poorer, in the physical and spiritual sense, than she would have, had the huge reservoir of manpower and talent within European Jewry attended her birth and kept watch over her cradle. In her internal structure, in her spiritual life, even in her relationships with her surroundings and in her position among the nations of the world, both as a state and as a people, Israel is still paying the price of the Holocaust."[96]

### Notes

1.    Malcolm J. Proudfoot, *European Refugees* (London: Faber and Faber, 1957), pp. 98-110.

2.    *The New York Times*, 4.22.45, Section IV, p. 5; 4.25.45, p. 1; 5.39.45, p. 6; Yehuda Bauer, *Flight and Rescue: Brichah* (New York: Random House, 1970), pp. 47, 50-51.

3.    Proudfoot, *Refugees*, p. 324.

4.    *The Jewish Spectator*, November 1945, p. 22; *The Indiana Jewish Chronicle*, 2.1.46, p. 2; *The New York Times*, 4.17.45, p. 4; 6.27.45, p. 6; *Time*, 4.30.45, p. 43.

5.    Yehuda Bauer, *A History of the Holocaust* (New York: Franklin Watts, 1982), pp. 337-338.

6.    Leo Schwarz, *The Root and the Bough* (New York: Rinehart and Company, 1949), p. 310; *Yiddisher Kempfer*, 6.16.45; *Forward*,

6.15.45; *T'khias Hamesim*, 5.4.45, a newspaper published by the Jews in Buchenwald, World Jewish Congress Archives, New York, Drawer 272, no file number.

   7.    Dorothy Rabinowitz, *New Lives* (New York: Alfred A. Knopf, 1976), p. 61; *Atlantic Monthly*, July 1945, pp. 87-90; *Jewish Telegraphic Agency Daily News Bulletin*, 6.10.45, p. 4 and 6.22.45, p. 4; Bauer, *Brichah*, p. 50; Joseph S. Shubow to Stephen S. Wise, 5.23.45, World Jewish Congress Archives, New York, Drawer 272, File 56.

   8.    *Congress Weekly*, 11.30.45, pp. 7-8.

   9.    Edward N. Peterson, *The American Occupation of Germany: Retreat to Victory* (Detroit: Wayne State University Press, 1977), pp. 54-55.

   10.    William Hardy McNeill, *Survey of International Affairs 1939-1946* (London: Oxford University Press, 1953), p. 582.

   11.    Leonard Dinnerstein, *America and the Survivors of the Holocaust* (New York: Columbia University Press, 1982), p. 11.

   12.    Schwarz, *The Root and the Bough*, p. 311.

   13.    Dinnerstein, *America*, p. 28.

   14.    Dinnerstein, *America*, p. 13.

   15.    Interviews with Abraham J. Klausner, Ann Borden (Liepah), and Marvin Linick. Oral History Division of the Institute of Contemporary Jewry, Hebrew University, Jerusalem (hereafter referred to as Jerusalem, OH).

   16.    Administrative Memorandum Number 39 (Jerusalem, OH) Revised 4.16.45, Adviser on Jewish Affairs Archives—Property of Abraham Hyman, Jerusalem, Israel.

   17.    Interview with Abraham J. Klausner (Jerusalem, OH); Dinnerstein, *America*, p. 13.

   18.    Abraham J. Klausner, "A Detailed Report on the Liberated Jew As He Now Suffers His Period of Liberation under the Discipline of the Armed Forces of the United States," 6.24.45. Central Archives for the History of the Jewish People, Hebrew University, Jerusalem, Israel (hereafter referred to as CAH).

   19.    Peterson, *American Occupation*, p. 87; Interviews with Sylvia Neulander, Herschel Schacter, and Eli Bohnen (Jerusalem, OH).

   20.    Peterson, *American Occupation*, pp. 86, 90.

   21.    Peterson, *American Occupation*, pp. 86, 90.

   22.    Dinnerstein, *America*, p.12.

   23.    Earl Stone to Philip Bernstein, 10.5.43, Jewish Chaplaincy Archives at National Jewish Welfare Board Archives, New York, Box 3, File A.

   24.    Alex Grobman, "The American Jewish Chaplains and the Remnants of European Jewry: 1944-1948"(Ph.D. diss., Hebrew University), pp. 51-53.

   25.    Interview with Abraham J. Klausner (Jerusalem, OH); Leo Schwarz, *The Redeemers* (New York: Farrar, Straus, and Young, 1953), pp. 17-23; Yehuda Bauer, "The Initial Organization of the Holocaust Survivors in Bavaria," *Yad Vashem Studies* VIII (1970): 148-151.

26.   Interviews with Abraham J. Klausner, Ann Borden, and Sidney Burke (Berkowitz) (Jerusalem, OH).

27.   Interviews with Abraham J. Klausner, Ann Borden, Marvin Linick, and Zalman Grinberg (Jerusalem, OH).

28.   Arieh Tartakower to Judah Nadich, Robert Marcus, Joseph S. Shubow, 6.25.45, World Jewish Congress, New York, File 64, Drawer 272.

29.   Leonard Dinnerstein, "The United States Army and the Jews: Policies Toward the Displaced Persons After World War II," *American Jewish History* (March 1979), p. 356; Dinnerstein, *America*, pp. 34-36; Harry S. Truman, *Memoirs: Years of Decision* (New York: Doubleday and Company, 1955), p. 311; Gemma Neuman, "Earl G. Harrison and the Displaced Persons Controversy: A Case Study of Social Action" (Ph.D. diss., Temple University, 1973), p. 160.

30.   Interview with Abraham J. Klausner (Jerusalem, OH).

31.   *The New York Times*, 9.29.45, p. 38.

32.   Peterson, *American Occupation*, p. 55; Harold Zink, *American Military Government in Germany* (New York: Macmillan Co., 1947), p. 25.

33.   *The New York Times*, 9.29.45, p. 8.

34.   *The New York Times*, 9.29.45, p. 8.

35.   *The New York Times*, 9.29.45, p. 8.

36.   *The New York Times*, 9.29.45, p. 8.

37.   *The New York Times*, 9.29.45, p. 38.

38.   *The New York Times*, 9.29.45, p. 38.

39.   Dinnerstein, *America*, p. 75.

40.   Francis Williams, ed., *Twilight of Empire: Memoirs of Prime Minister Clement Attlee* (New York: A.S. Barnes and Company, 1962), p. 188.

41.   Michael J. Cohen, *Palestine: Retreat from the Mandate* (New York: Holmes & Meier, 1978), pp. 183-186, 224.

42.   Bauer, *Brichah*, pp. 3-42; Yehuda Bauer, "Zionism, the Holocaust and the Road to Israel," in *The Jewish Emergence from Powerlessness*, Yehuda Bauer (Toronto: University of Toronto Press, 1979), pp. 62-63.

43.   Bauer, *Brichah*, pp. 3-42; Bauer, *Jewish Emergence*, pp. 62-63.

44.   Ephraim Dekel, *B'riha* (New York: Herzl Press, n.d.); *Encyclopedia Judaica*, Vol. 4 (Jerusalem: Keter Publishing House, 1972), pp. 622-630.

45.   Schwarz, *The Redeemers*, p. 15.

46.   Koppel S. Pinson, "Jewish Life in Liberated Germany," *Jewish Social Studies* IX (April 1947), p. 117.

47.   Herbert Agar, *The Saving Remnant* (London: Rupert Hart-Davis, 1960), p. 181.

48.   Interviews with Eugene Lipman, Abraham J. Klausner, Yosef Miller, Abraham Haselkorn, Eugene J. Cohen, Herbert Friedman, and Meyer Abramowitz (Jerusalem, OH).

49.   Bauer, *Brichah*, pp. 66-99.

50.   *The New York Times*, 12.7.45, p. 8.

51. Bauer, *Brichah*, p. 84. Nahum Goldmann to Stephen S. Wise, 1.8.46, and Gruenbaum to Stephen S. Wise, 1.8.46, World Jewish Congress, New York, File 56, Drawer 272.

52. Bauer, *Jewish Emergence*, pp. 68-69.

53. Bauer, *Jewish Emergence*, pp. 68-69.

54. Yehuda Bauer, "The Holocaust and the Struggle of the Yishuv as Factors in the Establishment of the State of Israel," in *The Catastrophe of European Jewry: Antecedents, History, Reflections*, ed. Yisrael Gutman and Livia Rothkirchen (Jerusalem: Yad Vashem, 1976), p. 620.

55. Leo Srole, "Why the DPs Can't Wait," *Commentary* (January 1947), pp. 20-21.

56. Gutman and Rothkirchen, *Catastrophe*, p. 620.

57. John Marlowe, *The Seat of Pilate* (London: The Cresset Press, 1959), pp. 206-210; Bauer, *Brichah*, pp. 242-243.

58. Bauer, *Jewish Emergence*, p. 74.

59. Marlowe, *Seat of Pilate*, pp. 206-210.

60. Mark Wischnitzer, *Visas to Freedom: The History of HIAS* (Cleveland: The World Publishing Company, 1956), pp. 207-208, 212-213; *Jewish Telegraphic Agency Daily News Bulletin*, 5.8.46, p. 4; S.R. Mickelsen to Joint Anglo-American Committee of Inquiry, n.d., CAH; Irwin Rosen to Philip Rosen, 12.30.46, CAH; *The New York Times*, 12.23.45, p. 1.

61. Bauer, *Jewish Emergence*, p. 65.

62. Bauer, *History*, pp. 341-342.

63. Bauer, *Brichah*, p. 291.

64. Bauer, *History*, pp. 343-344.

65. Srole, "Why the DPs," p.22.

66. Srole, "Why the DPs," p. 22.

67. Dinnerstein, *America*, pp. 102, 114.

68. Dinnerstein, *America*, p. 115.

69. Dinnerstein, *America*, p. 117.

70. Dinnerstein, *America*, p. 255.

71. Dinnerstein, *America*, p. 251.

72. Dinnerstein, *America*, pp. 217-253.

73. Howard M. Sachar, *A History of Israel* (New York: Alfred A. Knopf, 1976), p. 263.

74. Zvi Ganin, *Truman, American Jewry and Israel, 1945-1948* (New York: Holmes & Meier, 1979), p. 65.

75. Ganin, *Truman*, p. 67.

76. Ganin, *Truman*, p. 65.

77. Sachar, *History*, p. 247; Bauer, *Jewish Emergence*, p. 72.

78. Sachar, *History*, p. 257; Bauer, *Jewish Emergence*, p. 73.

79. Sachar, *History*, p. 265.

80. Bauer, *Jewish Emergence*, p. 73; Bauer, *History*, p. 346.

81. Sachar, *History*, pp. 270-271; Ganin, *Truman*, p. 77.

82. Ganin, *Truman*, pp. 79, 85, 93.

83. Ganin, *Truman*, p. 85.

84. Ganin, *Truman*, p. 93.

85. Ganin, *Truman*, pp. 104, 107.

86. Ganin, *Truman*, pp. 118-119.
87. Cohen, *Palestine*, pp. 190-191.
88. Bauer, *Jewish Emergence*, pp. 75-76.
89. Walter, Laqueur, ed. *The Israel/Arab Reader* (London: Weidenfeld and Nicolson, 1969), pp. 109-112; Sachar, *History*, pp. 280-287.
90. Laqueur, *The Israel/Arab Reader*, pp. 113-122.
91. Bauer, *History*, p. 348.
92. Bauer, *History*, pp. 347-348.
93. Ganin, *Truman*, pp. 178-179.
94. Bauer, *Jewish Emergence*, p. 76.
95. Bauer, *Jewish Emergence*, p. 76.
96. Evyator Friesel, "The Holocaust and the Birth of Israel," *The Wiener Library Bulletin* XXXII (1979): 59.

### For Further Reading

Bauer, Yehuda. *Brichah: Flight and Rescue.* New York: Random House, 1970.

―――. "The Initial Organization of the Holocaust Survivors in Bavaria." *Yad Vashem Studies* VIII (1970): 127-157.

―――. *The Jewish Emergence from Powerlessness.* Toronto: University of Toronto Press, 1979.

Cohen, Michael J. *Palestine: Retreat from the Mandate.* New York: Holmes & Meier, 1978.

Dinnerstein, Leonard. *America and the Survivors of the Holocaust.* New York: Columbia University Press, 1982.

Eliach, Yaffa, and Gurewitsch, Brana, eds. *The Liberators: Eyewitness Accounts of the Liberation of Concentration Camps.* Vol. I. New York: Center for Holocaust Studies Documentation and Research, 1981.

Ganin, Zvi. *Truman, American Jewry and Israel, 1945-1948.* New York: Holmes & Meier, 1979.

Peterson, Edward N. *The American Occupation of Germany: Retreat to Victory.* Detroit: Wayne State University Press, 1977.

Pinson, Koppel S. "Jewish Life in Liberated Germany." *Jewish*

*Social Studies* IX (April 1947): 101-126.

Proudfoot, Malcolm J. *European Refugees*. London: Faber and Faber, 1957.

Sachar, Howard M. *A History of Israel*. New York: Alfred A. Knopf, 1976.

Schwarz, Leo. *The Redeemers*. New York: Farrar, Straus, and Young, 1953.

# The European Jewish Communities After the Holocaust

## JOEL S. FISHMAN

The reconstruction of the European Jewish communities took place after the greatest tragedy that ever befell the Jewish people. The Holocaust resulted in an enormous loss of population, of leaders, of the traditional great centers of the Jewish faith and learning—not to speak of theft, vandalism, the destruction of private and communal property, and the personal suffering of the survivors. Individuals, families, communities, as well as Jews throughout the world, had to come to terms with this unprecedented disaster. Both the survivors and the communities which were spared were obliged to reconsider the place of the Jew in the modern world.

The Holocaust and the bitter disappointments of the postwar years made it clear that even in countries where Jews had lived for centuries, they did not share the same destiny as the local Gentiles. Jewish survivors were confronted with new struggles and exacerbated forms of the old antisemitism. Frequently, local populations were far from hospitable to Jews returning from concentration camps and hiding. Many had assumed that Jews would cease to live within their midst. Displeasure at their return was reported even in Denmark, where the population had helped save its Jewish citizens. In Kielce, Poland, a planned pogrom of horrifying proportions took place in July, 1946, as part of a campaign to drive Jewish survivors out of the country. It was organized by the police, and the Catholic church in Poland refused to condemn it. In the first two years after the liberation, more than 800 Jews lost their lives in Poland.[1]

It was a time of widespread violence with tendencies towards political polarization, efforts at international and interfaith reconciliation, and heightened consciousness of human rights; a time when political and social confrontations that had been postponed during the war took place to challenge all the established structures, from conventional class structures to colonial empires.

During these years of new-found hope for universal social justice, the Jewish people in the Diaspora and in the *Yishuv* waged bitter battles for individual and collective enfranchisement. Large numbers of stateless Jews, hoping to immigrate to what was then British Mandate Palestine, were accumulating in the displaced persons camps of Europe and detention camps of Cyprus. In the *Yishuv*, the battle for the state was underway. In far-off corners of the Diaspora, surviving Jewish populations, decimated, weakened, and disoriented, had to battle for reinstatement amidst largely indifferent and even hostile societies. Jews, both in the Diaspora and in the *Yishuv*, were clearly given to understand that they should not "get too much at the head of the queue."

# Western Europe

The process of reconstruction for the Jewish communities of western Europe was essentially comprised of three phases: care for urgent and pressing matters directly associated with the Nazi occupation and the Holocaust; evolutionary development and general rebuilding of the community; and accommodation to the modern welfare state. The first stage involved the search for missing friends and relatives, caring for orphan children, rebuilding of synagogues and communal buildings (when such property could be recovered), resumption of *shehitah* (ritual slaughter of animals in accordance with Jewish dietary laws) and, where possible, the recovery of personal and communal property. This last item created much tension and frequently resulted in violence because non-Jews who came into possession of plundered or abandoned Jewish property were frequently hostile when confronted with the prospect of relinquishing that property which had either been placed in their care for safekeeping or were simply ill-gotten. It should be noted that, in fact, not all efforts to recover stolen or expropriated property succeeded, and in many cases, local governments were not interested in helping their Jewish communities.

It was not only Jewish property that was difficult to restore. One major problem that confronted European Jews was the recovery of Jewish orphans who had been given to non-Jews for the duration of the war. After the liberation, there was a general reluctance throughout Europe to return these children, particularly if the parents had been killed. Many argued that there was no reason to break the bond between the children and their foster parents. When children had been baptized, foster parents wanted them to remain Christian. The Jews viewed this as a continued assault and fought by whatever means were at their disposal to regain custody. Such efforts were often futile.

The second phase, evolutionary development, took place roughly during the mid-fifties. With the increasing general stability of western Europe, Jewish communities, in step with the general populations, began to build new buildings and to make their first move into newly developed neighborhoods and future suburbs. Younger leaders now began to assume positions of responsibility. (The great loss of a generation of leaders and continuity would be felt most acutely about a decade later.)

During this period, developments in Israel inspired the Jews of western Europe. It could be said that the recovery and rehabilitation of European Jews partially took place in Israel, although this group of Holocaust survivors (of European origin) had left Europe to rebuild their lives in new surroundings. Ties of family and sentiment linked the two groups, and many European Jews, after liberation, decided to build their futures in Israel. Others emigrated to other countries, the United States, Canada, and Australia being the most favored.

The third phase, accommodation to the modern welfare state,

extends roughly from the mid-sixties to the present. The mid-sixties marked the advent of two prominent trends: the challenge to organized authority associated with youth culture and the New Left and the rise of the European welfare state, which followed new prosperity and the success of the European Community. The combination of a challenge to organized authority and the mentality of the welfare state had mixed effects on patterns of Jewish communal affiliation.

The former had a negative impact on the views of the younger generation towards established religion, including Judaism. At the same time, Israel did not stand very high in the cosmos of the New Left. In the ideology both of the New Left and of the European Community, nationalism was frowned upon as being backward and feelings of national loyalty ceased to attract the same personal allegiance as in the past. Such general attitudes caused some confusion in the minds of young Jews: whether to affiliate positively with their local Jewish communities and to give their unreserved support to Israel. This period witnessed a general continued trend of Jews moving to the suburbs, of the disintegration of the smaller communities, and of Jewish families living further apart. These trends presented challenges to the cohesiveness and viability of the individual communities. Demographically, the era presented a continuation of the previous decline of Jewish birth rates. This was coupled with a rise in divorce and a rate of intermarriage so high that many communities could no longer effectively cope with this development.

The advent of the welfare state throughout the continent also influenced attitudes towards established religion, while governmental funding policies conceived within this administrative framework gradually influenced Jewish communal structure in many localities. Within the scheme of the welfare state, religion is a cultural matter, rather than primarily spiritual. There has been an increasing tendency, especially in the wake of the pioneering progress of Protestant churches in psychological pastoral work, to classify and subsidize denominationally sponsored programs within the context of "culture and recreation." Where such funding opportunities were to be found, local communities pragmatically changed their structures in order to become eligible for funding. Gradually, a change of emphasis may be taking place, where the orientation of community activity is becoming increasingly directed to social care and secular Jewish educational programs at the expense of Jewish spiritual content. Similarly, the launching of communal umbrella organizations and other rationalized communal structures may have much to do with the desire to comply with eligibility requirements for local government funding.

There is, however, a force which may encourage increased individual affiliation, and that is the effects of recent manifestations of European antisemitism—which since the war have been present in latent form but currently have been more open. Perhaps, in reaction to new expressions of antisemitism, individual Jews will increasingly turn to their communities for comfort and support, but it is a questionable proposition at best to seek genuine benefits from this inherently evil and negative force.

## Eastern Europe

The experiences of Jews in eastern Europe bears occasional similarity to that of western Europe. They differ in that those countries that fell under Soviet Communist domination had other political, social, and economic developments. We can identify a number of periods of change and stability affecting the development of eastern European Jews: 1) immediate postwar flux and uncertainty; 2) the Communist takeovers of eastern European countries; 3) the demise of Stalin; 4) the evolution after Stalin's death; 5) the challenge to established authority, parallel to that in the West, but culminating roughly with the Soviet invasion of Czechoslovakia; 6) the development of internal dissent, the era of the Helsinki Accords (1975), and legal emigration from Russia[2]; and 7) as of 1982, the closing of doors once again.

An era of flux and uncertainty took place immediately after the Red Army's liberation of eastern Europe. Surviving Jews returned to their native lands from concentration camps or Soviet Russia, for the most part, in hopes of finding relatives and friends. Generally, their hopes were met with bitter disappointment, and Gentiles who had plundered or otherwise appropriated Jewish property turned violently hostile at the prospect of relinquishing the ill-gotten gains. Salo W. Baron considered that two of the major factors behind the strong postwar antisemitic feeling was the refusal to give up stolen property and the unwillingness to return children and orphans who survived the Holocaust in Gentile custody.[3] He reported that, during the first two years after the liberation, some 800 Jews were murdered in postwar Poland.[4] The Kielce pogrom, which took place on July 4, 1946, in which forty-two Jews lost their lives, was supported by the police and condoned by the Catholic church.[5]

During this period of flux, when civilian governments had not been firmly entrenched, Jews and other displaced persons could still cross international borders, legally or semilegally. The horrifying violence done to Jews in postwar Poland—and particularly the shock of the Kielce pogrom—prompted a mass exodus whose ultimate destination was British Mandate Palestine. However, even in countries committed to legality and the principle of minority rights, there was an inclination to encourage Jews either to assimilate or emigrate. President Benes of Czechoslovakia, in an interview on August 10, 1945, declared:

The Establishment of a Jewish Home in Palestine is a necessity for all nations, because antisemitism is a regrettable, but practically inevitable social phenomenon. It will not vanish till the creation of a Jewish country granting citizenship to all Jewry. It will be difficult to repatriate all Jews there, but it could be done soon at least for the European Jews. Those who would not leave for Palestine ought to be assimilated completely to the people of the country they want to live in, or live as citizens of a foreign state.[6]

Clearly, a change of mood had taken place, even among the more democratically inclined leaders in eastern Europe.

The following stage, from 1948 to 1953, witnessed the Communist takeovers of the eastern European countries. This development did not augur well for Jewish communal life. In general terms, many Jewish Communists were prominent in this first generation of takeovers. Ideologically, they opposed the reestablishment of Jewish communal life *and* Jewish emigration. Many rose to prominent positions, but with Stalin's increasingly harsh attitudes towards the Russian Jews late in his life, even their positions became uncertain.

During this period in Russia, almost all leading Jewish intellectuals were either liquidated or imprisoned. Such persecution reached its peak during the episode of the "doctors' plot," when a number of Jewish physicians who treated Stalin were charged with hastening his physical decline. It was also reputed during these tense times that plans had actually been prepared for the mass deportation of Russian Jews. But Stalin's death stayed the decree and a number of repressive measures were relaxed, although a long-term policy designed to bring an end to the Jewish religion and nationality remained in force.

There was no restoration of Jewish cultural rights or reversal in the systematic policy of supressing Yiddish-language publications and reducing the number of synagogues. The government did not give additional rights to the Jews at a time when more relaxed attitudes towards Christian faiths were adopted. The fact that a number of Jewish party members actively and visibly participated as political shock troops in the Communist takeovers of eastern European countries did not endear them to their non-Jewish compatriots. A number of prominent Jewish Communists met dreadful fates when their mentors, Stalin and Beria, passed from the political stage.

Once the eastern European regimes became moderately secure, the fate of each community, for the most part, depended upon the local conditions and policies of each government. In Hungary and Rumania, some form of *modus vivendi* was achieved. Hungary, for example, has a rabbinical seminary, while Rumanian Jews claim to enjoy a spiritual freedom and the opportunity to cultivate a Jewish communal life. In the revitalization of these communities, financial support from abroad, particularly from the American Jewish Joint Distribution Committee (JDC) and the World Jewish Congress, has been of considerable importance. Many communal programs have been directed towards social welfare, particularly the care of the elderly, a development which parallels developments in western

Europe. From the recent publications and public pronouncements of the Jewish community of the German Democratic Republic,[7] it appears that its position may be similar to that of Hungary and Rumania, reaching some accommodation with the authorities and achieving some form of administrative independence.

In other parts of Europe, such as Poland, Czechoslovakia, and Russia, relations between the local communities and the existing regimes were far more problematical. Jewish religious, cultural, and communal activities were systematically suppressed. A large-scale, relentless campaign against Zionism and Israel followed the Israeli victory in the Six-Day War (June, 1967) and the corresponding embarrassment to the Soviet cause. Despite all protests to the contrary, expressions of virulent anti-Zionist feelings had antisemitic ramifications in domestic policy. Furthermore, newly arising forces of general dissent in eastern Europe began to identify with Israel, a small power which succeeded in crushing and humiliating the Soviet Union's Arab clients. Ideologically, opposition to Israel became an important cause for those committed to safeguarding state authority.

In the context of the new constellation of relations which followed the Six-Day War, a second exodus of Jews from Poland took place. In 1967, Poland had 25,000 Jews; by 1970, that number dwindled to 15,000; 1975, to 8,000; 1981, to 6,000. And in Poland itself, an ironic anomaly was identified: a state of "Antisemitism without Jews." In the wake of the Six-Day War, many Russian Jews took courage and began their campaign for the right to leave the Soviet Union. This program was occasionally associated with the activities of Soviet dissidents and the world campaign for human rights (Helsinki Final Act, August, 1975.) It may be said that, in part, as a consequence of world public opinion, a large-scale Jewish emigration from the Soviet Union took place roughly during the decade of the seventies. Recently, however, Soviet authorities have restricted this exodus. The future prospects for Soviet Jews maintaining their identity and Jewish character are considered to be endangered by the government's long-term policy of bringing about their elimination through a process of attrition.

In countries of the Eastern Bloc, where the materialistic ideology of communism has been imparted to several generations by means of the state educational system and the skillful distribution of society's rewards, the spiritual content of Judaism has been neglected. The basis for Jewish identification has become increasingly a negative association, whereas those of Jewish descent have become objects of discrimination, singled out through the instrument of the official identity card. It has been noted that in countries such as Lithuania, which had a briefer exposure to the effects of the Soviet education, the Russian influence has been less profound. Frequently, emigrants from this area still bear the mark of its outstanding educational and cultural traditions.

On the whole, the condition of the Jews living in the Eastern Bloc varies from country to country, ranging from relations which have been moderately decent to those which may have been oppressive. Many factors influence the policies of governmental authorities in these countries, not the least of which is world public opinion. As of 1982, a certain feeling prevailed among international Jewish philanthropic organizations that the coming challenge would be to campaign for the right of Jews to exercise religious freedom within the countries in which they reside rather than to press exclusively for emigration.

## Consequences

As we consider the direct consequences of the Holocaust, we must note that the most obvious injury to Jewish life has been the decrease in size of the European communities, which effectively means that many medium-sized and smaller communities have ceased to exist on a viable basis. This has brought about an accelerated process of concentration and centralization in urban centers (a movement to be distinguished from the development of suburbs). In addition, Jewish life suffered a loss of leaders. Many had perished during the Holocaust, and a new leadership of the younger generation was also lost. Similarly, many individuals with strong initiative decided to build their futures in Israel.

European Jewish cultural life (as well as that of world Jewry) became impoverished through a severe shortage of teachers, trained rabbis, shohatim (ritual animal slaughterers), and hazzanim (cantors). Much of this personnel came from the yeshivot (talmudic academies) of eastern Europe or from the great German rabbinical seminaries. After the Holocaust, eastern Europe could no longer furnish such trained teachers and communal functionaries. Furthermore, the prolonged period of the German occupation and its anti-Jewish measures interrupted Jewish education for a whole generation. This break in continuity has had both serious educational and psychological consequences. On the personal level, the shock and suffering of the Holocaust resulted in prolonged psychological trauma for a whole generation and its offspring. In this way, the devastation of the Holocaust is so extensive that its ramifications simply cannot be quantified.

Within a world perspective, the loss of numbers and the profound cultural devastation accelerated the ascent of American Jewry to its position as a leading community of world Jewry. In addition, American Jews, during the thirties and war years, were making slow but steady progress in improving their financial and social positions, enabling them to assert themselves with increasing political influence.[8] Taking account of these developments, Jacob Lestschinsky, a well-informed and highly talented observer of contemporary Jewish life, noted that while in 1850, 88 percent of the world's Jews lived in Europe, in 1950, 24.5 percent (less than a quarter) lived in Europe. He stated that the declining trend would continue.[9]

As of 1982, the tendency seems to have changed, and Europe— western Europe particularly—has become a region of Jewish immigration. Between 29 to 30 percent of Jews throughout the world now live there. Jewish populations have migrated from North Africa to metropolitan France, Spain, and Italy, and from Israel to all parts of Europe. On the European continent, displaced persons have relocated to the Federal Republic of Germany, Austria, Belgium, and Denmark. The movement of Jews to Spain from politically troubled countries in Latin America has also been noted. The arrival of such new populations may not necessarily strengthen the Jewish communities as such, because increasing numbers of individuals are no longer accustomed to or conform with traditional patterns of Jewish communal life. But, with their distinctive peculiarities, the rebuilt communities do exist, and a quantifiable repopulation has taken place. Both in the East and in the West, the future well-being of these communities will depend on their own evolution and the ebb and flow of external political forces, a factor upon which they have limited influence.

### Notes

1. For the background to the immediate postwar era see: Joel S. Fishman, "The Reconstruction of the Dutch Jewish Community and its Implications for the Writing of Contemporary Jewish History," *Proceedings of the American Academy for Jewish Research* 45 (1978): 67-101; Nehemiah Robinson, ed., *European Jewry Ten Years after the War* (New York: Institute of Jewish Affairs, 1956); Salo W. Baron, "Changing Patterns of Antisemitism: A Survey," *Jewish Social Studies* 38 (1976): 5-38; Salo W. Baron, "Anti-Semitism," *Encyclopedia Britannica* (1972): 87-90; Salo W. Baron, *The Russian Jew Under Tsars and Soviets*, 2nd edition (New York: Macmillan Co., 1967).

2. Joshua Rothenberg, "Jewish Religion in the Soviet Union," *The Jews in Soviet Russia since 1917*, 3rd ed., ed. Lionel Kochan (Oxford: Oxford University Press, 1978), pp. 182-183.

3. Baron, "Anti-Semitism," pp. 87-88. Baron wrote that "Many Germans who had acquired from the Nazis confiscated Jewish houses, factories, and other businesses were reluctant to return them to their rightful owners, and formed protective associations to resist restitution."

4. Baron, "Anti-Semitism," p. 88.

5. Michael Chichinski, "The Kielce Pogrom, 1946," *Soviet Jewish Affairs* 5 (1971): 57-72.

6. Salo W. Baron, "The Spiritual Reconstruction of European Jewry," *Commentary* 1 (1945): 10.

7. See: *Nachrichtenblatt der Judischen Gemeinde von Berlin*

*und des Verbandes der Judischen Gemeinden in der Deutschen Demokratischen Republik,* passim.

8.   Salo W. Baron, "The Year in Retrospect," *American Jewish Year Book* 49 (1947-1948): 103-122.

9.   Jacob Lestschinsky, "The Rise and Decline of European Jewry" (New York: 1953). [stencil]

### For Further Reading

Baron, Salo W. "Opening Remarks to the Conference on Problems of Research in the Study of the Jewish Catastrophe, 1939-45." *Jewish Social Studies* 12 (January 1950): 13-16.

———. "Changing Patterns of Antisemitism: A Survey." *Jewish Social Studies* 38 (Winter 1976): 5-38.

———. "From a Historian's Notebook, European Jewry Before and After Hitler." In *American Jewish Yearbook.* Philadelphia: The Jewish Publication Society, 1962.

———. *The Russian Jew under Tzars and Soviets.* 2nd ed. rev. New York: Macmillan Co., 1976.

———. "The Spiritual Reconstruction of European Jewry." *Commentary* 1 (November 1945): 4-12.

———. "The Year in Retrospect." In *American Jewish Yearbook.* Philadelphia: The Jewish Publication Society, 1947.

Chichinski, Michael. "The Kielce Pogrom, 1946." *Soviet Jewish Affairs* 5 (1975): 57-72.

Fishman, J. S. "The Annelce Beekman Affair and the Dutch News Media." *Jewish Social Studies* 40 (Winter 1978): 3-24.

———. "The Ecumenical Challenge of Jewish Survival: Pastor Kalma and Post-War Dutch Society, 1946." *Journal of Ecumenical Studies* 15 (Summer 1978): 461-476.

———. "Jewish War Orphans in the Netherlands: The Guardianship Issue, 1945-1950." *Wiener Library Bulletin* 26 (1973-1974): 31-36.

———. "The Reconstruction of the Dutch Jewish Community

and Its Implications for the Writing of Contemporary Jewish History." *Proceedings of the American Academy for Jewish Research* 45 (1978): 140-173.

————. "Some Observations on the Postwar Reconstruction of the Western European Jewish Communities." *Forum* 35 (Spring/Summer 1979): 111-116.

Kater, J. "Concentratiekamp-syndroom." *Algemeen Handelsblad* 30 May 1964, supplement, p. 1.

Kochan, Lionel, ed. *The Jews in Soviet Russia Since 1917.* 3rd ed. Oxford: Oxford University Press, 1978.

Lestschinsky, Jacob. *Crisis, Catastrophe and Survival: A Jewish Balance Sheet, 1914-1948.* New York: Institute of Jewish Affairs, 1948.

————. "Do Jews Learn from History?" *Jewish Journal of Sociology* 5 (December 1963): 245-254.

————. "New Conditions of Life Among Jews in the Diaspora." *Jewish Journal of Sociology* 2 (November 1960): 139-146.

Robinson, Nehemiah, ed. *European Jewry Ten Years After the War.* New York: Institute of Jewish Affairs, 1956.

# The Impact of the Holocaust on Sephardic and Oriental Jews

## JANE GERBER

All attempts to discuss the impact of the Holocaust on the Jewish people have been necessarily flawed. The scope of the catastrophe cannot be easily contained in words. The repercussions on Jews are so subtle and the implications so awesome that only the foolhardy or the prophets among us have ventured into such speculations. Yet, the Jewish world was so irrevocably altered, power relationships so fundamentally changed, and demographic developments so critically influenced that discussions of impact and implications are extremely important at this juncture in Jewish history.

At first glance, the impact of the Holocaust on Sephardic and Oriental Jews is not immediately apparent, since the largest percentage of Sephardic and Oriental Jews did not experience the *direct* effects of Nazi occupation. Yet, unlike American Jews, neither were they precisely on the sidelines, forced to wonder in retrospect whether they had done "enough" to rescue their fellow Jews. Sephardic Jews lost their most stable and dynamic community, that of Salonica, they were much more intimately touched by the tides of war, and their lives hung in the balance. In addition, the Holocaust sundered their millennial relationships and ties with their native lands and thrust upon them a new historical challenge and burden— one which they barely anticipated or truly comprehended.

Throughout the 1930s and 1940s, the rise of nazism and the triumphs of fascism uncovered the precarious state of Jewish security in what had been the longest and, in certain instances, among the most stable Diaspora communities. In Algeria and Tunisia, severe discriminatory legislation and forced labor of Jewish males was enacted. In Libya, all Jews suffered from Mussolini's attempts to woo the Arab world by singling out the Jews for severely discriminatory treatment while Libyan Jews of foreign nationality were interned or expelled. In Iran, the nationalistic and pro-Nazi regime of Reza Shah introduced a host of anti-Jewish laws after 1936. So great was the attraction of nazism on the Iranian shah that Arthur S. Millspaugh, the administrator general of Iran's finances from 1922 to 1927 and from 1943 to 1945, testified "to all intents and purposes, Reza Shah handed over Persia to Hitler."[1] The pro-Nazi Mufti of Jerusalem Haj Amin el-Husseini found refuge in the Japanese Embassy in Teheran in 1941, and continued his anti-Jewish propaganda from there. Iran's Jews could feel secure only after British and Soviet troops occupied the country in 1941, deposed Reza Shah, and replaced him with the pro-Allied Mohammed Reza Pahlavi.

Flirtation with nazism assumed more violent forms in Iraq, exploding in pogroms and devastation of the Iraqi Jewish community in the spring of 1941. Syria, too, served as a lively base of pro-Nazi propaganda, aimed at inciting the Arab masses against the

Jews and resulting in the economic ruination of Syrian Jewry. By 1946, 85 percent of Syrian Jews were living on the brink of poverty. The widespread attraction of nazism in the Muslim world had served to undermine the economic and social underpinnings of Jewish life in Muslim lands, a life which had managed to survive intact for over 1,000 years with a rich, indigenous culture of its own. While the Holocaust did not directly disrupt these communities in the manner that it did throughout Europe, it succeeded in unraveling the relationships, ties, and fragile balances which the Jews had carefully nurtured with their neighbors. The repercussions of the events in Palestine on the fate of Jews in Muslim lands was to lead to ultimate communal dismemberment, a process which had been greatly accelerated by the Holocaust. After all, one of the most telling implications of the Holocaust was that it revealed the extreme vulnerability of Jewish life in dispersion.

Any discussion of the impact of the Holocaust on Sephardic and Oriental Jews suffers from a paucity of materials on the subject. Neither literary treatments nor sociological studies have been undertaken to determine whether there is, in fact, a particular Sephardic Jewish perspective on the European destruction. Moreover, since most Sephardim now reside in the State of Israel, their attitudes towards the Holocaust have been influenced by Zionist ideology and Israeli education, or by the continuing ethnic tensions among Sephardic and Ashkenazic Jews. Despite these limitations, observers of the modern Jewish experience would certainly concur that the Holocaust was a global Jewish tragedy that had profound implications for the entire Jewish people.

With the destruction of the Jews of Europe, a new historic burden and responsibility was thrust upon the shoulders of Sephardic and Oriental Jews. Prior to 1948, only 10 percent of the population of Palestine's Jewish community was Sephardic and Oriental. This segment was confined to deeply religious settlers in the four so-called Holy Cities of Hebron, Safed, Tiberius, and Jerusalem, or to workers in the British civil service and a small elite group of bankers and merchants. The ideology of Zionism, with its heavy emphasis on Socialist principles and the restorative powers of agricultural endeavor, were dreams conjured up in eastern Europe in response to the needs and perceived problems of eastern European Jews.

With the end of World War II and the revelations of the mass destruction of European Jews, the sole biological reservoir remaining to build the fledgling Jewish State was the population mass of Sephardic and Oriental Jews. Both western and eastern European Jews, the former by choice and the latter as a result of the Iron Curtain, showed no possibility of serving as the actors in the Zionist drama. The creation of the State of Israel, however, tapped deep messianic stirrings among the Jews of Muslim lands, and they assumed the historical role of replacing their lost brethren in providing the manpower for a precarious Zionist enterprise. Before long, the State of Israel became a state whose majority was constituted of Sephardic and Oriental Jews. This unanticipated development has raisêd a host of questions for the evolution of both the State of Israel and the actors in this historic undertaking.

The fact that the culture of the State of Israel had been formed before the arrival of Sephardic and Oriental Jews, and was built upon a perception of Jewish life in Europe, that the Holocaust, in fact, destroyed, has precipitated a profound crisis on a variety of levels for both the old and new communities of Israel. One doesn't easily disengage oneself from a 2,000-year-old traditional Middle Eastern culture, patriarchal in family structure, traditional in economic patterns, and religious in outlook, and assume a new twentieth-century personality. Moreover, the rapid dénouement of Jewish life in Muslim lands, which the Fascists had precipitated, followed by the xenophobic independence movements of the 1940s and 1950s, appeared to emphasize the lesson of the Holocaust—that Jewish minority status was no longer tenable. If the Holocaust abruptly severed the millennial ties of Sephardic Jews with their host cultures, it did so without the necessarily concomitant ideological adjustment to facilitate a smooth transition to a radically new society. The "predicament of homecoming," as the anthropologists have so perceptibly suggested, was not softened by a preparatory period before emigration.

Sephardic and Oriental Jews have, as a result of the Holocaust, become the prime actors in the building of a Jewish State. Neither they nor the Ashkenazic founders of the State had foreseen that history would assume this form. The meeting of Sephardic and Oriental Jews in Israel with their coreligionists from Europe has been a meeting of relatives who are virtual strangers to one another on many levels. The potentially mediating force of such communities as that of the European Sephardic Salonica was lost in the embers of Poland. It is still too early to predict what the ultimate cultural amalgam of Israeli society will be, but surely the Sephardic and Oriental majority will have an increasing voice in its creation as a result of the Holocaust.

One of the more subtle consequences of the Holocaust, a consequence that falls under the purview of the psychologist rather than the historian, is that of constructing an integrated view of the Jewish past. For Ashkenazic Jews, the Holocaust has erroneously been depicted as an exclusively European and Ashkenazic tragedy. It was, in fact, a Jewish tragedy of incalculable dimensions whose impact on Sephardic and Oriental Jews was enormous. Not only did the Holocaust provide the coup de grace, extinguishing ancient societies and cultures, but it thrust Jews into new, totally unanticipated, and radically revolutionary roles which will alter the destiny of the entire House of Israel. In the rewriting of Jewish history after the Holocaust, the impact of the Holocaust on the lives and destinies of Sephardic and Oriental Jews will surely form a prominent and important chapter.

## Notes

1. Arthur C. Millspaugh, *Americans in Persia* (New York: Da Capo. 1976), p. 8.

## For Further Reading

Deshen, Shlomo, and Shokeid, Moshe. *The Predicament of Homecoming*. Ithaca, NY: Cornell University Press, 1974.

Patai, Raphael. *Israel Between East and West*. Westpoint, CT: Greenwood Press, 1970.

# Renewal of Religious Life After the Holocaust

## DANIEL LANDES

In the aftermath of the Holocaust, Jews attempted to recreate their religious life.[1] They sought to rebuild educational institutions and religious communities destroyed during the war. Moreover, there was the urgent need to renew Jewish scholarship. The situation in the newly enlarged Soviet Union proved to be bleak. General religious repression combined with traditional antisemitism to supress the movement of many of the three million Jewish citizens towards Jewish tradition and Jewish identity. In other Communist countries, such as Rumania, which had an active chief rabbinate, and Hungary, where the tiny Jewish Theological Seminary of Budapest was rebuilt, conditions were significantly better. Jewish life there, however, was barely a pale reflection of its prewar glory.

Western Europe today contains a few viable Jewish communities in Switzerland and France; in the latter nation, an influx of North African Jews in the 1960s spurred a revitalization of Jewish life. In England, the immigration of the late 1930s and 1940s added to an already highly structured religious life. While these three communities developed their own indigenous institutions and leadership, Europe no longer held the center stage of Judaism. The scene shifted to America (the United States and Canada) and to Israel. It is in these two areas that one must search for the transplanting and renewal of the European legacy.

Israel and America had sufficient Jewish populations necessary for creativity, with the political and social freedoms for its expression. Israel, as the Jewish homeland, inspired and supported religious growth. America had the advantage of enormous economic opportunities for the private support of scholarship, synagogues, and educational institutions. Both had long histories of modern Jewish religious life, which greatly affected, in differing ways, the reception of various European religious forms, communities, and leadership.

## Liberal Judaism

Europe's Liberal Judaism (centered in Germany) was a movement with wide variations in principles and practices. In general, it employed the "scientific study of Judaism" *(Wissenschaft des Judentums)*, utilizing modern philological, historical, comparative religion, and critical methodologies. In addition, Liberal Judaism had a strong emphasis on ethics, and did not *a priori* consider any formulation of traditional beliefs or practices as authoritative. Some of the more radical branches discarded significant rituals, while others maintained major observances and an attachment, if not total congruence, to *halakhah* (Jewish law).

Liberal Judaism was also split on whether the Jews constituted a national group. Some viewed Judaism as only a religion and saw themselves as "Germans of the Mosaic persuasion." A few embraced Jewish nationalism to the extent of being fervent Zionists.

Europe's Liberal Judaism was devastated by the Holocaust. Its synagogues and educational institutions were destroyed, and many of its rabbis, scholars, and adherents perished. Those who either escaped or survived found difficulties in transplanting this form of Judaism on new soil. The Germanic flavor and style of Liberal Judaism was foreign and not attractive to the very different Israeli and American scenes.

European Liberal Judaism, except for a few small congregations, could not transfer to *Erez Israel.* Not one European Liberal educational institution reopened there in any guise. This failure was partly due to the hostile reception Liberal Judaism received from Orthodox Judaism—the only reorganized and viable religious Jewish community. This was not the major reason. Secular Zionism, which was generally antireligious, and the rebuilding of the land claimed primary attention. Secular Zionism was itself a "religion," providing identity, homeland, history, and Scripture through the Bible (especially the Prophets) and various Socialist and Zionist texts. It also established values, ceremonies (for example, the celebration of traditional holidays from a national and agricultural perspective), a language (modern Hebrew), and moral values. Many erstwhile Liberal Jews found fulfillment, a focus for creativity, and a healing of their wounds in Zionism.

Martin Buber's career after the Holocaust was indicative of this process. Buber, a lay personality associated with Liberal Judaism, was famed as the exponent of existential philosophy of dialogue.[2] Inspired mainly by his reading of the Jewish Bible and stories of the Hasidim, Buber understood the world through a theory of relation. Man, as an "I," usually meets his fellow man as an object, an "it." This is a limited and pragmatic relation in which neither the "it" nor the "I" truly reveal themselves. Man can choose, however, to encounter the other as a "thou"—a full subject having his own "I" identity. In the "I-thou" relation, both "I"'s discover themselves in the process of encountering the other. It is also in the "I-thou" relation that one can begin to glimpse and encounter the Eternal Thou (God), who stands behind and supports all human relations. The "I-thou" encounter does not take place in any lofty spiritual, romantic, or abstract intellectual dimension. It is to be found in the here and now, in real, concrete life situations. There is no rule, law, or *halakhah* that can instruct one in how to encounter the thou or the Eternal Thou. It must rise spontaneously from the particulars of the situation. It is crucial to note that Buber himself personified and lived his program of dialogue; an open person, "present" to the other he was meeting, he was even wary of intellectual "concepts" and fearful that they may "step between myself and the thou, the other person."[3] Similarly, he was not at all *halakhically* observant, refusing any patterned response to ever-changing situations.

While in Germany, Buber was one of the most influential thinkers of the twentieth century. His influence upon the thought of Liberal Judaism was especially profound, with many Liberal thinkers incorporating Buber's theology into the notion of Judaism. A long-time Zionist (Buber as a young man had been the secretary to Theodor Herzl, the founder of modern political Zionism), he escaped Germany in 1938 and joined the faculty of the Hebrew University of Jerusalem. His concern was now directed to the real problems and challenges in the creation of a new society in the Jewish homeland. He explored options in Arab-Jewish relations and was especially drawn to the Socialist and formally nonreligious *kibbutz* (commune) experiment as he had been to biblical and Hasidic community models. He saw *kibbutz* members as possessing an "amazing positive relationship—amounting to a regular faith," which penetrated "to the innermost being of their commune."[4] For Buber, as for many Liberal Jews, spirituality and religious meaning and action was to be enacted within the secular life of the Jewish community in *Erez Israel.* The re-creation of German Liberal Judaism was of no great concern or interest.

In America, Liberal Jews generally joined Reform Judaism,[5] originally formed in America in the 1800s by European Liberals. Reform Judaism's liturgy, rabbinical seminary (Hebrew Union College), and ideology had strong German roots adapted to a distinctively optimistic and vigorous American style. From the 1930s on, newly arrived European Liberal Jews, overwhelmed by their traumatic experiences, sensed a kinship with American Reform Judaism. They assimilated into the strong and highly organized American Reform Judaism, which welcomed them and also provided a home (the Hebrew Union College) for a number of their scholars and students.

Despite the benefits, European Liberal Judaism paid a high price in merging into American Reform. Eager to follow the "custom of the locale" where they now resided and lacking their own educational institutions, traditionalist tendencies of Liberal Judaism towards Jewish ceremonies and rites were muted or discarded in the face of the radically nonobservant temper of American Reform Judaism. Additionally, European rabbis, in general, did not have a leadership role in this country. The case of Rabbi Leo Baeck[6] is instructive. A towering presence, Baeck was the leader of German Liberal Judaism and a major theologian. He understood Judaism as "ethical monotheism," and the belief that even ritual laws were directed towards the creation of a moral individual. His extreme rectitude and dedication to the Jews of the Theresienstadt ghetto (Baeck refused opportunities to escape Germany, choosing to remain with his flock), rendered him a major figure in American Reform Judaism and the World Union for Progressive Judaism (an international group of Liberal synagogues). Yet, one receives the impression that Baeck, at this point very old, was more a symbolic presence than a leader. His teaching at the Hebrew Union College in Cincinnati was not successful: Students did not understand the method and direction of his scholarship (largely based on careful readings of rabbinic texts and classical Greek philosophy) and felt personally distant from the man.[7]

In the 1940s and 1950s, American Reform saw Dr. Baeck as a symbol of European Judaism's greatness. European Judaism, however, was a memory to be treasured but not necessarily emulated. A new development, commencing in the late 1960s, was the growing influence of a number of rabbis educated wholly or partially in European Liberal institutions. These included Emil Fackenheim,[8] philosopher; W. Gunther Plaut,[9] congregational rabbi and author of the official Reform English language commentary to the Bible; and Jakob J. Petuchowski,[10] a scholar of liturgy and theology. They encouraged an increased interest in traditional (albeit not Orthodox) prayer, observances,[11] beliefs, and text study—the hallmarks of European Liberal Judaism. This approach opposed other Reform tendencies towards greater assimilation into the surrounding culture and radical theological postures.

## Conservative Judaism

Conservative Judaism[12] emerged after World War II as the largest movement of religiously affiliated Jews in America. It has been popularly viewed as a cross between Orthodoxy and Reform. Conservative traditionalism is present in the espousal and public celebration of religious observances. The generally traditional *halakhic* observance of its rabbinical seminary (The Jewish Theological Seminary of America—J.T.S.) and a number of its graduates, along with the primacy given to the study of classic texts such as the Talmud at J.T.S., also contributed to this tendency. Its "liberal" side was evidenced by the lack of private religious standards on the part of most of conservative synagogue members and the lax observance of many of its rabbis, as measured against the standards of the Rabbinical Assembly (the "trade union" of Conservative Rabbis); the liberal theology of many of its exponents; and a commitment to the "scientific study of Judaism" by its scholars. Conservative Judaism does not accept the label of compromise. It views itself as conserving the forms of Judaism, both through evolving, legislating, or imposing changes in Jewish law to fit contemporary society and through reinterpreting major beliefs and religious symbols.

In general, Conservative Judaism was not hospitable to European Judaism. In the thirties and forties, Conservative Judaism was too traditional for European Liberal Jews. At the same time, it meant to distance itself from the European versions of Orthodoxy. Conservative Judaism meant to create an *American* Judaism:

> Hasidic Jewry in Poland did not seek to integrate itself into Polish life and did not grapple with the problems of its relationship to Poland. Hence, it was not Polish Judaism. On the other hand, in America, Judaism and surely the Jews

wish to be at home on the American scene . . . [where it has the] promise of being a permanent and well-integrated element in American life.[13]

The one major exception to the almost solely American leadership was Rabbi Abraham Joshua Heschel,[14] a scion of a major Hasidic dynasty and graduate of the *Hochschule* (the Liberal rabbinical seminary in Berlin) and the University of Berlin. Brought to America by the Reform Hebrew Union College, he eventually left for the Jewish Theological Seminary in New York. Heschel became a powerful figure in Conservative Judaism, contributing a liberal social consciousness as an activist in civil rights, interfaith, and nuclear disarmament movements, as well as championing the causes of Soviet Jews and the State of Israel. He also espoused a philosophy of Neo-Hasidism.

Heschel's thought was original and erudite, with a strong command of biblical, rabbinic, philosophical, and mystical Jewish thought.[15] His language (Heschel wrote in German, English, Hebrew, and Yiddish) was lyrical and poetic. Heschel sought to evoke as much as he intended to prove. His major concern was man's relation to God. According to Heschel, not only man but also God is affected by the relationship. The Jewish Bible reveals a loving God's search for man and the often sensitive, but too-frequently insensitive, responses by man. To understand the Bible correctly one must see it not as a book of man's theology, but, rather, as a record of God's anthropology—what God wishes and intends for His creatures.

Heschel urged that man respond to God by discovering His ineffable or sublime presence in all things, including nature. Man acts through holy deeds or *mitzvot*, which sanctify life and prayer. If performed vitally and fully—infusing feeling within the established forms—they can serve as a ladder leading to God. In popular lectures throughout America and in numerous published works, Heschel presented a religious vision and program for modern man. Heschel earned international acclaim for his thought and was a greatly beloved figure.

The European Heschel was overshadowed in Conservative Judaism by his seminary colleague, the American Mordecai Kaplan.[16] Dr. Kaplan, who was no match for Heschel as a scholar and was almost unknown in non-Jewish circles, enunciated a positivistic and pragmatic interpretation of Judaism that was devoid of "supernaturalism."[17] For Kaplan, God was a useful term denoting all natural strivings for the moral good and personal meaning. Kaplan's ideological framework emphasized Jewish peoplehood above theology and the retention of such Jewish ceremonies, customs, and rites as were relevant to the creative expression of a people's "folkways," rather than to the Law.

Kaplan and his followers eventually created another denomination of Judaism—the tiny school of Reconstructionism. His ideology, nevertheless, helped to create a Conservative Judaism that could be liberal or even radical in its theology, strongly committed to Jewish peoplehood and Zionism—although not to American *aliyah* (emigration) there—and attached to Jewish ceremonies and American celebrations (e.g., Thanksgiving). It could even incorporate the evocative and traditionally oriented Neo-Hasidic poetry of Heschel as a spice to the mix. This proved to be a potent attraction to many European Jews settling in America, who could adapt their religious observances and family lifestyle to the generally areligious demands of American society without feelings of regret or remorse for abandoning the faith of their parents. This Conservative Judaism as practiced by its adherents—although perhaps not as envisaged by some of its more rigorous traditional thinkers—emphasized key family ceremonies, the use of Yiddish idioms in speech, the retention of Hebrew in prayer, and the strict observance of dietary laws in public religious events. Observance on a private level, on the other hand, dwindled considerably among second-generation Conservative Jews and presented a crisis of identity and perhaps even of survival.[18] As sociologist Peter Berger stated, "Despite all sorts of traditional loyalties and nostalgias, the whole edifice of traditional piety takes on the character of a museum of religious history. People may like museums, but they are reluctant to live in them."[19] In any event, many second- and third-generation American Conservative Jews felt ethnically very *Jewish*, with warm but vague ties to the European religious experience.

## The Science of Judaism and Judaic Studies

The European Science of Judaism, which was closely associated with the development of Liberal Judaism and segments of German Orthodoxy,[20] succeeded in mapping out and investigating significant areas of Jewish research. At the same time, it was marked by an apologetic tone. It often attempted to prove Judaism's "worth" through measuring up to the standards of the surrounding and hostile non-Jewish world. In general, there was a bias towards rationality. Any manifestation of Judaism or of Jewish history that proceeded along nonrational lines was considered an aberration and was, therefore, ignored or dismissed. This led, obviously, to a distorted view of Jewish history. As one example, any minor Jewish philosopher merited attention, while the whole complex and rich phenomenon of *Kabbalah* (Jewish mysticism) was disavowed.

The Science of Judaism, transplanted to the more secure environments of Israel and America, underwent a new and more sophisticated stage as Judaic studies. In Israel, Judaic studies found a home at the Hebrew University of Jerusalem. The ferment of a developing Jewish nation constructed from the "ingathering of the exiles" inspired the confidence and enthusiasm to approach long-neglected areas of research. In addition, the results of scholarly investigation into Jewish history and culture were considered an important means of national self-understanding.

The work of the German-trained Gershom Scholem,[21] historian of the *Kabbalah,* is a significant example of this process. Scholem was not concerned with the "truth" or rationality of the *Kabbalah.* A major focus was on its historical and social significance as a potentially disruptive, antinomian, revolutionary, and often messianic force in Judaism. Scholem's scholarship combined with his passionate Zionism as he searched for parallels, antecedents, and even causes of what he considered to be anarchic elements in the character of the Zionist revolution that had violently wrenched itself free from the traditional life patterns of European Judaism. Scholem, along with other Judaic scholars at the Hebrew University, was a significant Zionist thinker whose scholarly research had an impact on the direction of his ideological work.

In America, Judaic studies were housed in secular universities[22] and in the rabbinical seminaries.[23] The study of Judaica in a non-Jewish setting had two important results. First, parallel to the world prominence given the Jewish people by the Holocaust and the rise of the State of Israel was the forum given to Jewish thought and history within the academy. Judaism as an area of research was no longer limited to biblical studies and as a background to early Church history. For the first time, the whole range of Judaic studies, including Jewish law, philosophy, modern Hebrew literature, and Holocaust studies, became a significant presence in general academic life. Secondly, at the same time, Judaic scholars rapidly began to approach their areas not as subjects isolated from the course of general history, but rather from a crosscultural perspective.

The academic career of Professor Salo W. Baron both reflected and contributed to these changes. Baron was a graduate of the Liberal seminary in Vienna and held doctorates in jurisprudence, political science, and history from the University of Vienna. His erudition in Jewish and non-Jewish sources enabled him to compose a synoptic *Social and Religious History of the Jewish People,*[24] which analyzed Jewish history within the general historical setting. In addition, while Baron taught rabbinical students at the Jewish Institute of Religion (which later merged with the Hebrew Union College), and at the Jewish Theological Seminary, his principal position was as a member of the history faculty at Columbia University. There, he taught a generation of scholars who subsequently held major university positions in America and abroad and continued his wide-ranging approach.

What Baron accomplished for Jewish history, Harry A. Wolfson[25] did for Jewish philosophy. An alumnus of the Lithuanian Slabodka Yeshivah, Wolfson was trained at Harvard, where he continued to teach. His work showed that medieval philosophy was essentially of one piece—sharing common methodologies and presuppositions—with Christian, Islamic, and Jewish branches. His work, and that of his students, demonstrated the impossibility of studying Jewish philosophy in a vacuum. One had to master the entire range of Greek, Latin, Arabic, and Hebraic sources.

The second area of Judaic studies in America took place in the rabbinical seminaries. Of special interest is the impact of a small group of graduates of the traditional European *yeshivot* (talmudic academies), subsequently trained in modern methodologies, who taught there. One such individual was Samuel Atlas[26] (also a graduate of the Slabodka Yeshivah) of the Hebrew Union College-Jewish Institute of Religion. His work combined *lamdanut* (traditional analytic and conceptual scholarship), the modern study of comparative texts, and German rationalist philosophy. Atlas' unique synthesis of these disparate elements left no major effect upon his Reform rabbinical students, who perhaps were uninterested in the man and his work, or insufficiently sophisticated in Talmud and philosophy to appreciate it.

At J.T.S., Saul Lieberman[27] (another graduate of the Slabodka Yeshivah and the Hebrew University) wrote on the influence of classical culture and civilization on the Talmud. Dr. Lieberman also edited major rabbinic texts. He produced a number of scholars but his relation to Conservative Judaism was problematic. While serving as both provost of J.T.S. and its recognized scholar *par excellence*, the scrupulously observant Dr. Lieberman's direct involvement with Conservative Judaism mainly extended to conserving traditional *halakhic* standards in the school in which he taught. Conservative rabbis, however, often drew implications from his scholarship and methodology for change in the *halakhah*. This evidently is not a unique pattern. A younger contemporary of Lieberman's, Professor David Weiss-Halivni (a graduate of the Hungarian Sighet Yeshivah), alluded to this disjunction in discussing critical approaches to the Bible and Talmud. Weiss-Halivni cautioned:

> Perhaps it should be noted that acceptance of criticism does not necessarily curtail changes in the Halakhic practice. Halakhic practice is determined by a process that may not go hand in hand with the historical reality which criticism seeks to discover.[28]

Many of Weiss-Halivni's students, however, have wished to effect change based precisely on their assessment of contemporary historical reality. Modern critical study of Jewish texts usually assumes the historical conditioning of a text—that it was formed, at least in significant part, by specific conditions of a particular era. This may imply that the law or theology based on that text is possibly deficient when confronted by new historical circumstances. That, indeed, is what many who viewed Jewish texts in the modern manner believed, and that, in turn, is what they believed to be their warrant for change in Jewish practices.

## Orthodox Judaism

Orthodox Judaism, which maintains a faithful allegiance to the entire corpus of traditional *halakhah*, practice and belief, was severely damaged by the Holocaust. Nevertheless, it underwent a rebirth in America and in *Erez Israel.* It rebuilt European institutions and communities and developed a new generation of leaders and scholars largely trained by the surviving remnant of the European rabbinate. This renaissance was not an easy process. In both the United States and Israel, Orthodox Judaism had been long established prior to the Holocaust period. Orthodoxy in both countries, nevertheless, was dependent upon the European communities for leadership, members (through continuous immigration), and inspiration. Pre-Holocaust Orthodoxy paved the way for the new European arrivals by establishing indigenous institutions and attempting resolutions of cultural conflicts. The new arrivals, however, still had to face the harsh challenges posed in each country.

European Orthodox Judaism was out of step with the American melting pot.[29] Even if one did not wear the distinctive garb favored by many Hasidim, the religious practices of the Orthodox Jew, such as the dietary laws and Sabbath observance, tended to isolate him. Confronted with the challenge of making it in America, many chose to leave Orthodoxy, while others compromised. Those who remained Orthodox and wanted to be successful in American society had to excel in order to find equal employment and educational opportunities.

In Israel,[30] the Jewish State had a nonreligious character, and the attraction of secular Zionism posed further problems. Zealots from both camps perceived the alternatives as an either-or situation. In response, a large number left Orthodox Judaism, while others retreated from any active participation in the building of the State. In general, the vast majority found themselves in the middle—fully involved in the life of Israel with varying degrees of enthusiasm and hostility to the secular manifestations of its culture.

Orthodox Judaism in both countries had serious internal difficulties. It lacked a central authority and organization. America, for example, had four relatively powerless Orthodox rabbinical organizations, with many Orthodox rabbis not affiliated with any; Reform and Conservative Judaism each had one powerful central group whose organizational decisions had great impact upon their respective memberships. Israel had an official rabbinate that provided unity in the area of personal status (marriage, divorce, conversion, and so on). With regard to other substantive issues, however, Orthodox Jews tended to follow a number of *halakhic* authorities who were not necessarily members of the official rabbinate. In both countries, Orthodoxy split on a number of important issues, including Zionism and secular studies (the three major positions being almost complete separation from, utilitarian use of, and synthesis with), and relations to the non-Orthodox. The bewildering array of positions, combined with a general tendency towards consistency and absolutism, led to bitter internecine controversies.

Orthodox Judaism did have a number of advantages. It possessed a clear sense of identity and its confidence in its beliefs and practices kept the movement united. Accepting and continuing the European tradition afforded Orthodox Jews varying models—from the synthesis with the outside culture (as approached by Samson Raphael Hirsch or Esriel Hildeshimer), the pietistic *Musar* Movement with its emphasis on ethics, and the warm and vibrant practices of Hasidism, to the intellectual dialectics of classical Jewish learning. These models were re-established in Israel and America in endless permutations.

A major strategy of right-wing Orthodox Judaism was to focus its energies on the rebuilding of its *yeshivot*. Rabbi Aron Kotler, a former leader of European Orthodoxy and considered one of its leading talmudists, wanted to recreate the intensity of study found in the best European *yeshivot*. Disdainful of the contemporary American *yeshivot*, which were largely directed towards the training of professional rabbis and learned laymen, the fiery Reb Aron built America's largest *yeshivah* in Lakewood, New Jersey. This dedication to *Torah Lishmah* (the study of Jewish teachings for its own sake) was also the goal of the former Lithuanian Rabbi of Ponevezh (Lithuania), Rabbi Joseph Kahaneman, who embarked upon a mission to rebuild the major *yeshivot* of Lithuania in Israel. The Ponevezh Yeshivah in Bnei Brak, under the guidance of the saintly Ponevezher Rav, along with such European-trained scholars as Rabbi Shmuel Rossovsky, emerged as the dominant *yeshivah* in Israel.

This pattern was duplicated in size and form by the former heads and alumni of other European *yeshivot*. The Mir Yeshivah, which survived the Holocaust in Shanghai, is worthy of note. It was rebuilt both in America and in Israel. The Mir's senior students subsequently formed the nucleus for the faculty of other emerging schools.

The growth of the *yeshivot* transformed Orthodox Judaism. It created a strong infrastructure of alumni whose loyalty to their *roshei yeshivah* (deans of the *yeshivot*) contributed to making them perhaps the major force within Orthodoxy. This was especially true in America, where the congregational rabbinate was generally no match for them in either scholarship or charisma. The talmudic knowledge imparted by the *yeshivot*, combined with their religious fervor and general ivory tower ambiance, moved their graduates towards greater isolation from the rest of the Jewish (and even Orthodox) community, whose religious standards were not considered high enough. Despite the isolation, a small but vital religious revival among secularized Jews, commencing after the Six-Day War (June, 1967), led many to explore the deeply religious Orthodox *yeshivot*. A number of special *yeshivot* for the *ba'al teshuvah* ("returnee" to Judaism) were successful. The majority of Orthodoxy, however, chose to ignore this phenomenon or presented the potential *ba'al teshuvah* with an all-or-nothing choice that he or she could not accept.

Many *yeshivah* graduates went on to build elementary and secondary schools and teachers' seminaries for women. In Israel, a religious track offering both secular and religious studies was part of the public school system, along with a number of privately run (although partially publicly supported) schools that generally were more conservative on religious issues, provided less time to secular studies, and were either less or not Zionistic. In America, intensive day school education[31] was totally privately supported through high tuitions and philanthropy. Although offering both religious and secular studies, it was initially hampered by the lack of support from the general Jewish community, who attacked it as sectarian and "anti-American." Eventually, the success of these schools in creating highly educated and committed Jews, as well as loyal Americans, became the sole system for precollege Orthodox schooling and has been copied to some degree by the Conservative and Reform movements.

On the post-high school level, modern Orthodoxy's most influential institution was Yeshiva University of New York. Yeshiva University, the oldest and largest university under Jewish auspices, combined a secular college with classical talmudic study under some of the foremost European scholars who were able to escape or evade the Holocaust. It was a forum for the synthesis of Western culture and science with Torah. The major figure at Yeshiva University from the 1940s on was Rabbi Joseph B. Soloveitchik,[32] scion of the Brisk dynasty of talmudists, who developed a precise conceptual-analytical method applied to rabbinic texts, and was a philosophy graduate of the University of Berlin. The Rav, as he is known in the community, was too creative a talmudist and thinker to be considered merely an ideologist for the modern Orthodoxy of Yeshiva University. A master teacher and eloquent lecturer, he combined selective involvement in public affairs with a personal shyness and reticence. Through a synthesis of such diverse intellectual stands as Neo-Kantianism, existentialism, biblical insights, *Kabbalah,* and *halakhic* analysis, he developed a profound explication of Jewish observance and thought. His teachings and personal example inspired students and admirers in many intellectual and leadership activities in the confrontation of tradition with modernity.

Rabbi Soloveitchik's thought confronted an American Jewish community in danger of being overwhelmed by modernity. The problem, as the Rav saw it, was not the claims of conflicting truths, but, rather, that a thoroughly secular modernism seemed to render religion irrelevant. At best, Judaism was reduced to a pleasant retreat where one fled from the conflicts of "real life" to achieve peace of mind. The Rav rejected this emasculation of Judaism. Torah demanded man's full intellectual creativity, effort of will, and emotional sensitivity to be properly understood, observed, and experienced. The Rav's unstated proposition, derived from the mystical formulation of his ancestor, Ḥayim of Volozhin (1749-1821),[33] is that the Torah is intimately connected to divinity and constitutes the foundation of the universe, for which the latter was created and is currently maintained. For the Rav, Torah has ultimate ontological significance—that is, it is the very basis of existence.

A proper understanding of the Torah and its *halakhah* can be no less sophisticated than research into the nature of the universe. In the latter, Aristotelian physics, which catalogued empirical and commonsense impressions of reality, was replaced by the Galilean-Newtonian revolution, which demonstrated that reality was better penetrated and grasped by mathematical, conceptual models. Surface judgments gave way to scientific laws. The Torah is also more than a collection of ceremonies, ritual behavior, quaint customs, and rabbinic texts. Behind the *halakhah* is a profound theoretical realm. Like the physicist, the student of *halakhah* must also intuit and postulate conceptional models, engage in rigorous argumentation and careful refinement of ideas, and seek various means of validation. Surviving theories, applied with a sensitive heart and a keen mind, will often enter as law into man's life.

The profound religious life evinces the same dynamism as Torah study. It starts with the precise observance of the details of the *halakhah*, but it also transcends it. The practices of Judaism induce within man a wide range of moods and emotions. The religious man alternately feels God's closeness and abandonment (or estrangement), which inspires him to return and re-seek the encounter. Self-affirmation (freedom of will) and self-denial (in surrender to God), love of God and fear of Him, joy and mourning, nostalgia and messianic yearnings, are parts of the dialectics of the religious experience. Judaism has no one mode or tone. A harmony of these opposing and valid feelings is maintained within the *halakhic* system.

This emphasis on the vitality of Torah study and observance does not necessarily lead to a rejection of social, economic, and cultural endeavors. The Rav saw man as existing within two dimensions. Man is, first of all, an aggressive being who seeks to build, dominate, and succeed. This majestic desire to introduce order is exhibited not only by the construction foreman but also by the artist, who imposes a design within the aesthetic realm, the jurist, who structures law and maintains society, and the physicist, who creates his own universe out of mathematical symbols on a blackboard. Majestic man does not work alone. He needs society not only as an ally for his creative endeavors but also as an audience before whom he can demonstrate his accomplishments and dignity.

Man also exists, however, as a solitary being. This man, aware of his loneliness, frustratingly seeks meaning within an absurd and silent universe. Ultimately, this leads him to God, through whom he achieves a redeemed existence. On this ground of meaning he can meet another solitary being who has also emerged from loneliness to commune with the divine. This covenantal community, consisting of I, thou, and God, is constructed on the basis of trust and commitment crystallized into external deeds and meaningful action between all three partners. It is important, finally, to consider that for Rabbi Soloveitchik both the majestic and covenantal man are valid experiences of humanity. To exist without either dimension is to live a tragically truncated existence.

Post-Holocaust Israeli Orthodoxy, lacking an institution to parallel Yeshiva University and a thinker of Rabbi Soloveitchik's caliber, was initially hampered in the development of a modern

Orthodoxy. Several developments, however, proved encouraging. Following the Six-Day War, there was a rapid growth of the *Yeshivot Hesder,* whose combination of superior talmudic education with service in the Israel Defense Force resulted in a new type of traditional scholar intimately engaged in his country's development. A number of these graduates have continued to combine their talmudic studies with a university education. Another development was Bar Ilan University, sponsored by the Religious Zionists, which served to continue the Orthodox version of the Science of Judaism (presently, Judaic studies) associated with Berlin's Hildesheimer *Rabbiner-Seminar.* Finally, an entire discipline—*Mishpat Ivri* (Hebrew or Jewish law)—emerged, seeking to integrate *halakhah* into the legal system of the modern secular state. Within this context, it is important to note that many archtraditionalist talmudic scholars have responded to the new ethical challenges of modernity with a continued effort to examine Judaism for answers. Jerusalem's modern Sha'arei Zedek hospital, for example, directs all questions of medical ethics to a traditional *halakhist.*

Perhaps the most astonishing recovery was achieved by the Hasidic groups.[34] It is within the Hasidic movement that the eastern European ethos and lifestyle, including distinctive dress and complete use of Yiddish as a spoken language—not just for the presentation of formal lectures in Talmud, as in the more right-wing Hasidic *yeshivot*—was restored. Customs and etiquette specific to Hasidic groups—in addition to strict *halakhic* observance—became commonplace. Although many Hasidim were economically well off, they showed an ability to sacrifice for their ideals and an indifference to the scorn of others for looking "foreign." The leadership of charismatic *rebbeim* (masters) took Hasidism into a variety of distinct directions.

The Rumanian Satmar Hasidim, based in the Williamsburg section of Brooklyn, New York, were led by Rabbi Joel Teitlebaum. The Satmar Rav was a recognized *halakhic* authority in Europe who exerted tremendous influence over his flock. A fervent European anti-Zionist, he continued in America to oppose the secular State of Israel in the strongest language, believing that only the Messiah would restore the Jewish homeland. In the same fashion, he fought any accommodation with modernity. By force of personality, he built his group to become the largest Hasidic community in America and perhaps the most organized, providing a full range of spiritual, educational, and social services. The extreme nature of their views rendered the Satmar Hasidim isolationists, even from the overwhelming majority of the Orthodox.

Very different and often at odds with the Satmar Hasidim were the Russian Lubavicher Hasidim, mainly located in the Crown Heights section of Brooklyn. Although the movement was originally opposed to Zionism, Lubavicher Hasidim who lived in Israel became active participants in all areas of Israeli society. Furthermore, their leader, Rabbi Menaḥem M. Schneersohn, was a hardliner about Israel's relation to the Arab states. The Lubavicher Rebbe, educated in European universities, made extensive use of modern technology and media to spread his Hasidic philosophy. He turned his flock towards an enthusiastic, if good-natured, evangelism, attempting to rekindle the divine spark that rests in all Jews, no matter how estranged, and that makes them all brothers. The Lubavich educational system spanned the globe and penetrated through the underground even into the Soviet Union. The Lubavicher Rebbe attracted an array of scholars, scientists, and the "common Jew," so prized by Hasidic thought, to his movement. Many American and Israeli Jews had a certain love-hate relationship with this group that was ready to go to extraordinary lengths to benefit their fellow Jews and to introduce them to such observances as the Sabbath, *tefillin* (black leather boxes containing Scriptural passages worn on the forearm and head of the Jewish men during morning prayers), and the *sukkah* (the hutlike structure in which the Jews dwell during the holiday of Sukkot). They were simultaneously attracted to and somewhat repelled by the vigor (and perhaps the success) of the movement, its adherents (who usually disregarded general polite behavior for a direct earthiness), its messianic tone, and the outspoken and noncompromising views it enunciated.

A third and perhaps more typical approach of most Hasidic groups was taken by the Polish Hasidim of Gur, centered in Jerusalem. Under the leadership of Rabbi Israel Alter, they established a strong and harmonious presence in Israel. They were faithful to the traditions of their group but simultaneously were politically and economically well-integrated into the country. Their major efforts extended to furthering their own spirituality and to encouraging the general ethical and Jewish dimension of the country.

European Orthodox leadership, institutions, and communities were to a remarkable degree reestablished in America and in Israel. A few Orthodox thinkers have suggested that Orthodoxy has been at the expense of total involvement in the concerns of the larger Jewish community. These critics have maintained that a continued concern only for the Orthodoxy's own spirituality and for the few that it can attract to a full Orthodox life was spiritually and morally insufficient. They have argued that Orthodox Jews would have to respond to their own claim that the tradition has much to say to the contemporary situation by assuming responsibility and exerting active concern for their fellow Jews. While Orthodoxy, by its very nature, cannot compromise on its religious principles, it may have to rethink its ideological posture in order to implement those principles within a larger social context. They hoped that Orthodoxy would abjure an understandable tendency towards smugness and fanaticism, acquired in its triumph over the forbidding situation faced after the Holocaust, that prevented it from moving to new levels of maturity and influence.[35]

Principles and strategies alone are never enough; it is people who implement them. The accepted *halakhic* authority for American Orthodox Jews is Rabbi Moshe Feinstein,[35] who came to America in the late thirties, having served as a rabbi for almost twenty years in Belorussia. Reb Moshe's opinion is sought on every major ritual and moral question, even by those who may disagree with him. He was not elected to the position, nor did he acquire it through any special charismatic endowment—Reb Moshe is an unassuming and quiet man. He was "selected" by the people as the one to turn to with a *sheilah* (legal question). They respect his faithfulness to the tradition, his readiness to address modern challenges, and his technical scholarship. More than anything else, however, they trust his sensibility and sensitivity to the human condition. The knowledge and empathy for man is the hallmark of the European rabbi who stood at the head of an organic community. One criterion of the success of Orthodox renewal in Israel and America will be whether it will create and respond to leaders of such caliber.

The course of renewal of European Judaism within America and Israel should not obscure several points. The first is that the specific situations of these two countries—respectively, America as the freest and wealthiest Diaspora land that Jews have resided in and Israel as the first Jewish homeland in 2,000 years—have produced their own challenges. One would imagine that "even" apart from the Holocaust, unique responses to Jewish identity and tradition would have emerged. Secondly, the sudden devastation of Europe's Jews has been of incalculable loss to Judaism. Much that has been accomplished in the post-Holocaust years has been by a surviving remnant of scholars, leaders, and adherents, faced by the terrifying and potentially paralyzing recognition that this could easily have been the last act of the Jewish epic. Finally, Judaism has always incorporated the major experience of its history into its life. We can expect Judaism to learn lessons from the Holocaust and to be influenced by that event. At the same time, Judaism has always been a religion of life. An element of its European legacy is to seek its meaning, identity, and fulfillment not in temporal defeats but in the value of its Torah.

### Notes

1. See "The European Jewish Communities After the Holocaust," by Joel S. Fishman, in this volume; Arnold Mandel, "The Jews in Western Europe Today," *American Jewish Yearbook 1967*, vol. 68 (New York: American Jewish Committee, 1967): 3-28.
2. Martin Buber, *Good and Evil* (New York: Charles Scribner's Sons, 1953); Buber, *I and Thou*, transl. Ronald Gregor Smith (New

York: Charles Scribner's Sons, 1970); Arthur A. Cohen, "Martin Buber and Judaism," *Leo Baeck Year Book* (1980): 287-300; Maurice Friedman, *The Life of Dialogue*, 3rd ed. rev. (Chicago: University of Chicago Press, 1976).

3.   Nahum N. Glatzer, "Reflections on Buber's Impact on German Jewry," *Leo Baeck Year Book XXV* (1980): 308.

4.   Martin Buber, *Paths in Utopia* (Boston: Beacon Paperback, 1958), p. 140.

5.   See "Jewish Religious Leadership in Germany: Its Cultural and Religious Outlook," by David Ellenson, in this volume; Theodore I. Lenn, Ph.d., and Associates, *Rabbi and Synagogue in Reform Judaism* (New York: Central Conference of American Rabbis, 1972); Michael A. Meyer, "Reform Judaism," in *Movements and Issues in American Judaism*, ed. Bernard Martin (Westport, CT: Greenwood Press, 1978), pp. 158-170. Bernard Martin, ed., *Contemporary Reform Jewish Thought* (Chicago: Quadrangle Books, 1968); Leonard J. Fein, et al, *Reform Is a Verb: Notes on Reform and Reforming Jews* (New York: Union of American Hebrew Congregations, 1972); Samuel E. Karf, ed., *Hebrew Union College— Jewish Institute of Religion—At One Hundred Years* (Cincinnati: Hebrew Union Press, 1976); Sefton D. Temkin, "A Century of Reform Judaism in America," *American Jewish Yearbook*, vol. 74 (1973) (New York: The American Jewish Committee, 1973); W. Gunther Plaut, *The Growth of Reform Judaism: American and European Sources until 1948* (New York: World Union for Progressive Judaism, 1965).

6.   Albert H. Friedlander, *Leo Baeck: Teacher of Theresienstadt* (New York: Holt, Rinehart and Winston, 1968); Leonard Baker, *Days of Sorrow and Pain: Leo Baeck and the Berlin Jews* (New York: Macmillan Co., 1978).

7.   Baker, *Days of Sorrow and Pain*, pp. 319-338.

8.   Emil Fackenheim, *Quest for Past and Future: Essays in Jewish Theology* (Bloomington: Indiana University Press, 1968); Fackenheim, *Encounters Between Judaism and Philosophy* (Philadelphia: The Jewish Publication Society of America, 1973).

9.   W. Gunther Plaut, *The Torah: A Modern Commentary (Genesis, Exodus, Numbers, Deuteronomy)* (New York: Union of American Hebrew Congregations, 1974, 1980, 1980, 1982).

10.   Jakob J. Petuchowski, *Heirs to the Pharisees* (New York: Basic Books, 1970); Petuchowski, *Prayerbook Reform in Europe: The Liturgy of European Liberal and Reform Judaism* (New York: World Union for Progressive Judaism, 1968).

11.   See W. Gunther Plaut, "New Directions for Reform Rabbis," *Central Conference of American Rabbis Journal* 18:4 (October 1971): 24-27.

12.   Moshe Davis, *The Emergence of Conservative Judaism* (Philadelphia: The Jewish Publication Society of America, 1963); Mordecai Waxman, *Tradition and Change: The Development of Conservative Judaism* (New York: Burning Bush Press, 1958); Marshall Sklare, *Conservative Judaism: An American Religious*

*Movement* (New York: Schocken Books, 1972); Bernard Martin, "Conservative Judaism and Reconstructionism," in Martin, *Movements and Issues,* pp. 103-157; Lawrence J. Kaplan, "The Dilemma of Conservative Judaism," *Commentary* (November 1976): 44-47; Elliot Dorf, "Towards a Legal Theory of the Conservative Movement," *Conservative Judaism* 27:3 (Spring 1973): 68-77.

13.  Robert Gordis, "A Response," *Conservative Judaism* 2:4 (June 1946): 27.

14.  See the Commemorative Issue to Heschel of *Conservative Judaism* 28:1 (Fall 1973).

15.  Abraham Joshua Heschel, *God In Search of Man: A Philosophy of Judaism* (New York: Farrar, Strauss, and Cudahy, 1956); Heschel, *The Prophets* (Philadelphia: The Jewish Publication Society of America, 1962); Heschel, *Theology of Ancient Judaism* [Hebrew] (London: Soncino, 1965).

16.  Charles S. Leibman, "Reconstructionism in American Jewish Life," *American Jewish Yearbook 1970* 71: 3-99; Mordecai Kaplan, *Judaism as a Civilization* (New York: Schocken Books, 1967); Milton Steinberg, *Anatomy of a Faith,* ed. and introd. Arthur A. Cohen (New York: Harcourt, Brace and Company, 1960).

17.  Eliezer Berkovits, *Major Themes in Modern Philosophies of Judaism* (New York: Ktav, 1947), especially his articles on Kaplan and Heschel, pp. 149-224.

18.  Charles S. Liebman and Saul Shapiro, *A Survey of the Conservative Movement and Some of Its Religious Attitudes* (New York: The Jewish Theological Seminary of America in cooperation with the United Synagogue of America, November 1979) [Xerox].

19.  Peter L. Berger, *A Rumor of Angels* (New York: Anchor Books, 1962), pp. 14-15.

20.  Benzion Dinur, *"Wissenschaft Des Judentums,"* Encyclopedia Judaica 16: 570-584.

21.  Gershom Gerhard Scholem, *From Berlin to Jerusalem: Memories of My Youth* (New York: Schocken Books, 1980); Scholem, *The Messianic Idea in Judaism* (New York: Schocken Books, 1971); Scholem, *On Jews and Judaism in Crisis,* ed. Werner J. Dannhauser (New York: Schocken Books, 1976); David Biale, *Gershom Scholem: Kabbalah and Counter-History* (Cambridge, Mass.: Harvard University Press, 1979).

22.  Arnold J. Band, "Jewish Studies in American Liberal Arts Colleges and Universities," *American Jewish Yearbook 1966* 67: 3-30; Paul Ritterband and Harold S. Wechsler, "Judaica in American Colleges and Universities," *Encyclopedia Judaica Yearbook 1977-1978,* pp. 73-77.

23.  Charles S. Liebman, "The Training of American Rabbis," *American Jewish Yearbook 1968* 69: 3-114.

24.  Salo W. Baron, *A Social and Religious History of the Jews,* 17 volumes (New York: Columbia University Press, 1952-1980); Baron, *Steeled by Adversity: Essays and Addresses on American Jewish Life,* ed. Jeannette Meisel Baron (Philadelphia: The Jewish Publication Society of America, 1971).

25. Harry Austryn Wolfson, *From Philo to Spinoza: Two Studies in Religious Philosophy*, introd. Isadore Twersky (New York: Behrman House, 1977); Wolfson, *Repercussions of the Kalam in Jewish Philosophy* (Cambridge, Mass.: Harvard University Press, 1979); Wolfson, *Studies in the History of Philosophy and Religion*, vols. I,II, ed. Isadore Twersky (Cambridge, Mass.: Harvard University Press, 1973, 1977); Leo W. Schwartz, *Wolfson of Harvard: Portrait of a Scholar* (Philadelphia: The Jewish Publication Society of America, 1978).

26. Samuel Atlas, *Pathways in Hebrew Law (Nitivim Be Mishpat Haivri)* (New York: American Academy for Jewish Research, 1978).

27. Saul Lieberman, *Greek and Hellenism in Jewish Palestine* [Hebrew] (Jerusalem: Bialik Institute, 1962); *Tosefta Ki-Peshutah* (11 volumes), 1955-1973.

28. David Weiss-Halivni, "Revelation and Zimzum," *Judaism* 21:2 (Spring 1972): 206.

29. See "Impressions of Religious Life Before World War II," by Zalman F. Ury, in this volume; Shubert Spero, "Orthodox Judaism," *Movements and Issues in American Judaism* (Westport, Ct.: Greenwood Press, 1978), pp. 83-102; Charles S. Liebman, "Orthodoxy in American Jewish Life," *American Jewish Yearbook 1965* 66: 21-98; Lawrence Kaplan, "The Ambiguous Modern Orthodox Jew," *Judaism* 28:4 (Fall 1979): 439-448; Samuel Heilman, *Synagogue Life: A Study in Symbolic Interaction* (Chicago: University of Chicago Press, 1976); Samuel Heilman, "The Many Faces of Orthodoxy," *Modern Judaism* vol. 2, no. 1: 23-52 and no. 2: 171-198.

30. Shlomo Deshen, "Two Trends in Israeli Orthodoxy," *Judaism* 27:4 (Fall 1978): 397-409; S. Zalman Abramov, *Perpetual Dilemma: Jewish Religion in the Jewish State* (Rutherford, N.J.: Fairleigh Dickinson Press, 1976); Gary Schiff, *Tradition and Politics: The Religious Parties of Israel* (Detroit: Wayne State University Press, 1977); Menachem Friedman, *Society and Religion: The Non-Zionist Orthodox in Eretz-Israel* [Hebrew] (Jerusalem: Yad Izhak Ben-Zvi Publications, 1977); I. Warchaftig, *Techumin: Torah, Society, State* [Hebrew] (Jerusalem: vol. A, 1980, vol. B, 1982); Geulah Bat Yehudah, *HaRav Maimon* [Hebrew] (Jerusalem: Mossad HaRav Kook, 1979); Emanuel Marx, ed., *A Composite Portrait of Israel* (New York: Academic Press, 1980).

31. Alvin I. Schiff, "Jewish Day Schools in the United States," *Encyclopedia Judaica Yearbook 1974*, pp. 136-147.

32. Joseph B. Soloveitchik, *In Aloneness, in Togetherness (Bisod Hayahid Vehayhad)*, ed. Pinchas H. Peli (Jerusalem: Orot, 1976); Soloveitchik, "The Lonely Man of Faith," *Studies in Judaica*, ed. Leon D. Stitskin (New York: Yeshiva University Press, 1974), pp. 69-133; Eugene B. Borowitz, "The Typological Theology of Rabbi Joseph B. Soloveitchik," *Judaism* (Spring 1966), p. 205; Lawrence Kaplan, "The Religious Philosophy of Rabbi Joseph Soloveitchik," *Tradition* 14:2 (Fall 1973); David Hartman, *Joy and Responsibility*

(Jerusalem: Ben Zvi Posner Publishers, Ltd.), pp. 198-231.

33.   *Nefesh ha-Ḥayim;* Norman Lamm, *Faith and Doubt* (New York: Ktav, 1971), pp. 212-246.

34.   See "Aspects of Hasidic Life Before World War II," by Nehemiah Polen, in this volume; Louis Jacobs, "The Lubavich Movement," *Encyclopedia Judaica Yearbook 1975/76,* pp. 161-165; Solomon Poll, *The Hasidic Community of Williamsburg* (New York: The Free Press, 1962); Israel Rubin, *Satmar: An Island in the City* (Chicago: Quadrangle Books, 1972); Jerome R. Mintz, "Ethnic Activism: The Hasidic Example," *Judaism* 28:4 (Fall 1977); Allan L. Nadler, "Piety and Politics: The Case of the Satmar Rebbe," *Judaism* 31:2 (Spring 1982): 135-152.

35.   Emanuel Rackman, "A Challenge to Orthodoxy," *Judaism* 18:2 (Spring 1969): 143-158; Eliezer Berkovits, *Crisis and Faith* (New York: Sanhedrin Press, 1976), pp. 54-147; Shlomo Riskin, "Orthodoxy and Her Alleged Heretics," *Tradition* (Spring 1976).

36.   Aaron Kirschenbaum, "Moses Feinstein's Responsa," *Judaism* 15 (1966).

### For Further Reading

Deshen, Shlomo. "Two Trends in Israel Orthodoxy." *Judaism* 27:4 (Fall 1978): 397-409.

Editors of *Commentary. The Condition of Jewish Belief.* New York: Macmillan Co., 1966.

Liebman, Charles S. *The Ambivalent American Jew: Politics, Religion, and Family in American Jewish Life.* Philadelphia: The Jewish Publication Society of America, 1973.

Martin, Bernard, ed. *Movements and Issues in American Judaism.* Westport, CT: Greenwood Press, 1978.

Sklare, Marshall. *Conservative Judaism: An American Religious Movement.* New augumented edition. New York: Schocken Books, 1972.

# Aspects of Psychological Trauma in Holocaust Survivors and Their Children

## ROBERT KRELL

Most people who see a powerful film and/or read eyewitness accounts of the Holocaust soon realize that this event was devastating and total for those involved. In a single moment, individuals lost their entire families, their freedom, their privacy, their individuality; they faced a variety of cruel tortures and almost certain death. It was undeniably the most massive assault on physical and psychological well-being. No survivor escaped its impact. And no survivor escaped without psychological scars.

But the manner in which survivors have dealt with the experience is as varied as other responses to situations of extreme stress. Some people are totally defeated. Some are inspired to compensate for the experience. There are survivors who deny the event, either fully or partially, and relegate it to the mind's recesses; for others it remains the centerpiece of life, either as a negative or positive force. Some survivors fantasize revenge, others have long ago forgiven their former tormentors. While many turned away from religion as a result of the Holocaust, others held on to or even developed greater faith. The Holocaust remains a complicated event, and often one response to this complexity has been to overgeneralize. It is undeniable that all survivors were affected, but it is an overgeneralization to imply that all suffer from a crippling psychopathology. In fact, it is remarkable that so many survivors have adjusted to new lives, new lands, and new languages, and have been successful in their careers despite their suffering and memories.

Initially, the psychological impact on the survivors was overlooked. Very few observers commented on the psychiatric aspects of incarceration in the camps.[1] This latency period can, to some extent, be explained. In the initial stages of liberation, the focus was to restore physical health and to search for lost relatives. Hopelessness was rampant and suicide common as most survivors found no one left alive. At the same time, there was hope for a better world to follow. There were a great many marriages in the DP (displaced persons) camps and desperate attempts to reconstruct families. For a number of years survivors were very busy: As immigrants to Israel, the United States, Canada, South America, and Australia, they had to learn new languages, acquire new skills, and rebuild their personal and family lives.

It was not until the early 1950s that the psychological repercussions showed en masse. By the late 1950s, sufficient clinical data had been gathered to suggest the existence of a "survivor syndrome"[2]—a constellation of symptoms observed by many different professionals who evaluated survivors with psychiatric problems or examined those who applied for restitution payments. This delay in the appearance of recognizable symptoms and their subsequent manifestation is now well-recognized in survivors of other catastrophes. Survivors of Hiroshima and Nagasaki, Vietnam War veterans, and victims of torture are all now considered as likely to have permanent psychological trauma from their experiences. And while some demonstrate symptoms quite early, for others more immediate preoccupations delay the onset of any overt symptoms. This phenomenon has been legitimized in psychiatric diagnostic terminology as the "post-traumatic stress disorder, acute, chronic, or delayed."[3]

For several years in the postwar period, psychiatrists remained focused on the physical trauma sustained in the camps as the primary cause of various disabilities. But these disabilities were soon accompanied and even overshadowed by the psychological problems. The latter persist to this day, and sometimes intensify with age.

In order to understand why these problems persist, one must take into account not only the viciousness of the original assault, but also the age of the victim to whom it occurred. Very few elderly people or children survived the camps.[4] It is self-evident that young survivors were often bereft of an adolescence and of an education. In addition to the loss of family, they suffered the loss of opportunities for learning how to be a member of a family, how to deal with the opposite sex, and how to develop life goals. Their classroom was the concentration camp and their social life a horrifying series of life-threatening experiences. Death was far better understood than some aspects of life. And these youngsters, deprived of much that was good and decent, faced a new world where they were forced to educate and virtually raise themselves. Nor was it a receptive world. For even after that darkness, the survivors faced hostility and suspicion: "If it was as bad as you say, what did you have to do to survive?"

## The Study of Survivors

The initial studies on survivors consisted of clinical observations. It is not easy to study survivors. In psychological studies of various kinds, objectivity is a prized and frequently essential prerequisite. Who, however, can remain objective in face of the Holocaust and its survivors? Indeed, we should perhaps be wary of the clinical opinions of those who claim to be objective. Objectivity in this unique situation would betray the clinician's own psychological denial in an effort to be protected from the overwhelming nature of the survivors' descriptions and problems. Such denial may counteract the compassion and understanding so necessary to the psychiatric evaluation and treatment of survivors. It is not totally clear what qualifications are needed to write about the survivor experience and to speculate about its dimensions, impacts, and consequences. It is interesting to note that a great deal of medical-psychiatric literature has been contributed by psychiatrists who are survivors themselves: e.g., Leo Eitinger, Henry Krystal, Hillel Klein, Viktor Frankl, to name a few. It would be logical to assume that some psychiatrists are drawn to the Holocaust because of their own experiences.

An often overlooked bias is the use of psychoanalytic theory to explain survivor behavior and survivor psychopathology without acknowledging the limitations of that theory. In fact, it is the psychological sequelae of the Holocaust that casts doubt on some fundamental psychoanalytic concepts.[5] It is not surprising, then, that there exist major problems with research methodology that is used to describe survivors: Some consequences of surviving simply defy description; survivor samples are select in terms of age and extraordinarily varied in terms of background; and prewar life is frequently idealized, while postwar life is sufficiently understood as having been influenced by such variables as the adjustments to the host country, family support systems, educational opportunities, etc. In fact, the *only* variable reflecting some constancy is the degradation and horror experienced in the camps.

Several authors have indicated greater need for control groups, and the very few who have used such groups find evidence for normalcy within a number of parameters used to compare survivor with nonsurvivor groups.[6]

It is, perhaps, important to point out that there may be differences in the consequences of surviving, depending on the nature of the survivor's individual experiences. In some writings, for example, those who were in hiding, partisans, prewar displaced persons, and concentration camp inmates are all lumped together and their experiences treated as universal. This is a serious mistake.[7]

## The Second Generation

There is little doubt that many survivors retain some residue of problems from their encounter with Nazi persecution. Has the experience of their suffering in turn affected their children, the so-called "second generation"? If we return to earlier observations on missed adolescence, the lack of opportunity for learning, both socially and educationally, the premature marriages in DP camps to "restore" the family, then we have identified a host of potential problem areas for children of survivors. Survivors who became parents had been themselves deprived of crucial parenting experiences during formative years as adolescents and young adults. Their children were born into conditions still unsettled and primitive, of parents still homeless and unemployed. Others, born after the parents had emigrated to new countries to begin new lives, nevertheless faced similar difficulties traceable to parental experiences. The children were prized beyond belief, overprotected and overfed, and raised in an atmosphere of understandable secrecy and mistrust. To raise children in such a dangerous world created a situation fraught with ambivalence for the survivor. In addition, there is a parental preoccupation with the Holocaust and its attendant depressions; it seems reasonable to assume that this interferes with normal child-rearing.[8] And yet, once again, the tendency to overgeneralize overshadows the very real accomplishments of the second generation. For despite the obvious handicaps, most children of survivors have good relationships with their parents.[9] While there are children with severe problems derived from the parental experience,[10] others have derived, from that very same experience, a dedication to the oppressed, a love for Jewish learning and the Land of Israel, and a determination to inspire their children. An often asked question is whether second generation children suffer from the normal problems associated with the complexities of growing up in America, Europe, or Israel, or whether these life problems are Holocaust-derived. From my own clinical experience, I have found that every second generation child with problems sufficiently severe to warrant therapeutic attention suffers additional complications deriving from parental Holocaust experiences. The child may not be aware that a measure of his difficulty derives from the Holocaust, and the parents surely hope it does not.[11] The therapist may, indeed, conspire to keep it out of the child's awareness by not pointing out the possible connections and potential importance of the parental Holocaust-derived experience. Even worse, some therapists do not inquire at all about such experience, and thereby remain personally unaware.[12] But it is there, even if ignored. We do a great disservice to children of survivors if we fail to assist them to sort out the relationship of this extra burden to the more mundane, typical, and acceptable problems of daily life.

It is unfortunate, yet understandable, that the second generation maintains an extremely ambivalent relationship to the psychiatric profession. First of all, many members of the second generation feel justifiably prejudged and thus labeled as defective. Second, many have required therapy[13] and, in a sense, have been accused of failing to get well. Of these, a large number have actually been misunderstood or their treatment mismanaged, and their therapeutic failures can be attributed, in part, to the limitations of some therapists. Third, some members of the second generation have entered the helping professions and recognize that their motivation is, at least in part, to obtain personal help.

Naturally, this also reflects the wish to help those less fortunate. It is not surprising that some of the best work on survivors is being produced as master's and Ph.D. theses by the sons and daughters of survivors educated in social work, psychology, and other helping professions.

While attacking psychiatry and psychology with some justification, children of survivors seldom organize a second generation conference where the panelists are historians and humanists, rather than psychiatrists and psychologists. At the Second Generation Conference in New York in 1979, for example, a particularly angry outburst was aimed at the panel of psychiatrists, three of whom themselves were survivors of the concentration camps (Leo Eitinger, Hillel Klein, and Henry Krystal[14])!

What has not yet been resolved, and perhaps could be with more careful studies, is whether the legacy of the survivors might endow the second generation with a special mission rather than simply a special burden. The two are not mutually exclusive. The negative effects are well-described in clinical samples. After all, psychiatrists and psychologists describe the persons who desire care, and who usually manifest symptoms. The positive effects must be investigated more vigorously among nonclinical samples of second generation children.

The latter are now between twenty and thirty-five, and many are already parents to a third generation. For evidence of transmissions between the generations, the following nonclinical example is instructive. A five-year-old boy came to play with one of my children. He excitedly told me about Jews who were burning, that he might die, that he was not afraid, but that Jews were falling from buildings. He then reminded me that he was Jewish.

I asked him where he learned all these things, knowing his parents were second generation. The night before, he had seen "The Wall"[15] on television. "But that was at nine o'clock at night. Who told you about it?" His answer was, "My grandmother phoned me and told my babysitter to allow me to stay up and watch it." The little boy dutifully followed his grandmother's instructions. As it turned out, this grandmother had seldom spoken to her own daughter about the camps. But her grandchildren have heard little else from her. Their initiation is taking place right now. Perhaps the grandmother's aging, her fears that history is being distorted or forgotten, the greater comfort of being able to tell her grandchild one generation removed, all these factors might allow her the liberty to instruct. Only time will tell with what effect.

## Conclusion

The Holocaust was an enormous event with a lasting effect on those who experienced it. Decades later, it remains a powerful factor in contemporary life. For the survivors, the memories remain vivid and there are daily triggers to remind the survivor of those days. The images of the camps can be recaptured by the mere barking of a dog, or a police siren in the night. When those images predominate to the exclusion of a life lived productively and satisfactorily, there is recognizable psychological impairment. Survivors must somehow integrate their unique experience and measure its importance to their children. Some opt for silence, others for full disclosure. Either way, the Holocaust experience does not escape the notice of their children and grandchildren and their destinies may become intricately interwoven with the effects on the parents and grandparents. For the second generation, the Holocaust remains an intimate event lived with its eyewitnesses. To some, the parents are larger than life; to others, pitiful wrecks who should not have borne them. To most, they are just parents with all that entails, yet imbued with a unique background.

The second generation might offer a key to the constructive

possibilities of this awesome legacy. How the second generation interprets their parents' experience to their own children might well determine in what manner future generations will grapple with the responsibility of remembering and assigning the Holocaust to its legitimate place in history and religion.

## Notes

1. Paul Friedman, M.D. was one of the very few early observers to comment on the psychological consequences. He examined 190 adults and children interned in Cyprus, many of whom were former concentration camp inmates. The physical complaints were predominantly psychosomatic and in the children, 50-60 percent sought medical help for complaints where no organic cause was evident. In his article, "The Effects of Imprisonment," *Acta Medica Orientala* 7 (1948): 163-167, Dr. Friedman is prescient in his comment that "for once the usual relationship between patient and psychiatrist was reversed: it was the psychiatrist who became emotional when these stories were told."

2. Dr. William G. Niederland, among others, has described the clinical findings common to many, but not all, survivors. This "syndrome" consists of a chronic state of tension, vigilance, irritability, depression, unrest, and fear, usually with sleep disturbances, anxiety dreams, and nightmares. Dr. Niederland has also summarized the main characteristics of the concentration camp trauma. See "Psychiatric Disorders Among Persecution Victims," *Journal of Nervous and Mental Disorders* 139 (1964): 458-474.

3. *The Diagnostic and Statistical Manual of Mental Disorders,* Third Edition (DSM III), 1980, of the American Psychiatric Association, now includes the post-traumatic stress disorder. The DSM III definition emphasizes, "The essential feature is the development of characteristic symptoms following a psychologically traumatic event that is generally outside of the range of usual human experience." The disorder was well-known to physicians and mental health professionals who worked with survivors. The more recent awareness of similar conditions in victims of torture, Vietnam veterans, and Southeast Asian refugees has bolstered the recognition and diagnosis of this particular disorder.

4. For a rare account of a follow-up of fourteen children who survived Buchenwald, Shalom Robinson and Judith Hemmendinger, "Psychosocial Adjustment 30 Years Later of People Who Were in Nazi Concentration Camps as Children," in *Stress and Anxiety,* Vol. 8, ed. Norman Milgram (Washington: Hemisphere Publishing Corporation, 1982). It is noteworthy that the coauthor described these

children in terms similar to those in Dr. Friedman's 1948 paper (see footnote 1)—as apathetic and indifferent, meeting efforts to communicate with them with hostility and tension. Of the eight who settled in Israel, seven served with the Israel Defense Forces, six have white-collar jobs, and two are blue-collar workers. All married and seven are with their first wives. All acknowledge psychosocial problems, but none required psychiatric treatment. The other six children who settled in France were also reported to be well-adapted to work and family.

In August, 1945, permission had been obtained from the British Home Office for the entry into England of 1,000 child survivors. But only 300 could be assembled. Dr. Sarah Moskovitz writes, "Of these, only 17 were under eight years old. It was difficult to find child survivors. They were rare, these little ones who had been strong enough to survive disease, separation from parents, the traumatic conditions of ghettoization and the death camps themselves." In *Love Despite Hate: Child Survivors of the Holocaust and Their Adult Lives* (New York: Shocken Books, in press), Dr. Moskovitz describes the lives into adulthood of twenty-four children initially cared for in a home run by Alice Goldberger.

5.  As Dr. Paul Chodoff points out, the psychoanalytic view held that objective danger alone cannot give rise to neurosis without significant childhood predisposition. He correctly notes that the neurotic symptoms so common to survivors reflect a traumatic neurosis "almost entirely the result of the trauma itself," without evidence for neurotic predisposition. Chodoff adds that an "ironic consequence of acceptance of the original view about the linkage connection between earlier psychopathology and traumatic neurosis was its use by certain German forensic psychiatrists to deny the causative role of the persecution when evaluating reparations claims"—*American Handbook of Psychiatry*, ed. Silvano Arieti (New York: Basic Books, 1975), Chapter 41.

6.  Dr. Norman Solkoff, in a critical review—"Children of Survivors of the Nazi Holocaust," *American Journal of Orthopsychiatry*, 51 (1981): 29-42—exposes a number of shortcomings in the complex psychosocial investigations concerning survivors and their children. He notes that in one of very few controlled studies, Rustin found no evidence that the experiences of survivors generated psychopathology in their children—S. Rustin, "Guilt, Hostility and Jewish Identification Among a Self-Selected Sample of Late Adolescent Children of Jewish Concentration Camp Survivors: A Descriptive Study," *Dissertation Abstracts International* 32 (1971): Order No. 71-24, 810. This is in strong contrast to most of the clinical literature.

Another study with control groups also revealed "no significant differences between the survivor and control group children on any of the psychological variables [in the study] or in their attitudes and behaviors towards their parents." Among other things, the authors question the "extremely maladaptive psychological influence" of the parental experiences—Gloria R. Leon, James N. Butcher, Max

Kleinman, Alan Goldberg, and Moshe Almagor, "Survivors of the Holocaust and Their Children: Current Status and Adjustment," *Journal of Personality and Psychology* 41 (1981): 503-516. And yet, in clinical studies such influences can be inferred (See footnote 10).

7. In an otherwise interesting and informative article, Dr. David M. Berger describes "three cases of psychotherapy only peripherally affected by the persecution." In his words, one only "spent time—and then only briefly—in a concentration camp." It turns out, however, that Mr. K. was in fact in Auschwitz for six months, certainly not a peripheral experience. But conclusions are drawn from this clinical sampling on the basis "that all victims of the Nazi racial persecution, in and out of concentration camps, suffered identical complaints," the latter quote attributed to V. Venzlaff, "Mental Disorders Resulting from Racial Persecutions Outside of Concentration Camps," *International Journal of Social Psychiatry* 10 (1964): 77, in "The Survivor Syndrome: A Problem of Nosology and Treatment, *American Journal of Psychotherapy* 31 (1975): 238-251.

Dr. Yael Danieli appropriately attempts to delineate survivor groups into at least two: the families of victims and the families of fighters. ("Families of Survivors of the Nazi Holocaust: Some Short- and Long-Term Effects," in *Stress and Anxiety*). The victims were forced into roles of extreme passivity and dependency while fighters (partisans, members of the underground, and even those in hiding) retained the capacity to make some decisions concerning their destiny. As a consequence, the messages conveyed to the children in each type of family are quite different, as are the apparent results of these messages.

And, finally, a distinguished Holocaust researcher, Professor Leo Eitinger, has pointed out that the group of people known as concentration camp survivors "are not a homogeneous group." His own studies initially focused on Norwegian concentration camp survivors. See "Preliminary Notes on a Study of Concentration Camp Survivors in Norway," *Israel Annals of Psychiatry* 1 (1963): 59-67. This and subsequent work was taken to be representative of concentration camp experiences and consequences. In fact, these were Norwegian non-Jews. Eitinger has recently written about the eleven Norwegian-born Jewish survivors, of which he is one. There are noteworthy differences in the two groups, particularly in respect to postwar adaptation—"Jewish Concentration Camp Survivors in Norway," *Israel Annals of Psychiatry* 13 (1975): 821-834.

8. These problems were postulated and discussed in an article by John J. Sigal and Vivian Rakoff, "Concentration Camp Survival. A Pilot Study of Effects on the Second Generation," *Canadian Psychiatric Association Journal* 16 (1971): 393-397.

9. See Gloria Leon (footnote 6).

10. A journal article of interest, in respect to the transmission of effects, analyzes data of thirty (hospitalized) patients who are the children of survivors. Two patients, "experienced the hospital as a concentration camp following admission," and ten of thirteen

patients in a follow-up therapy group revealed they had perceived the hospital "as if they were in a concentration camp." The authors postulate that for survivors' children, hospital admission could be an "unconscious reenactment of their parents' Holocaust experiences." See Sylvia Axelrod, M.D., Ofelia L. Schnipper, M.D. and John H. Rau, M.D., "Hospitalized Offspring of Holocaust Survivors," *Bulletin of the Menninger Clinic* 44 (1980): 1-14.

11. Survivor parents may shield their children from their Holocaust experiences but inevitably reveal a sufficient amount of information to arouse the curiosity of their offspring. The intensity and mystery of these "hints," the secrecy and subsequent fantasies, invariably contribute to the child's psychological make-up and most certainly accentuate any psychological problems. See Robert Krell, M.D., "Holocaust Families: The Survivors and Their Children," *Comprehensive Psychiatry* 20 (1979): 560-567.

12. In a study conducted by Dr. Judith Kestenberg among psychoanalysts, she reports, on the basis of a questionnaire survey, "A vast majority of those questioned revealed an amazing indifference to the problem. Some regretted that parent-survivors who consulted them did not follow through on their recommendation for analyses of their children. Some were startled by the questions because it never occurred to them to link their patients' dynamics to the history of their parents' persecution"—"Psychoanalytic Contributions to the Problem of Children of Survivors of Nazi Persecution," *Israel Annals of Psychiatry* 10 (1972): 311-325.

13. Despite the ongoing debate as to positive and negative effects of the Holocaust on the second generation, and the favorable controlled studies (G. Leon, et al, S. Rustin), it is noteworthy that Dr. Shamai Davidson reports, "we have found that as many as 20 percent of the children referred to some of the child psychiatric and adolescent outpatient services in Israel had at least one parent who was a CCS [concentration camp survivor]"—"The Clinical Effects of Massive Psychic Trauma in Families of Holocaust Survivors," *Journal of Marital and Family Therapy* 6 (1980): 11-21.

14. Harvey Peskin, Ph.D. provides some insights into this "confrontation"—"Observations on the First International Conference on Children of Holocaust Survivors," *Family Process* 20 (1981): 391-394.

15. The TV adaptation of John Hersey's novel about the Warsaw ghetto.

### For Further Reading

Bergmann, Martin S., and Jucovy, Milton E., eds. *Generations of the Holocaust*, New York: Basic Books, Inc., 1982.

Dimsdale, Joel. E., ed. *Survivors, Victims, and Perpetrators*, Washington, New York, London: Hemisphere Publishing Corporation, 1980.

Epstein, Helen. *Children of the Holocaust*. New York: G.P. Putnam's Sons, 1979.

Krystal, Henry, ed. *Massive Psychic Trauma*. New York: International Universities Press, Inc., 1968.

# Nuernberg and Other Trials*

## HENRY FRIEDLANDER

On November 1, 1943, the Allied leaders—Roosevelt, Churchill, and Stalin—issued the Moscow Declaration. In it, they warned the "Hitlerite Huns" that there would be retribution for Nazi crimes. They vowed to punish those who had committed "atrocities, massacres, and executions" in the occupied territories. They listed the crimes and the victims; but they did not mention the murder of the Jews. After the German capitulation, the four occupying powers— France, Great Britain, the United States, and the Soviet Union— signed the London Agreement of August, 1945. It established the International Military Tribunal for the trial of the major war criminals.

The International Military Tribunal, sitting in Nuernberg from October, 1945, to October, 1946, eventually tried twenty-two leading Nazis, sentencing twelve to death, three to life in prison, and four to long prison terms; three were not convicted. The twelve sentenced to death included Hermann Goering, chief of the *Luftwaffe* and of the Four Year Plan, who had transmitted Hitler's order for the killing of the European Jews; Hans Frank, the governor of occupied Poland; Ernst Kaltenbrunner, who had succeeded the assassinated Reinhard Heydrich as chief of the SS Central Office for Reich Security; Keitel and Jodl, the chiefs of the *Wehrmacht;* Julius Streicher, the editor of the pornographic and antisemitic *Stuermer;* and, in absentia, Martin Bormann, chief of Hitler's party chancellery. The tribunal also convicted as criminal a number of Nazi organizations, including the SS, SD, and Gestapo.

The indictment against the Nazi leaders and their subsequent conviction was based on three types of crimes. "Crimes against peace" involved the planning and waging of aggressive war. "War crimes" involved violations of the laws and customs of war, including the killing of POWs and hostages. "Crimes against humanity" involved crimes against civilian populations, including the persecution and murder of the European Jews. Before the International Military Tribunal, the first two crimes were more important for the prosecution than the third one; however, in later trials, "crimes against humanity" came to be considered central for conviction. Unfortunately, the terms "war crimes" and "war criminals," used by the Allies at Nuernberg, remained attached in the popular mind to all Nazi crimes, including the mass murder of the Jews, which was completely unconnected with the necessities and conditions of war. The Nazi defendants always considered themselves "not guilty" of "crimes against peace" and even of "war crimes," because no formal international law before 1945 had limited the rights of sovereign states to wage war. The defendants could not make this claim against

---

* *Prior to reading this article, it is useful to read "The SS and Police," by Henry Friedlander, in this volume.*

"crimes against humanity," which had been criminal even under German law; instead, they offered the excuse that they had merely followed the orders of their superiors.

The trial of the major war criminals was only the beginning of the judicial process. The Moscow Declaration had provided for extradition; therefore, many Nazi leaders were returned for trial to countries formerly occupied by Germany. For example, those convicted and executed in Poland and Czechoslovakia included Rudolf Hoess, the commandant of Auschwitz; Arthur Greiser, the governor of the annexed Polish territories who had established the killing center at Chelmno; Juergen Stroop, the SS leader who had destroyed the Warsaw ghetto; and Kurt Daluege, the chief of the German uniformed police. Altogether, approximately 75 Nazis were convicted in Belgium, 68 in Luxemburg, 204 in Holland, 80 in Denmark, 80 in Norway, thousands in Poland, and an unknown number in Czechoslovakia and Yugoslavia. Finally, in 1961-1962 Israel tried, convicted, and executed Adolf Eichmann, the chief of the Jewish Office in the headquarters of the Gestapo, who had been responsible for the deportations of the European Jews.

The largest number of Nazi criminals were judged by tribunals of the four occupation armies. In December, 1945, the Allies issued Control Council Law No. 10 "in order to establish a uniform legal basis . . . for the prosecution of war criminals and other similar offenders." This law, modeled on the London Agreement for the International Military Tribunal, was used in all subsequent trials.

Most prominent and widely publicized were the trials held under Law No. 10 at Nuernberg in the American zone of occupation. There, ten United States military tribunals judged cabinet and subcabinet Nazi leaders in twelve trials between October, 1946, and April, 1949. (These later Nuernberg trials have often been confused with the earlier trial of the major criminals at Nuernberg. Pictures from the earlier trial are usually used to illustrate war crime trials; the later trials, however, served as the basis for the popular film about Nuernberg, starring Spencer Tracy.) These trials included those against the state secretaries in various ministries; senior generals in the supreme command of the armed forces; judges and physicians guilty of judicial abuses, medical experiments, and the Euthanasia killings; and senior managers in the industrial concerns of Krupp, Flick, and I. G. Farben, guilty of employing slave labor. Two trials were of particular concern: the trial of the *Einsatzgruppen* commanders, responsible for the murder of Jews in the occupied Soviet territories, and the trial of the senior officials of the SS Central Office for Economics and Administration, responsible for the administration of the concentration camps. In these later Nuernberg trials, 177 offenders faced their judges; all but 35 were convicted. Ninety-eight received prison terms, 20 life terms, and 24 death sentences. Of these, only 12 were actually executed, including Oswald Pohl, the master of the concentration camps, Otto Ohlendorf, the commander of *Einsatzgruppe* D and Paul Blobel, the SS officer responsible for the massacre at Babi Yar outside Kiev.

In addition, United States military commissions, using officers as judges, tried large numbers of Nazi criminals at Wiesbaden, Ludwigshafen, and Dachau. These trials included the proceedings against the staffs of the Hadamar Euthanasia institution, the concentration camps Dachau, Buchenwald, Mauthausen, Dora, Flossenbürg, and numerous subsidiary camps. The remaining trials involved killings of Allied soldiers. The British and French also tried large numbers of Nazi criminals under Control Council Law No.10. These involved military commanders, industrial managers, and concentration camp guards. Most prominent was the British trial in Lueneburg of staff members from Auschwitz and Bergen-Belsen. Altogether, the three Western Allies convicted more than 5,000 Nazis, sentenced 800 to death, and executed almost 500. Although no accurate figures are available, the Soviet Union probably convicted even more Nazi criminals.

No Nazi criminal was executed by the Western Allies after 1952. After that date, all death sentences were commuted to life in prison. But even those sentenced to life did not remain in jail for long. The Western Allies released all Nazi criminals by the end of the 1950s. This policy of clemency applied also in the Soviet Union and other eastern European countries formerly occupied by Germany. Almost everywhere, Nazi criminals were released during the 1950s and 1960s. Those released from the jails of the Western Allies could not be tried again in German courts; the treaty between France, Great Britain, the United States, and the German Federal Republic prohibited the trial in a German court of any person previously tried, convicted, and pardoned by the Western Allies. No such treaty protected Nazis tried, convicted, and released in the Soviet Union, Poland, or any other eastern European country; they often faced a German court after their return to the German Federal Republic.

After the Allies ended their trials, the successor states of Hitler's German Reich—the Republic of Austria, the German Democratic Republic (East), and the German Federal Republic (West)— continued to try Nazis under German law for crimes committed during World War II. Thousands of Nazi criminals have been convicted in the three German successor states. The trials in the Federal Republic have received the most publicity; they include the *Einsatzgruppen* trial in Ulm, the Auschwitz trial in Frankfurt, the Chelmno trial in Bonn, the Treblinka trial in Düsseldorf, the Belzec trial in Munich, the Sobibor trial in Hagen, and the Maidanek trial in Düsseldorf.

### For Further Reading

Rückerl, Adalbert. *The Investigation of Nazi Crimes, 1945-1978: A Documentation.* Heidelberg: C. F. Müller, 1979.

Smith, Bradley F. *Reaching Judgment at Nuremberg.* New York: Basic Books, 1977.

———. *The Road to Nuremberg.* New York: Basic Books, 1981.

# Simon Wiesenthal:
# The Man, the Mission, His Message

## ABRAHAM COOPER

Some of you may have read about Simon Wiesenthal in the newspapers, seen him on television, or even heard him lecture. Still others may only have heard about the famed "Nazi hunter."

Since 1977, I have had the honor of traveling with Mr. Wiesenthal in Europe and the United States on numerous occasions. During these trips, we have spent many hours together discussing his life before the war; his experiences in the camps; his efforts in tracking down the murderers of his people; and his goals for the Simon Wiesenthal Center, which will carry on his legacy.

In many ways, Simon Wiesenthal's personal story closely parallels the tragedy and rebirth of the Jewish people. At the end of World War II, millions of the victors and the vanquished tried to piece together their dislocated personal, communal, and national lives. For the remnant of European Jews, this was especially difficult. Two out of every three Jews on the continent had been murdered in the Final Solution, and a once-vibrant European Jewish life and culture had been effectively wiped out.

A large number of the survivors left Europe, looking to start anew in Israel, the Americas, and Australia. One of those who chose to remain was Simon Wiesenthal. Living in Vienna, he could most effectively hunt the murderers and obtain the documents necessary to prosecute them.

## The Man

Simon Wiesenthal was born in Lvov, Galicia (today the Soviet Union) in 1908 and was educated as an architectural engineer at the University of Prague. A politically involved student, he recalls that in the 1920s, the response of his circle of friends to Adolf Hitler was to tell jokes: "No one was prepared to take Hitler seriously—then."

At the outset of World War II, the world changed rapidly and prospects for the Wiesenthal family deteriorated, as they did for all European Jews. Simon's stepfather was arrested by the Soviet secret police and eventually died in prison; his stepbrother was shot; he barely managed to save his mother, wife, and himself from deportation to Siberia. When the Germans invaded Russia in 1941, he was interned in a concentration camp near Lvov. Both Simon and his wife were then assigned to a forced labor camp. In Europe, the Final Solution had begun. It exacted a heavy toll on the Wiesenthal family—eighty-nine members perished without a trace. Simon Wiesenthal arranged for the Polish underground to spirit his wife, Celia, out of the camp in the fall of 1942. For two years, the blonde woman passed as an Aryan in Warsaw.

# The Escape

Wiesenthal escaped in October, 1943, but was recaptured in June, 1944. He was then sent to a camp where he certainly would have been murdered, had it not been for the German retreat from the eastern front. The SS guards, fearing that they would be transferred to the front if they had no prisoners to guard, kept a handful alive. Out of an original population of 149,000, only thirty-four remained. Wiesenthal was one of them.

Very few survived the long winter march west that ended for Wiesenthal at Mauthausen concentration camp in upper Austria. It was there, on May 5, 1945, that an American armored unit liberated him.

# The Mission

"First you will go to a sanitorium, then you will go home, and then you can build houses again." Such was the friendly advice of a United States Army captain to Mr. Wiesenthal just weeks after liberation. Not knowing that his wife was alive, Wiesenthal cried for the first time in years. There was no one from the prewar period "with whom or for whom I could live. . . . People like me don't need houses. We lost more than houses. We lost more than families—we lost belief in humanity, in friendship, in justice, and without these, I couldn't begin anew."

It was then that he decided to devote "a few years" to bringing the murderers to justice. "When justice would be served—then I can go back to building houses again," Wiesenthal explained. Within weeks, working for the War Crimes Section of the United States Army, along with the OSS (Office of Strategic Services) and OIC (Counter-Intelligence Corps), Wiesenthal captured the first of over 1,100 Nazi murderers.

The "few years" have evolved into half a lifetime. It has been a long and lonely journey. Many eyewitnesses never survived; tons of incriminating evidence were destroyed by the Nazis before the Allied victory; criminals often escaped prosecution after the war through Nazi underground groups such as Odessa, Six, Star, and Spider to safe havens in the Americas and elsewhere. The most frustrating fact was that, for the crucial years following the Nuernberg trials, most countries, including the United States, not only did not actively bring these people to trial, but, under the pressure of the cold war, opened their doors to thousands of these newfound "anti-Communists."

By 1954, Wiesenthal's volunteers and coworkers at his Jewish Historical Documentation Center in Linz, Austria, drifted away, and he closed his office there. Although Wiesenthal sent most of his files to Israel, he kept the dossier of Adolf Eichmann. Wiesenthal never relaxed his efforts and, with information provided by him and others, Israeli agents captured Eichmann in Argentina (May, 1960) and brought him to Israel for a trial that received international attention and coverage. Eichmann was found guilty of mass murder and crimes against humanity, and was executed in May, 1962.

Encouraged by this startling success, Wiesenthal reopened the Jewish Documentation Center in Vienna, Austria, yards away from the former Gestapo headquarters. Wiesenthal now works in a country which was home to countless, unrepentant "ex"-Nazis and within a postwar society which, unlike West Germany, has never systematically tried its compatriots for crimes related to the Holocaust.

One case that has given Wiesenthal a great sense of satisfaction was his pursuit and arrest "in the name of the Jewish people" of the SS officer responsible for the deportation of Anne Frank, the young diarist whose family hid in a false attic in Amsterdam.

Wiesenthal has chosen additional formats to delineate his views. He lectures extensively in West Germany, Holland, and the United States, primarily to university students. He is also a noted author. Four of his most prominent works have been translated into English: *The Murderers Among Us* deals with Nazi war criminals; *Sails of Hope* is an historical novel, which speculates on Christopher Columbus' Jewish roots and the possible connection between his journey to discover America and the Inquisition in Spain; *Sunflower* is a moving narrative on the questions of justice, forgiveness, and personal responsibility; *Max and Helen* is the story of a Nazi who was not turned over to the authorities for prosecution.

## The Message

People have often asked, "What motivates Wiesenthal? Why does he persist in hunting Nazis so many years after the Holocaust? What purpose can it serve?"

"I am neither a Jewish James Bond nor a crazy Don Quixote," Wiesenthal declares. Revenge is not his aim. Wiesenthal has always opposed vigilante justice. What measure of revenge can match the crimes of a Dr. Joseph Mengele, the infamous "Angel of Death" responsible for the death of 200,000 children at Auschwitz? Wiesenthal states that "It is impossible to punish these crimes. No, we need Mengele today as much as a witness as we do to try him for his unspeakable crimes. While arranging someone's death on a street in South America may be simple, it would serve no useful purpose. What we need are sentenced criminals, not martyred Nazis."

## I Am My Brother's Keeper

Another way to explain Wiesenthal's motivation is by recounting the following story:

He had just delivered his third lecture in as many days. This last appearance in a moderate-sized Midwestern city drew an audience larger than the total local Jewish population. Counting the initial flight from Vienna, Wiesenthal had flown over 20,000 miles in a week. Although forty years his junior and having only to join him from Los Angeles for this tour, I was exhausted. Yet, as we sat in another airport lounge, Wiesenthal clearly relished the challenge of another appearance 800 miles away that night. My face must have betrayed my thoughts, because it was then that he told me the story of the *siddur* (prayer book).

"Six months after the war, I was approached by an American Polish-born rabbi serving as a chaplain in the United States Army. He had heard a rumor that somewhere deep in the forests of Bavaria, there existed a medieval castle which housed Jewish holy objects, memorabilia, prayer books, and Torah scrolls.

"It was rumored that the Nazis had planned to create museums for the 'Thousand Year Reich,' which would teach future generations about an extinct group known as Jews. The army had finally allowed them to travel there and they asked me to go along as translator. Eight hours later, after driving through the snow, we reached this castle. As the door swung open, we knew instantly that the rumor was true. Thousands of volumes, candelabra, and other holy objects were stacked to the ceilings throughout the vast rooms. For some time, we said nothing, standing in awe of the only surviving remnants of entire communities. Finally, it was decided that we would each review a section of the castle.

"But as I ascended the staircase to check out the second floor, I heard a crashing sound. I rushed downstairs to find that the rabbi had collapsed with a small *siddur* in his hand. When I revived him, he could not speak—he only pointed to the Yiddish inscription in the book. It read in part: 'Whoever finds this *siddur*, please give it to my brother. The murderers are among us. They are in the next house. I do not know how much longer I will remain alive. *Please, do not forget us—and do not forget our murderers.*' "

Wiesenthal turned to me and added, "It was signed by the chaplain's sister.

"Some years later the chaplain passed away and his family sent me that precious book. It is the only prayer book in my home—I keep it on my night table next to my bed. . . . "

The final scene of the film, *Genocide,* shows Simon Wiesenthal in Israel (where his only daughter and grandchildren live) at the Western Wall, the holiest of Jewish shrines, placing between the cracks of the Wall his prayer: "I am my brother's keeper." This is an apt summary of Wiesenthal's calling and his hope for young people everywhere not to allow the repetition of the tragedies of past generations. Ultimately, it is they who stand to gain the most from his incredible odyssey.

**For Further Reading**

Wiesenthal, Simon. *Max and Helen*. New York: William Morrow, 1982.

―――. *The Murderers Among Us: The Wiesenthal Memoirs.* Edited by Joseph Wechsberg. New York: McGraw-Hill, 1967.

―――. *The Sunflower*. New York: Schocken Books, 1976.

# World War II Nazis in the United States

## MARTIN MENDELSOHN

For millions of displaced persons (DPs) in Europe, the prison conditions of Nazi concentration camps were exchanged for the more benign but, nonetheless, still primitive and harsh surroundings of the displaced persons camps. The whole continent of Europe had many urgent problems. The ravages of war had left it desolate and barely able to house, feed, clothe, and provide sanitary services for its populations. Without outside help, economic and social services were at a standstill.

In 1949-1950, the United States began relaxing its rigid immigration quotas to allow the victims of World War II to enter this country. By 1952, approximately 400,000 Europeans had entered America. But in the wake of the tidal wave of refugees seeking comfort and security, many former Nazis also were able to come to the United States, sometimes under the guise of anti-Soviet or anti-Communist refugees. Those who fought the United States now came to reap the benefits of its victory—and their defeat.

They came because the United States either did not know or did not care who they were or what they did. This combination of ignorance and apathy planted and nurtured the seeds of the problem with Nazi war criminals residing in the United States. Today, hundreds of individuals are under investigation, suspected of concealing their Nazi past. In the confusion of postwar Europe, visas were granted to thousands. A thorough investigation was a rarity, even if the records had survived, or if the investigators knew what to look for. Many displaced persons—both Jews and non-Jews—had no papers and no way to verify their identities. A significant number came from villages where the town hall's records were lost under German occupation or Allied bombardments. Lack of records meant that many could assume new bogus identities. With these new unverifiable identities, Nazis sometimes applied for visas to enter the United States as victims of aggression—and such visas were granted.

Many Nazis came to the United States in 1948 and 1949, claiming that they spent the war years in central and eastern Europe in such nonmilitary and nonpolitical positions as foresters and dairymen. In 1950, the Displaced Persons Act was changed to specifically exclude Communists. However, in the course of amending the act, the language prohibiting the entrance of Nazis and Fascists into the United States was dropped, either accidentally or deliberately. Between 1950 and 1978 even an avowed Nazi (including, one must assume, Hitler if he were alive) could have legally entered the United States as an immigrant and become a citizen.

In 1950, the Korean War started and anti-Communist hysteria was commonplace. United States intelligence agencies intensified existing programs to bring politically active, known anti-

Communists into the country to gain firsthand knowledge of the conditions, terrain, and people living in the Soviet Bloc. Many of these politically active, known anti-Communists were actually Nazis, Nazi sympathizers, or Nazi collaborators. Even in some cases where security and background investigations were made, known Nazis were allowed to enter this country. The rationale was that these Nazis were anti-Communists or had useful scientific skills.

As far back as 1944, the Joint Intelligence Activities Board began planning the "Paperclip Program," which admitted hundreds of Nazi scientists and administrators into the United States to assist American space and military development—especially rockets, missiles, jet engines, and airplanes. Nazis who had useful scientific skills were acceptable if they were deemed of use in fighting the Communists. The expediency of this shortsighted crusading logic was obvious to intelligent observers and critics at the time.

The Communists retaliated by releasing politically embarrassing information showing the Nazi backgrounds of these new Americans. The United States, with justification, dismissed most of these charges as Communist propaganda designed to discredit those who had historically opposed the imposition of Communist domination on their homelands. No one, to this day, knows how many Nazis the Communists used (and may still be using) in their military research programs.

Very few prosecutions of Nazi collaborators took place in the United States in the 1950s and 1960s. These prosecutions were either of notorious Nazis, such as the Rumanian Nicolae Malaxa and the Croat Andrija Artukovic, or they were Jewish *kapos*, such as Jonas Lewy. For different reasons these failed.

Nicolae Malaxa, for example, was a major industrialist in steel and heavy industry in prewar Rumania. Soon after the Nazi invasion, *Reichsmarschall* Hermann Goering nationalized and took control of all means of Rumanian industrial production. Originally Malaxa lost all his holdings. In a short period, however, he resumed control under Nazi protection and produced machinery for the German occupiers. Malaxa was also a strong financial backer of the collaborationist and native Fascist Iron Guard and the government of General Ion Antonescu. When the war was over, Malaxa transferred millions of dollars into New York banks. Even after the Communists took control in Rumania, Malaxa continued to have enormous influence. He arrived in the United States as part of a trade delegation and defected. When his past activities were discovered, the United States government moved to deport him. Through complex and intricate political and legal maneuvers, he was able to stymie deportation until his death in 1963, at which time he was residing on Park Avenue in New York City.

Andrija Artukovic, minister of the interior of Croatia, entered the United States under a false name in 1948. Since 1949, efforts have been under way to extradite him to Yugoslavia. On the narrow question of extradition, the case reached the United States Supreme Court. He was ordered deported to Yugoslavia in 1958 but that order has been judicially stayed. In 1959, the Justice Department tried to have Artukovic deported. The stay was lifted but he has appealed that order to the Circuit Court of Appeals. The court has not rendered a decision and as of the summer of 1982, Artukovic remains in the United States.

Perhaps the most tragic prosecution during this embarrassing period was the one directed against Jonas Lewy. Lewy was a Polish Jew who served as a *kapo* in a Nazi concentration camp. He was identified after his arrival in the United States as an overzealous guard who enjoyed his work, maltreating and brutally beating Jewish prisoners. Although he was found guilty and ordered deported, the United States government stayed his deportation to Poland because of justifiable fears that the Polish government would persecute him.

Yet, even these cases were isolated examples of unofficial attempts to remove the Nazis from the United States. For the most part, the American people and their government were not interested in pursuing these cases. The war was over and they had other priorities. The enormity of the Holocaust could not easily be dismissed. In May, 1960, Israel arrested Adolf Eichmann, the man responsible for implementing the Final Solution. He was tried in April-December, 1961. This nondescript Austrian SS officer personified Nazi evil. The Eichmann trial, which drew world attention, culminating in his execution in May, 1962, was high drama and led to renewed attention to Nazis hiding in our midst.

In 1974, the dam broke. Elizabeth Holtzman, a young Jewish congressperson from Brooklyn, learned of the problem of Nazis in America. As a member of the House Judiciary Committee she asked the Justice Department for information and was disturbed by its half-hearted response. Ms. Holtzman learned that for twenty years there had been evasion and equivocation with respect to Nazis in the United States. A policy of silence and indifference to Nazis in America prevailed in the United States government. Bureaucratic inertia made this policy as effective as tacit protection of ex-Nazis. There were no centralized records, no coordinated investigations, and individual cases were accorded very low priorities. No agency had the authority, mandate, or legal responsibility to investigate or arrest Nazi war criminals. Each branch of government had its own priorities—and none was interested in Nazis.

In 1977, the Justice Department responded favorably to Representative Holtzman's demands. For the first time since the Nuernberg prosecutions a single, centralized unit was created in the Justice Department with the mandate to investigate and prosecute individuals accused of concealing their Nazi past in order to obtain a visa allowing them to enter the United States. The investigative unit was first a part of the Immigration and Naturalization Service and was later incorporated into the Criminal Division of the Justice Department.

Since its inception, the unit (now called the Office of Special Investigations) has conducted research into hundreds of cases and has litigated all of the more than twenty cases brought against alleged Nazis. People such as Bishop Valerian Trifa, the student leader of the

Rumanian Iron Guard, Treblinka guard Feodor Fedorenko, and others have now been brought to justice. But justice in the American system is frustratingly slow due to constitutional safeguards. Despite their heinous deeds, these men and women are not, nor can they be, accused of violating any section of the United States criminal code, since their crimes are not covered by American law. Moreover, the United States has not been a signatory or ratifier of any treaty on the subject of genocide since 1945, and only under political pressure have prosecutions against Nazi criminals living in the United States begun. These Nazis can only be prosecuted for lying on their immigration forms about their Nazi pasts; as understood in the doctrine of defective immigration, their entry into the United States is invalidated by such substantial untruths as membership in a Fascist party or the holding of a criminal record. Their only punishment is denaturalization for citizens and deportation for aliens. Sometimes, as in the Ryan Case, in which Hermine Braunsteiner Ryan, a former guard at Maidanek concentration camp, was extradited from the United States, prosecution subsequently has taken place in West Germany. However, it is not known if the United States would deport to such countries as Poland and Soviet Bloc nations, where the political climate is undesirable but where Nazi war criminals are prosecuted. Despite the relative leniency of the American punishments, the effort is still to be supported for its educational value.

Today, efforts to find and prosecute Nazi war criminals continue. Officially, the governments of Israel, the United States, and West Germany cooperate and share information. There is limited cooperation between those governments and some Communist countries, such as the Soviet Union, the German Democratic Republic, Yugoslavia, and Poland. Other Western countries, such as Canada and France, are now also beginning to examine their own Nazi immigrant problem.

**For Further Reading**

Blum, Howard. *Wanted!: The Search for Nazis in America.* New York: Quadrangle Books, 1977.

Borkin, Joseph. *The Crime and Punishment of I. G. Farben.* New York: The Free Press, 1978.

Dinnerstein, Leonard. *America and the Survivors of the Holocaust.* New York: Columbia University Press, 1982.

Klarsfeld, Beate. *Wherever They May Be!* New York: Vanguard Press, 1975.

Knoll, Erwin, and McFadden, Judith Nies, eds. *War Crimes and the American Conscience.* New York: Holt, Rinehart, and Winston, 1970.

Knoop, Hans. *The Menten Affair.* New York: Macmillan Co., 1978.

Loftus, John. *The Belarus Secret.* Edited by Nathan Miller. New York: Alfred A. Knopf, 1982.

Lyttle, Richard B. *Nazi Hunting.** New York: Franklin Watts, 1982.

Rückerl, Adalbert. *The Investigation of Nazi Crimes, 1945-1978: A Documentation.* Heidelberg: C.F. Müller, 1979.

Wiesenthal, Simon. *The Murderers Among Us: The Wiesenthal Memoirs.* Edited by Joseph Wechsberg. New York: McGraw-Hill, 1967.

\* *For children.*

**10**

# IMPLICATIONS

# Escape

*In my heart I was still convinced that the only refuge for us was to join the partisans in the forest.*

*"I've got to go," I told Papa, who I knew, deep down, shared my view. "Okay," he finally said. "We'll leave Radom. Then if there is no other way, we'll go to the forest."*

*We went to tell Mother. I believe she had always known it would one day come to this. But we were not prepared for her answer.*

*"No," she said. "You'll have to go without me. Grandmother could never make the journey. I must stay here to look after her." We begged her to change her mind, but she remained adamant. "You go and save yourselves," she said. "This is my decision. You are not responsible. You must go and live. But please understand—Grandmother has no one but me. My obligation is to stay with her."*

*For four days we argued but we could not sway her. She wanted to come, but nothing could deter her from the obligation she felt.*

*Our parting will remain forever on my mind and conscience. We hugged and kissed goodbye again and again; then at the door, I turned to look back, to take one last mental picture of my dear mother. I can still see her, her dark wavy hair now prematurely gray, but her beautiful strong features unchanged. I was torn between my fear of dying and my conviction that I was betraying her, letting her down when she needed me. A hundred times I told myself to stay, a hundred times my terror forced me to leave my adored mother, the one to whom I had turned with my troubles ever since I was a tiny child, and who, with a single kiss, made me whole again.*

*To this day, I still wonder if had we insisted more, or begged just a little longer, maybe she would have relented. My only comfort is the prayer that in those last moments before she and Grandmother were led into the gas chamber, she found consolation in the thought that her husband and children were still alive—alive to carry on the tradition and commitment for which she gave her life.*

# How Unique Is the Holocaust?

## HENRY L. FEINGOLD

There is one question that always arises in discussions about the Holocaust and its importance to Western civilization: Is the Holocaust merely one in a series of genocides to be found in virtually every historical epoch, or is there something unique about the systematic murder of European Jews? Quite often the Holocaust is compared with the sufferings of other groups, such as American Blacks, American Indians, Cambodians, and the Vietnamese boat people. These facile comparisons are not only misleading; they also conceal the real meaning of the Holocaust.

The Holocaust was a unique historical event, a *novum*, partly because its primary victims, the European Jews, were a unique people in the context of European history. In consuming them by fire, Europe, not Nazi Germany alone, destroyed its own most representative children in a massive and unprecedented act of cannibalism. As a central historical event—like the French Revolution, the discovery of America, or the discovery of the wheel— it has changed the course of subsequent history. Such an event always has historical echoes.

This approach might be labeled both Judeocentric and Eurocentric. It is my response to those who believe that the Jews are touting the Holocaust to garner a psychic income or a sacred prestige based on their suffering. It is true that genocide has happened before in history and that Jews were not alone in the extermination camps. The particularist view can easily be mistaken for a kind of ethnic conceit. But that is not what is intended. By claiming a historical uniqueness for the Holocaust, there is no intention of detracting from the suffering of other victimized groups in the long history of human cruelty. The ability to fully fathom one's own group's crucible actually enhances the possibility of feeling some empathy for the pain of others.

The Judeocentric position is not an effort to garner a special group prestige, as recently suggested by a noted sociologist. In a world where the powerful control events, there can be no prestige in being powerless and victimized. A community that touts its victimization denies itself the possibility of having a "usable past." How does one teach Jewish children that at a certain historical juncture their people were considered bacilli and eradicated like so much vermin? Can such a page of history be ingested without lacerating the Jewish self-image? No child willingly accepts membership in a community that has seemingly lost so radically. It is better to be the hero in history. I suspect that the reason Jewish teachers have placed such an inordinate emphasis on the question of Jewish resistance during the Holocaust is in order to furnish our youth with something beyond an image of their kinfolk waiting on line for the gas chamber. We seek a kernel of courage to redeem ourselves and to create a tradition of resistance in case it happens again.

There are perils in claiming uniqueness for the Holocaust by linking it to the character and historical role played by the Jewish victims. It brings us perilously close to Nazi demonology, which assigns to Jews unique attributes: They are satanic, dangerous, evil, *ein Gegenvolk*—an antipeople. Yet, to deny Jewish uniqueness is to allow oneself to be limited by the antisemitic imagination. Shall we stop speaking of the Holocaust because Arab, Neo-Nazi, and Communist propagandists all claim that Jews are using the Holocaust to garner good will for Israel? There is, after all, nothing unique in claiming uniqueness. Every people identifiable as a separate group feels that its cohesive identity is unique, not quite the same as the rest of mankind. Paradoxically, the Nazi concept of Nordic racial superiority mistranslates the biblical idea of chosenness into pseudo-scientific biological terms. But such a claim is at the very heart of group formation and, when it does not take a perverse form as it did in Nazi Germany, it is able to acknowledge the suffering of other groups in history.

It is not difficult to understand those who insist on comparing the Holocaust with other catastrophies. Educators, for example, would experience difficulty in making local school boards see the validity of a Judeocentric-Eurocentric approach. It appears too ethnocentric, too centered on one group experience to serve the needs of a variegated, pluralistic student population. At the same time, it raises a question whether the emerging pattern of Holocaust education, which subsumes it beneath a generalized ethnic scream of pain, is really an improvement which brings us closer to the truth. History simply does not lend itself to equal distribution. At times some groups seem to be at the center of its forces and seem to have a heavier valence than others.

The trivialization of the Holocaust occurs when categories are mixed and various groups reach out for the Holocaust metaphor to express real or imagined oppression. Angela Davis is transformed into a Jewish housewife en route to Dachau; a cut in the food stamp program becomes an exercise in genocide; the Vietnamese boat people become the hapless Jewish refugees of the 1930s. It is not difficult to understand why spokesmen for such groups slip so easily into the use of the Holocaust metaphor. In a perverse way it is, in fact, the clearest evidence that we are dealing with an extraordinary event. The use of the Holocaust metaphor signals the danger they feel, and, truly, after Auschwitz all vulnerable and defenseless groups must feel danger.

The Holocaust is an event of magnitude which deserves examination in its own right; its truth is concealed by facile comparisons. The distillation of a lesson is best achieved and derived from the uniqueness of the event rather than from what it shares with other atrocities. Some have pointed out that the uniqueness of the Holocaust lies in the radicalness and the scale of the evil involved. During those bitter years, death was not an incidental by-product of a greater purpose—it was *the* product. The Jews were not civilians killed in a particularly cruel war. Rather, the full energy of a formidable bureaucratic apparatus was devoted to identifying them, searching them out even in the remotest mountains of Bulgaria, and, finally, murdering them on an assembly-line process. The victims, western European Jews in particular, were slow to understand, since they did not think of themselves only as Jews but also as Germans, Frenchman, Dutch, etc. They did not see themselves as a people earmarked for destruction. It is difficult to understand and believe even today: A modern nation turned on a minority of its own citizens, which had made enormous contributions to European civilization, imagined itself to be at war with a weak, vulnerable people, and destroyed them using modern industrial techniques for which European civilization was celebrated. It was so incredibly demonic that, in some subconscious way, those in our own society who wish to project the image of evil find the appropriate paraphernalia in the outfit of the SS—black leather jackets, Nazi medals and helmets, jack boots, motorcycles, and always the color black. It has reinforced group paranoia until there is no certainty that a conspiracy for murder is not in the air. Jews, after all, once lived in a world that wanted to kill them and offered them no quarter or shelter. That is a classic paranoid nightmare; but it really happened.

The uniqueness of the Holocaust does not lie merely in the radicalness of evil, nor even in the immensity of its scale. The Holocaust is a central historical event that has radically altered the flow of Jewish as well as Western civilization. It did so in two ways. The Final Solution marked the juncture where the European industrial system went awry; instead of enhancing life, which was the original hope of the Enlightenment, it began to consume itself. It was by dint of that industrial system and the ethos attached to it that Europe was able to dominate the world. Secondly, by destroying the Jews of Europe, it destroyed the communities which produced a good portion of the modernizing elite who helped push Western civilization forward.

Let us turn to the first point. Auschwitz, the symbol of the Holocaust, has been called another planet. But it was also a mundane extension of the modern factory system. Rather than producing goods, the raw material was human beings and the end-product was death, so many units per day marked carefully on the manager's production charts. The chimneys, the very symbol of the modern factory system, poured forth acrid smoke produced by burning human flesh. The brilliantly organized railroad grid of modern Europe carried a new kind of raw material to the factories. It did so in the same manner as with other cargo. In the gas chambers, the victims inhaled noxious gas generated by prussic acid pellets, which were produced by the advanced chemical industry of Germany. Engineers designed the crematoria; managers designed the system of bureaucracy that worked with a zest and efficiency more backward nations would envy. Even the overall plan itself was a reflection of the modern scientific spirit gone awry. What we witnessed was nothing less than a massive scheme of social engineering, of "redoing" society on the basis of "scientific" racial eugenics. That was not true of the murders of the Armenians, the Ibos, the Burundians, the Indonesians, the Cambodians, the Kulaks, and the many other groups who have been victims of massive barbarity.

I have said that the second major factor differentiating the Holocaust is the uniqueness of the Jews, who were its primary victims. I do not mean here the uniqueness a group assigns to itself but the unique position of Jews in the culture of the West, the special relationship that Jews and the modernizing elite they produced had in European culture. Whether one calls them "creative wanderers" as George Steiner does, or "conscious pariahs" as Hannah Arendt did, or a "universalizing elite" as I do makes little difference. What is important is that Europe would simply not be able to think of itself the way it does without the conceptualizations of Marx, Freud, Wittgenstein, von Neumann, and the hundreds of other Jewish intellectuals and thinkers with Jewish sensibilities. The principal characteristic of this opinion-making elite was its universalizing, global, transnational view of things. That was true for the neutral science, whose truths were everywhere the same, the Espéranto movement, the psychoanalytic movement, and socialism. That tendency towards transnationalism may, in the end, have been based on the fact that while there existed a *K'lal* or *Knesset Yisrael* (the Jewish people), Jews were, in fact, dispersed among the nations. Much of the development of Jewish secular organizational life after the mid-nineteenth century—the French *Alliance*, the British Board of Deputies, the German *Hilfsverein*, and the American Jewish Committee—addressed themselves to persecuted Jewish communities wherever they might be. Jewish globalism was a physical as well as an ideological datum.

The idea of an internationally guaranteed world order was staunchly supported by Jews, whose own vulnerability required its protection. The Holocaust period was not the first instance when Jews turned to the "international community" with a special plea for help. Jewish leaders had, in fact, been asking for some form of international protection at every major international conference since the Congress of Vienna in 1815. One might almost conclude that the very idea of an international order was a projection of the Jewish imagination based on a Jewish need. Jews were perennially asking the world to be better than it wanted to be.

Jewish thinkers and organizations did not only project their universalism outward. It had enormous impact on the interior life of Jews as well. Virtually every ideology accepted by the Jewish masses in the post-Enlightenment period possessed a strong universalist component. This was true of the Zionism of Achad Ha'am, the cultural nationalism of Simon Dubnow, the socialism of Medem's Bund (General Union of Jewish Workers in Lithuania, Poland, and Russia), and the universalism of the Liberal-Reform movement in Germany.

By perverting the very ethos and technology which allowed

Western civilization to dominate the world, Europe set the stage for itself to become the backwater of history. Indeed, Raymond Aron is accurate in observing that Europe has lost its elan, its self-confidence. It no longer even possesses the will to defend itself. How could it be otherwise with Auschwitz in its closet?

What happened at Auschwitz *is* different. What happened there is a portent. The ideology and system which gave rise to it remains intact. This means that the nation-state itself is out of control and capable of triggering acts of social cannibalism on an undreamed-of scale. If not checked, it can consume an entire civilization in fire. It cannot carry a humanitarian mission; its trespasses cannot be checked by legal and moral codes; it has no conscience.

### For Further Reading

Bauer, Yehuda, and Rotenstreich, Nathan. *The Holocaust as Historical Experience.* New York: Holmes & Meier, 1981.

Fein, Helen. *Accounting for Genocide.* New York: Macmillan Co., 1979.

Feingold, Henry L. "Determining the Uniqueness of the Holocaust: The Factor of Historical Valence." *Shoah* 2 (Spring 1981): 3-11.

Kren, George M., and Rappoport, Leon. *The Holocaust and the Crisis of Human Behavior.* New York: Holmes & Meier, 1980.

Rubenstein, Richard. *The Cunning of History: The Holocaust and the American Future,* New York: Harper Colophon Books, 1978.

# The Threefold Covenant:
# Jewish Belief After the Holocaust

## DANIEL LANDES

Analysis of Jewish religious self-understanding after the Holocaust must begin with a consideration of Jewish belief before this event. Since the Destruction of the Temple and the subsequent Exile, Jews have existed outside the mainstream of majority history. This position resulted from persecution and the majority's lack of interest in the spiritual life of a formerly great but presently obscure and somewhat mysterious minority. As individuals, Jews continuously contributed to Western civilization, but there was an acquiescense to their communal passivity and invisibility. The lack of prominence had certain advantages: It often kept them out of harm's way; visible, they were endangered. Since they existed outside of power, they did not participate in the violent excesses of the West (even if they were often its victims). Jews did not have to compromise their ideals or distort their faith in the battle for temporal control and earthly wealth.

Even survival, often at crisis, was only seen as a necessary condition for Israel's vocation and not a goal in its own right. Jews considered themselves God's chosen people.[1] This entailed the creation of a society that believed man to be created in the *zelem elokim* (image of God; "Let us make man in Our image, after Our likeness"—Genesis 1:26). To further this ideal, *halakhah* (Jewish law) promoted peace, justice, equity, and congenial relations between men; it also sought to connect man in prayer, ritual, and study with the transcendent. While this was accomplished within the Jewish covenantal community, there was an implicit albeit little proclaimed significance for mankind. *Zelem elokim*, as man's inheritance and imperative, would at some date be learned from Israel. In exchange for this faithful preservation of *zelem elokim*, it was the covenantal responsibility of the non-Jew to allow the people of Israel to live. At the same time, it was the pledge of God to preserve Israel for this future destiny.[2]

The Holocaust threatened to sever the bonds tying the Jew with the rest of mankind, his own people, and God. A Jew today knows that in the twentieth century he (or his fellow Jew) stood alone, bereft of support and comfort as a strange "other" in the face of unwarranted, ruthless, and total destruction. This knowledge corrodes trust and fundamental commonality that must serve as the basis of constructive cooperation between Jews and non-Jews in the post-Holocaust world. It is not merely Israel's relationship to mankind that has been imperiled. Ideally and romantically, one expects that shared adversity would lead to complete unity among Jews. Families that suffered major trauma during the war underwent great internal stress with guilt, recrimination, and assignment of blame for the tragedy upon other family members. These intense pressures, which can destroy a family, can also wreak havoc on a people, especially if they expect little or no respite from further trials. Furthermore, the Jew who believes in a God whose providence extends over the world, cannot bear His abandonment of the chosen people during the Holocaust. The convenant that binds Israel to God appears violated by God's refusal to rescue them during their most desperate need.

In fact, many laymen and theologians have concluded that one or more of these bonds were severed. Some gave up hope in Israel and its God and have sought sanctuary in assimilating into other nations. Others committed to Israel felt that salvation was only to be found within, and angrily rejected spirituality as a dead-end leading to irrelevance, quietism, and death. Still others affirmed their bond with God but turned away from the world that rejected them. They are content to await a more propitious moment in history (or messianically, at the end of history). Their radical suspicion of the world extends even to fellow Jews who are active participants in contemporary society.

Jewish belief in the post-Holocaust era is based on an overwhelming choice to maintain these bonds either partly or fully. This resilient faithfulness must be explored. Those who have remained within the Jewish community accept the inescapable condition of their Jewishness, finding succor and support within their own community. The Holocaust is converted from a threat into a prod to Jewish existence. Indeed, in a strange transfiguration it has become a badge of honor: "The people of Israel lives," even if only as a saving remnant. While these feelings have, at times, dissolved into an easy and eventually empty triumphalism, they express the desire not to opt out of Israel and thereby "complete Hitler's work."[3] This essentially negative commitment is transformed when the Jew explores the significance of his peoplehood. Studying its history, he becomes aware of more than a lachrymose account of suffering and persecution: An epic of many dimensions and a rich heritage is revealed. The Jew thus hopes for a meaningful future, despite the stark and contrary evidence of the Holocaust.

Israel's bond with the rest of mankind similarly has an imposed quality. The Jewish community is inextricably connected economically, politically, and socially with the rest of the world. The nationalistic Jew who wishes the State of Israel to pursue an independent course—for "after the Holocaust, we owe the world nothing"—must acknowledge the web of international relationships and interdependencies that affect, shape, and often govern national policies and decision-making. Even the separatist Jew must react to the values and culture of the "outside world" which inexorably penetrates every household. The only real alternative for the Jew and his community is to participate intelligently within Western society, benefiting from and contributing to its technological and intellectual progress while exerting their own autonomous moral influence. This must be accompanied by a skepticism for the ideological roots of Western civilization, knowing the violent excesses they have either led to or condoned. The Jew recognizes, nonetheless, the greater danger that ensues when he is isolated from the rest of humanity.

Many Jews have also felt desperately compelled to remain faithful to their God. They understand Judaism to enhance life and to affirm its worth. Clinging to Judaism is thus identical with clinging to life. The source of values and meaning within life stems from God. Only He, in His majesty transcendent to the world, is beyond the radical pessimism of the Holocaust and the moral void it has opened. Jews fear that the utter negativity, futility, and deep nihilism that this event represents and induces may engulf all that survives. Their response is to seek meaning grounded in a reality totally distinct from despair. This approach is often interpreted as escapism. Even the most mystical approach to Judaism, however, leads man back to the world, the arena where his Torah is to be fulfilled. In any event, the believer feels compelled to accept God even with the awesome question raised by Auschwitz, rather than reject Him and the basis for value within life.

Jews have felt driven to renew the threefold covenant with mankind, their own community, and God, but this has not resolved the tensions resulting from the Holocaust. The strains are more evident in the affirmation of the covenant "in spite of all that happened" than by its denial. The threefold covenant cannot evade an honest (and not just professed) confrontation with the Final Solution. Refusal, in the long run, is devastating: It denies the Jew's own self-worth, dismissing his significance as a historical being. It is a religious failure, implying that the resources of Judaism are insufficient to meet the harsh challenges of threatening nature. It is dangerous, because it prevents a community from learning the lessons of the past in order to prepare intelligently for future risks. It is morally insensitive, for it closes one's heart to the suffering of the powerless and the innocent. Finally, this leads to the invalid assumption that one can understand the Jew's vocation in post-capitalist civilization without considering its major public event.

The most readily available theory to account for the Holocaust is the traditional teaching of reward and punishment,[4] whose major application until now has been to the Destruction and Exile. In this doctrine, Jews are of central interest to God. He rewards and punishes them according to the morality of their deeds and the purity of their service. The people of Israel's worldly persecutors are unknowing rods of His wrath, but they are not excused for their malicious zeal and ruthless behavior. The doctrine of reward and punishment functions as a theodicy, explaining the existence of evil, shaping events, and clearing God of any fault. The onus is upon Israel, who bears the responsibility for its own actions and thus for its own fate. Despite the harshness of this teaching, there is an implied optimism: Just as a nation can deserve punishment, it can also merit reward. The suffering of the Destruction and Exile was accompanied by prophecy, through which the people of Israel were exhorted to examine their deeds and move to a higher plane in their relationship to others and to God.

The doctrine of reward and punishment applied to the Holocaust results in bizarre and disturbing conclusions. It necessitates the search for a sin that merited the attempted extermination of an entire people. Since a sin of such magnitude is obviously not present, it would have to be manufactured. Speculation in this direction leads to paralleling the antisemitic assumption of the Nazis: The Jews deserve the cruelest of fates. Additionally, the assignment of this responsibility to Israel is inherently a crushing burden, causing inner fragmentation and mutual recrimination.[5] It is not surprising that the most vigorous exponents of this view have distanced themselves from the Jewish community.

This theory also fails as a defense of God, attributing actions to Him which could be ascribed to a monster. It is not adequate to respond that God's punishment of Israel is "beyond our understanding." This ascribed action runs *counter* to our understanding of morality, as formed and shaped by His own Torah. Finally, the application of this doctrine to the Holocaust fails to account for the fact that the Nazis were not unknowing instrumentalities but self-motivated haters whose world program had a unique intentionality directed against the Jews.

No religious doctrine can "explain" why the Holocaust happened. Prior Jewish suffering has been subsumed under the Destruction and Exile. These twin episodes, however, were accompanied by prophecy, which first warned and later determined the reason for punishment. The Holocaust, as a unique occurrence, cannot be understood as a part of these other tragedies. At the same time, no heavenly voice has broken Divine silence to elucidate its meaning. We are left with an historical event which can only be analyzed in those terms. This does not suggest that the Holocaust lacks religious importance. It does mean that a religious understanding of the Holocaust cannot ignore, but must rest on, a profound historical inquiry into the complex and confusing components of the event.

A major element in this approach is the realization that, unlike the Destruction and Exile, the Holocaust was not inevitable. Things could have happened differently if participants and bystanders had made other decisions. The Holocaust as history presumes full human responsibility. It is only within this context that a contemporary meaning of the threefold covenant and Israel's vocation can be found.

An approach to this threefold covenant is suggested by a passage describing the essence of Israel in the writings of Abraham Isaak Kook, the early twentieth-century European talmudist, thinker, and later chief rabbi of *Erez Israel* (the Land of Israel). Rabbi Kook's works are not readily accessible to many readers. The writing is allusive, evocative, and mystically charged. It posits an underlying unity to reality having been created by One God. His thought, in addition (or, in consequence), conveys an unbounded optimism. Writing before the Holocaust, Rabbi Kook held what in retrospect was a naive confidence in the progress and moral ascent of man.

Rabbi Kook's theory of Israel, nevertheless, presents a vivid depiction of its chosenness in relation to mankind. Further, Kook's mysticism does not obscure but rather heightens Israel as an immanent entity, acting out its destiny within this world. Any definition of chosenness will entail a transcendent purpose, but Rabbi Kook's formulation of this doctrine is accomplished not at the expense of history but rather through it. With this acceptance of history, Kook's theory allows for the Holocaust to be confronted. It does so at the risk of the theory itself being transformed from a spirited optimism to a sober realism redeemed by a radical belief in God and His promise.

> *Knesset Israel* (the people of Israel) is the microcosm of all existence. This refers, in a worldly context, to Israel's material and spiritual dimensions—both its saga and it's faith. Israel's history is the ideal microcosm of universal history. There is no social fluctuation among the peoples of the world that you will not find its prototype in Israel. Its faith is the well-sifted essence as well as the influential source of the good and the ideal of all faiths. In this sense, Israel's faith serves as a resource that reviews belief systems with the goal of elevating their discourse so that all may call in the Name of the Lord; your God, "the Separate One of Israel, shall be called the God of the entire earth."
>
> *Knesset Israel* is the sublime revelation of the spirit, within human existence. One does not doubt that the manifestations of life contained within the brain and the heart are not to be found to a similiar degree elsewhere in the body. Identically, one cannot doubt—although a sensitive soul and a thoughtful mind will marvel at—the manifestations of life, wonders, miracles, prophecy, the highest degree of divine inspiration, eternal hope, victory over every obstacle, revealed in an exalted form within Israel. *Knesset Israel* is the revelation of the arm of the Lord within the world, His hand in existence, and His participation within the development of nations. It is intimately connected to all that is exalted, venerable, holy, and lofty within the entire physical and spiritual scope of reality. It is impossible to think otherwise.[6]

Underneath Rabbi Kook's extravagant language is the rejection of any absolute disjunction between Israel and mankind. Israel is not a different form of man; he is man. This is more than a state of being. Israel's vocation and destiny is *to be* human and to share in all that is human, both materially and spiritually. The truth of the Torah is not separate from the truths contained within other systems, nor are the latter considered to be deviant forms of Torah. Rather, it is Israel's task to engage in a critical dialogue with mankind in order to declare monotheism—man's responsibilities to one another and to God. All nations and peoples share in the *ẕelem elokim* in that reality is a creation of God, and man the crowning jewel. The meaning of Israel's election is to be the flesh-and-blood bearer of monotheism's message: to cherish the human and the transcendent.

Israel's election does not assure an easy triumph for *ẕelem elokim*, despite Rabbi Kook's colorful messianic expectations. The Jewish people were not incidental victims of World War II. The attempt to exterminate them went beyond political expediency and was even counterproductive to the German war effort. Nazi hatred for the people of Israel had a unique intentionality[7] and was the very basis of its ideology and purpose. Standing at the center of mankind, Israel became the target. The Nazi attack upon Israel was thus an attack upon man himself. Nazi hatred of Israel was hatred turned against the image of man. By denying humanity to the Jews, the Nazis denied their own. Ultimately, it was a self-hatred.

From where does this self-hatred derive? Judaism has maintained that violence perpetrated upon man is rebellion against God, in that man is God's image upon earth. The refusal to consider another as in His image is the desire to cast off the yoke of His image that the hater himself bears and the manifold ethical responsibilities that he is charged with. It is a rejection of meaning and responsibility and a descent into nihilism. A religious understanding of the Final Solution yields this cursed equation: hatred of Israel = hatred of man = self-hatred = hatred of God.

The Holocaust is a paradigmatic event for all mankind. It is a microcosm of ultimate violence and tragedy within the modern nation-states of the West.[8] The Holocaust was not a sacrificial event in which the death of six million Jews expatiates the possibilities of such murder of others. It was, rather, a breakthrough event that threatens its own uniqueness by setting a genocidal pattern for other peoples in other situations. The Holocaust is a dark revelation of man's capacities for participating in (the Nazis and their followers) and acquiescing to (the Allies and others) systematic and total destruction. The Holocaust of that people dedicated to bearing the human and divine image heralds the Nuclear Age, where man's self-destruction is contemplated, planned for, and even played at in wargame scenarios. It announces a technological era in which means of dehumanization and methods of torture are mass produced, increasingly sophisticated, and generally ignored. What befell the Jews now threatens all people.

The Holocaust is revelational *of* man but also *to* man. In that sense, its religious understanding is an historical understanding. Its significance is historical in that it not only provides the background for contemporary society but also points the path where the future may lead. The exploration and teaching of the Holocaust becomes a religious obligation of Israel, who, seeking the continuation of *ẕelem elokim*, is the exposed and vulnerable arm of God in history. Man, a morally autonomous and free agent, may reject God and His people.[10] Israel, as the servant of the Lord, has suffered the wrath of those who rebelled against its master. Grieviously hurt, Israel has chosen to renew its threefold covenant. For Israel, the Holocaust has imperiled the mission of the chosen people but, paradoxically, has also confirmed it. The renewal of His service takes on a new dimension of desperate urgency in an age when man stands in mutual threat and self-alienation. Israel draws stength from the prophet who charged that he (Israel) "shall not fail nor be crushed until he has rectified the world, for the islands await his teachings" (Isaiah 42:4).

### Notes

1.   Judah Haleui, *Kuzari* (standard editions) 3:36.
2.   Isaiah 54:10.
3.   Emil Fackenheim, *God's Presence in History* (New York: New York University Press, 1969), p. 84.
4.   Eliezer Berkovits, *Faith After the Holocaust* (New York: Ktav, 1973), pp. 86-94.
5.   Yoel Teitelbaum, *Sefer Vayoel Moshe.* Brooklyn: 5721. p. 5.
6.   Abraham Isaac Kook, *Orot* (Jerusalem: Mossad HaRav Kook, 1961), p. 138.
7.   Steven T. Katz, "The Unique Intentionality of the Holocaust," *Modern Judaism* (September 1981): 161-183.
8.   See "How Unique Is the Holocaust?" by Henry L. Feingold, in this volume.
9.   Irving Greenberg, *Voluntary Covenant* (Monograph) (New York: National Jewish Resource Center, 1982), pp. 21-28.
10.   Joseph B. Soloveitchik, *Lessons in Jewish Thought: Adapted from the Lectures of Rabbi Joseph B. Soloveitchik,* ed. Abraham Besdin (Jerusalem: World Zionist Organization, 1979), pp. 31-39; Berkovitz, *Faith,* pp. 94-113.

### For Further Reading

Berkovits, Eliezer. *Faith After The Holocaust.* New York: Ktav, 1973.

Fackenheim, Emil. *God's Presence in History.* New York: New York University Press, 1969.

————. *The Jewish Return into History: Reflections in the age of Auschwitz and New Jerusalem.* New York: Schocken Books, 1978.

Greenberg, Irving. "Cloud of Smoke, Pillar of Fire: Judaism, Christianity, and Modernity After the Holocaust." In Eva Fleishner, ed., *Auschwitz: Beginning of a New Era?* New York: Ktav, 1977.

Rubenstein, Richard L. *After Auschwitz.* Indianapolis: The Bobbs-Merrill Company, Inc., 1968.

Soloveichik, Joseph B. *Lessons in Jewish Thought: Adapted from the Lectures of Rabbi Joseph B. Soloveichik.* Edited by Abraham Besdin. Jerusalem: World Zionist Organization, 1979.

# Implications of the Holocaust for the Christian Churches

## JOHN T. PAWLIKOWSKI

The impact of the Holocaust has been felt only slowly, one might even say grudgingly, in Christian theological and educational circles. Dr. Eva Fleischner's study of the postwar theological scene in Germany concludes that few, if any, of its leading theologians had taken the Holocaust with any seriousness.[1] Similar results would generally be the case for the rest of Europe and North America. Professor Alice Eckardt's survey is confirmation of this. She writes:

> Whatever aspect of response one looks at—historical, theological, psychological, existential—it is overwhelmingly that of Jews, individually and collectively. If we say that this is to be expected and is quite normal, we are only giving away the very problem: that nothing normal should prevail after the most fearful abnormality in human history. It further assumes that the Holocaust is primarily a *Jewish* problem— whereas in fact it is, in far deeper respects, a Christian problem.[2]

In the field of popular religious education within the churches, silence again appears as the rule rather than the exception. A scientific study of Catholic schools (primary through seminary) throughout the country undertaken by the American Jewish Committee and the Institute of Judaic-Christian Studies in 1970 showed virtually no consideration of the topic at Catholic colleges and only slightly better exposure at other levels.[3] And if we examine the international and regional statements on Christian-Jewish relations issued over the last two decades by various Christian bodies, hardly any mention of the Holocaust is found.[4] When postwar Christianity was challenged about its stance during the Nazi era, the responses were, usually, defensive. The preference was to bury rather than to probe. The churches were incapable of seriously examining their collective conduct during the Nazi era, which some Christian and Jewish voices were beginning to call a serious challenge to Christianity's moral integrity.

Fortunately, the silence about Auschwitz in the Christian churches was not total. Pioneering names like Gordon Zahn, in his sociological study *German Catholics and Hitler's Wars*,[5] and in his prize-winning biography of the Austrian peasant resister Franz Jagerstatter.[6] and Guenter Lewy in *The Catholic Church and Nazi Germany*,[7] were beginning to lift the veil. Rolf Hochhuth's *The Deputy* also opened discussion. This play, which engendered much controversy, including public demonstrations against its performance in several American cities, helped, without doubt, to force the issue of the Holocaust into the consciousness of a growing number of Christians.[8]

These initial responses were still limited in scope. Even today's more advanced studies on the Holocaust may need further revision as new archival materials become available. But the Christian community owes these early writers on the Holocaust a profound debt of gratitude for helping us to remember.

Over the past decade, the scene has changed considerably, and for the better. Admittedly, indifference to the theological and moral challenge of the Holocaust continues unabated in some sectors of Christianity. Among Third World Christians, there is the often-expressed view that this is not their problem, but one confined to the Western churches. Nonetheless, there has emerged a steadily growing willingness on the part of Christian leaders to address the implications of the Holocaust experience. Figures like Franklin Littell, A. Roy Eckardt, and Edward Flannery have led the way, with new scholars entering the subject on a regular basis. The following statement of Protestant theologian Elwyn Smith captures well the spirit of these new Christian investigations into the challenge of Auschwitz:

> Was not the Holocaust a terrible test—which the church failed? ... It may be ... that the question whether Christianity is to remember the Holocaust or dismiss it is a question of the ability and the right of Christianity to survive in a form in any way conformable to the Scriptures.[9]

In addition to intensified scholarly research on the Holocaust within the Christian community, many Holocaust conferences have been held throughout the country during the last few years, and the NBC and other network television specials have brought Christian educators to a new awareness of this pivotal event for both the Church and the Jewish people. Without exaggeration, there is little doubt that the Holocaust and its implications are beginning to receive a serious hearing within a broad spectrum of the Christian community. Liberated from the extreme defensiveness characteristic of the immediate postwar decade, an increasing number of faithful Christians are willing to probe the subject rather than bury it.

As the Christian community continues to examine the Auschwitz experience, the following themes are emerging. A number of present-day theologians have begun to ask what difference the Holocaust makes for basic Christian faith affirmations, such as Christology. Questions like this are raised by such leading figures as Johannes Metz, David Tracy, Gregory Baum, and Jurgen Moltmann. Moltmann, more than any other Christian theologian thus far, has tried to incorporate Auschwitz into the core of his interpretation of the Christ Event. This is developed especially in his volume *The Crucified God*,[10] in which he maintains that Auschwitz shows us, perhaps more dramatically than any other reality, the root meaning of the Christ Event—God can save people, including Israel, because through the cross he participated in their very suffering. Post-Auschwitz theology would be an impossibility in Moltmann's thinking . . .

> ...were not the Sch'ma Israel and the Lord's Prayer prayed in Auschwitz itself, were not God Himself in Auschwitz, suffering with the martyred and murdered. Every other answer would be blasphemy. An absolute God would make us indifferent. The God of action and success would let us forget the dead, which we still cannot forget. God as Nothingness would make the entire world into a concentration camp.[11]

The Lutheran ethicist, Franklin Sherman, expresses the Christology-Auschwitz connection in a way that closely parallels Moltmann's position:

> For Christianity the symbol of the agonizing God is the Cross of Christ. It is tragic that this symbol should have become a symbol of division between Jews and Christians, for the reality to which it points is a Jewish reality as well, the reality of suffering and martyrdom.[12]

The cross, as Sherman understands it, reveals to us, in the first instance, a profoundly Jewish reality. Subsequent interpretation by Christians of the sufferings of Jesus must always be conscious of this Jewish reality. The God of the post-Auschwitz age is the God who calls all people into a new unity, not only a unity between Jews and Christians, but one in which that unity bears a particular significance.

The Israeli Catholic scholar, Dr. Marcel Dubois, follows much the same line as Moltmann and Sherman in his analysis of the Holocaust. He is not unaware of the difficulties in trying to locate Auschwitz within a theology of the cross. Such a linkage may, indeed, seem blasphemous to Jews, given Christianity's role in the Holocaust. Nonetheless, he feels compelled to affirm the connection:

> . . . . In the person of the Suffering Servant, there appears to take place an ineffable change. Our vision of Jewish destiny and our understanding of the Holocaust, in particular, depends on our compassion; the Calvary of the Jewish People, whose summit is the Holocaust, can help us to understand a little better the mystery of the Cross.[13]

These attempts to set Auschwitz within a Christian theology of the cross have met with mixed reactions from several other theologians. Professor A. Roy Eckardt has taken strong exception, particularly to Moltmann. He feels that there is no way Christians can assert that the Jewish victims of the Holocaust were *liberated* from death or from any suffering through Christ's Crucifixion. To make such a claim in light of Christian involvement with the Nazi Final Solution amounts to blasphemy. He writes:

> What does it mean to tell the inmates of Buchenwald or Bergen-Belsen, as this Christian theologian does, that "through his suffering and death, the Risen Christ brings righteousness and life to the unrighteous and the dying?"[14]

For Eckardt, Moltmann simply claims too much for the sufferings of Christ. "It may be contended," he argues, "that in comparison with certain other sufferings, Jesus' death becomes relatively nonsignificant."[15]

A Canadian theologian, Douglas J. Hall, is generally much more sympathetic to Moltmann's perspective and the Holocaust theology of the cross-link. It remains his conviction that the development of the theology of the cross is the only way to finally overcome the type of Christological thinking in the churches which inevitably winds up in the antisemitism manifested in the Holocaust. A Christology built around the reality of the cross establishes what Hall terms a "soteriology of solidarity," which by definition sets up the cross of Jesus as a point of fraternal union (which does not mean conversion) with the Jewish people, and with all in need of liberation and peace:

> . . . The faith of Israel is incomprehensible unless one sees at its heart a suffering God whose solidarity with humanity is so abysmal that the "cross in the heart of God" [H. Wheeler Robinson] must always be incarnating itself in history. Reading the works of Elie Wiesel, one knows, as a Christian, that he bears this indelible resemblance to the people of Israel.[16]

Undoubtedly, this theme of the Holocaust-Crucifixion link will continue to be debated by Christian scholars. It is my opinion that while there is some merit in positing the link, it should not be made the center of Christian theology after the Holocaust.

The meaning of the Church, or ecclesiology as theologians call it, has also undergone new scrutiny in the light of the Holocaust. The Austrian Catholic philosopher, Frederich Heer, locates the main problem in a theological vision of the Church, long dominant in the Church and attributable to St. Augustine, which removes the Church from the sphere of history:

> The withdrawal of the church from history has created that specifically Christian and ecclesiastical irresponsibility towards the world, the Jew, the other person, even the Christian himself, considered as a human being—which was the ultimate cause of past catastrophes and may be the cause of a final catastrophe in the future.[17]

Unless Christianity reestablishes a link with the Hebrew Bible's roots of Christ's own piety, the antihistorical conception of the Church that caused Christian indifference to the plight of the Jews under Hitler may engender the same unconcern about the growing threat of a worldwide nuclear catastrophe.

Gordon Zahn has also reflected on the implications of the Holocaust for the Christian conception of the Church. For him, the one overriding lesson to be gained from an examination of Auschwitz is that:

> . . . the religious community must never again become so enmeshed in its support for a given socio-political order that it loses its potential to be a source of dissent and disobedience. In other more familiar terms, the church must recognize that it has a stake in maintaining a separation of church and state as that separation is defined from its own perspective.[18]

The attempt to construct a theological vision that will conceive of the Church as sufficiently part of history to see that human suffering—like that endured by the Jewish people at the hands of the Nazis—poses a definite threat to its own meaningful existence, while at the same time standing in critical judgment over particular movements in history, as Gordon Zahn urges, will prove a difficult task. But it is one that remains a primary obligation after the Auschwitz experience.

The Holocaust also forces the Christian community to examine more thoroughly the possible roots of antisemitism in the New Testament. None of the current Christian commentators on the Holocaust wishes to draw a straight line from negative New Testament portrayals of Judaism to the Final Solution. Most would stress that the primary origins of nazism are to be found in modern secular racial theories. Nonetheless, it is being increasingly admitted by Christian scholars that the architects of nazism found their targets well-primed for the formulation of their racist theories because of centuries of antisemitism in the churches going back to New Testament times. Dr. Edward Flannery expresses this perspective well:

> The degraded state of the Jews, brought about by centuries of opprobrium and oppression, gave support to the invidious comparisons with which the racists built their theories. And in their evil design, they were able to draw moral support from traditional Christian views of Jews and Judaism.[19]

There is little doubt that traditional Christian antisemitism provided an indispensable seedbed for the popular support accorded in many Christian quarters to nazism's attack on the Jewish people.

Another area that is being explored by Christian scholars in collaboration with their Jewish colleagues is the impact of the Holocaust on the religious and political fabric of Western society. Franklin Littell and the various conferences held in Philadelphia under the auspices of the Philadelphia Coordinating Council on the Holocaust have addressed this point.[20] It has also been a special focus of my own writings on the Holocaust.[21] The realization is emerging that the Holocaust was not an isolated example of insane human brutality. Rather, it marked the coming together of many of the major forces shaping contemporary Western society: bureaucracy, technology, and the loss of transcendent morality. The Holocaust has shattered not only much of Christianity's traditional moral base, but that of Western liberal society as well. It has truly marked the beginning of a new era in human history.

Other more specific problems will also need the attention of the churches. The question of evil and the Holocaust explored recently by A. Roy Eckardt, Gregory Baum, and André LaCocque is one of these. In addition, a recent volume by Harry James Cargas spells out some fourteen areas that require Christian response in light of Auschwitz. Among them is the formal excommunication of Adolf Hitler by the Catholic church, and a plea that:

> . . . . the heavy Christian emphasis on missionizing should be redirected toward perfecting individual Christian lives. Missionary efforts, however well-intentioned, are generally not as well received by the presumed beneficiaries as they are enthusiastically endorsed by those of the performing group. Perhaps Christians might comprehend this better if they tried to convert us to Judaism. The true missionary activity, we must realize, is in the perfection of our individual, personal lives. If what we do, if how we live, is worthy of emulation, that will be missionary activity enough.[22]

One final point. The increase in Holocaust awareness within Christianity has produced some negative reactions, particularly within sections of the Catholic community. Basically, the objections have focused on what some Catholics believe to be an overly negative image of the Church portrayed in Holocaust studies and the failure to deal adequately with the non-Jewish victims. On the first point, Christians must be prepared to examine critically the actions of their church. This is a sign of mature faith. But there needs to be greater attention given to those "righteous Christians" who did respond to the Jewish plight. As for the non-Jewish victims, while the special nature of the Jewish suffering under the Nazis must be preserved—for them there was no escape—the extermination and oppression of Slavs, Gypsies, the mentally and physically handicapped, and homosexuals must also receive a better hearing. They, too, were victims of the genocidal thrust that was at the heart of the Nazi desire to "purify" humanity.

**Notes**

1. Eva Fleishner, *Judaism in German Christian Theology Since 1945* (Metuchen, NJ: The Scarecrow Press, 1975).
2. Alice Eckardt, "The Holocaust: Christian and Jewish Responses," *Journal of the American Academy of Religion* 42 (September 1974): 453.
3. See John T. Pawlikowski, "The Teaching of Contempt: Judaism in Christian Education and Liturgy," in *Auschwitz*, ed. Eva Fleischner (New York: Ktav, 1972), p. 160.
4. See Helga Croner, ed., *Stepping Stones* (London: Stimulus Books, 1977).
5. Gordon Zahn, *German Catholics and Hitler's Wars* (New York: Sheed & Ward, 1962).
6. Gordon Zahn, *In Solitary Witness* (New York: Holt, Rinehart, and Winston, 1964).
7. Guenter Lewy, *The Catholic Church and Nazi Germany* (New York: McGraw-Hill, 1964).
8. Rolf Hochhuth, *The Deputy* (New York: Grove Press, 1964). See also Eric Bentley, ed., *The Storm Over The Deputy* (New York: Grove Press, 1964).
9. Elwyn Smith, "The Christian Meaning of the Holocaust," *Journal of Ecumenical Studies* 6 (Summer 1969): 421-422.
10. Jurgen Moltmann, *The Crucified God* (New York: Harper & Row, 1974). For a condensation, see "The Crucified God," *Theology Today* 31 (April 1974).
11. Moltmann, "The Crucified God," p. 10.
12. Franklin Sherman, "Speaking of God after Auschwitz," *Worldview* 17 (September 1974): 29. See also Sherman's essay on the same theme in *Speaking of God Today*, eds. Paul D. Opsahl and Marc H. Tanenbaum (Philadelphia: Fortress Press, 1974).
13. Marcel Dubois, "Christian Reflections on the Holocaust," *Sidic* 7 (1974): 15.
14. A. Roy Eckardt, "Christians and Jews along a Theological Frontier," *Encounter* 40 (Spring 1979): 102.
15. Eckardt, "Christians and Jews," p. 103.
16. Douglas J. Hall, "Rethinking Christ," in *Antisemitism and the Foundations of Christianity*, ed. Alan T. Davies (New York: Paulist Press, 1979), p. 183.
17. Frederich Heer, *God's First Love* (New York: Weybright and Talley, 1970), p. 406.
18. Gordon Zahn, "Catholic Resistance? A Yes and a No," *The German Church Struggle and the Holocaust*, eds. Franklin H. Littel and Hubert G. Locke (Detroit: Wayne State University Press, 1974), p. 234.
19. Edward Flannery, "Anti-Zionism and the Christian Psyche," *Journal of Ecumenical Studies* 6 (Spring 1969): 174-175.
20. See, for example, Franklin H. Littell, "The Credibility Crisis of the Modern University," in *The Holocaust: Ideology, Bureaucracy, and Genocide*, eds. Henry Friedlander and Sybil Milton

(Millwood, NY: Kraus International Publications, 1980), pp. 271-284, and Glora Coleman, SHCJ, ed., *Proceedings of the Fifth Philadelphia Conference on the Holocaust* (1979).

21.  See John T. Pawlikowski, *The Challenge of the Holocaust* (New York: Anti-Defamation League, 1978); Pawlikowski, "Christian Perspective and Moral Implications," in Friedlander and Milton, *The Holocaust*, pp. 295-308; and Pawlikowski, "The Holocaust: Its Implications for Church and Society Problematics," *Encounter* (Spring 1981).

22.  Harry James Cargas, *A Christian Response to the Holocaust* (Denver: Stonehenge Books, 1981).

23.  See, for example, Bohdan Wytwycky, *The Other Holocaust: Many Circles of Hell* (Washington, D.C.: The Novak Report, 1980).

### For Further Reading

Bentley, Eric, ed. *The Storm Over The Deputy*. New York: Grove Press, 1964.

Cargas, Harry James. *A Christian Response to the Holocaust*. Denver: Stonehenge Books, 1981.

———. *When God and Man Failed: Non-Jewish Views of the Holocaust*. New York: Macmillan Co., 1982.

Croner, Helga, ed. *Stepping Stones to Further Jewish-Christian Relations*. Lodon: Stimulus Books, 1977.

Fleischner, Eva, ed. *Auschwitz: Beginning of a New Era?* New York: Ktav, 1977.

Friedlander, Henry, and Milton, Sybil, eds. *The Holocaust: Ideology, Bureaucracy, and Genocide*. Millwood, NY: Kraus International Publications, 1980.

Heer, Frederich. *God's First Love*. New York: Weybright and Talley, 1970.

Hochhuth, Rolf. *The Deputy*. New York: Grove Press, 1964.

Lewy, Guenter. *The Catholic Church and Nazi Germany*. New York: McGraw-Hill, 1964.

Littell, Franklin H., and Locke, Hubert G., eds. *The German Church Struggle and the Holocaust*. Detroit: Wayne State University Press, 1974.

Moltmann, Jurgen. *The Crucified God.* New York: Harper & Row, 1974.

Pawlikowski, John T. *The Challenge of the Holocaust for Christian Theology.* New York: Anti-Defamation League, 1978.

―――. *Christ in the Light of the Christian-Jewish Dialogue.* Ramsey, NJ: Paulist Press, 1982.

Wytwycky, Bohdan. *The Other Holocaust: Many Circles of Hell.* Washington, D.C.: The Novak Report, 1980.

Zahn, Gordon. *German Catholics and Hitler's Wars.* New York: Sheed & Ward, 1962.

―――. *In Solitary Witness.* New York: Holt, Rinehart, and Winston, 1964.

# A Jewish Reflection on Christian Responses*

## DANIEL LANDES

Every Jew has ambiguous feelings when reflecting upon Christian responses to the Holocaust. For centuries, the suffering of the Jews has been significant for the Church, but only as proof of the punishment by God for their rejection of Jesus as the Savior. It is with bitterness that a Jew notes that it took the Holocaust to allow sensitive Christians to see the sufferings of Jews not as a testimony to the Church Triumphant, but rather as a spiritual challenge of the highest order to Christianity. Nonetheless, we must welcome serious and sensitive responses on the part of the Christian community. It is our belief that no man can ignore the Holocaust and its lessons. To do so is to invite future catastrophe. If this is true for the modern secular humanist, it is certainly no less true for the committed Christian. We share, in this nuclear world, a perilous existence as the shadow of the crematorium smokestack falls on us all.

A Jew has certain constraints as he considers the previous articles by Christian scholars. The Christian theological matrix is not his own. He shares neither its language not its symbols. His own faith-community has different presuppositions and different expectations. It takes a certain *chutzpah* (gall), therefore, to comment upon an understanding emanating from a different and "other" experience of faith. Still, a reflection that casts light upon certain basic concerns might be attempted.

I am bothered by Douglas Hall's statement that, "reading the works of Elie Wiesel, one knows, as a Christian, that he bears this indelible resemblance to the people of Israel." "Indelible resemblance" has a ring of "identity." An early trend of Christianity was to replace the identity of the People Israel with that of True Israel—that is, the Church. This allowed for the Jewish experience—the forefathers, the Exodus from Egypt, the writings of the prophets, and such symbols as the paschal lamb—to be assimilated into Christianity as the Jews themselves were disenfranchised.

Hall and others, such as Moltmann, may be leading to a parallel route with the Holocaust. The experience of the Jewish people from 1933 to 1945 is transformed into a Christian experience of the "mystery of the cross." True, the Jews are not disinherited from their experience. Indeed, they share in it in a "soteriology of solidarity" with Christians and with "all in need of liberation and peace." On one level, this may be looked upon as hopeful and healing. The cross now is no longer, in Douglas Hall's words, the "battering ram"[1] that

---

* This article refers to the preceding essay, "Implications of the Holocaust for the Christian Churches," by John T. Pawlikowski.

attempted to compel Jews to conform to Christian norms. A few points, however, must be considered by the Christian theologian:

1) Obviously, the Jew will never see the cross in Christian terms. This is not his symbol and its theology will never enter his language.

2) For the Jew, the Holocaust is not to be elided into any other framework of suffering. Indeed, he sees the Holocaust as a paradigmatic experience of suffering.

3) Most importantly, it is the experience only of the flesh-and-blood Jewish people. Others may participate to some degree, empathetically, in what took place. But it is those who died in the Holocaust and those who survived it, their children, and the future generations, who bear the scars of what took place on their own flesh and on their community.

4) Finally, as the sensitive non-Jew participates in the plight of the sufferers, he must remember his other role. He is a member of Western civilization, shaped in great measure by Christianity, which participated in or allowed for the death of six million Jews.

There were faithful Christians who undertook great risks to save Jews during the Holocaust. A number of them died in the attempt. I may suggest that these instances of heroism and of martyrdom be explored by Christian thinkers. They are also of great importance educationally. Young people encountering the Holocaust need to know these men and women who, acting from the dictates of their faith, embraced the difficult path of preserving life. Clearly, these individuals and few communities do not "balance out" the perpetrators and the bystanders; they do, however, offer powerful role models and symbols for the future.

### Notes

1.   Douglas Hall, "Rethinking Christ," in *Antisemitism and the Foundations of Christianity*, Alan T. Davies (New York: Paulist Press, 1979), p. 182.

### For Futher Reading

Baeck, Leo. *The Essence of Judaism*. Philadelphia: The Jewish Publication Society, 1958.

Berkovits, Eliezer. *Faith after the Holocaust.* New York: Ktav, 1973.

Borowitz, Eugene. *Contemporary Christologies: A Jewish Response.* New York: Paulist Press, 1980.

Davies, Alan T. *Antisemitism and the Foundations of Christianity.* New York: Paulist Press, 1979.

Greenberg, Irving. "Cloud of Smoke, Pillar of Fire: Judaism, Christianity, and Modernity after the Holocaust." In *Auschwitz: Beginning of a New Era?,* edited by Eva Fleischner. New York: Ktav, 1977.

McGarry, Michael B. *Christology after Auschwitz.* New York: Paulist Press, 1977.

Soloveitchik, Joseph B. "Confrontation." In *Studies in Judaica,* edited by Leon D. Stitskin. New York: Ktav and Yeshiva University Press, 1974.

# The Holocaust and Israel

## DANIEL LANDES

> On that long coast, we, the refugees and survivors, parted
> to go our various ways. Opposing impulses were intertwined
> there. Some turned their backs and left everything behind;
> others held tight to every remaining fragment and Jewish
> memory.
>
> I have not come to judge anyone. But let it be said that the
> desire of those who made the choice of *Erez Israel* was for a
> recovery beyond that of the body.[1]

The two significant events of the past 2,000 years of Jewish
history are the Holocaust and the establishment of the State of Israel.
We may consider them as events that mirror each other. The
Holocaust denied life and existence to anyone and anything Jewish.
Israel protects and affirms Jewish existence on every conceivable
level. As the Holocaust can be understood as Jewish powerlessness
and victimization, Israel is the expression of Jewish power and self-
determination.[2]

## Powerlessness and Power

The impotence of the Jews during the Holocaust does not deny
their many courageous decisions and actions. It does mean not only
that whatever power the Jewish people did exhibit was symbolic or
tragically limited, but that it also failed to accomplish the minimal
task of the protection of one's family. Thus, the Jewish partisan was
inspirational both to his generation and later to Israel, by inflicting
damage upon the enemy. But to fight effectively as a hunted Jewish
partisan in the forests and mountains of Europe, one had to be bereft
of or prepared to abandon one's family.[3] This contrasts sharply with
Israel, where a soldier's chief motivation is the defense of family.[4]

The story of the *Judenräte* (Jewish Councils) in the ghettos has
exposed the tragedy of limited autonomy. Within the framework of
implementing Nazi orders, they were able to assist and benefit their
brethren.[5] They could sometimes delay death, but their lack of real
power precluded them from saving lives. The bureaucracy of the
*Judenräte* was often implicated in the destruction. Here, too, the
situation in Israel is starkly different. A sovereign nation, Israel
makes its own decisions, even if it sometimes displeases its vastly
more powerful allies. While room is always open for negotiation and
compromise, Israel refuses to acquiesce to life-and-death decisions
made by others.

Included in the dismal sketch of Jewish impotence during the
Holocaust is the response of the American Jewish community. Its
failure—however it is understood—to exert greater and more effective
pressure upon the United States government indicates an enormous

weakness. With the establishment of Israel, this has also changed. American Jews have grown more vigorous in pursuing support for their endangered brothers. They know that a too-quiet diplomacy will only be ignored. American Jews no longer fear using American political sophistication to defend Israel.[6]

One could argue that this concern for Jewish power is naïve in thinking that it is a guarantee against tragedy. Obviously, there are no guarantees. But it is worth noting that the imagined power of the Jews was one element during the Holocaust that served to save some Jews.[7] Japan, Germany's ally, spared the lives of some 18,000 European Jews. Reading *The Protocols of the Elders of Zion* and remembering the loan granted to Japan by the American Jewish philanthropist Jacob Schiff during the Russo-Japanese War, the Japanese believed that the Jews controlled the United States. Wanting to keep an edge for possible peace negotiations, they left their hostages alone. Virulently antisemitic Rumania, which also believed that the Jews had some secret world power, delayed the deportation of its Jews, thereby saving the community from full destruction. There are a few other examples of perceived Jewish power amidst their actual powerlessness.

Israel's ability to make autonomous decisions supported by armed might is not a guarantee of ultimate protection. But without it, we are left with the tragic equation of the Holocaust: Antisemitism and Jewish powerlessness equals Mass Murder.[8] The State of Israel has eliminated the crucial factor from this equation: Jewish powerlessness.

At the same time, the experiences of 1933-1945 teach that a nation cannot stand alone. Early in the Holocaust, Jews were systematically and progressively set apart from the rest of society. This isolation set the stage for the Jews' ultimate murder by their enemies and their being ignored by the rest of the world.[9] International cooperation along with coalition building with countries who share mutual interests is an essential lesson of the Holocaust for Israel. Through strong political, social, economic, and cultural linkage with other nations, this small and potentially isolated country can voice its right to exist and reject the efforts of other nations to render it an outcast and pariah. Israel, therefore, fights to participate in all international political forums, athletic competitions, scientific seminars, and so on, in the face of Arab pressure to boycott them. Israel also often has to cooperate with nations which, in a more ideal world, it would have no dealings with.

The Holocaust additionally warns of the abuse of power. In Israeli policy, swift retaliation to aggression has always been balanced by restraint. The Israel Defense Force has pioneered the concept of *Tohar HaNeshek* (Purity of Arms). This term signifies a concrete application of ethics to the battlefield. It expresses concern for moral issues far beyond those sanctioned by international convention and practice, often involving considerable risk-taking.

The concern for the lives of others has often meant needless deaths of Israeli troops. Reflecting upon the death of two officers who were ambushed in an Arab hut by terrorists hiding behind a woman villager, a soldier writes: "They were fully aware of our weakness and exploited it—that damned hesitation that keeps us from playing to the hilt. That is the hesitation that says you must remain a human being, always decent, always defeating the enemy while endangering yourself to the utmost."[10] The exercise of power within a moral framework ensures that this tension of action and hesitation will remain unresolved until the time arrives that the Jew is no longer looked upon as a potential victim.

## Theological Impact

The dialectic of Jewish powerlessness and power has had a profound impact upon theology. Christianity has traditionally understood the Jew's low and essentially defenseless status in the Diaspora as justifiable punishment by God for his stiff-necked rejection of Christian faith. There was considerable interest in preserving the wretched state of the Jew in order to serve as a witness for the truth of Christianity. In reaction, the Jew took inward satisfaction in his religion and in his community.[11] He responded with philosophic argumentation that tried to account for the sad empirical reality of his situation in "an apology for a despised faith," as one eminent medieval theological work was subtitled.[12]

After the Holocaust, sensitive Christian thinkers were appalled at the destruction resulting from Jewish inferior status in Western society. They noted that Nazi antisemitism incorporated Christian anti-Jewish hatred and that the Final Solution took place in Christian Europe with the participation of identifying Christians and the indifference of many more. In addition to claiming *mea culpa*, they have seen the need to fundamentally rethink the Christian attitude to Jews and Judaism.[13]

The Holocaust, however, does not have to be seen as a challenge to traditional Christian attitudes towards the Jews. Witness the response of a high Church cleric to the plea of a rabbi for the lives of innocent Jewish children: "There is no innocent blood of Jewish children in the world. All Jewish blood is guilty. You have to die. This is the punishment that is awaiting you because of that sin."[14] In this view, the Holocaust is a confirmation of the Jew's inferiority and powerlessness resulting from his accursedness.

Strikingly parallel to this Christian position is the approach of one noted Jewish thinker, who asserts that, after Auschwitz, the Jewish faith can no longer claim the doctrine and vocation of the chosen people. The Jew must be normalized so that any distinctiveness and therefore attention is removed from him. According to this theologian, the Holocaust has destroyed any positive notion of Jewish specialness or destiny.[15]

These views of the Jew, stemming directly from the condition of his powerlessness, are altered decisively in light of the establishment of the State of Israel. No other nation can approach the story of the

Jews' return after 2,000 precarious years of exile, which culminated in destruction, to rebuild a devastated homeland. Jewish autonomy has removed their inferior status, and with the change in status comes a change in self-perception. The Jew no longer has to respond to charges of God's rejection with either complicated philosophic apologetics or with a plea for ordinariness. He is free to explore the meaning of his destiny.

Christianity is split in its reactions to Israel.[16] Some, unable to let go of centuries of prejudice, are threatened by the Jew who is no longer homeless and uprooted. They can't adjust to Christian holy places being guarded by Jewish soldiers and the earthly Jerusalem as once again the Jewish capital. Others, ostensibly friends who have decried Jewish suffering at the hands of Christendom, are "concerned" about the contemporary expression of Jewish power in Israel. They would rather the Jews bear a burden of suffering for some idealistic creation of Christian conscience than sully themselves with the hard decisions and responsibilities of a modern nation. While bewailing the Holocaust, they still prefer their Jews to be powerless.

Finally, there are Christians who recognize that Jews can no longer survive on Christian charity. They see in Israel not only a haven and refuge for a shattered people but also the redemptive quality of the rebirth of a people on its ancestral soil. These Christians find in their support for Israel a concrete response to the Holocaust. By their support of Israel, they participate in an undertaking in the Holy Land that has great meaning for their own faith.

# Particularism and Universalism

The Holocaust and the existence of the State of Israel have had a significant effect upon Jewish expressions of particularism and universalism. Judaism has traditionally felt that its distinctive and particular mode of religious life and close communal identity contained a messianic significance. In the modern era, many Jews have rejected this belief. They consider Jewish particularism to be an anachronism in a new age when barriers between men are lessening. They claim that Jews only have a future in the context of a more universal structure than Judaism, such as that of the surrounding nation or culture, international justice, science, or the creation of a universal language.[17]

Both universalism and particularism failed the Jews during the Holocaust.[18] Universalism offered no protection; in fact, it was an excuse not to get involved with the specific Jewish situation. On the other hand, the Holocaust was a unique case of a people being tragically singled out and chosen for death. Indeed, it can be taken as a wholly negative and perverse confirmation of Jewish identity.

The State of Israel redeems Jewish particularism. If the nations of the world could allow Jews to be chosen for death, then there must be one nation that will choose them for life. That nation is Israel. A Jew today is not homeless; he can automatically become a citizen of Israel merely by entering its borders. A Jew today is not abandoned; his brethren in Israel will exert whatever military, economic, and diplomatic power they have to save him.

Conscious of the Holocaust, the Jewish State also makes Jewish universalism a real possibility once again. Israel provides educational and economic aid to developing nations. Its hospitals and research facilities produce cures and inventions that benefit the world. As a state with its own navy, it sent the first ships to pick up the Indochinese boat people for resettlement in Israel. The State of Israel redeems both particularism and universalism for the Jewish people.

# Jewish Spirituality

Jewish spirituality underwent a significant change with the Holocaust and the establishment of the State of Israel. Jews in Europe had developed a religious life of intense intellectuality, scrupulous piety, and punctilious observance of the commandments in every area of personal and communal concern. To protect this life, the majority of the Orthodox chose to isolate themselves from the currents of modernity, which they judged as hostile to traditional Jewish values. They especially separated themselves from Zionism, which was unabashedly modern in its program, generally antispiritual, and "materialistic."[19]

Rabbi Zvi Pesah Frank, the chief rabbi of Jerusalem and son of the religious pioneering family that founded the agricultural settlement of Hadera, understood the possibilities that the return to *Erez Israel* meant for Jewish spirituality. Writing to his cousin, Rabbi Issar Zalman Melzer—famed European talmudic luminary and dean of the *yeshivah* at Slutzk, Lithuania—after World War I, he urged him:

> . . . to find a way to ascend to the holy mountain [immigrate to Jerusalem] with the holy *yeshivah*. Why should we not be inspired by the correct ones from the camp of the free thinkers [secular Zionists] who although far from our holy Torah [Law] . . . sacrifice their bodies and souls to improve our beloved land, according to their understanding and ideology, while the bearers of the flag of our holy Torah stand from a distance? . . .
>
> It is a holy duty charged to the great leaders of our generation to hasten . . . to establish in the holy city [Jerusalem] a spiritual center and a factory for the production of Torah and service to God. Perhaps we shall merit to return the crown [of Torah] to its former glory and fulfill the Scriptural verse "for from Zion shall come forth Torah and the Word of the Lord from Jerusalem."[20]

Between the world wars, a number of scholars and their schools did return to *Erez Israel* to join the old Orthodox community. They were involved in all facets of rebuilding the land and made a significant contribution. The majority of Orthodoxy, however, could foresee only spiritual corruption in joining forces with secular Zionism. They would rather forego the opportunity to emerge from powerlessness than risk contamination by modernity.

Abraham Isaac Kook, arguably the preeminent scholar of the Talmud, mystic, and charismatic religious leader of the century, rejected the isolationist policy. He argued that Judaism in the Diaspora had grown overly spiritualistic and ethereal, favoring the *neshama* (soul) and neglecting the *guf* (body). According to Rabbi Kook, the rejection by the Zionists of spirituality in favor of an earthy materiality was tragic but understandable. After the long Diaspora, Jews were unprepared for a direct encounter with the land and the challenge of rebuilding a nation. Caught up with this rediscovery of the body of the Jewish people, they could not incorporate traditional spirituality with their practical efforts.

Rabbi Kook believed that the exclusive nature of the concern for the material needs of the nation and the exploration of its physicality would eventually be tempered by a return to the age-old Jewish commitment to the development of the soul. In the meantime, however, he dismissed the possibility of a meaningful spirituality that continued to reject the newfound vibrant physicality of the Jewish people. He believed that Jews were religiously charged to come to terms with modernity in order to build a full and integrated life of the body and of the soul in their homeland.[21]

Rabbi Kook's insights have been confirmed by history. Spirituality alone is not sufficient to preserve a people. Indeed, intense spirituality coupled with the refusal to exploit the material opportunities afforded by modernity—the Zionist movement— proved catastrophic. The martyred Rabbi Isacher Solomon Teichthal, a noted Hasidic *dayan* (judge of religious court), wrote during the Holocaust of the consequences of the isolationist policy:

> . . . if only they had influenced the people of Israel and persuaded them to participate in it [rebuilding the land of Israel]—then how many Jews would have settled in the land of Israel, and how the land would have developed! How many Jews would have been saved thus from death, and, given life, could have saved more Jews, thereby fulfilling the injunction "to save those escaped from death!" But because they opposed it—and not only opposed it but awakened such hate for the building of our land in the hearts of simple, pious Jews, that anyone who opened his mouth to speak of it or became excited about it himself was considered disgusting and despicable. . . . And what was their fate? That they caused generations to lament their deeds . . . [because of their opposition] we have arrived at the situation we are in to day. . . .[22]

It is important to understand that Rabbi Teichthal is not blaming Jews for their own death. He means something different. The assumption of Jewish law is that acts have results, not only spiritually but concretely in this world. Rabbi Teichthal is working here within a natural framework. The performance of the commandment to return to the Land of Israel would have led to the beneficial result of Jews being saved. The refusal to recognize and perform this commandment has led to the opposite. Indeed, in the Kovno ghetto, the spiritual director of the Slobodka Yeshivah, Rabbi Abraham Grodzinsky, listed the neglect of *Erez Israel* as one of the factors leading to the destruction.[23]

The State of Israel has contributed to Jewish spirituality in two ways. First of all, it has provided the freedom and support for the rebuilding of the *yeshivot* (talmudic academies) and indigenous religious communities. Both have flourished in Israel. Jerusalem and Bnei Brak, among other cities throughout Israel, are home to hundreds of *yeshivot* that rival in numbers the ones of pre-Holocaust Europe. The level of their scholarly attainment is steadily on the rise. Hasidic courts, which were virtually destroyed, have been resurrected with all the color, warmth, piety, and enthusiasm as when their seats were in Poland, Hungary, and Russia. The vibrant and various Sephardic communities have been transferred to a new home, where they are rebuilding their unique ways of life. In addition, the success and struggles of the State have inspired a worldwide movement among alienated Jews to reidentify with their spiritual heritage. The map of Israel is dotted with centers, schools, and projects for these *ba'alei teshuvah* (returnees).

The opportunity to confront the material challenges of Israeli daily life has been significant for Jewish spirituality. In every area of a modern society—agriculture, economics, social policy, criminology, and so on—Jewish law and ethics are being consulted.[24] Not every problem has been "solved," and the strains of implementing solutions are often great. Israel, after all, is a democratic country and predominantly nonreligious. The Torah of modern Israel, however, is a Torah of life, unbounded by the limitations of a truncated exile existence. Its task is no longer how to exist within a situation of general communal powerlessness, but rather how to translate the moral and spiritual heritage of Judaism for a vital and growing nation.

### Notes

1. Aharon Appelfeld, "Witness," *Jerusalem Quarterly* No. 16 (Summer 1980): 96.

2. For an historical treatment of the issues, see Yehuda Bauer, *The Jewish Emergence from Powerlessness* (Toronto: University of Toronto Press, 1979). For theological reflections, the major works are: Eliezer Berkovits, *Faith after the Holocaust* (New York: Ktav, 1973); Eliezer Berkovits, *Crisis and Faith* (New York: Sanhedrin Press, 1976); Emil L. Fackenheim, *The Jewish Return into History* (New York: Schocken Books, 1978); Irving Greenberg, "Cloud of Smoke, Pillar of Fire," in *Auschwitz: Beginning of a New Era*, ed. Eva Fleischner (New York: Ktav, 1976); Irving Greenberg, "The Interaction of Israel and American Jewry—After the Holocaust," in *World Jewry and the State of Israel*, ed. Moshe Davis (New York: Arno Press, 1977); and Joseph B. Soloveitchik, "Kol Dodi: Dofek," in *Ish HaEmuna* (Jerusalem: Mossad HaRav Kook, 1975), pp. 65-106.

3. See "Rebellions in the Camps: Three Revolts in the Face of Death," by Yisrael Gutman, in this volume.

4. "A World: Whole, In Ruins and Rebuilt—Radio Dialogue with Abba Kovner . . . " [Hebrew] *Yalkut Moreshet* 22 (November 1976): 7-30.

5. Isaiah Trunk, *Judenrat* (New York: Macmillan Co., 1972); Richard L. Rubenstein, *The Cunning of History: The Holocaust and the American Future* (New York: Harper & Row, 1975), pp. 22-35.

6. Irving Greenberg, "Interaction," in *World Jewry and the State of Israel*, ed. Moshe Davis (New York: Herzl Press, 1977), pp. 259-282.

7. David Kranzler, *Japanese, Nazis and Jews* (New York: Yeshiva University Press, 1976); Yehuda Bauer, *The Holocaust in Historical Perspective* (Seattle: University of Washington Press, 1978), pp. 64-66.

8. Fackenheim, *The Jewish Return*, pp. 273-286.

9. See Christopher R. Browning's article, "The German Bureaucracy and the Holocaust," in this volume.

10. Meir Pa'il "The Dynamics of Power: Morality in Armed Conflict after the Six Day War," in *Modern Jewish Ethics*, (Columbus, Ohio: Ohio State University, 1975), p. 206; Shaul Yisraeli, "The Kibya Incident in the Light of the Halacha" [Hebrew], in *Ha'Torah Ve'Hamedinah*, Volumes 5-6 (1954).

11. Jacob Katz, *Exclusiveness and Tolerance, Jewish-Gentile Relations in Medieval and Modern Times* (New York: Schocken Books, 1962), pp. 67-113.

12. Yehuda Even Shmuel, *The Kosari of R. Yehuda Halevi* [Hebrew] (Tel Aviv: Dvir Publishing Company, 1972).

13. See "Implications of the Holocaust for the Christian Churches," by John T. Pawlikowski, in this volume.

14. Rabbi Michael Dov-Ber Weissmandel, *Min Hamezar*. Quoted by Eliezer Berkovits, *Faith*, p. 17.

15. Richard L. Rubenstein, *After Auschwitz* (New York: Bobbs-Merrill, 1966), pp. 47-60. Rubenstein's position is a legacy from Mordecai M. Kaplan, who first wrote about this in 1934. See Mordecai M. Kaplan, *Judaism As a Civilization* (New York: Schocken Books, 1967), p. 43.

16.    See "Response to John Pawlikowski by Claire Hutchet-Bishop," in *Auschwitz: Beginning of a New Era?*, ed. Eva Fleischner (New York: Ktav, 1977), p. 184; A. Roy and Alice L. Eckardt, "Again, Silence in the Churches," *The Christian Century* (July 26 and August 2, 1967); Walter Brueggemann, *The Land* (Philadelphia: Fortress Press, 1977.)

17.    Gershom G. Scholem, *The Messianic Idea in Judaism* (New York: Schocken Books, 1971); Haim Hillel Ben-Sasson, ed, *A History of the Jewish People* (Cambridge: Harvard University Press, 1976), pp. 825-833; Henry L. Feingold, "Determining the Uniqueness of the Holocaust: The Factor of Historical Valence," *Shoah* (Spring 1981): 6-11.

18.    Both Fackenheim and Greenberg deal extensively with this issue.

19.    Arthur Hertzberg, *The Zionist Idea* (New York: Atheneum, 1977), pp. 15-100.

20.    *Hazevi Yisrael* (Jerusalem: Machon Harav Frank, 1971), p. 280.

21.    Abraham Isaac Kook, "Orot Yisrael," in *Orot* [Hebrew] (Jerusalem: Mossad HaRav Kook, 1961). The best English anthology of his work is Ben Zion Bokser, trans., *Abraham Isaac Kook—The Lights of Penitence, The Moral Principles, Light of Holiness, Essays, Letters, and Poems* (New York: Paulist Press, 1978).

22.    Isaachar Teichthal, *Sefer Em Habanim S'mehah* (Budapest: Zalman Katz Karburg, 1943), pp. 16-17. This translation is from Pinchas H. Peli, "In Search of Religious Language for the Holocaust," *Conservative Judaism 32* (Winter 1979): 3-24. See also Peter Schindler, *Responses of Hasidic Leaders and Hasidim During the Holocaust in Europe* (Ph.D. diss., New York University, 1972), especially pp. 81-108.

23.    Abraham Grodzinsky, *Torat Abraham* [Hebrew] (Bnei Brak: Kollet Avrechim Torah Abraham, 1979), p. 17.

24.    *Dine Yisrael* Vols. 1-9 (Tel Aviv); *Noam*, Vols. 1-29 (Jerusalem).

### For Further Reading

Bauer, Yehuda. *The Jewish Emergence from Powerlessness.* Toronto: University of Toronto Press, 1979.

Berkovits, Eliezer. *Crisis and Faith.* New York: Sanhedrin Press, 1976.

Fackenheim, Emil L. *The Jewish Return Into History:*

*Reflections on the Age of Auschwitz and a New Jerusalem.* New York: Schocken Books, 1978.

Greenberg, Irving. *On the Third Era in Jewish History: Power and Politics.* New York: National Jewish Resource Center, 1980.

Soloveitchik, Joseph B. "Kol Dodi Dofek." In *In Aloneness, In Togetherness: A Selection of Hebrew Writings,* edited by Pinchas H. Peli. Jerusalem: Orot, 1976.

# Postscript:
# The Making of the Film
## *Genocide*

### MARVIN HIER

In the fall of 1979, I proposed to the Board of Trustees of the Simon Wiesenthal Center that we produce a major multimedia presentation on the Holocaust. My reasons were twofold. A new generation too young to remember the Holocaust now makes up the majority of the population and they need to know about the nature of the world they have inherited. Perhaps even more importantly, most of the films on the Holocaust, while careful to document the horrors, fail to capture the essence of the lives that were lost—who these people were and what values they lived by. I felt that this approach was essential, since it was the only way we could motivate young people to study the Holocaust. Unless the viewers could personally identify with the victims, it would be difficult for them to empathize with their fate.

With these presuppositions, and with no formal background in movie-making, Chairman of the Simon Wiesenthal Center Board of Trustees Samuel Belzberg, a leading Canadian financier, philanthropist, and community leader, along with Chairwoman Esther Cohen, a Holocaust survivor and member of the United States Holocaust Memorial Council, accompanied me to an appointment with Saul Bass, a multimedia specialist who had been highly recommended to us. We went to Bass hoping to persuade him to take on the assignment, or at the very least, to ascertain his view on a potential film. As it turned out, Bass could not fit our film into his schedule, but he did give us some very good advice: "Don't compromise on quality, and don't tell me that someone who belongs to your organization has a camera so he will direct, and you know someone who is a musician and he will write you a score. To do your film properly and professionally will cost a few million dollars; that's life, and if it's important enough to you, then you will find the money."

With Bass' words still fresh in mind, we tried to adjust to the idea of a multimillion-dollar budget. It was clear to us that unless we could raise that kind of money, we had no business even attempting the project.

I then proposed that we ask Simon Wiesenthal to undertake a national fundraising drive, which would take him to at least half a dozen cities to raise the money for this project. At the same time, I began the search for a professional writer and director. The search led us to Arnold Schwartzman, who was then working for Saul Bass. Bass recommended Schwartzman, because in addition to filmmaking, he had an international reputation as a graphic designer. Schwartzman was hired for the project.

At this phase of development, I thought the film should be a multimedia presentation—that is, the combined usage of film and stills on multiple screens. I felt that this would open up new possibilities in presenting the many dimensions of the Holocaust which could otherwise not be shown through a single lens. I was convinced that it would be ideal for an exhibit at the Wiesenthal Center's museum and at other major cultural institutions. Indeed, a multimedia presentation about the universe at the Smithsonian in Washington, D.C., has never diminished in timeliness.

The project gained new momentum when Martin Gilbert, official biographer of Sir Winston Churchill and professor at Oxford University, was asked to write the historical script. Gilbert, author of a number of books on the Holocaust, was then writing another study on this topic. In our first meeting in London in early 1980, Gilbert agreed that *Genocide* be written from a combined historical and personal perspective, and that the factual material be balanced by selected verified testimonies. We proposed that these personal accounts derive from the last wills, testaments, poems, and admonitions found at Birkenau or Bergen-Belsen.

Soon after the meeting in London, Schwartzman assembled a team to accompany him on research trips to archives located in Europe, the United States, and Israel.

Simon Wiesenthal had, meanwhile, arrived in the United States for a two-week lecture tour to help raise funds for the project. Wiesenthal, who had given his name to the Center and is considered a major spokesman for Holocaust survivors, was both excited and apprehensive about this undertaking. He was worried about asking for financial support. He remembered his own negative experience with American Jews who, in the 1960s, failed to perceive the importance of his work. When he really needed their help, they did not respond. Once the tour started, Simon saw the excitement the film concept generated. His own excitement mounted when Esther Cohen and John Francis (a producer and promoter of Hollywood shows), arranged for Simon Wiesenthal to meet Frank Sinatra in San Francisco in the middle of his lecture tour. Sinatra, who had an immediate rapport with Wiesenthal, told Simon that he had been his hero for many years, and had always looked forward to meeting him. Sinatra was interested in Simon's life and work, particularly the 1,000 Nazis he brought to trial. Sinatra wanted to know how he could help now. Sensing Simon's reluctance, he pressed Esther Cohen, who told Sinatra about the Center and its new film project. "Why would you want to hide something like that from me?" Sinatra asked. "Although I'm not Jewish, the Holocaust is important to me." Sinatra donated the first $100,000 to the project at this meeting and became a member of the Wiesenthal Center's Board of Trustees. Earlier that evening he had told 3,000 people attending his San Francisco concert that his personal hero was seated in the audience. He then introduced Simon to a five-minute standing ovation. Since that day, Sinatra has made four appearances for the Center and was directly responsible for raising an additional $400,000 for the film. When Simon returned to

Vienna in late June, $1 million had been raised and committed to the project. In addition, a Simon Wiesenthal Fellows Society was created with twenty-five Fellows pledging more than $2.5 million over a period of five years.

The funding was more certain and our attention now turned to the production. Gilbert sent me a first draft of the script, and Schwartzman returned from his trip bringing with him enormous photo and document files. It was now time to talk about narration and music. Gilbert's script sketched the history of the Third Reich, incorporating Wiesenthal's concern for the suffering of non-Jews trapped in Nazi Europe. Although our main aim was to show the uniqueness of the Jewish tragedy, Simon felt it a major mistake not to mention Nazi persecution of other ethnic groups. I felt that the script also needed a poetic, personal style that would communicate the suffering more profoundly. Both Gilbert and Schwartzman agreed that I should revise the script to reflect this.

Schwartzman was asked by Samuel Belzberg to coordinate the entire production, and he arranged for production work to begin at Quantum Leap Studios in Venice, California. One of our first tasks was to find two narrators, one for the historical portion and the other for the personal testimony. Elizabeth Taylor and Orson Welles were our first choices, because as recognizable personalities and voices, they would lend enormous credibility to *Genocide*.

Several other decisions were also made at this point in production. We concluded that the project merited an original score and that the Academy Award-winning composer Elmer Bernstein would be a natural choice. We also decided that the film should be introduced by Simon Wiesenthal at the Mauthausen concentration camp, where many members of his family were murdered. Wiesenthal, standing beneath the barbed wire fence of Mauthausen, would engage the conscience of the viewer.

When the script was complete, I flew to Washington, D.C., to ask United States Senator John Warner if he would show the script to his then wife, Elizabeth Taylor. Warner, a good friend of the Center, had worked closely with us on a number of social action issues; he promised he would take the script home to Elizabeth, but cautioned me against overoptimism. "You know stars; you can't tell which scripts they will accept. I'll call on Monday either way," Senator Warner promised.

On Monday, Warner called excitedly. "Rabbi, I've got both good and bad news. The good news is that Elizabeth will do it without remuneration. The bad news is you ruined my weekend—she couldn't stop crying from Friday to Sunday night."

A week later, Elizabeth Taylor and I had lunch at the Polo Lounge in the Beverly Hills Hotel. A Greyhound bus driver spotted her coming in and alerted his busload of tourists, who soon found the secluded window table where we were seated. When Elizabeth noticed them and turned around to wave, I told her that they did not come to see her, but that what attracted them was the sight of an Orthodox rabbi at the Polo Lounge! At this meeting, Elizabeth made it clear that this project was very special to her, since she regarded the Jewish people as her people, and wanted to identify personally with the tragedy of the Holocaust. She asked if we could record in London while she was filming Agatha Christie's *The Mirror Cracked.* She also asked if I could coach her in the correct Yiddish and Hebrew pronunciations that were part of her narration. We agreed to record in London in June with two days set aside for rehearsal.

By June, Orson Welles had also read the script and agreed to donate his services without remuneration. He felt it was a tribute to Jewish history and continuity. Welles, who is very fussy about scripts and a stickler for precise English usage, said that the *Genocide* script was the finest to cross his desk in a long time. He insisted on using his own studio to record, so that the Center could save any additional costs.

With Welles' narration completed, Schwartzman and I flew to London to record Elizabeth Taylor's segments. Elizabeth Taylor pronounced *"Mir velen zei iberleben"* ("We shall outlive them") like a Jewess from Warsaw, and her perfectly accented *"Hazak V' Amatz"* ("Be Strong and Brave") drew compliments from Israel's ambassador to the United States. She was deeply moved during the recording of one of the stories. She wept and could not continue recording Leon Kahn's description of the murder of the residents of Eisiskes at the hands of their Ukrainian tormentors.

Elmer Bernstein recorded his score one week later with the Royal Philharmonic Orchestra, and *Genocide* thus moved into the final phase of production. The multimedia project was screened at Quantum Leap Studios in June, 1981. In addition to the trustees of the Simon Wiesenthal Center of Yeshiva University of Los Angeles, a group of distinguished members of the motion picture industry were present. The effect of the presentation was astounding. Fay Kanin, president of the Academy of Motion Picture Arts and Sciences, said, "Rabbi, this should be transferred to film. Everyone should have the opportunity to see this." The more I considered her idea, the more convinced I became that Mrs. Kanin was right. By limiting ourselves to a multimedia format with multiple projectors and computers, we would restrict our audience outreach. If the presentation was powerful, then it deserved more exposure than museums and cultural institutions could provide for us.

With the help of a challenge grant from Atlantic Richfield Company, we moved rapidly to convert the multimedia into a 35mm film. A group from the Center, consisting of Marvin Segelman, Leslie Belzberg, Bob Jenkins, and Jeff Karoff, performed the herculean task of creating the film, which was completed in December, 1981. Three months later, on the evening of March 29, 1982, *Genocide* won an Academy Award for the Best Documentary Feature. An unbelieveable dream had come true. As I walked up with Arnold Schwartzman to accept the Oscar, I thought of many people who helped me accomplish this: Samuel Belzberg, who had the courage and gave me the opportunity to create such an institution; Bill Belzberg, who opened so many doors for me; Esther Cohen, who devoted two-and-a-half years of her life to the project; Alan Casden, who demonstrated such sound judgment and loyalty; Roland Arnall, the first person who helped me when I came to Los Angeles in 1977; the dedicated staff of the Center, especially my assistant Rabbi Abraham Cooper and Efraim Zuroff, the historical consultant on *Genocide*; and my dear wife, Marlene, and our children, Ari and Avi, who experienced with me both the anguish and the joy. As I received the Oscar, I thanked those people and the Board of Trustees, and Simon Wiesenthal, who all these years stood alone, and then I told the 360 million viewers, "*Genocide* is dedicated to the millions of victims of Hitler's Holocaust. They have no graves, but their memory will live on until the end of time."

# Appendix: Selected Documents

1

## Instructions by Heydrich on Policy and Operations Concerning Jews in the Occupied Territories, September 21, 1939

The Chief of the Security Police

Berlin, September 21, 1939

*Schnellbrief*
*To Chiefs of all Einsatzgruppen of the Security Police*
Subject: *Jewish Question in Occupied Territory*

I refer to the conference held in Berlin today and again point out that the *planned total measures* (i.e., the final aim—*Endziel*) are to be kept *strictly secret*.

Distinction must be made between:
1. the final aim (which will require extended periods of time) and
2. the stages leading to the fulfillment of this final aim (which will be carried out in short periods).

The planned measures require the most thorough preparation with regard to technical as well as economic aspects.

It is obvious that the tasks ahead cannot be laid down from here in full detail. The instructions and directives below must serve also for the purpose of urging chiefs of the *Einsatzgruppen* to give practical consideration [to the problems involved].

*I*
*For the time being, the first prerequisite for the final aim is the concentration of the Jews from the countryside into the larger cities.*

This is to be carried out speedily.

In doing so, distinction must be made
1) between the zones of Danzig and West Prussia, Poznan, Eastern Upper Silesia, and
2) the other occupied zones.

As far as possible, the areas referred to under 1) are to be cleared of Jews; at least the aim should be to establish only few cities of concentration.

In the areas under 2), as few concentration centers as possible are to be set up, so as to facilitate subsequent measures. In this connection it should be borne in mind that only cities which are rail junctions, or are at least located on railroad lines, should be selected as concentration points.

On principle, Jewish communities of *less than 500 persons* are to be dissolved and transferred to the nearest concentration center.

This decree does not apply to the area of *Einsatzgruppe* 1, which is situated east of Cracow and is bounded roughly by *Polanice, Jaroslaw*, the new line of demarcation, and the former Slovak-Polish border. Within this area only an approximate census of Jews is to be carried out. Furthermore, Councils of Jewish Elders *(Jüdische Altestenräte)*, as outlined below, are to be set up.

## II
### Councils of Jewish Elders

1) In each Jewish community a Council of Jewish Elders is to be set up which, as far as possible, is to be composed of the remaining authoritative personalities and rabbis. The Council is to be composed of up to 24 male Jews (depending on the size of the Jewish community).

The Council is to be made *fully responsible*, in the literal sense of the word, for the exact and prompt implementation of directives already issued or to be issued in the future.

2) In case of sabotage of such instructions, the Councils are to be warned that the most severe measures will be taken.

3) The Judenräte (Jewish Councils) are to carry out an approximate census of the Jews of their areas, broken down if possible according to sex (and age groups): a) up to 16 years, b) from 16 to 20 years, and c) above; and also according to the principal occupations. The results are to be reported in the shortest possible time.

4) The Councils of Elders are to be informed of the date and time of the evacuation, the means available for evacuation, and, finally, the departure routes. They are then to be made personally responsible for the evacuation of the Jews from the countryside.

The reason to be given for the concentration of the Jews in the cities is that the Jews have taken a decisive part in sniper attacks and plundering.

5) The Councils of Elders in the concentration centers are to be made responsible for the appropriate housing of the Jews arriving from the countryside.

For reasons of general police security, the concentration of the Jews in the cities will probably call for regulations in these cities which will forbid their entry to certain quarters completely and that—but with due regard for economic requirements—they may, for instance, not leave the ghetto, nor leave their homes after a certain hour in the evening, etc.

6) The Councils of Elders are also to be made responsible for the suitable provisioning of the Jews during the transport to the cities.

There is no objection to the evacuated Jews taking with them their movable possessions in so far as that is technically possible.

7) Jews who fail to comply with the order to move into cities are to be

given a short additional period of grace where there was sufficient reason for the delay. They are to be warned of the most severe penalties if they fail to move by the later date set.

### III

*All necessary measures are, on principle, always to be taken in closest consultation and cooperation with the German civil administration and the competent local military authorities.*

In the execution [of this plan], it must be taken into consideration that economic requirements in the occupied areas do not suffer.

1) Above all, the needs of the army must be taken into consideration. For instance, for the time being, it will scarcely be possible to avoid, here and there, leaving behind some trade Jews who are absolutely essential for the provisioning of the troops, for lack of other possibilities. But in such cases the prompt Aryanization of these enterprises is to be planned and the move of the Jews to be completed in due course, in cooperation with the competent local German administrative authorities.

2) For the preservation of German economic interests in the occupied territories, it is obvious that Jewish-owned war and other essential industries, and also enterprises, industries and factories important to the Four Year Plan, must be maintained for the time being.

In these cases, also, prompt Aryanization must be aimed at, and the move of the Jews completed later.

3) Finally, the food situation in the occupied territories must be taken into consideration. For instance, as far as possible, land owned by Jewish settlers is to be handed over to the care of neighboring German or even Polish farmers to work on commission to ensure the harvesting of crops still standing in the fields, and replanting.

With regard to this important question, contact is to be made with the agricultural expert of the Chief of the Civil Administration.

4) In all cases in which it is not possible to coordinate the interests of the Security Police on the one hand, and the German civil administration on the other, I am to be informed by the fastest route and my decision awaited before the particular measures in question are carried out.

### IV

The Chiefs of the *Einsatzgruppen* are to report to me continuously on the following matters:

1) Numerical survey of the Jews present in their areas (according to the above classifications, if possible). The numbers of Jews evacuated from the countryside and of those already in the cities are to be listed separately.

2) Names of the cities which have been designated as concentration centers.

3) The dates set for the Jews to move to the cities.

4) Surveys of all the Jewish [owned] war and other essential industries and enterprises, or those important to the Four Year Plan in their areas.

If possible, the following should be specified:

a) Type of enterprise (with a statement on possible conversion to really vital or war-important enterprises or ones of importance to the Four Year Plan);

b) which factories should be most urgently Aryanized (in order to forestall possible losses);

What kind of Aryanization is proposed? Germans or Poles? (the decision to depend on the importance of the enterprise);

c) The number of Jews working in these factories (specify those in leading positions).

Can operations at the enterprise be continued without difficulty after the removal of the Jews, or will it be necessary to allocate German or possibly Polish workers in their place? In what numbers?

If Polish workers have to be used care should be taken that they are drawn mainly from the former German provinces so as to begin to ease the problem there. These matters can be carried out only by means of coordination with the German Labor Offices which have been set up.

## V

In order to reach the planned aims, I expect the fullest cooperation of the whole manpower of the Security Policy and the SD.

The Chiefs of neighboring *Einsatzgruppen* are to establish contact with each other immediately in order to cover the areas in question completely.

## VI

The High Command of the Army; the Plenipotentiary for the Four Year Plan (attention: Secretary of State *Neumann*), the Reich Ministry for the Interior (attention: State Secretary *Stuckart*), for Food and the Economy (attention: State Secretary *Landfried*), as well as the Chiefs of Civil Administration of the Occupied Territories have received copies of this decree.

Signed Heydrich

PS-3363.

## 2

# From a Speech by Frank on the Extermination of the Jews, December 16, 1941

...One way or another—I will tell you that quite openly—we must finish off the Jews. The Führer put it into words once: should united Jewry again succeed in setting off a world war, then the blood sacrifice shall not be made only by the peoples driven into war, but then the Jew of Europe will have met his end. I know that there is criticism of many of the measures now applied to the Jews in the

Reich. There are always deliberate attempts to speak again and again of cruelty, harshness, etc.; this emerges from the reports on the popular mood. I appeal to you: before I now continue speaking first agree with me on a formula: we will have pity, on principle, only for the German people, and for nobody else in the world. The others had no pity for us either. As an old National-Socialist I must also say that if the pack of Jews *(Judensippschaft)* were to survive the war in Europe while we sacrifice the best of our blood for the preservation of Europe, then this war would still be only a partial success. I will therefore, on principle, approach Jewish affairs in the expectation that the Jews will disappear. They must go. I have started negotiations for the purpose of having them pushed off to the East. In January there will be a major conference on this question in Berlin,[1] to which I shall send State Secretary Dr. Bühler. The conference is to be held in the office of SS *Obergruppenführer* Heydrich at the Reich Security Main Office *(Reichssicherheitshauptamt)*. A major Jewish migration will certainly begin.

But what should be done with the Jews? Can you believe that they will be accommodated in settlements in the *Ostland?* In Berlin we were told: why are you making all this trouble? We don't want them either, not in the *Ostland* nor in the *Reichskommissariat;* liquidate them yourselves! Gentlemen, I must ask you to steel yourselves against all considerations of compassion. We must destroy the Jews wherever we find them, and wherever it is at all possible, in order to maintain the whole structure of the Reich... The views that were acceptable up to now cannot be applied to such gigantic, unique events. In any case we must find a way that will lead us to our goal, and I have my own ideas on this.

The Jews are also exceptionally harmful feeders for us. In the Government-General we have approximately 2.5 million [Jews], and now perhaps 3.5 million together with persons who have Jewish kin, and so on. We cannot shoot these 3.5 million Jews,[2] we cannot poison them, but we will be able to take measures that will lead somehow to successful destruction; and this in connection with the large-scale procedures which are to be discussed in the Reich. The Government-General must become as free of Jews as the Reich. Where and how this is to be done is the affair of bodies which we will have to appoint and create, and on whose work I will report to you when the time comes....

PS-2233
1. *See following document.*
2. *The figures are not based on facts.*

# 3
# Protocol of the Wannsee Conference, January 20, 1942

*Reich Secret Document*
*30 Copies*

## Protocol of Conference

I. The following took part in the conference on the final solution *(Endlösung)* of the Jewish question held on January 20, 1942, in Berlin, Am Grossen Wannsee No. 56-58:

| | |
|---|---|
| *Gauleiter* Dr. Meyer and Reich Office Director Dr. Leibbrandt | Reich Ministry for the Occupied Eastern Territories |
| Secretary of State Dr. Stuckart | Reich Ministry of the Interior |
| Secretary of State Neumann | Plenipotentiary for the Four Year Plan |
| Secretary of State Dr. Freisler | Reich Ministry of Justice |
| Secretary of State Dr. Bühler | Office of the Governor General |
| Undersecretary of State Dr. Luther | Foreign Ministry |
| SS *Oberführer* Klopfer | Party Chancellery |
| Ministerial Director Kritzinger | Reich Chancellery |
| SS *Gruppenführer* Hofmann | Race and Settlement Main Office |
| SS *Gruppenführer* Müller | Reich Security Main Office |
| SS *Obersturmbannführer* Eichmann | Reich Security Main Office |
| SS *Oberführer* Dr. Schöngarth, Commander of the Security Police and the SD in the Government-General | Security Police and SD |
| SS *Sturmbannführer* Dr. Lange, Commander of the Security Police and the SD in the *Generalbezirk* Latvia as representative of the Commander of the Security Police and the SD for the *Reichskommissariat* for the *Ostland* | Security Police and SD |

11. The meeting opened with the announcement by the Chief of the Security Police and the SD, SS *Obergruppenführer* Heydrich, of his appointment by the Reich Marshal[1] as Plenipotentiary for the Preparation of the Final Solution of the European Jewish Question. He noted that this Conference had been called in order to obtain clarity on questions of principle. The Reich Marshal's request for a draft plan concerning the organizational, practical and economic aspects of the final solution of the European Jewish question required prior joint consideration by all central agencies directly involved in these questions, with a view to maintaining parallel policy lines.

Responsibility for the handling of the final solution of the Jewish question, he said, would lie centrally with the *Reichsführer* SS and the Chief of the German Police (Chief of the Security Police and the SD), without regard to geographic boundaries.

The Chief of the Security Police and the SD then gave a brief review of the stuggle conducted up to now against this foe.

The most important elements are:

a) Forcing the Jews out of the various areas of life *(Lebensgebiete)* of the German people.

b) Forcing the Jews out of the living space *(Lebensraum)* of the German people.

In pursuit of these aims, the accelerated emigration of the Jews from the area of the Reich, as the only possible provisional solution, was pressed forward and carried out according to plan.

On instructions by the Reich Marshal, a Reich Central Office for Jewish Emigration was set up in January 1939, and its direction entrusted to the Chief of the Security Police and the SD. Its tasks were, in particular:

a) To take all measures for the *preparation* of increased emigration of the Jews;

b) To *direct* the flow of emigration;

c) To speed up emigration in *individual* cases.

The aim of this task was to cleanse the German living space of Jews in a legal manner.

The disadvantages engendered by such forced pressing of emigration were clear to all the authorities. But in the absence of other possible solutions, they had to be accepted for the time being.

In the period that followed, the handling of emigration was not a German problem alone, but one with which the authorities of the countries of destination or immigration also had to deal. Financial difficulties—such as increases ordered by the various foreign governments in the sums of money that immigrants were required to have and in landing fees—as well as lack of berths on ships and continually tightening restrictions or bans on immigration, hampered emigration efforts very greatly. Despite these difficulties a total of approximately 537,000 Jews were caused to emigrate between the [Nazi] assumption of power and up to October 31, 1941.

These consisted of the following:

| | | |
|---|---|---|
| From January 30, 1933: | from the *Altreich* [Germany before 1938] | Approx. 360,000 |
| From March 15, 1938: | from the *Ostmark* [Austria] | Approx. 147,000 |
| From March 15, 1939: | from the Protectorate of Bohemia and Moravia | Approx. 30,000 |

The financing of the emigration was carried out by the Jews or Jewish political organizations themselves. To prevent the remaining behind of proletarianized Jews, the principle was observed that wealthy Jews must finance the emigration of the Jews without means; to this end, a special assessment or emigration levy, in accordance with wealth owned, was imposed, the proceeds being used to meet the financial obligations of the emigration of destitute Jews.

In addition to the funds raised in German marks, foreign currency was needed for the monies which emigrants were required to show on arrival abroad and for landing fees. To conserve the German holdings of foreign currency, Jewish financial institutions abroad were persuaded by Jewish organizations in this country to make themselves responsible for finding the required sums in foreign currency. A total of about $9,500,000 was provided by these foreign Jews as gifts up to October 30, 1941.

In the meantime, in view of the dangers of emigration in wartime, and the possibilities in the East, the *Reichsführer* SS and Chief of the German Police has forbidden the emigration of Jews.

III. Emigration has now been replaced by evacuation of the Jews to the East, as a further possible solution, with the appropriate prior authorization by the Führer.

However, this operation should be regarded only as a provisional option; but it is already supplying practical experience of great significance in view of the coming final solution of the Jewish question.

In the course of this final solution of the European Jewish question approximately 11 million Jews may be taken into consideration, distributed over the individual countries as follows:

| Country | Number |
|---|---|
| **A.** | |
| *Altreich* | 131,800 |
| *Ostmark* | 43,700 |
| Eastern Territories[2] | 420,000 |
| Government-General | 2,284,000 |
| Bialystok | 400,000 |
| Protectorate of Bohemia and Moravia | 74,200 |
| Estonia—free of Jews | |
| Latvia | 3,500 |
| Lithuania | 34,000 |
| Belgium | 43,000 |
| Denmark | 5,600 |
| France: Occupied territory | 165,000 |
| France: Unoccupied territory | 700,000 |
| Greece | 69,600 |
| Netherlands | 160,800 |
| Norway | 1,300 |
| **B.** | |
| Bulgaria | 48,000 |

| | |
|---|---:|
| England | 330,000 |
| Finland | 2,300 |
| Ireland | 4,000 |
| Italy, including Sardinia | 58,000 |
| Albania | 200 |
| Croatia | 40,000 |
| Portugal | 3,000 |
| Rumania, including Bessarabia | 342,000 |
| Sweden | 8,000 |
| Switzerland | 18,000 |
| Serbia | 10,000 |
| Slovakia | 88,000 |
| Spain | 6,000 |
| Turkey (in Europe) | 55,500 |
| Hungary | 742,800 |
| U.S.S.R. | 5,000,000 |
| Ukraine | 2,994,684 |
| Byelorussia, without Bialystok | 446,484 |
| | Total: over 11,000,000 |

As far as the figures for Jews of the various foreign countries are concerned, the numbers given include only Jews by religion *(Glaubensjuden)*, since the definition of Jews according to racial principles is in part still lacking there. Owing to the prevailing attitudes and concepts, the handling of this problem in the individual countries will encounter certain difficulties, especially in Hungary and Rumania. For instance, in Rumania the Jew can still obtain, for money, documents officially certifying that he holds foreign citizenship.

The influence of the Jews in all spheres of life in the U.S.S.R. is well known. There are about 5 million Jews in European Russia, and barely another 250,000 in Asiatic Russia.

The distribution of Jews according to occupation in the European area of the U.S.S.R. was roughly as follows:

| | |
|---|---:|
| Agriculture | 9.1% |
| Urban workers | 14.8% |
| Trade | 20.0% |
| State employees | 23.4% |
| Professions—medicine, press, theatre, etc. | 32.7% |

Under appropriate direction the Jews are to be utilized for work in the East in an expedient manner in the course of the final solution. In large (labor) columns, with the sexes separated, Jews capable of work will be moved into these areas as they build roads, during which a large proportion will no doubt drop out through natural reduction. The remnant that eventually remains will require suitable treatment; because it will without doubt represent the most [physically] resistant part, it consists of a natural selection that could, on its release, become the germ-cell of a new Jewish revival. (Witness the experience of history.)

Europe is to be combed through from West to East in the course of the practical implementation of the final solution. The area of the Reich, including the Protectorate of Bohemia and Moravia, will have to be handled in advance, if only because of the housing problem and other socio-political needs.

The evacuated Jews will first be taken, group by group, to so-called transit ghettos, in order to be transported further east from there.

An important precondition, SS *Obergruppenführer* Heydrich noted further, for the carrying out of the evacuation in general is the precise determination of the groups of persons involved. It is intended not to evacuate Jews over 65 years old, but to place them in an old-age ghetto—Theresienstadt is being considered.

In addition to these age groups—about 30% of the 280,000 Jews who were present in the *Altreich* and the *Ostmark* on October 31, 1941, were over 65 years old—Jews with severe war injuries and Jews with war decorations (Iron Cross, First Class) will be admitted to the Jewish old-age ghetto. This suitable solution will eliminate at one blow the many applications for exceptions.

The start of the individual major evacuation *Aktionen* will depend largely on military developments. With regard to the handling of the final solution in the European areas occupied by us and under our influence, it was proposed that the officials dealing with this subject in the Foreign Ministry should confer with the appropriate experts in the Security Police and the SD.

In Slovakia and Croatia the matter is no longer too difficult, as the most essential, central problems in this respect have already been brought to a solution there. In Rumania the government has in the meantime also appointed a Plenipotentiary for Jewish Affairs. In order to settle the problem in Hungary, it will be necessary in the near future to impose an adviser for Jewish questions on the Hungarian Government.

With regard to setting in motion preparations for the settling of the problem in Italy, SS *Obergruppenführer* Heydrich considers liaison with the Police Chief in these matters would be in place.

In occupied and unoccupied France the rounding-up of the Jews for evacuation will, in all probability, be carried out without great difficulties.

On this point, Undersecretary of State Luther stated that far-reaching treatment of this problem would meet with difficulties in some countries, such as the Nordic States, and that it was therefore advisable to postpone action in these countries for the present. In view of the small number of Jews involved there, the postponement will in any case not occasion any significant curtailment. On the other hand, the Foreign Ministry foresees no great difficulties for the south-east and west of Europe.

SS *Gruppenführer* Hofmann intends to send a specialist from the Main Office for Race and Settlement to Hungary for general orientation when the subject is taken in hand there by the Chief of the Security Police and the SD. It was decided that this specialist from the

Race and Settlement Main Office, who is not to take an active part, will temporarily be designated officially as Assistant to the Police Attaché.

IV. In the implementation of the plan for the final solution, the Nuremberg Laws are to form the basis, as it were; a precondition for the total clearing up of the problem will also require solutions for the question of mixed marriages and *Mischlinge*.

The Chief of the Security Police and the SD then discussed the following points, theoretically for the time being, in connection with a letter from the Chief of the Reich Chancellery:

1. *Treatment of first-degree* Mischlinge

First-degree *Mischlinge* are in the same position as Jews with respect to the final solution of the Jewish question. The following will be exempt from this treatment:

a) First-degree *Mischlinge* married to persons of German blood, from whose marriages there are children (second-degree *Mischlinge*). Such second-degree *Mischlinge* are essentially in the same position as Germans.

b) First-degree *Mischlinge* for whom up to now exceptions were granted in some (vital) area by the highest authorities of the Party and the State. Each individual case must be re-examined, and it is not excluded that the new decision will again be in favor of the *Mischlinge*.

The grounds for granting an exception must always, as a matter of principle, be the deserts of the *Mischling himself*. (Not the merits of the parent or spouse of German blood.)

The first-degree *Mischling* exempted from evacuation will be sterilized in order to obviate progeny and to settle the *Mischling* problem for good. Sterilization is voluntary, but it is the condition for remaining in the Reich. The sterilized *Mischling* is subsequently free of all restrictive regulations to which he was previously subject.

2. *Treatment of second-degree* Mischlinge

Second-degree *Mischlinge* are on principle classed with persons of German blood, *with the exception of the following cases,* in which the second-degree *Mischlinge* are considered equivalent to Jews:

a) Descent of the second-degree *Mischling* from a bastard marriage (both spouses being *Mischlinge*).

b) Racially especially unfavorable appearance of the second-degree *Mischling*, which will class him with the Jews on external grounds alone.

c) Especially bad police and political rating of the second-degree *Mischling*, indicating that he feels and behaves as a Jew.

Even in these cases exceptions are not to be made if the second-degree *Mischling* is married to a person of German blood.

3. *Marriages between full Jews and persons of German blood*

Here it must be decided from case to case whether the Jewish spouse should be evacuated or whether he or she should be sent to an old-age ghetto in consideration of the effect of the measure on the German relatives of the mixed couple.

4. *Marriages between first-degree* Mischlinge *and persons of German blood*

   a) *Without children*

   If there are no children of the marriage, the first-degree *Mischling* is evacuated or sent to an old-age ghetto. (The same treatment as in marriages between full Jews and persons of German blood, [see] para. 3.)

   b) *With children*

   If there are children of the marriage (second-degree *Mischlinge*), they will be evacuated or sent to a ghetto, together with the first-degree *Mischlinge, if they are considered equivalent to Jews.* Where such children *are considered equivalent to persons of German blood* (the rule), they and also the first-degree *Mischling* are to be exempted from evacuation.

5. *Marriages between first-degree* Mischlinge *and first-degree* Mischlinge *or Jews*

   In such marriages all parties (including children) are treated as Jews and therefore evacuated or sent to an old-age ghetto.

6. *Marriages between first-degree* Mischlinge *and second-degree* Mischlinge

   Both partners to the marriage, regardless of whether or not there are children, are evacuated or sent to an old-age ghetto, since children of such marriages commonly are seen to have a stronger admixture of Jewish blood than the second-degree Jewish *Mischlinge.*

   SS *Gruppenführer* Hofmann is of the opinion that extensive use must be made of sterilization, as the *Mischling*, given the choice of evacuation or sterilization, would prefer to accept sterilization.

   Secretary of State Dr. Stuckart noted that in this form the practical aspects of the possible solutions proposed above for the settling of the problems of mixed marriages and *Mischlinge* would entail endless administrative work. In order to take the biological realities into account, at any rate, Secretary of State Dr. Stuckart proposed a move in the direction of compulsory sterilization.

   To simplify the problem of the *Mischlinge* further possibilities should be considered, with the aim that the Legislator should rule something like: "These marriages are dissolved."

   As to the question of the effect of the evacuation of the Jews on the economy, Secretary of State Neumann stated that Jews employed in essential war industries could not be evacuated for the present, as long as no replacements were available.

   SS *Obergruppenführer* Heydrich pointed out that those Jews would not be evacuated in any case, in accordance with the directives approved by him for the implementation of the current evacuation *Aktion.*

   Secretary of State Dr. Bühler put on record that the Government-General would welcome it if the final solution of this problem *was begun in the Government-General,* as, on the one hand, the question of transport there played no major role and considerations of labor supply would not hinder the course of this *Aktion*. Jews must be removed as fast as possible from the Government-General, because it was there in particular that the Jew as carrier of epidemics spelled a great danger, and, at the same time, he caused constant disorder in the economic structure of the country by his continuous black-market dealings. Furthermore, of the approximately 2½ million Jews under consideration, the majority were in any case *unfit for work*.

Secretary of State Dr. Bühler further states that the solution of the Jewish question in the Government-General was primarily the responsibility of the Chief of the Security Police and the SD and that his work would have the support of the authorities of the Government-General. He had only one request: that the Jewish question in this area be solved as quickly as possible.

In conclusion, there was a discussion of the various possible forms which the solution might take, and here both *Gauleiter* Dr. Meyer and Secretary of State Dr. Bühler were of the opinion that certain preparatory work for the final solution should be carried out locally in the area concerned, but that, in doing so, alarm among the population must be avoided.

The conference concluded with the request of the Chief of the Security Police and the SD to the participants at the conference to give him the necessary support in carrying out the tasks of the [final] solution.

NG-2586-G.

1. *Reich Marshal Hermann Göring.*
2. *The reference is to the districts of western Poland annexed to the Reich.*

# 4
# The Jewish Population Disbelieves Reports of the Extermination*

... The liquidation of the Jews in the Government-General began at Passover 1942. The first victims were the Jews of the city of Lublin, and shortly after that the Jews of the whole District of Lublin. They were evacuated to Belzec, and there they were killed in new gas-chambers that had been built specially for this purpose. The Jewish Underground newspapers gave detailed descriptions of this mass slaughter. But [the Jews of] Warsaw did not believe it! Common human sense could not understand that it was possible to exterminate tens and hundreds of thousands of Jews. They decided that the Jews were being transported for agricultural work in the parts of Russia occupied by the Germans. Theories were heard that the Germans had begun on the productivization of the Jewish lower-level bourgeoisie! The Jewish press was denounced and charged with causing panic,

* *From a report by Yitzhak Cukierman in Warsaw in March 1944, and sent to London on May 4, 1944, through the Polish Underground.*

although the *descriptions* of the "rooting out" of the population corresponded accurately to the reality. Not only abroad were the crimes of the Germans received with disbelief, but even here, close by Ponary, Chelmno, Belzec and Treblinka, did this information get no hearing! This unjustified optimism developed together with the lack of information, which was the result of total isolation from the outside world and the experience of the past. Had not the Germans for two and a half years carried out many deportations of Jews—from Cracow, from Lublin, from the Warsaw District and from the "Reich?" Certainly there had been a few victims and blood had been shed during these deportations, but total extermination?

There were some people who believed it, however. The events at Ponary and Chelmno were a fact, but—it was said—"that was just a capricious act of the local authorities." For, after all, the German authorities in the Government-General did not have the same attitude to the ghettos in the cities and the small towns, not until death brought an equal fate to all. More than once, in various places, the reaction to the information we had about the liquidation of the Jews was: "that cannot happen to us here."

It was of course the Germans themselves who created these optimistic attitudes. Through two and a half years they prepared the work of exterminating the three and a half million Jews of Poland with German thoroughness. They rendered the Jewish masses helpless with the aid of individual killings, oppression and starvation, with the aid of ghettos and deportations. In years of unceasing experiments the Germans perfected their extermination methods. In Vilna they had needed several days to murder a thousand Jews, in Chelmno half an hour was enough to kill a hundred, and at Treblinka ten thousand were murdered every day!...

Yad Vashem Archives, 0-2596.

# 5

# Survey of Problems of Jewish Resistance by an AK Officer in charge of the Jewish Affairs Department[1]

...In the military field the demands of the Jews were directed towards obtaining arms and technical instruction for the preparation of the last, final battle for the Warsaw ghetto. The Jewish Fighting Organization took a decisive stand, saying that the fate of the Warsaw ghetto, like the fate of all the other concentrations of Jews, had been decided, and that total annihilation awaited it sooner or later. In view of this they asked to die with honor, that is—with arms in their hands. In December (1942), after insistent requests, the Jewish Fighting Organization received 10 revolvers and a limited amount of ammunition, by order of the Central Command. These weapons were in very poor condition and only a part were fit for use. The Jewish

Fighting Organization considered this gift as covering only a very small part of their requirements. It therefore demanded incomparably more efficacious help, and said it was willing to budget a large part of the funds[2] which it had at its disposal at its central offices for the purchase of arms. This request could be satisfied only in very small part. Prior to January 17,[3] 1943 (the date of the liquidation of the Warsaw ghetto, which then numbered 50,000 souls), the Jewish Fighting Organization received another 10 revolvers,[4] instructions for sabotage action, a formula for the production of bottle fire-bombs and instruction in military operations. The period up to January 17, 1943, was marked by feverish preparations by the Jewish Fighting Organization for the coming struggle, persistent, continuous calls for help to the army, which reacted to these appeals with lack of confidence and much reserve. The liquidation of the ghetto, which began on January 17, 1943, met with stubborn armed resistance that undoubtedly caused consternation among the German troops and caused the *Aktion* to be stopped after four days. The Jewish Fighting Organization judged its success to mean the postponement for a time of the final liquidation, and with unshaken vigor continued preparations for a second struggle, all the while with growing persistence demanding help from the army. By order of the Chief Commander I held three consultations with the Commander of "Drapacz,"[5] Mr. Konar.[6] Konar agreed to aid the Warsaw ghetto with materials and instructions and spoke of the possibility of our units helping from outside the ghetto. Work was begun immediately under the direction of Chirurg.[7] Contact was established between Jurek[8] of the Jewish Fighting Organization and our officers. The Jewish Fighting Organization received 50 revolvers, a large quantity of bullets, about 80 kgs. [170 lbs.] of material for the preparation of "bottles" and a certain number of defensive grenades. A workshop was put into operation in the ghetto for the manufacture of bottles. In addition it was made easier to obtain the arms which the Jewish Fighting Organization was providing for itself. The plan for the struggle in the ghetto was worked out jointly, and took into account help to be given by our unit. On March 6, 1943, Jurek was arrested (in the apartment in Wspolinej Street). This fact stopped the work process which had been carried out jointly by the Jewish Fighting Organization and "Drapacz." More than ten days after the arrest I had a conversation with Konar. The subject of the conversation was defining the aims of the cooperation between our units and the ghetto fighters. The aim had been supposed to be to get as many Jews as possible away from Warsaw and give them shelter, something that I could do at any time. This plan was not carried out. No units moved out into the designated area. The Jewish Fighting Organization decided that it was to be avoided that their people should have to force their way through a distance of hundreds of kilometers, and the base for materials and shelter established by the order of Edward of "Len"[9] for "Hreczka"[10] proved to be insufficient help. It proved to be impossible to take Jews into our military units in the areas of "Drapacz" and

"Cegielnia."[11] Instead, Konar agreed to organize the Jews into units for passive resistance. One such unit was set up in Warsaw. One of the officers was appointed to train this unit. He came to the place where the training was to be carried out, and arranged a meeting, but failed to come to the meeting. As the result of many interventions the above officer did come once more to the training area, but he arrived drunk. Further requests failed to produce results. The Jewish rebel unit received no military training and ceased to exist...

B. Mark, *Powstanie w getcie warszawskim* ("The Warsaw Ghetto Revolt"), Warsaw, 1963, pp. 345-347.

1. *The man in charge of Jewish affairs in the AK was Henryk Wolinski, whose name in the Underground was "Waclaw."*
2. *The reference is to funds obtained by the Jewish Fighting Organization in the ghetto for the purchase of arms.*
3. *The date is incorrect; it should read January 18. January 18 also was not the date of the final liquidation of the ghetto, which began only on April 19, 1943.*
4. *Receipt of this consignment is not confirmed by Jewish sources.*
5. *The secret name of the AK in the Warsaw District.*
6. *The Underground name of General Antoni Chrusciel, Commander of the AK forces in the Warsaw District.*
7. *The AK Chief of Staff in the Warsaw District, Stanislaw Weber.*
8. *Arie Wilner, representative of the Jewish Fighting Organization on the Aryan side of Warsaw.*
9. *AK, Lublin District.*
10. *AK, Volhynia District.*
11. *A district in the neighborhood of Warsaw.*

# 6
# The Last Letter from Mordecai Anielewicz, Warsaw Ghetto Revolt Commander,* April 23, 1943

It is impossible to put into words what we have been through. One thing is clear, what happened exceeded our boldest dreams. The Germans ran twice from the ghetto. One of our companies held out for 40 minutes and another—for more than 6 hours. The mine set in the "brushmakers" area exploded. Several of our companies attacked the dispersing Germans. Our losses in manpower are minimal. That is also an achievement. Y [Yechiel] fell. He fell a hero, at the machine-gun. *I feel that great things are happening and what we dared do is of great, enormous importance....*

Beginning today we shall shift over to the partisan tactic. Three battle companies will move out tonight, with two tasks: reconnaissance and obtaining arms. Do remember, short-range

* Written to Yitzhak Cukierman

weapons are of no use to us. We use such weapons only rarely. What we need urgently: grenades, rifles, machine-guns and explosives.

It is impossible to describe the conditions under which the Jews of the ghetto are now living. Only a few will be able to hold out. The remainder will die sooner or later. Their fate is decided. In almost all the hiding places in which thousands are concealing themselves it is not possible to light a candle for lack of air.

With the aid of our transmitter we heard a marvelous report on our fighting by the "Shavit" radio station. The fact that we are remembered beyond the ghetto walls encourages us in our struggle. Peace go with you, my friend! Perhaps we may still meet again! *The dream of my life has risen to become fact. Self-defense in the ghetto will have been a reality. Jewish armed resistance and revenge are facts. I have been a witness to the magnificent, heroic fighting of Jewish men of battle.*

M. Anielewicz

Ghetto, April 23, 1943

[M. Kann], *Na oczach swiata* ("In the Eyes of the World"), Zamosc, 1932 [i.e., Warsaw, 1943], pp. 33-34

# 7
# Hitler Bans Public Reference to the "Final Solution of the Jewish Question," July 11, 1943

National-Socialist German Workers' Party
Party Secretariat
Head of the Party Secretariat
Führer Headquarters, July 11, 1943
*Circular No. 33/43 g.*
Re: *Treatment of the Jewish Question*

On instructions from the Führer I make known the following:

Where the Jewish Question is brought up in public, there may be no discussion of a future overall solution *(Gesamtlösung)*.

It may, however, be mentioned that the Jews are taken in groups for appropriate labor purposes.

signed M. Bormann

Distribution: *Reichsleiter*
     *Gauleiter*
     Group leaders

File Reference: Treatment/Jews

NO-2710

# 8

# From a Speech by Himmler before Senior SS Officers in Poznan, October 4, 1943

### Evacuation of the Jews

...I also want to speak to you here, in complete frankness, of a really grave chapter. Amongst ourselves, for once, it shall be said quite openly, but we will never speak about it in public. Just as we did not hesitate on June 30, 1934,[1] to do our duty as we were ordered, and to stand comrades who had erred against the wall and shoot them, and we never spoke about it and we never will speak about it. It was a matter of natural tact that is alive in us, thank God, that we never discussed it. Each of us shuddered and yet each of us knew clearly that the next time he would do it again if it were an order, and if it were necessary.

I am referring here to the evacuation of the Jews, the extermination of the Jewish people. This is one of the things that is easily said: "The Jewish people are going to be exterminated," that's what every Party member says, "sure, it's in our program, elimination of the Jews, extermination—it'll be done." And then they all come along, the 80 million worthy Germans, and each one has his one decent Jew. Of course, the others are swine, but this one, he is a first-rate Jew. Of all those who talk like that, not one has seen it happen, not one has had to go through with it. Most of you men know what it is like to see 100 corpses side by side, or 500 or 1,000. To have stood fast through this and—except for cases of human weakness—to have stayed decent that has made us hard. This is an unwritten and never-to-be-written page of glory in our history, for we know how difficult it would be for us if today—under bombing raids and the hardships and deprivations of war—if we were still to have the Jews in every city as secret saboteurs, agitators, and inciters. If the Jews were still lodged in the body of the German nation, we would probably by now have reached the stage of 1916-17.

The wealth they possessed we took from them. I gave a strict order, which has been carried out by SS *Obergruppenführer* Pohl, that this wealth will of course be turned over to the Reich in its entirety. We have taken none of it for ourselves. Individuals who have erred will be punished in accordance with the order given by me at the start, threatening that anyone who takes as much as a single Mark of this money is a dead man. A number of SS men—they are not very many—committed this offense, and they shall die. There will be no mercy. We had the moral right, we had the duty towards our people, to destroy this people that wanted to destroy us. But we do not have the right to enrich ourselves by so much as a fur, or a watch, by one Mark or a cigarette or anything else. We do not want, in the end, because we destroyed a bacillus, to be infected by this bacillus and to die. I will never stand by and watch while even a small rotten spot develops or takes hold. Wherever it may form we will together burn it away. All in all, however, we can say that we have carried out this most difficult of tasks in a spirit of love for our people. And we have suffered no harm to our inner being, our soul, our character...

PS-1919; Gutman translation, as amended by the Simon Wiesenthal Center.

*1. The reference is to "the night of the long knives"—murder of Röhm, SA leaders and other purges.*

# 9
# From Notes Made by Kurt Gerstein, an Engineer Working for the SS, on the Extermination Camp at Belzec*

...In Lublin, SS *Gruppenführer* Globocnik was waiting for us. He said: This is one of the most highly secret matters there are, perhaps the most secret. Anybody who speaks about it is shot dead immediately. Two talkative people died yesterday. Then he explained to us that, at the present moment—August 17, 1942—there were the following installations:

1. Belzec, on the Lublin-Lvov road, in the sector of the Soviet Demarcation Line. Maximum per day: 15,000 persons (I saw it!).
2. Sobibor, I am not familiar with the exact situation, I did not visit it. 20,000 persons per day.
3. Treblinka, 120 km. NNE of Warsaw, 25,000 per day, saw it!
4. Maidanek, near Lublin, which I saw when it was being built.

Globocnik said: You will have very large quantities of clothes to disinfect, 10 or 20 times as much as the "Textiles Collection," which is only being carried out in order to camouflage the origin of the Jewish, Polish, Czech and other items of clothing. Your second job is to convert the gas-chambers, which have up to now been operated with exhaust gases from an old Diesel engine, to a more poisonous and quicker means, cyanide. But the Führer and Himmler, who were here on August 15, that is, the day before yesterday, gave orders that I am to accompany all persons who visit the installations. Professor Pfannenstiel replied "But what does the Führer say?" Then Globocnik, who is now Higher SS and Police Leader in Trieste on the Adriatic Coast, said "The whole *Aktion* must be carried out much faster." Ministerial Director Dr. Herbert Lindner [Linden] of the Ministry of the Interior suggested "Would it not be better to incinerate the bodies instead of burying them? Another generation might perhaps think differently about this?" Then Globocnik, "But, Gentlemen, if we should ever be succeeded by so cowardly and weak a generation that it does not understand our work, which is so good and so necessary, then, Gentlemen, the whole of National Socialism will

* Gerstein wrote down his evidence on May 26, 1945.

have been  in vain. On the contrary, one should bury bronze plaques [with the bodies], on which it is inscribed that it was we who had the courage to complete this gigantic task." Hitler said to this, "Well my good Globocnik, you have said it, and that is my opinion, too."

The next day we moved on to Belzec. There is a separate little station with two platforms, at the foot of the hill of yellow standstone, due north of the Lublin-Lvov road and rail line. To the south of the station, near the main road, there are several office buildings with the inscription "Belzec Office of the *Waffen*-SS" [Military Unit of the SS]. Globocnik introduced me to SS *Hauptsturmführer* Obermeyer from Pirmasens, who showed me the installations very much against his will. There were no dead to be seen that day, but the stench in the whole area, even on the main road, was pestilent. Next to the small station there was a large barrack labelled "Dressing Room," with a window that said "Valuables," and also a hall with 100 "Barbers' Chairs." Then there was a passage 150 m. long, in the open, enclosed with barbed wire on either side, and signs inscribed "To the Baths and Inhalation Installations." In front of us there was a house, the bath house, and to the right and left large concrete flower pots with geraniums or other flowers. After climbing a few steps there were three rooms each, on the right and on the left. They looked like garages, 4 by 5 m. and 1.90 m. high. At the back, out of sight, there were doors of wood. On the roof there was a Star of David made of copper. The front of the building bore a notice "Heckenholt Institution." That is all I saw that afternoon.

Next morning, a few minutes before 7 o'clock, I was told that the first train would arrive in 10 minutes. And in fact the first train from Lvov arrived a few minutes later. There were 45 carriages with 6,700 persons, of whom, 1,450 were already dead on arrival. Through small openings closed with barbed wire one could see yellow, frightened children, men and women. The train stopped, and 200 Ukrainians, who were forced to perform this service, tore open the doors and chased the people from the carriages with whips. Then instructions were given through a large loudspeaker: The people are to take off all their clothes out of doors—and a few of them in the barracks—including artificial limbs and glasses. Shoes must be tied in pairs with a little piece of string handed out by a small four-year-old Jewish boy. All valuables and money are to be handed in at the window marked "Valuables," without any document or receipt being given. The women and girls must then go to the barber, who cuts off their hair with one or two snips. The hair disappears into large potato sacks, "to make something special for the submarines, to seal them and so on," the duty SS *Unterscharführer* explained to me.

Then the march starts: Barbed wire to the right and left and two dozen Ukrainians with rifles at the rear. They came on, led by an exceptionally pretty girl. I myself was standing with Police Captain Wirth in front of the death chambers. Men, women, children, infants, people with amputated legs, all naked, completely naked, moved past us. In one corner there is a whimsical SS man who tells these poor people in an unctuous voice, "Nothing at all will happen to you. You must just breathe deeply, that strengthens the lungs; this inhalation is necessary because of the infectious diseases, it is good disinfection!'' When somebody asks what their fate will be, he explains that the men will of course have to work, building streets and houses. But the women will not have to work. If they want to, they can help in the house or the kitchen. A little glimmer of hope flickers once more in some of these poor people, enough to make them march unresisting into the death chambers. But most of them understand what is happening; the smell reveals their fate! Then they climb up a little staircase and see the truth. Nursing mothers with an infant at their breasts, naked; many children all ages, naked. They hesitate, but they enter the death chambers, most of them silent, forced on by those behind them, who are driven by the whip lashes of the SS men. A Jewish woman of about 40, with flaming eyes, calls down [revenge] for the blood of her children on the head of the murderers. Police Captain Wirth in person strikes her in the face 5 times with his whip, and she disappears into the gas chamber....

PS-1553; Gutman translation, as amended by the Simon Wiesenthal Center.

# 10
# The Revolt at the Sobibor Extermination Camp*

...as though in response to an order, several axes that had been hidden under coats appeared and were brought down on his head. At that moment the convoy from the second camp approached. A few women who were frightened by what they saw began to scream, some even fainted. Some began to run crazily, without thinking and without purpose. In that situation there was no question of organizing or maintaining order, and therefore I shouted at the top of my voice: "Forward, comrades!"

"Forward!" someone echoed behind me on the right.

"For the Fatherland, for Stalin, forward!"

The proud cries came like thunder from clear skies in the death camp. In one moment these slogans united the Jews of Russia, Poland, Holland, Czechoslovakia, Germany. Six hundred men who had been abused and exhausted broke into cries of "Hurrah!" for life and freedom.

The assault on the arms store failed. Machine-gun fire barred our way.

Most of the people who were escaping turned in the direction of the main gate. There, after they finished off the guards, under cover of fire from the rifles that a few of them had, they threw stones and scattered sand in the eyes of the Fascists who stood in their way, broke

* *The author, Alexander Peczorski, a Jewish Soviet prisoner of war, was one of the organizers of the uprising in the Sobibor Camp on October 14, 1943.*

through the main gate and hurried in the direction of the forest.

One group of prisoners turned left. I saw how they attacked the barbed-wire fence. But after they had cleared away this obstacle, they still had to cross a mine-field that was about 15 meters wide. Many of them surely fell here. I turned towards the Officers' House with a group of prisoners; we cut the barbed wire there and so made an opening. The assumption that the area near the Officers' House would not be mined proved correct. Three of our comrades fell near the barbed wire, but it was not clear whether they stepped on mines or were wounded by bullets, as salvoes were fired at us from various directions.

We are already on the far side of the fence, and the minefield is behind us. We have already gone 100 meters, then another 100... fast, still faster... we must cross the bare open area where we are exposed to the bullets of the murderers... fast, still faster, we must get to the forest, get among the trees, get into shelter... and already we are in the shade of the trees.

I stopped for a moment to catch my breath and cast a glance backwards. Exhausted, with their last srength, running bent over, forwards... we were near the forest. Where is Loka? Where is Shlomo?

...It is difficult to say for certain how many people escaped from the camp. In any case, it is clear that the great majority of the prisoners escaped. Many fell in the open space that was between the camp and the forest. We were agreed that we should not linger in the forest, but divide up into small groups and go in different directions. The Polish Jews escaped in the direction of Chelm. They were drawn there by their knowledge of the language and the area. We, the Soviets, turned east. The Jews who had come from Holland, France and Germany were particularly helpless. In all the wide area that surrounded the camp there was none with whom they had a common language.

The shots from machine-guns and rifles that rattled behind us from time to time helped us to decide on our direction. We knew that the shooting came from the camp. The telephone line had been cut, and Franz had no way of calling for help. The echo of the shots became more distant and disappeared.

It was already beginning to get dark when we once more heard shots echoing far away. Probably they came from our pursuers...

We began to march.

From time to time, from one side or the other, we were joined by new people. I questioned all of them whether they had seen Loka or Shlomo. Nobody had seen them.

We emerged from the forest. We walked for 3 kilometers over open fields, until we reached an open canal about 5 or 6 meters wide. The canal was very deep, and it was not possible to cross it on foot. When I tried to walk around it, I observed a group of people at a distance of about 50 meters from us. We dropped flat on the ground and sent out Arkadiosh to reconnoiter. At first he crawled on his stomach, but after a minute he got to his feet and ran up to the people.

A few minutes later he was back.

"Sasha, they are some of our people. They found tree trunks by the side of the canal and are crossing on them to the other side. Kalimali is there among them."

That is how we crossed the canal....

A. Peczorski (Sasha), "Ha-Mered be-Sobibor" ("The Revolt in Sobibor"). *Yalkut Moreshet*, No. 10 (1969), pp. 30-31. Gutman translation, as amended by the Simon Wiesenthal Center.

# 11
# Extract from Evidence Given at the Nuremberg Trials on the Auschwitz Extermination Camp*

M. Dubost: What do you know about the Jewish transport that arrived from Romainville about the same time as you?

Vaillant-Couturier: When we left Romainville the Jewish women who were together with us remained behind. They were sent to Drancy, and finally arrived in Auschwitz, where we saw them again three weeks later. Of 1,200 who left, only 125 arrived in the camp. The rest were taken to the gas chambers immediately, and of the 125 not a single one was left by the end of the month.

The transports were carried out as follows: at the beginning, when we arrived, when a Jewish transport came there was a "selection." First the old women, the mothers and the children. They were told to get on trucks, together with the sick and people who looked weak. They kept only young girls, young women and young men; the latter were sent to the men's camp.

In general, it was rare for more than 250 out of a transport of 1,000 to 1,500 to reach the camp, and that was the maximum; the others were sent to the gas chambers straight away.

At this "selection" healthy women between 20 and 30 years old were also chosen, and sent to the Experimental Block. Girls and women, who were a little older or not chosen for this purpose, were sent to the camp and, like us, had their heads shaved and they were tattooed.

In the spring of 1944 there was also a block for twins. That was at the time of the immense transport of Hungarian Jews, about 700,000[1] persons. Dr. Mengele, who was carrying out the experiments, kept back the twin children from all transports, as well as twins of any age, so long as both twins were there. Both children and adults slept on the floor in this block. I don't know what experiments were made apart from blood tests and measurements.

M. Dubost: Did you actually see the "selection" when transports arrived?

* *From the evidence of a Frenchwoman, Marie-Claude Vaillant-Couturier, who was a prisoner in the Auschwitz concentration camp, where she arrived on January 1, 1943.*

Vaillant-Couturier: Yes, because when we were working in the Sewing Block in 1944, the block in which we lived was situated just opposite the place where the trains arrived. The whole process had been improved: Instead of carrying out the "selection" where the trains arrived, a siding took the carriages practically to the gas chamber, and the train stopped about 100 m. from the gas chamber. That was right in front of our block, but of course there were two rows of barbed wire between. Then we saw how the seals were taken off the trucks and how women, men and children were pulled out of the trucks by soldiers. We were present at the most terrible scenes when old couples were separated. Mothers had to leave their daughters, because they were taken to the camp, while the mothers and children went to the gas chambers. All these people knew nothing of the fate that awaited them. They were only confused because they were being separated from each other, but they did not know that they were going to their death.

To make the reception pleasanter there was then—in June and July 1944,—an orchestra made up of prisoners, girls in white blouses and dark blue skirts, all of them pretty and young, who played gay tunes such as the "Merry Widow," the Barcarolle from the "Tales of Hoffmann," etc. when the trains arrived. They were told it was a labor camp, and since they never entered the camp they saw nothing but the small platform decorated with greenery, where the orchestra played. They could not know what awaited them.

Those who were taken to the gas chambers—that is, the old people, children and others—were taken to a red brick bulding:

M. Dubost: Then they were not registered?
Vaillant-Couturier: No.
Dubost: They were not tattooed?
Vaillant-Couturier: No, they were not even counted.
Dubost: Were you yourself tattooed?
Vaillant-Couturier: Yes.
(The witness shows her arm)

They were taken to a red brick building with a sign that said Baths. There they were told to get undressed and given a towel before they were taken to the so-called shower room. Later, at the time of the large transports from Hungary, there was no time left for any degree of concealment. They were undressed brutally. I know of these particulars because I was acquainted with a little Jewess from France, who had lived on the Place de la Republique...
Dubost: In Paris?
Vaillant-Couturier: In Paris; she was known as "little Marie" and was the only survivor of a family of nine. Her mother and her seven sisters and brothers had been taken to the gas chambers as soon as they arrived. When I got to know her she worked on undressing the small children before they were taken into the gas chamber.

After the people were undressed they were taken into a room that looked like a shower room, and the capsules were thrown down into the room through a hole in the ceiling. An SS man observed the effect through a spy-hole. After about 5 to 7 minutes, when the gas had done its job, he gave a signal for the opening of the doors. Men with gas-masks, these were prisoners too, came in and took the bodies out. They told us that the prisoners must have suffered before they died, because they clung together in bunches like grapes so that it was difficult to separate them....

*Trial of the Major War Criminals before the International Military Tribunal, Nuremberg 14 November 1945-1 October 1946, VI, Nuremberg, 1947, pp. 214-216. Gutman translation, as amended by the Simon Wiesenthal Center.*

*1.The correct number of Hungarian Jews sent to Auschwitz was about 430,000.*

# Glossary

## HANNA GUNTHER

**Allies.** In World War II, the nations fighting Nazi Germany and Fascist Italy, mainly the United States, Great Britain, and the Soviet Union.

**Anielewicz, Mordecai.** Leader of one of the organizations of Jewish resistance during the uprising in the Warsaw ghetto. Killed May 8, 1943.

**Antisemitism.** Prejudice against and fear of Jews, either religiously or racially—or both. The term was first applied to a movement of opposition to Jews in the second half of the nineteenth century.

**Aryan Race.** "Aryan" was originally applied to people who spoke any of the Indo-European languages—which had nothing to do with race. The Nazis, however, applied the term to people of "proven" non-Jewish, purely Teutonic "racial" background. Their aim was to avoid the bastardization of the German race, and they considered the main task of the state to preserve the ancient racial elements. (*See* Nuernberg Laws)

**Auschwitz.** Concentration and extermination camp in Upper Silesia. Established in 1940 as a concentration camp, it became an extermination camp in early 1942. Eventually, it consisted of three sections: Auschwitz I was the main camp; Auschwitz II, Birkenau, was an extermination camp; Auschwitz III, Monowitz, was the I. G. Farben labor camp, also known as Buna. In addition, there were numerous subsidiary camps.

**Austro-Hungarian Empire.** After the collapse of the Holy Roman Empire in 1806, the Habsburgs became emperors of Austria until 1867, when the Hungarian Compromise created the Dual Monarchy of Austria-Hungary, which existed until 1918. Between 1867 and 1918 it included substantial parts of what later became Czechoslovakia, Yugoslavia, and Poland, as well as parts of the Soviet Union.

**Axis.** The Axis powers were originally Nazi Germany and Fascist Italy (the Rome-Berlin Axis). When Japan entered World War II, this pact was extended to include that country, too (the Berlin-Rome-Tokyo Axis).

**Leo Baeck.** Chief rabbi of Berlin at the time the Nazis came to power. He became chief of the Reich Association of Jews in Germany, an organization that dealt with the Nazi regime in all Jewish questions. Baeck refused to emigrate and leave his flock. In 1943, he was deported to the ghetto of Theresienstadt (Terezin), where he became head of the Council of Elders and spiritual leader of the Jews imprisoned there. He survived and emigrated to London after the war.

**Belz.** A town in Galicia, formerly part of the Austro-Hungarian Empire; now on the Russian-Polish border.

**Belzec.** One of three killing centers (extermination camps) in eastern Poland (the other two were Sobibor and Treblinka), established in 1942 under SS and Police Leader of the Lublin District Odilo Globocnik, for the express purpose of concentrating, pillaging, deporting, and killing the Jews of occupied Poland. Belzec opened in March, 1942, and closed in January, 1943, during which time, more than 600,000 persons were killed there.

**Bund.** *Allgemener Yiddisher Arbeter-Bund* or *Der Bund*—Yiddish. General Union of Jewish Workers in Lithuania, Poland, and Russia. Founded in Vilna, Lithuania, in October, 1897, the Bund was a popular Socialist party—antireligious and anti-Zionist—which was active in the workers' trade union struggle. Originally seeing itself as a part of Russian social democracy, the Bund eventually became a national Jewish movement pressing for Jewish group rights in eastern Europe, not only for Jews as individuals. The Bund organized Jewish self-defense units during the 1903-1907 pogroms and played a role in the 1905 revolution. With the subsequent repression of political parties in Russia, the Bund focused on Yiddish secular cultural activities. A large part of its leadership and active membership migrated to America. The Bund participated in the Russian Revolution but its opposition to the eventually dominant Bolshevik party led to its suppression. It became a mass movement in Poland between the world wars, but it was essentially powerless. Although outlawed, the Bund continued to play an active role in the ghettos during the Holocaust. In the Warsaw ghetto, the Bund delayed resistance, waiting for support from Polish Socialists that never materialized. Eventually, the Bund was a major participant in the Warsaw ghetto uprising.

**Chamberlain, Neville.** British prime minister, 1937-1940. He concluded the Munich Agreement in 1938, which, he believed, would bring "peace in our time."

*Hazak V'Amatz.* "Be strong and courageous"—Hebrew. Words of encouragement to soldiers going into battle, and for similar occasions.

**Chelmno.** A special extermination camp established in late 1941 in the Wartheland (the incorporated region of western Poland), where the SS killed the Jews from Lodz and the Poznan province, using mobile gas vans.

**Christ Killers.** A term applied by religious antisemites to Jews, accusing the Jews of being responsible for killing Christ.

**Chrysostom, St. John.** Greek Church father, born in Antioch. He hated the Jews for their refusal to convert to Christianity.

**Churchill, Winston.** British prime minister, 1940-1945. He succeeded Chamberlain on May 10, 1940, at the height of Hitler's conquest of western Europe. Churchill had been one of the very few Western politicians who, early on, recognized the threat Hitler posed to Europe and strongly opposed Chamberlain's appeasement policies.

**Communists.** Members of the ruling party of the Soviet Union; also members and adherents of the International Communist movement, who believed in the success of the future worldwide Communist revolution.

**Concentration Camps.** Immediately after their assumption of power on January 30, 1933, the Nazis established concentration camps for the imprisonment of all kinds of "enemies" of their regime: actual and potential political opponents (Communists, Socialists, Monarchists, etc.), Jehovah's Witnesses, Gypsies, homosexuals, and other so-called asocials. The general roundup of Jews did not start until 1938. Before then, only Jews who fit one of the other categories were interned in camps. The first three concentration camps were Dachau (near Munich), Buchenwald (near Weimar), and Sachsenhausen (near Berlin).

**Cossacks.** Peasant-soldiers in the Ukraine and in several other regions of the Russian Empire who, until 1918, held certain privileges in exchange for military service. They were responsible for many antisemitic outbursts and pogroms. After the Bolshevik victory in the Russian Revolution of 1917, the majority of the Cossacks fought against the Red armies in the civil war of 1918-1920. In 1920, the Soviet government abolished all their privileges, but in 1936, their status was partly restored, and they were permitted to serve in the Red Army.

**Diaspora.** The dispersion of the Jewish people outside *Erez Israel* (the Land of Israel) after the destruction of the Jewish community of 586 B.C.E.* and the subsequent settlement in other lands. The term generally refers to Jewish communities living outside of *Erez Israel.*

**Dreyfus Affair.** In an atmosphere of French antisemitism in 1894, Alfred Dreyfus, a member of the French General Staff, was convicted of espionage on fraudulent evidence and sentenced to life imprisonment on Devils Island. This was seen by antisemites as proof of "Jewish treachery." A public outcry (1897-1899), including Emile Zola's famous "J'Accuse," reopened the case and the falsity of the charges became public. Dreyfus was eventually pardoned but only exonerated in 1906. The Dreyfus affair led to a diminution of church and military influence in France and resulted in a law mandating the separation of church and state. While it damaged the credibility of the antisemitic movement, it led to intransigence by die-hard antisemites. The Dreyfus affair helped turn Theodor Herzl from an assimilated Jewish journalist into the leader of modern political Zionism.

**Eichmann, Adolf.** Lieutenant-colonel and head of the "Jewish Section" of the Gestapo. Instrumental in implementing the Final Solution, organizing transportation of Jews from all over Europe (first from Austria, later from Hungary, and still later from all western European countries). He was a participant at the Wannsee Conference (January 20, 1942) and was arrested at the end of World War II in the American zone, but escaped, went underground, and disappeared. On May 11, 1960, members of the Israeli Secret Service discovered him in Argentina and smuggled him to Israel. He was tried in Jerusalem (April-December, 1961), convicted, and sentenced to death. He was executed on May 31, 1962.

**Einsatzgruppen.** The mobile units of the Security Police and SS Security Service that followed the German armies into the Soviet Union in June, 1941. Their charge was to kill all Jews, as well as

* *Before the Common Era; equals B.C.*

Soviet commissars, mental defectives, and Gypsies. They were supported by units of the uniformed German Order Police, and used auxiliaries (Ukrainian, Latvian, Lithuanian, and Estonian volunteers) for the killings. The victims were executed by shooting and buried in mass graves (later the bodies were dug up and burned). At least a million Jews were killed in this manner. There were four *Einsatzgruppen* (A to D), and they were subdivided into *Einsatzkommandos*. In 1942, these mobile units were transformed into stationary offices of the Security Police and Security Service.

**Eisenhower, Dwight D.** American general and thirty-fourth president of the United States, 1953-1961. In 1942, he was named United States Commander of the European Theater of Operations. He commanded the American landings in North Africa and in February, 1943, became chief of all Allied forces in North Africa. After successfully directing the invasions of Sicily and Italy, he was called to England to become chief commander of the Allied Expeditionary Forces. He was largely responsible for the cooperation of the Allied armies in the battle for the liberation of the European continent.

**Enlightenment.** *See Haskalah.*

***Erez Israel.*** Land of Israel. During the biblical period, the narrow strip of land at the southwestern point of the Fertile Crescent. Bounded by the Arabian Desert to the east, Mediterannean Sea to the west, Syria to the north, and the Nile Valley to the southwest, it was thus situated at the intersection of Asia, Africa, and the Aegean worlds. "A land flowing with milk and honey," *Erez Israel* is the traditional national, cultural, and religious homeland of the Jewish people. Currently, the State of Israel grants immediate refuge and citizenship to any Jew who so desires as he enters the land.

**Euthanasia.** The original meaning of this term was the easy and painless death for the terminally ill. However, the Euthanasia program under the Nazis took on quite a different meaning: the taking of eugenic measures to improve the quality of the German "race." This was the beginning of a development that culminated in enforced "mercy" deaths for the incurably insane, permanently disabled, deformed, and "superfluous." In due course, three major classifications were developed: 1) euthanasia for incurables; 2) direct extermination by "special treatment"; and 3) experiments in mass sterilization.

**Evian Conference.** President Franklin D. Roosevelt called a conference to discuss the problem of refugees in July, 1938. Thirty-two states met at Evians-les-Bains, Switzerland. However, not much was accomplished, since most Western countries were reluctant to accept Jewish refugees.

**Extermination Camps.** Nazi camps for the mass killing by gas of Jews and others (Gypsies, Russian prisoners-of-war, ill prisoners). Also known as "death camps." These camps were: Auschwitz-Birkenau, Belzec, Chelmno, Lublin-Maidanek, Sobibor, and Treblinka. All were located in eastern Europe.

**Final Solution.** The cover name for the plan to destroy the Jews of Europe, the "Final Solution of the Jewish Question." Beginning in

1941, Jews were rounded up all over Europe and sent to extermination camps in the East. The transports were disguised as "resettlement in the East."

**Frank, Hans.** Governor-general of occupied Poland. A Nazi from the earliest days; SA Storm Trooper. He announced: "Poland will be treated like a colony; the Poles will become slaves of the Greater German Reich." By 1942, more than 85 percent of the Jews in Poland had been transported to extermination camps. Frank was tried at Nuernberg, convicted, and executed in 1946.

**Frick, Wilhelm.** Appointed Minister of the Interior in 1933. A loyal bureaucrat, trained as a jurist, in 1935 he drew up the Nuernberg Laws on Citizenship and Race. He was tried at Nuernberg, convicted, and executed.

**General Government.** The official name for Nazi-occupied Poland, not including the incorporated areas in the West (Upper Silesia, West Prussia, Poznan-Lodz) and Bialystok in the East. Its capital was Cracow. It included the districts of Warsaw, Radom, Cracow, Lublin, and, after 1941, Galicia (Lvov).

**German Empire.** In 1871, after the Franco-Prussian War, the German confederated states were united and William I of Prussia was proclaimed emperor of Germany. From then until 1918, after its defeat in World War I, Germany was ruled by a succession of emperors. In 1918, the last emperor, William II, fled and abdicated, and Germany became a republic, the so-called Weimar Republic, named after the city where the new German constitution had been proclaimed.

**Gerstein, Kurt.** Chief disinfection officer in the Office of the Hygienic Chief of the *Waffen* SS, he purchased the gas needed in Auschwitz, officially for fumigation purposes, but actually used for the killing of Jews. He passed on information about the killings to Swedish representatives and Vatican papal *nuncios.* He hanged himself in a French jail after the war. He is the author of a widely quoted description of a gassing procedure in Belzec, protagonist of Rolf Hochhuth's *The Deputy,* and subject of Saul Friedländer's biography, *The Ambiguity of Good.*

**Ghetto.** The Nazis revived the medieval term "ghetto" to describe their compulsory "Jewish Quarter" *(Wohnbezirk).* These were poor sections of a city where all Jews from the surrounding areas were forced to reside. Surrounded by barbed wire or walls, the ghettos were sealed and no one could leave. Established mostly in eastern Europe (Lodz, Warsaw, Vilna, Riga, Minsk, etc.), the ghettos were characterized by overcrowding, starvation, and heavy labor. All were eventually dissolved and the Jews killed.

**Globocnik, Odilo.** SS major-general in Poland during World War II. In 1938, he had worked for the *Anschluss* of his native Austria and was made *Gauleiter* of Vienna. In Poland, he became head of the police of the Lublin district, where he established the extermination camps Belzec, Sobibor, and Treblinka (as well as Maidanek in the Warsaw district). By 1941, he was head of all extermination camps in Poland.

Arrested by Allied troops in Austria in May, 1945, he committed suicide.

**Goering, Hermann.** An early member of the Nazi party, he participated in Hitler's "beer-hall putsch" in Munich, 1923 (*see* Hitler, Adolf). After its failure he went to Sweden, where he lived until 1927. In 1928, he was elected to the Reichstag and became its president in 1932. When Hitler came to power in 1933, he made Goering air minister of Germany and prime minister of Prussia. He was responsible for the rearmament program and especially for the creation of the German air force. In 1939, Hitler designated him his successor. During World War II, he was virtual dictator of the German economy and was responsible for the total air war Germany waged. On July 31, 1942, he wrote the letter to Heydrich that ordered Heydrich to organize the Final Solution. In May, 1945, he surrendered to American troops and was the chief defendant at the Nuernberg War Crimes Trials (1945-1946). He was convicted and sentenced to death. Two hours before his scheduled hanging, he committed suicide by swallowing a poison capsule.

**Greater German Reich.** Designation of an expanded Germany that was intended to include all German-speaking peoples. It was one of Hitler's most important aims. After the conquest of most of western Europe during World War II, it became a reality for a short time.

**Grynszpan, Herschel.** A Polish-Jewish youth who had emigrated to Paris. He brooded over the fate of his parents who, in the course of a German-wide deportation of Jews with Polish citizenship, were deported to Poland, where they were not accepted but shoved back and forth in the no-man's land between the two countries. On November 7, 1938, he went to the German Embassy and shot and mortally wounded Third Secretary Ernst vom Rath. The Nazis used this as an exucse for the *Kristallnacht* (Night of Broken Glass).

**Gypsies.** A nomadic people believed to have come originally from northwest India, which they left for Persia in the first millennium. They became divided into five main groups that are still extant today. Traveling mostly in small caravans, their bands are still ruled by Elders. Gypsies first appeared in western Europe in the fifteenth century. By the sixteen century, they had spread to every country of Europe. Alternately welcomed and persecuted, they were considered enemies of the state by the Nazis and persecuted almost as relentlessly as Jews. It is assumed that approximately 500,000 perished in the gas chambers.

**Hasid.** Member of an old Jewish religious sect. The Hasidic movement was founded in Poland in the eighteenth century by Baal Shem Tov in reaction to the academic formalism of rabbinical Judaism. The talmudists (whom the Hasidim called Mitnaggedim—opponents) were strongly opposed to it and in 1781 pronounced these modern Hasidim heretics. Hasidism stresses the mercy of God and encourages joyous expression through music and dance. The Baal Shem taught that purity of heart is more pleasing to God than learning. His teachings were largely based on Jewish legends and influenced by the Kaballah and its mysticism. The Hasidic movement developed into a popular mass movement. Largely destroyed by the Holocaust, it has undergone a remarkable resurgence in Israel and the United States.

**Haskalah.** Enlightenment. A movement starting in the eighteenth century as Jews began to have wider contact with and participation in European culture. A branch of the general European Enlightenment, it prized reason, individual autonomy, and a universal spirit. As the Jewish people adapted to European civilization in many ways, the *Haskalah* was not a uniform phenomenon. In general, however, *Haskalah* meant an attempt to reform the individual and community away from traditional modes of behavior. Secular knowledge (especially natural sciences, philosophy, history, and literature) competed with the study of Torah and Talmud. Many were able to effect a synthesis between the two (with varying weights given to secularity and tradition). For others, the *Haskalah* was the cultural bridge allowing them to secularize and even leave Judaism for assimilation to the prevailing national culture.

**Hatikvah.** The unofficial national anthem of Israel. Sung since the turn of the century at Zionist congresses, it has become the official Zionist anthem.

**Hess, Rudolf.** Hitler's deputy; was at his side from the earliest days of the Nazi movement. On May 10, 1941, he flew alone from Augsburg and parachuted to earth in Scotland, where he was promptly interned. The purpose of this flight has never become clear. He probably wanted to persuade the British to make peace with Hitler as soon as he attacked the Soviet Union. Hitler promptly declared him insane. Hess was tried at Nuernberg, found guilty, and was sentenced to life imprisonment. He is the only Nazi still in Spandau Prison.

**Heydrich, Reinhard.** Former naval officer who joined the SS in 1932, after he was dismissed from the navy. He headed the SS Security Service (SD), a Nazi party intelligence agency. In 1933-1934 he became head of the political police (Gestapo) and then also of the criminal police (Kripo). He combined Gestapo and Kripo into the Security Police (Sipo). In 1939, he combined his SD and Sipo into the Reich Security Main Office. He organized the *Einsatzgruppen* that killed Jews in occupied Russia in 1941-1942 and was asked by Goering in 1941 to implement the Final Solution. In January, 1942, he presided over the so-called Wannsee Conference, an interdepartmental meeting to coordinate the Final Solution. In 1941, he was also appointed protector of Bohemia and Moravia. On May 29, 1942, he was assassinated by Czech partisans parachuted by Britain. (For consequences of this assassination, *see* Lidice).

**Himmler, Heinrich.** An old Nazi who participated in the "beer-hall putsch." Appointed Reich leader of the SS in 1929. Built the SS into the elite Nazi party paramilitary organization and made his black-shirted SS independent of the brown-shirted SA. Was used by Hitler to eliminate the SA as a political force and kill its leaders. In 1933-1934, Himmler took over control of German police forces and eventually became chief of the German police. Early in World War II, he presided over a vast empire: all SS formations, including the

*Waffen* SS army; all police forces, both uniformed Order Police and the nonuniformed Security Police; all concentration and labor camps and the Death Head Units guarding them; the SS intelligence units (SD); and various offices for resettlement of racial Germans. In the course of the war, his powers increased. In 1943, he became minister of the Interior; 1944, commander of the Home Army; 1945, commander of the army on the Vistula. Himmler was the senior SS leader responsible for the implementation of the Final Solution. In his Posen speech in 1943, he discussed the killing of the Jews and told his senior SS officers that he was executing Hitler's order. In late 1944, he ordered an end to the gassings; early in 1945, he attempted to negotiate with the Allies. He tried to flee but was captured by British troops. While being examined by a British military physician, he swallowed cyanide and died almost immediately.

**Hitler, Adolf.** Fuehrer and Reich chancellor. Although born in Austria, he settled in Munich in 1913. At the outbreak of World War I, he enlisted in the Bavarian army, where he became a corporal and received the Iron Cross First Class for bravery. Returning to Munich after the war, he joined with a few nationalist veterans in the German Workers' party. In 1920, the party was reorganized under his leadership and became the National Socialist German Workers' party (NSDAP). In November, 1923, he attempted the "beer-hall putsch" in Munich, which was supposed to bring Germany under nationalist control. When the coup failed, Hitler fled but was arrested and sentenced to five years in the Landsberg fortress. He served only nine months. In prison he dictated to Rudolf Hess his book *Mein Kampf*, which became the bible of National Socialism. When the Nazis were elected the largest party in the Reichstag (July, 1932), President von Hindenburg offered Hitler a subordinate position in the cabinet. However, Hitler held out for more power. In January, 1933, Hindenburg made Hitler chancellor of a coalition cabinet but refused him extraordinary powers. Hitler took office on January 30, 1933. However, he immediately began to set up a dictatorship, although he won a bare majority in the Reichstag elections on March 5, 1933. In 1934, the chancellorship and presidency were united in the person of the Fuehrer. Soon all parties were outlawed and opposition brutally suppressed; liberal newspapers banned; and Communists, Socialists, Jews, and many other actual or potential "enemies" relentlessly persecuted. In 1938, Hitler implemented his dream of a "Greater Germany" by first annexing Austria, then (with the agreement of the Western democracies) the Sudetenland (the German province of Czechoslovakia), and finally Czechoslovakia itself. On September 1, 1939, Hitler's army invaded Poland. By then the Western democracies realized that no agreement with Hitler could be valid, and World War II had begun. In the blitzkrieg of 1941, he defeated France, invaded Belgium and Holland, and occupied Denmark and Norway. In June, 1941, he invaded Russia, but he did not succeed in conquering it, although the Germans had occupied extensive territory. England also held out and fought back. When America joined the war in December, 1941, the tide slowly began to turn. Although the war was obviously lost by early 1945, Hitler insisted that the Germans continue to fight to the death. He remained in his bunker in Berlin when it was stormed by the Red Army. On April 29, 1945, he married his long-time friend, Eva Braun. On April 30, he committed suicide with her in the underground shelter of the Chancellery, having ordered that their bodies be burned.

**Holocaust.** The destruction of some six million Jews by the Nazis and their followers in Europe between the years 1933 and 1945. Other individuals and groups suffered grievously during this period, but only the Jews were marked for complete and utter annihilation. The term "genocide" is not a preferred term for this event. "Genocide" was coined by Raphael Lemkin in 1944 to refer to atrocities and policies of destruction perpetrated against a number of peoples. As such, it tends to obscure the unique experience of the Jewish people between 1933 and 1945. It has been noted that the term "Holocaust"— literally meaning "a completely burnt sacrifice"—tends to allow a sacrificial connotation to what occurred. The Yiddish term *"hurbn"* (derived from the Hebrew), meaning "destruction," has associations with the destruction of the First and Second Temples in Jerusalem. The Hebrew term *"Shoah"* is a biblical term meaning widespread disaster.

**Jehovah's Witnesses.** A sect originating in America, organized by Charles Taze Russell, whose doctrine centers on the Second Coming of Christ. The Witnesses base their teachings on the Bible. They have no official ministers of the Gospel. Regarding governments as the work of Satan, the Witnesses refuse to salute the flag, bear arms in war, and to participate in the affairs of government. This doctrine obviously brought them into conflict with National Socialism. They were considered enemies of the state and relentlessly persecuted.

**Jews.** According to Jewish law, all those born of a Jewish mother and those converted to Judaism. Mostly considered members of the religion of Judaism; also, those considered members of the Jewish nation. Also known as Hebrews, Israelites, and those of the Mosaic persuasion. Falsely considered as members of a race by Nazis and other antisemites.

**Kaddish.** A Jewish prayer for the dead, recited by mourners.

**Keitel, Wilhelm.** A career officer, connected with the War Ministry since 1935. In 1938, when Hitler personally assumed supreme command of all the armed forces, he promoted him to full general and made him chief of the High Command of the Armed Forces. He was Hitler's chief military adviser during World War II. After the fall of France in 1940, he took part in the signing of the armistice at Compiègne. He was made field marshal. Although he threatened to resign in 1941 because he was opposed to the invasion of Russia, he still believed in Hitler and remained loyal to him, even agreeing to issue such orders as the Night and Fog Decree (*see* Night and Fog Decree). On May 8, 1945, he ratified in Berlin the unconditional surrender of Germany. He was convicted at Nuernberg and executed.

***Kristallnacht.*** Night of Broken Glass. Pogrom unleashed by the SA on November 9-10, 1938. All over Germany, synagogues and other

Jewish institutions were burned down, Jewish stores destroyed and their windows smashed, Jews mistreated, and approximately 35,000 Jewish men sent to concentration camps. The "excuse" for this action was the assassination of Ernst vom Rath in Paris, and the Nazi leaders tried to disguise this highly organized pogrom as "spontaneous" demonstrations.

**Krupp Munitions Plant at Auschwitz.** When the Krupp fuse plant in Essen was bombed in March, 1943, plans were made to move the remaining machinery to Auschwitz. Five hundred Jewish workers from two Berlin firms were "recruited" and deported to Auschwitz to be made available to Krupp. Other workers were selected from the camp.

**League of Nations.** An international organization founded after World War I, with headquarters in Geneva, Switzerland. Predecessor of the United Nations, its purpose was the promotion of international cooperation and the achievement of international peace and security. President Woodrow Wilson incorporated the proposal in his Fourteen Points and was the chief figure in its establishment at the Paris Peace Conference of 1919. Some of its allied bodies were the Permanent Court of International Justice and the International Labor Organization (which later became affiliated with the United Nations). Although at first the League was successful in settling minor disputes, especially in the economic sphere (financial aid to needy states, health surveys, aid to refugees, etc.), it started with a major handicap when the United States refused to join. Its failures in the political sphere were due to the hostility of the great powers, who preferred to make their own unilateral decisions, as well as weaknesses of organization. By 1938, the League had more or less collapsed, but it lingered on until 1946, when it dissolved itself.

**Lehman, Herbert.** Governor of New York State, 1932-1942. During his administration, much liberal legislation was enacted. In 1943, he was appointed director of the United Nations Relief and Rehabilitation Administration (UNRRA). From 1949 to 1956 he was a United States senator.

**Lidice.** A Czech mining village (population 700). In reprisal for the assassination of Reinhard Heydrich, the Nazis "liquidated" the village in 1942. They shot the men and older boys, deported the women and children to concentration camps, razed the village to the ground, and struck its name from the maps. After World War II, a new village was built near the site of the old Lidice, which is now a national park and memorial.

**Lodz.** City in western Poland (incorporated territory), renamed Litzmannstadt, where the first major ghetto was created in April, 1940. By September, 1941, the population in the ghetto was 144,000 on an area of 1.6 square miles; it had 25,000 rooms, which averages 5.8 people per room. In October, 1941, 20,000 Jews from Germany, Austria, and the Protectorate of Bohemia and Moravia were sent to the Lodz ghetto. Deportations from Lodz during 1942 and June-July, 1944, led to the extermination camp Chelmno. In August-September,

1944, the ghetto was dissolved and the remaining 60,000 Jews sent to Auschwitz.

**Lublin.** City in eastern Poland (General Government). Headquarters of SS and Police Leader Odilo Globocnik, who headed Operation Reinhard. Site of a ghetto, with many smaller ghettos surrounding it, at one time it was considered by the Nazis as a possible "Jewish reservation." Many German Jews were deported to the Lublin region (Piaski, Itsbica, etc.). Surrounding Lublin were many forced labor camps, the Trawniki training camp for Ukrainian and other volunteer SS, and the concentration camp Maidanek.

**Luther, Martin.** Leader of the German Reformation and founder of the Lutheran church. In 1517, he posted his ninety-five theses on the door of the castle church in Wittenberg. Luther hoped that his understanding of Christianity would help convert the Jews. When this failed, he returned to a virulent medieval anti-Judaism with all the chimeric fantasies about the Jews, such as the ritual murder of children. In 1935, the Nazis published a popular edition of his pamphlet *The Jews and Their Lies,* in which he wrote: "So we are even at fault in not avenging all this innocent blood of Our Lord and of the Christians which they shed for 300 years after the destruction of Jerusalem. . . . We are at fault in not slaying them."

**Mauthausen Concentration Camp.** A camp for men, opened in August, 1938, in Austria, near Linz. Established to exploit the nearby quarries, it was classified by the SS as a camp of utmost severity, and conditions there were brutal even by concentration camp standards. Many were killed by falling or being pushed down into the quarries.

**Maidanek.** Lublin-Maidanek in eastern Poland (General Government) was opened in late 1941. At first a labor camp for Poles and a POW camp for Russians, it was classified as a concentration camp in April, 1943. Like Auschwitz, it was also an extermination camp, holding large numbers of Jews, who were all killed in November, 1943. Maidanek was liberated by the Red Army in July, 1944.

***Mein Kampf.*** The autobiographical book Hitler wrote while he was imprisoned in the Landsberg fortress after the "beer-hall putsch" in 1923. It was published in the fall of 1925. In this book, Hitler propounds all his ideas, beliefs, and plans for the future of Germany. Everything, including his foreign policy, is permeated by his "racial ideology." The Germans, belonging to the "superior" Aryan race, have a right to "living space" (*Lebensraum*) in the East, which is inhabited by "inferior" Slavs. Throughout the book he accuses Jews, whom he considers the source of all evil, and equates them with Bolshevism and at the same time with international capitalism. Unfortunately, those people who read the book (except for his admirers) did not take it seriously but considered it the ravings of a maniac.

**Mengele, Josef.** SS physician at Auschwitz, notorious for pseudomedical experiments, especially on twins and Gypsies. He selected among new arrivals, by simply pointing to the right or left, thus separating those considered able to work from those who were not. Those too weak or too old to work were sent straight to the gas chambers after all their possessions, including their clothes, were taken for reuse by the Germans. After the war he spent some time in a British internment hospital but disappeared, went underground, and escaped, presumably to Argentina. Apparently, he is now in Paraguay, where he became a citizen in 1957. Although he has been hunted by Interpol, Israeli agents, and Simon Wiesenthal, he has not yet been caught.

**Niemoeller, Martin.** Born in 1892, he was a U-boat captain during World War I. Afterwards he became a Protestant pastor in Berlin-Dahlem. As a German nationalist he first welcomed the Nazis but soon became disillusioned, and was one of the founders (in the fall of 1933) and guiding spirits of the Confessing Church. This became a minority group among German Protestant churchmen opposed to the so-called German Christians who wanted to combine National Socialism and Protestantism. The members of the Confessing Church objected to what they considered anti-Christian tendencies and to the Aryan clause, which prohibited Christians of Jewish descent from holding office in the Church. In 1938, Niemoeller was arrested and spent the years until the end of World War II in Sachsenhausen and Dachau concentration camps. In 1947, he became president of the Evangelical church in Hesse-Nassau.

**Night and Fog Decree.** Issued on December 7, 1941, by Hitler to seize "persons endangering German security" who were not to be executed immediately but were to vanish without a trace into night and fog. (*See* Keitel, Wilhelm)

**Nuernberg Laws.** During the party rally in Nuernberg in the fall of 1935, the Law for the Protection of German Blood and Honor was promulgated. It prohibited marriages and extramarital intercourse between Jews and "citizens of German or related blood"; employment in Jewish households of female citizens of "German or related blood" under the age of forty-five; and the raising of the Reich flag by Jews. Two months later (November, 1935), a second law was enacted, the Reich Citizenship Law, which stated that only persons of "German or related blood" could be citizens. This law also defined various categories of people of mixed blood *(Mischlinge)*. It established three categories of "non-Aryans": (1) Jews: persons with two Jewish grandparents, persons belonging to the Jewish religion or married to a Jewish person on September 15, 1935, and persons with three or four Jewish grandparents; (2) *Mischlinge* of the first degree—persons with two Jewish grandparents who did not belong to the Jewish religion and were not married to a Jewish person on September 15, 1935; (3) *Mischlinge* of the second degree—persons with one Jewish grandparent. *Mischlinge* suffered basically three discriminations: (1) they were excluded from the civil service and the party; (2) they were restricted in the army to service as common soldiers; (3) they could not marry Germans without official consent.

**Olympic Games in Berlin.** In 1936, the Summer Olympic games were held in Berlin. The Nazis were determined to impress the many foreign visitors and organized and staged these games with lavish displays. They even downplayed the anti-Jewish slogans and signs in the vicinity of the stadium.

**Owens, Jesse.** Black American athlete who won the 100-meter and 200-meter runs in the Olympic games in Berlin in August, 1936. Hitler stormed out of the stadium quickly in order to avoid having to present two gold medals to a black man. Owens died in 1981.

**Pale of Settlement.** The defined limited area in Russia where Jews were allowed to live. Established in 1804 under the reign of Alexander I, this area included sparsely populated sections on the Black Sea and in the southern Ukraine. It also included parts of Poland which had been annexed by Russia. The Pale of Settlement ended in 1917.

**Partisans.** Members of groups of irregular troops engaged in guerrilla warfare, often behind enemy lines. During World War II this term was applied to all resistance fighters in Nazi-occupied countries, first to those in Yugoslavia and later to Jewish resistance fighters who fought with Russians in the forests and those in the ghettos of eastern Europe.

**Pesah.** Passover. The eight-day (seven in *Erez Israel*) festival commemorating the Exodus from Egypt of the children of Israel. It is observed with the elimination of all leavened food stuff—*hamez*— from one's diet and possession; the eating of *matzah* (unleavened bread), commemorating the quick bread baked by the children of Israel when they departed hastily; and the celebration on the eve of the holiday of the festive ritual meal, the *seder,* during which the *Haggadah* is recited recounting the process and significance of the Exodus.

**Pinsk.** City in Belorussia, in the Pripet Marshes. It had belonged to Poland since 1921 but was ceded to the Soviet Union in 1939, after the conquest of Poland. More than half its population was Jewish and practically all were killed by mobile killing units, especially *Einstazgruppe* A, which closely followed the invading German army.

***Pogroms.*** Devastation—Yiddish. Violent riots against Jews in villages, towns, and large urban areas in the nineteenth and twentieth centuries. While usually "spontaneously" carried out by hooligans, they were supported and planned by antisemitic elements who sought pretexts (e.g., blood libels) for attacks. Typically the police—often bribed—turned a blind eye, only interceding after murder, rape, and looting had occurred and passions were temporarily abated. A terrible pogrom took place in Kishinev in April, 1903, in which over fifty people were killed. This created a backlash of sentiment for the Jews in certain segments of the Russian population (and spurred the growth of Jewish self-defense units).

***Protocols of the Elders of Zion.*** A major piece of antisemitic propaganda written in Paris by members of the Russian secret police. Essentially, it was a copy of a French polemic written by the French lawyer, Maurice Joly, which was directed against Napoleon III. Substituting Jewish leaders, the *Protocols* maintained that Jews were plotting world dominion by setting Christian against Christian, corrupting Christian morals, and attempting to destroy the economic and political viability of the West. It gained great popularity after

World War I and was translated into many languages. It encouraged antisemitism in Germany, France, Great Britain, and the United States. It has long been repudiated as an absurd and hateful lie. The book currently has been reprinted and widely distributed by Neo-Nazis, those Third World countries who are committed to the destruction of the State of Israel, and the Soviet Union.

**Radom.** 1) The city in Poland (General Government), where a ghetto, surrounded by a massive wall, was established in April, 1941; 2) the name of district in the General Government in which the city was located; 3) the ghetto, later a labor camp, which still later became a subsidiary of Maidanek.

**Rath, Ernst vom.** Third Secretary at the German Embassy in Paris, who was assassinated on November 7, 1938, by Herschel Grynszpan. (*See* Grynszpan, Herschel)

*Rebbe.* Literally, "my master." A version of the term *"rabbi,"* it often refers to one's teacher or a Hasidic master or *zaddik* (righteous one).

**Ribbentrop, Joachim von.** Champagne merchant who joined the Nazi party very early. He was ambassador to Great Britain, 1936-1938 and German foreign minister, 1938-1945. He was influential in forming the Rome-Berlin Axis and in concluding the Russo-German nonaggression pact in August, 1939. He was convicted at Nuernberg and executed.

**Rosenberg, Alfred.** A Baltic German born in Estonia, he came to Germany in 1919, a rabid anti-Bolshevik. In 1923, Hitler made him editor of the party organ *Voelkischer Beobachter.* Author of the anti-Christian, antisemitic, neo-pagan book, *The Myth of the 20th Century (Der Mythos des 20. Jahrhunderts),* which provided Hitler with a spurious philosophical and scientific basis for his racial ideology, he became the official Nazi party "philosopher." In 1933, he became foreign affairs secretary of the party. After 1940, he headed the *Einsatzstab* Rosenberg, whose purpose it was to loot art works in the occupied countries of western Europe, especially France and Holland. In 1941, he became minister for the Eastern Occupied Territories. He was tried at Nuernberg, convicted, and executed.

**Rosh Hashanah.** Jewish New Year. A two-day holiday marked by solemn celebration, prayer, and supplication. The *shofar* (ram's horn) is sounded a number of times during the synagogue service with the intention of arousing the congregation to *teshuvah* (penitence).

**Sabbath.** *Shabbes*—Yiddish; *Shabbat*—Hebrew. The day for rest, prayer, study, and three festive meals. It begins at sundown on Friday and lasts until after dark on Saturday. Religiously observant Jews refrain from performing any physically creative tasks on that day (e.g., use of electricity, kindling a fire, writing, or cooking).

**Scapegoat.** A goat over the head of which the high priest of the Hebrews confessed the sins of the people on the Day of Atonement, after which it was allowed to escape (*see* Lev. 16:8-22). In general usage, the term is applied to persons or groups who are blamed for the mistakes or misfortunes of others for which they bear no responsibility.

**Selection.** Euphemism for the process of choosing victims for the gas chambers in the Nazi camps by separating them from those considered fit to work whenever a new transport arrived. (*See* Mengele, Josef)

***Shtetl.*** Yiddish name for a small town. It is used to describe the Jewish communities in eastern Europe. These were cohesive communities, mostly Orthodox, living according to Jewish law, where the *shul* (synagogue) was the spiritual center and the rabbis settled disputes.

**Simhat Torah.** Jewish feast day (following Sukkot), celebrating the annual end of the weekly readings of the Torah and the beginning of the new cycle.

**Slavs.** Largest ethnic and linguistic group of peoples in Europe, belonging to the Indo-European linguistic family; inhabiting mainly eastern, southeastern, and east-central Europe, or religiously belonging either to the Roman Catholic or the Orthodox Eastern church. Another distinction: the eastern Slavs use the Cyrillic alphabet; the western Slavs, the Roman alphabet.

**Sobibor.** Extermination camp in the Lublin district in eastern Poland (*See* Belzec; Extermination Camps). Sobibor opened in May, 1942, and closed one day after a rebellion of the Jewish prisoners on October 14, 1943. At least 250,000 Jews were killed there.

**Social Democrats.** Members and adherents of the Social Democratic party. The Social Democratic party in Germany was founded in 1875 by the merger of the General German Workers' Association (founded in 1863 by Ferdinand Lassalle) and the Social Democratic Workers' party (founded in 1869 by August Bebel and Wilhelm Liebknecht). Outlawed by the Nazis, its members were persecuted. After World War II, it emerged again under the same name (SPD).

**SS.** Abbreviation, usually written with two lightening symbols, for *Schutzstaffel* (Protective Units), the Nazi paramilitary, blackshirted storm troops. It was built into a giant organization by Heinrich Himmler, including, among others, the police, the camp guards, and the fighting units (*Waffen* SS). (*See Einsatzgruppen*)

**SS St. Louis.** The steamship *St. Louis* was a refugee ship that left Europe in the spring of 1939, bound for Cuba. When the ship arrived there, the refugees were not allowed to go on land. No other country accepted them, and the ship finally had to return to Europe. Some of the refugees were later granted entry into Holland, France, and Belgium.

**Stalin, Joseph.** Absolute ruler of the Soviet Union, Lenin's successor. Although Communists and Nazis were arch enemies, Stalin concluded a nonaggression pact with Hitler in August, 1939. After the Nazis had defeated Poland, Stalin took his share of the spoils. After Hitler invaded Russia in June, 1941, Stalin joined the war on the side of the Allies, constantly urging them to help him by opening a second front in the West. He attended several international conferences with the Allied leaders. However, it was an uneasy alliance that barely lasted to the end of World War II and soon deteriorated into the cold war.

**Star of David.** *Mogen David*—Hebrew; literally, shield of David. A six-pointed star formed of two equilateral triangles. A symbol of Judaism. Used by the Nazis as an identification mark for Jews. After September 1, 1941, all Jews in Germany over the age of six had to wear this badge whenever they appeared in public: a black star on yellow background with the word *Jude* (Jew) inscribed in black in the center of the star. According to specifications, it had to be as large as the palm of a hand and sewn tightly on the left front of the clothing. In other countries of western Europe, it was imposed (with "Jew" written in the native language) during 1942. In the East, it was imposed in 1939, in former Soviet territories in 1941, and was worn there on armbands or on the front and back of clothing.

**State of Israel.** On May 14, 1948, the independent Republic of Israel was proclaimed in Tel Aviv. The Declaration of Independence stated that the Land of Israel had been the birthplace of the Jewish people and that it would be open to all Jews who wished to come there. Before independence, when it was the British Mandate of Palestine, Jewish immigration had been severely restricted.

**Streicher, Julius.** Early member of the Nazi party and *Gauleiter* of Franconia. Editor of the notoriously vicious antisemitic weekly, *Der Stuermer,* he was Nazi Germany's leading antisemitic propagandist. In his articles and speeches he combined racial fantasies and pornographic antisemitism to produce vicious diatribes. He was convicted and executed at Nuernberg.

**Sukkot.** The eight-day holiday (seven in *Erez Israel*) of "Tabernacles," commemorating the wandering of the children of Israel in the desert after the Exodus from Egypt. One of the chief observances of the holiday is dwelling in the *sukkah*—a hutlike structure with an impermanent semiopen roof, reminding one of God's continuing providence.

**Synagogue.** *Shul*—Yiddish; *Beit ha-kenest*—Hebrew. Jewish house of worship, for prayer and religious study. At times, it is also a cultural and intellectual center.

*Tallit* (*taliyot,* pl.). Ritual prayer shawl with four corners, symbolizing the 613 laws of the Torah. The *arba kanfot* is a poncho version worn either over or under the shirt the entire day.

**Talmud.** Compilation of the rabbinic tradition of the Jews with rabbinical elucidations, elaborations, and commentaries. It consists of two parts: the Mishnah, or text of the rabbinic tradition; and the Gemarah, the expansive elucidations and discussions of the apodictic Mishnah. The Talmud is the accepted authority for Orthodox Jews everywhere, and the subject of intensive study.

*Tefillin.* Phylacteries—black leather boxes containing Scriptural passages specially written on parchment. Attached to leather straps, they are worn on the left forearm (the right forearm if the wearer is lefthanded) and head of the religiously observant Jewish man during morning prayer.

**Terezin (Theresienstadt).** Established in early 1942 in Bohemia as a "model" ghetto, it differed from all other ghettos. It was not a sealed section of a town but was located in an eighteenth-century Austrian garrison. It became a Jewish town governed and guarded by the SS.

When the deportations from central Europe to the extermination camps began in the spring of 1942, certain groups were excluded: invalids, and those over sixty-five; decorated and disabled war veterans; those of mixed marriages and their children; and prominent Jews with special connections. These were sent to the ghetto in Terezin. They were joined by old and young Jews from the Protectorate, and later by small numbers of prominent Jews from Denmark and Holland. Its large barracks served as dormitories for communal living; they also contained offices, workshops, infirmaries, and communal kitchens. The Nazis used Terezin to deceive public opinion. They tolerated a lively cultural life: theater, music, lectures, and art. Thus, it could be shown to foreign visitors from the International Red Cross. However, Terezin was only a station on the road to the extermination camps; about 88,000 were deported to their deaths in the East. In April, 1945, only about 17,000 Jews remained in Terezin, where they were joined by about 14,000 Jewish concentration camp prisoners, evacuated from camps threatened by the Allied armies. On May 7, 1945, the Red Army liberated Terezin.

**Tishah be-Av.** The ninth of Av (Jewish month during the summer). Commemorating the destruction of the First and Second Temples in Jerusalem and, to a lesser extent, other tragedies in Jewish history, it is a national day of mourning (preceded by three weeks of public mourning, during which no weddings are performed). It is celebrated with a fast and the solemn reading of the Book of Lamentations and various elegies.

**Torah.** Literally, "teaching." Minimally, it refers to the Pentateuch (Five Books of Moses). The *Sefer Torah* (Scroll of the Torah) is the specially written Pentateuch on rolled parchment. It has a special sanctity in Jewish law. In an expanded meaning, the Torah refers to the entire corpus of Jewish law, commentary, and tradition (through present times) based on the Pentateuch.

**Treblinka.** Extermination camp on the river Bug (General Government). Opened in July, 1942, it was the largest of the three killing centers of Operation Reinhard. Between 700,000 and 900,000 persons were killed there. A revolt of the inmates on August 2, 1943, destroyed most of the camp and it was closed in November, 1943. (*See* Belzec; Sobibor; Extermination Camps)

*Umschlagplatz.* German word meaning "reloading place." It was a square in the Warsaw ghetto where Jews were herded together for deportation to Treblinka.

**Vienna.** Capital of Austria; once the capital of the entire Habsburg Empire. Hitler had a special hatred for Vienna because as a young man he was not admitted to the academy to study art and architecture. After the *Anschluss* he demoted it as much as possible to a provincial city.

**Wannsee.** Lake near Berlin where the so-called Wannsee Conference was held on January 20, 1942. It was an intramural meeting to coordinate the Final Solution and was attended by Heydrich, Eichmann, and other Nazis.

**Wallenberg, Raoul.** Swedish industrialist who, in 1944, went to Hungary on a mission to save as many Jews as possible by handing out forged Swedish papers, passports, and visas. He is credited with saving thousands of people. After the liberation of Budapest, he was seen in conference with the Russians, and that is the last that is known of him. It is not known whether he died in a Russian prison or whether he is still alive and a prisoner. Recently there have been rumors that he had been seen. There is now an international effort being made to find out what really happened.

**Warsaw.** Before World War II, the capital of Poland. After Poland was defeated by the Nazis, it became a city in the General Government.

**Warsaw Ghetto.** Established in November, 1940, it was surrounded by a wall and contained almost 500,000 Jews. Almost 45,000 Jews died there in 1941 alone, due to overcrowding, hard labor, lack of sanitation, insufficient food, starvation, and disease. A revolt took place in the ghetto on April 1943, when the Germans, commanded by General Juergen Stroop, attempted to raze the ghetto and deport the remaining inhabitants to Treblinka. The defense forces, commanded by Mordecai Anielewicz, included all Jewish parties. The fighting lasted twenty-eight days.

**Weissmandel (Rabbi Michael Dov-Ber).** Head of the rescue committee of Bratislava (Slovakia), 1943-1944, *Va'adat Hazala*. He passed the information about the deportation of Hungarian Jews on to Jewish groups in Switzerland.

**Wilson, Woodrow.** Twenty-eighth president of the United States, 1913-1921. He tried very hard to keep the United States out of World War I, but after the Germans renewed their unrestricted submarine warfare early in 1917, which sank several American ships, it became impossible, and the United States declared war on Germany in April, 1917. He felt that the war was necessary "to make the world safe for democracy" and drew up a program of Fourteen Points, which he considered essential for the future peace of the world. He headed the American delegation to the Paris Peace Conference; however, the resultant Treaty of Versailles was far removed from his dreams. (*See* League of Nations)

**Wirth, Christian.** A Stuttgart police officer and captain (later, major) in the SS. He was involved in the Euthanasia Program, 1940-1941, which involved the killing of mental patients in Germany. In 1942-1943, he was commander of the extermination camps of Operation Reinhard: Belzec, Sobibor, and Treblinka. He was killed by partisans in Yugoslavia.

**World War I (1914-1918).** A worldwide war fought between the Central Powers of Germany and Austria-Hungary, with their satellites, against England, France, and, later, the United States. It was supposed to be "the war to end all wars," and to make the world "safe for democracy." It ended with the defeat of the Central Powers, but did not live up to President Woodrow Wilson's idealistic Fourteen Points. (*See* Wilson, Woodrow; League of Nations)

**Yeshivah** *(yeshivot, pl.).* Academies for the traditional study of Talmud. (*See* Talmud)

**Yiddish.** Literally, "Jewish." The popular language of Ashkenazic (of German descent) Jews from the tenth century on. Its grammar is derived from German, while its vocabulary also stems from Hebrew, Aramaic, Slavic, Romance, and other languages. Whatever its origins and sources, Yiddish is a language in its own right. With the destruction of European Jewish life in the Holocaust, the existence of Yiddish has been imperiled. In recent years, there has been a new rise in the academic study of Yiddish in Israel and the United States. As a vital living language passed on to a new generation, it can be found chiefly among Orthodox Jews of eastern European origin, especially the Hasidim.

**Yom Kippur.** Day of Atonement. Occurring ten days from the beginning of Rosh Hashanah, it is the holiest day of the Jewish year. Spent in prayer in the synagogue, the fast commences the (preceding) evening and ends the next day after sunset.

# Suggested Reading

Abella, Irving, and Troper, Harold. *None Is Too Many: Canada and the Jews of Europe, 1933-1948.* Toronto: Lester and Orpen Dennys, 1982.
    Well-researched study of Canadian failures to rescue European Jews.

Arad, Yitzhak; Gutman, Yisrael; and Margaliot, Abraham. *Documents on the Holocaust: Selected Sources on the Destruction of the Jews of Germany and Austria, Poland, and the Soviet Union.* Jerusalem: Yad Vashem (in cooperation with the Anti-Defamation League and Ktav Publishing House), 1981.
    This volume contains a collection of documents from Germany, Austria, Poland, the Baltic countries, and areas of the Soviet Union occupied by the Nazis during World War II. It includes Nazi ideology and policy towards Jews and Jewish response to Nazi persecution in these countries.

Bauer, Yehuda. *The Holocaust in Historical Perspective.* Seattle: University of Washington Press, 1978.
    In a scholarly and lucid contribution to Holocaust historiography, Bauer places the Holocaust in an historical perspective that enables the reader to understand the uniqueness of this event; he attacks those who attempt to transform the Holocaust into a mystical experience. There are important essays on: The Holocaust and American Jewry; Jew and Gentile; The Holocaust and After; and the Mission of Joel Brand.

Berkovits, Eliezer. *With God in Hell.* New York: Sanhedrin Press, 1979.
    This book vividly recounts stories and instances of Jewish spirituality in the camps and the ghettos. The author analyzes these responses psychologically, philosophically, and in terms of the cultural-religious background of European Jews. This work also raises the question of believing after the Holocaust.

Blatter, Janet; Milton, Sybil; and Friedlander, Henry. *Art of the Holocaust.* New York: W.H. Smith-Rutledge, 1981.
    This is the first survey of the artistic records of Jewish and non-Jewish victims of Nazi terror—from the initial response in 1933, through the ghettos, transit camps, concentration camps, resistance, hiding, and postwar survival. Focusing on professional artists, the book emphasizes the value of the art of the Holocaust as historical documents for investigating the history of the Holocaust. Contains over 350 illustrations and over 100 biographies.

Borowski, Tadeusz. *This Way for the Gas, Ladies and Gentlemen and*

*Other Stories.* New York: Viking Press, 1967; paper, Penguin, 1976.
A Polish poet's short stories, based on his experiences in Auschwitz.

Dawidowicz, Lucy S. *A Holocaust Reader.* New York: Behrman House, 1976.
Selection of many important documents translated from German, Yiddish, Polish, French, and Hebrew sources. Both official and private papers, including diaries, communal records, and folk literature, trace the growth of antisemitism in the twenties and thirties, the preparation for the deportation of Jews, and the eventual program for their murder.

Des Pres, Terrence. *The Survivor.* Oxford: Oxford University Press, 1976.
This book is an analysis of the concentration-camp experiences and the dynamics of survival. Evidence of humane behavior and conscience contradicts current ideas about the survivors. The author establishes the link between staying alive and staying human in a world ruled by death.

Dinnerstein, Leonard. *America and the Survivors of the Holocaust.* New York: Columbia University Press, 1982.
Dinnerstein sheds new light on the response of the Truman administration, the Congress, and the American military to the plight of the remnants of European Jews. This pioneering study adds much to our understanding of the DP (displaced persons) period.

Donat, Alexander. *The Holocaust Kingdom.* New York: Holocaust Library, 1965.
An autobiographical account of a Jewish couple who smuggled their son out of the Warsaw ghetto and were later separated as they were shunted through a succession of concentration camps. Their survival and eventual reunification is the subject of this book. Donat chronicles life in the ghetto, the uprising, and concentration camp experiences.

Eliach, Yaffa. *Hasidic Tales of the Holocaust.* New York: Oxford University Press, 1982.
Collection of eighty-nine Hasidic stories about the Holocaust based on interviews and oral histories; contains much material on the role of women.

Feingold, Henry. *The Politics of Rescue: The Roosevelt Administration and the Holocaust, 1938-1945.* New Brunswick, NJ: Rutgers University Press,1970.
In recent years, President Roosevelt has come under harsh criticism for failing to make the rescue of Jews a priority during the Holocaust. United States policy for the rescue of Jews during the Roosevelt administration is the main subject of this book. The

volume tells about the Roosevelt administration and its priorities, as well as the positions of American Jews on the complex issues of relief and rescue.

Friedlander, Henry, and Milton, Sybil, eds. *The Holocaust: Ideology, Bureaucracy, and Genocide.* Millwood, NY: Kraus International Publications, 1980.
    A scholarly, interdisciplinary collection of incisive essays by leading experts grouped around six topics: 1) Before the Holocaust (ancient, medieval, and modern antisemitism); 2) The Setting of the Holocaust, including essays on the "Artists in the Third Reich" and "Manipulation of Language"; 3) The Professions in Nazi Germany and the Holocaust (lawyers, doctors, civil servants, clergy, professors, etc.); 4) Anti-Jewish Elites in Occupied Europe; 5) The United States and the Holocaust; and 6) After the Holocaust (the impact on art, theology, and education).

Friedman, Philip. *Their Brothers' Keepers.* New York: Holocaust Library, 1978.
    A Pan-European survey about those non-Jews who helped rescue Jews, 1939-1945.

Gutman, Yisrael. *The Jews of Warsaw, 1939-1943: Ghetto, Underground, Revolt.* Bloomington, Ind.: Indiana University Press, 1982.
    The Warsaw ghetto revolt of April, 1943, remains the best-known act of resistance during the war. Professor Gutman, a survivor and participant in the ghetto uprising, has written a comprehensive and scholarly analysis of Jewish life during the occupation of Warsaw, the story of the ghetto, and the development of the resistance movement. He also analyzes the motivations and behavior of the Germans, using a large number of primary sources.

Hilberg, Raul. *The Destruction of the European Jews.* Chicago: Quadrangle Press, 1961.
    This monumental study of the Nazi perpetrators analyzes the systematic murder of European Jews. It is the most comprehensive study of the "machinery of destruction."

Langer, Lawrence L. *The Holocaust and the Literary Imagination.* New Haven: Yale, 1975.
    Critical approach to literature and the Holocaust.

Levi, Primo. *If This Is a Man.* New York: Orion Press, 1959; paper (ed. with title: *Survival in Auschwitz*), Collier, 1961.
    An objective and dispassionate report about an Italian Jewish chemist deported to Auschwitz. The best eyewitness account of the camp world.

Poliakov, Leon. *Harvest of Hate: The Nazi Program for the*

*Destruction of the Jews of Europe.* Wesport, Conn.: Greenwood Press, 1971. Paper, New York: Holocaust Library, 1978.

The best survey of the European Catastrophe; brief, concise, and comprehensive, with extensive quotes from original sources.

Reitinger, Jacob. *The Final Solution: The Attempt to Exterminate the Jews of Europe, 1939-1945.* New York: A.S. Barnes (Perpetua Paperback), 1961.

The earliest comprehensive history, first published in 1953. Provides a detailed country-by-country account of the Nazi plan and its implementation.

Rosenfeld, Alvin H. *A Double Dying: Reflections on Holocaust Literature.* Bloomington & London: Indiana University Press, 1980.

Clearly written study about the issues of Holocaust "literature."

Ryan, Michael D., ed. *Human Responses to the Holocaust: Perpetrators and Victims, Bystanders and Resisters.* New York and Toronto: Edwin Mellen Press, 1981.

Anthology including essays by Robert G.L. Waite on Hitler; Henry Friedlander on "The Nazi Concentration Camps"; on Holland and Denmark; on German resistance of von Moltke and von Trott; and ethical and theological reflections.

Schoenberner, Gerhard. *The Yellow Star.* London: Corgi, 1969.

Earliest and most comprehensive illustrated documentation about the persecution of Jews in Europe, 1933-1945.

Skloot, Robert, ed. *The Theatre of the Holocaust.* Madison, Wis.: University of Wisconsin Press, 1982.

In this anthology, a penetrating essay on the moral and aesthetic problems of writing a play about the Holocaust introduces four remarkable plays: *Resort 76,* by Shimon Wincelberg; *Throw a Straw,* by Harold and Edith Lieberman; *The Cannibals,* by George Tabori; and *Who Will Carry the Word?,* by Charlotte Delbo.

Trunk, Isaiah. *Jewish Response to Nazi Persecution.* New York: Stein and Day, 1978.

In sixty-two eye-witness accounts of physical and spiritual resistance to the Nazis, this book tells of the uprisings in the ghettos, resistance in the camps, and the experiences of the Jewish partisans. This book should be read in conjunction with *They Chose Life,* by Yehuda Bauer (New York: American Jewish Committee, 1973), which refutes the unjustified accusation that Jews went to their death like "sheep to the slaughter."

Trunk, Isaiah. *Judenrat: The Jewish Councils in Eastern Europe Under Nazi Occupation.* New York: Macmillan Co., 1972.

Some historians have charged that the Jewish Councils, which were established by the Nazis, were responsible for hastening the destruction of European Jews. This indispensable study addresses this issue in an objective and scholarly fashion, examining the role of the Jewish Councils in several ghettos of eastern Europe.

Wells, Leon W. *The Death Brigade* (originally titled *The Janowska Road*). New York: Macmillan Co., 1963; paper, Holocaust Library, 1978.
    Memoir by a young Jewish boy about the murder of Jews in eastern Galicia, including the Janowska camp in Lvov (Lemberg) and its "death brigade."

Wiesel, Elie. *Night.* New York: Avon, 1969.
    *Night* is the compelling story of Elie Wiesel's experiences in several concentration and extermination camps (Auschwitz and Buchenwald). It is a classic in Holocaust literature, eloquently raising basic issues about life and death.

Wiesenthal, Simon. *The Sunflower.* New York: Schocken Books, 1976.
    While an inmate in a concentration camp, Wiesenthal had an encounter with a dying soldier in the *Waffen* SS. The soldier begged Wiesenthal to forgive him for murdering Jews. Wiesenthal discussed the question with his fellow inmates and together they decided that no one could speak on behalf of the victims. After the war, Wiesenthal still wondered whether this was an appropriate response, and sought the views of various intellectuals and laymen throughout the world. This book contains this encounter with the German soldier and the contemporaneous reactions to Wiesenthal's response.

Wiesenthal, Simon. *The Murderers Among Us: The Wiesenthal Memoirs.* Edited by Joseph Wechsberg. New York: McGraw-Hill, 1967; paper, Bantam, 1973.
    Profile of Simon Wiesenthal, his documentation center, and work tracing German war criminals. Includes a biographical essay by Joseph Wechsberg.

# List of Contributors

**Solon Beinfeld** was born in New York. He received his A.B. from New York University and his A.M. and Ph.D. from Harvard. He is Associate Professor of History at Washington University in St. Louis, where he is also a member of the Jewish Studies Committee. His teaching and research interests include Modern European History and Modern Jewish History, with an emphasis on East European Jewry. His publications include articles and reviews in the *McGraw-Hill Encyclopedia of Biography*, *The American Historical Review*, *Present Tense*, and *The Simon Wiesenthal Center Annual*. He has edited *A History of Our Own Times* by Ford Madox Ford and is currently completing a study of the Vilna ghetto.

**Christopher R. Browning** was born in 1944. He received his A.B. from Oberlin College (1967) and his Ph.D. from the University of Wisconsin-Madison (1975). He has been a member of the History Department at Pacific Lutheran University in Tacoma, Washington, since 1974. His book, *The Final Solution and the German Foreign Office*, was published in 1978. He has undertaken research on the Final Solution in German archives and court records with the support of fellowships from the German Academic Exchange Service (DAAD) and the Alexander von Humboldt Foundation.

**Abraham Cooper** was born in New York in 1950. He received his B.A., M.A., in History, and his rabbinic ordination from Yeshiva University. Long active in the Soviet Jewry movement, he has traveled throughout the Soviet Union, worked with Soviet immigrants in Israel and the United States, and lectured extensively in the United States and Canada. Rabbi Cooper has served as the Assistant Dean and Director of Outreach Programs of the Simon Wiesenthal Center, Los Angeles, since its inception in 1977. In this capacity, he has conducted the Center's campaign for abolition of the Statute of Limitations on Nazi War Crimes. He coordinated the visit of twenty-five prominent Americans to Germany, culminating in a meeting with West German Chancellor Helmut Schmidt. In 1980, during the Cambodian crisis, Rabbi Cooper coordinated the Center's Mission of Concern, which traveled to Washington and New York for meetings with White House and Congressional representatives and for discussions with United Nations Secretary General Kurt Waldheim. He later served as liaison to Auschwitz survivor, Fania Fenelon, author of *Playing for Time*, in her battle against CBS' casting of Vanessa Redgrave in the TV production of that story. Rabbi Cooper has compiled two works on Raoul Wallenberg, *Lost Hero of the Holocaust: Report and Analysis to United States Congress* (1981) and *Raoul Wallenberg: A Chronicle of Courage* (1981). His article on Sweden's mishandling of the Wallenberg case was published by the *Los Angeles Herald Examiner* (1981) and his articles about the Statute of Limitations on Nazi War Crimes have appeared in the *Los Angeles Times* and *Jewish Living Magazine* (1979). He has co-authored (with Rabbi Marvin Hier) an article on Idi Amin in Saudi Arabia (*Los Angeles Times*, 1981) and compiled (with Rabbi Daniel Landes) a Candidate's Questionnaire on Jewish Issues for *Jewish Living Magazine* (February, 1980). Rabbi Cooper currently serves as Editor of the Wiesenthal Center's *Social Action Update* and is Contributing Editor for "Page One," a weekly radio magazine on contemporary Jewish life.

**David Ellenson** is Assistant Professor of Jewish Thought and Director of the Jerome Louchheim School of Judaic Studies at Hebrew Union College-Jewish Institute of Religion, in Los Angeles, where he was ordained. He received his B.A. from the College of William and Mary; his M.A. from the University of Virginia; and his Ph.D. from Columbia University. He is the author of the soon-to-be-published *Continuity and Innovation: Rabbi Esriel Hildeshemier and the Creation of a Modern Jewish Orthodoxy* and of numerous articles published in a variety of Judaic and other academic journals.

**Henry L. Feingold** is Professor of History of Baruch College and the Graduate School of the City University of New York. He is the author of *The Politics of Rescue: The Roosevelt Administration and the Holocaust, 1938-1945*, which won the Leon Jolson Award as the best book on the Holocaust in 1974, and *Zion in America: The Jewish Experience from Colonial Times to the Present*. He is the Editor of *American Jewish History*, the oldest scholarly journal in the field; serves on the editorial boards of *YIVO Annual, Shoah,* and *Reconstructionist;* is a member of the Academic Council of the American Jewish Historical Society; and serves on the executive committee of the Jewish Historical Society of New York. He has spoken and written widely on themes in American Jewish and Holocaust history.

**Joel S. Fishman** was born in Winston-Salem, North Carolina, on May 4, 1943, and grew up in Brookline, Massachusetts. He received his B.A. from Tufts University in Medford, Massachusetts, and his M.A. and Ph.D. in Modern European History from Columbia University in New York City. During his years as a Fulbright Scholar at the University of Utrecht, the Netherlands (1968-1970), he became interested in the postwar problems of the Dutch Jewish community. In 1972, he made *aliyah* to Israel. From 1975 to 1978, he was the guest of the Netherlands State Institute for War Documentation in Amsterdam, where he carried out research on his forthcoming book on the postwar Dutch Jewish community. Dr. Fishman is presently the Executive Secretary of the Israel Association for American Studies and manager of Quality Photography of Jerusalem.

**Henry Friedlander** was born in Berlin in 1930, and was deported to the Lodz ghetto in 1941 and to Auschwitz, Neuengamme, and

Ravensbrück in 1944. He came to the United States in 1947, and received his Ph.D. in German History from the University of Pennsylvania. He served on the Captured German Documents Project of the National Archives in Alexandria, Virginia; taught history at the Louisiana State University, McMaster University (Canada), the University of Missouri, and the City College of New York; and is currently Professor of Judaic Studies at Brooklyn College of the City University of New York. He is the author of several *Guides to German Records* (1958-1961); *On the Holocaust* (1973); and a number of important articles, including "Toward a Methodology of Teaching about the Holocaust" (in *Teachers College Record*, 1979), "The Nazi Concentration Camps" (in M. Ryan, ed., *Human Responses to the Holocaust*, 1981), and "The Language of Nazi Totalitarianism" (in *Shoah*, 1978). He is one of the authors of Vol. 2 of *Jewish Immigrants of the Nazi Period in the USA* (1981); coeditor (with George Schwab) of *Detente in Historical Perspective* (1975); coeditor (with Sybil Milton) of *The Holocaust: Ideology, Bureaucracy, and Genocide* (1980); and coauthor (with Janet Blatter and Sybil Milton) of *Art of the Holocaust* (1981). He wrote the Introduction to Vol. 12 of *The Holocaust: The Final Solution and the Extermination Camps* (1982). He also served as Chairperson of the Annual Scholars Conference on Church Struggle and the Holocaust of the National Conference of Christians and Jews (1980-1982). He is currently working on the legal implications of the postwar trials of the Nazi criminals in Germany and the United States (Fedorenko case).

**Jane Gerber** is Associate Professor of Jewish History at the Graduate School of the City University of New York and President of the Association for Jewish Studies. She is the author of *Jewish Society in Fez, Jews in Muslim Lands*, and *The Jewish People: Ethnographic Studies* and has served as Editor of *Shoah*.

**Martin Gilbert** is a Fellow of Merton College at Oxford University. He was educated at Highgate and Magdalen College, Oxford, and has published over thirty books and atlases. Among his publications are *Auschwitz and the Allies* and *Final Journey*. Since 1968 he has been the official biographer of Sir Winston Churchill. He coauthored the script of the film, *Genocide*.

**Alex Grobman** graduated with a B.A. in Sociology from the University of Wisconsin. He received an M.A. *(cum laude)* and Ph.D. in Contemporary Jewish History from the Hebrew University. His doctoral dissertation was *The American Jewish Chaplains and the Remnants of European Jewry*. He was a lecturer at School for Overseas Students, Hebrew University, and at Yad Vashem, and was the first Director of the St. Louis Center for Holocaust Studies. He is a member of the Yad Vashem World Council and is on the editorial board of *Shoah: Review of Holocaust Studies and Commemorations*. He has published scholarly and popular articles on the Holocaust, and has served as a technical consultant for film and television productions related to the Holocaust. In 1980, he was appointed Director of Holocaust Studies at the Simon Wiesenthal Center. He is a lecturer at Yeshiva University of Los Angeles and coeditor of *The Simon Wiesenthal Center Annual.*

**Hanna Gunther,** freelance translator, editor, researcher, has had considerable experience in publishing: as Senior Editor at Frederick A. Praeger, Inc., from 1957 to 1965, and as Managing Editor of Schocken Books, Inc., from 1965 to 1971. She has also worked on various projects for the Leo Baeck Institute in New York. Her special fields are political science and history (mainly east-central European history, especially World War II and the Holocaust).

**Yisrael Gutman,** Professor of Jewish History at the Hebrew University, Jerusalem, and Director of the Research Center, Yad Vashem, has written (in Hebrew) *Men and Ashes: The Story of Auschwitz, The Revolt of the Besieged,* and *The Jews of Warsaw, 1939-1943: Ghetto, Underground, Revolt.* An inmate of the Warsaw ghetto, at the age of twenty he took an active part in the uprising as a member of the Jewish Fighting Organization.

**Marvin Hier** received his rabbinic ordination at the Rabbi Jacob Joseph Theological Seminary, New York. He became Assistant Rabbi at the Schara Tzedek Congregation, Vancouver, where he later assumed the pulpit and served as Rabbi for fifteen years. Concurrently, he was Hillel Director at the University of British Columbia. In 1975, he became the first Vice President of the Canadian Zionist Federation. In 1977, he founded the Yeshiva University of Los Angeles (YULA) and the Simon Wiesenthal Center, the center of Holocaust studies in Los Angeles. In April, 1979, he led an American delegation to West Germany to meet with Chancellor Helmut Schmidt about extending the Statute of Limitations for Nazi War Crimes. In February, 1980, he served as cospokesman for the American Jewish delegation that met with Secretary General Kurt Waldheim about the Cambodian genocide. In 1982, Rabbi Hier received the Academy Award for Best Documentary Feature of 1981 for the Simon Wiesenthal Center's film, *Genocide,* which he coauthored and coproduced. Subsequently, he was elected as a member of the Academy of Motion Picture Arts and Sciences.

**Stuart Kelman** received a B.S. from Columbia University; a rabbinic ordination, M.H.L. and B.R.E. from the Jewish Theological Seminary of America; an M.A. from the California State University at Northridge; and a Ph.D. in the Sociology of Education from the University of Southern California. He has been Director of United Synagogue Youth and of Camp Ramah; Principal of Herzl Schools; and is currently Assistant Professor in Jewish Education at Hebrew Union College, Los Angeles. Dr. Kelman frequently lectures and conducts training sessions in Jewish education throughout the country and has been Western Region Chair and Conference Cochair

(1978, 1980) for the Coalition for Alternatives in Jewish Education. He has published a number of papers in the field of Jewish religious education.

**Robert Krell** was born in The Hague in 1940 and survived in hiding. After receiving his M.D. in 1965 at the University of British Columbia, he interned at the Philadelphia General Hospital and completed psychiatric residencies at the Temple University Hospital, the Stanford University Hospital, and the University of British Columbia Health Sciences Hospital. He is currently Associate Professor of Psychiatry at the University of British Columbia, where he also serves as Director of psychiatric postgraduate education and the Child and Family Psychiatry Outpatient Clinic. Dr. Krell has lectured at the Hebrew University in 1975 and the UCLA Neuropsychiatric Institute in 1982. His numerous scholarly articles and contributions to books focus on the fields of child psychiatry; the consequences of divorce, custody, and one-parent families; psychiatric education; and Holocaust survivors. His recent publications include: "Holocaust Families: Survivors and their Children," in *Comprehensive Psychiatry* 20 (1979); "Family Therapy with Children of Concentration Camp Survivors," in *American Journal of Psychotherapy* 36 (1982); and together with Professor Leo Eitinger of Norway, he is currently preparing a bibliography of medical and psychiatric literature pertaining to survivors of the Holocaust. Since 1976, Dr. Krell has organized annual Holocaust symposia for Vancouver high school students and in 1980, he initiated the Canadian Holocaust Documentation Project.

**Daniel Landes** studied in Yeshivat Mercaz HaRav Kook in Jerusalem. A graduate of Yeshiva College, New York, in Philosophy, he was ordained by the Rabbi Isaac Elchanan Theological Seminary. After receiving his M.A. from Yeshiva University, New York, he continued as a Bernard Revel Fellow in Jewish Philosophy. Rabbi Landes was a founding faculty member of Yeshiva University of Los Angeles (YULA) and the Simon Wiesenthal Center. He is Assistant Professor of Talmud and Jewish Thought at YULA and Director of Research Projects at the Simon Wiesenthal Center. He is Coeditor of *The Simon Wiesenthal Center Annual* and is author of a forthcoming study of responses to violence in Jewish law.

**Dov Levin** is Senior Research Editor, Research Fellow, and Project Director at the Institute of Contemporary Jewry, Hebrew University, Jerusalem. Born in Lithuania, he fought in the Zionist underground of the Kovno ghetto and then in the forests. He came to Israel in 1945, where he received an M.A. and Ph.D. from Hebrew University, Jerusalem. He has been Chairman of the Editorial Board of *Sefer Yahudut Litta* (4 vols.) and Vice Chairman and Secretary of "Lehanchalat Moreshet Ha-sho'a." He is a member of the executive of the National Social Work Association. He fought with Israeli defense forces in four wars. He is the author of over 120 articles and of

*The Story of an Underground* (Jerusalem, 1962); *They Fought Back* (Jerusalem, 1974); and *With Their Backs to the Wall* (Tel Aviv, 1978). He is the recipient of the Yitzhak Sade Prize for Military Literature, 1972.

**Steven M. Lowenstein** received his B.A. from the City College of New York (1966) and his M.A. (1969) and Ph.D. (1972, History) from Princeton University. He was Assistant Archivist and Research Associate at the YIVO Institute for Jewish Research, 1973-1975; Archivist at the Leo Baeck Institute, 1975-1979; and, since 1979, Assistant Professor of Modern Jewish History at the University of Judaism, Los Angeles. He is the author of many publications on various aspects of German Jewish social history, including "The Pace of Modernization of German Jewry in the Nineteenth Century" (*Leo Baeck Institute Yearbook*, 1976), "The 1840s and the Creation of the German-Jewish Religious Reform Movement" (*Revolution and Evolution, 1848 in German-Jewish History*), "The Rural Community and the Urbanization of German Jewry" (*Central European History*, 1980), and "The Readership of Mendelssohn's Bible Translation" (*Hebrew Union College Annual*, 1982). He is currently working on a book on the German-Jewish community of Washington Heights in New York City.

**Martin Mendelsohn** was Chief of the Special Litigation Unit of the United States Department of Justice, Immigration and Naturalization Service, from October, 1977, to May, 1979. At that time the unit was transferred to the Criminal Division and became the Office of Special Investigations. Mendelsohn was then appointed Deputy Director of Litigation of the Office of Special Investigations. He was responsible for the prosecution of all individuals alleged to be Nazi war criminals living in the United States. He was transferred from that position on January 7, 1980. Mendelsohn is a graduate of Brooklyn College and George Washington Law School. He is a member of the District of Columbia and Illinois Bars. He has worked on Capitol Hill and in Legal Aid, as well as in government service. He is presently a member of the Board of Directors of the National Legal Aid and Defender Association and is on the faculty of the Illinois Institute for Continuing Legal Education. He serves as the legal counsel for the Simon Wiesenthal Center.

**Sybil Milton** was born in 1941 and educated at Barnard College, the University of Munich, and Stanford University, where she received her Ph.D. in Modern European (German) History. She served on the Historical Commission in Berlin and the Commission for Parliamentary History in Bonn, taught at Stanford, and is currently Chief Archivist of the Leo Baeck Institute in New York. Dr. Milton is a recipient of the National Jewish Book Award (Visual Arts Category), May, 1982. She is the author of numerous scholarly and bibliographical articles about Czechoslovakian history, German Labor and Socialist politics, captured German documents, Jewish archives, and art of the Holocaust. She is coauthor of the text for the national Albert Einstein Centennial Exhibit, distributed by the American Institute of Physics and the State Federation of the Humanities (1979); editor and translator of *White Flags of Surrender: Memoirs of a Half-Jew in Frankfort on the Main, 1933-45* (1974); editor and translator of *The Stroop Report* (1979); and coeditor (with Henry Friedlander) of *The Holocaust: Ideology, Bureaucracy, and Genocide* (1981). She is also coauthor (with Janet Blatter and Henry Friedlander) of *Art of the Holocaust* (New York: Rutledge, 1981) and is Associate Editor of *The Simon Wiesenthal Center Annual*. She wrote the introduction to Vol. 16 of *The Holocaust: Rescue to Switzerland* (1982) and has contributed an essay on "Women and the Holocaust" to Kaplan, Bridenthal, and Grossmann, eds., *Women in Weimar and Nazi Germany* (1983). She is a member of the Society of American Archivists, the International Council on Archives, a founding member of the International Council on Jewish Archives, and the American Committee for the History of the Second World War. She has participated in the conferences of the National Institute on the Holocaust, the Scholars' Conference of the National Conference of Christians and Jews, and has lectured widely on various aspects of the Holocaust and World War II. She is currently preparing a volume on the photographic record of the Holocaust.

**John T. Pawlikowski** is Professor of Social Ethics at the Catholic Theological Union, a constituent school of the Chicago Cluster of Theological Schools. For over a decade, he has been prominently involved in the Christian-Jewish dialogue as lecturer, writer, advisor to the American Bishops' Secretariat for Catholic-Jewish Relations, and as a member of the Israel Study Group of Christian Scholars. In 1980, he was appointed by President Carter to the United States Holocaust Memorial Council, a position he continues to hold.

**Nehemia Polen** was ordained at Ner Israel Rabbinical College in Baltimore, Maryland. In addition, he holds degrees in mathematics from Johns Hopkins University and in counseling from Northeastern University. He is currently a University Scholar at Boston University, pursuing research on Hasidism during the Holocaust period under the direction of Elie Wiesel and Nahum Glatzer. He is Rabbi of Tifereth Israel Congregation in Everett, Massachusetts.

**Sheryl Robbin** is a graduate in psychology and English from the University of Michigan. She has graduate degrees from the University of Chicago in Social Work and Human Development. She is a member of the American College of Social Workers and is a Licensed Clinical Social Worker (California). Robbin has been on the staff of University of California, Los Angeles Hospitals and Project Step (National Institute of Mental Health). A consultant at the Simon Wiesenthal Center, she has taught a course on Literature and the Holocaust.

**David G. Roskies** teaches literature at the Jewish Theological Seminary of America. He is a founder and Editor of *Prooftexts: A Journal of Jewish Literary History* and is currently finishing a book on responses to catastrophe in modern Jewish culture.

**Franklin Sherman** received his A.B. from Muhlenberg College, his M. Div. from Chicago Lutheran Theological Seminary, and his Ph.D. from the University of Chicago. In 1961, Oxford University conferred upon him the degree of M.A. (Oxon). Dr. Sherman has been Tutor and Dean of Lutheran Students at Mansfield College, Oxford, England; a member of the Faculty of Theology of Oxford University; and Associate Professor, Professor of Christian Ethics, and Director of Graduate Studies at the Lutheran School of Theology in Chicago, where he is currently Dean of Faculty. In addition, he has served as Visiting Professor in the Graduate School of Ecumenical Studies at Bossey, Switzerland, in the Department of History and Literature of Religions at Northwestern University, and in the Divinity School of the University of Chicago; as Visiting Lecturer at the Japan Lutheran Theological College and Seminary in Tokyo; and as Scholar in Residence at the Ecumenical Institute for Advanced Theological Studies in Jerusalem, where he conducted a seminar on "Current Issues in the Jewish-Christian Dialogue." Dr. Sherman is a Fellow of the Society for Values in Higher Education and a member of the American Society for Christian Ethics, and from 1972 to 1976 served as Executive Secretary of the latter organization. He has written extensively in theological journals and was Editor of "Facet Books, Social Ethics Series," published by Fortress Press, and the volume *Christian Hope and the Future of Humanity* (Augsburg, 1969), and *Luther's Works* (Fortress, 1971). Dr. Sherman has also contributed articles and essays to several books dealing with the thought of Dietrich Bonhoeffer, and is the author of the article on Bonhoeffer in the current edition of the *Encyclopedia Britannica.* Among his recent publications are an essay in the volume *Speaking of God Today: Jews and Lutherans in Conversation* (Fortress, 1974) and a pamphlet entitled *The Problem of Abortion: After the Supreme Court Decision,* published by the Department for Church and Society of the Lutheran Church in America. His translation of Paul Tillich's book *Die Sozialistische Entscheidung (The Socialist Decision)* was published by Harper and Row in 1977.

**Zalman F. Ury** was born in Stolpce, Poland, and studied at Yeshiva Etz Hayim in Kletzk and Vilna (Lithuania) from 1938-1941. During World War II, he was interned in a Siberian Concentration Camp, and after the war returned to Poland. Later, he lived in Prague, Czechoslovakia, and emigrated to the United States in 1947, where he received his rabbinic ordination at Beth Medrash Gavoha in Lakewood, New Jersey. Rabbi Zalman received his B.S. from Washington University, St. Louis, Missouri; his M.A. in Education from Loyola University, Los Angeles; and his Doctor of Education at the University of California, Los Angeles. He has taught extensively and has held many administrative educational posts in Russia and the United States. He is the author of over 100 articles and educational materials for journals and books and of *The Musar Movement* (New York: Yeshiva University Press, 1970). Currently, he writes a column in the *Jewish Community Bulletin* of the Jewish Federation Council of Greater Los Angeles, teaches at the Jewish Studies Institute of Yeshiva University of Los Angeles, and is Rabbi of Young Israel Congregation of Beverly Hills, California.

**Shelly Usen** is a freelance editor, copy editor, and production editor in Los Angeles. She has been Production Editor at E. P. Dutton, New York; Editor of *Crafts Bulletin* at New York State Craftsmen; Managing Editor of Pinnacle Books and J.P. Tarcher, Los Angeles; and Executive Editor of Dana/Corwin Enterprises, Los Angeles.

**Paul M. van Buren,** Doctor of Theology, Professor at Temple University in the Department of Religion, was educated at Harvard College, the Episcopal Theological School, and the University of Basel. He has taught at the Episcopal Seminary of the Southwest, and was Visiting Professor at Oxford University, Austin Presbyterian Theological Seminary, Princeton Seminary, and the Harvard Divinity School. He has received Fulbright, Guggenheim, and National Endowment for the Humanities fellowships, and has published six books and numerous articles. He is a member of the Consultation on the Church and the Jewish People of the World Council of Churches, and is on the Advisory Board of The American Friends of the Israel Interfaith Association.

**Efraim Zuroff** graduated with a B.A. in History and a B.H.L. from Yeshiva University, New York. He went on *aliyah* in 1970 to Israel and received an M.A. from the Institute of Contemporary Jewry of the Hebrew University, Jerusalem, where he is currently completing a Ph.D on the "Response of Orthodox Jewry in America to the Holocaust." He was Director of the Department for Overseas Activities at Yad Vashem, Assistant Editor of *Yad Vashem Studies* Vols. 10 and 11 (Hebrew and English editions), and coeditor of *Rescue Attempts During the Holocaust: Proceedings of the Second Yad Vashem International Historical Conference* (1977). He has published a number of scholarly articles on the Holocaust. From 1978 to 1980, he was the first Director of the Simon Wiesenthal Center for Holocaust Studies and a lecturer at Yeshiva University of Los Angeles. Currently, he is Israel Liaison to U.S. Department of Justice, Office of Special Investigations and correspondent for *Page One,* the Wiesenthal Center's national radio news program.

## AUTHOR INDEX